The Gastronome . . . The Gourmet . . . The Epicurean . . . What is he?

A DEFINITION / LUDWIG BEMELMANS

The popular concept of the gourmet is that of a seal-like, happy creature of Gargantuan appetite, who sticks a napkin inside his collar, dunks bread into the sauces and throws on the floor plates that are not properly heated. His nourishment is catalogued as caviar, pâté de foie gras, truffles, pheasant and crêpes Suzette. He drinks only the proper wine, but on closing his eyes and rinsing it in and out through his teeth he is able to tell you not only the age of the wine but also the number on the barrel in which it has been aged. He is thought of as a middle-aged man (never a woman), portly and jolly, given to reciting toasts that are spiked with French terms. His extravagant dinners take on the aspect of an eating contest rather than a good meal.

Actually, the true gourmet, like the true artist, is one of the unhappiest creatures existent. His trouble comes from so seldom finding what he constantly seeks: perfection.

To be a gourmet you must start early, as you must begin riding early to be a good horseman. You must live in France; your father must have been a gourmet. Nothing in life must interest you but your stomach. With hands trembling, you must approach the meal about which you have worried all day, and risk dying of a stroke if it isn't perfect.

—from "On Innkeeping"

HOLIDAY MAGAZINE BOOK OF

The World's Fine Food

a treasury of adventures in gastronomy

by	*Roger Angell*	*Pierre and Renée Gosset*
	Herbert Asbury	*Eric Newby*
	Lucius Beebe	*Frank Schoonmaker*
	Ludwig Bemelmans	*Silas Spitzer*
	Paul E. Deutschman	*Phil Stong*
	Clifton Fadiman	*Joseph Wechsberg*
		and others

With an Introduction by *Ted Patrick*
·
Recipes by *Florence Brobeck*

SIMON AND SCHUSTER / NEW YORK / 1960

FIRST PRINTING

Frontispiece by Arnold Newman

LIBRARY OF CONGRESS CATALOG CARD NUMBER: 60–6735
MANUFACTURED IN THE UNITED STATES OF AMERICA
BY RAND MC NALLY, CONKEY DIVISION

Contents

Introduction / *Ted Patrick*

Everyone carries an almost exact memory of any event which has had an overwhelming impact on his life. I remember the day a great change came into my own life, and the exact words that brought forth that change. It was in the depraved days of Prohibition. I was sitting at a table in Zani's, one of New York's better speakeasies, on East 50th Street, with a close friend, an older man named Doug Smith. He was regaling me with tales of memorable meals he had had at Mouquin's, and Sherry's, and Bustanoby's, and of lavish banquets at the old Waldorf—the Lucullan parade of oysters, fish, roast, game, cheese, dessert, white wine, red wine, champagne, coffee, liqueurs, cigar. Then he said, "We ought to try to bring some of that back. For a long time I've had an idea for putting together a dining group and calling it The Brillat-Savarin Club. Let's do it." We did. And a new dimension came into my life.

At first glance, the Prohibition era appeared to be the worst time in history to start an epicurean society. Oddly enough, it wasn't. There were some superb chefs in New York, heartsick because no one knew or used their knowledge

and their gifts, and they responded ecstatically to the challenge of preparing meals of epicurean proportions and quality, to be served with the proper wines or the closest possible approximation, unhurriedly, to only six or eight black-tied men.

The experiment was eminently successful. And from this somewhat hazardous start has come an association with food which includes pilgrimages through the wine countries of Burgundy, Bordeaux, Germany, Italy, and California, a partnership in a restaurant, a partnership in a wine-importing company, friendship with a number of the greatest chefs and restaurateurs in the world, a high office in the most venerable of all wine societies, a consummate collection of books on food and cooking, an ability to cook, and a waistline kept in bounds only by the most spartan disciplinary measures.

This affinity with food was quickly brought into the editing of *Holiday*, and food has been and is a major editorial subject for the magazine. This is most appropriate, for we look upon the world as our province, and it is impossible to adopt such a vista without seeing food loom large. Food is a determining factor in where to go, where to stop. Food is a determinant in the enjoyment of any place or on any carrier. Food can make or mar any trip, any holiday. Food can play a potent part in making life dull or exciting.

The realization of all this has been growing mightily in the United States, and strange, wonderful things have been happening here to food and to eating.

Enlightenment and sophistication have finally brought their benevolent influence to American eating habits. We eat elegantly and imaginatively in our own homes; we bring a worldly knowledge to the selection of food in our markets (which themselves have brought worldliness to their counters); we choose restaurants judiciously; in fact, if we continue on the path of progress and wisdom in food, there is the heady prospect that we'll become a nation of epicures.

Another manifestation of our maturing attitude toward food is the voracious way in which we're reading about it. Cookbooks are best sellers. Beautiful, copious, expensive books about dining in France, in Italy, in Vienna, in Britain, inspire quick and enthusiastic response and sell vigorously. The newspaper food page has left behind the plebeian period when it gave the day's prices of potatoes and similar drab information, and it now bedazzles its faithful readers with news of snails, and Brie, and *foie gras,* and mussels, and crêpes, and all the other magical curiosa of haute cuisine. Then there are the magazines, including *Holiday;* you will find in this book of pieces which appeared in *Holiday* an intelligent effort toward a different and comprehensive treatment of food, wine, malts, and spirits.

The first food piece we tackled was called "All about Seafood." "*All* about Seafood" might seem a somewhat pretentious approach, but it's probably a better philosophy under which to start than "A *Little Bit* about Seafood." Since then, other generic foods have been given the 'A'll about' treatment, foods such as soup and bread and pasta and candy and beef and pork. Individual restaurants have also been treated,

restaurants such as the best of them all, the superb Pavillon in New York, and musty old Gage & Tollner's in Brooklyn, and nostalgic Galatoire's in New Orleans. Restaurants also have been done in a multiple way, by areas, such as in the "Little Wonders of New York," the posh places of San Francisco, and the restaurants, big and small, of France. We've commissioned New Yorkers to write about New York food, Chicagoans to write about Chicago food Englishmen to write about English food, Frenchmen to write about French food, Chinese to write about Chinese food. We've explored the intricacies and goodness of food on land, on the sea, and in the air. We've called upon the talents and knowledge of some of the best writers in the English language— Clifton Fadiman (an old wine-importing partner), Frank Schoonmaker (another old wine-importing partner), Silas Spitzer (a fellow Brillat-Savarin member), Joe Wechsberg (a companion on a French Line crossing and on gastronomic tours of Paris and Vienna), and others who are equally adept with pen and fork.

As said before, American people have become vastly enlightened about food. Perhaps the repeal of the silly Prohibition amendment started it, prosperity helped, increased leisure helped a bit more, and the coverage by magazines and newspapers and books such as this helped immeasurably more. Not too long ago it was almost impossible to find a good restaurant in the United States outside New York, Chicago, San Francisco, Boston and New Orleans. Today you will find excellent restaurants in Los Angeles, Pittsburgh, Cincinnati, eastern Long Island, and even in such unlikely places as Marshall, Michigan, and Meridian, Mississippi. Supermarkets, which not too long ago offered little more unusual than a loaf of bread and a can of soup, now have dazzling gourmet counters, and the sharp-eyed young housewives who visit them patronize these counters and know exactly what they are choosing from them.

So much for the appetizer; now for the main course.

PART I: *The Gourmet in the Kitchen*

1. SOUP AND SEA FOOD

All about Soup / *Silas Spitzer*

A real French onion soup . . . or a tangy cream of sorrel . . .
a hot, exotic mulligatawny . . . or a winy-tasting borsch.
A soup lover of the old school evokes
unforgettable aromas and some tender memories . . .

AMONG Central Europeans there is a saying that goes something like this: "If you meet a girl who cooks good soup, marry her." Indeed, there is nothing more beautiful to a hungry man at mealtime than a tureen brimming with old-fashioned soup. And so the big kettle was once kept simmering seven days a week in most American homes. But nowadays it is considered neither elegant nor fashionable to indulge a passion for soup of the kind that is thickly reinforced with meat, beans, noodles, vegetables or other substantial cargo. In polite dining circles, soup is either eliminated or offered in a cup. Clear consommé or an ethereal cream soup is served, not to satisfy the appetite, but as an interlude to more important courses.

Not long ago, the maître d'hôtel of a smart New York restaurant made a characteristic reply to my question about the

◀ One of the classic soups of France is *petite marmite*—the slow-cooked liquid soul of meat and vegetables, unadorned and only lightly seasoned. One recipe, cooked in an earthenware stockpot, calls for a strong bouillon made from a knucklebone, a shinbone and the juicy round of beef. Chicken may go into it, too, with gizzards, wings, necks and feet (which are gelatinous and improve the broth). Other basic ingredients are leeks, carrots, white turnips, onions, white cabbage, parsley and cloves. The items shown here were assembled in a little restaurant in Pont l'Evêque, the heart of Normandy.

ARNOLD NEWMAN

popularity of soup among the well-heeled and worldly. "Me—I love soup," he said. "What Frenchman doesn't? We always have one or two good, thick *potages* on the menu every day. *Mais, alors!* Who orders them? Only the older men, the big eaters. And maybe a few Europeans. Ladies? They're too worried about their waistlines. But we serve soup every day, anyway. No matter how much is left over, the help eats it up. If we stopped making soup they'd quit!"

A few unreconstructed eaters—among whom please include me—still dote on soup, especially the kind that needs hours of unhurried preparation and often makes an entire meal. Earlier generations of Americans were brought up on soups of that description.

The eloquent perfume of soup, simmering slowly at the back of the stove, permeated most kitchens of that earlier time. No smell gave off more glorious promise or made good so completely. There was never anything fancy about the contents of the big soup kettle. Usually there was meat of some kind and always a big bone, with scraps of leftovers from previous meals and vegetables in lavish profusion. Onions and herbs contributed a poetic note to the steaming exhalation. If one yearns these days to sniff once again that honest, unassuming aroma, he would be most likely to find it in households where foreign influences still prevail. It may also be detected in restaurant kitchens which maintain a respect for quality. The cook with the second tallest bonnet in most good French or Italian restaurants is usually custodian of the stockpot, wherein simmers the soul of all good soups, stews

9

and gravies. An experienced chef with a European background should be adept in about a hundred soups, some of them simple, many so complicated that two days are needed to prepare them properly.

Up to about thirty years ago, many farmers and small tradespeople in provincial France ate soup three times a day, the year round. It was generally a simple bouillon of vegetables in which floated ample pieces of bread. A bowl of such soup for breakfast was the logical foundation upon which to build a long forenoon of labor. It was only shortly after the close of the First World War that coffee, often laced with strong home-distilled spirits, began to replace it.

In the French Army the principal meal of the day is still known as "*La Soupe*," even though it may be followed by other courses. It is not difficult to understand this popularity in a country where thrift is regarded as a national asset. Home-made soup is not only healthful, it is also economical. It can be made from almost any leftovers at hand. But apart from its practical side, soup is also a dish of wonderful flavors and has never lost its appeal to people who sit down to the table with a keen sense of hunger and anticipation.

Long ago, while serving as a soldier with our Army in France, I learned how important soup could be. It was in the little market town of Mont-sûrs, center of a once-prosperous agricultural region in the northwest. It was shortly after the armistice of November 11, 1918. We had been moved back from the combat zone and I had been detached for special duty vaguely connected with the entertainment of the troops, who were marking time before shipment home.

Most of my meals were depressingly Army type, but occasionally I escaped from the Headquarters Company mess line to dine at the Boule d'Or, an unpretentious little hotel on the market place. The countryside around was gaunt and frozen and had a stricken look after four long years of war.

On Sundays and market days, the dining room of the Boule d'Or was crowded. Regular guests of the hotel ate at a few small tables, but for transients like myself there was a long board set with a white cloth, with room for twenty or more. Every meal I ate there followed the same general pattern. A stout, red-cheeked woman in a black dress waddled from place to place and ladled steaming soup into deep bowls for each guest.

Platters of sliced bread and a jug of the native hard cider were also passed around and occasionally there would be coarse pork liver *pâté* and a leaf-wrapped soft cheese as powerful as a bomb. But these were incidentals. Soup was the meal and it came around two or three times for those who wanted it. For my taste, it was a fine soup, but that may be only because it was so different from Army chow and also because it reminded me a little of home. Besides the liquid, there were masses of green cabbage in it, a few carrots or turnips, broken bits of potato and hunks of the heavy wartime bread, made of three different grains, with a crust like armor. No meat ever appeared in my soup bowl. But undoubtedly a few bones and some fat had gone into the pot to supply a faint but reminiscent meaty overtone.

A great many years later, I revisited that same northwestern part of France on a sentimental journey. To my surprise, I learned that what I had eaten had not been an emergency soup for wartime, but was still the favorite of the region.

After many happy years of adventurous eating at home and abroad, I am convinced that the best soup is a family affair. The family soups of the world have much in common. They are usually thick, they stick to the ribs and often are eaten as a complete meal. Every European country has at least one national soup that fulfills this basic description. But the contents and seasoning vary from province to province, from town to town, and even from family to family. It is all a matter of what edible ingredients are available in the immediate neighborhood. The skill, imagination and personal whims of each cook also have a lot to do with it.

Vegetable soups are the most common, and of these perhaps the best known and certainly the most popular in the United States is Italian minestrone. But there is no such thing as *the* minestrone of Italy. In all of the different kinds, there are vegetables and either beans or chick peas. There is also the unmistakable native taste of olive oil and cheese and perhaps a haunting evidence of ham or some other cured meat. Minestrone of the northern provinces is usually lighter and more subtle than the massive near-stews of Naples, Calabria and Sicily. The cooks of Genoa and Bologna often simmer fresh vegetables and dried beans in water for an hour or so, then add a few spoons of *pesto*, a dark-green, odorous paste made by pounding garlic, fresh basil, parsley, Parmesan cheese and oil in a mortar. When this is stirred into the soup, the resulting flavor is the very soul of Italian cooking, which is not far from the best in the world.

Minestrone Milanese is a bulkier preparation, closely resembling the sort we are most familiar with in this country. It starts by browning salt pork, garlic, onions, herbs and seasonings in oil in a capacious vessel. A little tomato paste is added, then stock or water is poured on top of the fried mixture, and, at a later stage, at least seven or eight kinds of fresh vegetables and dried beans are put in. The last touch is a handful or two of elbow macaroni or pasta in some other substantial form. Grated Romano cheese is served at the table.

In Tuscany, all the usual vegetables are present, but the seasoning is different, a special kind of plump white bean is included and the tureen is garnished with a dozen round slices of toast. Rice is often used instead of macaroni in Venice and northern Italy. Yellow, mealy chick peas are mated with blunt cuts of macaroni in Naples, where soup, goes an old saying, is no good unless a spoon will stand straight up in it. Odd notions in other country types of minestrone are the tiny buds and blossoms of the zucchini vine, escarole or Swiss chard, sweet sausage and smoked spareribs.

France is a land where soups have never lost their ancient standing. In typical French homes it would be thought peculiar to begin the big meal of the day with anything except soup. And the French cook has so many wonderful recipes to choose from that she need not repeat herself often. Many of them originated in regional cookery and have the veritable taste and smell of their surroundings. One of the best of these is a luxurious sort of vegetable-and-meat mélange called *garbure*. At least four different provinces claim it, but the best known is probably *garbure Béarnaise*, which contains white beans, pork, many vegetables and a local delicacy called *confit d'oie*, or a preserved goose meat.

A typically French cream soup which never attains its true delectability in alien parts is cream of sorrel, a magical blend of acidity with velvety smoothness and richness. Leek and potato is another creamy affair, immensely popular because it can be prepared from the humblest of farm products, but is as delicious as the most expensive soup.

There is no such thing as a national soup of France. Perhaps the closest to it is *petite marmite*, which was the soup referred to by King Henri IV when he expressed the wish that every citizen in his kingdom might rejoice in chicken in the pot every Sunday. Known also as *Poule au Pot*, it is still widely popular in all parts of the country, though more often beef takes the place of fowl, in which case the soup is the equally famous *"pot-au-feu."* Whether chicken or beef, or both, go into the pot, this is a hearty soup, but never a thick one. Actually, it is the slow-cooked liquid soul of meat and vegetables, unadorned and only lightly seasoned. Yet the late Curnonsky, and other cultivated French gastronomes, considered it typical of the finest French cuisine, which, contrary to the belief of most Americans, is simple, not elaborate or contrived, and which "tastes of the thing of which it is made."

A good old-fashioned recipe for *pot-au-féu* calls for a strong bouillon made from a knucklebone, a shinbone and the juicy lower round of beef. With this goes a substantial piece of the firm-textured *"platecote,"* for eating at the table. It is the custom to serve the meat separately, at the same time as the soup. For gala occasions, chicken is cooked with the beef, including such flavorsome bits as the gizzard and liver, the neck, last joint of the wings, the head and the feet. These last are especially important, as they are gelatinous and do much to improve the quality of the broth. Besides the necessary water, other basic ingredients are leeks, carrots, white turnips, white cabbage and onion, parsley, cloves and seasoning. The cook may indulge a personal taste, like a drop of bottled sauce or a pinch or two of garden herbs. The meat is always started in the pot with cold water. The liquid is carefully skimmed to keep it clear of fat during the cooking. The vegetables go in at a later stage and the simmering continues for three hours. Then the white parts of the leeks are added and the soup is simmered one hour longer. The bouillon is meticulously strained, small oven-toasted rounds of bread are floated on top, the tureen is brought to the table and the guests fall to with sighs of ecstasy. When the last spoonful has been eaten, the meat is served, garnished with parsley and accompanied by tiny sour gherkins and a saucer of coarse marine salt.

There are so many fine soups in the world that it would take a stout book to do them justice. Luckily it is not necessary to travel abroad to get acquainted with the most worthy examples, as these are usually available in more or less authentic form at most of the foreign restaurants in our larger cities. Italian minestrone and French onion soup are the two most highly esteemed by Americans, or so I am told by my foreign restaurant friends. For many returned tourists, *soupe à l'oignon* is regarded with sentimental affection because it recalls Paris in its most romantic mood. Vacationists and honeymooners always devour bowls of onion soup at four o'clock in the morning in noisy little restaurants of Les Halles. It is the favorite soup, apparently, of lovers, market men and drunkards—perhaps because it is supposed to soothe and uplift the weary and the exalted. Indeed, in its true form, served in a brown earthenware bowl, smoking hot, golden with melted cheese and toasted bread, it has a tonic effect which restores one's faith in tomorrow.

Americans have also made friends with the ruby-tinted borsch, which originated in Russia and Poland, but is now an international dish. In the old Czarist regime there were several extravagant versions, including one that was built around duck and vintage Burgundy. But at its best it is a family soup, ruggedly simple, containing beets, cabbage and odds and ends

of meat. At the moment of serving, heavy sour cream is spooned into the plate and the dark red tint of beet juice changes to a lovely blush pink. Good borsch should have a winy taste, faintly acid and refreshing. When strained and whipped in a mixer with sour cream and a sprig of fresh dill, it makes a wonderful iced drink for hot weather. Borsch is familiar to Jewish cuisine and rivals such other savory and strengthening soups as mushroom and barley, Lima bean and farfel, and golden chicken broth with noodles, *kreplech* or *mandlen*.

Our restaurant menus frequently offer us the dried pea soups of Holland, Sweden and French Canada. Their heaviness seems suitable mainly for lumberjacks or foot soldiers, but ordinary city folk of modest appetite love them equally.

Fish soups are closely related, but each is influenced by regional resources and personal tastes. The best known, certainly the most widely exploited in literature, is bouillabaisse, a soup which is also a dinner.

A bouillabaisse ordered a day ahead and served to me at a little restaurant on the coast near Toulon was made from an astonishing variety of fish. They were identified for me in a richly garlic-scented voice by the corpulent proprietor. He said they were *rouget, rascasse, St. Pierre, daurade, baudroie, vive,* and *merlan*. Also some lobster and a few shellfish whose names I have forgotten. All of these had been caught and brought in that morning, he said, by his father-in-law. In my mood of that particular moment, which owed much to the optimistic influence of two *pastis* and a chilled bottle of the local white cassis, I had no reason to doubt his word. An ineffable aroma of the south steamed upwards from the broth and the fish, which were served separately. A trained nose could detect the presence of garlic, onions, fennel, tomatoes and saffron. Thick slices of coarse, crusty bread, fresh from the village baker's oven, were there to soak up the gold-flecked ambrosial liquid. For dessert, after this piscatorial banquet, I had five large black grapes and a small cup of black coffee. Anything more substantial would have been disgraceful to record.

In Europe, wherever fish are taken with net or line, there are certain to be generously composed soups which taste of the regions where they originate. The *matelote* of Normandy is made with red wine, spices, chunks of conger eel and a bouquet of freshwater fish. The *ttoro* of the Basque country has even more ingredients than bouillabaisse and for added potency a deep draught of old Armagnac. The solid portion of the Breton soup called *cotriade* is eaten with a *sauce vinaigrette*. The *brandade* of Provence is a cream soup made from pounded dried codfish, milk, olive oil and a fistful of garlic.

Italy has its own various *zuppa di pesce*, some of them mysterious and even disquieting to the outlander. Once, at a Sunday dinner on the Ligurian seacoast near Livorno, an adventurous compatriot ordered a local fish soup called *cacciucco*. It came to the table in an immense bowl. The color of the soup matched the murky crimson of the cliff upon which the restaurant was perched. The bowl was full of bits and pieces, floating or submerged, all apparently contributed by the sea nearby, but none of an identifiable nature. Gamely, my friend ate the entire contents of his plate, rejecting only some small rubbery items which might have been squid and avoiding a leathery green substance that was probably seaweed. He partook of none of the fine food that followed, however, and remained oddly silent and thoughtful for some time later. However, since he returned to the States, he has never stopped talking about *cacciucco Livornese.*

If there is a national soup of England, it is probably the ubiquitous mock turtle, served with unrelenting loyalty at boardinghouses, seaside hotels, family restaurants and at most comfortable "non-U" dinner tables. This background may sound depressing, but the fact is that mock turtle, when prepared from honest ingredients such as shin beef and bones, a calf's head, vegetables, country butter, spices and sherry, can be quite a tasty dish. Most visitors to England would probably prefer the genuine article. There is nothing more heartening than clear green turtle soup with a glass of old Madeira, as served up at the annual Lord Mayor's dinner, or at those London clubs for gentlemen which keep a good kitchen. This was the soup which inspired the immortal verses in *Alice in Wonderland:*

> *Beautiful soup, so rich and green, .*
> *Waiting in a hot tureen!*

In sharp contrast to the placid nature of much English cookery is mulligatawny, a soup with the exotic flavors of the East. In Kipling's time, it was the favorite first course of dinner at the officers' mess in the old British Indian Army. Very much in the Kipling tradition is a wondrous recipe for mulligatawny which is one of the treasures of my culinary file. To cook it properly required the skill of Escoffier and the patience of Job. The most important element was a kitchen-compounded curry powder that needed ten separate spices and condiments, few of them known to the western world. For the rest, there were such diverse edibles as the head and shoulders of a large cod, sliced green apples, a brown *roux* (flour and butter stirred over medium heat until light brown; for thickening), much hot red pepper and long-grained Patna rice.

Americans today are not a soup-loving people. Complicated, long-cooked soups are rare in an age when the dominating compulsion is to save time, space and labor in the kitchen. We have come to rely more and more upon packaged soups that are stocked compactly in the pantry or freezer and when called upon go straight into the pot. This widespread national preference has been prompted by the really remarkable improvement in canned, frozen and dehydrated soups.

The repertoire and resources of the average commercial soup maker cannot be duplicated by even the wealthiest or most talented home cook. It is a simple and easy trick today to serve an oyster stew, Scotch cock-a-leekie, or a sea-food bisque, all of high quality and delightful flavor, without extending one's self beyond opening a can and turning on the range.

Intelligent housewives frequently improve upon the original by combining two or more kinds of prepared soups, adding extra touches such as hard-cooked eggs to black bean purée, chopped almonds or salted peanuts to creamed pea or chicken, fresh chives to iced vichyssoise, or a topping of lightly browned cream to boula boula, which is half pea and half turtle.

Yet, in spite of the tremendous and well-deserved popularity of ready-made soups, there are still homes in this nation where the big soup kettle is kept simmering, at least part of the time. And lucky families are still pampered occasionally with such justly famous regional soups as New Orleans crab

gumbo, New England or Long Island clam chowder, Maryland oyster soup or the beer soup of Wisconsin. Particularly irresistible to male appetites is navy bean soup of the smoky, hambone-scented variety which is served daily at the Senate restaurant in Washington, D.C. Another fine local soup is Philadelphia pepper pot, a succulent mixture of honeycomb tripe, onions, celery, green peppers, cubed potatoes and butter. In Colonial times, the vendor of pepper pot went through the streets of Philadelphia, according to local historians, singing:

> *All hot! All hot!*
> *Pepper pot! Pepper pot!*
> *Makes backs strong,*
> *Makes live long,*
> *All hot! Pepper pot!*

I am quite sure that this fine soup is still eaten in many Philadelphia homes, but it would be nice to know what local restaurant can offer a stranger a dish of the original and genuine, full of tripe, onions and sentimental memories.

The best of all American soups, or so it seems to my taste, is still old-fashioned vegetable. Making the home-cooked kind that I remember from my youth calls for meat, marrow bones and at least a dozen different vegetables and dried legumes, as well as some other starchy component, like macaroni or dumplings. This is a vegetable soup, not a soup for vegetarians. It needs meat and bones to give it power and poetry. The kettle should be big enough to hold five or six quarts, and the simmering goes on for most of a day. Vegetables limited only by the season and the state of the cook's larder are showered into this fragrant, bubbling stock, each in its own proper time. A parsnip, or so my mother was convinced, was indispensable to the final bouquet of flavors.

It is impossible in this space to pay tribute to all the fine soups of every land. Certainly there should be a place here for a great summer soup like the ice-cold but spicily seasoned *gazpacho* of Spain. It is never made exactly the same way and is really a "wet" salad. However much it may vary, the usual essentials are tomatoes, onions, olive oil, peppers, cucumbers and plenty of garlic. Sometimes it is thick with bread crumbs; often it has a block of ice in it; but always it is as reminiscent of Spain as the sound of castanets.

Other foreign soups which deserve more than casual mention are Belgian *waterzoie,* German lentil-and-smoked-frankfurters, Spanish *olla podrida,* Jewish chicken broth with matzoh balls, English oxtail. Also the formidably caloric Dutch pea soup called *snert,* the Swedish ditto known as "Thursday Soup" because it is made on the cook's day off, Russian *chlodnik,* Scottish toasted oatmeal soup called brose, and the sturdy potato soups of country people everywhere. For the delicate eater, there are soups of purest fantasy like Chinese winter melon, bird's nest and shark's fin. A special tribute ought to be paid to the inventive minds that dreamed up West Indian chip-chip, French *velouté* of frog's legs and water cress, Hungarian *gulyas* soup, Norwegian huckleberry, the creamed peanut-butter soup of Virginia, which tastes better than it sounds, Scandinavian fruit soup and that cluster of herb-garden brews which are flavored whimsically with marigold buds, portulaca and nasturtium leaves. Perhaps the limit of refinement is reached in Norman Douglas' recipe for almond soup, which calls for pounding almonds in a mortar with the yolks of hard-cooked eggs, then nursing this daffodil-colored paste with stock in a saucepan until it becomes a thin cream. To be eaten, I suppose, with a silver spoon in the moonlight, under a willow tree.

But the roster of international soups is just about endless. In André Simon's *Encyclopaedia of Gastronomy* there are more than a hundred separate recipes alone for classical French consommés. The great Carème was the master of five hundred different soups, mainly his own inventions or adaptations. No wonder Alexandre Dumas once wrote: "France is one great soup tureen."

There is something homelike and cozy about the thought of good soup, and these qualities seem to attach themselves to the cook. Today's ambitious housewife would do well to return, if only occasionally, to the big soup pot and the old-fashioned recipes of grandmother's day. The best time to prepare a soup of that kind is on a cold day, when appetites are razor-keen and the masculine interior yearns for solid sustenance.

Ladle it generously from a big tureen that will retain the heat and odor of its contents until the last spoonful is eaten. The soup plates should be deep and wide and the conscientious cook will preheat them. Nothing is more discouraging than tepid soup, unless it be soup that is watery and insipid. Let your soup be strong, therefore. Do not, as the French say, heat a pot of water and drive a cow past the door.

Soup lovers, it seems to me, are usually happy mortals, with a serene outlook upon life. Soup haters, on the other hand, are likely to be thin-blooded and on the neurotic side. The conclusion is obvious. Let us return to soup on a national scale. Not, however, because it is the virtuous thing to do, or with any thought of restoring family life as it used to be, but simply because soup is one of the best things life affords, worth cultivating for its own sake.

NEW ENGLAND CLAM CHOWDER

1 quart fresh, shucked clams	Grind of fresh pepper
2 cups cold water	4 cups boiling water
¼ pound salt pork, sliced	1 quart hot milk
1 onion, peeled and sliced	4 tablespoons butter
4 cups cubed and peeled potatoes	2 teaspoons flour
	10 large chowder crackers
1½ teaspoons salt	Large soup tureen

Remove any bits of shell from clams. Pour the cold water over clams, then strain and set liquid aside. Cut salt pork in small pieces, heat in a 4-quart soup kettle until browned. Add onion and cook until soft. Cover with layer of potatoes. Then add the clams. Season with salt and pepper; add boiling water and cook for 15 minutes over moderate heat. Add hot milk and 3 tablespoons butter, cook 3 minutes longer, lower heat. Reheat the 2 cups strained liquid from clams. Stir in flour and remaining tablespoon of butter, which have been kneaded together; cook, stirring, until thickened. Add to chowder, stir well, let come to a boil and pour at once over crackers in warmed tureen. Makes 8 to 10 servings.

OHIO SATURDAY NIGHT BEAN SOUP

1½ cups navy beans	8 peppercorns
1 ham bone, or 4 slices lean bacon or salt pork	6 cups hot beef stock, bouillon or hot water
½ cup diced pared turnip	¾ teaspoon sugar
3 small potatoes, pared and diced	½ teaspoon salt
2 celery stalks, diced or 1 parsnip, pared and sliced	6 tablespoons toast crumbs

Look over beans, wash and drain. Cover with cold water, let soak 12 hours. Drain, combine with ham bone and bacon or salt pork in 4-quart kettle; add vegetables, peppercorns, and hot stock, bouillon, water, or a mixture of these liquids. Cover and cook over low heat about 30 minutes; reduce heat to simmer, and cook, stirring occasionally, for at least 1 hour or longer if possible. Remove bone. Force soup through a sieve and reheat, adding sugar and salt. Or season and stir but do not sieve. Serve hot with spoonful of toast crumbs on each serving. Makes 6 servings.

MINESTRONE MILANESE

1 tablespoon olive oil
2 slices fat salt pork, chopped
½ clove garlic, peeled and chopped
½ medium-size onion, peeled and chopped
1 tablespoon chopped parsley
1 teaspoon crumbled dried sage
1 teaspoon salt
½ teaspoon pepper
1 tablespoon tomato paste stirred into 1 cup water

3 stalks celery, scraped and chopped
2 carrots, scraped and sliced thin
2 potatoes, pared and diced
2 cups cooked dried peas
¼ head cabbage, shredded
2 zucchini, diced
1 cup green peas
1¾ quarts water or stock
1 cup elbow macaroni
Grated Romano or Parmesan cheese

In a 4-quart marmite or soup pot combine olive oil, salt pork, garlic, onion, parsley, sage, salt and pepper; heat slowly; stir and let onion brown a little. Stir in the tomato paste and the water. Cook for about 5 minutes. Add all vegetables and the stock or water. Cook slowly for 45 minutes to 1 hour. Add macaroni; let soup boil 10 minutes longer. Serve into warm soup plates; sprinkle top lightly with cheese. Makes 6 servings.

PARKER HOUSE PHILADELPHIA PEPPER POT

3 pounds fresh honeycomb tripe
Salt
Large meaty veal knuckle
1 each, leek, large peeled onion, carrot and celery stalk, sliced
3 sprigs parsley
8 cloves
½ teaspoon freshly ground pepper

1½ teaspoons salt
1½ teaspoon sweet marjoram
1 teaspoon each, summer savory, basil, thyme
1 small slice fresh hot red pepper
3 potatoes, pared, diced and boiled 10 minutes
Flour
Butter
Small dumplings

Wash and scrub tripe thoroughly. Rinse, drain, place in a 4-quart kettle with 3 quarts cold water. Add 1 teaspoon salt. Bring to boil and cook over low heat for 5 hours or until tripe is tender. Add more water from time to time if necessary.

In another 4-quart kettle place the veal knuckle, vegetables and parsley. Cover with water, add ½ teaspoon each salt and pepper. Bring to boil, lower heat and simmer about 1 hour. Add cloves and herbs, correct seasoning, and continue simmering about 1 hour or until meat falls from bone. Strain, let stock cool. Remove fat from top.

When tripe is done remove it from its cooking liquid and save liquid. Cut tripe in very small dice. Combine veal and tripe stocks in a 3-quart marmite or soup kettle, heat, add diced tripe, the small piece of hot pepper, and the potatoes. Let boil slowly about 5 minutes. Blend about 1 tablespoon flour with 2 tablespoons butter, add in small bits to soup, stirring constantly. Make any preferred small dumplings and serve at once. Makes 3 quarts soup or 12 servings.

SIMPLE FLOUR DUMPLINGS

1 cup all-purpose flour
1 teaspoon baking powder

¼ teaspoon salt
2 teaspoons butter

Sift flour, baking powder and salt 3 times. Blend in butter, mixing with fingers; gradually add just enough water to make a dough. Pinch off and roll tiny balls about the size of a pea. Drop into the boiling soup 10 minutes before serving.

NEW ORLEANS CRAB GUMBO

1 pound crab meat, cooked, canned or quick-frozen
3 tablespoons butter
4 tomatoes, skinned and chopped
1 onion, peeled and chopped
1 teaspoon dried thyme or a sprig of fresh thyme
1 tablespoon chopped parsley

1 teaspoon salt
Grind of fresh pepper
1 teaspoon Worcestershire sauce
½ pound okra, thinly sliced
1 bay leaf, crumbled
2 cups hot fish stock
2½ cups boiling water
Cayenne
4 cups hot, boiled rice

Some New Orleans cooks use about a dozen hard-shell crabs in place of ready-to-use crab meat in this gumbo. The crabs are cleaned, cut in quarters, claws removed and cracked and all thrown into a heavy soup kettle to cook in butter for 10 minutes. If you use just the crab meat, flake it and remove all shells and bones. Heat butter in kettle, cook crab meat 5 minutes. At this point, whether you are using crabs or crab meat, add tomatoes, onion, herbs, salt, pepper and Worcestershire. Cook 5 minutes, stirring occasionally. Add okra, stir and cook until okra is browned. Add bay leaf, hot stock and water. Cover kettle, reduce heat, cook slowly about 1 hour. The soup should now be thick. If it isn't, uncover kettle and let cook down. Season lightly with cayenne. Spoon hot rice into 4 large soup plates. Pour gumbo over rice. Makes 4 large servings.

GERMAN BEER SOUP

2 12-ounce bottles beer
1 tablespoon butter
2 tablespoons flour
1 tablespoon sugar
3 tablespoons lemon juice
2 tablespoons grated lemon peel

½ teaspoon cinnamon
1 beaten egg
3 slices pumpernickel, diced and toasted

Open beer and let stand 2 hours or longer. Melt butter in soup kettle, stir flour and sugar into hot butter until lightly browned. Stir in beer, lemon juice, lemon peel and cinnamon. Cook slowly until boiling. Stir in beaten egg. Serve at once, in warmed soup bowls. Garnish generously with diced toast. Makes 4 servings.

LA PETITE MARMITE

2 pounds lean beef plate
5-pound chicken, cleaned, ready for cooking
6 quarts water
3 teaspoons salt
2 medium-sized leeks, cut in inch pieces
3 medum-sized carrots, scraped and cut in inch pieces
2 white turnips, pared and quartered
3 stalks celery, scraped and cut in inch pieces
½ small head green cabbage, quartered

1 medium-sized onion, peeled, halved, and 1 clove stuck in each half
½ tablespoon beef suet or butter
Grind of black pepper
Bouquet garni (1 large bay leaf, 8 sprigs parsley, 1 sprig thyme)
8 slices raw beef marrow
1 teaspoon finely minced chervil or parsley
Toasted French bread
Grated Swiss cheese

A 10-quart earthenware soup marmite is traditional for this soup, but a metal soup pot can be used. Place beef, chicken and water in marmite or pot; add salt and cook over low to moderate heat, slowly, until boiling. Lower the heat and let simmer for 3½ hours or longer if desired. Remove the scum from the surface of the soup from time to time. When meat and chicken are tender, add leeks, carrots, turnips, celery, cabbage and the onion which has been lightly browned in the suet or butter. Correct the seasoning, adding a quick grind of pepper and the bouquet garni. Cook slowly for ½ hour longer. Remove beef and chicken; let them cool slightly and then cut in cubes or 2-inch lengths. Return meats to the marmite or kettle, continue cooking slowly for about 1 hour longer. Just before serving remove the onion and bouquet garni and discard them. Add beef marrow and chervil or parsley to the soup and serve into large warmed soup plates. Toasted French bread is usually served with this soup. Makes 12 or more servings.

GAZPACHO A LA BADAJOZ

On hot days in Spain, this so-called soup is served very cold as a main dish for luncheon.

4 tomatoes, skinned
1 cucumber, chopped
1 sweet red pepper, seeded
1 onion, peeled and chopped
3 or 4 stalks parsley
3 cloves garlic, peeled and chopped
1 teaspoon salt
Grind of fresh pepper

1 cup dry bread crumbs
3 tablespoons olive oil
2 tablespoons wine vinegar
2 or 3 tablespoons ice water
4 to 6 tablespoons cracked ice
Extra vegetables and cubed fried bread

Chop vegetables and garlic as finely as possible. Put in electric blender or mixer with seasonings, crumbs, oil, vinegar, and ice water. Blend to a fine purée. Serve at once in chilled soup bowls with spoonful of cracked ice added. Provide separate small dishes of chopped cucumber, onion, green pepper and cold squares of fried bread to be added to the gazpacho by guests as desired. Makes 4 to 6 servings.

CALIFORNIA GARDEN SOUP

2 tablespoons butter
2 tablespoons each chives, basil, thyme and parsley, minced
½ cup finely diced cucumber
½ cup finely diced Belgian endive
1½ quarts bouillon or chicken stock

½ teaspoon salt
Grind of fresh pepper
¼ teaspoon grated nutmeg
½ cup white wine
6 slices French bread spread with grated Romano or Parmesan cheese

Melt butter in a 2-quart kettle. Add herbs and cook slowly for 3 minutes. Add cucumber and endive, stir, add bouillon or stock. Cover, cook over moderate heat for about 20 minutes. Season, add wine, stir. Place a slice of the prepared French bread in each soup bowl. Pour in hot soup at once. Makes 6 servings.

GARLIC SOUP FROM CADIZ

3 large tomatoes, skinned and seeded
4 cups water
5 cloves garlic, peeled
½ teaspoon salt
2 green peppers, sliced and seeded

1 teaspoon paprika
2 tablespoons olive oil
2 slices whole-wheat bread without crust

Place tomatoes in 2-quart kettle or marmite, cover with 4 cups water, and bring to boil. Boil about 8 minutes. Remove tomatoes, save liquid. Pound garlic in mortar or heavy bowl with salt. Continue pounding and add green peppers, paprika, olive oil and the drained cooked tomatoes. Pound until smooth (or use an electric mixer or blender). Add to boiling tomato liquid alternately with crumbled bread. Stir until bread is absorbed. Serve this thick, hot soup in small bowls. Makes 4 servings.

Bouillabaisse / *Joseph Wechsberg*

It has a lot in common with the Stradivarius—
no one really knows what makes it so good

BOUILLABAISSE is the name of a Provençal dish—a fish soup. And, as in the cases of other regional dishes that have achieved world-wide acclaim—Serbian pilaf, Hungarian goulash, Russian beef Stroganoff, Viennese apfelstrudel—fame has not necessarily brought improvement to the original recipe. Today "bouillabaisse" more often than not is merely an unscrupulous chef's answer to the question of what to do with leftover fish before he has to throw it away.

According to the *Larousse Gastronomique*, the bible of all French chefs, *cordon bleu* and otherwise, bouillabaisse is "a Provençal dish, made of various kinds of fish cooked in water or white wine, with oil, tomatoes, garlic, saffron, parsley, pepper, laurel (bay) and other spices added."

This definition is, of course, as lofty as a statement by Talleyrand, and wide open to interpretation.

The best bouillabaisse of my experience was not eaten in one of the many restaurants along the Côte d'Azur where this most famous of all fish soups is a time-honored tradition on the daily bill of fare; or in such swank places as Prunier in Paris, or Isnard in Marseille. I had my best bouillabaisse on the fo'c'sle deck of the *Azay-le-Rideau*, in the middle of the blue Mediterranean, and it was made by my friend Etienne-Marcel, who is a strictly nonprofessional cook.

As a rule, Etienne-Marcel, the parchment-faced carpenter aboard the *Azay-le-Rideau*, was as loquacious as an old lobster. But he could get awfully mad when passengers came to his quarters, where they had no business anyway. They would stare suspiciously at his saucepan, which contained specimens of the entire fauna of the Mediterranean, and ask what he was cooking there, *pour l'amour de Dieu*.

Etienne-Marcel would stare right back at them and say, "Not that it is any of your business, but let me tell you—I would not mind eating my own grandmother, God bless her, if she were properly cooked in white wine and seasoned with garlic, fennel and saffron." It was his version of a well-known Provençal proverb and it silenced even the most persistent kibitzers.

Etienne-Marcel, like most seafaring men, had no use for passengers and their silly questions. Aboard the *Normandie*, God bless her, too, a few ladies of uncertain age once asked me whether the excellent *Filet de Sole Dugléré* which they'd had for lunch had been caught that morning presumably through a porthole on C deck. I was only a ship's musician, so I tactfully referred them to M. Olivier Naffrechoux, the impeccable maître d'hôtel, a man who has become patient and gray-haired in the faithful service of the Compagnie Générale Transatlantique. Monsieur Naffrechoux explained with all the finesse at his command that it would be extremely difficult to fish for Channel sole while going at twenty-nine knots through the western Atlantic. The ladies were bitterly disappointed and walked away mumbling that maybe the sole wasn't so fresh, after all.

Fishing from a luxury liner is not encouraged by the steamship companies any more than cooking in staterooms or running around in one's underwear. The only vessel on which I ever saw crew members take their own dinner straight out of the ocean was the *Azay-le-Rideau*, a dilapidated Messageries Maritimes boat that had only one funnel and no serviceable lifeboats to speak of. The *Azay-le-Rideau* steamed morosely between Marseille and the French possessions in Asia, such as Pondicherry, India, and Hanoi, Indo-China. The

16

Maritime harvest: French fish form an appetizing still life against the ancient harbor of Marseille, home port of bouillabaisse and much Mediterranean history.

crew was an odd assortment of disgruntled misanthropes who would have made a fine cast for a remake of *Mutiny on the Bounty*. At one time or another most of us had served aboard the Messageries Maritimes' floating palaces, *Mariette Pacha* and *Champollion*, but we had misbehaved. We had insulted passengers—both male and female—or been insubordinate to our officers, or—worst of all—damaged company property such as mirrors and chairs. So we had been transferred to the *Azay-le-Rideau*, the company's mobile Devil's Island.

The ship's machinery frequently broke down at the most inopportune place and moment—in the Red Sea in July, or the Indian Ocean during a monsoon. While the engineers struggled with the tired turbines, the deck crew started fishing. One night in July, 1930, we had an unscheduled halt in the middle of the Mediterranean somewhere between Northern Corsica and St. Tropez. Etienne-Marcel threw out his net and came up with a catch that would have made a fine collection for a course in ichthyology.

He built a fire in the *mécanicien's* shop, sent for saucepans, soup plates and various ingredients, and then and there cooked the best bouillabaisse I have ever eaten. It was a glorious meal, made even more memorable by a few bottles of fine Moselle and Chablis which two resourceful stewards had been able to procure.

I asked Etienne-Marcel for his recipe. Shrugging, he said, "Remember just two things about bouillabaisse, *mon petit*. First, never make it for less than a dozen people. Second, never use fish that is merely fresh. Only the *very freshest* is good enough."

He was right. The secret of bouillabaisse is to blend the different *parfums propres* of all kinds of fish while they still have the wonderful aroma of salt water, algae and seaweed.

Since then, I have eaten bouillabaisse several times with Etienne-Marcel in Marseille, where he and his wife lived in a small house overlooking the Bassin de la Joliette. He had his fishing boat in the Vieux-Port and often invited his friends to go fishing with him, after which he cooked his bouillabaisse.

There were a few drawbacks, however. Etienne-Marcel insisted on going out at two in the morning—too early for musicians, who traditionally sleep late. And he expected you to consume vast amounts of wine out there in his boat. At dawn you came back, cold and tired and hangoverish, and then you had to scale the fish and wash it in sea water. Personally, I would have preferred a pot of coffee, but Etienne-Marcel was contemptuous of what he called "the bad Anglo-Saxon habit" of drinking tea or coffee in the morning. "The only way to start a new day is with fish and wine," he always said.

We carried the cleaned fish on large wooden plates to his house, where his wife, a big friendly woman, was already encouraging a brisk fire in the coal stove. It was only a few minutes' walk, but it was much too long for Etienne-Marcel.

"Let's hurry, *mon petit*," he would say. "Fish must be fresh. It is more important to get the right fish for bouillabaisse than to cook it right. When you have to buy fish, look right into its eyes. They must be clear and round and they ought to stare straight at you the way those *imbécile* passengers look at you. If the fish's eyes are sunken and clouded, don't touch it. The flesh should be firm, the skin shiny and the odor that of the tide coming in. Don't think absence of odor means freshness. After being washed a few times and iced, most fish gives out little odor, but does that mean that they are fresh?

And watch the gills. They ought to be reddish. There are some fishmongers around the Vieux-Port who are not ashamed to inject the blood of some animal into the gill covers so they will look fresh. Don't ever trust a fishmonger."

I have often sat in Etienne-Marcel's kitchen, watching him while he prepared his bouillabaisse. There are as many recipes for the *bonne soupe* as varieties of fish that ought to go into it. Etienne-Marcel started by separating the firm-fleshed fish—gurnet, conger eel, *chapon*, dory, *rascasse*, as the French call the hogfish, bass, weever, *boudreuil*, lobster, crabs—from the tender-fleshed varieties such as whiting, *roucaou*, *saint-pierre* and that supreme delicacy called *loup de mer* (sea perch), which, according to Etienne-Marcel, was the finest fish of all, devoid of all muddy aftertaste.

"If you cook them all together," he said, "either the firm-fleshed fish will be half-cooked, or the tender-fleshed varieties will dissolve."

He cut the larger fish into slices two inches wide, eliminating heads and tails. The small fish he left whole. Then he took one of those deep saucepans that the French call casseroles and put into it three finely minced onions, four crushed cloves of garlic, two peeled, crushed tomatoes, a sprig of thyme, savory, a laurel (bay) leaf, some orange peel, fennel and parsley. He placed the firm-fleshed fish on top, added half a pint of olive oil and enough boiling water to cover the fish. He spiced the whole with salt, pepper and half a tablespoonful of powdered saffron, and cooked it over a brisk fire. He removed a stove lid and set the casserole so that flames licked its sides. This, too, was important, said Etienne-Marcel.

After five minutes—no more—he put in the tender-fleshed fish and let everything cook together four or five minutes longer. Meanwhile, he prepared one-inch-thick slices of toast with a few drops of oil on each to keep them from getting soggy and placed them in hot soup plates.

When the soup was finished—the whole preparation lasted no longer than nine or ten minutes—he strained the broth over the toast. Then he arranged the fish on a big, warm plate so each of us might choose whatever kind of fish he liked to put into his soup, and sprinkled it with chopped parsley.

On one occasion he wrapped the heads and tails in linen, cooked them five minutes in boiling water and used this liquor, instead of boiling water for the preparation of the bouillabaisse.

"Nothing to it," he would say, when we complimented him on his masterpiece. "Just be sure to separate the various kinds of fish, and to cook everything on a very hot fire—otherwise, oil and water won't mix."

And there it is, as simple a recipe as most of the world's great dishes. As long as you stick to the general principles you can make a good fish soup wherever you are and forget the Mediterranean. Just get a few varieties of white-fleshed fish at your nearest and most trustworthy fish market: sole, flounder, skate, whiting, mullet, haddock. The more varieties, the better. Don't forget lobster, crab and scallops. Be sure to set aside the whiting, mullet and other tender-fleshed varieties that cook fast. Speed is imperative. "Bouillabaisse" means "boil-stop."

I do not maintain Etienne-Marcel's recipe to be the best. Connoisseurs of bouillabaisse can talk about the "correct" preparation for hours on end. But I think it is a fine recipe. Bouillabaisse has a lot in common with the Stradivarius:

everybody has heard of it, but no one really seems to know what makes it so good.

One of the difficulties of arriving at a basic recipe is the mystery of Provençal nomenclature. The same kind of fish may have three or four different names along the thirty-five miles of coast between Marseille and Toulon, so that even French ichthyophagists are not too sure about them. Bouillabaisse, incidentally, is called *bouiabaisso* by the Provençals, which is close enough.

Practically everything about bouillabaisse is problematic—and no one seems to agree about its origin, either. Some of my atheist French friends maintain that Venus, the goddess of love, invented the "saffroned soup" in order to put her jealous consort Vulcan to sleep whenever she was pleasantly occupied elsewhere. However, I have never felt any soporific effects from bouillabaisse.

The more devout connoisseurs maintain that you ought to eat it on meatless Fridays and they quote:

> *Pour le vendredi maigre*
> *Un jour, une certaine abbesse*
> *D'un couvent Marseillais*
> *Créa la bouillabaisse.*

I have never found out how much historical truth there is about this bit of gastronomic poetry. No one seems to know the name of the good abbess nor of the convent where she "invented" bouillabaisse. Neither is there any proof of the theory that the Carthaginians, across from Marseille on the coast of North Africa, were the original inventors.

Perhaps the most notable tribute to bouillabaisse was written by Thackeray, who got so enthusiastic about the soup that he gave a rhymed, though not very complete, recipe in his *Ballad of Bouillabaisse.*

> *This bouillabaisse a noble dish is—*
> *A sort of soup, or broth, or brew,*
> *Or hotchpotch of all sorts of fishes*
> *That Greenwich never could outdo,*
> *Green herbs, red peppers, mussels, saffern,*
> *Soles, onions, garlic, roach and dace:*
> *All these you eat at Terre's tavern,*
> *In that one dish of bouillabaisse.*

Most people will always associate bouillabaisse with Marseille, but today Marseille is no longer the capital of Bouillabaisse County.

"Everything's been different since the war and the Boches were here," an old friend from the *Azay-le-Rideau* told me one night a few years ago when we sat in a café on the Cannebière in Marseille. It was only ten P.M. but the lights were dim and the café terraces deserted. It was hard to realize that not so long ago this had been one of the happiest, merriest, noisiest streets on earth.

"During the Occupation no one was allowed outdoors after seven P.M. Now people have got used to staying at home," my friend continued. "Besides, there is always trouble lately, strikes and riotings, and too many *flics* around. The lights go out early and there isn't enough to eat and besides—who's got the money to pay for it? Ah, *mon vieux*, it's a good thing that our old Etienne-Marcel died one day in 1939. I'm sure he is now cooking the bouillabaisse for the angels in heaven.

Bon Dieu, he wouldn't recognize his Marseille today. Time was when you couldn't offend a man more than by telling him, 'You're so stingy you put only half a dozen kinds of fish in your bouillabaisse.'"

My friend shook his head sadly. "Today they put potatoes in the good soup. They use *sardines!*" He almost wept. "What's happened to our bouillabaisse? *Tout le monde s'en fiche!*"

I told him to cheer up, there were still plenty of fish in the Mediterranean and there must be a few places left where one could find a passable bouillabaisse.

"That's true," he admitted. "You get a good soup in La Napoule, Chez la Mère Terrace. And at Testou, in Golfe-Juan, a few miles out of Cannes, they know how to cook it. Or at Justin, in Toulon. But Marseille is *fini.*"

Fortunately, things aren't that bad. The old fights are still raging and people will argue for hours about whether you should put lobster (or, as the smaller variety is called there, *langouste*) into your bouillabaisse or not; whether it is permissible to use wine instead of water (it is); whether you should throw in mussels as they do in Nice. Personally, I have no violent objections, but the orthodox bouillabaisse gourmets have never recognized the area east of Toulon and are contemptuous of "the vague concoction called bouillabaisse" which they serve in Nice, Antibes or Villefranche.

In Paris there are restaurants where absinthe is put into fish soup to impress the innocent gastronomes. However, Paris is considered barbarous by the true Provençal.

"In Paris they even mix water *with* wine," said a housewife in Hyères. "Imagine!"

Yet the Provençal housewives, who are just as thrifty as the rest of the French *ménagères*, cook an eccentric soup called bouillabaisse *borgne* (in Provençal, *Aigo-sau-d'iou*). Here is the recipe: Place the chopped white of a leek and a minced onion in a saucepan, fry in olive oil; add a crushed tomato, three minced cloves of garlic, fennel and orange peel; add one quart of cold water, spice with pepper, salt and half a tablespoonful of saffron. Add one pound of potatoes, peeled and cut in round slices not thicker than a third of an inch. Cook on a brisk fire until the potatoes are tender, but don't let them fall apart. While the potatoes are cooking, poach five eggs in the liquid that covers them. Strain the liquid over pieces of toast; take out all herbs and spices, arrange the potatoes on a warm plate and put the poached eggs on top of them; sprinkle with chopped parsley and serve.

Almost every coastal region of France has its own fish soup. Along the Atlantic Ocean they make bouillabaisse à *la Coran d'Ys*, with white wine *and* Pernod, served over toasted garlic bread. In Normandy they don't use saffron in their fish soup but put in plenty of noodles for consistency. Speaking of consistency, I should, perhaps, mention the *Schifferin-Suppe*, or Sailor-Woman's Soup of the Germans along the North Sea coast, which is prepared with sherry and white wine, and with loads of spaghetti to take the place of toasted bread crusts. And if you ever travel through Bretagne ("the only part of France from where you really see the ocean," as Jean Richepin said), be sure to go to the coast of Cornouaille, or to Pont-Aven or Concarneau, and order that delicious Breton fish soup called *Cotriade*. It is made with potatoes and shallots, and, of course, with all the fish teeming along the coast, and eating it is quite a ritual. You take a bite of boiled fish dipped in vinegar, then a bite of potato, then a swallow of cider. The bouillon is eaten afterwards.

If you prefer the milder taste of fresh-water fish to the sharper flavor of sea fish, there is no reason why you shouldn't make a fine fish soup entirely of fresh-water fish. In fact, the *Larousse Gastronomique* authorizes *Pochouse* (also called *Pauchousse*). Monsieur Emile, the maître d'hôtel of Le Bec Rouge, in Beausoleil, just five minutes' walk from the Monte Carlo Casino and one of the finest restaurants in France, prefers it to bouillabaisse.

Emile uses any kind of fresh-water fish that has arrived at the nearby fish market in the morning—pike, perch, eel, crayfish, trout, anything. He puts in the same herbs and spices that go into bouillabaisse, but cooks his fish in wine—any dry white wine will do—and adds fried mushrooms and small onions and, after the soup is served, fried bread crusts.

Bouillabaisse people are a strange and wonderful species of mankind. I'll never forget the day Etienne-Marcel told us, during one of his bouillabaisse breakfasts, that a friend of his was going to get a divorce. In Marseille people don't divorce so easily and frequently as in Hollywood or Manhattan, and everybody was stunned. "What happened?" we asked.

"He found out that his wife has a lover," Etienne-Marcel said.

Everybody protested. *Mince alors*, one need not break up on account of a silly little *affaire!*

"And besides," Etienne-Marcel said with finality, as though he didn't expect any argument, "I've been told that the woman puts sardines and toadfish into her bouillabaisse."

There was no argument.

BOUILLABAISSE CREOLE

6 *slices red snapper*	½ *teaspoon ground allspice*
6 *slices any mild fish*	*Olive oil*
3 *onions, peeled and sliced*	6 *large tomatoes, skinned*
Herb bouquet (thyme,	*and sliced*
bay leaf, parsley)	½ *lemon, sliced very thin*
Salt and pepper	1½ *cups white wine*
3 *sprigs each thyme and*	*Cayenne*
parsley	½ *teaspoon saffron*
3 *bay leaves*	12 *slices French bread fried*
3 *cloves garlic, peeled*	*in butter*

Ask fish dealer to clean snapper and other fish, cut off heads, tails, any fins, and slice each fish crosswise in 6 pieces. Save red snapper head. Rinse head, drain, place in a 3-quart kettle with 1 onion and the herb bouquet. Add 2 quarts water, bring to boil and boil fast until liquid is reduced to 4 cups. Remove fish head and herb bouquet, strain liquid and set aside. Rub fish slices thoroughly with salt and pepper. Use blender and mince thyme, parsley, bay leaves, garlic, and allspice together thoroughly. Rub this herb mixture into fish slices until every portion is permeated with the herbs, spice, and garlic.

Heat 2 tablespoons oil in a wide kettle, lay seasoned fish slices side by side in the hot oil, add remaining 2 onions. Cover and cook gently 10 minutes. Turn each piece of fish once. Remove fish and set aside. Add tomatoes to kettle and cook for 8 minutes, stirring. Add lemon slices and the 4 reserved cups fish stock, and the wine; add dash of cayenne. Stir, boil gently 10 minutes. Lay fish slices side by side in the hot mixture and let boil about 5 minutes. Mix a little of the liquid with the saffron and stir into the kettle. Place 2 slices fried bread in each of 6 large soup plates.

Remove fish slices from kettle, placing one on each piece of bread. Pour the hot soup over and serve immediately. Makes 6 generous servings.

Like all other bouillabaisse, this creole soup may have a few shelled and cleaned raw shrimp boiled with the fish head, and 1 or more cups cooked crab lumps added to the final mixture with the fish stock and wine. With such additions, the reserved stock should be 5 cups, and the original amount of water 3 quarts.

PORTUGUESE BOUQUET OF THE SEA

1 *quart fish stock*	1 *stalk celery with leaves,*
2 *cups white wine*	*chopped*
12 *large raw shrimp*	1 *onion, peeled and chopped*
12 *scallops*	2 *sprigs parsley, coarsely*
1 *cup cooked, canned or*	*chopped*
quick-frozen crab	12 *shucked oysters and*
meat	*their liquor*
1 *cup cooked, canned or*	
quick-frozen lobster	
or lobster-tail meat	

For this bouillabaisse combine stock and wine in a 4-quart kettle and let it heat slowly. Shell and clean shrimp, remove heads, cut shrimp into small pieces. Slice or quarter scallops. Remove any bones from crab meat. Add shrimp and scallops to hot stock and wine. Add celery, onion, and parsley, cover, cook gently about 12 minutes, or until shrimp and scallops are done. Add crab and lobster meat, let simmer gently. Cut drained oysters in quarters, add with oyster liquor to kettle. Boil about 5 minutes. Serve at once in deep soup plates, with plenty of crusty bread and butter. Makes 6 to 8 servings.

GULF COAST BOUILLABAISSE

1 pound each, perch, red snapper and mackerel or pompano
2 2-pound lobsters
2 or 3 scallions, cut in half
1 or 2 large yellow onions, peeled and quartered
2 cloves garlic, peeled and sliced
2 large tomatoes, skinned and quartered
2 tablespoons chopped parsley
1 tablespoon chopped fresh dill
2 teaspoons salt
½ teaspoon saffron
Grind of fresh pepper
1 teaspoon orégano
¼ teaspoon thyme
½ cup olive oil
Boiling water
1 cup dry white wine
6 to 8 slices French bread, buttered

Have fish dealer clean fish, cut off heads, tails and large fins and remove large bones. Cut fish crosswise in 2½-inch pieces. Cut through spinal cord of lobsters with sharp knife between head and body, cut lobster crosswise through shell into large chunks.

Place scallions, onions, garlic, and tomatoes in large kettle, add parsley, dill, salt, saffron, pepper, orégano and thyme. Place fish and lobster pieces on vegetables and herbs. Pour oil over. Add enough boiling water to cover mixture with 2 or 3 inches of water above foods. Cover kettle; bring to a boil quickly over high heat; let boil hard for 10 minutes. Reduce heat, boil gently for 15 minutes. Add wine, continue gentle cooking 5 to 8 minutes. Remove pieces of fish and lobster to large warmed platter and place in center of table. Lay buttered bread slices in deep soup plates and fill with the hot soup. Serve immediately. Everyone helps himself to fish, either adding a few pieces to his soup or eating them from a side dish with additional bread and butter. Makes 6 to 8 servings.

CORNISH COAST BOUILLABAISSE

5 leeks
6 medium-sized potatoes
4 tomatoes
2 or 3 parsnips
1 quart water
1 teaspoon salt
½ teaspoon pepper
½ teaspoon dried thyme or sprig fresh thyme
3 or 4 sprigs parsley, coarsely chopped
4 pounds fish, cleaned and cut in thick slices (mullet, mackerel, tuna, rock salmon, etc.)
2½ cups white wine
3 egg yolks
¼ cup light cream
¼ cup croutons fried in butter

Wash vegetables, cut white part of leeks into inch lengths. Pare and quarter potatoes. Skin tomatoes, remove seeds, quarter. Pare parsnips and slice thin. Combine vegetables in marmite or deep soup casserole, add water, salt, pepper and herbs. Cook for 30 minutes over moderate heat. Add fish and wine, cover and cook for 15 to 20 minutes or until fish is done. Beat egg yolks until light, mix with cream, stir lightly into marmite. Continue to cook for 2 minutes. Cover top with hot croutons and serve at once. Makes 8 or more servings.

BOUILLABAISSE PROVENCALE

4 large Spanish onions
1 cup plus 3 tablespoons olive oil
1 sprig thyme
2 cloves garlic, peeled and sliced
½ cup flour
2 cups dry white wine
1½ quarts fish stock or consommé
3 cleaned cod, whiting, or any other mild fish
12 fresh mussels in their shells
Salt and pepper
3 cups water
1 tablespoon chopped tarragon
1 teaspoon chopped chervil
½ teaspoon saffron
Juice 1½ lemons
3 beaten egg yolks
Cayenne
¼ cup grated Parmesan cheese
2 cups croutons fried in olive oil

Peel and slice onions and yellow slightly in 3-quart kettle in about ¾ cup oil. Add thyme and garlic, mix, sprinkle with flour, stir and cook until flour is browned. Add wine and consommé, stir until boiling. Reduce heat, cover kettle, let simmer 30 minutes. Pour soup through sieve and return it to kettle over very low heat.

Cut cleaned fish in small chunks to make 3 cupfuls. Place in saucepan. Season with salt and pepper. Place mussels on rack in steamer containing 3 cups water, cover kettle tightly, bring to boil and steam until all shells open. Remove mussels from shells and add with liquor from the steamer to the fish in the saucepan. Add 3 tablespoons oil, the tarragon, chervil, saffron, and juice of ½ lemon. Bring to boil, lower heat, cook for 10 minutes or until fish is done. Add mussels. Pour this mixture into a warmed soup tureen.

Increase heat under soup kettle. Stir a little warm soup into the beaten egg yolks; then stir into the soup; add dash of cayenne and juice of remaining lemon. Mix, add cheese. Stir and heat about 3 minutes. Pour at once into tureen. Float croutons on top. Serve in large soup plates. Makes 6 servings.

The World of the Oyster / *Joe McCarthy*

For a taste thrill spiced with dashes of humor,
join a true Blue Pointer as he makes a bivalvular tour

CHARLIE ROBINSON, the painter and paperhanger in our village, is a good and reasonable craftsman but it is sometimes difficult to get him to work regular hours during the months that have an R in them. Charlie comes from a proud line of baymen, as the shellfishermen are called here on Long Island, and he loves boats and the water. He puts aside his stepladder and paintbrush when there is an excuse to go oystering.

"Afraid I won't be here tomorrow morning," Charlie will explain as he knocks off at the end of a day. "Have to run over to Old Field Bay and get a few oysters. I'll try to get back in the afternoon. If not, I'll be here Friday morning for sure, rain or shine."

Sometimes these interruptions disturb my wife but they do not bother me at all. Because when Charlie returns from the North Shore, he brings with him, as a sort of peace offering, a bucket of the lovely oysters that grow more or less wild in the free public beds near Port Jefferson. Still cold from the water of the Sound, they are fat and firm and full of flavor. In our sunny kitchen, along about three o'clock on a December afternoon, a dozen of Charlie's oysters, with a tall glass of beer, enables a man to face life again with a restored faith in human nature. At that point I don't care if it takes the rest of the winter to get the living room painted.

It is rather hard for Charlie and the other baymen on this part of the South Shore to realize that the nearest oysters are now at Port Jefferson, clear over on the opposite side of the island. This village where we live happens to have the world-famous name of Blue Point and it looks out on Great South Bay, the home of generations of the finest oysters that graced the menus at Rector's, Delmonico's and the old Waldorf-

Astoria. Growers used to pay as high as $60,000 a year for the right to gather up baby oysters off Smith Point, at the eastern end of the bay, for transplanting in beds a few miles to the west near Blue Point, Bayport and Sayville, where they were matured for the market. These were the small Blue Points that were never duplicated in any other body of water.

But the sad fact of the matter is that the Blue Point oyster has become almost extinct since World War II. A storm in 1931 opened an inlet in Moriches Bay that brought a new ocean current into Great South Bay from the east. This, in the course of about ten years, changed the tidal system and salt content of the bay and introduced a growth of algae and coral that eventually made the raising of edible oysters impossible. The Bluepoint Oyster Company is still in business and still maintains an address in Sayville but, like all the other big Long Island growers, it now raises its oysters in Peconic Bay. As every oysterman knows, nobody ever brought up a true Blue Point in Peconic Bay. The precise and delicately balanced mixture of minerals and vegetable and animal food matter that gave the Blue Point its unique size, substance and flavor existed only in Great South Bay before the fatal storm of 1931.

Similarly, the deliciously hearty Peconic Bay oyster, which many men preferred, even in the old days, to the dainty Blue Point, cannot be grown anywhere except in the water of

A Robbins Island Salt from the cool waters of Peconic Bay, ▶
Long Island, ready for the table.

DAVID E. SCHERMAN

Peconic Bay. And only the shallow, brackish mud flats near Lynnhaven, Virginia, can develop the large and bland Lynnhaven oyster that was Diamond Jim Brady's favorite. A vine from France can grow the same grape in California as it grew in Bordeaux and a sirloin steak in Buenos Aires may taste the same as one in Chicago. But two oysters from two bays that are only a few miles apart on the same peninsula will differ radically in taste, appearance and texture. An oyster is a product of environment.

This makes oyster growing a fascinating, but sometimes unpredictable, business. All the oysters on the Atlantic and Gulf coasts of the United States, where 89 per cent of our harvest is reaped, belong to the same species (*Ostrea virginica*) and at birth are identical. How each oyster turns out in later life depends on the temperature of the water in which it grows and on the water's mineral and food content. Oysters spawn in warm water and hibernate in cold. During the spawning season, they are soft and filmy. During the time of hibernation, they are fat, firm and delectable. The longer the period of hibernation, the more solid the oyster. Thus an oyster from Long Island, Cape Cod or Chesapeake Bay that hibernates all through the R months will tend to be more meaty than one from the Gulf coast that spawns most of the year.

"That's why they knock themselves out in New Orleans cooking that Oysters Rockefeller stuff," a Greenport, Long Island, grower observed recently. "Them Louisiana oysters ain't fit to eat raw, the way God intended us to eat oysters. And when somebody in New Orleans does get up enough courage to tackle an uncooked oyster, they cover it with Tabasco sauce to give it some kind of a taste."

American oysters are not found in really cold water, like that off the coast of Maine or New Hampshire, because they go through their fertilization in the water outside of the parent's body and the larvae do not flourish in less than 65° of warmth. The European oyster (*Ostrea edulis*), on the other hand, can survive in colder water because it retains its fertilized eggs for quite a while within the mantle cavity of its body. So does the small Pacific oyster in the chilly tides of Puget Sound. In 1949, the United States Fish and Wildlife Service imported 9000 European oysters from Holland to see if they could be cultivated in Maine and Washington State. The experiment proved not only the viability of the European oyster in American waters but has suggested that its introduction in certain areas could lead to the founding of a new shellfish industry.

Incidentally, there is nothing poisonous about a spawning oyster. The law in New York State that forbids the selling of oysters during the summer months is a conservation measure, not a health precaution. The law was passed at the suggestion of the growers themselves to protect the reproduction of the oyster crop.

Water temperature is by no means the only factor to be considered in oyster growing. Some coastal areas are excellent for the breeding and early development of oysters but no good at all for the important late maturing that makes them look tempting on the half shell. This leads to involved trading between growers in different localities. An oyster that spends its childhood at a river mouth on the Connecticut side of Long Island Sound will pass the next three or four years in Peconic Bay or Delaware Bay. A crop of oysters will be placed in a certain bed to be fattened and then shifted to another part of the same bay where the water will make the meat solid. Most of the celebrated Cape Cod oysters that are featured at Dinty Moore's in New York and at Boston's venerable Union Oyster House do not become acquainted with the waters of Cape Cod until they are three years old. They are shipped at that age from Connecticut and Long Island, planted during the early spring in the beds at Cotuit and Osterville and dug up for the market in the next autumn and winter. But during that short stay in Massachusetts, they lose their Long Island Sound or Peconic Bay characteristics and acquire the definite flavor and distinctive green shell of the Cape Cod oyster.

One of the first oyster lovers to learn that quality depends on environment was Julius Caesar. During his invasion of Britain, he found oysters that were superior to the ones he had known in Italy. Caesar shipped the British oysters, packed in ice and snow, all the way across Europe to Rome, pausing for repacking in the Alps. The ancient Romans seem to have mastered the controlling of reproduction of oysters by artificial methods, something which modern growers have never been able to do on a large, commercial scale. Oysters were a favorite dish at the lavish Roman banquets, where they were regarded as an aphrodisiac. This belief, of course, is still widely held. "It's an established scientific fact," a Long Island oysterman told me recently, in all seriousness. Actually, most scientists have not gone so far as to establish oysters as a love potion but it is agreed that the meat of an oyster, being high in content of valuable food properties, should give vigor.

Men were eating oysters long before the days of the Roman Empire. There is evidence that they were being consumed as early as the era of the Piltdown Man, who might have been the courageous fellow James the First of England had in mind when he dropped his often misquoted remark: "He was a very valiant man who first adventured on eating of oysters." One theory, probably borrowed from Charles Lamb's tale of the first tasting of roast pig, holds that the whole thing started as an accident, rather than as a bold adventure. A youngster, it is said, was playing one day on a seashore and happened to stick his finger into an open oyster shell. The shell closed quickly on the finger and, to relieve his pain, the boy put his finger in his mouth. The taste of oyster juice pleased him and, in no time at all, everybody in his clan was eating oysters.

But many fingers must have been pinched by the shells of annoyed oysters in many widely separated parts of the world. Oysters were eaten centuries before the coming of Christ—in China, Japan, Australia and North America. The early white settlers in Rhode Island fell upon the native oysters with such greed that a law was passed in 1766 forbidding dredging in the beds. In colonial times and during the first half of the nineteenth century, the choice oysters in the London market came from New York Harbor and the lower Hudson River. Good-looking oysters still grow thickly around Bedloe's Island, where the Statue of Liberty stands, and in the slips and channels of Staten Island, but, because of pollution, the taking of shellfish is banned in the harbor waters. However, there are several Staten Islanders, apparently in the best of health, who claim that they eat New York Harbor oysters regularly.

One of the first freight trains to cross the continent carried a load of Staten Island and Newark Bay seed oysters that were planted in San Francisco Bay, but Eastern oysters have never thrived in Pacific waters. The prevailing oyster in California, Oregon and Washington is another species, *O. lurida*, commonly known as the Olympia oyster. It is not much bigger than a man's thumbnail. There is also a large Pacific oyster, the Japanese Gigantic (*O. gigas*), which was brought from Japan in 1902. These two Western species account for only 11 per cent of the national production, and great quantities of Eastern oysters are shipped daily to Pacific Coast dealers. Ask an oysterman on Long Island or Delaware Bay what he thinks of the two Western oysters and he will answer you by stoutly maintaining that oyster cocktail sauce originated in California.

Old-timers in Greenport regard cocktail sauce as a concoction of the devil. "If you've got a real good oyster," a veteran Long Island grower told me, "you don't need to spoil the taste with sauce gook. A little lemon juice, sometimes, perhaps a dab of horseradish—that's all."

Needless to say, the Eastern oysterman feels that oysters are at their best alive and raw. I know one whose daughter, an exceptionally strong and beautiful girl, was fed chopped, raw oysters at the age of six weeks. "For a teething ring," he says, "we gave her the neck of a clam."

On cold days, however, the average grower will allow his oysters to be stewed or fried. ("No matter how you're cooking them, cook them quick. Otherwise they'll get hard as bullets.") All hands generally agree that it is hard to beat the oyster stew served at the famed Oyster Bar in New York's Grand Central Terminal.

"The secret of our stew," says Andrew McClurg, manager of the bar and its adjoining restaurant, "is the steam-heated pan in which each dish of stew is separately cooked. We use forty pounds of steam pressure on one stew and it cooks in a minute and a half. That heats the oysters all the way through, but they stay soft and juicy. It has to be done very fast, from start to finish, and I don't know anybody who can do it with ordinary kitchen equipment."

Nick Petters, head oysterman at the Grand Central bar, starts an oyster stew by tossing into his hot steam pan—right before the customer's eyes—a dash of Worcestershire sauce, paprika, celery salt and a pat of butter. When this mixture boils into foam, he adds to it eight freshly opened oysters and a half cup of clam juice. As the edges of the oysters begin to curl, he pours in a cup of milk, or, if the customer wants it, cream, or half and half. When this rises to a boil, he pours it into a bowl and serves it with another pat of butter and another sprinkling of paprika. Yummy.

McClurg has an adaptation of the Grand Central Oyster Bar's stew which he makes at home sometimes, and it has never been known to disappoint his guests. The ingredients are the same, and the procedure only a little different. He starts it in the top of a double boiler (instead of the matchless steam pan) over hot, not boiling, water. He puts in two teaspoons of butter, a quarter teaspoon each of Worcestershire sauce, paprika and celery salt and a quarter cup of clam juice (instead of adding it later). He stirs until the butter melts and the mixture is thoroughly heated, then adds eight medium-sized oysters. When the oysters begin to curl, he adds a cup of milk, or light cream, or half and half. He continues heating until the stew is piping hot, then pours it into a warm bowl and tosses in a pat of butter and a dash of paprika. This makes one serving—about a cup and a half.

An increasingly popular dish at the Oyster Bar is the establishment's "Oyster Pan Roast," which isn't a roast at all. It's merely a stew with chili sauce poured over a piece of toast in the bottom of the bowl. The pan roast begins like a stew, in a hot pan with a pat of butter, one teaspoon each of Worcester-

shire sauce, paprika and celery salt, and one quarter of a cup of clam juice. Stir and heat this mixture and add eight medium-sized oysters. When the oysters begin to curl, add one tablespoon of chili sauce and half a cup of cream. When the cream comes to a boil, pour the whole "roast" over a slice of dry toast in a soup plate and serve immediately. Charlie Robinson and the other baymen on Long Island would consider the chili sauce a sacrilege, but it adds character to the oyster flavor.

McClurg and Petters do not take the classic stand-offish view of cocktail sauce, but it irks them to see a customer adding globs of horseradish or Tabasco to his cup of sauce before diving into a plate of oysters on the half shell. "We make our sauce very carefully in a blend that brings out the flavor of the oyster without spoiling it," McClurg says. "If you make it hotter, you ruin the whole effect."

The Grand Central Oyster Bar is undoubtedly the busiest oyster bar in the country, if not the world. It serves an average of 25,000 oysters daily (some days 35,000), about half of them on the half shell and most of the other half in stews. A lot of travelers from the Middle West and Far West head straight for the Oyster Bar as soon as they get off the train and fill up on oysters before they even think about checking into their hotels. "We can tell when a man's from out of town," Petters says. "A New Yorker sits back in his chair while he eats his oysters. A man from the Middle West leans forward. He's trying to make up for lost time. He can't get enough. He eats a dozen or two on the half shell. Then he has a stew. Sometimes, after the stew, he goes for a plate of fried oysters." In the great output of oysters at the Grand Central's bar, quite a few pearls turn up. A few years ago a lady who had never eaten an oyster was escorted to the bar by her husband, an old and faithful customer. Putting her spoon into her first oyster stew, she found thirty-two pearls in the bowl and thereby established a new Grand Central record. But pearls of the Eastern oyster, like those of most table oysters, are valueless.

A visitor from the interior of the country is likely to lose his head about the oysters in a seacoast restaurant such as the Grand Central's because, unlike the ones he gets at home, they are served fresh from the shell. The average housewife today does not know how to open an oyster shell. To make it easy for her, and for shipping convenience, most of the oysters on the market are shucked by the grower and shipped in gallon containers without their shells. Sanitary regulations require the shipper to wash shucked oysters thoroughly, and much of the juice and flavor is lost. The superior-tasting oysters in the shell are sent only to the better hotels, restaurants and clubs, and to first-class retail fish markets. Consequently, only 15 per cent of the nation's crop is eaten from the half shell.

When it comes to raw oysters, there is a strong school of gourmets that favor the small Chincoteagues which are sold at the better sea-food places in Baltimore and at Twenty One in New York. They are a sort of sweet Southern version of the old Blue Point. The fame of the Chincoteague was spread originally by wealthy sportsmen who discovered it while hunting at Chincoteague Island off the Virginia coast, just below the Maryland line. Other Baltimoreans remain loyal to the Chesapeake Bay's Tangier oyster.

The most popular half-shell oyster in New York, though, is the Peconic Bay. All the oysters served at the Grand Central's bar are Peconic Bays, shipped from Greenport, and they are also used for oyster cocktails at such elite spots as The

Colony. Visitors from Europe, by the way, are somewhat puzzled by the small, round oyster crackers that are served here with oysters. In England and France, as in ancient Rome, raw oysters are eaten with buttered slices of coarse brown bread. European oyster connoisseurs do not swallow raw oysters whole as so many Americans do. They chew them.

There is a Great South Bay breakfast called Oysters and Onions that makes fine eating if you like onions and oysters. Slice enough small white onions—about a pound—to cover the bottom of a ten-inch frying pan. Pour a half pint of oyster liquor over the onions and let them simmer until they are transparent. Add about a quarter teaspoon of pepper and a teaspoon of salt and a good-sized chunk of butter—couple of tablespoons—and cook until the butter melts. Then cover the onions with a blanket of medium-sized oysters—about forty. Let them cook uncovered for five minutes and then cover the pan until the oysters begin to curl around the edges.

Serve each portion on a slice of toast, removing it from the pan with a pancake turner, so that the layers of oysters and onions will not be disarranged. The late Bob Davis, popular columnist of the old New York Sun, once ate such a breakfast at Massapequa before going duck shooting and described it as one of the great experiences of his life.

Plain fried oysters, without onions, are an old American stand-by. Some like them pan fried; others prefer deep fat, about 385° F. There are two things to remember about fried oysters. Before rolling the oysters in batter, make sure that they are dry. Drain them well and pat them between two towels. And don't fry them too long. Serve as soon as they are a light golden brown.

I was discussing oysters one afternoon recently with Royal Toner, of Greenport, a jovial man who has been growing and shipping them for many years. We talked about the poachers who prey on private beds and the Maryland law that requires oystermen to use sailboats and the preference in France for oysters with bright green shells. Toner held forth for a while on the value of the oyster as a source of protein. He feels strongly that the nation with the most protein will come out on top in today's muddled world. After an entertaining digression about the temptations to which Greenport oystermen were subjected by rum runners during prohibition, the conversation swung around to the future of the oyster.

"When I was a boy," Toner said, "there was an oyster bar on the corner of almost every city street. You'd walk in and the man would open an oyster and put it down on the bar in front of you. No nonsense about plates or cocktail sauce. When you ate that oyster, he'd open another one. As long as you kept on eating oysters, he'd keep on opening them. But not many young fellows in their twenties went into the oyster bars. Only older people. After I got into the oyster business, this worried me. I figured that after the older people died off, there wouldn't be any more call for oysters."

Toner puffed on his cigar and smiled.

"Well, I found out there's always a new generation of older people coming along," he said. "Youngsters don't know or care about good food anyway. Their idea of something to eat is a hot dog or a hamburger. When they get along toward thirty-five, they find out about oysters and begin to eat them. I got nothing to worry about. There'll always be enough people over thirty-five to keep me busy."

BAKED OYSTERS BORDELAISE

12 large oysters
12 deep half shells
1 teaspoon salt
½ teaspoon pepper
½ teaspoon orégano
4 tablespoons finely chopped
    shallots or green
    onions
1 teaspoon chopped
    tarragon
½ cup dry red wine
¾ cup bread crumbs
4 tablespoons butter

Start oven at hot (450° F.). Drain oysters, place one in each deep half shell, and arrange shells evenly in shallow baking pan. Mix salt, pepper and orégano and season oysters. Scatter chopped tarragon and shallots or onions over oysters, sprinkle each with a little red wine. Cover with crumbs and dot with butter. Bake in hot oven 5 to 8 minutes, or until surface is bubbly. Serve at once. Use 2 large spoons to lift hot shells to serving plates. Pour any pan sauce over oysters. Makes 4 appetizer servings.

NEW ORLEANS STUFFED BAKED OYSTERS

8 tablespoons butter
1 tablespoon flour
1 clove garlic, peeled and
    minced
1 tablespoon parsley, minced
1 tablespoon green onions,
    minced
24 large oysters, drained
    and finely chopped
3-ounce can chopped
    mushrooms
2 tablespoons sherry
24 deep half shells
1 cup fine cracker crumbs
1 tablespoon butter
Lemon wedges

Start oven at hot (425° F.). Melt butter in large saucepan, stir flour in smoothly and cook until lightly browned. Add garlic, parsley, and onions. Cook gently for 3 minutes, stirring. Add chopped oysters and drained mushrooms. Cook slowly 8 minutes, add sherry, mix. Fill shells, arrange in shallow baking pans. Cover with crumbs and dabs of butter. Bake for about 8 minutes or until tops are browned and bubbly. Serve at once, with wedges of lemon and a fine cold Chablis or dry Vouvray. Makes 6 servings.

VIRGINIA OYSTER AND TURKEY PIE

Puff pastry to cover top of
    deep pie dish
1 pint medium-sized oysters
    and their liquor
2 cups bite-sized pieces cold
    cooked turkey
Salt and pepper
Celery salt

Grated nutmeg
Butter
Few slices truffles or
    ripe olives
¼ cup turkey broth or
    oyster liquor
2 or 3 tablespoons heavy
    cream or sour cream

Make pastry, roll out to fit top of deep oval or round baking dish. Start oven at hot (425° F.). Scald oysters about 5 minutes in their liquor, drain, saving liquor. Place alternate layers of turkey and oysters in dish. Season each layer lightly with salt, pepper, celery salt, and a few grains nutmeg. Add small dabs of butter between layers and a few truffles and olives. Pour turkey broth or oyster liquor over, add cream. Fit pastry top in place and make decorative edge, crimping well to dish. Gash top in leaf-and-stem pattern to let steam escape. Bake for about 15 minutes or until pastry is golden and done. Makes 6 servings. When baked in individual casseroles, this is a favorite buffet supper or Sunday-brunch dish.

BUFFET OYSTERS WITH MUSHROOMS

12 large oysters, drained
4 tablespoons butter
12 thin slices hot buttered
    toast
16-ounce jar pâté de foie gras

6-ounce can sliced
    mushrooms
2 cups heavy cream
½ teaspoon celery salt
Paprika

Place butter in chafing dish, heat until slightly brown. Add oysters and cook 3 minutes or until edges curl. Spread hot buttered toast with pâté, place an oyster on each piece of toast. Arrange on warmed serving platters. Heat drained sliced mushrooms in cream, add seasonings, stir until steaming, but do not boil. Pour mushrooms and cream over oysters on toast. Serve at once. Makes 12 hors d'oeuvre.

OYSTERS EN COQUILLE

12 medium-sized oysters and
    their liquor
6 tablespoons butter
2 tablespoons minced
    parsley

½ cup chablis or other
    white wine
4 buttered scallop shells
½ tablespoon flour
½ cup bread crumbs

Start oven at moderate (375° F.). Pour oysters and their liquor into small saucepan, add 2 tablespoons butter, the parsley and wine. Heat to steaming, and continue cooking until oyster edges curl. Spoon 3 oysters into each scallop shell. Let sauce boil 1 or 2 minutes to reduce slightly. Blend flour and 2 tablespoons butter, stir into sauce and cook it until slightly thickened. Pour over oysters. Cover with crumbs. Add remaining 2 tablespoons butter in dabs over crumbs. Bake for about 10 minutes or until browned and bubbly. Serve at once. Makes 4 servings.

BAKED OYSTERS MORNAY

1 cup Mornay Sauce
Shallow baking pan half
    filled with coarse salt
6 large oyster shells
12 large oysters and their
    liquor

⅜ cup grated Parmesan
    cheese
¼ cup melted butter

Make Mornay Sauce. Start oven at very hot (475° F.). Place oyster shells (deep halves only) firmly on salt in baking pan. Place generous spoonful of Mornay Sauce in each shell. Heat oysters in their liquor in a saucepan until steaming and oyster edges begin to curl. Drain oysters, place 2 in each half shell, cover with an additional tablespoon of Mornay Sauce. Sprinkle with cheese, add dabs of melted butter and set in very hot oven about 6 minutes, or until top is glazed. Serve at once, using 2 large spoons to lift shells to guests' plates. Makes 6 servings.

MORNAY SAUCE

1 cup hot Béchamel Sauce,
    made with fish stock
1 tablespoon grated Gruyère
    cheese

1 tablespoon grated
    Parmesan cheese
2 tablespoons butter

Beat into the Béchamel Sauce the cheeses. Let sauce remain over heat, but do not boil, until cheese melts. Stir, remove from heat and beat in gradually butter in bits. Makes about 1¼ cups sauce.

HERB-SEASONED OYSTER PANCAKES

12 oysters and their liquor
¼ cup thick Béchamel
    Sauce, made with fish
    stock
Salt and pepper
1 tablespoon minced parsley
¼ teaspoon grated nutmeg
½ teaspoon mixed basil and
    orégano

1½ cups sifted all-purpose
    flour
2½ teaspoons baking
    powder
¾ teaspoon salt
1 egg, well-beaten
1¼ cups milk
4 tablespoons shortening,
    melted

Poach oysters in their liquor 5 minutes. Drain; cut in small dice; mix with just enough thick Béchamel Sauce to hold together. Add salt, pepper, nutmeg and the herbs. Blend well. Let stand.

Make pancakes. Sift flour, baking powder and salt together twice. Combine egg, milk, and melted shortening. Pour into flour mixture and stir just enough to blend with dry ingredients. Do not beat. Bake on hot griddle, about ¼ cup batter to each cake. Makes 1 dozen large cakes, 1½ dozen smaller ones.

Start oven at hot (425° F.). Spread each pancake with layer of oyster mixture, roll up, place rolls in buttered ovenware serving dish. Brown in hot oven about 10 minutes. Serve at once. One small or 2 large rolls make a serving. Recipe makes 6 servings. A spoonful of any preferred sauce, such as light curry-flavored cream sauce, Mornay or mushroom sauce is usually served with these pancakes.

Caviar: The Costliest Food / *Lucius Beebe*

**A celebrated bon vivant explores the romance
of one of the oldest epicurean delights—caviar**

WHEN the late Ernest Byfield, genius of the Ambassador Hotels and the Sherman in Chicago, died, the "office" of Caliph of Caviar in the United States was briefly without occupant. For years Byfield, whose Pump Room and Buttery at the Ambassadors and Well of the Sea at the Sherman had come to be national shrines of good living, had a way with caviar, a commodity which lends itself to specialized exploitation and with which the name of a fervent amateur or promoter may become forever associated like Daniel Webster and Medford rum or Dr. S. Weir Mitchell and Madeira.

Byfield cherished caviar. He loved to eat it himself in liberal quantities and he delighted in seeing patrons at the Pump Room order it, preferably accompanied by the best Latvian vodka and served from special rolling tables decorated with a likeness of a Russian mosque.

Byfield's interest in the promotion of caviar, despite his own cynical comments to the contrary, wasn't entirely commercial. There is little profit in the sale of so perishable a commodity and one which has so limited a market. He liked to see it on his patron's plates because of the cachet of elegance associated with sturgeons' eggs. They appear on menus of the classic age of Roman imperialism along with sows' udders, thrushes' tongues and other delicacies valued by such spenders as Trimalchio, the fictional parvenu and glutton of note, and they achieved immortality in Elizabethan pentameter when Shakespeare, in Hamlet, remarked that an intelligent play "was caviare to the general," implying that its appeal was to the educated alone.

Not everyone could appreciate caviar even though he might be able to afford it, and Byfield went the competition one better by serving his beluga with shredded pheasant's breast, an exclamatory panache quite in keeping with the Pump Room's haughty décor, which includes footmen in knee breeches.

After Byfield's untimely passing (there is a legend that he died as a result of dieting so as to be able to get behind the wheel of a Jaguar) the post of Caviar Caliph was only briefly vacant, for almost immediately the choice of gourmets everywhere had lighted on Henri Soulé, proprietor of the irreproachable Pavillon Restaurant in New York's Fifty-seventh Street. It is probable that Soulé, who is the ranking perfectionist of the American restaurant scene, actually knows more about caviar and possesses more feeling for it than did Byfield, who was strictly a promoter.

Soulé doesn't print the price of his "fresh beluga" on the menu, but it comes to better than $7.50 a serving, if you are interested, and he sells, it is said, $36,000 worth of it a year. For special customers like the Duke of Windsor and Bernard Baruch, he opens a new five-pound tin with each serving on the theory, perhaps demonstrable to such exalted diners, that once exposed to the air the eggs have a tendency to adhere slightly to one another.

Soulé personally purchases caviar for the Pavillon, selecting

Caviar feast on the high seas. Halfway between Southampton ▶ and New York, an officer aboard the luxury liner SS *United States* entertains at a magnificent repast built around beluga malossol.

ARNOLD NEWMAN

28

on an average of one tin out of every half-dozen submitted by wholesalers. "Those are for you," he says arbitrarily, in rejecting samples that don't live up to his rigorous standards. "This one is for my patrons."

Even though its appreciation by gourmets and the initiated goes back to the banquet couches of imperial Rome, caviar in the United States hasn't always been in such exalted brackets as it now occupies. Many old-time New Yorkers remember when, along with the Kentucky ham, Cape Cod oysters and dark rye bread, caviar was on free-lunch counters at such well-remembered institutions as the Knickerbocker, the old Waldorf and the Holland House. In the writer's file is a Denver & Rio Grande dining-car menu from the days when the railroad's entire trackage was narrow gauge, advertising caviar at two bits, the same price as queen olives and celery, while oysters commanded twice as much.

These footnotes to an ample era stem from the time when processing sturgeon for its roe was a considerable American industry and by no means a monopoly of Russia and Persia as it is today. The caviar industry in the United States was a victim of the industrial age as waters became polluted and the sturgeon became fewer in the Great Lakes and the coastal rivers of the Atlantic seaboard.

Virtually all the caviar served in American restaurants today comes from inside the U.S.S.R. or from the Caspian waters under the sovereignty of the Iranian government. Probably more than 90 per cent of the caviar, both the so-called fresh and the processed eggs, is imported to the United States by four agencies: the Romanoff Caviar Company of New York, Jules Weber of West Forty-second Street, the Iron Gate Corporation, which is an offshoot of Jack and Charlie's celebrated "21" Club, and Vita Food Products, also in New York.

Carrying inventories which in the case of Romanoff may run as high as $300,000, these four firms import all the lightly salted sturgeon roe which appears in the several classifications of fresh caviar and distribute it to retailers and restaurants throughout the United States. Romanoff also imports vast quantities of the more heavily salted eggs which are processed, pasteurized and sold in sealed containers by delicatessen shops and grocers everywhere. Jules Weber and the Iron Gate company specialize in the costly and highly perishable fresh caviar which may appear on menus in New York, Hollywood and Palm Beach at $7.50 or even $10 a portion.

An hour spent some time ago with Charles Aubry, then with the firm of Jules Weber, constituted a liberal education in the realm of caviar.

"Even among experts appearance and eye appeal in caviar may be highly deceptive," said Mr. Aubry. "The size of the eggs and the type of fish from which they are taken determine their classification. Beluga, which comes from Caspian sturgeon weighing up to 2000 pounds, is the largest egg. A medium size called osetra is taken from fish running up to 300 pounds and the smallest size, sevruga, comes from a sturgeon weighing no more than 150 pounds. Malossol is Russian for 'little salt' and the product sold everywhere in the United States as 'fresh' caviar is beluga, osetra or sevruga to which has been added no more than two per cent salt, the absolute minimum necessary to preserve it for export. In most European countries borax rather than salt is used to preserve fresh caviar, but this is forbidden in this country by the Pure Food and Drug Act."

The word caviar itself is not Russian, but Turkish: *khavyah*,

and applies only to sturgeon roe after it has been salted. Until preservative is added, it is simply roe. *Paiusnaya* is the Russian name for pressed caviar much favored by Continental gourmets and Russians themselves, but not frequently encountered in America, although sold by Romanoff in their Gold Seal and Blue Seal packages. *Schipp* is the medium-size sturgeon which yields osetra caviar and there is a so-called red caviar obtained from salmon, but it is not caviar in the precise meaning of the word. Sterlet is the almost legendary gold caviar, all of which was once reserved for the tables of the Czars, and which today is probably served only to high-ranking Soviet officials.

"I have been served sterlet," says Colonel Malcolm K. Beyer of the Iron Gate firm, "but it was in Russia many years ago. It is truly a very superior product, but it's one with which we simply don't concern ourselves in this country. On the other hand, the borax-preserved beluga and osetra are familiar to many Americans.

"The vast quantities of caviar that used to be served at parties at the Russian embassy in Washington were all of this type, and it is sweeter than the eggs preserved with salt."

Most of the fresh caviar now coming to America arrives via Leningrad packed in tins holding two kilos or about four and a half pounds each. The tins are placed in wooden casks of crude construction, bound in willow hoops with woven reeds for insulation. Everything is covered with ice from the Volga, which lasts all the way to New York. Each tin is numbered, the number corresponding to that of a particular fish, and fanciers such as Mr. Soulé are thus able to place repeat orders for the roe of a specific sturgeon which excites their admiration.

Temperature is the great risk factor in selling all fresh caviar. It must be stored between 27° and 30° F.; it does not freeze at these temperatures because of its large oil content. Once frozen, it is worthless—it disintegrates on thawing out. Fresh caviar reaching a temperature above 40° for more than a few hours is spoiled.

Caviar en route to America is insured at fairly moderate rates, but everyone connected with the trade remembers with a shudder the great caviar catastrophe which shook the trade the year before World War II. In some manner never yet explained a shipment valued at more than $100,000 was stowed in the refrigerated hold of a trans-Atlantic liner and arrived in New York frozen solid. Cream of the spring catch, too, and not an ounce of the precious stuff was edible. The insurance companies paid—almost literally—on the barrel-head, and shipping circles heard about the matter for months.

Considering its de luxe implications and the accustomed elegance of its service, fresh caviar arrives in almost no style at all. The two-kilo tins are beat up, unsightly, and their joints are sealed with broad bands of rubber. This permits flexibility, and allows the eggs to settle during passage, which they frequently do.

Asked what restaurateur was the most sophisticated of his firm's customers, Charles Aubry unhesitatingly named Henri Soulé, with the parenthetical addition that he was also the most difficult to please. When Mr. Soulé needed fresh stock for Le Pavillon, Mr. Aubry in person was likely to wait upon him, Mr. Soulé having a short way with anyone except the heads of firms.

"Another excellent customer is Dave Chasen from Hollywood," said Mr. Aubry. "He will wait until an hour before his plane is scheduled to leave for the Coast and then come over here to the warehouse, pick out half a dozen tins and take them back with him personally. In this way he can be sure it's handled properly."

The New York market is by far the most important in the United States, according to Aubry. Florida is good but, of course, seasonal. Soulé, the Pierre, Chateaubriand and the St. Regis are prized Manhattan customers.

In Manhattan the leading outlets for fresh caviar, at the current market bringing $32 a pound, are Shaffer's Market, the Madison Grocery, Ellen Grey, Martin's Fruit Shop, Vendôme and Charles & Co., all of which, except the Madison Grocery, are on Madison Avenue, making it the world's most opulent beluga bazaar.

Colonel Beyer, whose Iron Gate firm customarily handles a big share of the country's malossol imports, is a sevruga fan, although he admits that the biggest demand, especially at "21," is for the big, gray, well-separated eggs of the beluga category. He recommends a spread made with about equal parts of the pressed product and thick sour cream, which he says tops all cocktail canapés he has ever encountered.

"Our firm has about half a dozen real caviar aficionados who aren't dealers," says Colonel Beyer. "They rush over as soon as they hear we have a fresh shipment and take home a few tins after sampling and comparing for hours at a time."

Something of a mystery to executives of the Iron Gate company is a French gentleman named Joseph Gerney who turns up at Christmas-time and sends one-pound gifts of the best beluga to about 100 friends. Between seasons he's never seen in Fifty-second Street.

Details of the service of caviar vary with different establishments, although not widely. With the exception of the Ambassador Hotels in Chicago, which perpetuate the memory of Ernie Byfield by serving a side dish of shredded breast of pheasant or guinea hen, general practice demands that the eggs appear packed in a container on ice flanked by chopped onions, shredded whites and yolks of eggs, sliced lemon and grated parsley. The caviar is spread generously on slices of not-too-dry white-bread toast and flavored with the egg, lemon and parsley to taste.

Purists maintain that anything but lemon juice and perhaps a tiny touch of parsley spoils the flavor of really fine caviar, and just wave a quarter of lemon vaguely over their eggs in the manner in which extra-dry-Martini fanatics wave the vermouth in the general direction of the shaker.

A variation favored by many knowing gourmets is to pile the best eggs liberally on wafer-thin Russian pancakes called *blini*, and douse the arrangement with quantities of sour cream and melted butter. In fact, the caviar-aux-*blini* school of thought embraces many notable gastronomes and may be said to be the last word in sophisticated appreciation of the product. Delicatessen fans like to encase pressed caviar between slices of rich black bread liberally flavored with raw onion. Reuben's in New York runs up a very tasty sandwich for $5.50 which finds favor with theatrical celebrities.

What to drink with caviar occasions endless debate among true believers. Cognoscenti hold out for vodka, preferably the Latvian variety that runs to 120 proof and will start a fire if carelessly handled. Others say soubrovka, aquavit or any of the Scandinavian and Slavic schnapps will do very well indeed. Great numbers of folk find no trouble in going along with a dry Martini.

"Best of all drinks with caviar," says Fred Wildman, a celebrated New York *viveur* and wine salesman of the old school, "is the very driest champagne, preferably I'd say a vintage Perrier-Jouet." Mr. Wildman should know. He sells the stuff.

SAUCE RUSSE, CARÊME

2 tablespoons sieved or pounded cooked lobster
2 tablespoons fresh black caviar
1 cup mayonnaise
1 teaspoon prepared French mustard

Blend and mash lobster and caviar together in mixing bowl. Put through sieve. Mix into mayonnaise with mustard. Chill. Makes 1¼ cups sauce. Serve with cold sea food, cold fish mousse and on hot boiled or broiled salmon, broiled lobster tails and crab cakes.

SOLE VARSOVIENNE

1½ pounds fillets of sole
Salt and pepper
2 cups court bouillon
2 or 3 tablespoons Béchamel or cream sauce
2 tablespoons Caviar Butter

Season fillets, place in saucepan, add court bouillon, and bring to boil. Reduce heat and poach gently for 15 minutes, or until fish is done. Remove fish to warmed serving dish. Strain sauce, reheat rapidly to reduce to about one cup. Add Béchamel or cream sauce, stir; add Caviar Butter, stir and heat for 1 or 2 minutes over low heat. Pour over sole and serve. Makes 4 servings.

SOLE À LA SOYER

1 pound very thin fillets
  of sole
Salt and pepper
½ cup very thick creamed
  fish or lobster
2 cups court bouillon
Aspic
2 large cucumbers

Boiling water
Fresh caviar
1 cup mayonnaise
3 tablespoons finely diced
  cold boiled lobster
2 tablespoons caviar

Season fillets lightly with salt and pepper. Spread each fillet with a little creamed fish or lobster and roll up with the filling inside. Tie round once or twice with white thread so rolls hold their shape. Place rolls in saucepan, pour court bouillon over them and bring to boil over moderate heat. Reduce heat and poach gently 15 minutes, or until fish is done. Drain rolls, let cool. Cut thread and remove. Coat rolls with aspic, chill.

Wash cucumbers, score from top to bottom with prongs of kitchen fork. Cut cucumbers in 1-inch chunks, cover with boiling water, let stand 5 minutes. Drain, hollow out slices, chill. Fill each hollowed slice with roll of sole, place on chilled serving platter. Surround rolls with mounds of caviar. Serve with a cold sauce made by combining mayonnaise, lobster and 2 tablespoons caviar. Makes 6 or more servings.

ASPIC

1 tablespoon plain gelatin
½ cup cold fish stock
  or bouillon
1 cup boiling stock
  or bouillon

⅛ teaspoon salt
¼ cup lemon juice

Sprinkle gelatin on cold stock or bouillon to soften. Add boiling stock or bouillon, salt, and stir until dissolved. Add lemon juice, stir. Let stand until the consistency of egg white then use as called for in recipe. Makes about 1½ cups aspic.

Caviar in small puff paste tart shells is used as garnish for various cold dishes of fish in aspic.

RUSSIAN EMBASSY VEAL
WITH CAVIAR SAUCE

4-pound boned roast from
  leg of veal
¼ pound sliced salt pork
2 small shallots, peeled
  and sliced
2 sprigs parsley
2 stalks celery and leaves,
  chopped
2 bay leaves
3 cloves

1 tablespoon grated lemon
  peel
Grind of pepper
1½ cups dry white wine
Flour
1 teaspoon lemon juice
1 tablespoon water
2 or 3 tablespoons fresh
  black caviar

Have meat dealer lard the veal roast with a few thin strips of fat salt pork. Place sliced salt pork, vegetables, herbs, spice and lemon peel in heavy pot. Place veal on top of these. Cook over high heat for 20 minutes, stir pork frequently to prevent burning. Turn veal to brown all sides. Add grind of fresh pepper. Pour on wine, cover pot and cook over low heat for 1½ hours. Turn veal 2 or 3 times.

When meat is done remove roast to a hot platter, slice it. Re-form roast, do not spread slices out on the platter. Keep roast in warm oven, with door open. Strain the pot sauce, skim off excess fat. Reheat and thicken with a little flour, stir and let boil for 1 or 2 minutes. Add lemon juice and water, stir and boil 1 minute. Strain quickly, reheat, add caviar, stir and pour over meat. Serve at once. Makes 8 servings.

CAVIAR SAUCE STALINGRAD,
FOR SALMON STEAKS

2 salmon steaks about
  1½ inches thick
Olive oil
Salt
Freshly ground pepper
1 cup thick hot cream sauce

2 beaten egg yolks
1 teaspoon lemon juice
2 tablespoons anchovy
  butter
2 tablespoons fresh caviar
1 tablespoon butter

Rinse salmon, pat dry. Rub steaks with a little oil, then rub salt and pepper well into both sides. Broil under moderate heat 10 minutes. Turn steaks once or twice, adding a little oil if they seem dry. Beat egg yolks and lemon juice into hot cream sauce. When steaks are done, place them on warm serving platter and spread top side with anchovy butter. Stir caviar and butter into cream sauce, pour over steaks and serve at once. Makes 2 to 4 servings.

CAVIAR-AUX-BLINI

Russian cooks say that their pancakes—blini—are no different from well-made American pancakes; but most Russians prefer their pancakes made with yeast-raised buckwheat batter and baked in thick cakes 3 inches wide. To eat these blini the Russian way, spread them, hot from the griddle, with melted butter, and then add a spoonful of caviar and a dab of sour cream. Serve very hot.

CAVIAR BUTTER, CARÊME

4 tablespoons fresh black
  caviar

6 tablespoons butter

Mash caviar thoroughly with spoon in mixing bowl. Cream thoroughly with butter. Press through fine sieve. Chill. Makes 10 tablespoons caviar butter. Add to sauces for fish. Also spread on thin buttered toast cut for canapés, garnish with fresh or pressed caviar, surround with narrow piped ruffle border of creamed butter.

◄ Henri Soulé, the perfect restaurateur, serving caviar Malossol at what to many is the perfect restaurant, Le Pavillon.

His Highness the Lobster / *Joe McCarthy*

*There is no substitute for the Down-East lobster—
boiled and steaming hot—and served with plenty of melted butter*

JONESPORT is a village on the far Down-East extremity of the Maine coast that makes its living on fish, lobsters and sardine canning. People who remember the A & P Gypsies and Tony Wons and Singin' Sam, the Barbasol Man, may recall Jonesport as the town that was used as the setting for Seth Parker's hymn and prayer meetings, a popular Sunday-evening radio program of many years ago. It sticks in my mind for another reason. At lunchtime one September day, in the sunny kitchen of John Young, the Jonesport doctor, I ate the best lobster I ever tasted.

That morning I had gone along with Dr. Young in a motorboat when he made calls at the homes of the fishermen who live on nearby Beals Island. When we came back to the mainland, he drove to a weatherbeaten cottage at the water's edge where an old man in heavy rubber boots was sitting in the sun, mending a lobster trap. Dr. Young playfully asked him a highly intimate question about his marital life, which amused the old man immensely. The people along that part of the coast think Dr. Young is wonderful.

When Dr. Young went into the cottage to talk with the old man's wife about her diabetes diet, the old man walked down to the water. Standing upright in a small rowboat and pushing on the oars with short, gentle strokes, he rowed out to his lobster pound. In a few minutes he was back with half a dozen black-green lobsters, shining and squirming in a cardboard box. He placed the box in the back of Dr. Young's car. When the doctor came out of the cottage, he talked seriously with the old man about his wife. In characteristic Maine fashion, the old man did not mention the lobsters. Dr. Young did not discover them until we arrived back at his office.

We ate them an hour later, the way lobsters are always served in Maine homes and the way they are almost never served in restaurants—boiled and steaming hot, right out of the bubbling pot of sea water, with plenty of melted butter. When I order a boiled lobster in a restaurant, the waitress usually misunderstands my pronunciation and brings a broiled one. I prefer plain boiled lobster, either hot or cold, to broiled lobster. Very few cooks know how to broil a lobster without cooking away the sea water that gives it taste and flavor. Practically everybody I know in Maine feels the same way.

Those lobsters from the old man's traps were incredibly good, sweet, firm and full of the clean taste of the ocean. Eating them was one of the great experiences of my life. But when I exclaimed over them, Barbara Young, the doctor's wife, assumed that I was merely being a polite guest. Her father runs a smack that carries lobsters from Jonesport and Nova Scotia to the national dealers on McLoon's Wharf in Rockland and she has been eating the best lobsters in the world since she was a baby.

"If you think *these* lobsters taste good," Mrs. Young said, "you ought to eat lobsters the way we like to eat them down

A small short-tined fork, an implement to crack the claws, and ▶ lemon cut in quarters are the only paraphernalia necessary to enjoy this feast from the sea—the boiled lobster.

ARNOLD NEWMAN

here. We get a gang of friends together and build a fire on the rocks beside the ocean. We fill up a couple of big kettles with sea water and throw in some rock weed for flavor and then boil the lobsters. And we dump a few pecks of steamer clams into the same pots with the lobsters. Then we sit around on the rocks, with the wind blowing on our faces, and eat lobsters and clams until we're ready to burst. There's nothing like it."

"By the way," Dr. Young added, "don't believe that stuff about the vein in the lobster being poisonous. The lobstermen around here will tell you there's no part of the lobster you can't eat. They're right."

The waters of Maine supply only a fraction of the lobster America consumes. The Maine name, when used as an adjective to describe a lobster, has become a loose, generic term. Any North Atlantic lobster, either from New England or the Maritime Provinces of Canada, is now called a Maine lobster. More than half our live lobsters come from Canada, which catches and sells twice as many as Maine. And most of the canned lobster meat is shipped from New Brunswick, Nova Scotia, Prince Edward Island, Newfoundland and Quebec. The Canadians have an advantage over our canners because they can cook baby lobsters below the minimum size required by the Maine conservation law.

Another considerable portion of the lobster meat being eaten in America is the frozen rock-lobster tails that are imported from South Africa, Australia, South America and Mexico at the rate of 20,000,000 pounds a year—as much as the native Maine catch. Maine lobstermen refer scornfully to the imported rock lobster as "crayfish." This is not accurate. Crayfish is a fresh-water crustacean. Rock lobster is the salt-water shellfish that some sources identify as spiny lobster, or salt-water crayfish, and that the French call *langouste*. As anybody who has eaten *langouste* in Paris knows very well, rock lobster can be delicious when it is cooked alive and fresh. Whether a rock lobster could ever compete, even in its freshest condition, with any of the world's three regular lobsters—the American, or Maine lobster, the European lobster and the Norwegian lobster—is a matter of warm dispute.

However, the crustacean cannot be frozen without losing much of its original flavor. The blood that gives a lobster's meat its distinctive taste is composed mostly of sea water. When the meat is frozen, the blood turns into ice which melts and runs out when the lobster is thawed. The freezing of the imported rock-lobster tail makes it, in the opinion of fussy sea-food cooks, a product that lacks a first-class taste and texture. New York's oldest seafood restaurant, Sweet's, on Fulton Street, refuses to serve imported tails.

Other restaurants and dealers like the frozen rock-lobster meat because it is less expensive and easier to handle and store than thrashing live lobsters and because it can be kept indefinitely. Some eating places use South African tails for lobster salads and Newburgs, figuring that the customers will never know the difference, and one restaurant has even had the effrontery to advertise frozen tails on its menus as "Cape Cod Lobster."

Despite its spreading popularity, the lobster still occupies an aloof position in the upper crust of the American food world. Outside of a few parts of New England, where it is cooked as casually as ham and eggs, people are in awe of it. They think of it as a luxury that should be reserved for special and extravagant occasions, like champagne and Baked Alaska. Most of the lobsters that are eaten in the United States are

served in restaurants to visitors from out of town who are in a celebrating mood. The restaurant that probably does the biggest lobster business in the world is Hackney's in Atlantic City, which is purely a holiday resort. Places like Ireland's in Chicago, Pieroni's in Boston and The Lobster, on 45th Street off Times Square in New York, all say that tourists eat lobsters heavily on trips to conventions and sporting events because they seldom get a taste of it at home.

Most housewives claim that cooking lobster at home is too much trouble. They are afraid that a lobster will bite them. A lot of women also say that the act of plunging a live lobster into a pot of boiling water, or splitting it with a knife to broil it, makes them feel like murderers. The Massachusetts Society for the Prevention of Cruelty to Animals has delved into the problem of how to cook a lobster humanely. The Society recommends soaking the crustacean first in a mixture of two quarts of cold water and a pound of salt. Softhearted cooks are assured that the lobster will pass out cold in this anesthesia and can be boiled or sliced within the next five minutes without "visible signs of discomfort."

Fortunately, my own wife has no scruples about slaying a lobster. We eat lobsters often at our house when we are alone and my wife regards cold boiled lobster as an ideal meal to serve to company.

"I hate to be working in the kitchen when everybody else is having drinks in the living room," she says. "I hate to miss all that conversation. When we have lobsters, I can boil them early in the afternoon and set them out to cool and forget about them. All I need to serve with them is a mixed green salad and baked potatoes, or potato chips, and melted butter. I don't need to worry about gravy or sauces. If we decide to have another drink, there is nothing in the oven or under the broiler that might spoil. So I can sit in the living room and mingle. And when the guests see a whole lobster on their plates, they feel they're getting something very de luxe."

There is nothing more simple than boiling a lobster. You take the whole lobster, without cracking the shell or removing any of the insides, and drop it into a pot of briskly boiling salted water. After the water comes to a boil the second time, leave the lobster in the pot from 10 to 15 minutes, depending on its size. That's all there is to it.

Broiling a lobster is something else again. It is like broiling a steak—it depends on the heat of the broiler, the size of the lobster and, most of all, on your own judgment. There is no hard-and-fast rule. The recipe books tell you to split the lobster down through the middle of the body and the tail, to crack the claws and to remove the roe and the dark vein that runs through the tail, and to broil it eight or ten minutes on the exposed meat side and six or eight minutes on the shell side. Some people spread a seasoned cracker-crumb or bread dressing on the meat. Others prefer to smear it with plenty of butter.

But every cook seems to have his own method. Take, for example, the late Aristides Bordone, who worked for many years at Christ Cella's, one of the very best steak and lobster restaurants in New York, and later with his brother, Euclide, ran the Casa Bordone, a fine country dining room at Coram, Long Island. He sprinkled the split lobster with olive oil, salt and pepper and a touch of A.1 Sauce and put it under the flame for ten minutes. Then he put it in the oven for another ten or fifteen minutes. It came out moist and delectable. At Hugo's and Kimball's in Cohasset, Massachusetts, two of the most famous New England lobster houses, they follow the same system—ten minutes of broiling to seal in the juices and then the oven to cook it through.

This keeping the moisture in the meat is, of course, the difficult part of broiling a lobster. John Carzis, the proprietor of both Hugo's and Kimball's, feels that retaining the moisture is not so much a trick of cooking. "You've got to keep them in a tank of freshly pumped ocean water until a few minutes before you broil them," Carzis says. "The longer they're out of water, the dryer they'll be."

I asked Carzis a while ago why seafood restaurants serve so many broiled lobsters and so few of the hot boiled lobsters that are preferred by the folks in Maine.

"I think that most customers have gotten into the habit of ordering broiled lobsters simply because they look more attractive on the plate," he says. "It is true that the real connoisseurs prefer plain hot boiled lobster, with the shell whole and unopened. But we get very little call for them. It must be because they don't look as pretty as broiled lobsters."

Anyway, broiling a lobster takes a delicate touch. If I were you, I'd boil it instead.

If you have time on your hands, a Maine-style lobster stew is a great dish. At the big-city seafood bars, a lobster stew is thrown together in a few minutes, like an oyster stew. Up in Maine it takes a couple of days. To serve four people, you first boil a pound-and-a-half lobster. Remove the green tomalley—which is the liver—and the white, fatty stuff, which happens to be blood, and the red roe and simmer them in a large pot with a half cup of butter for eight minutes. The lobster meat, cut in large pieces, is added to this mixture and cooked over slow heat 10 minutes.

Then you push the pot back on the stove and let it cool. After it is cooled, you pour in a quart of creamy milk very slowly, a dribble at a time, while you stir the stew constantly. Then you let it stand in the pot in a cool place for at least six hours. Maine people say that every extra hour of standing improves the flavor. They recommend two days. After it has been standing, you simply reheat it and serve it.

"You got to remember to pour that milk into the kettle ever so slowly," a character in Gouldsboro once told me. "Just a little trickle now and then while you keep astirring. After a while the stew comes up a handsome pink. That's when it's ready to be aged, like whisky."

Many people order lobster Newburg or lobster salad instead of boiled or broiled lobster because they think that taking a lobster apart is too much trouble. Once you get the hang of it, digging out a lobster is a pleasure.

We break off the tail by bending it back, and twist off the claws from the body. The claws are broken open with a nutcracker. Some people get the meat from the tail by breaking off the tail flippers and pushing the meat out with a small fork. We usually split the tail before we serve the lobster and the meat can then be lifted out easily.

There is not much meat in the remaining upper part of the body, but don't be afraid to eat the soft green tomalley. It is wonderful. Tomalley, by the way, makes a fine hors d'oeuvre to serve with cocktails when it is mixed with a little Worcestershire sauce and spread on crackers. And, of course, you finish the lobster by breaking off the small claws and sucking the sweet strands of meat out of them.

Lobsters in North America are found along the Atlantic coast from Cape Hatteras to Labrador. Because those waters have been getting warmer in recent years, hard-shelled cherrystone and littleneck clams and the destructive green crabs have been advancing from Long Island and Cape Cod into the shores of New Hampshire and Maine and the lobsters, along with cod, have been retreating farther north. They are now caught in quantity only above Cape Ann in Massachusetts. New York and Long Island used to have busy lobster fleets. Up until 1930, traps were set daily in New York Harbor, from the Statue of Liberty to Sandy Hook. The only lobstering in New York today is done by a few boats from Brooklyn that work in the Mud Hole, a fishing ground in the ocean southeast of Ambrose Lightship. The once-famous Montauk lobster is a thing of the past. The biggest lobster firm in Montauk—Perry Duryea and Son—brings its lobsters by boat from Maine and Nova Scotia. The last lobsterman in Port Jefferson, on Long Island Sound, went out of business years ago. The local lobsters that are sold on Long Island are mostly caught unintentionally in the nets of fishing trawlers.

Fishing nets often snare huge lobsters that cannot be bought from lobster dealers. The Maine law forbids the taking of lobsters less than three and one-eighth inches and more than five inches from eye sockets to the beginning of flippers. A five-pounder is too big to enter a lobster trap, anyway. My wife bought a mess of lobsters from a fisherman on the south shore of Long Island a few months ago and one of them was a monster of seven and a half pounds. A lobster that big does not broil well, but this one boiled excellently and the meat was fine. My wife and I had all we could do to finish the tail between us. The claws made a good-sized salad for lunch the following day.

The biggest American lobster on the record book is a forty-two-pounder caught off Virginia in 1935. Its shell is now in the Boston Museum of Science. Fully formed lobsters in the ocean measure as small as five-eighths of an inch in length. When they are born, they float on top of the water until they grow a shell and most of them are eaten in infancy by fishes. After the shell forms, they dive to the bottom and find a home under a rock. In his first year, a lobster will shed his shell and grow a larger one as often as twenty times. It takes about six years for him to reach the weight of one pound. A mature lobster molts, or sheds its shell and grows a new one, once a year, in the spring or early summer.

Lobstering is a rugged and risky way of earning a living. A man with a hundred traps may haul up 300 lobsters in a morning, but the next day he is likely to find only a few, and these may be smaller than the legal minimum size. A bad storm can wreck or wash away his traps and put him out of business for many weeks. A loss of forty traps, at today's prices, can be a loss of several hundred dollars. The traps are cratelike semicylindrical boxes, about thirty by twenty-six inches, that are lowered to the rocky bottom of the ocean. They are baited with dead fish.

From March until July, when the lobsters are shedding and mating, they hibernate and are hard to catch. After their shells harden, they come out of retirement searching for food. The catch becomes plentiful for the next four months, but the price goes down.

In the winter, the prices are high but the work is punishing and discouraging. A man who works 150 traps on a summer morning is doing well if he can handle 60 traps in a whole day in January. As the cold weather sets in, the lobsters move away from the shore into deeper water. The lobsterman travels in the freezing wind and angry waves three or four miles out to sea and, because the bottom is twice as deep, the hauling of each trap takes twice as much time and labor.

State of Mainers are calm and independent people, to whom money is unimportant. Most of them prefer not to be bothered with the hardships and dangers of winter lobstering. " 'Taint worth it," an old salt at Small Point observed recently. "Last winter Guy Johnson at Cundys Harbor tied up that boat he built himself, the Laura E., and worked ashore as an automobile salesman. Freeman Young over at Popham Beach, he took a job in Bath and didn't set a trap until the last week in April. Can't blame 'em. If them dealers in Rockland want lobsters in winter, let 'em buy 'em from the crazy Nova Scotians and Newfoundlanders. Why should we risk our necks so a millionaire can dress up in a Tuxedo suit and buy his lady friend lobster thermidor at the Waldorf-Astoria?"

Along with the housewife's reluctance to cook it, a strong factor that has kept the lobster from becoming a home dish is the suburban supermarket's reluctance to sell it. The stores are leery of live lobster and fresh lobster meat because it can-

not be stored for a length of time. It is likely to turn into a dead loss overnight. A group of leaders in the lobster industry have recently formed The North Atlantic Lobster Institute, which is promoting long-overdue improvements in shipping and storing lobsters. Progress has been made in the development of chemically salted water tanks for maintaining lobsters in stores and in restaurants. "The tank is going to make a big change in this business," one Institute man says.

In the past, lobsters have been shipped successfully only when packed in ice. Dry ice, like fresh water, kills them. Ice packing is not ideal, because ice is heavy and bulky and has a tendency to melt. Some lobsters are now being shipped as far as California in hermetically sealed cans that have no ice. The cans have a chemical solution that keeps the temperature of the water inside constant. It seems that the lobster does not have to be kept especially cold; the thing that injures him is a sudden change in temperature. After six or seven days in the sealed can, the lobster comes out alive and sparring.

LOBSTER NEWBURG

1 2-pound lobster, freshly boiled or 2 cups canned or quick-frozen lobster	1 cup light cream (approximately)
3 tablespoons butter	¼ cup heavy cream
⅛ teaspoon salt	1 egg yolk, beaten
¼ teaspoon cayenne	6 or 8 toast points or a crisp puff-paste ring shell
3 tablespoons sherry	
1 tablespoon cognac	Few slices truffles

The lobster for this dish should be cooked in court bouillon (recipe on p. 39). When done, let cool in cooking liquid. Remove, cut and crack shells, remove all meat and cut in slices. Sauté meat gently in butter in a chafing dish or saucepan until golden. Add seasonings. Sprinkle with sherry and cognac; let sauce cook down slightly; then add enough light cream to cover lobster. Cook gently for 3 or 4 minutes. Mix heavy cream and beaten egg yolk together and pour into lobster mixture. Stir for 1 or 2 minutes until hot. Do not boil. Serve at once on toast points or in puff paste shell. Garnish with truffle slices. Makes 4 or more servings.

LOBSTER PAELLA

2 lobsters, freshly boiled	1 teaspoon salt
¼ cup olive oil	½ teaspoon ground pepper
2 cloves garlic, peeled and chopped	1 teaspoon saffron
4 tomatoes, skinned, seeded and chopped	2 cups hot water or fish stock
4 sweet red peppers, seeded and chopped	1 cup cooked peas
1 cup rice, uncooked	6 small artichokes, trimmed and cooked

Remove all lobster meat from shells, cut into good-sized chunks. Heat oil in deep saucepan or flame-proof casserole. Sauté garlic 5 minutes, remove and discard it. Brown lobster lightly in same hot oil. Remove lobster. Add tomatoes and peppers to hot oil and cook 8 minutes. Add rice and salt and pepper and stir well to absorb oil. Add saffron and hot water or stock, increase heat and boil 5 minutes. Add lobster, reduce heat and cook slowly 15 minutes. Stir gently as it cooks, adding more liquid if needed. Just before serving, stir peas in. Spoon into hot soup plates, garnish with artichokes. Makes 4 to 6 servings.

LOBSTER, HOTEL KAISERHOF

2 1½-pound lobsters, freshly boiled	3 tablespoons butter
	½ cup light cream
½ cup Madeira	2 tablespoons minced parsley
2 tablespoons meat glaze	
3 tablespoons fresh bread crumbs	1 tablespoon lemon juice
	Toast points

The lobsters for this delicious German dish should be boiled in court bouillon. When done, let cool in cooking liquid, drain, crack shells and remove all meat. Cut meat in slices and place in sauté pan. Add Madeira and meat glaze, heat slowly to boiling. Stir bread crumbs and butter together; then stir them into sauce in pan until well combined. Dilute sauce with cream; then add parsley and lemon juice. Stir and cook for 1 or 2 minutes. Spoon lobster out into shallow warmed timbale (French white-ware) or serving dish lined with toast points. Cover with the hot sauce. Serve at once. Makes 4 or more servings.

Meat glaze—can be bought at fine gourmet food shops. Usually prepared by a local chef and sold in small glass jars.

COLD LOBSTER, MAYONNAISE

2-pound live lobster	Mayonnaise
2 quarts court bouillon	4 narrow anchovy fillets
(recipe below)	4 narrow strips pimiento
1 tablespoon tomato paste	1 tablespoon chopped capers
1 teaspoon each finely	
chopped fresh chervil,	
chives and tarragon	

Boil the live lobster in court bouillon until shell is red. Let cool in cooking liquid. Remove lobster and chill it. To serve, split lobster lengthwise, remove meat, cut into bite-sized pieces. Remove claws, crack, and remove meat. Save shell halves. Chop finely all meat from claws, add to it the tomato paste, herbs, and 2 tablespoons mayonnaise. Spread mixture in half shells. Cover with the bite-sized pieces of lobster meat. Decorate with mayonnaise forced through pastry bag with small fancy tube. Add strips of anchovy, pimiento and few capers to each filled shell. Serve on cracked ice. Makes 2 servings.

COURT BOUILLON FOR SHELLFISH

1 large carrot, sliced	Bouquet of fresh herbs:
2 onions, peeled and minced	parsley, bay leaf,
3 tablespoons butter	thyme, celery leaves
3½ cups white wine	Peppercorns
4½ cups water	

In large kettle lightly brown carrot and onions in butter. Add white wine and water. Add bouquet of fresh herbs and a few peppercorns all tied together in cheesecloth. Bring to boil, add lobsters or other shellfish and after liquid comes to boil again, let lobsters boil for 10 to 15 minutes or until shells are red; 20 minutes or longer if the lobsters are larger.

LOBSTER À L'AMÉRICAINE

1½-pound live lobster	3 tablespoons white wine
2 tablespoons olive oil	About ½ teaspoon each
2 tablespoons butter	minced fresh parsley,
Small sliver crushed garlic	chervil and tarragon
1 tablespoon chopped onion	1 tablespoon of either
or shallot	consommé, fish stock
Cayenne	or cream sauce
2 tablespoons tomato paste	3 tablespoons cognac

Cut through lobster behind head, and then cut lengthwise in half and into pieces. Crack claws and remove meat. Remove liver and coral and set these aside. Heat oil and butter in large frying pan. Add garlic and stir 2 or 3 minutes. Add lobster pieces and claw meat, sprinkle with onion or shallot and a few grains cayenne. Cover and cook 5 minutes. Mix tomato paste and wine together and stir into pan. Cover again and cook over low heat 10 to 15 minutes or until shells are red.

Remove lobster to warmed serving dish. Strain sauce. Pound liver and coral to a paste and add to sauce, as well as the herbs and the consommé, fish stock or cream sauce. Cook and stir until thickened. Pour brandy into large cooking spoon, light and stir into sauce. Pour over lobster and serve at once. Makes 2 servings.

LOBSTER SOUFFLÉ, HOTEL CRILLON

2 cups Béchamel Sauce made	½ cup grated Parmesan
with fish stock	cheese
½ cup sifted soft bread	3 egg yolks
crumbs	4 egg whites
2 cups finely ground cooked	
lobster meat	Butter
2 tablespoons finely chopped	1 tablespoon ground cooked
truffles	lobster
½ teaspoon salt	
Cayenne	

Start oven at moderately hot (400° F.). Butter oval 2-quart soufflé dish and butter a 2-inch strip of white paper to put around top edge of dish so it extends above the rim.

Make the sauce and while it is still hot, beat in crumbs, lobster, truffles, salt, few grains cayenne and the grated cheese. Beat egg yolks until lemon colored and combine with lobster mixture. Whip egg whites until stiff; fold into mixture. Pour at once into prepared dish. Bake for 30 minutes. Remove paper carefully and serve at once. Pass with it hot melted butter in which the tablespoon of ground lobster and few grains of cayenne are mixed. Makes 4 to 6 servings.

LOBSTER BOMBAY

3 1½-pound lobsters,	Grind of fresh pepper
freshly boiled	¼ teaspoon salt
6 tablespoons butter	2 cups fish stock or bouillon
3 onions, peeled and sliced	2 tablespoons lemon juice
1 tablespoon curry powder	½ cup boiled rice
8 fresh mint leaves	

Remove all meat from lobsters. Cut in bite-sized pieces. Melt butter in a 2-quart chafing dish or flame-proof casserole and cook onions until golden. Add lobster meat and stir for about 1 minute. Sprinkle curry powder over lobster, stir well. Bruise mint leaves in bowl of cooking spoon by mashing with smaller spoon. Stir leaves into curry pan. Add small grind of pepper. Cook gently for 5 minutes. Stir in salt and stock or bouillon; let simmer a few minutes until sauce thickens and is reduced slightly. Add lemon juice and rice and serve. Makes 6 servings.

MALIBU BEACH DEVILED LOBSTER

1 large live lobster	¼ teaspoon A.1 or soy sauce
4 tablespoons melted butter	1 teaspoon dry mustard
or olive oil	½ teaspoon celery salt
1 teaspoon Worcestershire	Cayenne
sauce	

Cut through lobster behind head. Then split it for broiling. Place halves in shallow pan. Spread meat generously with seasoned melted butter or olive oil. Favorite mixture in some gourmet kitchens: mix melted butter or oil with Worcestershire, A.1 or soy sauce, mustard, celery salt and a few grains cayenne. Broil under moderate heat for 10 minutes. Baste again with remaining seasoned butter or oil and place in a moderate oven (375° F.) for another 10 minutes. Makes 2 servings.

2. MEAT AND FOWL

Beef: America's Favorite Meat / Morris Markey

This is the story of steaks and roasts of beef, from the open range to your table

S IR, the porterhouse steak is the noblest of all eating objects. I resist your desire to tell me vulgar facts about it."

"But the esteemed Brillat-Savarin wrote a hundred thousand words explaining why and how you are able to taste its flavors."

"A useless labor. Res ipsa loquitur."

"Then you really do not wish to understand the rather interesting process which brings you a porterhouse steak whenever your appetite calls for one?"

"Sir, inquiries into perfection are trifling. Do I care to know how many strokes of the chisel were needed to produce the Venus de Milo?"

"Very well. Then you do not care to learn that only four porterhouse steaks can be taken from a thousand-pound steer."

"Sir! You have no right to terrify me in this fashion!"

"I am sure . . ."

"Of what are you sure? That I am at the mercy of an animal?"

"Compose yourself. There is little need to fear."

"For the love of heaven, sir, explain the matter!"

◀ One culinary art raised to near perfection by American men is the outdoor barbecue. This meal also includes top loin steak, beef brisket, chuck-wagon potatoes, smoked beans, sourdough biscuits and fried pies.

JOHN LEWIS STAGE

Down in the Osage country, which is in Oklahoma, the roads run in long, lifting curves over endless hills that are tufted with grass of a hundred colors—shades of orange and saffron, green and red and brown and blue. Little streams run through the lush draws, and here and there stands a clump of trees. But on that day all the land seemed curiously empty of life, of habitation. Doc Mundy drove his new Cadillac slowly. His head turned now to one side of the road, now to the other, and he made no effort to hide his relish in the sight of the 32,000 acres of this grass that belonged to him.

He chuckled. "I guess you think I'm fooling you. You come all the way out here to look at cattle and I just show you a lot of grass."

I remarked it was handsome grass, anyway.

"It's full of cattle too." He chuckled again.

We drove into the little town of Pawhuska and met some of Doc's friends there; then on toward Bartlesville.

"Tell me, Doc," I said as we went along. "You're a beef man from way back. What's the best way of all to eat beef?"

He lit up a cigarette. "Well, barbecue is a good way. It's fine if you've got somebody knows how to make barbecue sauce, and if you get the meat served hot. Some of the best steaks I ever ate were right out of a steer we'd slaughtered about an hour before chow time. That may sound wrong to you, because you've heard a lot about hanging beef and letting it season. But if you eat it right quick, it's tender and sweet. Don't leave it over to the next day, though. If you do,

41

then you've got to hang it a while or you can't eat it at all. Talking about hanging beef, I'll tell you the best hung meat in the world.

"Along in December you dress a young steer—maybe one that weighs about eight hundred pounds. You put a cloth around it to keep the flies away, and you hang it high up at the top of your windmill, where the wind can keep blowing through it. About six weeks later you've got something that tastes better than any damn meat you ever put in your mouth."

It must be said at once that Osage County, Oklahoma, is not typical of the beef-producing country in America. It is one of the half dozen small areas in the land where cattle may be bred, raised, fattened and finished for the market without ever seeing any other acres. It would be a fine thing if we had enough such land to produce all our beef, because it is certainly the most economical and satisfactory way. But most of our beef cattle moves to maturity, to "finish" in a much more complex manner.

Something more than one half of all the land area in the United States is grass country—grass country only, and unfit for any other use. On about 950,000,000 acres of our soil, no grains or other foods suitable for human consumption are produced. The most logical way this vast expanse of earth can be utilized is through grazing: the production of livestock. As might be expected, the great reach of these grasslands lies in the West, beyond the Mississippi River. The breeder herds of that western country produce more than two thirds of American beef.

There are today more than 118,000,000 cattle in the United States, and over 21,000,000 of these are milk cows.

"Sir, you fill me with an inexpressible sense of relief."

"I suggest that you do not jump to conclusions."

"I never jump. Will you pause while I calculate the number of porterhouse steaks . . ."

"But so many things must be explained."

"Among them, if you please, the best way to obtain a windmill."

"If you are bored . . ."

"Not excessively. Pray go on."

There were no cattle at all in America when the first white men came, and all these Western ranges were grazed by bison and antelope, deer and elk. The New England Pilgrims and the Virginia adventurers both imported small herds, but these were needed for milk and butter. For some years, in fact, it was a capital offense in Virginia to slaughter any sort of domestic cattle. Earlier settlers, however, the Spaniards to the south, liked beef and brought seed herds from Europe in 1540. These herds were first grazed in Mexico, but ultimately they spread northward across the Rio Grande. A hundred years ago there were great herds of these animals in the Southwestern United States. They were changed somewhat by adaptation to climate, but the mark of the original Spanish strain was still upon them. Half wild, half domesticated, they were the Texas longhorns—and they were rugged.

They had to be, to survive the crushing summer heats, the savage winters, the periodic droughts, and, finally, the long drive along the Chisholm Trail or the Shawnee Trail to market—a drive that sometimes took four or five months. They got to the slaughter pens of Kansas City or Chicago or Omaha as lean and sinewy as mules, and it took a man of outstanding strength and determination to work his way through a longhorn steak.

The Civil War of the 60's was hardly over, however, before America began to import the basis of the ideal type: square, straight back, small head, short limbs—heavy in the loins and quarters—a minimum of bone to carry the maximum of muscle tissue (which is beef). Herefords are greatly predominant in numbers, and the Angus is the newest importation. Either of these, as well as shorthorns, will produce about the same proportion of perfect specimens and of culls.

In the early frontier days of America, we were the greatest meat-eating country in the world. The average man and woman, outside the crowded Eastern settlements, probably ate more than 300 pounds of meat a year. But that was not Hereford beef nor even longhorn beef. It was wild meat from the teeming forests and plains, and the supply of it must have seemed almost without limit. But the plow and the forester's ax and the fabulous growth of population changed that. Nowadays, the average American eats 145 pounds of meat a year. Almost exactly half of that is beef. (Forty-six per cent is pork and the remaining four per cent lamb and mutton.)

When World War II began, the men responsible for feeding our troops decided that the national average of meat consumption was not nearly enough for a fighting man. They undertook to provide a pound of meat a day for every man in uniform—365 pounds a year, and half of that to be beef.

Under the pressure of this almost overwhelming demand, it was obvious that new methods would have to be devised to hurry beef along from the ranges of the West, and through the feeder farms, and into the Army's kitchens, the Navy's galleys.

The only point at which a speed-up seemed remotely possible, without great deprivation for the civilian populace, was in the feeder farms. And thus began the quick-feeding practice which has been almost universally adopted today, which undoubtedly will affect our meat consumption in the future.

Before the war, steers would spend six or seven months on the feeder farms, slowly acquiring that perfection which goes by the name of finish.

Experts working under pressure from Washington found out that by feeding, quickly, large amounts of corn or meal cake, the appetites of the animals would be greatly stimulated. They would, in short, eat the same amount of protein feed in two months or, at the most, three, that they formerly ate in half a year. So, in these days, the feeder puts about thirty-five bushels of corn into a steer in less than three months, and has him ready for the market in the minimum of time. There is probably no other business on earth which bends to the law of supply and demand so instantly and positively as the meat business.

The daily auction of cattle at the big union yards of Chicago and Kansas City and Omaha, Fort Worth and St. Paul and East St. Louis and a score of other public markets is a complex affair that looks simple because it happens so swiftly. It is an odd sort of auction. A union stockyard, as the name suggests, is a place where all packers have plants, and to which the marketers of live cattle are invited to send their stock. There are thousands of pens, each holding thirty or forty head of cattle. They are built in streets, so that it is easy to look into them. Just after dawn, the buyers from all the packing companies at the yard set out on horseback to look at the day's supply, and to make their purchases.

Let us say that the buyer for Swift & Co. reaches a penful of young steers that catches his eye—the kind that the market is demanding back East. From his saddle he judges the quality of the steers, asks the owner or his commission agent to move them about, perhaps even gets down to peer at them from ground level. Then he offers a price. The owner may decide to accept the price at once, but it is more likely that he will wait to hear the offers of the other buyers. The Swift man rides away, and in due time men on horseback from Armour and Cudahy, Morris and Libby and all the rest will come up to make their bids. No two buyers will ever talk to the owner of the cattle at the same time.

Nutritionally, there is very little difference between the costly "Prime" beef—coming from a steer or heifer that is perfect in conformation, quality and finish—and the lowest grade of all, "Canner" beef (which, like "Cutter" beef, is not sold as butcher meat at retail). But in flavor, appearance, tenderness and texture there is a mile-wide gulf.

Take, for example, the problem of "finish." Look at the rim of fat; it should be very white and brittle. Look at the bone; it should be red and porous. Look at the meat itself; it should be neither staring bright pink nor veering toward blue. Above all, the meat should be marbled. That is the true sign of finish: the little streaks or lines of fat interlacing the tissue like veins of color in a slab of marble. It is the sixty or ninety days of finishing off at the feeder lots which marbles beef. The fat makes the meat tender and succulent and easy to prepare.

Hanging permits the enzymes in the meat to break down the solid walls of the cellular structure, release flavors that otherwise would remain latent, and make the meat tender. To be perfect, beef should hang from eight to twelve weeks. But only a minute fraction of American beef receives this prolonged aging, only the very finest of loins and ribs. That is because hanging is expensive, and it is also difficult to manage. Temperatures in the big coolers must be carefully controlled, humidity must be kept at a fixed level. There must be a constant movement of air. The hanging meat should not touch anything at all. There is a considerable degree of shrinkage and since beef is bought and sold by the pound, the man who does the hanging sells fewer pounds than he paid for in the first place. The price per pound to the consumer must be raised accordingly.

It is impractical to attempt the "hanging" or aging of beef in the home refrigerator. Temperature control is too doubtful. Air movement is almost impossible to manage. And in the nature of things the joint or roast would be touching against something else. If properly wrapped in porous paper, a roast or steak may improve with two days in the icebox before cooking. Beyond that time there is danger of spoilage, of mold, or even the growth of microorganisms that could cause illness. (Meat placed in the freezer compartment and frozen solid will keep almost indefinitely, but its flavor is impaired rather than improved.)

"Sir, I hesitate to imply that you become prolix. But when shall we proceed to important matters?"

"You refer to——"

"The kitchen, sir! Gad, sir, let us get to the kitchen!"

The fine cuts of choice beef bear immemorial names. Of these, perhaps the most universally known is the sirloin. It is, of course, a magnificent steak, a magnificent roast. There is a witty legend that the name was given it by James I of England —that on the occasion of a particularly splendid dinner he rose heavily from his chair, drew his court sword, touched the joint with it and cried, "You are the noblest of us all. I dub thee Sir Loin." Alas, it did not happen. The word is the usual Anglicization of the French term for the cut—*surlonge*—or top of the loin.

The tenderloin steak is, in the opinion of most males, a feminine dish. Taken from the boneless roll of tissue which lies alongside the backbone of the animal, it is extremely tender but somewhat lacking in flavor. Like most feminine affairs, it is expensive, and the French name for it, *filet mignon*, probably suits it best.

To most connoisseurs, the porterhouse really is the choicest of all steaks. It is not particularly large (though it should be cut at least an inch and a half thick); it includes a nugget of the tenderloin—for dessert, as it were—and it embodies all the flavors of the sirloin plus a texture of its own. The name, and the cut for that matter, originated in New York just after the American Revolution. The alehouses specialized in sirloin steaks. The houses serving porter—or porterhouses—were not to be outdone, and devised a special cut of steak for themselves.

The T-bone steak is, among one group of critics, considered the best of all. It is, actually, a small porterhouse—differing therefrom in that it carries only a fragment of the tenderloin.

The three great beef cities—New York, Chicago, and Kansas City—differ in their methods of cutting a side of beef. Each of the cities has given its name to its own way of dressing out a loin. Thus there will be some small variation between the division of the less important cuts. Minute steaks, club steaks, Delmonico steaks—they are not identical in the three cities. They are, for the most part, individual steaks of high quality, more often found in restaurants than in homes.

It is an odd thing that what would seem the simplest of all cookery—a broiled steak or a roast of beef—is least often accomplished even to a passable degree of perfection. For ten thousand housewives who can turn out the trickiest of cakes or the most impressive of casseroles, less than a dozen can really broil a steak or bring a proper juicy roast to the table.

Outdoor broiling has improved vastly but it still doesn't guarantee a finished steak that hasn't cooled in the evening breeze. And indoor (range) broiling often produces enough smoke to bring out five hook-and-ladder trucks and has been known to dry or toughen an otherwise good cut of beef.

Pan broiling on an iron skillet (there is no substitute for iron here!) is, on the other hand, an art that warrants rediscovery. You cannot, it is true, cook a two-inch steak this way. But a perfect one-inch steak is better than a so-so two-inch.

Cut the steak up or leave it whole, doctor it with mustard or leave it pure, but in any case, when the skillet has been heated until it begins to turn gray, shut all doors and windows, wrap a Turkish towel around your head, take a deep breath of pure air, and throw a few ounces of suet into the pan. An unholy squall of blue smoke will come up, but that only proves that the pan is hot enough. Then the steak—all in one piece or cut into individual servings—is laid in with tongs, or with a blunt fork and a spoon.

It will brown superbly, almost with the true charcoal crust, in a very few moments. If it sticks, toss in a few more bits of suet. When the bottom side is really brown, turn the steak over, but do not do it with a fork. Use the tongs or a spatula. And do not keep digging into the steak with a knife to see how done it is. Once the searing is pierced, the juices flow out and are lost, and disaster is at hand.

Of course it should be said that well-done steak—well-done

beef of any kind—is a barbaric misuse of a fine food. It is to the credit of the taste of the American people that less than 10 per cent of the steaks ordered in restaurants are requested well done. Once overcooking is rejected, the degree of rareness is a matter of taste. But if the color of the steak within the casing of crust is touched with gray or brown, the steak should be thrown away.

People who have fireplaces may, of course, try their hands at a charcoal broil under the chimney piece. It is not difficult, but it demands patience—patience to wait until the bagful of charcoal has really settled into red-hot heat. When that happy stage is set, the steak may be put on, with the assurance of admiring cheers from the assembled guests. The meat may be laid upon a four-legged standing spider, adjusted so that it barely clears the coals—or it may be held in a long-handled clamp-style broiler.

No steak of any sort should be carved until it has been away from the fire for four or five minutes. Put it on the back of the stove to keep warm, or in a warm but turned-off oven. This brief period of waiting allows the juices, which have been struggling to escape as steam, to settle back into the fibers. Any steak that is two inches or more in thickness should be carved in slices. Lay it on a board or a warm platter, and cut downward to make the slices—making them a little more than a quarter-inch thick.

All sorts of sauces, bottled ones and ones that the cook can make up out of butter and parsley and garlic and such matters, may be poured over a serving of steak. The best sauce of all for a steak is made by raising some salt butter in the juices that remain in the broiling pan or the skillet.

There are several basic things to remember in the matter of roast beef. First: If you can afford rib roast (though the sirloin tip is almost as good) do not make your butcher remove the rib bones and roll the meat with a lacing of string. Leave the ribs in, and the flavor will be greatly enhanced. Second: Never cover a roasting pan. Roasting, by definition, is dry cooking. A covered pan or patent roaster will steam the meat, not roast it. For all roasting, use low temperatures, because high temperatures dry the meat too rapidly. And do not sear the joint before putting it into the oven.

RUSSIAN EMBASSY BEEF STROGANOFF

1½ pounds fillet of beef	1 teaspoon prepared English
1½ teaspoons salt	mustard or mushroom
2 teaspoons pepper	ketchup
3 tablespoons butter	1 onion, peeled and sliced
1 tablespoon flour	¼ cup thick sour cream
1 cup bouillon or stock	

Cut fat and gristle from meat. Slice in strips about ¼ inch thick and 1½ to 2 inches long. Season with salt and pepper. Let stand 2 hours at kitchen temperature.

Melt half of the butter in a saucepan, stir flour in and cook 1 or 2 minutes, add bouillon or stock, stirring, and let boil. Stir mustard or mushroom ketchup in, remove from heat.

Heat remaining butter in a skillet, add onion, and brown lightly. Remove onion and discard, add meat and sauté until all pieces are lightly browned. Stir sour cream into the mustard or mushroom sauce, reheat to boiling, then pour over meat. Cover pan, heat but do not boil. After 20 minutes turn heat up for about 2 minutes, and serve the Stroganoff at once. Makes 4 to 6 servings.

SPANISH GARLIC STEAK

2-pound steak, cut 2 inches thick	1 cup white wine vinegar
1 teaspoon salt	½ cup olive oil
4 cloves garlic, peeled and chopped	Butter or oil for skillet

Have meat dealer slice steak crosswise into thin slices. Place them in a bowl. Combine salt, garlic, vinegar and oil and pour over the meat. Cover and let stand for 6 hours. Turn slices of meat from time to time. Remove meat from marinade, drain. Sauté in hot butter or oil a few minutes until lightly browned on both sides. Makes 4 servings.

Serve with mixed green salad and small hot potato or red-bean pancakes.

SWEDISH CHAFING-DISH CUTLETS

2 pounds lean beef	¼ cup thick sour cream
2 tablespoons chopped chives	½ cup fresh bread crumbs
1 teaspoon salt	3 tablespoons melted butter
¼ teaspoon pepper	1 pound mushrooms, sautéed in butter
½ teaspoon celery salt	Au Gratin Potatoes, or
1½ tablespoons onion, peeled and grated	Potato Soufflé to serve 6
1 teaspoon minced fresh dill	

Chop beef and chives together, add salt, pepper, celery salt, onion and dill. Mix well, add just enough thick sour cream to moisten. Shape into 6 cutlets or oblong cakes. Coat lightly with crumbs. Cook in a very small amount of hot butter in a chafing dish or skillet; baste frequently with melted butter as the meat cooks. The cutlets should be browned on both sides and well done throughout. Serve at once on hot plates, with hot sautéed mushrooms and Au Gratin Potatoes or Potato Soufflé. Makes 6 servings.

GOVERNOR'S MANSION POT ROAST

3-pound chuck roast
Flour
2 tablespoons beef suet or fat
2 tablespoons salt
Grind of fresh pepper
1 cup chopped canned
    tomatoes
½ cup water
1 clove garlic, peeled and
    quartered
1 large Bermuda onion,
    peeled and sliced very
    thin

2 tablespoons brown sugar
¼ teaspoon paprika
2 teaspoons prepared
    mustard
¼ cup ketchup
¼ cup lemon juice
¼ cup wine vinegar
1 tablespoon Worcestershire
    sauce
Corn-Meal Dumplings

Dredge meat with flour, rubbing it well into all sides of the roast. Heat fat in Dutch oven or other heavy roasting pot. Brown roast on all sides. Add salt, pepper, tomatoes, water and garlic (with wooden pick through each piece), cover and cook over low heat about 2 hours. At end of first 30 minutes remove garlic and discard it. At the end of 2 hours' cooking cover top of meat with onion slices and combine remaining ingredients (except dumplings) and pour over meat. Cover pot again, continue cooking another half hour or until tender. Serve very hot, sliced, with pot gravy and small Corn-Meal Dumplings. Makes 6 servings.

CORN-MEAL DUMPLINGS

¾ cup sifted all-purpose
    flour
1½ teaspoons baking
    powder
½ teaspoon salt
½ cup yellow corn meal

½ cup milk
2 tablespoons green pepper,
    finely chopped
2 tablespoons melted
    shortening
1 quart bouillon

Combine flour, baking powder, salt and yellow corn meal; sift twice. Stir in milk, green pepper and melted shortening. Mix. Drop by spoonfuls into boiling bouillon. Cover, boil rapidly for 15 minutes. Lift dumplings out with a slotted spoon. Serve with pot roast. Makes 6 to 12 small dumplings.

MINUTE STEAK BON VIVANT

6 minute steaks
½ cup thick sour cream
¼ cup chopped parsley
2 tablespoons chopped
    chives

1 teaspoon orégano
1 tablespoon onion juice
1 tablespoon grated lemon
    peel

Start oven at moderate (350° F.). Place steaks in shallow pan, broil on each side until well browned. Combine sour cream with herbs, onion juice and lemon peel. Spread on steaks and place pan in moderate oven about 10 minutes. Serve very hot with shoestring potatoes and sliced tomatoes. Makes 6 servings.

STEAK FILLETS DUQUESA

6 filet mignons
1 clove garlic, peeled and
    chopped
Olive oil
Salt and pepper
6 artichokes
Juice 1 lemon
2 cups water
Chopped peel ½ lemon

6 potatoes
3 tablespoons butter
1 beaten egg yolk
6 slices bread
1 tablespoon flour
1 tablespoon tomato purée
¼ cup sherry
6 fresh mushrooms, cleaned
    and sliced

Place fillets in wide dish, sprinkle with chopped garlic, about 3 tablespoons oil and a little salt and pepper. Wash artichokes, remove all hard outer leaves, hollow center of artichokes, cut out choke and discard it. Sprinkle artichokes with juice of ½ lemon. In a large kettle, combine the 2 cups water, juice of the remaining ½ lemon, the lemon peel, 1 tablespoon oil, and ½ teaspoon salt. When boiling, add artichokes, cover tightly, bring to boil again, reduce heat and cook slowly for 20 minutes. When artichokes are tender (test with fork) remove and drain. Return artichokes to drained kettle and keep them hot.

Scrub and pare potatoes, dice them, cover with lightly salted cold water and boil for 20 minutes. Drain, let stand for a few minutes, then mash, beating into them the butter and egg yolk. Cover, keep warm over hot water.

Fry bread slices golden brown in hot oil. Remove and drain. Sauté beef fillets in same pan over high heat, cooking about 8 minutes on each side. Shake the pan from time to time. Place fried bread on hot platter, a cooked fillet on each piece of bread. Set platter in hot oven with door left open. Quickly pour away all but about a tablespoon of the fat in the pan, stir in 1 tablespoon flour smoothly and let brown. Stir in tomato purée, add sherry, ¼ cup water, mix and heat. Add mushrooms, season with salt and pepper, stir and cook 10 minutes. Pour mushroom mixture over fillets on platter, surround with artichokes and mounds of potato purée. Serve at once. Makes 6 servings.

In place of mashed potatoes, mix and shape potato croquettes ahead of time. Egg and crumb them, and while steaks are cooking brown the croquettes in hot oven (450° F.). Serve with artichokes on platter with fillets.

HUNGARIAN STEAK ESZTERHÁZY

2½-pound steak, cut 1 inch
    thick
1 teaspoon salt
Grind of fresh pepper
2 tablespoons fat

1 cup chopped fresh
    (peeled) or canned
    tomatoes
1 cup thick sour cream
Hot buttered noodles or rice
    cooked with peas

Make cuts in edge of steak every 2 inches so it will not curl in the skillet. Rub meat well on both sides with salt and freshly ground pepper. Brown on both sides in hot fat; pour tomatoes over meat; cover skillet and let simmer for 25 minutes or until meat is almost tender. Add sour cream, cover and cook for 8 minutes more. Serve at once with hot buttered noodles or hot rice cooked with peas. Makes 6 servings.

The Tasty Pig / Morris Markey

*From it come hams of simple or exotic variety, chops, roasts
and 2000 delicacies—smoked, dried or spiced*

An amiable controversy has long engaged the more fastidious epicures, to wit: Is the left ham of the hog more tender, more juicy, more gracious to the palate than the right ham? Champions of the left ham have a specific argument which they advance: The pig, taking its rest, almost invariably lies upon the right side. Thus most of the weight of the animal is upon that ham, making the muscles stronger, more fibrous, and therefore tougher. Defenders of the right ham hold stubbornly that both hams are such wondrous victuals that it is mere preciosity to make a distinction. There is considerable doubt that a conclusive decision in the matter will ever be reached.

It is no great cause for wonder that so large a body of lore and anecdote, joke and jingle, should be built about the simple pig. Everybody, even the humblest peasant, could always contrive to keep a pig, for the plain reason that it could subsist upon anything that it could swallow—roots and acorns, ground nuts and weeds, and scraps from the family table.

Yet, despite the obvious fact that the most dim-witted yokel can manage to raise a pig or two for the winter's meat, raising a hundred for market is a ticklish and somewhat chancy undertaking. It requires a far greater variety of knowledge, more skill and more hard work than raising a hundred steers for market. You would know why, if you wandered around for a while in that region of sweeping prairies and low rolling hills, of black earth and blinding sun, which is called the Corn-Hog Belt of the Middle West. That country is the ham factory of America—the bacon factory and the lard factory, the sausage factory and the pork-chop factory. It produces the hogs, millions of hogs, that labor with industrious greed to turn the fields of tall corn into meat. And it

has devised ways of handling that meat in the great packing houses so that we get hams when we want them, and fresh pork when we want it.

Despite their appearance of total imperturbability, hogs are nervous, temperamental beasts and demand a great deal of human attention. Unlike a cow, which calves on the open range and brings her offspring up without the help of man, a sow has to be brought indoors to a special pen for farrowing. And, under the pressures of modern hog production, it is a rare sow which can provide milk for her young that is a proper balance of proteins, fats, minerals and vitamins.

The suckling pig must have its diet augmented, and the best way to do it is to paint the sow's teats with a palatable vitamin compound every day until the pig is weaned.

Pigs cannot thrive unless they have dirt to eat—not mud or filth, but simple earth. It is an essential in their diet because of the minerals in it, and so barrows full of it are brought into the sheds where the little pigs are nursing. The shallow pool of oil is in lieu of the outmoded hog wallow. All the pigs bathe in it regularly; it kills vermin and makes their coats supple.

The whole purpose of a pig's brief life is to eat corn. It takes about thirteen bushels of corn (fifty-five pounds is reckoned as a bushel) to put a hundred pounds of weight on a pig.

The preferred weight at the markets, the packing plants, is about 225 pounds. And so, to give us this much of meat and lard, a pig must eat about 1600 pounds of corn. There have been economists and dietitians who complain that this is an absurdly extravagant way for human beings to get nourishment from grain. To the dietitians, it may be remarked that

Flanked by a brace of pheasants, the suckling pig is presented here in regal splendor by M. Joseph Castaybert, chef of the St. Regis Hotel in New York.

SLIM AARONS

pork meat contains proteins in an ideal balance—which corn does not. To the economists there is one simple answer: Put down on a table a corn pone and a roast loin of pork—a loin with the sweet steam rising and the white meat falling away at the mere touch of the carving knife—and ask them to take their pick.

It is actually a pig, and not a hog, that goes to market. For he accomplishes his destiny of turning corn into meat at a very early age. The pork we eat, the hams and the bacon and the chops, comes from pigs that are, on the average, six months old.

If any of the usual breeds were allowed to reach full maturity, the boar would weigh about 1000 pounds. It is not necessary to point out the ruinous wastefulness of feeding an animal to such size. Each of its hams would weigh about 100 pounds, and not even Gog, not even Magog (who were giants in the earth in the old days) could manage that sort of dish. A sow at full maturity would weigh about 700 pounds and require corn in proportion. So it is that sows farrow once as a rule, twice at the limit, before they too are sent off to market.

In the husbandry of swine there is no such insistence upon purity of breed as there is in cattle raising. The cattleman with his Herefords or Shorthorns or Aberdeen Angus must be very careful to keep his strains pure, or the animals of his herd will lose their quality. That is not the case with pigs. Indeed, the great majority of the animals on the hog farms are hybrids, crossbreds.

Unlike cattle upon another count, the pigs of America are not merely improvements upon strains of stock imported from Europe. They are, in the most actual sense, American developments. The Poland China, for example (the most numerous and important strain of swine we have), was originated and brought to perfection in Ohio. It was the result of crossbreeding and inbreeding for many generations of many types of pigs: the Bedford and the Woburn, the Russian and the Irish Grazier, smoothed off with blood from the Berkshire. The Duroc-Jersey was developed in New Jersey and Pennsylvania. Our Chester Whites and Hampshires are native Americans. The Tamworth was evolved by the Canadians, who were intent upon producing a long-sided pig that would provide quantities of lean bacon—the preference in the English market.

Instead of fancy bloodlines, the hog farmer wants a good, quick feeder, an eager corn burner, and he makes up his own hybrids as he goes along. He buys new boars at frequent intervals and he is quite likely to vary the breed from time to time. All he wants is 225 pounds of pig at the end of six months, with the lard on that pig in the ideal proportion: one fifth of the total weight.

There flows through today's American pig no blood at all of the first swine this continent saw. There is a legend that Christopher Columbus brought a few pigs from Spain on his second voyage, but no record supports the tale. It is an established fact, however, that Ferdinand De Soto landed thirteen hogs in Florida in 1539, long before the first English settlements at Jamestown and Plymouth. The romantically inclined associate the razorback hogs of Virginia with these early immigrants, but there is little to justify the notion.

There are now in the land only about 57,201,000 hogs, a figure that does not meet the country's needs and therefore keeps pork prices high.

The term "meat packer" had its origins in simple realism. The first meat packers were farmers, preparing their own lard-

ers against the unproductive winter months. In Pilgrim days, they used to put away venison and bear meat, and ultimately hog meat, in salt. They packed it in barrels and boxes.

The first commercial meat packer—the first man to pack meat to sell it, rather than eat it himself—was Captain John Pynchon of Springfield, Mass. He flourished in 1662, and his packing process was confined to the simple pouring on of salt. Even this crude method of preserving meat for shipment was enough, however, to cause the Midwest, nearly two centuries later, to become a meat-producing area.

Cincinnati was the first big pork-packing town. Indeed, as far back as 1840, the natives called it "Porkopolis," and it was not until later that Chicago and St. Louis and Milwaukee got interested in the meat business.

All of this Midwestern meat-packing industry that grew up before the Civil War was concerned with cured and preserved meats, yet it was strictly a winter industry. When summer came, the slaughtering of animals ceased. It is rather astonishing to realize that the huge meat industry of our time, with the Midwest producing fresh meat and the packers distributing it, still fresh, to all the world, is less than seventy-five years old.

The marketing of live pigs is, for the most part, quite different from the marketing of cattle—where all stock is sold at auction in the big union yards. The Rath Company sends out four radio programs a day to the hog country. They quote the price they will pay for hogs that day.

The farmer, listening at home, decides when he wants to sell. He telephones to the Rath office in Waterloo, saying how many hogs he has ready for market and also saying he will accept the latest price quoted by radio. The Raths make the purchase then and there, over the phone. It may be that they do not wish delivery of the hogs for a day or two. If the price declines during this brief delay, the farmer is protected.

Fresh pork does not improve with hanging, as beef does. Generally speaking, fresh pork is on somebody's dinner table within three or four days from the time the pigs reach the packing plant.

Fresh pork is, of course, an important element in the packer's business, but it is not his chief concern. His biggest job is to cure meat, to make hams and bacon and sausages by a variety of processes that run into the hundreds.

There is only one essential ingredient in the curing of pork. That ingredient is salt—as it always was. Up to the time of World War I, it was the general practice to soak hams in barrels of strong salt brine for sixty or seventy days. This meant that the housewife, when she bought such a ham, had to soak it in clear water to reduce the saltiness. Several methods were used to counteract some of the salty flavor. The packers added sugar to the brine. They also employed the ancient device of smoking the meat, for a smudge of hardwood smoke modifies the saltiness to a marked degree and also is probably of some usefulness in preserving the meat.

In recent years, however, pork packers have perfected an entirely new method of pickling, or curing, hams. The brine is compounded of salt and sugar and saltpeter—the purpose of that last ingredient being to make the meat red and appetizing, since pure salt has a tendency to turn it dark and hard. But the ham is not immersed in this pickle. Instead, the solution is injected into the main artery of the ham and spreads quickly through the microscopic capillaries; in two weeks, instead of two months, the ham is uniformly preserved against spoiling.

Nearly all packers smoke their hams too. At Rath's there

are scores of smoke rooms where the hams are hung on racks. A smudge of hardwood chips is fired in the basement of the building and the smoke rises through flues to fill each room. This is less than a cooking process, as the temperatures in these vaults are not high. Precooked, or tenderized, or ready-to-eat hams are actually cooked by steam after the smoking.

Whether they are to be precooked or sold in the raw state, hams at Rath's are smoked for twenty-four hours. So is bacon. But the salt-curing process is different for bacon. It is impracticable to pump brine into bacon slabs, and so the formula of salt and sugar and saltpeter is rubbed into the meat from the outside. The slabs are then piled upon boards, and heavy boards are laid on between layers of bacon, and finally a heavy weight is placed on top of the whole stack. The resulting pressure forces salt into the slabs, and forces moisture out.

Of all the methods for processing meat so that it can be preserved without refrigeration, one of the most ancient—far older than the making of ham and bacon—is the manufacture of sausage. It is impossible to say where or when sausage-making began, but the Chinese were writing about it centuries before the Christian era began.

Nearly 2000 varieties of sausage are made in America. About a billion and a half pounds of meat are used every year to make them—pork, beef and veal. In the packing industry, sausage is divided into three main categories. There is the thing they call domestic sausage, there is dry sausage, and finally there are the so-called sausage specialties.

The best generalization for domestic sausage is that it is soft to the touch, and also moist—like frankfurters (a modification of the sausage first made at Frankfurt am Main) and bologna (something like the stuff they make at Bologna, Italy) and pure fresh-pork sausage (the finest breakfast dish in the world), which is native American.

Dry sausage, as distinguished from domestic sausage, is a food of almost infinite variety. There are the salamis that originated in Greece and were brought to perfection in Germany. There are the German and Scandinavian cervelats—the highly seasoned mortadellas and capicolli and peperoni from Italy—the Genoas and the Romas, the Frisse and the Milanos and hundreds of other regional European types. All of them now have their American versions, manufactured by the packers. They make Polish-style sausage and bockwurst (which has milk and eggs added to the meat mixture), they make mettsausage and braunschweiger and liverwurst and hundreds of other sorts.

The majority of the dry sausages are sold, and eaten, raw. But before they are sold they are subjected to a prolonged curing process. Some of them are smoked. All of them are hung in curing rooms for long periods. They become, in due time, the dense, compact, and highly flavored food that looks so handsome on our plates of cold luncheon cuts.

In the third category, sausage specialties, most of the meats look and taste nothing whatever like the things we call sausage. They get their name for no better reason than that the responsibility for their manufacture is generally left to the sausage departments of the packing plants. Under the heading come meat loaves and jellied meats, packed tongues and souse and headcheese. Chile con carne is called a sausage specialty. And so, oddly enough, are Canadian-style bacon, prosciutto and Westphalian hams, and preserved pigs' feet.

Canadian bacon is not really bacon at all—since true bacon comes from the side and belly of the hog. The Canadian style is actually the loin of pork, with all the bone and most of the fat removed. The loin is rolled until it looks rather like a salami. Then it is salt-cured and smoked in precisely the way that true bacon is treated.

Prosciutto and Westphalian hams had their respective origins, of course, in Italy and Germany. But the made-in-America variety of both these hams is virtually the same product. The only difference is in the mechanical treatment they receive in the packing plant, which results in a marked difference in appearance and perhaps some slight difference in flavor. Both hams are eaten raw. The secret of their preparation lies in the curing.

The hams themselves come from the same Midwest pigs that produce all the other hams we eat. Those destined to become prosciutto are treated somewhat like bacon slabs. That is to say, they are laid out upon a platform, and weighted down with extremely heavy blocks of iron. The pressure makes the hams become almost flat as the moisture is forced out of them to be absorbed in the dry air. They remain under this pressure for much longer periods of time than are necessary for bacon, and they hang in the smoke rooms for days instead of hours. The meat that results is curiously delicate in flavor, and very tender when served in extremely thin slices. A classic use of prosciutto calls for the spreading of these almost transparent slices upon wedges of iced honeydew melon. Nobody ever invented a better hot-weather appetizer.

Westphalian ham, to all intents and purposes, is prosciutto with the bone removed—prosciutto bound into a roll resembling a rolled roast of beef, and then treated with more smoke. The flavor is almost identical with the Italian prototype, which means that it is almost perfect.

It is the custom of our times for restaurants and delicatessen stores to put the label "Virginia Ham" upon any hind leg of a pig which is baked with a few cloves rather than boiled in a kettle. As a matter of fact, the state of Virginia produces very few hams. It is not hog country, except for a small region on the peninsula between the James River and the York, where a relatively small quantity of Smithfield hams is produced. The hog they raise there is a lean and hungry chap, the razorback—which is to the Poland China hog what the Longhorn steer is to the Hereford. The important thing, however, is that his diet is almost wholly confined to acorns and peanuts.

This forage gives a curiously compact and faintly oily quality to its flesh, and these qualities are exploited to the fullest possible extent in the process of curing. Salt, of course, is an essential to the Smithfield ham as it is to the ham from Iowa. But when the salting is done, the ham is rubbed with great handfuls of ground black pepper. And then the ham goes to the smokehouse to hang for weeks in the rich, heavy fumes of hickory wood. Finally, it spends an almost interminable time in the cool, dry curing rooms, losing the last few drops of its moisture. The finest Smithfield hams are likely to be four or five years old, though some connoisseurs insist that they are at their best after ten years of aging.

Because of its age, the Smithfield ham is likely to appear moldy and forbidding from the outside, but this does not discourage the epicure. It merely puts him to work. For the ham must be soaked and scrubbed with the utmost care. A stiff brush is essential, and many cooks use strong yellow laundry soap to help remove the outer crust. After that, of course, the ham must be rinsed in running water, and then soaked in cold water overnight.

The best Smithfield ham I ever ate was treated like that and then put on to cook in cold water with two pounds of brown sugar and six green apples in the pot. It was boiled slowly for three hours (this was a twelve-pound ham) and then allowed to cool off in the cooking stock. When it was cold, the cake of fat was taken off the top of the pot.

Then the cook made up a mixture of pastelike consistency —brown sugar and prepared mustard and sherry—just enough to cover the ham as if it were a cake being iced. The roasting, in a medium oven, took about an hour, with frequent basting from the stock that was left in the boiling pot.

There is another sort of Virginia ham which has not gained the universal *réclame* of the Smithfield but which still is wonderful to eat. That is the simple farm-cured ham—not from razorbacks but from ordinary pigs fed upon an ordinary diet of corn and table scraps and buttermilk from the kitchen churn. It is cured in a variety of ways, most of them secret, in the smokehouses of farms in every county of Virginia.

It is not mere chance or legend which gives the Smithfield ham honorable acclaim throughout the world. The rich, pervading flavor of the slices is quite unlike anything else in the way of pork.

Something more than a hundred years ago, Queen Victoria of England ordered for Buckingham Palace a shipment of six hams a week from Smithfield, Virginia. The order has never been canceled. The shipments have never been interrupted, even in times of war.

There is nothing romantic about a pig. It is a stupid and comical and greedy creature, by any definition. Swineherds are not glamorous fellows like their opposite numbers, the cowboys. They do not play the guitar or wear fancy clothes. But Tom, Tom, the Piper's son, had his head on his shoulders when he swiped a pig instead of a calf. They say that at the end, Tom went crying down the street. But I do not believe his yells were invoked by the beating they gave him. I believe he was shouting with delight, because after all he had eaten the pig.

Please, if you don't mind, pass the pork chops.

The fabled Virginia ham is a main attraction in this sumptuous Christmas repast set out at the King's Arms Tavern in Williamsburg. ▶

ARNOLD NEWMAN

BOILED HAM DIJONNAISE

8- to 10-pound smoked
    Virginia or Smithfield
    ham
3 or 4 peeled onions
Cloves
4 carrots, scraped and
    quartered
2 bay leaves
Bunch of celery, root end and
    almost all leaves cut
    off, the rest chopped
1 small clove garlic, peeled
    and halved
4 sprigs parsley
Sprig fresh thyme, or ½
    teaspoon dried thyme

2 teaspoons chopped fresh
    tarragon or 1 teaspoon
    dried tarragon
2 tablespoons white vinegar
2 cups dry white wine
1 quart consommé
1 teaspoon each chopped
    parsley and chervil
1 tablespoon butter
1½ teaspoons prepared
    French mustard
1 tablespoon capers
1 tablespoon chopped
    gherkins

Scrub ham thoroughly, rinse trim off any black or smoke discolorations. Cover with cold water and let soak for 12 to 14 hours. Drain, place skin side up in a large kettle. Cover with boiling water, add onions, each stuck with a clove, and carrots, bay leaves, celery, garlic, parsley and thyme. When water is boiling again, reduce heat and cook slowly for 25 to 30 minutes per pound. Remove garlic and discard it after first half hour. When ham is done, let it cool in its liquor; then remove and skin. (Pot liquor makes fine base for soup.) Remove all excess fat from ham. Place ham in roasting pan and start oven at moderate (350° F.).

Prepare sauce. Combine tarragon, vinegar and wine in an enamel saucepan; let boil gently until reduced by one half. Add consommé and boil gently until sauce is again reduced by about one half. This leaves about 3 cups. Add parsley, chervil, butter and mustard. Stir for about 3 minutes. Place ham in oven and let heat and brown about ½ hour; baste every few minutes with the sauce. For final bastings add capers and gherkins to sauce. Place ham on hot platter, pour all sauce from baking pan over it. Makes 20 or more servings.

BAKED HAM SLICE IN MADEIRA

2-pound slice of ham
2 small onions, peeled and
    chopped
1 tomato, skinned and
    chopped
1½ cups Madeira

1 clove
½ teaspoon orégano
1 cup bouillon or stock
2 tablespoons flour
2 tablespoons butter

Start oven at moderately hot (400° F.). Cut rind off ham. Place in casserole, cover with vegetables, wine, seasonings and bouillon or stock. Bake for about 30 minutes or until meat is tender and browned. Serve at once, or if gravy topping is preferred, remove the ham slice to a warmed platter. Stir flour smoothly into casserole, add the butter, and if too thick, add a tablespoon or two of Madeira. Stir and boil for 1 or 2 minutes. Pour over ham on platter and serve immediately. Makes 4 or more servings.

HOTEL BLACKSTONE HAM TIMBALES

1½ cups bread crumbs
4 tablespoons butter
1¾ cups milk
4 beaten eggs
2 cups minced cooked
    ham
1 tablespoon parsley,
    chopped

1 teaspoon chopped
    onion
Salt and pepper
Mushroom Sauce
3 tablespoons sautéed
    chopped mushrooms

Start oven at moderate (350° F.). Butter 6 or 8 small molds for individual service. Combine crumbs, butter, and milk in saucepan and cook 5 minutes, stirring. Remove from heat. Add eggs, ham, parsley, and onion and light seasoning of salt and pepper. Mix and pour into molds. Place molds in a shallow pan containing very little water. Bake for about 45 minutes. Unmold on warmed platter or serving plates; add a spoonful Mushroom Sauce to each timbale and top with sautéed chopped mushrooms. Makes 6 to 8 servings.

MUSHROOM SAUCE

½ pound fresh mushrooms
3 tablespoons butter
½ teaspoon pepper

¼ teaspoon Worcestershire
    sauce
1 cup Medium White Sauce

Wash, dry and slice the fresh mushrooms. Sauté mushrooms in butter with seasonings about 5 minutes, or until lightly browned. Add with pan butter to white sauce. Stir to blend. Makes about 1½ cups sauce.

HUNGARIAN PORK CHOPS, NÉUMÁNNY

2 small onions, peeled and
    chopped
2 tablespoons fat
1 teaspoon paprika
1 pound (2 cups) drained
    sauerkraut

½ teaspoon salt
6 thin pork chops
1¼ cups sour cream
12 slices dill pickle

Cook the onions in the fat in a flameproof casserole until golden. Add paprika and sauerkraut. Cover and simmer while browning chops.

Start oven at moderate (350° F.). Salt the chops on both sides and pound well with a meat mallet. Brown chops slowly in their own fat in a skillet. When browned on both sides, place chops on top of sauerkraut; cover and cook in oven for 1 hour. Five minutes before serving, stir sour cream into kraut. Garnish tops of chops with pickle slices. Serve in casserole. Makes 6 servings.

BAKED HAM SIMON

8-pound, boned, ready-to-eat
    baked ham
2 cups sifted all-purpose
    flour
2 teaspoons baking powder
2 tablespoons sugar
½ teaspoon salt
½ pound butter

½ cup milk (approximately)
1 cup finely chopped
    parsley
¼ cup finely chopped
    chives
1 cup prepared mustard
¼ cup mayonnaise or sour
    cream
Lemon juice

Remove skin from ham. Prepare dough by sifting the flour, baking powder, sugar, and salt together twice. Cut the butter into the flour mixture with pastry blender, add milk gradually and work into dough. Turn out on bread board and knead a few minutes then roll lightly out to about ¼ inch thickness in a sheet large enough to wrap the ham and fold ends over.

Start oven at hot (425° F.). Combine parsley, chives, mustard, and mayonnaise or sour cream. Add a little lemon juice if needed to improve spreading consistency. Spread this mixture on dough, place ham on this coated surface, wrap dough around ham, turning dough in at ends. Place in baking pan. Bake for 2½ hours. Reduce heat to 350° F. when pastry begins to brown. To serve, use thin, sharp knife and cut crust away. Slice ham and serve hot or cold garnished with pieces of the crust. Makes 20 or more servings.

CREAMED HAM IN CHEESE RING

2½ cups soft bread crumbs
1 teaspoon salt
Grind of fresh pepper
Dash of cayenne
½ teaspoon dry mustard
1 teaspoon chopped shallot
    or onion
1½ teaspoons Worcester-
    shire sauce
2 drops Tabasco sauce

2 cups grated Cheddar
    cheese
3 cups milk
6 slightly beaten eggs
2 tablespoons melted butter

2 cups cubed cooked ham
3 cups medium white sauce
3 tablespoons browned
    buttered bread crumbs

Start oven at moderate (350° F.). Grease 6- or 7-cup ring mold. Pour crumbs into mixing bowl, add all seasonings, shallot or onion, Worcestershire, Tabasco and cheese. Mix well. Pour milk over cheese-crumb mixture and stir. Add eggs and butter. Mix well and pour into greased mold. Set mold in shallow pan of warm water. Bake for 45 minutes. Combine ham and white sauce. Unmold baked cheese ring on large warmed platter. Fill center with creamed ham, sprinkle browned crumbs on top. Makes 8 or more servings.

PORK CHOPS BRAISED IN WINE

6 pork chops
Salt and pepper
6 tablespoons prepared
    mustard
3 tablespoons butter
1 cup white wine

3 tablespoons sour cream
3 tablespoons browned
    buttered crumbs
2 tablespoons finely chopped
    fresh dill

Rinse chops, pat dry. Season well on both sides, rubbing salt and pepper into the meat. Spread chops with mustard, place on a platter, cover and let stand in refrigerator several hours.

Start oven at moderate (325° F.). Melt butter in flameproof casserole, brown chops on both sides. Add wine, cover and cook in oven for about 45 minutes or until pork is well done. During last 15 minutes of cooking baste chops with the sour cream. Spread crumbs and dill over all and serve immediately. Makes 6 servings.

HONG KONG BARBECUED SPARERIBS

3 pounds fresh pork
    spareribs
1½ cups soy sauce
2 cloves garlic, peeled and
    crushed

1½ teaspoons salt
2 tablespoons honey
2 tablespoons sherry

Have meat dealer chop the large piece of ribs into short pieces. Wash, remove gristle, pat dry with towel. With thin sharp knife, cut in small servings of two or three ribs each. Combine remaining ingredients in large bowl, mix well. Place spareribs in this marinade. Let stand 30 minutes, turning occasionally to coat all pieces. Drain; broil under moderate heat until cooked through and both sides are browned. Makes 6 or more servings.

LOIN OF PORK, CHILEAN STYLE

2 pounds pork tenderloin
    cut in thin steaks
1 cup vinegar
2 cloves garlic, peeled and
    mashed
Small sliver red pepper

½ teaspoon ground cumin
    seed
Fresh grind black pepper
½ teaspoon salt
¼ teaspoon sage
Butter or lard

Rinse steaks, pat dry. Combine vinegar, garlic, seasonings and sage in earthen bowl. Place steaks in marinade and let stand 1 hour. Drain. Rub generously with butter or lard and then grill, or sauté in flameproof casserole for about 10 minutes or until golden brown on both sides. Start oven at moderate (350° F.). Place casserole in oven and bake for about 45 minutes. Remove garlic from marinade and baste steaks with marinade a few times while they cook. Makes 6 servings.

IOWA-FARM PORK TENDERLOIN

2 pounds pork tenderloin
    cut in thin steaks
Juice 1 lemon
Salt and pepper

6 tablespoons butter
¾ cup currant jelly
1 cup Medium White Sauce

Rinse steaks, pat dry. Sprinkle with lemon juice and add enough water to just cover and let stand 30 minutes. Drain, season lightly all over with salt and pepper.

Cook steaks in a flame-proof casserole for 5 to 10 minutes in 2 tablespoons butter. When golden brown, add 4 tablespoons butter and the jelly. Start oven at moderate (350° F.). Set casserole in oven and bake for 40 minutes, basting frequently with white sauce. Stir pan gravy well after each basting. Serve very hot. Makes 6 servings.

LINK SAUSAGES WITH WINE

¾ pound link sausages
    (12 sausages) or
1 pound bulk sausage in 6
    flat patties
2 tablespoons white wine

2 tablespoons water
Parsley or mixed fresh herbs
    such as chervil,
    tarragon, basil

Place sausages in cold skillet. Mix wine and water; add to skillet. Cover and cook for 8 to 10 minutes. Remove cover and pour off fat. Brown the links over medium heat, turning as necessary. Do not pierce links with fork. When cooked and brown, remove sausages to thick paper toweling, let drain for 1 or 2 minutes. Serve hot on platter garnished with parsley, or sprinkle finely chopped herbs over the sausage before serving. Makes 4 to 6 servings.

The Feast of Christmas / *Silas Spitzer*

Today it may not be 104 peacocks escorted to the table
by candle bearers, minstrels and baying hounds,
but it's the richest, sweetest, most heart-warming feast of the year

THE Christmas dinner of my youth was the longest, most lavish repast of the year. It took several days to prepare, needed extra help in the kitchen, and was so elaborate that it always strained the family's finances. It began with a crunching of salted nuts and a munching of celery at about two o'clock, and drifted, without coming to any definite conclusion, into a sort of contented stupor as the late afternoon shaded into twilight.

Even on ordinary occasions we were a tribe noted for our uninhibited appetites. But on Christmas, our number supplemented by relatives and close friends, we sat down to a table so heavily laden that it can only be described as medieval. If turkey or goose were the major element of this unbuttoned orgy, it was always a bird of monumental proportions, the largest the local market could supply. If roast beef held the place of honor, it was seven ribs thick, and loomed in its platter like Gibraltar.

Gravy was served in depth, homemade bread in huge, sweet-smelling loaves. Quantities of vegetables and minor accompaniments were handed around in overflowing bowls and tureens. In the largest of these vessels was a snowy pile of whipped potatoes, with rivulets of yellow butter running down its sides from a large chunk melting in a cavity at its peak. Another fixture was our mother's wonderful red cabbage, spicy with caraway seeds, rich with goose or chicken fat and piquant with the tart-sweet taste of green apples and sugar.

From year to year, there were few surprises in this most traditional of holiday menus, except on those last few occasions when the family still assembled in force. At these later gatherings, I seem to recall several new dishes of a spectacular modern sort, introduced by the eldest sister, who had sud-denly become aware of the fascinations of fashionable living as reported in the glossy periodicals of that day. With her own fair hands, she prepared and served orange-flavored sweet potatoes buried under a froth of toasted marshmallow, odd-tasting artichokes with a thick yellow sauce that was slightly curdled, and a complicated dessert involving lady fingers, jelly, whipped cream and candied violets.

These innovations, however, were consumed with curiosity rather than gusto, and were tolerated mainly to keep the family peace. For the greater part, our Christmas dinner progressed happily through the old familiar edibles and was crowned not only by mince pie and apple pie but by a sleek jet-black plum pudding that looked like an old-fashioned anarchist's bomb, and was just about as heavy. During the final languid hour, while the grownups smoked cigars and sipped muscatel or brandy, the younger element snapped frilly favors which blossomed into frivolous paper hats.

Many Americans no longer eat on such a formidable scale, but in spite of the present generation's daintier appetites, our native Christmas food and customs still largely follow the traditions established by our English forebears. In England's earlier times there were feasting and pageantry so magnificent that even Hollywood, in its gaudiest moments, has never quite succeeded in capturing their grandeur. For hundreds of

Christmas in Lüchow's Restaurant in New York: two roasted ▶ Watertown geese surrounded by the dishes that make this traditional dinner a high point in the gastronomical year for gourmet and gourmand alike.

ARNOLD NEWMAN

years the great moment of these banquets was the joyous entrance of the cavalcade which brought in the boar's head garlanded with rosemary and bay, a lemon or a rosy apple clenched between its bristling tusks. It was carried aloft on a great platter to the sound of harps and the singing of carols. I had always conceived of the boar's head as having only symbolical significance, but I learned from recent reading that it was also a dish relished for its own sake. In its preparation, the head itself was boned and the inside coated with minced pig's liver, chopped apples, onion, sage and rosemary. It was then solidly stuffed with sausage meat, ox tongue, truffles, mushrooms, pistachio nuts and spices, moistened liberally with apple brandy and then boiled in a cloth for the better part of a day.

A hundred and four roasted peacocks were served at one famous feudal feast, borne in single file by a procession of a hundred and four servants, with an escort of candle bearers, minstrels and baying hounds. Each peacock had been stuffed with spices and wild herbs, its beak gilded, and its tail feathers replaced and fanned out to their full spread of opulent color. Less spectacular, but perhaps more satisfying in a gustatory sense, was a celebrated pie that once graced the banquet of an English nobleman. Under its mountainous crust it was laden with geese, rabbits, wild ducks, woodcocks, snipe, partridges, curlews, pigeons and blackbirds, and was brought to the guests on a cart that was specially built to carry it.

A poet of Elizabeth's time, boasting of country Christmases, writes of "their thirty pound butter'd eggs, their pies of carps' tongues, their pheasants drenched with ambergris, the carcasses of three fat wethers bruised for gravy, to make sauce for a single peacock." As may be imagined, it took floods of drink to wash down these unctuous and heavily flavored courses—a circumstance that did nothing to hamper the boisterousness of the occasion. The wassail bowl was an early English tradition which has just about disappeared, together with the classical thirsts which inspired it. Usually prepared by the host, its contents were a mixture of powerful wines, sweetened and spiced, with roasted apples swimming on the heady tide. The custom was to pass this heavy bowl around the table so that each guest, if he were muscular enough, could lift it to his lips, to drink deeply with an appropriate toast.

In Washington Irving's genial account of an English feast of his own day, the Squire kept to the ancient custom of the nut-brown wassail "a potation, indeed, that might well make the heart of the toper leap within him." But, due to a shortage of peacocks in that season, the host, somewhat to his embarrassment, was forced to offer, instead of this resplendent creature, a pie decorated with peacock's feathers, but actually made with pheasant. As you may recall from your school reading, the head of an enormous pig was served instead of the grinning boar, while an elderly harper twanged out a discordant flourish and an old carol was recited by the Young Oxonian.

The English still take pride in serving a Christmas repast of noble proportions, overflowing with good things to eat and drink and warmed by the glow of the human spirit in its happiest and most grateful mood. The pattern still follows, in greater or lesser degree, the memorable dinner of the Cratchits in Dickens' *A Christmas Carol*.

Preparations for such a spread are not lightly undertaken. An English writer on cooking advises that early November is the proper time to make Christmas cake, mincemeat and puddings "if they are to be of the rich spirituous variety that improves with keeping."

All three of these delights need much coddling and draw, in return, an abundance of respect, but in the opinion of virtually all Englishmen and most Americans the plum pudding is not only the noblest of its race but the only dessert blessed with the authentic look and flavor of Christmas. When it is brought in with fitting ceremony on a silver tray, its swelling façade decked with holly and enveloped in a blue nimbus of blazing brandy, it never fails to awaken a chorus of joyful praise, whether the diners resemble Dickens' humble Cratchits or look more like characters plucked all aglitter from the pages of the Social Register.

The earliest recorded version of plum pudding was much eaten, appropriately enough, during the reign of Queen Anne, that indulgent, overstuffed monarch who suffered from the gout. It was a sort of porridge made by thickening mutton broth with brown bread, contained raisins and spices, and was served in great smoking tureens as a first course at feasts. From this rude beginning evolved the plum pudding as we know it today—firm and solid, sleekly rounded, dark and gleaming of complexion, and filled to bursting with every sort of fruit and sweetmeat except—and this is rather odd—plums.

In the family recipe favored by the British Royal Household, there are more than twenty separate ingredients, each sanctified by generations of use. To create a dish of such magnificence is not a simple or casual undertaking, especially when it involves the resources of the average modest home. According to classic admonition handed down from early-Victorian times, a proper Christmas pudding "takes three days to cook, three weeks to set and ripen." Its preparation usually calls for the loving cooperation of all the family, not excepting small boys and girls, with or without the assistance of their pets.

Many Americans of an older generation will recall with sentimental fondness the childish parts they once played in their own domestic version of this preholiday orgy of wonderful sights, sounds and smells. They needed little urging to rally round, to run swift errands, or to help in the actual kitchen tasks. There was work enough for everybody during those jolly, bustling days. Small boys cracked and picked nuts and, if they could be trusted to wield a knife, were put to slicing and shredding chunks of translucent, sugar-crusted citron and the ruddy peels of candied fruit. Fat, gleaming raisins and golden currants were washed and picked, then segregated in neat piles for weighing and mixing. A faint but persistent fragrance lingers in the memory of cinnamon and mace, of ginger and cloves, not to mention the exciting bouquet of brandy and rum which had been boldly filched from Papa's treasured supply.

Many families clung to an old custom which proclaimed that everybody, from the head of the house to the smallest high-chair tenant, took turns at stirring the pudding, "for luck." The culminating act took place when the dark, suety mixture was tied tightly in a floured cloth or pressed into a bowl and lowered into a kettle of furiously boiling water for at least six hours.

Certain cynics maintain that plum pudding is a decorative symbol, not a delicacy for the gourmet, and that it is frequently eaten only because of the spirits which saturate it, or the hard sauce which bears it company. Any attempt, they add, to do it justice after a man has packed away several ample helpings of soup, roast turkey and the usual fixings, is a simple invitation to calamity. But less delicate and more capacious mortals sharply disagree, among them some of the great names of English literature.

Nobody has ever written of food or feasting as well as Charles Dickens, and the classic description in *A Christmas Carol* of the anxiously awaited pudding that blessed the Cratchits' Yuletide dinner forever captures the excitement and glory of that wonderful occasion:

In half a minute Mrs. Cratchit entered—flushed, but smiling proudly—with the pudding, like a speckled cannon ball, so hard and firm, blazing in half of half-a-quartern of ignited brandy, and bedight with Christmas holly stuck into the top.

Indeed, the costliness of this opulent dessert and the time consumed in its making are mitigated by the fact that, like all things of character and worth, it actually improves with age. As most good cooks know, it should be wrapped carefully, put away in the pantry and given occasional refreshing draughts of brandy or rum to keep its spirits up.

Meanwhile the well-organized housewife will have begun a few other foresighted activities, like ordering snapdragons and table decorations or baking shortbread and other plain cakes that can be kept well in airtight tins or jars. Beginning about a week before Christmas and continuing until the morning of the great day, still other tasks should proceed in their correct sequence—the making of almond paste for the cake, the glazing of nuts and the sugaring of plums. Small items like salted nuts and cheese straws may now be undertaken, stock put on to simmer for the soup, and if there is to be a ham, it must be put in to soak. Finally, in a last burst of activity, the bird will be stuffed and trussed, jellies and other sweets whipped up, hard sauce confected for the pudding, holly and mistletoe hung and the cloth laid with the best silver and plate. With these ministrations completed, the hostess may await with serenity the arrival of the guests and pray for a day lightly frosted with snow and laced with the sweet music of distant bells.

Household habits are changing. There are not many cooks today who begin to prepare Christmas dinner six weeks before the event. Or who will undertake the making of a mince pie that requires twenty-eight separate ingredients of the richest and most exotic variety. The English feast has become simpler, though it is still built around such traditional dishes as oysters, turkey, roast beef or goose with a dressing of sage and onion. Elegant modern embellishments are now often served, like shrimp cocktail or iced caviar, *pâtés*, whitebait, pheasant, venison and—though this strikes me as heresy—flaming crêpes suzette instead of the massive pudding that delighted Dickens.

A great many American families are loyal to the Christmas stand-bys of their foreign ancestors. In German-American neighborhoods, the shops at Yuletide are festooned with *wursts* of every imaginable shape and content. There are piles of tongue-tingling *pfeffernuesse*, frosted gingerbread churches, strawberries of marzipan paste, and the towering *Baumkuche*, an edifice of cake in a dozen layers, heavily iced and built to resemble a Christmas tree.

For the Swedish people, the true taste of Christmas is in lutfisk, made of salt codfish which has been creamed and seasoned with dill, and *Julgröt*, rice porridge cooked in milk, and containing a single almond which is a marriage omen for the one lucky enough to find it in his helping. The most highly esteemed Christmas course is a young roast pig, meltingly sweet under its russet crust of crackling. Other Scandinavian treats are almond cakes, tiny crullers and ginger cookies. Floods of coffee are kept hot on the stove for all who drop in during the day to pay their holiday respects.

Italian markets in New York keep live eels in tanks for the much-loved Christmas *capitoni* which, sizzled in olive oil and garlic, fills the lower East Side with an exciting smell that recalls the teeming streets of Naples and Palermo. *Zabaglione*, whipped up from egg yolks, sugar and Marsala wine, is a Latin version of eggnog. It is often served with the fruit-filled bread called *panettone*, a specialty of Milan.

In all lands and among all people who celebrate Christmas, time and fashion may work their inevitable changes, but the good things eaten are still essentially the old favorites, and dinner is never less than a feast. Wonderful food is an important part of the day. But the true meaning of Christmas attains its deepest significance in the gathering of family and friends, the sharing in mutual love and understanding of a happiness which belongs only to that season.

HOLIDAY PLUM PUDDING

1 cup finely chopped beef suet (¼ lb.)	1 cup sliced blanched almonds
1 cup plus 2 tablespoons brown sugar	1¼ cups sifted all-purpose flour
½ cup milk	1 teaspoon baking soda
2 eggs, well beaten	1 teaspoon salt
1 cup currants	½ teaspoon nutmeg
1 pound chopped mixed dried fruits (cherries, citron, orange peel, lemon peel)	1 teaspoon cinnamon
	¼ teaspoon mace
	1 cup soft bread crumbs
	½ cup brandy

Combine suet, brown sugar, milk and eggs. Mix fruit and almonds with ¼ cup of the flour. Sift remaining flour with soda, salt and spices. Add fruits, crumbs and flour-and-spice mixture to suet mixture. Mix well. Turn into a well-greased 2-quart covered pudding mold. Steam for 3 hours. (Steaming directions: Use steamer or deep covered kettle. In using kettle, place filled and covered mold on trivet or wire rack in kettle. Pour in boiling water to ½ depth of mold. Place cover on kettle and steam, replenishing the boiling water when necessary to keep the proper level of ½ depth of mold.) Turn out on hot platter; heat brandy in small saucepan, pour over pudding, light brandy and bring pudding to the table flaming. Serve with hard sauce.

HARD SAUCE

½ cup butter	2 cups sifted confectioners' sugar
Dash of salt	Brandy if desired

Soften butter; beat in salt and sugar until light and fluffy. Add brandy to taste, beating it in thoroughly.

ROAST TURKEY, PLANTATION STYLE

8-to-10-pound young turkey	¾ cup dry white wine
Salt	¾ cup melted butter
Olive oil or butter	2 cups heavy cream
Virginia Stuffing	Freshly ground pepper

Have poultry dealer dress turkey, clean it, singe and wash it well. In your kitchen rinse the bird, wipe it dry inside and out, rub cavity with salt, using ⅛ teaspoon per pound of turkey. Rub cavity with a little oil or butter. Fill loosely with stuffing about ¾ full. Do not pack stuffing in. Fasten opening with small skewers or wooden picks. Use thin layer of stuffing between breast meat and (gently loosened) skin of breast to keep meat tender; add a little melted butter to the stuffing you place on the breast.

Truss the turkey: tie center of the string to the tail; pull the legs close to the tail and tie legs together. Bring wing tips onto back over neck skin; turn bird over on breast and bring each end of string forward over the front and tip of wings, then bring back and tie securely in the middle of the back.

Start oven at moderate (325° F.). For the first part of the roasting place the turkey, breast side down, on a rack in a shallow roasting pan. Brush bird all over with oil or butter. Roast for 20 to 25 minutes per pound for a small turkey (up to 10 pounds), 18 to 20 minutes per pound for a medium-sized 10-to-16-pound bird. Baste frequently with equal parts of wine and melted butter and, as it cooks, with the liquid in the pan. Turn the turkey after 2 hours and 45 minutes so the breast meat will cook evenly and brown gently. When turkey is done, remove roast to a warm platter, cut strings, and remove them and the vent skewers. Garnish platter lightly with something easy for the carver to serve onto the plates, such as rounds of cranberry jelly or thin slices of unpeeled orange with a dab of currant jelly on each.

Pour all of the fat but 2 tablespoonfuls out of the roasting pan. Place pan over low heat on top of the range. Stir the cream in slowly, heating gently. Stir continually, scraping the brown crust from the bottom and sides of the roasting pan into the hot cream. Do not boil; add a little salt if needed (taste it of course!) and a dash of pepper. Pour into hot gravy boat and serve with the turkey. Makes 10 to 12 servings.

VIRGINIA STUFFING

Turkey giblets	1 tablespoon salt
¼ cup peanuts, finely chopped	¼ teaspoon pepper
3 quarts day-old bread cubes	½ teaspoon thyme
1½ cups butter	¼ teaspoon marjoram
½ medium onion, finely chopped	

Simmer all the giblets, except the liver, in a little water about 2½ hours; add liver about 8 minutes before the end of the simmering time. Drain and chop coarsely. Add peanuts. Combine mixture with bread cubes. Mix and let stand for a few minutes. Heat 1½ cups butter in a large saucepan; add ½ medium onion finely chopped and stir until onion is golden. Add bread-and-giblet mixture and the seasonings. Mix and stir well until bread is lightly browned and butter is absorbed. Should be a dry crumbly dressing, enough for a 10-pound or slightly larger bird. For a moister stuffing, mix with a little heavy cream. Use as described in recipe above.

HOLIDAY GAME PIE

2 pheasants or quail, or 3 smaller birds	½ cup diced uncooked veal
Salt and pepper	2 (3-ounce) cans diced mushrooms
3 tablespoons chopped fat salt pork or bacon	¼ cup diced parsley
Pastry for Game Pie	¼ teaspoon thyme
2-cups Brown Sauce or gravy	½ bay leaf
½ cup sherry or Madeira	8 ripe olives, chopped
4 hard-cooked eggs, chopped	or
½ cup chopped shallots	2 or 3 truffles, chopped

Start oven at hot (450° F.). Have birds cleaned and drawn, ready to cook. Season with salt, place in baking pan, cover breasts of birds with chopped salt pork or bacon. Roast uncovered for 15 minutes, basting birds twice with the mixture of chopped fat and juices from pan. Remove birds from oven and turn off oven heat. Let birds cool. Remove meat from bones, cutting 3 slices from each leg and 3 (large slices) from each breast. (Reserve bones and scraps for soup kettle.)

Prepare pastry. Line pie dish. Combine Brown Sauce with sherry or Madeira. Combine hard-cooked eggs, shallots, veal, and moisten with a little sherried Brown Sauce. Mix well. Spread a little of the egg mixture over the pastry in the bottom of the baking dish. Add layer of sliced game, a few drained mushrooms, a little parsley. Add layer of egg mixture, a few spoonfuls of Brown Sauce, a layer of game; repeat until there are 3 layers of game and 4 of the egg mixture; sprinkle top-layer egg mixture with a few spoonfuls of Brown Sauce. Scatter thyme, crumbled bay leaf, olives or truffles over all. Cover dish with pastry, moisten edge of lower pastry and seal upper and lower crust together by pressing firmly with fingers; then shape into decorative edge.

Start oven at moderately hot (400° F.). Complete pastry top as described in pastry recipe below. Bake for about 1 hour or a little longer, until crust is golden brown.

PASTRY FOR GAME PIE

2 cups all-purpose flour, sifted	8 tablespoons lard
¼ cup sugar	¼ cup sherry
½ teaspoon salt	1 or 2 tablespoons water, if needed
4 tablespoons butter	1 egg

Sift flour, sugar and salt together into a mixing bowl. Use pastry blender to cut in butter and lard, until shortening particles are the size of peas. Sprinkle with sherry, about 1 tablespoon at a time. Mix lightly with a fork. Beat egg, and mix in with fork until all flour is moistened. Add water if necessary. Work dough together lightly with hands; press firmly into a ball, cut dough in half. Place one half on lightly floured board, flatten with hand, roll lightly to ¼ inch thickness. Line decorative orange or red oval baking dish, or a terrine with ornamental border for best effect. Dish should be 1½-quart size, larger if birds were plump and meaty. Fill dish as described in recipe above. Roll out second half of pastry, cover dish, make elaborate, thick decorative edge. Cut round hole in center of top pastry for steam. With paring knife make decorative leaf-and-stem or game-bird design in pastry top. With bits of pastry trimmings shape small flowers or other designs and press onto pastry top.

Bake as described, in moderately hot oven, one hour or longer. To serve, cut off piece of pastry for each plate and cut into pie, place a serving on each plate. If extra gravy is to be served with this pie, make a brown sauce, flavor with 2 tablespoons grated orange peel. Pie makes 6 or more servings.

Pastry note. English cooks double the amount of lard in the pastry recipe. This makes a difficult to handle, very rich topping, which is placed on top of the game mixture instead of on top of the dish. It is pressed onto the game mixture and literally bakes into it. Wonderful flavor, but not such a handsome pie as the one made with pastry top on the dish.

THE CHRISTMAS GOOSE

8- to 10-pound young goose, cleaned, ready for cooking	Stuffing:
	1 quart bread cubes
Boiling water to cover	2 tablespoons fat
1 bay leaf	Goose liver and heart, chopped fine
Grated peel 1 orange	¼ onion, peeled and chopped
1 cup orange juice	
½ cup lemon juice	¼ cup celery root, diced
Salt	1 teaspoon salt
1 teaspoon crumbled sage	⅛ teaspoon pepper
½ teaspoon thyme	½ teaspoon powdered ginger
½ teaspoon marjoram	⅛ teaspoon grated nutmeg
Flour	1 beaten egg
Orange juice	5 or more apples, pared, cored and diced
Gravy:	
2 tablespoons flour	1 cup currants, washed and drained
1 cup milk	
1 cup light cream	

Wash and drain goose. Place in kettle and cover with boiling water. Add bay leaf, orange peel and juice, and lemon juice. Bring to boil again, cover and boil gently about 1 hour, or longer if bird is large or mature. Drain. Season inside well with salt, sage, thyme and marjoram. Let stand while stuffing is prepared.

Brown bread cubes lightly in hot fat, stir, add chopped liver and heart, the onion, celery root, salt, pepper, ginger, and nutmeg; stir and heat together for about 5 minutes. Add beaten egg, mix, add apples and currants. Stuff goose, sew or skewer vent. Dredge goose generously with flour. Start oven at moderate (325° F.) and roast for 20 to 25 minutes per pound, about 3 hours and 20 minutes for an 8-pound bird. From time to time, prick skin with sharp fork to let fat run out. Baste with orange juice, or mixture of orange and other fruit juices.

If you want to make gravy, when goose is done, remove bird from the roasting pan to a large warmed platter. Skim off fat from pan juices, cook juices rapidly over direct heat until amount is reduced to about 2 tablespoons. Then stir in 2 tablespoons flour, cook and stir until smooth and bubbling. Add 1 cup milk and 1 cup light cream, stir and boil until slightly thickened. Taste and correct seasoning as preferred. Serve hot gravy with goose. Makes 10 or more servings.

To garnish the Christmas goose: Decorate the large platter on which the hot brown roast is placed, with fresh holly or a wreath of holly pushed over the roast around the bird's neck. For bird's head use an orange hollowed and filled with

chopped fresh and candied fruits such as sugared mint leaves, candied apricots, candied pineapple and cherries, and fresh white grapes and place similar filled oranges around the roast.

The carver must remove the holly wreath (and it can be taken from the table to the kitchen) before he carves, and he serves a little fruit from the oranges, as well as apple jelly, currant jelly, and spiced watermelon pickle with each serving of goose. A chestnut purée, sweet potato soufflé or sweet potatoes with rum, braised celery or leeks, and small oyster or wild-rice croquettes belong on this menu.

ROAST SUCKLING PIG

Young porker about 10-pound weight	1 cup boiling water
	Parchment cookery paper
Salt and pepper	1 red apple, baked, or left raw with slice cut from top and bottom
1 medium onion, peeled and sliced	
1 tablespoon caraway seeds	Raisins for eyes
8 cups Apple and Prune Stuffing	

Have meat dealer select a piglet which is about 6 weeks old and clean it thoroughly, making it ready for cooking. Rinse porker inside and out with running cold water. Wipe dry and season inside and out with salt and pepper, rubbing well into the meat. Scatter onion slices inside piglet and scatter caraway seeds over the onion. Mix stuffing and fill cavity loosely. Sew vent securely or fasten with several small skewers. Tie legs together, place roast in kneeling position in a large uncovered roasting pan. Open mouth of piglet and brace it open with short skewer or a few wooden picks, so apple can be inserted later.

Start oven at moderate (350° F.). Pour boiling water into the baking pan; cover porker loosely with parchment. Roast, basting every 15 minutes with hot water and pan drippings, for about 4 hours or longer, until the meat is tender throughout. Remove paper about 30 minutes before estimated end of roasting period. The skin should be evenly browned and crisp. If snout and ears brown too quickly, cover with parchment.

Place the hot roast on a warmed platter (two people are better than one for this; to lift the hot roast use wide pancake turners). Remove string from around pig's legs. Discard skewer or picks from mouth and place baked or raw apple in mouth and raisins in eye sockets. Garnish the platter with holly, spiced crabapples and stuffed baked onions. Makes 12 to 15 servings.

APPLE AND PRUNE STUFFING

9 strips lean bacon chopped fine	2½ teaspoons salt
⅜ cup chopped peeled onions	3 pared, cored and chopped apples
4 cups soft bread crumbs	2¼ cups chopped cooked prunes

Cook bacon in skillet until browned, pour off some of the fat, add onion to skillet, mix and cook 3 minutes. Combine crumbs with salt, apples and prunes. Mix; then stir into bacon-onion mixture. If stuffing is too dry add a little hot water, wine or the liquid in which the prunes were cooked. Stuff piglet as described in recipe above. Makes 8 cups stuffing.

CHESTNUT PURÉE

2 pounds chestnuts
Boiling water
2 tablespoons butter or fat
2 or more cups hot water or
  bouillon

1 teaspoon salt
Grind fresh pepper
3 tablespoons heavy cream

With short, sharp, pointed knife cut gash in the shell of each nut. Cover nuts with boiling water and boil rapidly for about 1 minute. Drain, heat nuts in skillet with 2 tablespoons butter or fat, stirring and shaking pan over high heat until shells absorb the fat. When nuts are cool enough to handle, insert knife in the slits, remove skin and shells. Cover blanched nuts with hot water or bouillon and boil gently for 15 to 20 minutes or until nuts are soft. Drain, put through sieve. Season with salt and pepper and add the cream. Beat until light and fluffy. Keep hot in double boiler until time to serve. Makes 6 servings.

VIRGINIA SWEET POTATOES
WITH RUM

3 or 4 large sweet potatoes,
  boiled
2 tablespoons butter
2 tablespoons light brown
  sugar
1 tablespoon grated lemon
  peel

Lemon, sliced as thin as
  possible with peel
  left on
½ cup light rum
Additional butter

Cut potatoes lengthwise in thick slices. Sauté lightly in butter in wide flame-proof baking dish. Brown both sides lightly. Then sprinkle with sugar and grated lemon peel. Cover potatoes with lemon slices. Pour on rum. Add dabs of butter. Place under moderate broiler heat about 5 minutes or until butter melts and mingles with rum on potatoes. Makes 6 servings.

SWEET POTATO SOUFFLÉ

9 medium-sized sweet
  potatoes
Boiling water
2 teaspoons salt
5 tablespoons butter
¼ cup hot milk or light
  cream

½ teaspoon grated lemon
  peel
2 egg yolks, beaten
½ cup drained crushed
  canned pineapple
4 egg whites

Wash and scrub potatoes, pare them, cover with boiling water containing about 1½ teaspoons salt. Boil about 25 minutes or until potatoes are done. Drain, put through ricer or mash. Add 2 tablespoons butter, beat well, then add a little hot milk or cream and beat until fluffy and light. Let cool.

Start oven at moderate (350° F.). Grease 7-inch soufflé dish and grease a strip of paper 2 inches wide and long enough to wrap around upper rim of dish. Fasten in place with string. Beat 3 more tablespoons butter into mashed potatoes, add ½ teaspoon salt, ½ teaspoon grated lemon peel, and 2 beaten egg yolks. Mix well, fold in drained pineapple. Whip egg whites stiff, fold into potato mixture, pour at once into prepared soufflé dish. Set dish in shallow low pan of hot water. Bake for about 40 minutes. Remove paper rim and serve soufflé at once, from baking dish. Makes 6 servings.

CHRISTMAS DARK FRUIT CAKE

3 pounds seedless raisins
1 pound each candied
  cherries, citron,
  apricots and pineapple
1½ pounds currants
¾ cup cognac
2 cups all-purpose flour,
  sifted
½ teaspoon baking powder

1 teaspoon powdered
  cinnamon
½ teaspoon powdered cloves
1 teaspoon grated nutmeg
½ pound brown sugar
½ pound butter
6 eggs, separated
½ cup strong coffee
Extra brandy

Chop raisins coarsely. Slice cherries, citron, apricots and pineapple very thin. Wash currants, drain, cover with brandy and let soak about 30 minutes. Drain currants and save the brandy. Combine currants with other fruits, sprinkle with enough flour to coat them well.

Sift remaining flour, baking powder, and spices together. Cream butter and sugar together in a mixer bowl until light; beat in 1 egg yolk, add part of dry ingredients, beat; then add coffee and reserved brandy alternately with the egg yolks and remaining dry ingredients. Mix well. Add the fruits and mix thoroughly.

Start oven at slow (250° F.). Grease 2 large round funnel cake pans, line with 2 thicknesses of waxed paper and grease the paper. Whip egg whites stiff, fold into fruit batter. Pour batter into prepared pans filling them about three-quarters full. Bake for about 2½ hours or until cake tester inserted deeply comes out clean. Or use five 2-pound loaf pans and bake about 2 hours. When cakes are done, remove from oven, let pans stand on cake rack until cakes are completely cooled. Then remove from pans and peel off paper. Place each cake on a plate in a tin box with tightly fitting cover. If cake is to be stored a few weeks before use, wrap with cheesecloth, saturate cloth with brandy and pour a few tablespoons brandy on it once a week. Recipe makes two 5-pound round cakes, or five 2-pound loaf cakes, 50 or more servings.

CHRISTMAS BOMBE

1½ quarts pistachio ice
  cream
1 pint deep-red raspberry
  sherbet or strawberry
  ice cream full of
  crushed berries

Fresh frozen or canned red
  raspberries or
  strawberries
Red and green angelica
  berries and leaves or
  red and green candied
  cherries

Use 2-quart covered mold. Let pistachio ice cream soften just enough to press around inside of the mold in an even layer. Fill center with sherbet or strawberry ice cream. If you use red raspberry sherbet, add a generous spoonful of crushed raspberries. If you use strawberry ice cream add a generous spoonful of sliced strawberries. Cover filled mold with sheet of heavy waxed paper cut large enough to extend about an inch all around mold. Put metal cover in place, and seal cover with adhesive tape. Freeze for 2 or 3 hours or longer.

To unmold, wrap sealed mold in Turkish towel wrung out of very hot water. After about 2 minutes remove hot towel, rip adhesive tape off, remove mold's cover and peel off waxed paper. Invert serving platter over the ice cream, then turn mold and plate upside down; remove the mold. Garnish the ice cream with holly berries and leaves of angelica or with red and green candied cherries and other candied fruits. Makes 8 servings.

FRENCH APPLE TART WITH APRICOT GLAZE

Pastry for 1-crust pie	3 tablespoons sliced
2 cups very thick applesauce	blanched almonds
2 apples, pared and sliced	¼ cup apricot jam, melted
1 tablespoon butter	over hot water
2 tablespoons light-brown	¼ cup heavy cream
sugar	

Make puff paste or extra-rich pie crust dough and line a greased, 9-inch, round baking dish. Fill three-quarters full with thick applesauce. Start oven at moderate (375° F.). Sauté sliced apples in butter, sprinkle with sugar and cook until golden and sugar-coated. Arrange sautéed apples on top of applesauce; scatter almonds generously over apples. Bake in moderate oven about 12 minutes or until pastry is baked. Spread with apricot jam. Let cool. Serve cold with garnish of whipped cream piped on with a pastry tube. Makes 6 or more servings.

TURRÓN DE ALMENDRAS— CHRISTMAS CANDY

Actually a nougat, either soft or firm, this delicious candy is a perfect holiday sweetmeat to give in small boxes and to hang on the Christmas tree in little metallic foil bags, a variation on the boxes of homemade fudge and taffy American families make for their friends.

Spanish cooks let the turrón cool in an oblong mold about 1 inch deep, 6 inches long, 3 inches wide, or in a waxed paper mold of these same proportions, held in place by a wooden frame. Here is a recipe for this candy:

1 cup sugar	1 teaspoon vanilla extract
½ cup water	2½ cups blanched almonds,
3 tablespoons light corn	sliced or chopped
syrup	½ cup pistachio nuts,
2 egg whites	chopped
½ cup strained honey	Nougat rice wafers *

Combine sugar, water and half of the corn syrup in a sauce-pan, cook, stirring, until the sugar is dissolved. Continue cooking to 290° F. on a candy thermometer. Remove from the heat. Beat egg whites stiff in the upper part of a double boiler, add hot syrup gradually to the egg whites, beating steadily. Heat honey and remainder of corn syrup and vanilla together and cook to 290° F. on candy thermometer. Remove from heat, add at once to egg white mixture, pouring in gradually and beating steadily. Add the nuts; stirring continually, cook over hot water until mixture dries. Take a small amount out in a spoon and if it holds its shape when cooled and is not

* When you make turrón or nougat, you need nougat wafers for professional-looking results. These are Japanese rice wafers, purchased in large sheets from wholesale confectioners. They are similar to the wafers used as goldfish food and if nougat wafers are not available, these smaller sheets of rice wafers from the pet shop will do.

sticky to the touch, it is done. Pour into a shallow pan lined with nougat wafers, cover at once with additional nougat wafers. Place board or other smooth top over the candy and press with a heavy weight for 12 hours or longer. Remove the block of candy from the pan, cut into oblong pieces. Makes about 1¾ pounds, 48 pieces.

CHRISTMAS PARTY WALNUT CRUNCH

2 cups coarsely chopped	⅛ teaspoon salt
walnuts	¼ teaspoon powdered
3 tablespoons butter	cinnamon
1 egg white	⅛ teaspoon grated nutmeg
½ cup sugar	

Start oven at moderate (325° F.). Spread the walnuts in a 9-inch-square pan. Dot with 1 tablespoon butter. Bake for about 15 minutes, stirring frequently. Remove pan; let walnuts cool.

In the same pan, melt the remaining butter. Beat the egg white until stiff, fold the sugar into the egg white with salt and spices. Stir egg-white mixture into the cooled walnuts. Mix well. Spread nut mixture in pan in the melted butter. Bake for about 30 minutes. Remove from oven and let cool.

Break into pieces. Makes 16 or more pieces.

CHRISTMAS PRALINES

2 cups firmly packed brown	3 tablespoons butter
sugar	½ pound black-walnut meats
½ cup milk	1 teaspoon vanilla extract

Combine sugar, milk and butter in a saucepan. Cook, stirring constantly, to 236° F., or to slightly under the soft-ball stage. Add the nuts and vanilla extract. Let cool to lukewarm (110–122° F.). Beat until creamy but still soft. Drop in mounds on a heavily buttered baking sheet. When the pralines are cold, wrap each in waxed paper. Makes about 12 medium-sized pralines.

These make a fine dessert for any buffet supper. They are often served with a sherry- or cognac-flavored sauce, or centers are filled with sliced, brandied fruits.

CHRISTMAS-NIGHT WINE JELLY

2 tablespoons gelatin	2 tablespoons cognac
½ cup cold water	⅜ cup kirsch
1½ cups boiling water	⅓ cup orange juice
1 cup sugar	3 tablespoons lemon juice
½ cup sherry	Cold baked custard

Soften gelatin in the cold water for 5 minutes. Then stir into boiling water until dissolved. Add sugar, liquors and fruit juices. Pour into 1-quart ring mold rinsed with cold water. Chill until firm. Unmold on chilled serving dish. Fill center with cubes of firm, cold, baked custard. Makes 6 servings.

Wine jelly for Christmas-night supper is a tradition in some parts of the South. It is always served with warm gingerbread, as the finale to cold sliced turkey or a ham-and-turkey pie, served with assorted salads and relishes.

3. BREAD, GRAIN AND PASTA

Break Bread with the World
/ Silas Spitzer

*As old as written history, as diversified as human personalities,
bread is still the world's staff of life*

THE French, whose love of bread is deep and abiding, have a well-worn phrase which sums up the character of a man. "He is as good as bread," they say. There is a finality about the words that tells everything. For what could be better than bread, more honest, less pretentious? No other food has kept its hold so long upon the good will of the earth's millions. In 6000 years, men have never lost their hunger for bread.

There are crumbs of bread scattered through all the pages of history. Wars have been fought for it. Famine or plenty have hinged upon its harvesting. Revolutions have flamed because of the manner of its distribution. And from the very beginning, most of the world's religious faiths have chosen bread as their holiest symbol.

The story of bread begins with the earliest records of the human family. Charred and stony hunks of bread, baked some 10,000 years ago, have been found in the household litter of prehistoric dwellers in the Swiss lake region. They were made from crushed grains of wheat and barley, baked on hot stones in the ashes of an open fire. Flat cakes of unleavened bread are prepared today in much the same way by nomadic Arabs and natives of Central Africa.

It is generally accepted that the raised wheaten loaf was first baked in Egypt, long before the Christian Era. In the British Museum, there are both leavened and unleavened breads, round, square or triangular in shape, some a foot across and more than an inch thick. Nobody has determined exactly how the ancient Egyptians first made their dough rise. We do know that they mixed salt and water with meal that was stone-ground from good wheat raised in the Nile Valley. Probably a mess of this stuff was left standing one day, exposed to the hungry bacteria of the air. After a time, natural fermentation set in, and the dough, aerated with bubbles of carbonic gas, rose to twice its original volume. We can imagine some puzzled Egyptian peasant kneading and slapping this ball of dough, only to see it rise again in the familiar phenomenon since repeated in all ages and in every land. The miracle of bread was accomplished when the heat of the oven transformed the self-risen dough into a puffy loaf, ventilated with irregular holes and covered with a brown crust that smelled richly of the earth's generous bounty. It must have dawned eventually upon some observant person that when a bit of the soured dough was saved and added to the next

◀ The world's bread comes in many delightful shapes, sizes—and tastes.

ARNOLD NEWMAN

batch, the same fermentation took place in less time. And so the art of bread-baking began.

From earliest times, white bread made from pure wheat has been preferred by the wealthy and the well-born, while black bread of mixed origin was the fare of the lower classes. The true lover of bread, however, judges a loaf not by its color but by its taste and texture. But to most of us white bread is softer, sweeter, more attractive and costlier than bread made of rye, oats, millet, corn or barley. And these are sufficiently good reasons why white bread has always appealed to the instincts of snobbery.

White bread is still associated with the better things in life, but it is no longer only the rich who consume it. More than 40,000,000 loaves of white bread are baked and sold every day in the United States. Yet there is an articulate and growing minority, only partially made up of people of foreign blood, that rejects white bread in favor of darker or more rugged varieties, not only because they are better for the health but because they taste better.

It is my own personal conviction that the so-called "humbler" breads, even the blackest and roughest, furnish more interesting work for the teeth and more pleasure to the palate than fine white breads of highly milled, bleached white flour. I am thinking of nut-sweet whole-grain bread, made with milk, salt, butter, yeast and honey, kneaded by hand, and baked in a kitchen filled with the warm familiar smell that has never lost its fascination. And of the sour black bread called pumpernickel, the tough-crusted bread of the Italians, German rye with caraway seeds, or the unleavened flat breads found on the shelves of Armenian and Syrian shops in our largest cities.

Probably the best bread I ever ate was in France during the years between the great wars. It was hearth-baked from native wheat and had a firm substance you could get your teeth into. You broke it off in irregular chunks, and two people could easily do away with a long, golden *flûte* at a meal, especially if there was rich gravy to be soaked up, in the sensible French manner. But even without butter or sauce, this was bread to be relished for its own sake. And that seems to me the highest test you can make of any bread. It was a test more than met by the wholesome, delicious bread my mother baked, long years ago. She used flour that came from the grocer in a sack with a familiar blue-and-red label.

While I watched, the dough was kneaded long and lovingly, on the kitchen table. Sometimes the loaves were square-sided with high, mushrooming tops. Or they might turn out moon-shaped, or roughly oval with pointed ends. And occasionally she would make a pan of hot rolls that were brown and crisp and sweet, and tasted of wheat, butter and molasses.

Ask any middle-aged male if he can recall his mother's oven-baked bread, and you will almost certainly be rewarded with a gush of nostalgic memories. A friend of mine who lived his boyhood in a small Polish village told me that bread made up at least half of the family diet. He remembers that his grandmother, a calm, slow-moving old lady in a white headcloth, kneaded a week's supply every Friday morning in a vast, wooden trough, shiny with age and use. When the mass of dough had risen grandma would carry the trough carefully to her bedroom and stow it underneath the mountainous feather mattress, where it would keep safe and warm. On days when she made strudel or pastry, she would spread layers of thin dough to dry on top of the bed sheets. About midday, the heavenly smell of baking bread would begin to drift through the little house like a benediction.

Another foreign-born friend recalled that in his boyhood he had been taught to regard bread with such respect that, whenever he dropped a piece of it, he picked it up from the floor and kissed it reverently. It struck me that this gesture of simple gratitude would look odd indeed in the typical American home where bread is no longer relished for its own sturdy goodness, but serves as a "pusher" for meats and vegetables, or to make sandwiches, *canapés* or toast. The home-baked bread of older generations has practically vanished from our tables. We are the only people in the world who subsist largely on commercial bread, manufactured by impersonal machinery on an assembly line—limp white bread that is presliced, prepackaged, and all but predigested.

But Europeans still eat the bread of their forefathers, baked in the immemorial forms of tradition. It follows that, here at home, the most interesting and appetizing breads are usually those with a foreign background. There is no shop so pleasant to visit as a busy Italian, German, French or Jewish bakery in one of our more cosmopolitan cities. The unaccustomed smell of fresh bread is rewarding enough, but there is the added excitement of seeing loaves of strange size and contour, quite unlike the standardized product we buy at the supermarket. In these colorful little shops, the art of the baker has managed to survive, in spite of our mania for mass production.

Italian breads are often imaginative to the point of fantasy. Clever hands shape the dough into curious designs. Some loaves are braided and twisted so intricately that no slice cut from the same loaf quite resembles the next one. The heavy brown crust is often thickly decorated with anise seeds, or embellished with a lustrous egg-white glaze that reflects light like a mirror. The most exuberant creations, as might be expected, are the work of Neapolitan bakers. Some of the decorative effects are inspired by fruit, flowers and religious symbols. Egg breads are traditional treats for feast days. The rich *panettone*, a specialty of Milan, is stuffed solidly with raisins and candied fruits.

To bring out its true flavor, this opulent holiday bread is best toasted and spread with butter while hot. But, as in all European countries, the most widely eaten bread of Italy is a plain loaf, either long and cylindrical or round and mound-shaped, deeply scored by hand to lend variety to the surface.

A sister loaf, now much in demand, is made of whole wheat. Tough and savory under its thick, uneven crust, it has a hearty flavor that is much livelier than our refined "graham" variety. Only the Italians seem to have mastered the art of baking *grissini*, those slender bread sticks that are all crust, and are the predestined companions of raw ham, salami and red wine.

German bakers have a light hand with breakfast rolls but are better known for their many versions of rye bread, from the bland, light-colored *bauernbrot* to weighty black pumpernickel that calls for beer, sausage or strong cheeses. Square-sided Westphalian pumpernickel, which blends rye and wheat, cuts daintily in paper-thin, moist slices for sandwiches. Germans delight in many variations of kuchen, made from plain bread dough twisted into rings, shells and braids, usually topped with sugary crumbs or fruited icing. Zwieback, a Hamburg invention, is nothing but ordinary bread baked twice. For festive occasions, the *hausfrau* is partial to gingerbread or a curious grayish loaf studded with bits of spiced pear, called *hutzelbrot*.

A great quantity of so-called "French" bread is sold and served in our cities. Most of it resembles the genuine article only in its narrow, elongated modeling. Even the expert French baker who has migrated to these shores never quite succeeds in capturing the hard, crunchy crust, the resilient crumb or the slightly salty, mildly sour flavor of his native product. The difficulty seems to lie in the fact that French wheat is different from our own, and is milled into a flour which is not only coarser but is usually not even sifted. Or it may be that in France dough is kneaded long and tirelessly to bring out the gluten content, a procedure which encourages elasticity. But, whatever the reason, the best French bread always has a "home-made" taste and texture. Large-scale commercial baking is unknown in that country. In many rural villages, the dough is mixed at home and carried to the baker once a day. In the larger towns, bread is baked in the cellar of small neighborhood shops, and sold by weight at the peak of its freshness.

The French long ago decided that the best part of any loaf was the crust, and they have created the longest, thinnest and noisiest-eating breads known to man. The *croissant*, a horn-shaped roll, has a buttery, flaky crispness that has converted many an American tourist to the meager Parisian breakfast. The thin, curving contour of this delectable creation is ingeniously adapted for immersion in a large glass of coffee or red wine. The brioche, a round, spongy roll with a ball-shaped top, has a fluffy yellow crumb endowed with an elusive flavor. It is delightful when sliced, toasted, buttered and eaten hot with a cup of creamy chocolate. A giant epicurean version from Perigord contains a stuffing of velvety *foie gras*.

Any man who has ever lived in a French town will understand the importance of good bread to a people who have raised eating to the level of love. A familiar French street spectacle that always diverts the foreigner is the transportation of bread of all types and sizes by homeward-bound citizens. Loaves a yard long, naked as the moment they left the baker's shovel, are carried jauntily like a flag, or clasped close to the bosoms of hurrying housewives. Respectably clad elderly gentlemen often thrust a golden brown *flûte* amid the ribs of a folded umbrella, and it is not unusual to see the rough, hollow-centered loaf known as a *couronne* dangling from the handlebars of a bicycle ridden by a black-smocked schoolboy.

The danger of exposure to the elements never seems to worry a people whose sanitary regulations are notoriously few, but whose bread is truly wonderful.

In America, snacks and sandwiches are a mainstay of home life, a fact which may have something to do with the increasing use of rye bread in every part of the nation except the South. Almost everywhere else, no sensible person would think of constructing a corned-beef sandwich of any less flavorsome bread than dark rye, with or without the extra zest of caraway. The best rye is Jewish. One of the oldest and most respected Brooklyn baking firms assures the freshness and hearty character of its product by grinding flour from whole rye grain every morning. The dough is prepared from a zealously guarded Old World formula, and baked on the open hearth to achieve the proper glazed dark-brown crust on all sides. Oval slices of this sour, spicy bread bring out the full smack of smoked and pickled meats, Swiss cheese, or salami that has been lightly kissed by the magic of garlic. The Jewish baking repertoire also includes oddities like the *bagel*, a flinty brown roll with a shiny exterior and a hole in the center. There is probably no more lethal missile than a stale bagel. But while fresh, it is a famous local treat when split laterally and layered with smoked salmon and cream cheese. Round, flat-cheeked rolls impregnated with oven-crisped onions and poppy seeds are another Lower East Side delicacy, so good that it has invaded the breakfast nooks of Park Avenue. The decorative *challah*, a braided egg bread of feathery lightness, makes its appearance on Fridays and is eaten traditionally at the Sabbath meal.

Many other fascinating foreign breads may be found in little shops and restaurants tucked away in odd corners of America's big cities. There are three busy bakeries in the Syrian quarter of Brooklyn that supply their compatriots with a flat disklike wheaten loaf which has come down unchanged from earliest times. A chef pointed out to me that the word for "bread" in Arabic was the same as the word for "life." And he added that it was once the custom, and may still be, for desert tribesmen to bake this same kind of bread on their circular shields over a campfire.

Guests of his colorful establishment tear off small pieces and use them with native skill to dig chunks of spicy lamb out of a stew. As in the Middle Ages, rounds of *khubz*, as this fine bread is called, were used in the Arab countries instead of plates. When the meat was finished, the gravy-soaked trencher was either eaten or thrown to the dogs. Among other Eastern breads is the Armenian *lavash*, thin as a wafer and made without leavening. It is as crisp and brown as toast, with an irregular surface broken up with air bubbles. Two delicious breads from India are *chapati* and *puri*—the first almost as thin as lace, and the second a kind of golden puffball, fried in deep fat, and always served hot.

Scandinavian rye crisps are so dehydrated that they can be filed away like phonograph records. They have a spicy flavor that contrasts magically with strong yellow cheese, as well as all the other piquant titbits of the *smörgåsbord* table. The heaviest and sourest of all foreign breads is the Russian *soldatsky*, a formidable black boulder of coarse unmixed rye. Soldiers of the Tsar's armies, when in the field, were issued a weekly ration of several pounds of this bread, with a gob of lard for spreading. This, with a basin of cabbage soup, made up their diet. Black peasant bread is not for dainty eaters, but it has meant life to many a man born to hunger and hard work. In direct flavor contrast are the English cottage loaf and the soda-risen bread of the Irish. These clean, floury breads cut evenly in capacious slices, fine for toasting and munching with butter and marmalade. Even milder and more delicate are the Scottish teatime clan of scones, muffins, oat cakes, bannocks and baps.

When it comes to really delicate table fare, the lightest and most elegant breads in the world were developed in old Vienna, and are still an important asset to any restaurant or hotel kitchen which aspires to the higher cuisine. They are a part of that sentimental tradition, dear to the nostalgic traveler, that is also compounded of light wines, whipped cream, blondes and gypsy violins. Not long after they first appeared, Viennese bread, rolls and buns conquered Europe like the waltzes of Strauss. No bread is whiter, more fragile, or so appealing to the eye and the appetite. The bakers of Vienna are a race apart, born with a light-fingered magic which transforms dough into a sort of delectable pastry that intrigues without cloying.

Any tourist who has ever enjoyed a long, leisurely café

breakfast in Vienna of the old regime will lovingly recall the classically laden tray, with its charming still-life arrangement of an egg, a mound of sweet butter, preserves, a pot of fragrant coffee, and most appetizing of all, a cluster of tiny rolls nestling crisp and golden in the fold of a napkin. The most enchanting of these rolls is the *kipfl*, only known rival of the Parisian *croissant*. It is made in the same crescent shape, but has a different crust, which seems both tender and crisp at the same time. There are a dozen different varieties of the *kipfl*. Among the most celebrated are the Radetzky, Uhl, Peregrini, Badener, Carlsbader, Kloster, Butter, Pressburger and Mohn—each distinguished by some special ingredient or embellishment, but all cunningly shaped for easy dunking in a cup of coffee.

Of the endless coterie of Viennese rolls, the most famous are the plump, rotund *Kaiser semmel* and *Kaiser weckerl*, so named because they were once cherished by the amiable Franz Josef. The *semmel* has a crunchy folded top and is usually strewn thickly with poppy seeds. The *weckerl* is shaped like two little pillows which split neatly apart for buttering. Other Viennese favorites which have been adopted by bakers of most civilized nations are: the *salzstangl*—baton-shaped, thickly encrusted with salt and caraway seeds, with a flavor that begs for goulash and beer; the *Wiener knopf*—shaped like a lover's knot; the *salzgschrade*—a fat double "pistolet" that breaks into four tiny rolls; the *beugel*—much like our East Side *bagel*, but easier on the teeth; the *Bosniaken*—a rye roll of peasant heartiness.

In mixing the dough for these famous enticements, a local yeast called *St. Marxner Pressheffe* is used to attain the airy texture so widely renowned. The characteristic "golden bloom" of the crust is made possible by baking with steam in specially constructed ovens. Rolls and bread in old Vienna were officially pronounced stale four hours after they had been exposed. But nothing is wasted by the Austrian housewife, who still uses every bit of stale bread to make stuffing, dumplings, rusks or desserts.

In our own American breadmaking, we have borrowed freely from all countries. But we do have a few types of bread distinctly our own. Corn bread is a true American product—as native as wampum or jazz. In spite of critical Yankee opinion, Southerners still dote on corn or white breads that are served and eaten smoking hot, usually with lavish additions of butter, sirup or jam. And it must be conceded that few edibles are more tempting than hot corn bread, or Maryland biscuit, fluffy from tireless beating, almost light enough to float unaided from platter to mouth.

Corn bread—whether called pone, dodger, hoecake, batter bread, Johnny cake or hush puppy—is almost invariably made from stone-ground white meal in the South, with the gritty consistency and characteristic flavor of the grain. In the North, corn bread is yellow and has a slightly sweet taste. The quarrel as to the correct color and best flavor is deep and ancient, and will probably never be satisfactorily resolved.

We have few genuinely regional breads of the sort common to European countries. Perhaps as well known as any is the brown bread of New England, rich with raisins and molasses, an indispensable adjunct of the sacred Saturday night supper of pork and beans. Sweet, milky Parker House rolls, invented at the venerable Boston hotel of that name, are about the size and shape of a child's pocketbook. A large man with a healthy appetite can eat a panful without pain. Most American housewives, when so inclined, can whip up breads of the "party" type, fancily enriched with things like fruits, cheese, nuts, dates, honey, citron and raisins.

These strike a nice balance between bread and cake, and make dainty sandwiches with the help of a cooky-cutter. Even quicker and easier to make are the new packaged frozen muffins, rolls and crumpets, which come all ready to slide into the oven. The dehumanization of baking, however, has achieved its ultimate triumph in the latest American invention—bread put up in hermetically sealed cans. To any man who still sits down to table with a sense of anticipation, the dismal notion of canned bread is enough to murder appetite.

Compared to the rugged and delicious bread of our forefathers, the commercial loaf consumed in vast quantities in the United States today is a puny specimen, with a taste and texture like cotton. It is made from flour so highly refined that the wheat germ and bran which contain most of the nutriment are lost. By Government regulation, specific doses of vitamins, minerals and milk solids are now added to the mix, thus compensating officially for the loss. This synthetic "enrichment" satisfies our national yearning for scientific embroidery. Nevertheless, modern bread never seems adequately to fill the hollow space inside a healthy human creature. The spokesman for one of the larger bakeries has stated that today's commercial loaf is carefully based upon consumer preferences. "We are giving the majority of the people exactly what they want," he says. "When enough of them demand a change to something else, we will follow their ideas as faithfully as before."

There are at least three bakeries in the East—one in Connecticut and two in Brooklyn—producing bread that compares favorably in texture, flavor and nutriment with the old-fashioned homemade product. These and other new breads are helping to restore respect for one of mankind's oldest and best foods. It is to be hoped that they will influence the spread of better commercial bread to every part of the country. In the meantime, there is nothing to prevent any housewife who is sincerely interested in good food from occasionally baking a few loaves at home for the special delectation of her family and friends. Not long ago, I was a guest at a private dinner party given by a lady known for the excellence of her table. A maid brought in a capacious wooden board covered with a white cloth. She set this before our hostess, who removed the cloth and revealed a bulging golden-brown loaf with a glazed crust that shone in the candlelight. A homely fragrance drifted to our nostrils, unlike any other in the world, and just about the best of them all.

When the loaf was cut into with a long knife, there was a crunchy, appetizing sound that has not been heard in most American homes for about forty years.

"What is it?" cried the guests. "Can it really be—"

"Yes," replied the lady of the house, trying to look modest —"it's homemade bread. I baked it myself, and it's still warm from the oven."

If she had unveiled a clutch of plover's eggs or a *pâté* of woodcock flown from Paris, the reaction could not have been more gratifying. The same sort of pleasant excitement is sure to reward any ambitious reader who cares to tackle the rather simple task of baking an honest loaf at home. Just ask any hungry man who happens to be listening.

GOLDEN BRAID

½ cup warm water (110° F.)	¼ cup soft butter
2 packages dry yeast	7½ cups all-purpose flour,
1½ cups lukewarm milk	sifted
¼ cup sugar	Extra butter for top
1 tablespoon salt	1 egg yolk
3 eggs	2 tablespoons cold water

Measure the warm water into a large mixing bowl; add yeast, stirring to dissolve it. Gradually stir in the milk, sugar, salt, unbeaten eggs and softened butter. Continue to stir until smooth. Add about half of the flour, slowly, mixing smoothly. Then add enough remaining flour to make an easily handled dough. Mix with the hand at this stage of the preparation. Turn the dough out on a lightly floured board; knead well. Grease mixing bowl; return dough to bowl; cover lightly with a folded towel, and let rise in a warm but not hot place until doubled in bulk.

Turn the dough out onto the lightly floured board and divide into three parts. With hands, shape each into a strand about 14 inches long. Place the three strands side by side on a greased baking sheet and braid them gently and loosely; do not stretch. Seal braid ends by pressing firmly together and then tucking them under. Brush braid with butter. Cover with damp cloth. Let rise in a warm place until doubled in bulk (about 50 minutes). Start oven at hot (425° F.). Beat egg yolk and cold water together and brush over loaf evenly. Bake for 25 to 30 minutes, until golden brown. Let cool before slicing. Makes 1 large braid loaf.

OATMEAL BREAD

2 packages active dry yeast	1 tablespoon salt
or 2 cakes compressed	1 cup hot double-strength
yeast	coffee
½ cup warm water	½ cup boiling water
1 cup uncooked rolled oats	5½ cups all-purpose flour,
⅔ cup molasses	sifted
½ cup shortening	2 eggs, well-beaten

If dry yeast is used, soften it in ½ cup warm water at 110° to 115° F. If compressed yeast is used, soften cakes in ½ cup water 80° to 85° F. Let stand for 5 minutes. Combine in large mixing bowl the oats, molasses, shortening and salt. Mix well. Pour over ingredients in the bowl the hot coffee and boiling water. Let cool to lukewarm. Then mix and beat until thoroughly blended. Sift in 1 cup flour, stir softened yeast in, mixing well. Add about 2 cups flour, beating well. Beat in the eggs and then enough of the remaining flour to make a soft dough. Turn dough into greased bowl, and turn dough over so as to grease its entire surface. Cover lightly with a towel and place in refrigerator to chill for 2 hours.

Grease bottoms of two 9½ x 5¼ x 2¾-inch pans. Turn chilled dough onto lightly floured board. Divide into two equal pieces and form each into a smooth ball; then shape into loaves. Place in greased pans. Cover pans lightly; let dough rise in warm, but not hot, place until doubled in bulk (about 2 hours). Start oven at moderate (350° F.). Bake loaves for about 1 hour. Make 2 loaves.

CHEDDAR BREAD

1¼ cups milk	1 tablespoon lukewarm
1 tablespoon sugar	water
1 teaspoon salt	2¾ cups all-purpose flour,
½ tablespoon butter or	sifted
margarine	1½ cups shredded Cheddar
½ cake compressed yeast	cheese
	Melted butter or margarine

Scald the milk, add sugar, salt and ½ tablespoon butter or margarine. Let cool to lukewarm. Crumble yeast into the tablespoon of lukewarm water and let soften a few minutes. Add to milk mixture. Stir and add 2 cups flour. Mix well and add cheese and remaining flour; mix into good dough. Turn dough out onto floured board and knead for 10 minutes. Grease mixing bowl, return dough to bowl, brush top with melted butter or margarine, cover lightly with towel. Let rise in a warm, but not hot, place until doubled in bulk. Knead or punch down well in bowl, then shape into a loaf and place in a greased 4 x 8-inch loaf pan. Brush with melted butter or margarine. Cover again with towel, let rise until double in bulk. Start oven at moderate (375° F.). Bake loaf for 50 minutes. Makes 1 loaf.

BANANA NUT BREAD

2½ cups all-purpose flour,	3 large ripe bananas, mashed
sifted	½ cup buttermilk
¾ teaspoon salt	½ cup shortening
1½ teaspoons baking soda	½ cup sugar
2 teaspoons baking powder	2 eggs
1 cup chopped pecans	

Start oven at moderate (350° F.). Grease 2 bread pans and sprinkle greased surfaces lightly with flour. Sift flour, salt, soda and baking powder together three times. Combine with nuts in mixing bowl. Blend mashed ripe bananas and buttermilk. Cream shortening and sugar together until fluffy. Add eggs 1 at a time, beating mixture until light after each addition. Add flour-nut mixture alternately with banana-milk mixture, mixing well into a light batter. Pour into prepared pans. Bake for 45 to 60 minutes. Let cool on wire rack before slicing and serving. Makes 2 loaves.

BROWN NUT BREAD

1½ cups graham flour	1½ cups sour milk
¾ cup all-purpose flour,	⅓ cup New Orleans
sifted	molasses
½ teaspoon salt	¼ cup broken walnuts
1½ teaspoons soda	

Start oven at moderate (325° F.). Grease 4 x 8-inch loaf pan. Mix and sift dry ingredients into mixing bowl. Add milk and molasses, stir well to smooth batter. Add nuts. Pour into greased pan. Bake for 1 hour. Makes 1 loaf.

POLISH RYE BREAD WITH CARAWAY SEEDS

2 cups of milk, scalded	4 cups rye flour, sifted
3 tablespoons shortening	2 cups all-purpose flour,
2 tablespoons molasses	sifted
1 tablespoon salt	1½ tablespoons caraway
1½ cakes compressed yeast	seeds
¼ cup lukewarm water	

Combine in a large mixing bowl the milk, shortening, molasses and salt. Let cool to lukewarm. Soften the yeast about 5 minutes in the lukewarm water. Add to mixing bowl. Slowly add flour, both white and rye, and caraway seeds, until dough is stiff enough to knead. Turn dough out on floured board and knead until smooth and elastic. Grease mixing bowl generously, place dough in bowl, cover lightly with towel and let rise in a warm, not hot, place until doubled in bulk. Punch down well in bowl, and then put into 3 well-greased loaf pans. Cover lightly with towel and let rise again in mildly warm place about 1 hour. Start oven at moderate (375° F.). Bake loaves for 1 hour. Makes 3 loaves.

HONEY, NUT AND ORANGE BREAD

2 cups all-purpose flour,	¼ teaspoon grated nutmeg
sifted	½ cup honey
1 teaspoon baking powder	1 slightly beaten egg
1 teaspoon soda	1 cup milk
1 teaspoon salt	½ cup chopped nuts
½ teaspoon powdered	¼ cup grated orange or
cinnamon	lemon peel
½ teaspoon powdered ginger	

Start oven at moderate (350° F.). Grease 5 x 9-inch loaf pan. Mix and sift dry ingredients together three times into mixing bowl. Add honey, egg and milk, and beat for 15 minutes. Fold in nuts and peel. Bake for 45 minutes. Makes 1 loaf.

DUTCH POPPY-SEED BREAD

1 cake compressed yeast	4 tablespoons butter, melted
1 cup milk, scalded and	and cooled
cooled to lukewarm	1 egg beaten with
¼ cup sugar	2 tablespoons water
1 teaspoon salt	¼ cup poppy seeds
1 well-beaten egg	
3¾ cups all-purpose flour,	
sifted	

Soften yeast in lukewarm milk in mixing bowl. Add sugar and salt and let stand 5 minutes. Beat egg in. Add flour and butter gradually to make dough. Turn dough out on lightly floured board and knead until smooth and elastic. Grease mixing bowl, place dough in bowl, and turn it around and over in the bowl to grease all surfaces of the dough. Cover lightly with towel and let rise in warm, not hot, place for 30 minutes. Punch down in bowl. Divide into 3 parts, shape gently into long ropes and braid them. Place braid on a greased baking sheet or in a greased wide pan. Cover lightly with towel and let rise again until doubled in bulk. Start oven

at moderate (350° F.). Brush braid with beaten egg and water. Sprinkle thickly with poppy seeds. Bake for 35 to 40 minutes. Makes 1 braided loaf.

GERMAN ONION BREAD

2 medium-sized onions,	2 cups all-purpose flour,
peeled and chopped	sifted
8 tablespoons butter or	3 teaspoons baking powder
shortening	¾ cup milk
1¾ teaspoons salt	1 cup thin sour cream
Grind of fresh pepper	3 egg yolks

Cook onions in 4 tablespoons butter or shortening until golden, but not browned. Season with ½ teaspoon salt and a grind of fresh pepper. Pour mixture into 1 3 x 9-inch baking pan. Keep pan warm.

Start oven at very hot (450° F.). Sift flour, baking powder and ½ teaspoon salt together 3 times. Cut in the remaining 4 tablespoons butter or shortening until mixture has the consistency of coarse meal. Stir milk in to make soft dough. Turn dough out on lightly floured board and knead for about 1 minute. Then roll dough to about ½ inch thickness and place on top of onion mixture in baking pan. Beat sour cream and eggs together; season with ¾ teaspoon salt and generous grind of fresh pepper. Pour over dough. Bake for 12 to 15 minutes. Serve hot, cut in squares. Makes about 20 servings. It is especially good with salad.

FRENCH GRUYÈRE CHEESE BREAD

2 cups water	6 eggs
¾ cup butter	1½ cups grated Gruyère
¾ teaspoon salt	cheese
1¾ cups all-purpose flour,	1 beaten egg
sifted	1 tablespoon water

Combine water, butter, and salt in a large saucepan and bring to a boil. When boiling, remove pan from heat and stir flour in smoothly. Return to heat, cook for about 30 minutes stirring vigorously with wooden spoon. Remove from heat again; add eggs, one at a time beating vigorously. Stir in cheese.

Start oven at hot (425° F.). Butter a baking sheet. Spoon dough onto baking sheet in a high ring. Brush top with beaten egg mixed with water. Bake in hot oven for 10 minutes. Reduce heat to moderate (350° F.) and continue baking for about 30 minutes or until browned and crusty. Let cool. Makes 10 or more servings. Wonderful as a Sunday-night bread to go with salad.

BUTTERMILK SODA BREAD

4 cups all-purpose flour,	1 teaspoon baking soda
sifted	2 teaspoons cream of tartar
¼ teaspoon salt	1 egg, beaten
1 teaspoon sugar	1½ cups buttermilk

Start oven at moderate (350° F.). Grease 4 x 8-inch loaf pan generously. Sift dry ingredients together three times into a mixing bowl. Add egg and buttermilk and mix well. Pour batter into greased pan. Bake for 35 minutes. Makes 1 loaf.

SAFFRON BREAD STOCKHOLM

About 7 cups all-purpose
   flour, sifted
2¼ cups slightly warm milk
3 cakes compressed yeast
1 teaspoon saffron
⅔ cup plus 1 teaspoon sugar
10 tablespoons butter
1 beaten egg
2 tablespoons ground
   almonds

⅔ cup seedless raisins or
   currants soaked in
   warm water and
   drained

Coating:
1 beaten egg
3 tablespoons chopped
   almonds
2 tablespoons sugar

Sift 5 cups flour into a large mixing bowl. Soften the yeast in 2 cups of the warm milk for about 5 minutes. Combine with the flour; work into a dough, adding more flour if needed. Cover lightly with a towel, let rise in a warm, not hot, place until doubled in bulk. Mix the saffron with 1 teaspoon sugar, stir into the remaining ¼ cup of warm milk. Cream butter and ⅔ cup of sugar until light, add the egg, and then the saffron mixture, almonds and raisins or currants. Work into the dough, adding more flour if needed. When well worked in, let dough rise again until doubled in bulk. Cover lightly with a towel and set bowl in warm, not hot, place until dough doubles in bulk.

Turn risen dough out onto a lightly floured board and knead well. Divide into 6 pieces. Roll out gently and shape into strands. Twist the strands into 2 braids, place on greased baking sheet, cover lightly and let rise about 30 minutes or longer if necessary to double their bulk. Start oven at moderate (350° F.). Mix coating of egg, almonds and sugar. Brush lightly over top of braids. Bake for about 30 to 40 minutes. Test for doneness. Let cool on bread rack. Makes 2 braids or 1 large braid ring. Makes 16 to 20 servings.

WISCONSIN POTATO BREAD

1 cake compressed yeast
⅓ cup lukewarm water
6 cups all-purpose flour,
   sifted
4 tablespoons lard or
   shortening
4 tablespoons butter

1 cup light cream
1½ cups lukewarm riced
   potatoes
¼ cup currants, soaked in
   hot water and drained
1 beaten egg
2 tablespoons water

Soften yeast in lukewarm water for about 5 minutes. Sift flour into large mixing bowl, cut in lard or shortening and butter. Add softened yeast, cream, riced potatoes and currants. Mix well, work with hands until a good dough texture is obtained. Turn out onto lightly floured board, knead until elastic. Grease mixing bowl, place dough in it, cover lightly with towel and let rise in warm, but not hot, place for 30 minutes. Punch down and knead for 1 or 2 minutes. Divide into 3 parts, shape gently into long ropes and braid. Place braid on baking sheet or in shallow pan. Cover lightly with towel and let rise in warm place until doubled.

Start oven at moderately hot (400° F.). Beat egg with the 2 tablespoons water and brush over braid. Bake in moderately hot oven for 10 minutes. Reduce heat to moderate (350° F.) and bake for 45 to 50 minutes more. Makes 1 braided loaf.

Everybody Loves Spaghetti / *Silas Spitzer*

You may serve spaghetti, ravioli, vermicelli, noodles—
of a hundred sizes and shapes—
in endless appetizing ways, all happily rewarding

Few experiences are more satisfying than finding one-self seated on the terrace of a Neapolitan water-front restaurant, gazing at the fantastically beautiful vista of bay and hills from behind a heap of steaming spaghetti, crested with scarlet sauce and topped with a snowy mantle of cheese.

Such an experience moves one to offer silent thanks to the unknown benefactor of mankind who first created spaghetti by forcing dough through holes in a metal plate. The thin yellow strands which resulted have become one of the world's great wheaten foods, forming the major diet of at least one large population, and rivaling bread itself in the esteem of hungry people everywhere.

Pasta, an Italian word embracing solid spaghetti, tubular macaroni, noodles, ravioli and all their multitudinous kinfolk of whatever shape or size, is as typically Italian as grand opera, old masters and tart red wine in wicker-bound flasks. But the truth is that the Italians did not invent *pasta.* According to reliable authority, *pasta* actually originated in China and there is a fable that the first specimens were brought to Europe by that tireless traveler, Marco Polo, packed away in what surely must have been the most capacious sample case that ever existed.

To this day, the Chinese are rapt eaters of noodles and deft manipulators of those threadlike tendrils, seemingly without beginning or end, which are known elsewhere as vermicelli. Both noodles and vermicelli play a prominent role in the Chinese dishes which have become so familiar in American cities. During the thrifty one-flight-up days of Chinese-American restaurants, twenty cents would buy a large bowl of Yat

Gar Mein, a soup which was loaded with a mass of noodles. An elderly horse player we once knew sustained himself on this soup when his luck was bad. He discovered a gaudy emporium on Third Avenue where it was served not only containing a heavy ballast of noodles but halves of hard-boiled eggs and chunks of chicken. In his opinion, it was the cheapest complete meal in America. *Won Ton* is an elegant Chinese conceit resembling ravioli, and is usually offered in chicken or vegetable broth, where it spreads its delicate wings like some fragile undersea fauna. *Chow Mein* owes its intricate texture to the addition of crisply fried rice noodles, now so well known to Americans that they are sold in most grocery stores.

The Italians, who are supposed to have first learned about *pasta* in the fourteenth century from the Chinese, elaborated upon the theme with typical Latin imagination and artistry. They became adept at extruding it in narrow lengths, or punching it out of sheets of dough with metal dies, at first by hand, later with ingenious machines. Meat has always been scarce in Italy, and it is easy to see why Italians took to eating vast quantities of this most satisfying substitute. It is cheap, easy to prepare, wonderfully filling, and practically imperish-

The Amalfi drive at Positano—and a dish of pasta at Miramare ▶
where the artistry of the spaghetti matches that of nature.

SLIM AARONS

70

able in storage. It has the honest wheat flavor of good bread, universally appealing to people of all races. But *pasta* has been developed by Italians until it has become an entire school of cookery, rich, infinitely varied and utterly unlike any other.

There are in America certain Italian restaurateurs who strive honestly to preserve the pure *pasta* tradition of their homeland and thus, little by little, educate the American palate to appreciate its undeniable merit. We are proud to claim the friendship, for example, of Toni Gugnoni, for many years master chef and owner of some of New York's better Italian restaurants. Toni was born near Forlì, well within the benign influence of Bologna, and not far from the Adriatic Sea. His mother was, of course, a famous cook—what Italian would ever admit to anything less? "But my father," he says, with a look of astonishment—"he was even better." As a boy, he watched them both at work in the kitchen and made careful mental notes which laid the foundation for his later career. When he came to this country, about thirty-five years ago, the most precious object in his trunk was the family rolling pin, four feet long and about half the diameter of the kind Americans use. Since that time, he has used this impressive implement six days a week to roll out his batches of noodle dough.

"In my restaurant," said Toni, "we serve only fresh noodles, fresh ravioli. Everything is homemade from high-gluten flour and the best eggs. The macaroni and spaghetti come ready-made in packages, of course. I would make them myself, like the noodles, but that is not possible. In my home in the old country, the noodles were always made fresh the same day they were eaten—and that's the way it has to be in my restaurant."

Early every morning, Toni works in a small room of his establishment—the San Marino, in East 53rd Street—using not only his remarkable rolling pin but several mysterious hand-operated "machines" which cut the dough in various widths, from the wispy *Capelli di Angelo* (angel's hair) to the broad-beamed *lasagne*. He keeps the door of his "laboratory" locked at all times, and no outsiders are permitted to assist in his secret rites. Among his specialties are green *tagliarini* and *lasagne*, made with fresh chopped spinach, cooked and served with a sauce or stuffing of beef, lamb and chicken livers, blended with tomato paste and Parmesan cheese. He is equally famous for his *Gnocchi alla Romana* and his *cannelloni* baked with cheese in individual casseroles.

"Maestro Toscanini used to come all the time to eat my green noodles and ravioli," said Toni, beaming modestly. "Many famous singers from the Met have eaten my food. But never Caruso. I cannot lie to you—I am the only Italian chef who never cooked for Caruso."

A puzzled expression clouds his broad, open countenance when he speaks of the difficulties he has had with less appreciative clients. "I don't know why it is," he says, "but most Americans must eat everything soft. The steak must be like butter. Boiled beef must fall apart when touched with the fork. Vegetables, too. I like to cook all spaghetti to order, eight, ten minutes—*al dente*, you know, slightly firm to the teeth. But too many customers still send it back. They like it only when it is soft like mush."

Most Americans are familiar with half a dozen patterns of *pasta*. Italians have more than a hundred and fifty shapes and sizes—from the tiny golden specks called *pastina* which are fed mainly to children and invalids in soups and puddings, to cavernous muff-shaped *tufoli* and *rigatoni*, so large that they are usually stuffed, one at a time, with meat, cheese and tomatoes, like individual tarts. The names Italians have invented for these different forms of *pasta* are sometimes charming, and always vividly descriptive of their shape or dimensions. Here are a few of the more picturesque and less familiar ones: *amorini*—cupids; *farfalle*—butterflies; *cappelletti*—little hats; *stellini*—little stars; *mostaccioli*—little mustaches; *tirabaci*—kiss catchers; *fidelini*—faithful ones.

These and many other types are widely known in Italy, but some American manufacturers, with an eye to efficiency, have stripped the list down to an essential few. The largest domestic firm, however, which has an important Italian-American trade, carries fifty-odd shapes and sizes, and does a brisk business with most of them. And this illuminates a fundamental difference between the eating habits of Italians and Americans. Although all varieties of *pasta* are made from the same basic formula of wheat and water, they do not all taste the same to an Italian.

Thin *vermicelli* or *spaghettini* does not taste like short, fat macaroni such as *ziti* or *rigatoni*. Besides the difference in length and thickness, one is quite smooth and the other is corrugated.

When one chews a mouthful of hollow shells, there is a spurting sensation, because each shell encloses some sauce. The same sauce forms a sort of coating on the outside of spaghetti or noodles—quite a different taste.

These fifty-odd shapes and sizes give the cook a chance to use different ideas in sauces, meat, fish and vegetables. She doesn't have to repeat herself in a month. The coarser patterns call for bulky meat mixtures and can make a whole meal. *Minestrone*—that's the vegetable soup into which you dump everything you find in the kitchen—is made different each time by adding little things like *ditalini*, alphabets or *farfalle*—or big ones like *mezzani* or *tortellini*. The wide, flat *lasagne*, with a rich filling between the layers, covered with cheese and sauce and then baked, is a fine meal in itself. Americans are learning how much more there is to *pasta* than spaghetti with meat balls.

All macaroni products of good quality are made of semolina, a granular meal ground from the heart of amber durum wheat. This is the hardest known variety of wheat, high in gluten and low in starch. Its flinty character is what enables *pasta* to stay firm and chewy after it has been cooked. There are a number of experimental versions, usually sold in "health-food" shops, which contain flour ground from rice, soybeans, artichokes or cornmeal as partial replacements for semolina, but they have not found much favor with devotees of conventional *pasta*. One leading manufacturer, however, has made a successful specialty of products with an unusually high gluten content. These are popular with diet-conscious women. A small portion of *pasta*, with a spoonful of cheese and a scanty teaspoonful of butter, contains no more calories than potatoes dressed in the same manner. But who wants to eat a small portion of *pasta*?

Macaroni products made from American semolina are said by authorities to be a match for the world's finest grades. Now and then, you may hear a minority opinion to the contrary. A veteran Italian restaurateur, when asked his views, shook his head sadly, recalling the spaghetti formerly imported from his native country.

"We used to serve the Abruzzi spaghetti years ago," he said nostalgically. "That was the real stuff, like I remember when I was a boy. It had a taste like . . . like nuts. Maybe on account of the water they used. Maybe because they made it out of the pure semolina, nothing else. Even if you boiled it for half an hour, it stayed *al dente*. It was long—long as your arm. They always made macaroni long in the old country. It tasted better that way." And he went on to talk about the little town in Southern Italy where he was born. In fair weather, they used to hang the freshly made macaroni outdoors to dry in the sun. It would fill the narrow, crooked street from wall to wall, and when you looked down from a hilltop near the town, it was like a winding river of gold. "The sea air and sunshine got into it while it was drying," he said, "and did something wonderful to its flavor."

Despite such nostalgic recollections of that fine old Italian *pasta*, Americans favor food products not exposed to dust and germs. In modern U. S. plants, most of the operations take place inside fully enclosed machines.

Our macaroni is dried with circulating purified air, in thermostatically controlled chambers, and packaged in airtight containers. A satisfactory strand of spaghetti is translucent, has a pale amber color, and is elastic enough to bend slightly under pressure, but will snap with a clean, glassy break. One of the best ways to test it is to watch how it behaves while boiling. In ten minutes, a good spaghetti will swell to at least twice its former size, yet retain its tubular outline, firmness and pleasant wheat odor.

Egg noodles, which constitute about 15 per cent of all *pasta* sold, are made by adding not less than 5.5 per cent of egg solids to a mixture of durum flour and water. Only egg yolks are used, as whites would make the noodles tough. Unlike other varieties of *pasta*, egg noodles are not pressed through dies, but ironed out in thin sheets between rollers, and then sliced into various widths. They take less than ten minutes to cook and can be mixed or mated with yesterday's leftovers of meat, fish or vegetables, and rushed to the table in a jiffy.

The conscientious housewife of yesteryear rolled out her noodle dough every morning and hung it up to dry in sheets behind the stove. There are still a few old-fashioned wives who make noodles in the old manner, but most people think the manufactured noodle of today is as good as its handmade ancestor.

The late Leo Lindy, that shining paragon among modern restaurateurs, however, used nothing but homemade noodles in the rich distillation identified on his menu as "Chicken in the Pot." And he was quite certain that his pampered clients would detect the presence of a manufactured noodle at the very first nibble.

We owe our most delectable *pasta* recipes to the Italians, who have specialized in this field of cooking for six hundred years. In Italy the heaviest eaters of spaghetti are those who are the hungriest. But *pasta* is much more than a humble form of provender for yawning stomachs. From the poorest Calabrian peasant to Roman or Florentine aristocrats who can afford to dine off gold plates there are few Italians who do not eat it in some form at least once a day. The fact is that this good wheat food seems to have been created expressly for the Italian style of cooking, which is distinguished by simplicity, robust flavor, and the gift of arousing and satisfying appetite without recourse to artificial fripperies.

The observant traveler in Italy perceives that *pasta* becomes increasingly important as he proceeds southward. In Naples, Calabria and Sicily, it is more often a full meal than a supplementary course. If you have a rugged appetite, you will find yourself unable to resist spaghetti or macaroni as it is served in the southern tradition—piled mountainously in deep plates, lavishly sauced and strewn with cheese and served steaming hot.

Ladies who boast delicate appetites usually prefer the more elegant type of North Italian cuisine, but when a man of sound digestion is confronted with a huge helping of *Vermicelli alle Vongole* or *Cannelloni all' Amalfitana*, the glutton within him is likely to take over.

Neapolitan spaghetti sauce is traditionally founded upon tomatoes. A pot of it simmers constantly on the stove of even the humblest household. It is thick and oily, with a powerful undertone of garlic and the aromatic fragrance of orégano, that delightful herb which is as characteristic of the region as the liquid accent of its inhabitants. Thick and ruddy, this tomato sauce of the south bears little kinship to the meager concoction of the same name which is prepared in so many American homes and restaurants.

Sicilians are a rugged people who do not look for fantasy in their *pasta*. They like their macaroni stubby and thick, and they delight in combining it with fried eggplant and tomatoes—a dish that is understandably attractive to a man who has been toiling all day in the fields, or hauling nets in a fishing boat. The people of Rome are fond of the shorter cuts of macaroni and like their *pasta* cooked with even more firmness than *al dente* implies elsewhere. They boil macaroni briefly, mix it with a zestful sauce made of ham or bacon and tomatoes, and often set the pot inside the oven for a few minutes to attain a light crust of brown. Their favorite cheese with *pasta* is either Pecorino, which is made from goat's milk, or the tingling Romano, which many Americans find a bit too sharp.

Visitors to Rome who have eaten Alfredo's *Maestose Fettuccine al triplice burro*—or "Majestic Noodles with a triple serving of butter"—will never forget it: a huge silver-domed platter rushed to your table by a panting major-domo, flanked on each side by two eager but quite useless flunkies, Alfredo bringing up the rear. He would lift the silver lid with a dramatic flourish and reveal a mess of plain egg noodles, writhing in their own steam. With his shining implements, he would toss and swirl the *fettuccine* into a frothing mass, working into it drifts of freshly grated cheese and a great chunk of sweet butter. The final seasoning of salt and pepper was an airy gesture executed at arm's length. We have eaten noodles at a hundred different boards since that time long ago, but none seem worthy of comparison with Alfredo's.

It is practically impossible to find inferior *pasta* in Bologna, a city which many knowing palates rank as the capital of fine Italian cooking. Meat sauce is Bologna's significant gift to the world. There is no definitive recipe for this savory mixture. The meat may be beef or ham, veal, lamb, chicken livers or sausage. Sometimes it is chopped coarsely and sometimes it is ground like hamburger. The choice of seasonings may be basil, thyme, bay leaf, tarragon or parsley, or a combination of several. It depends entirely upon the inspiration of the moment and the state of the larder. Often the sauce contains dried or fresh mushrooms, or the heart and liver of rabbits—even larks, quail, figpeckers or swallows. The only unvarying element of Sauce Bolognese is meat of some kind and, of course, garlic, tomatoes and olive oil. Whatever goes into it, this sauce is always dark, rich and thick, and makes the perfect companion for *pasta*.

Visitors to Bologna are advised to try the renowned Restaurant Pappagallo, where the importance of *pasta* is indicated by two separate and distinct classifications on the lengthy menu—*Al Brodo*, or cooked and served in soup, and *Asciutta*, or boiled, drained and eaten with a sauce. They will take your order for such local favorites as green *Tagliatelle* made with fresh spinach; *Cappelletti*, or "little hats," stuffed with minced chicken breast, ricotta cheese, butter and egg yolk, then cooked in a golden essence of capon; *Cannelloni* baked with prosciutto and fresh pot cheese—and, perhaps most satisfying of all, *Spaghetti Bolognese*, which looks much the same as you remember it back home, but somehow tastes as though it came straight from heaven.

In Genoa and the neighboring coast, a favorite meal for "lean" days in the religious calendar is *Pasta al Pesto*, the dressing for which is made very quickly by pounding leaves of basil, cloves of garlic and Parmesan cheese with oil in a mortar until it forms a paste. Even more typical regional dishes are those which combine *pasta* with practically everything that swims or wiggles in the salty waters of the Ligurian Sea.

We know certain gourmets who insist that spaghetti attains the rating of an international delicacy only when it is wedded to clams, in the Genoese manner. Two types of clam sauce, white and red, are usually offered on most menus. The true clam lover will prefer the white sauce, which contains no tomatoes, peppers or onions, and permits the inimitable smack of clams to come through unimpaired. At the top of its form, *Spaghetti alle Vongole*—or the equally seductive *linguine* or *vermicelli* prepared in the same style—is the pure unadulterated soul of the bivalve. It is made quite simply, by first coloring garlic and parsley in olive oil (heating in the oil until the garlic becomes golden and the parsley darker), then adding clam broth and letting it cook slowly until considerably reduced. Coarsely chopped clams, or tiny whole ones, are simmered in this mixture for about five minutes, and a plentiful seasoning of cracked black pepper is the final touch. It should be served at the very moment that sauce and spaghetti meet in sizzling communion.

One of the simplest *pasta* dishes, popular in all parts of the country, is *Spaghetti aglio olio*, literally "Spaghetti with garlic and oil." Not many Italian restaurants in America trouble to put it on the menu, but when you do find it there, you may be quite sure you are in a place where *pasta* is respected for its intrinsic goodness and where food is cooked without snobbery or pretense. We know at least one male amateur who has won a reputation for culinary skill solely on the perfect accomplishment of this simple but irresistible recipe. He selects his guests with discrimination and is careful to avoid the sort of eater who "can take garlic or leave it alone." For this food is designed for those rugged souls who are never troubled by inhibited notions of gentility when their appetites are aroused. If any fairly competent amateur would like to try the recipe on his friends, the procedure is not difficult.

To serve six reasonably ravenous eaters who plan to make spaghetti the mainstay of the meal, you will need not less than three pounds of spaghetti. Use the largest kettle you can find in the kitchen—a five-gallon stock pot is not too large, as spaghetti must swim in an ample bath to come out free of excess starch. Salt the water plentifully, about six level tablespoons (two for each pound of spaghetti), and when it has come to a violent boil, slide in your spaghetti a few pieces at a time. When a sample length of spaghetti feels tender yet springy between finger and thumb, it is cooked. This should take about ten minutes—or longer, depending upon your personal interpretation of the phrase *al dente*.

Meanwhile, you have been heating together in a heavy iron skillet one cup of olive oil and a quarter pound of butter. Now drop into the butter and oil five or six fat cloves of garlic which have been minced small. Do not allow the garlic to turn black and bitter—when it is lightly colored scoop the bits out with a strainer. (You can throw them away, or else reserve them for later addition to the spaghetti.)

Place a colander in the sink and, with a large fork, lift the spaghetti from the pot into the colander. (A few gentle shakes of the colander will drain the spaghetti.) While the spaghetti is still smoking hot, transfer it quickly to a warm tureen or other large-lidded vessel and pour over it the seething garlic sauce. (It is these last few hectic moments that test the skill of the cook, for no step may be overlooked and the final success of the dish depends on keeping everything as hot as possible.)

Add half a cupful of finely chopped fresh basil, half a pound of Parmesan cheese, freshly grated, salt to taste and plenty of freshly ground black pepper. (If fresh basil is not available, the next best thing is an equal quantity of finely chopped fresh parsley. Dried herbs are not recommended for this dish.) Lift and blend the spaghetti vigorously with a large fork and spoon. Then cover the tureen while the steam is still rising and rush it to the table. A bowl of grated Parmesan should be passed around while you are heaping soup plates with the fragrant, herb-flecked *pasta*.

In America, the best-known macaroni dish is the familiar home-style job, baked with yellow cheese. In its less admirable forms, it comes awash with a milky sauce which dilutes its natural zestfulness and robs it of character. But when made with a good quality of snappy Cheddar, a sharp seasoning of mustard, and a minimum of liquid content, it is a fine, wholesome course.

Once an appreciative visitor has sampled *pasta* in the better eating places of Italy, he will find it hard to reconcile himself to the overcooked, underseasoned and thinly sauced versions which are served without apology in so many American restaurants. Only in New York and San Francisco is the genuine Italian cuisine practiced and patronized on an ample public scale. Exceptions exist elsewhere, but it is evident that *pasta* worthy of its traditions is available only where there happens to be a large concentration of Italian citizens. If you ever discover a restaurant where you are greeted on entering by the pervasive aroma of garlic, hot olive oil and spices, and where the menu lists at least a dozen different *pasta* items under their authentic native titles, you may be reasonably sure that you are about to eat well.

BRANDIED CHICKEN LIVERS AND NOODLES

1 8-oz. package of thin noodles	¾ teaspoon salt
2 quarts rapidly boiling water	½ teaspoon celery salt
	Grind of fresh pepper
1 tablespoon salt	1 teaspoon chopped chives
Butter	1 teaspoon chopped parsley
2 tablespoons grated Swiss cheese	½ teaspoon thyme
	1 tablespoon flour
1 pound chicken livers	2 tablespoons cognac
1 pound sliced mushrooms	3 tablespoons heavy cream
	¼ cup bread crumbs

Cook noodles in rapidly boiling water to which salt has been added, about 10 minutes or until tender. Drain. Mix with about 1 tablespoon butter; pour into buttered, shallow 2-quart baking dish. Sprinkle with grated Swiss cheese.

Sauté livers and mushrooms lightly and quickly in 2 tablespoons butter. Reduce heat and season with salt, celery salt, pepper, chives, parsley and thyme. Sprinkle the flour over the mixture and stir it in well. Add cognac and cream and stir over low heat for a few minutes. Let stand over very low heat for 5 minutes. Start oven at moderately hot (400° F.). Pour mushroom mixture into center of noodles. Sprinkle crumbs over all. Place in oven for 15 minutes or until top is browned. Serve hot. Makes 6 servings.

ROMAN HOLIDAY SPAGHETTI

1 8-oz. box spaghetti	6 fillets anchovy, cut in small pieces
2 quarts rapidly boiling water	1 cup grated Parmesan cheese
1 tablespoon salt	
	1 tablespoon chopped chives
½ pound fresh mushrooms, thinly sliced	1 tablespoon chopped parsley
5 tablespoons butter or margarine	½ teaspoon sweet basil or orégano
	Extra cheese

Cook spaghetti in rapidly boiling water, with salt added, about 12 minutes or until tender. Drain in warm colander and keep warm over boiling water until sauce is ready.

Cook mushrooms in 3 tablespoons butter or margarine for 5 minutes. Add anchovies, stir, and mix with spaghetti. Add the cheese, chives, parsley, basil or orégano and remaining 2 tablespoons of butter. Serve at once with a bowl of grated cheese. Makes 6 servings.

MUSHROOM AND CLAM SAUCE

Substitute 6 fresh clams, finely chopped, for the anchovies, and complete recipe as described.

MUSHROOM AND CHICKEN LIVER SAUCE

Substitute 6 cooked chicken livers, chopped fine, for anchovies in sauce above; increase parsley to 2 tablespoons, add ½ teaspoon salt and a grind of fresh pepper. Complete recipe as described.

RIGATI WITH GARLIC AND TOMATO SAUCE

½ pound beef, chopped	Salt and pepper
½ pound pork, chopped	½ teaspoon sweet basil
2 tablespoons olive oil	2 bay leaves, crumbled
1 clove garlic, peeled and cut in half	1 tablespoon butter
	Grated Parmesan cheese
1 tablespoon chopped parsley	1 pound rigati, large macaroni cut diagonally in short lengths
1 No. 2 can tomatoes, chopped	
1 10½-oz. can tomato purée	6 quarts boiling water

Combine meats and brown slowly in hot oil in a deep saucepan. Add garlic and parsley, stir and cook 5 minutes. Remove garlic and discard it. Add tomatoes, tomato purée and a light seasoning of salt and pepper; cover the saucepan and let sauce simmer about 1 hour. Add basil and bay leaves; cook 1 or 2 minutes longer. Remove from heat, add butter, stir.

When sauce is nearly done, put rigati on to cook in 6 quarts of rapidly boiling water to which 2 tablespoons of salt have been added. Boil rapidly for 12 minutes or longer if very soft macaroni is preferred. Stir occasionally. Drain in colander. Pour onto hot serving platter; add above sauce. Top with grated Parmesan cheese and serve at once. Makes 4 servings.

Use same sauce and cooking instructions for the large-tube macaroni called ziti, the giant-sized occhi di lupo macaroni and the huge rigatoni tubes.

MANICOTTI

1 pound all-purpose flour, sifted	¼ pound prosciutto, finely ground
1½ tablespoons butter	Grind of fresh pepper
3 eggs, beaten	4 quarts boiling water
½ teaspoon salt	1 tablespoon salt
Stuffing:	1½ cups tomato sauce
1 pound ricotta (Italian cottage cheese)	½ cup grated Romano cheese
2 eggs, beaten	

Mix flour, butter, eggs and salt together. Add a little barely warm water, mixing with hands or wooden spoon to a fairly soft dough. Turn it out on a lightly floured board; knead into a smooth ball. Cut in half. Lightly roll each half out to the thickness of noodle dough. Cut in pieces about 5 x 6 inches.

Mix ricotta and eggs smoothly together; add prosciutto and pepper and mix until smooth and well blended. Spread about 1½ tablespoons of this mixture on each piece of dough, fold over securely or roll and close edges firmly by moistening the edges of the dough and pressing them tightly together.

Cook these "muffs," a few at a time, in about 4 quarts of rapidly boiling water with salt added. After about 10 minutes' boiling or when dough is tender, lift each muff out with a flat skimmer. Place on greased fireproof oven platter. Cover with tomato sauce and sprinkle with Romano cheese. Place under moderate broiler heat for about 5 minutes or until the sauce is bubbly and the edges of the manicotti are lightly browned. Serve at once. Makes 6 servings of 2 manicotti per serving.

RAVIOLI, TUSCAN STYLE

½ pound pork sausage,
    cooked
1 cup chopped and drained
    cooked spinach
1 tablespoon grated
    Parmesan cheese
1 egg yolk, beaten ·
Salt and pepper
3 tablespoons finely chopped
    prosciutto
2 tablespoons finely chopped
    Italian salami

½ teaspoon sweet basil
4 cups all-purpose flour,
    sifted
3 eggs, beaten
5 quarts rapidly boiling
    water
3 tablespoons salt
½ cup melted butter
3 tablespoons finely
    chopped parsley

Combine cooked sausage, spinach, cheese and egg yolk. Season lightly with salt and pepper. Add prosciutto, salami and basil. Mix well.

Sift flour 3 times. Combine with beaten eggs and about 1 teaspoon water to make dough. Knead dough in bowl until firm, turn it out onto lightly floured board and knead again. Then cut into 2 pieces. Roll each out into a very thin sheet. Cut each sheet into 2-inch squares using a pastry wheel or knife. Place about 1 teaspoon meat mixture in center of each square. With finger tip quickly moisten pastry around filling with a very small amount of water. Cover each filling topped square with another square of pastry, press all edges carefully with fingers or tines of fork, to seal filling in.

Add salt to boiling water; cook a few ravioli at a time. Let boil for about 20 minutes. Lift out with slotted spoon, drain in warmed colander. Serve at once in warmed serving dish with melted butter and parsley. Makes 4 or more servings.

ANOTHER RAVIOLI FILLING

2 cups finely chopped cooked
    chicken, turkey or veal
2 tablespoons grated
    Parmesan cheese
1 egg, beaten

½ teaspoon salt
Grind of black pepper
¼ teaspoon grated nutmeg
1 teaspoon grated lemon
    peel
1 tablespoon butter

Combine chicken, turkey or veal with the Parmesan cheese, egg, salt, black pepper, and nutmeg. Add the lemon peel and butter. Mix well. Use as filling for ravioli pastry as given in the recipe above.

GOURMET'S CHOICE FILLING

1 lamb's brain, cleaned by
    meat dealer
½ cup very thick sour cream
½ cup lumpy pot cheese
1 egg, beaten

½ teaspoon salt
Grind of black pepper
¼ teaspoon grated nutmeg
1 tablespoon grated
    Parmesan cheese

Parboil brain in slightly salted water 5 minutes. Drain and chop in bowl with sour cream and pot cheese; blend in the egg, salt, pepper, nutmeg and Parmesan cheese. Mix well. Taste and add more pot cheese if the mixture is too thin and more Parmesan cheese if it seems bland. Spread on ravioli pastry and cook as described.

SWEET RAVIOLI AS A DESSERT

½ pound lumpy pot cheese
1 egg plus 1 yolk, beaten
2 tablespoons granulated
    sugar
½ teaspoon vanilla extract

1 tablespoon finely ground
    orange peel or
    preserved ginger
Powdered sugar

Mix well together pot cheese, egg and extra yolk, granulated sugar and vanilla extract. Add the preserved ginger or orange peel. Spread on ravioli pastry as described and fry in deep hot lard or shortening, at 375° F. for about 5 minutes or until golden brown. Drain. Serve hot with powdered sugar.

SICILIAN BAKED VERMICELLI

½ pound vermicelli or thin
    spaghetti
4 quarts water, rapidly
    boiling
1 tablespoon salt
3½ tablespoons olive oil
2 tablespoons chopped
    parsley
½ cup bread crumbs

¼ cup tomato sauce
6 smelts, cleaned, split and
    boned
8 anchovy fillets, cut in
    small pieces
2 tablespoons capers
4 ripe olives, chopped with
    1 mushroom

Cook vermicelli in rapidly boiling water, with salt added, about 12 minutes or until tender. Drain in a colander. Mix with 2 tablespoons olive oil and the parsley. Start oven at moderate (325° F.). Butter an oblong casserole, sprinkle buttered surface with about 4 tablespoons crumbs. Pour about half of the vermicelli into the dish. Spoon about half of the tomato sauce over it, lay smelts on top, scatter anchovy fillets over all, add a few capers, and half of the chopped olives and mushroom. Pour on the remaining tomato sauce, olives and mushroom; then add the remaining vermicelli. Cover top with remaining crumbs; add 1½ tablespoons oil scattered over crumbs. Bake in moderate oven for about 1 hour and 15 minutes. If top browns too much and seems dry, scatter a little oil over it. Makes 6 servings.

Other small, cleaned fish or shrimp may be used. This makes a wonderful buffet supper dish to be kept hot over a candle warmer throughout supper.

VERMICELLI WITH FRIDAY SAUCE

½ pound vermicelli or
    thin spaghetti
4 quarts rapidly boiling
    water
1 tablespoon salt

3 anchovy fillets
¼ cup olive oil
2 tablespoons finely chopped
    parsley

Cook vermicelli in rapidly boiling water with salt added, for 12 minutes or until tender. Drain in warm colander. Chop and mash anchovy fillets in a large saucepan; add oil. Heat and stir until oil is golden. Add drained vermicelli to hot sauce, stir and mix, sprinkle with parsley, and serve. Makes 3 or 4 servings.

A Sicilian variation of this flavorful dish adds chopped olives and capers to the anchovy and oil, heating and stirring together until the oil is steaming. Then the drained cooked vermicelli is added, mixed, parsley added, and served.

FARFALLE WITH ITALIAN RAGOUT

¼ cup all-purpose flour, sifted	2 tablespoons chopped parsley
1½ teaspoons salt	1 cup water
Grind of fresh pepper	6 small whole onions, peeled
½ teaspoon paprika	
¼ teaspoon grated nutmeg	3 tablespoons tomato paste
1½ pounds beef, cut in serving pieces	1 pound farfalle (bow-knot) macaroni
1 or 2 tablespoons olive oil	6 quarts rapidly boiling water
1 clove garlic, peeled and finely chopped	2 tablespoons salt

Mix flour, salt, pepper, paprika and nutmeg. Sprinkle generously over meat, turning pieces until all are coated with the seasoned flour. Brown meat evenly in hot oil in kettle. Add garlic, parsley and water; cover kettle and turn heat low. Let simmer for 1½ hours. Add onions and tomato paste, mix, cover kettle again and continue cooking for 30 minutes or until meat is done.

When meat is nearly done, cook bow knots in rapidly boiling water with 2 tablespoons salt added. Boil rapidly for 12 minutes or until tender. Drain in warmed colander. Spoon hot meat stew onto a warmed serving platter, surround with hot cooked bow knots. Serve at once. Makes 4 to 6 servings.

Use same recipe with macaroni shells (maruzzelle).

SICILIAN MACARONI WITH EGGPLANT

1 medium-size eggplant	Salt and pepper
1 tablespoon oil	Cayenne
6 chicken livers, chopped	¾ pound macaroni
6 chicken hearts, chopped	4 quarts rapidly boiling water
2 tablespoons butter	
2 tablespoons tomato paste	1 tablespoon salt
½ to 1 cup hot water or tomato juice	3 tablespoons grated Parmesan cheese

Wash eggplant, pare, cut in thick slices. Sauté lightly in hot oil. Break up cooked eggplant with fork; do not mash. Cook chopped livers and hearts in hot butter for about 5 minutes, stirring and mixing. Add tomato paste and mix; then add either hot water or tomato juice to thin the mixture. Add salt, pepper and a dash of cayenne. Cook, stirring, for 15 minutes. Combine with eggplant and keep hot.

Cook macaroni in rapidly boiling water with salt added, for about 12 minutes or until tender. Drain in warm colander. Combine with the hot eggplant mixture. Pour into warmed serving dish, sprinkle with grated cheese and serve. Makes 4 servings.

LASAGNE, VILLA RONDI

⅔ pound beef, ground	½ teaspoon salt
⅓ pound pork, ground	½ teaspoon pepper
3 tablespoons olive oil	6 quarts rapidly boiling water
1 yellow onion, peeled and minced	2 tablespoons salt
1 clove garlic, peeled and halved	1 pound lasagne, cut in half
1 tablespoon minced parsley	1 pound mozzarella cheese, sliced thin
2 6½-oz. cans tomato paste	¾ pound ricotta
2 cups water	2 tablespoons grated Romano cheese

In a saucepan, brown meats in hot oil with onion, garlic and parsley. When meat is evenly browned, remove the garlic and discard it. Add tomato paste, 2 cups water, salt and pepper. Simmer about 1½ hours.

Cook lasagne in rapidly boiling water with 2 tablespoons salt added, for about 20 minutes or until tender. Stir constantly to prevent sticking. Drain lasagne in warmed colander. Start oven at moderate (375° F.). Butter 2½-quart casserole, arrange lasagne in layers, alternated with layers of sauce, mozzarella and ricotta, with the top layer being ricotta. Sprinkle top with Romano cheese. Bake for about 25 minutes or until brown and bubbly. Makes 6 or more servings.

BUFFET SUPPER NOODLES

1-pound package broad noodles	1½ cups milk
	½ cup oyster liquor
Boiling water	1 tablespoon chopped parsley
Salt	
2 cups drained shucked oysters	1 tablespoon lemon juice
	1 teaspoon celery salt
4 hard-cooked eggs	2 tablespoons sherry
2 tablespoons butter	⅓ cup bread crumbs
2 tablespoons flour	

Cook noodles as described on package, drain. Look over oysters, removing any bits of shell. Chop eggs coarsely. Melt butter in saucepan, smoothly stir in flour, stir milk in gradually; let cook for a few minutes, stirring, and then add oyster liquor, parsley, lemon juice and celery salt; stir until slightly thickened.

Start oven at moderately hot (400° F.). Butter large casserole, pour layer of drained noodles into dish, add half the oysters, cover with about half the chopped eggs and half the sauce. Repeat layers using remaining noodles, oysters, eggs and sauce. Sprinkle crumbs over top. Bake for 20 minutes or until top is lightly browned and dish is bubbly. Makes 12 servings.

Corn: Sweet, Tender, Wonderful
/ Phil Stong

There are tortillas and hoecake, Brunswick stew and fluffy corn soufflé;
fritters, dodgers and johnny cake—
but of all edibles derived from our most versatile grain,
perhaps the most delightful is new corn-on-the-cob

"Good corn weather" begins in the Midwest in June. That is what we call the kind of sun that beats down on us with brazen hammers, parches the roads to dust, practically boils the yellow catfish in the Des Moines River, which flows by my home town. People go on working in the fields; in the Farmers' State Bank, with wilted collars; in general stores like my father's, where in desperation men sometimes pull their collars off and the women's souvenir fans go faster and faster over the bolts of oilcloth and percale.

Dinner is in the middle of the day, with the sun right overhead—fried pork tenderloin or round steak with brown gravy, ham, fried chicken, mashed potatoes and cold milk or hot coffee by the potful—and the people eat it. There is no fruit-salad-Melba-toast nonsense in this country in hot weather. Out here, you can't work on that kind of fodder without getting weak—and maybe "upset"—before supper, though a plate of cold tomatoes, sliced with the skin on and served with salt and pepper, or sometimes a bowl of potato salad made with boiled dressing and lots of onion, is all right if you have plenty of solid food to go with it.

Maybe you think you're not hungry on a hot day, but after you've eaten you feel better, and you look at the blazing sky and you count up the bushels your acres will yield this year in corn—or if you have no acres and work in the bank, you feel sad because no farmer is going to need a mortgage this year—and yet you feel good because all around you are sunlight and success and the wealthy plumes of cornfields. Even a banker feels the warmth of money growing from the dirt—money which will turn into farmers' deposits in the fall, which

he can lend to the correspondent bank in Chicago, which can lend it to starving millionaires in New York.

Near the middle of July there is a special day, hot as the hinges, but with a whiff of a breeze toward evening. If you have been helping your father in the store, serving hot, damp farm women with lengths of gingham, fitting their squirming children with hot, sticky shoes, you will climb the hill from Main Street, which runs along the river, thinking, "I'll have a glass of iced tea and pull my bed out on the porch and go to sleep, and to hell with the mosquitoes."

But as soon as you have opened the side door into the parlor, closed all day against the heat, you are cooler, and you know what there is for supper—the first sweet corn! The house is full of the fresh, sweet smell of roasting ears. In the kitchen a pot of Golden Bantam is finishing its five minutes of boiling—and at once you are so hungry you could eat a horse.

An Iowa woman expects each member of her family to eat about five ears of Golden Bantam. (In my childhood, before Bantam was perfected, three or four of the larger ears then popular would do.)

In towns like Keosauqua, corn is picked from the stalk just

America as the land of plenty—symbolized in this panorama ▶ of her native bounty.

PAUL DOME

as the pot begins to boil—and that is why it needs only five minutes' boiling. Somebody runs to the garden with a half-bushel basket, races back, husks and silks the ears on the back porch, and drops them straight into the boiling water—without salt. Authorities argue this point, but I believe salt in the water toughens corn, and should be added only at the table, along with butter out of a silver dish surmounted by a small silver cow.

People who are unable to buy fresh corn in city grocery stores should remember that frozen corn—either whole on the cob or sliced off—is processed within a couple of hours after picking. However, in many U. S. areas, corn is picked at night and reaches stores just before dawn.

In Iowa butter is *not* spread with a fancy corn-butterer. Neither is the corn daintily grasped with silver or ivory holders—not while we have our strong two hands.

If Mother has cooked more corn than the family can eat, so much the better. There will be fried corn for noon dinner tomorrow, the kernels sliced from the ear and dropped into a skillet in which minced onions and green peppers have been lightly browning in butter; or the leftover corn will go into fritters or corn pudding or succotash, if the Lima beans are ripe. There will be corn to eat in one form or another at least once a day all through the roasting-ear season.

"Roasting ears" is one of those fossil phrases embedded in the language from three hundred years ago. Corn is seldom roasted any more, except by Boy Scouts and other campers-out, or by Societies for the Preservation of Folk Dancing and Primitive Indigestion—or occasionally by eastern politicians who inadvertently throw in a few ears of corn when they are steaming their clams and kissing babies for votes.

As a matter of fact, roasted corn is very good, and simple to cook, as I learned when I was a telephone "pole man" for Ma Bell, one summer. Old Snooky, the foreman, used to get the cook fire started while the rest of our gang went to pick some catfish and some corn. By "picking" catfish, I mean precisely what I say. Broody catfish ladies make their nests—or their mates do it for them, or they co-operate—between the bases of the glacial boulders of the Des Moines and the sand or mud on which they rest. Then the parents take turns watching the eggs. By swimming under water and following a likely boulder with your toe, you can easily find a nest. Then you gently slide your hand up along the back of the watcher and push a third finger into the gill. At this point the fish gets scared and struggles forward, biting, and you can push your thumb into its mouth—and then you have picked a catfish.

When we came back to the campfire with catfish, we would skin them; and by this time Snooky's fire would have settled into quiet embers and his skillet would be sizzling with fat salt pork. We would dust the fish with cornmeal and drop them in the pan.

Some of the boys would have picked some sweet corn on the nearest farm—the farmer didn't care, because we gave him fish. We threw the unhusked ears of corn into the fire and watched for steam to come from them. Even on red-hot coals corn doesn't *exactly* roast—it steams in its own broth, within the husk, and wood smoke adds its incomparable seasoning.

Nobody out home ever admits that he is tired of corn, though as the cornstalks in the garden get heavier and the tassels wither, you will see two women talking over a fence, and you can be sure that one is trying to give away a bushel or two of sweet corn before her neighbor gets the drop on her and offers *her* a bushel or two. If you can't give it away you've got to can it—or, in these days of scientific wonders, freeze it.

Or, you can dry it. Dried corn is one survival from pioneer days that has not become archaic. Throughout July and August, the porches of Iowa houses are full of hammocks made of flimsy muslin and spread with cut-off corn, which is covered against flies, but not against the sun, by the sheerest cheesecloth. In my childhood, in the early 1900's, this method of preserving corn was considered by far the safest.

It is a long corn season in the Midwest, and when you have planted, cultivated, picked, eaten, and helped put up corn one way or another, you are likely to think it will never end. But the earth does turn and the sun swings south and in September comes the equinox. Astronomers may talk about the ecliptic and Libra and Scorpio, but any Midwesterner knows that the summer is over on the day when he comes home and smells not boiling corn but hot spiced vinegar. That means putting up corn relish and pickled corn-stuffed peppers and other things that won't have to be eaten until later in the fall, when your taste for corn has revived.

Along about November, you begin to be interested again in dried corn. A hundred years ago a pocketful of it and a string of "jerky"—smoked venison—often took a man a few hundred miles. It never took my generation that far, but it did take me through geometry.

Bates ("Bakey") Peacock used to room in town like a good many other farm boys who lived a few miles outside of easy driving range of Keosauqua High School. Bakey always brought in some supplies on Sunday evening, and we city fellers settled on him like locusts. Bakey knew why right angles are right; but more important, he always had a bag of dried corn and plenty of sweet butter. We crisped the corn in the butter while Bakey explained the next week's theorems.

Our regular teacher was merely Helen Walker, now one of America's great mathematicians; but dried corn was not served in her classroom. Bakey would explain that if seven rectangles fell supine, the result would be Q.E.D., while we crunched the nice, hot, buttery stuff. I passed geometry on 74½ (75 was "passing"), which is why I am not attending Keosauqua High School at this moment.

This is how corn-eating goes in the Corn Belt. And though we feel as though we had invented corn, we know that we are actually latecomers to the cornfield. Long before us came the first tentative nibblings of John Smith's Virginia company, and of the Pilgrims at Plymouth, who, if they hadn't been so hungry, might have scorned the outlandish Indian grain, and so missed the most important—if not, as some think, the best—of all strictly American dishes.

Over the nation, corn followed the settlers, regional cookery developed and the trouble began: the three-hundred-year Corn Wars.

One of the most potent battle slogans is: "Fritters!" Here the war crosses geographical lines. In the South, as in the North, there are two schools of cookery. One fries the fritter on a griddle, and the other drops it into deep fat. If you like one of the types, you won't admit the other is a fritter, though you may eat it and think it tastes pretty good.

Quite apart from fritters, there is a type of corn griddlecake I have met in only one place in this vast country—my wife's Missouri home town. This is not the usual "corn pancake" made by substituting part corn meal for wheat flour in an ordinary batter. The Kansas City corn cake is made of a rich sour-milk-wheat-flour pancake batter, to which is added cold boiled corn, sliced to keep the kernels whole; and the cob is scraped to get the sweet milk too. These, with maple sirup or strained honey—or, if you are a real Missourian, light sorghum—can hold their own with any fritter.

There are skirmishes and squalls between cooks over succotash. The deep South puts crinkles of fried salt pork or bacon in it, and sometimes sins against Massachusetts by using green beans instead of Limas. But the true dish belongs to New England (nobody can deny that, since the word is from the Narraganset language) and it is simply a combination of stewed corn and Lima beans seasoned with salt and pepper and enriched by cream or butter or both. It tastes just as good now as it did on Plymouth Rock that first hungry winter.

New England claims chowder too—you know, lobster chowder, crab chowder, chowder of cod or haddock, clam chowder, without tomatoes—also corn chowder, or, for super de luxe occasions, corn-and-crab-meat chowder, which is guaranteed to wow your guests. In ours there is just salt pork and milk and onions and potatoes, and corn and fresh crab meat. I have heard that some cooks serve cheese croutons with this —but we stick to the orthodox pilot crackers.

We like our guests, but sometimes we do not like our current cook. Once we had a "superior" native one, named Ida, who belonged to a book club and wouldn't wear an apron; she always swiped the Double-Crostics from our *Saturday Review* before my wife could get them. Her cooking was strictly of the Wooden Nutmeg School. But after a year as captive employers, we fixed her. We got our friend, Bill Jenkins, of Norfolk, Virginia, to come up and, right in her kitchen and under her nose, make Brunswick stew.

Brunswick stew is one of the nobler Southern projects in the use of corn. In Virginia the base is squirrel, chicken, ham, beef, and/or any other kind of meat, simmered a while; but in Connecticut we settled for young chickens.

After two or three hours of cooking the chicken, you put in some other things—tomatoes, potatoes, onions, okra, seasonings—and corn. Then the pot cooks on, more or less all day. As the Williamsburg cookbook says, "this requires at least six hours' slow cooking," and you must stir frequently.

When all the stuff was in the pot, we took Bill, still in his apron—for he had no such prejudices as Ida's against covering his clothes from spatters—back to the living room to the sideboard toddies, another Virginia favorite. All that lovely hazy Sunday in October we spent around the fireplace; and Ida stirred the pot.

At half past seven the stew was ready, and Ida was a wreck. Her idea of a Sunday afternoon was to work the Double-Crostic, curl her hair, and read one of her club books. She plunked the tureen on the table, and retired to the kitchen to listen for the first groans of people eating such victuals. The Brunswick stew was superb, much to Ida's disbelief.

Corn pudding is another common American dish that varies from east to west, from north to south, and sometimes from town to town. But in general the pudding of the South is a baked custard stiffened only with eggs and the corn itself; in the Midwest it usually contains eggs, milk, corn and cracker or bread crumbs; and in the Southwest it has a Mexican tang with peppers, pimentos and minced onion—to say nothing of occasional ripe olives.

Whereas fritters and chowders cause a lot of guerrilla fighting, the Great Corn War that rages over the continent century after century is over corn breads. It is as safe to voice an opinion on corn bread, no matter where you are, as to mention General Sherman affectionately at an Atlanta dinner party.

These United States have never been able to unite on any single aspect of the subject. First of all, they disagree on the color of the meal—white in the South, yellow in New England, though water-ground and fairly coarse, in any section, if you can get it. Then there is the question of milk versus hot water, to soften the meal. Oddly enough, the lavish South uses water, and the "close" Yankees use milk.

Sugar is a very sore point between North and South. New England is unanimous in using it—or molasses—in corn cake, spider cake, corn, corn dodgers, or Johnnie, Johnny, Jonny cake. (There is a nice little internal war up here over the spelling, though probably "Jonny cake" is best, because in the beginning it was "journey cake," to be munched on horseback, and the "h" is plainly an interloper.)

The multitudinous and virtuoso corn breads of the South are alike in one respect—there is *never* a grain of sugar in any of them. This matter has been disposed of for all time by *The Williamsburg Art of Cookery*, published for The Williamsburg Society, which says: "Of prime importance in the Making of these Breads is the Selection of a proper Meal. Only the native Corn, ground slowly in a Water Grist Mill may be used and under no Circumstances should a Cook so far depart from the good Judgment of Generations of Virginia Housewives as to permit Sugar in any variety of Corn Bread."

There isn't anything you can do with corn meal that Southern cooks haven't done. From Virginia south and west you will meet endless varieties of corn bread: the primitive ash or hoe cakes (baked on the hearth or a hoe and washed and dried before eating), both called "pone"; batter bread or spoon bread or "soft egg bread," baked in a pudding dish and eaten with a fork—the best spoon bread I ever ate was baked by Oklahoma-born Dorothy Cameron Disney (Mrs. Milton MacKaye); Virginia corn-meal bread (with yeast!); Texas corn sticks, served in a bowl with a pitcher of buttermilk; "cracklin' bread" in Tennessee.

As you approach the real Southwest, corn-meal dishes grow stranger and more wonderful. Tamales begin in Kansas City. "Ho-o-ot tama-a-les!" goes echoing down the streets on black sultry nights under the trees, when by common sense nobody would touch anything but "i-i-ice cre-eam." Except that everybody does. The kids and a good many grownups go scrambling down the front steps, chasing the little cart to the corner lamppost, where its black-haired owner is bending over it fishing out the little cornhusk rolls—like the paper snappers used at children's parties, but dripping with a fiery red sauce. It happened one night when we were visting my wife's family. As if we hadn't a heat wave already—still 105° at nine P.M.— the heat rose under the breathless trees from the small steam wagon, and, I have no doubt, from the pepper too. I hadn't missed my wife from the dark porch, but suddenly I saw her on the sidewalk, paying out her money for a cardboard boat full of tamales.

"Oh, my Lord," said my father-in-law from the porch swing, "there she goes again. Can't you stop her?" Apparently he still doesn't know my wife. "Those things," he said, "are made over in the slums, out of heaven knows what——"

"Golly," said my wife, coming up the steps, "these are *really* hot!" It was just ten minutes since she had been swearing that the heat would *kill* her.

"And they've got plenty of chili pepper, and I shouldn't be

surprised if the stuffing was really chicken—or beef, at least." She glanced at her father. "He was a nice clean man."

"I managed to keep her from eating them all through her childhood," her father said to me.

"You did not. I've eaten dozens—whenever I had a nickel and you weren't on the porch. I ate them under the syringa bush. I could go out there now, I suppose."

But she was already eating them, sitting on the top step. I ate some too, and they were very good. Also, we felt cooler when we had finished them, though maybe it was on the same principle as that of the man who pounded his finger because it felt so good when he stopped.

As you travel on southwest, the tamales and the chili con carne get hotter by the mile, of course. In Neodesha, Kansas, where I taught school thirty years ago, every lunch counter and soda fountain sold tamales and chili, with three separate pots of sauce—mild for sissies, medium for the slightly braver, and hot for the lion-hearted.

The omnipresent tortilla of deep Texas, New Mexico, Arizona and Mexico is only a Latin-Indian version of the ash or hoe cake, mixed and baked in much the same way, but varied by a number of sauces and usually served as a base for a main dish rather than as a bread.

There is one strip of this country from St. Louis down to New Orleans where corn goes French. In many a house along the Mississippi, people who have not a drop of French blood are eating a slightly different corn bread from that of Kentucky or the Carolinas, merely because the fur traders and agents of Louis XVI brought their wives up the river by pirogue and flatboat, and the French women set about refining the coarse foodstuffs offered by the wilderness.

The corn-meal puffs of St. Louis and Cape Girardeau bear little resemblance to the solid Anglo-Saxon hoe cake.

They are light with stiffly beaten egg whites and are baked in a slow oven till they fluff. Here, too, corn pudding is a soufflé, sometimes enlivened by cheese and Tabasco.

Another step up the ladder of Creole elegance is the New Orleans soufflé of green corn and shrimp or crawfish—an inspired combination of flavors and textures that, to my mind, has all the shrimp-and-rice dishes licked off the map. The New Orleans fried oyster, too, is coated with corn meal and is much lighter and crisper than the Northern oyster wrapped in cracker crumbs.

There is something about corn.

In general, Europe has been a bit skittish about corn—except in meal, for the peasants; and on the cob, for cattle and hogs. Among early visitors to these shores, it seems to have been only the English who took a chance on eating it. The French and the Spanish noticed it as a phenomenon of Indian diet, but were slow to try it themselves. That prime adventurer, Columbus, does mention it in his journals, but there is no record that he ever tasted it himself.

As for corn-on-the-cob, I have yet to hear of any foreign visitor to America who has really liked it. A neighbor of ours in Connecticut entertained for week ends during the war a long series of service men from most of the Allied nations and, being of a nature both patriotic and persistent, each summer she tried corn on them, fresh from her garden, tender and sweet and milky in the bite, with fresh butter from her own cow. One and all they hated it. The Frenchmen chewed and gave her a look of sheer horror; a Netherlander took one cautious nibble and said nothing; the Australians and the lower ranks of Britishers said "It's delicious" and put the rest of the ear on their butter plates where they made a barricade of rolls to hide it; the "brass" from England said, "Int'r'stin' flavor," and laid it boldly on top of their rolls, where all could see.

It must be an awful thing to be a European; and there are times in America when it must be an awful thing to be an aristocrat. One of them is when the lower classes are eating. *The Williamsburg Art of Cookery* says: "The bread in Gentlemen's Houses is generally made of Wheat, but some rather choose the Pone, which is the bread made of *Indian Meal. . . .*"

In fact, the editors of the Williamsburg cookbook have conjured up an irresistible vision of gentlemen and ladies named Byrd or Randolph or Fairfax, creeping out through the back door of the manor house down to the slave quarters, to sniff the rich smell of hoe cake, or fried corn-meal mush with crisp salt pork—all the forbidden rude joys of slavery for which white men and women were supposed not to have the taste or the stomach.

Hominy and grits are another wide and tortuous subject. "Hominy" seems to have been, in its first phase, a name for what we would call cornstarch. William Byrd of Westover, in 1729, wrote in his recipe for "Veal Glue" or "Pocket Soup," which was a kind of large sheet of bouillon cubes, intended for foresters and other travelers, when game was scarce: "This Broth will be more heatening if you thicken every Mess with half a spoonful of Rockahominy, which is nothing but Indian Corn parched without burning and reduced to Powder."

Then—there is corn whisky. The southeastern Indians of the 16th Century used corn to make beer; but they knew nothing about distillation, a means of bringing out the splendid virtue of corn much exploited in later centuries by the Hatfields and the McCoys and a lot of other people in the Great Smokies and the Ozarks. I am willing to admit that without "cawn likker," American mythology and song would be the duller.

Rich, golden and succulent corn is truly an American delight ▶

FOSTER ENSMINGER

WESTCHESTER BUFFET CORN PUDDING

6 fillets from chicken breasts
Salt and pepper
2 tablespoons fine crumbs
2 tablespoons butter
2 cups (No. 303 can)
   cream-style corn or 2
   cups cooked green
   corn

3 beaten eggs
2 cups milk
1 teaspoon salt
½ teaspoon paprika
¼ cup buttered crumbs
6 crisply cooked bacon curls

Season chicken lightly with salt and pepper; coat with fine crumbs and sauté in butter about 20 minutes or until golden and almost done. Mix the corn, eggs, milk, salt, and paprika. Start oven at moderate (350° F.). Grease narrow, oblong baking dish. Pour about a sixth of the corn mixture into the dish, place a cooked fillet next and with it push the corn to one end of the dish. Add another sixth of corn, then another fillet and continue until dish is filled with alternating corn and chicken in horizontal rows. Cover all with buttered crumbs and a light sprinkling of paprika. Set dish in a shallow pan of hot water. Bake in moderate oven for about 1 hour or until a knife inserted in corn pudding comes out clean. Serve in baking dish. Garnish with bacon curls. Keep hot on table warmer. Makes 6 servings.

SWEET CORN CROQUETTES WITH CHEESE SAUCE

3 tablespoons butter
1 tablespoon chopped leeks
   or scallions
2 tablespoons chopped green
   pepper
¼ cup all-purpose flour,
   sifted
½ teaspoon salt
¼ cup tomato purée or
   mushroom ketchup

1 cup cooked young sweet
   corn
1 cup bread crumbs
1 beaten egg
1 tablespoon water
2 or 3 tablespoons finely
   chopped water cress
Fat for deep frying

Heat butter in saucepan, cook onion or leeks and pepper about 5 minutes, stirring until softened and lightly browned. Stir flour and salt in, mixing well. Cook until bubbling. Add tomato purée or mushroom ketchup, stir until boiling; add corn, mix, let come to a boil; then remove from heat. Pour onto a buttered platter to cool. When cold, form into eight croquettes, first roll lightly in crumbs, and then in beaten egg mixed with water. Let croquettes stand a minute or two; then roll again in remaining crumbs mixed with water cress. Lower, in frying basket, into hot fat (375° to 385° F.) and cook from 2 to 4 minutes or until evenly browned all over. Drain croquettes on thick brown paper. Serve with cheese sauce. Makes 4 or 8 servings.

CORN WITH SAUTEED ONIONS

2 tablespoons butter
8 small onions, peeled and
   sliced thin
1 teaspoon flour
Salt and pepper
1 teaspoon white-wine
   vinegar

2 cups freshly cooked green
   corn
2 or 3 tablespoons heavy
   cream
1 tablespoon finely chopped
   parsley

Sauté onions lightly in hot butter until golden. Sprinkle with flour and a light seasoning of salt and pepper; stir, add vinegar and stir again. Let simmer 15 minutes. Pour hot corn mixed with a little heavy cream into a warmed serving dish, cover with onions and sprinkle with parsley. Makes 4 servings.

Should be served hot with cold cuts, broiled ham or Canadian bacon. This is also a fine accompaniment for an omelet; or it can be made into a delicious casserole: Pour the creamed corn into a buttered 1-quart baking dish, cover with onions, add 2 or 3 tablespoons buttered crumbs. Bake in moderate oven (350° F.) for about 20 minutes or until browned and bubbling.

CASSEROLES OF TOMATOES AND CORN

4 large firm ripe tomatoes
1 cup bread crumbs
½ teaspoon curry powder
3 tablespoons sugar
2 cups cream-style canned
   corn

2 tablespoons finely chopped
   onion
¼ teaspoon salt
Grind of fresh pepper

Start oven at moderate (350° F.). Butter 4 individual baking dishes. Skin tomatoes, cut off slice at top and bottom; then slice crosswise in half. Mix crumbs with curry powder and sugar. Dip tomato slices in crumb mixture and lay 1 slice of tomato in each of 4 individual baking dishes. Pour over each tomato slice 4 tablespoons of the corn mixed with onion, salt and pepper. Cover each serving with another slice of tomato. Then top with remaining crumb mixture. Bake for 20 minutes or until bubbling and browned. Makes 4 servings.

A half-cooked bacon strip or some finely minced smoked ham or chopped oysters can be added to the final crumb topping before the casseroles go into the oven to make delicious variations. Excellent for buffet parties.

CORN GRIDDLE CAKES WITH CREAMED CHICKEN

2 cups finely diced cooked
   chicken
2 cups white sauce made
   with chicken stock
2 tablespoons finely chopped
   pimiento
2 tablespoons finely chopped
   ripe olives or truffles

1 cup water-ground corn
   meal
½ teaspoon salt
½ teaspoon soda
1 to 1¼ cups thick
   buttermilk
1 beaten egg
1 tablespoon butter or
   margarine

In upper part of a double boiler over hot water or in chafing dish on a buffet table, combine the chicken, white sauce, pimiento and olives or truffles. Add seasoning of salt, pepper and celery salt if desired.

Sift corn meal, salt and soda together 2 or 3 times into a mixing bowl. Add the buttermilk, egg and melted butter. Stir vigorously until well mixed. The batter should be thin. Bake on hot griddle in cakes about 4 or 5 inches in diameter. Turn cakes with pancake turner or wide spatula to brown on other side. As soon as a cake is ready to serve, slip it onto a warmed serving plate and spoon a generous serving of chicken onto one half of the cake; then fold the other half over. Makes 12 servings.

BAR HARBOR GREEN CORN PIE

Pastry for 9-inch pie pan
2 tablespoons butter or
    margarine
1 cup milk
2 cups fresh green corn
½ teaspoon salt
¼ cup heavy cream
2 tablespoons soft bread
    crumbs

Quick grind of pepper
¼ teaspoon paprika
2 beaten eggs
¼ cup French-fried
    onions, crisped in
    oven
½ cup buttered cracker
    crumbs

Make puff paste or rich pie pastry and line pie dish. Combine butter or margarine, milk, corn and salt in saucepan and bring to a boil. Lower heat, cook and stir for 3 minutes. Slowly add cream to mixture, stirring constantly. Add crumbs, pepper and paprika and cook for 2 or 3 minutes, until thickened. Let cool slightly, add eggs and stir until thick.

Start oven at moderately hot (400° F.). Pour half the corn mixture into the pastry-lined pan; cover with crisp fried onions. Pour in rest of corn, sprinkle with cracker crumbs and bake for 20 minutes or until browned. Makes 6 servings. Serve hot with oysters or roast chicken.

GREEN CORN PUFFS, DEEP FRIED

3 or 4 ears tender young
    sweet corn
1 cup sifted cake flour
½ teaspoon salt
Grind fresh pepper

1½ teaspoons baking
    powder
2 eggs, separated
Fat for deep frying

With a sharp knife score the kernels of the corn lengthwise of the cob; then press out the pulp into a measuring cup. Continue until cup is full. Sift dry ingredients together twice. Combine with corn, beating well. Beat egg yolks until thick and lemon colored. Combine with corn and dry ingredients, beating well. Whip egg whites stiff and fold into yolk mixture. Drop by the tablespoonful into hot fat (365° to 375° F.) and cook for 2 to 5 minutes, until puffs are browned all over. Turn puffs during cooking. Lift out with slotted spoon, drain on thick paper towels. Makes 8 large puffs. Serve hot, 2 per person, with broiled breast of chicken and new asparagus or an endive salad.

CHINESE CORN AND CODFISH CAKES

1 pound dried codfish,
    freshened, drained,
    cooked and flaked
1 cup canned or cooked corn
2 eggs, well beaten

1 teaspoon sugar
1 tablespoon soy sauce
Butter, margarine or peanut
    oil
Grated fresh horse-radish

Combine fish, corn and eggs. Add sugar and soy sauce and mix well. Chill. Shape into small cakes. Sauté in hot butter, margarine, or oil for 3 or 4 minutes or until lightly browned on all sides. Serve very hot with a little grated fresh horse-radish. Makes 6 to 8 servings.

SATURDAY NIGHT CORN SOUFFLÉ

1 tablespoon butter
2 tablespoons flour
1 cup milk
1¼ teaspoons salt
Fresh grind of pepper
¼ teaspoon celery salt

2 cups freshly grated new
    sweet corn or drained
    canned corn
2 egg yolks, beaten
4 egg whites
6 slices lean bacon, cooked
    until crisp

Heat butter in saucepan, stir flour in smoothly, and, when well blended, stir milk in slowly. Bring to a boil; then add seasonings, corn and beaten yolks. Mix, remove from heat, and let cool for 10 minutes.

Start oven at moderate (350° F.). Whip egg whites stiff, fold into corn mixture and pour at once into an unbuttered 1½-quart soufflé dish in which crisply cooked bacon has been crumbled. Place in shallow pan of hot water and bake for 30 minutes. Serve immediately on taking soufflé from oven. Makes 6 servings.

EASTERN SHORE CORN AND CRAB CHOWDER

1 small onion, peeled and
    sliced
5 tablespoons butter
2 cups fresh green corn or
    canned kernel corn
3 cups milk
1½ cups light cream

1 teaspoon salt
Quick grind of pepper
⅛ teaspoon grated nutmeg
1½ cups flaked crab meat,
    all bones removed
6 round soda crackers

Sauté onion in 2 tablespoons butter until soft. Combine with corn, milk and cream; heat slowly, stirring frequently. Simmer until very hot. Do not boil. Add remaining 3 tablespoons butter and seasonings, stir; increase heat slightly, but do not boil. Add crab meat; stir only until crab is hot. Serve at once in warmed soup bowls each containing a cracker. Makes 6 servings.

CORN-MEAL PECAN STICKS

2 cups water-ground corn
    meal
1 teaspoon salt
½ teaspoon baking soda

2 cups thick buttermilk
2 eggs
¼ cup melted fat
½ cup sliced pecans

Start oven at hot (425° F.). Grease 18 cast-iron or cast-aluminum corn-stick pans.

Sift corn meal, salt and soda together 3 times. Combine milk and unbeaten eggs, mixing well. Sift dry ingredients into milk mixture beating well. Add the melted fat, mix thoroughly. Add pecans and mix. Fill prepared corn-stick pans ¾ full. Bake for about 20 minutes. If done, but not brown enough, place pan under broiler for 2 or 3 minutes. Makes 18 sticks. Serve hot with soup or salad.

The cheese market at Alkmaar. Porters haul Edam on a special cradle slung from the shoulders; all wear white drill overalls and picture hats whose colors designate the various workmen's teams. The yellow cannonballs are for domestic use; those for export are dyed red.

ELLIOTT ERWITT

4. CHEESE, SPICE AND TRUFFLES

Cheese / Clifton Fadiman

An appraisal of the fine arts of making,
and eating, one of the most universally prized
of all the world's foods

SOME years ago, having resolved to write a book about cheese, I collected data on upwards of 500 varieties and accumulated specimens (often quite lively) from many of the countries of the world—literally from China to Peru. (China's soybean yields a courtesy cheese, *hoi poi*; Peru's cheeses I cannot recall.) The specimens have long since gone the way of all flesh and dairy products. The data, however—so vast is the field—I have never been able to digest, and so the book remains an unfulfilled dream of my youth. For consolation I call to mind one whom I resemble in no other outstanding respect, Casanova, who also found his powers unequal to the task of writing a dictionary of cheese. Yet I think a man should from time to time, in whatever poor phrases he may command, laud those gifts of God which have filled him with most joy. Let these rough notes, therefore, so ill-matched to the altitude of my theme, serve as a kind of thanks offering.

Universal hungers are few: who dreams hotly of soufflé? But wine, once loved, remains a passion; so too with bread, salt, perhaps meat. As for cheese, I range myself with the great connoisseur P. Morton Shand, who deemed a love of it inherent in humanity. The Chinese, it is true, like it little, linking all milk products with their herdsmen-conquerors, the Tartars and Mongols. Yet Ben Gunn, marooned on

Treasure Island, with his pitiful "Many's the long night I've dreamed of cheese—toasted mostly," emblems much of mankind; and I have heard that our men on besieged Corregidor, reduced to mule meat, split into two groups—those who dreamed of chocolate, those who dreamed of cheese.

Like its great brethren, bread and wine, cheese is born of a miracle. At the very instant when the milk is on the road to ruin, mysterious lactic acid or that more mysterious ferment, rennet (extracted—who knows first by whom?—from the fourth stomach of the suckling calf), works like grace upon it and raises it to the higher life of curd. Curd, pressed and treated, is touched again by grace, this time in the guise of bacteria or mold. Time passes. Now the curd, like Odysseus before Penelope, throws off its grossness, growing godlike in form and feature. It has become Cheese.

Cheese is not the gift of the cow alone, but of the ewe, the goat, the reindeer, the zebu, the buffalo, the camel, the llama, the mare, the ass, the zebra, the yak. It may even be, if we are to trust Maurice des Ombiaux's droll anecdote in his *Les Fromages*, the gift of the human female. In color it shades from the delicate rose of a virgin's blush to the grand severity of Pentelic marble. In form it is protean: the ball and the brick, the cube and the cucumber, the disc and the dumbbell, the melon and the millstone, the bologna and the ostrich egg, the pineapple and the parallelepiped. On New York's First Avenue, near East 116th Street, there used to be and perhaps still is a veritable Cellini of cheesemongers who would fashion your cheese to your fancy.

The eye of the turophile may consider the 18 basic varieties of cheese or the thousand variations on those varieties. In either case he tries to classify. He may arrange them according to the quality of their resistance to life's onslaught: yielding, such as the chaste cream, the mold-matured Camembert, the bacteria-ripened Roquefort; firm, such as Gorgonzola or Münster; obdurate, such as Parmesan. Or, with André Simon, he may view them in terms of their aggressiveness: the gentle Petit Suisse, the strong Roquefort, the brutal Limburger or Marolles. Or he may borrow the late Edward Bunyard's division, based on their poetical style: the romantic cheese, like Brie, given to excess, even to tears; the classic cheese, such as Stilton, growing like Nestor nobler as it ages.

Ancient is the lineage of cheese. A legend, deeply unreliable, has it that some thousands of years ago an Arab merchant named Kanana, wandering over the desert, stopped for lunch, poured out the milk that he had kept in a skin bottle made from the lining of a calf's stomach, and found an odd but attractive-tasting mess, now known as curd. As a child, Queen Semiramis was fed cheese by the birds. Zoroaster, who flourished about 1000 B.C., lived, says Pliny, exclusively on à cheese for 20 years. (It has been deduced that this could only have been a Gibraltar of a Parmesan weighing about 1 ton, 12½ cwt.) The Old Testament (see I Samuel, 17:18) speaks well of cheese. When British soil first shook under the tread of Caesar's legions, Cheshire cheese was already being made there. His affection for Roquefort, first mentioned in a monkish chronicle of 1070, ennobles the character of Charlemagne.

Cheese is what Hilaire Belloc said it is, a profound matter. Only countrymen, leading quieter, wiser lives than ours, still know this. In England's remoter countryside, when a birth is expected, a vast cartwheel of cheese is piously set aside. Day by day it is cut out at the center so that at last there remains a large ring through which on his christening day the fortunate babe is ritually passed. Switzerland's Saanen, an Emmenthal cheese, takes six years to ripen and will keep till the blast of Gabriel. In our culture, a privileged child is at birth put down for Groton and Harvard, but in Switzerland, when a baby is born, a wheel of Saanen is marked with his name. On all the holiest occasions of his mortality—christening, betrothal, marriage—his private cheese is served; and when he dies the mourners consume the last of this ceremonial Wheel of Life.

Provided it be well and truly made there is really for the confirmed turophile no such thing as a *bad* cheese. A cheese may disappoint. It may be dull, it may be naïve, it may be oversophisticated. Yet it remains cheese, milk's leap toward immortality.

Edam's crimson cannon balls, for example, may seem, like their solid Dutch creators, a bit plodding. But a thick round of Edam or Gouda on the blackest of bread companioned by the blackest of coffee makes a muscular breakfast that puts to shame epicene toast-and-orange-juice. Nor does the more reflective palate disdain that rarity, Edam that is sharp, dry and two years of age.

"Swiss" cheese, Emmenthaler or Gruyère, would seem to have too obvious an appeal. But there is virtue in simple candor. (Simple candor is particularly good with beer.) Look

to it, however, that your Gruyère betrays around its eyes that trace of lachrymose moisture which announces its ripeness, its readiness to be yours. Hardest of all to come by is the supreme Gruyère long past its salad days when it was green in judgment, Gruyère that is rich, salty, nutlike and virtually holeless.

I will confess Bel Paese a neutral affair at best but Taleggio shows to what it may aspire, and Pont l'Evêque seems to me the highest avatar of the type. Pont l'Evêque now appears rarely, but it has an attractive cousin in Mont Dore, a Rhône valley whole-milk cheese I have found in many New York shops. Soft, yellow, delicate without effeminacy, Mont Dore was the favorite cheese of Pascal, whose *Pensées* must owe some of their powerful grace to its ingestion.

Parmesan, the carborundum of cheeses, is humble fare. Marry it to onion soup—and it is royal. One bows the head in gratitude to Louis XV's father-in-law, the exiled Polish king Stanislaus Leszczynski, who made it famous. Mark well, however, that God did not make it in canisters. It was not born grated; it does not achieve gratedness; it must virtually at table have gratedness thrust upon it.

Gentlemen, let us raise our sights. Let us praise the immortal French triad, the Three Musketeers: Roquefort, Camembert, Brie.

Ewe-born, cave-educated, perfected by moldy bread, greenish-blue-veined Roquefort was called by Grimod de la Reynière "the toper's biscuit." So joyfully does it mate with wine that wine buyers will not use it as a palate cleanser lest it mask the wine's poorer qualities. The poet Baudelaire, liking perhaps its faint tantalizing hint of decay, was an amateur of Roquefort, pairing it with that Burgundy of beautiful balance, Corton. We receive great Roquefort rarely, for it is often oversalted for export purposes. Though it lacks the true Roquefort texture, our native Langlois Blue from Colorado is no bad substitute.

Esteeming Roquefort, I view it without passion. Yet I can conceive why Emile Zola, in describing a cheese market, speaks of "majestic Roqueforts looking down with princely contempt upon the others, through the glass of their crystal covers."

For full persuasion Camembert, like a good orator, should stop short just this side of fluency. Before this stage it speaks of chalk; past it, of ammonia. For perfect Camembert the recipe is simple: go to Normandy. Our present law demands pasteurization of the milk before the cheese may be exported to us: the equivalent of assassination.

Perhaps this law is being slyly evaded, for I have recently eaten good Brie. (Domestic Brie, pleasant enough, is not Brie at all.) When you speak of Brie, uncover: Talleyrand called it the King of Cheeses, the only King, it has been noted, to which he remained faithful. In its subtlety, its delicacy, its beauty and its appeal to the intellect, Brie might quite as aptly be called the Poet of Cheeses. Like many fine poets, it is hard to get at. The ordinary cheese knife, an abomination, is powerless; a razor blade has been suggested; I have found a small demi-tasse spoon the very thing for those precious, cryptic corners. A perfect Brie cannot be produced by standardized methods; it is the end product of a series of miracles. Essays are writ by fools like me, but only God can make a Brie.

As for English cheeses, only one (but that the lordliest, Stilton) seems to reach our shores today. Cheddar, Cheshire, Gloucester, Double Gloucester—all could after patient research once be found. Now, I hear, supreme examples of these cheeses are even on their native heath hard to come by. Pity; for, while England may well survive the falling away of her colonies, a falling off in her cheese whispers of some deep and stanchless inner wound.

Great Cheddar, I hope, Englishmen still enjoy. As for ourselves domestic Cheddar lies around us in its infancy, and some in its maturity. But even at its shelf-cured, three-year-old Vermont best, it cannot equal a fine English Farmhouse Cheddar. (Farmhouse Cheddar is satisfactory; the other kind merely Factory.) A good Cheddar, like a human being, needs nine months to round into decent enough shape to make a public appearance. I prefer a more elephantine period of gestation. A knowledgeable Englishman, John Houghton, once suggested two to five years—but his counsel was offered two and a half centuries ago when both men and cheese were allowed time to live. To Cheddar—as to all cheeses of character—Edgar's wise words in *King Lear* must apply: "Ripeness is all."

Of Stilton it is hard to speak without emotion. Its azure veins avouching its noble lineage, it is enthroned as the world's most regal Blue, exerting, like any true aristocrat, authority without aggressiveness. A Stilton's self-confidence springs from its past (the richest milk and cream) and its future, which can only be one of glory. John Jay Chapman recalls a morsel "that was like Agincourt. It was sonorous, undying." Here Chapman strikes the right note. There's such divinity doth hedge a Stilton as aureoles no other cheese. It is magisterial.

See, however, that your Stilton be of a healthy cream color, not anemic, with a hint of greenish-yellow, its edges brownish, its veins wide-branching, its texture not over-flaky, its vast interior uncrevassed. If you can, buy a whole Stilton or at least a half. The grandiose gesture will repay you; properly kept at room temperature a well-bought, well-bred Stilton will for many months share with you its nobility. With careful stroke remove the crown. Then cut out a wedge perhaps 1½ inches high, and further wedges as required of exactly the same height, until a new smooth top is exposed. Replace the crown so that it fits tightly; keep truncating your Stilton in this manner till you have disposed of the last bit. Then buy another Stilton.

Stilton, as I say, does reach us, as do many other fine cheeses. Phil Alpert, the master cheesemonger of Fulton Street, New York, offers hundreds of "cheeses of all nations," but most of them are made here in excellent imitation of their originals. To secure, however, a wide and deep understanding of cheese one must and should travel. The pleasures of a cheese tour are subtler than those of a châteaux tour, for there is always the chance that you will make a great discovery. Besides, cheeses taste better on the home grounds.

We come now to our own land, with which from the cheese-lovers' viewpoint we may merge our good neighbor Canada. Let us joyfully aver that we have a God's plenty of sound, decent domestic cheeses, most of it Cheddarish in nature, some of it an excellent aping of greater European originals, such as Gruyère or Roquefort.

Our basic trouble is that we are in a hurry and cheese is not. Honest, edible Cheddar is easily found, but really mature, shelf-cured Cheddar, dry and on the point of the crumble, is rare. Still, I have eaten good Cheddar from Canada, Vermont, New York and Wisconsin; and I once tasted an Oregon Tillamook filled with both the goodness and severity of God. Sage Cheddar—Vermont's pride—can be a wondrous thing. It eats supremely well on a hot summer afternoon in the country (circumstances alter cheeses), especially if you mate it incestuously with its mother, milk, and load it on cracker-barrel crackers—even though for the most part crackers are the enemy of cheese, just as bread is its friend. (I mean real bread—pumpernickel, dark rye, stone-ground whole-grain bread, or crusty French loaf.)

The great war, as in other areas, is between the urge to standardize and the urge to create. More often than one would think, the creator wins. One of our finest native cheeses is the work of a creative artist, Emil Frey, of Monroe, New York. This cheese offers a good example of serendipity. Frey was experimenting with a formula for a German-type cheese (probably Limburger, which is originally Belgian) and accidentally came up with something new. But it takes greatness to recognize greatness, and Frey, being great, knew he had something. He called it Liederkranz—one of the most beautiful (and odorous) soft cheeses in the world, and named after a famous New York singing society.

The roll of individualistic, ruggedly independent American cheeses is a long one. (No "process cheese," of course, can be included in the list.) Let me mention only a few. There is, for carefree nibbling, the plain, honest Jack from California. From the Colorado Rockies comes a little flattened sphere of black-rinded whole-milk Cheddar, Bellows Blackie —an utterly delicious, subtly acid eating cheese, imperfect for wine but otherwise a fresh and lovely thing. Poona, a Pont l'Evêque-like cheese made in New York State, has extraordinary breeding. Canada's Oka, lineally descended from Port Salut, can be superior, though I fear it is cured too quickly. The secretary of the Cistercian Abbey of la Trappe d'Oka (where the cheese is made) writes me that its unique flavor is due "partly to the special bacteria of our cellars, and partly to the rich pasture ground of our hilly country."

Certain strange and wonderful cheeses of Europe I may never taste—Sweden's Prestost or Saaland Pfarr, whose curd is washed in whisky; Rumania's Branja de Cosulet, a creamy sheep's-milk cheese, resinous from its pinebark casing; Septmoncel from the Jura, ranked by some experts above Roquefort; England's esoteric Blue Vinny and Wensleydale . . . But no matter: there is enough fine cheese in my own country to last my time and give it edge, savor and unctuousness. And there is always the hope that, like a new planet, a truly supreme American cheese will swim into my ken, and that, like Cortez in Keats' sonnet, I shall at last look

"With a wild surmise,
Silent, upon a peak in dairyin'."

SWISS MUSHROOM CHEESE PIE

For a buffet supper, bake two of these in matching, French, white china baking dishes.

Enough rich pie pastry for
  2 crusts in an 8-inch
  baking dish
1 pound Swiss cheese,
  thinly sliced

4 tablespoons butter
1 cup thinly sliced
  mushrooms sautéed
  in butter
Light cream

Start oven at hot (425° F.). Line dish with pastry and chill for ½ hour. Arrange slices of cheese in bottom of lined dish, add dabs of butter and a few mushroom slices. Repeat layers, filling the dish. Cover with pastry and make a decorative crimped edge around the dish. Cut a few gashes in the top layer of pastry. Bake in a hot oven for 20 to 25 minutes; then lower the heat to moderate and bake for 5 or 10 minutes longer, until the pastry is browned. Makes 4 or more servings.

DELICATE CHEESE SOUP

1 large onion, peeled and
  sliced
2 cups water
2 tablespoons butter
2 tablespoons flour
1 teaspoon salt

½ teaspoon white pepper
2 cups milk
½ cup grated Parmesan
  cheese
Poppy-seed croutons
2 tablespoons chopped
  chives

Cook onion in the 2 cups water for 15 minutes or until tender. Drain, save liquid, discard onion. Melt butter in soup kettle; blend in flour, salt and pepper; add milk and onion liquid gradually. Cook, stirring constantly, over low heat until thickened and smooth. Add cheese and stir until melted. Serve at once in warmed cream-soup bowls. Add 2 or 3 poppy-seed croutons and about ¼ teaspoon chives to each bowl. Makes 4 servings.

Poppy-seed croutons—Cut French bread in ½-inch cubes, roll lightly in olive oil, sprinkle with poppy seeds; then sauté in a little hot oil until browned. Drain. Place on pan and crisp a few minutes in a hot oven.

SWISS AND CAMEMBERT POINTS

4 tablespoons butter
3 ounces ripe Camembert
  cheese
¼ cup grated Swiss cheese
3 eggs

1 teaspoon salt
Grind of pepper
¼ teaspoon paprika
2 cups all-purpose flour,
  sifted

Start oven at hot (425° F.). Grease baking sheet. Cream butter until soft; blend Camembert cheese into butter; add Swiss cheese and beat smooth. Add eggs, one at a time, beating well. Stir salt, pepper and paprika into the flour, sift together, stir into the cheese mixture until soft dough is formed. Pat dough out on a floured board in circle about 10 inches in diameter. Place on prepared baking sheet and cut dough into 16 pie-shaped wedges. Bake for 25 to 30 minutes or until lightly browned. Serve warm or cold with drinks. Makes 16 generous servings.

COUNTRY HOUSE BAKED BREAD
AND CHEESE

1 teaspoon orégano
2 tablespoons butter
12 slices day-old white bread
½ pound process Cheddar
  cheese, sliced thin
4 eggs
2½ cups milk

1 teaspoon prepared mustard
1½ tablespoons chopped
  onion
1½ teaspoons salt
Grind of black pepper
Dash of paprika

Grease a baking dish 12 x 7 x 2 inches with butter, dust orégano lightly over the butter coating. Arrange 6 slices of bread in bottom of dish. Cover with the cheese then with the remaining bread. Beat eggs until light; add the milk, mustard, onion, salt and pepper. Mix well and pour over the bread. Sprinkle lightly with paprika. Let dish stand for 1 hour. Start oven at moderate (325° F.). Bake for 1 hour. Serve immediately in baking dish. Makes 4 to 6 servings.

A good buffet supper dish. Prepare the recipe 2 or more times and bake in identical dishes for a big party. A green salad, small prosciutto horns filled with horseradish, chopped cucumber and sour cream, or assorted cold smoked meats, and coffee round out this supper.

SWISS FONDUE

1 pound (4 cups) imported
  Swiss cheese,
  shredded
3 tablespoons flour
½ clove garlic
2 cups dry white wine such
  as Riesling or Chablis
Salt, pepper, grated nutmeg

⅜ cup kirsch
  or
¼ cup cognac
2 loaves crusty French or
  Italian bread, cut into
  bite-sized pieces, each
  having some crust

This dish is made at the table, in a 2-quart flameproof casserole, over an easily adjusted alcohol lamp. If possible, also have an electric tray at hand. Dredge the cheese with flour. Rub the casserole or chafing dish with the garlic and discard the garlic. Pour the wine into the dish and set it over very low heat. Do not boil. When the wine is so hot air bubbles rise to the surface, stir with a fork and add cheese by the handful. Stir each handful until melted before adding the next.

Keep stirring until the mixture starts bubbling lightly. Add salt, pepper and few grains of nutmeg. Add kirsch or cognac. Remove from the heat and set the dish on a warm tray or electric plate with asbestos pad.

Each guest spears a piece of bread on his fork, through the soft part of the bread and the crust so he doesn't lose his bread in the mixture (for if he does, he must pay for the wine!). He dips his bread with a stirring motion through the hot cheese. Each person dips in turn, always with a stirring motion; the stirring helps maintain a good fondue consistency.

The fondue must remain hot, bubbling very lightly. If it becomes too thick a very small amount of heated wine stirred through it restores the texture.

Swiss gourmets say cold drinks are never served with fondue. A glass of kirsch or brandy may be taken and hot coffee served afterwards. Makes fondue for 4 people.

FOSTER ENSMINGER

BATON CLUB CHEESE SOUFFLÉ

4 tablespoons butter
4 tablespoons flour
1 teaspoon salt
Dash cayenne
1½ cups milk

½ pound Cheddar cheese,
    thinly sliced
6 eggs, separated
8 crisply cooked bacon curls
Broiled tomato slices

Start oven at moderately slow (300° F.). Melt the butter in the top of a double boiler over boiling water, stir in flour smoothly, adding salt and cayenne. Stir until blended; add milk and stir until thickened and smooth. Add the cheese and stir until melted. Remove pan from heat, add beaten egg yolks and mix well. Let mixture cool slightly. Whip egg whites stiff. Then slowly pour slightly cooled cheese sauce into the egg whites, thoroughly cutting and folding the two together. Pour into an ungreased 2-quart soufflé dish or casserole. Set dish in a shallow pan of hot water. Bake for 1 hour and 15 minutes. Serve at once. Serve crisp bacon curls and broiled tomato slices with the soufflé. Makes 4 to 6 servings.

FRENCH CHÂTEAU BAKED BREAD AND CHEESE

Puff paste to make 3 9-inch
    rounds of pastry
¾ cup butter
⅔ cup all-purpose flour,
    sifted
1 quart warm milk
6 beaten egg yolks

1 pound imported Swiss
    cheese, grated
½ teaspoon salt
Grind of black pepper
Paprika
2 tablespoons crumbs

Roll out puff paste about ⅛ inch thick and cut in 3 rounds each a little less than 9 inches in diameter. Place on baking sheets, prick surface all over with fork. Start oven at hot (450° F.) and bake rounds for 8 to 10 minutes or until crisp and browning. Remove from oven.

Melt butter in a 2-quart saucepan. Stir flour smoothly into it. Gradually add warm milk, stirring continually until smooth and thickened. Stir in egg yolks, mix, add cheese (all but 2 tablespoons) and the seasoning; mix and cook about 1 minute. Place a baked round of pastry in a round baking dish, cover with cheese sauce, repeat pastry and sauce layers, with sauce on top. Sprinkle top with the reserved 2 tablespoons of grated cheese mixed with crumbs. Bake for 8 to 10 minutes or until top is browned. Cut like pie in the hot dish and serve at once. Makes 6 or more servings.

CHEESE PIE FOR BRUNCH

Pastry for 1-crust
    9-inch pie
2 cups hot, seasoned
    mashed potatoes
2 cups (1 pound) cottage
    cheese
½ cup sour cream

2 tablespoons finely diced,
    peeled onion
1 teaspoon salt
Grind of black pepper
½ teaspoon paprika
Milk
2 tablespoons butter

Start oven at hot (425° F.). Line pie pan with pastry and chill it. Combine potatoes, cheese, sour cream, onion and seasonings. Pour into pie shell. Brush top with milk and dot with butter. Bake in hot oven for about 15 minutes. Then reduce heat to moderate and bake for 15 minutes longer or until top is browned. Makes 6 servings. This cheese pie also makes a good supper dish with tossed salad and coffee.

ITALIAN CHEESE CROQUETTES

½ pound mozzarella
    cheese
½ cup all-purpose flour,
    sifted

1 beaten egg
¼ teaspoon salt
Grind fresh pepper
1 cup olive oil

Mash and work mozzarella with wooden spoon or your hands until the cheese is soft. Add about 1 tablespoon flour, the egg, salt and pepper, and mix well. Shape into small croquettes, roll lightly in flour. Fry in hot oil (370° F.) for 5 to 6 minutes or until golden brown. Lift out carefully with slotted spoon or pancake turner. Let drain a few seconds on thick paper toweling. Serve as luncheon dish with hot tomato sauce, crusty bread and romaine salad. Makes 12 croquettes, 6 servings.

BAKED CRÈME LORRAINE

6 slices bacon
1½ cups grated Gruyère
    cheese
1½ cups grated Parmesan
    cheese
2 cups heavy cream

2 eggs, well beaten
1 teaspoon salt
½ teaspoon dried basil
Dash pepper and paprika
Toasted French bread

Start oven at moderate (350° F.). Butter 1½-quart baking dish. Fry bacon until crisp; drain and crumble. Combine bacon, cheese, cream, eggs and seasonings. Pour into baking dish. Place dish in shallow pan of warm water. Bake in preheated moderate oven about 35 minutes or longer, until set. It should be the consistency of thick custard, or slightly firmer. Serve warm, from baking dish, onto toasted French bread. Makes 4 servings.

CHEESE AND SMOKED TONGUE RAMEKINS

6 buttered individual
    casseroles or ramekins
3 tablespoons butter
2 eggs, plus 1 egg white
¾ cup grated Parmesan
    cheese

1 cup ground, cooked,
    smoked beef tongue
1 teaspoon prepared mustard
¼ teaspoon dried basil
¼ teaspoon celery salt

Start oven at moderate (350° F.). Butter casseroles or ramekins. Cream butter until light and fluffy; beat egg yolks until light, then combine with butter, beat cheese in, add tongue and seasonings and combine well. Whip egg whites until stiff, fold into tongue mixture, heap into casseroles or ramekins. Place in shallow pan with just enough water to cover bottom of pan. Bake in preheated oven until puffy and lightly browned. Serve as first-course appetizer or as a hot entrée with a salad supper. Makes 6 servings.

CRAB AND CHEESE SUPREME

6 or 8 thin slices bread,
   lightly toasted and
   buttered
2 cups freshly cooked crab
   meat, all fibers
   removed
½ pound Swiss cheese, grated
   or cut in thin slivers

3 eggs
1 cup light cream
1 cup milk
Salt, pepper, paprika

Start oven at moderate (325° F.). Butter an oblong baking-serving dish. Line dish with buttered toast. Cover toast with flaked crab meat. Sprinkle generously with cheese. Beat eggs until light, combine with cream and milk, and pour over contents of dish. Add dash of seasonings. Bake in preheated oven about 50 minutes, or until set. Makes 8 servings.

PARIS CHEESE-AND-LEEK PIE

Baked 8-inch pie shell
4 or 5 leeks
2 cups Cheese Sauce (recipe
   below)

1½ cups grated Swiss
   cheese
Grated nutmeg

Prepare pastry for 8-inch pie shell and bake until lightly browned. Wash leeks, trim, cook in slightly salted water to cover for 15 minutes or until tender. Drain, cut in 1-inch lengths. Pour into shell enough cheese sauce to make layer about ½ inch deep; you will probably use the entire 2 cups of sauce. Arrange leeks in layer in sauce. Cover with the grated cheese. Add light sprinkling of nutmeg. Start oven at slow (275° F.), and when oven is warm, put in the filled pie dish and bake 15 to 20 minutes, or until set and of the firmness and texture of custard. Use higher heat if necessary, but never more than moderate (350° F.). If preferred, instead of pastry, the baking dish may be lined with thin slices of buttered toast, then filled with sauce, leeks and cheese, and baked as described. Makes 4 or more servings.

NORMANDY ASPARAGUS WITH CHEESE SAUCE

16 stalks hot, freshly cooked
   asparagus
8 rounds hot, buttered toast
4 hard-cooked eggs, cut
   lengthwise in quarters

Salt, pepper
Paprika
Hot Cheese Sauce
Finely minced truffle

Arrange hot, drained asparagus in a warm serving platter. Surround it with the rounds of toast and place 2 quarters of hard-cooked egg on each toast round. Season egg lightly with salt, pepper, paprika. Add spoonful of Cheese Sauce to each egg-covered toast round and garnish with a bit of truffle. Serve at once, with bowl of extra sauce for those who like to spoon it directly over the asparagus. Makes 4 servings.

Cheese Sauce (actually a Mornay sauce; either plain cheese sauce or this Continental version is delicious on asparagus)

3 tablespoons butter
3 tablespoons flour
1 chicken bouillon cube
   dissolved in ¾ cup hot
   water, or
¾ cup chicken broth, heated

¾ cup light cream
1 thin slice onion
½ cup grated Parmesan
   cheese
½ cup grated Gruyère cheese

Melt butter, stir flour smoothly in, add hot bouillon or broth, then the cream, gradually, stirring meanwhile. Add onion slice, continue to cook and stir until thickened. Remove onion. Add cheese, a little at a time, stirring until all is well blended. Serve hot, as described. Makes about 2 cups of sauce.

Spice to Taste / *Morris Markey*

*The search for spices inspired great voyages of discovery
and profoundly affected human destiny*

You can go into the corner grocery with half a dollar in your hand and buy enough pepper or nutmeg or cinnamon to last your family for a year. The purchase will be, of course, an utterly commonplace transaction, and the stuff you take home will seem about as romantic as a glass of water. But if you are in a mood to think a little about your box of spice, tucked on the kitchen shelf with its bright new label, you might feel disposed to pick it up again and shake a few grains into your palm. And you might say to yourself: "What a fantastic thing that men have suffered inhuman hardship—have mortgaged their treasures and died miserable deaths—just to get their hands on two or three pounds of this spice."

Here is the plain fact of it: No trade in all the history of the world, neither gold nor grain, precious gems nor iron tools, has affected the course of human destiny in any way comparable to the spice trade. The finding and the shipping and the selling of spices—of pepper and cloves, cinnamon and nutmeg and ginger and all the rest—has built empires. The cultural patterns of whole races of men have been turned into fresh and sometimes startling channels by the spice trade. And finally a whole new world was discovered by men who were on the hunt for spices.

They were not, to be sure, looking merely for something that would add a dainty fillip to a favorite dish. Rather, they were looking for something which, in their own day and time, was almost essential to human survival. At any rate, men had come to think that it was, which amounts to the same thing.

All over the civilized world, spices were bent to a great variety of uses. First, of course, as a condiment for food, to make palatable the daily nourishment which generally lay between two extremes: the tasteless grain staples of the East and the half-spoiled meats of the West. But spices were also among the most important medicines that doctors possessed. They were (especially turmeric and saffron) invaluable dyestuffs. And spices, not flowers, were the base of nearly all the perfumes and ointments and incenses that were so widely employed to make everyday life endurable.

Nobody knows when man first used spice. The Bible abounds with references to spices, and perhaps the earliest mention of them that we have is in the words of the Lord God Jehovah himself. He had revealed Himself to Moses in Exodus, and in the thirtieth chapter of that book He gave Moses precise instructions for the preparation of anointing oil: ". . . Take thou also unto thee principal spices, of pure myrrh five hundred shekels, and of sweet cinnamon half so much, even two hundred and fifty shekels, and of sweet calamus two hundred and fifty shekels, and of cassia five hundred shekels . . . and of olive oil an hin."

Though the authority is by no means so exalted, records show that the Chinese were using spices, particularly cassia and ginger, 3,000 years before Christ. And the writings of the Sumerians and Egyptians seem at first glance to devote an unreasonable amount of space to these aromatic articles, until it is remembered that most of the records are concerned with commerce and that spices were, indeed, the most profitable of all goods in which a merchant might deal.

The spice trade between the Far East and the civilization of the Mediterranean had become a major business enterprise thousands of years before men discovered that the earth was round. The spice route was a well-beaten path. The spices were brought by sea from the remote spice islands to the Yemen and the Hadramant, and from there carried by

Cloves from Zanzibar, saffron from the Near East, curry from India. Spices from everywhere in the world bring delicate flavors and aromas to the kitchens of America.

SOMOROFF

camel caravan to Mecca, whose merchants took their profits and formed new caravans. They sent the sweet-smelling bags to the ports of Tyre and Sidon, whence they were shipped out again to the cities of Southern Europe and the African Coast.

It goes without saying that the first thing the Romans did when they won control of the Mediterranean sea lanes was to take over the spice trade. Since the Suez Canal had not yet been dug, there was no way for the Roman galleys to dominate the Persian Gulf or the Red Sea or the Indian Ocean. And so the middleman, bridging the gap between the far-off islands and the sophisticates of Rome, was still the Arab merchant. He kept secret, you may be sure, the sources of his precious wares.

Rome carried on an immensely active trade with the spice merchants, buying chiefly pepper and cinnamon, nutmegs and cloves. In exchange, Rome sold to the East glass, textiles and amber. But the balance of trade was so adverse to Rome that Pliny the Younger worried about it.

"The prospects for an economic collapse within the Empire must be considered," he said, "so dearly do we pay for our luxuries and our women."

With the fall of the Roman Empire and the disappearance of the Roman fleet, the Moslems of the Near East took over the world trade in spices. Their domination lasted until the beginning of the tenth century, when the little seaport town of Venice became, by reason of its geography and the cleverness of its merchants, the crossroads for a slowly reviving traffic between the Orient and Europe. It is no exaggeration to say that the Venice of the Doges, perhaps the most opulent society the world has known, was built upon spices. An almost countless merchant fleet plied in and out of its harbor, carrying spices and silk and ivory and coral and precious woods and a thousand other things. But the value of the spices, bought from the Arabs and resold to France and Portugal and Spain, to Germany and Holland and England, far exceeded that of all the other goods put together.

Spices did not reach England until about 900 A.D., but the moment they did they were acclaimed the most marvelous and useful objects that the bounty of the Lord had yet provided. The English, then as now, were a meat-eating people, but the art of storing foodstuffs for the winter had not been discovered. It was the custom, in the autumn, to slaughter all cattle except the seed stock, and try somehow to preserve the meat for the long months that lay ahead. Some of it was salted down. But when midwinter came, it was dubious meat indeed that was brought to England's festive boards.

With the arrival of the first shipment of spices from the Orient, all that was changed. The aromatic seeds and powders gave flavor and piquancy to even the most doubtful joint. And, more important, it was quickly discovered that pepper was an almost miraculous preservative of meat. They found that meat rubbed with black pepper did not spoil, and that its flavor was improved.

The appearance of spices in England stirred other imaginations too. The practice of medicine was a mystery rather than a science. The Orient was the most mysterious of all places. Here, wonderfully at hand, were some of the secrets of the East. Spices became the chief ingredients of miraculous nostrums and cure-alls. They were sold at fabulous prices, and by the hogshead. Love potions which carried

the aromas of the East were a high-class side line for doctors.

Not all the uses of spice in the materia medica were quackery, however, The oils of spices are still used in prescriptions filled at your drugstore today. Sometimes their only purpose is to mask the vile taste of some really curative concoction, but they have well-recognized therapeutic uses as well. The oils of cassia and cinnamon and cloves are carminatives of the first order. Oil of cloves is still the best thing to put on an aching tooth.

The almost incredible prosperity of the city of Venice naturally aroused the envy of other cities and kingdoms. Toward the middle of the fifteenth century men who did not live within the snug security of the Mediterranean began to think about the wealth that would be theirs if they could find a direct sea route to the spice islands and so eliminate the profits of the Arab merchants and of the merchants of Venice.

By 1492, the Spaniards had fitted out a voyage for Christopher Columbus, who believed that he could reach the spice islands by sailing westward. In Portugal, a sailor named Vasco da Gama convinced the crown that he could reach those islands by sailing toward the east. Christopher Columbus did not find the true Spice Islands, but he did find other spice islands. Five years later, in 1497, Vasco da Gama with four ships rounded the Cape of Good Hope, proceeded into the Indian Ocean, and found the East Indies, the Spice Islands themselves.

That was the beginning of the end for Venice. In an incredibly brief time Lisbon became the capital of the world's commerce, and thereafter for a hundred years the Portuguese and Spanish controlled the spice trade.

Soon, however, the Dutch decided that they would like to have the spice trade. They built a battle fleet, sailed it into the Indian Ocean, and between 1595 and 1600 they drove the Portuguese from the seas. They ran up the Dutch flag on all the spice islands they could find, laid down a brass-bound monopoly upon the commerce in spices, and thus founded one of the great empires of modern times. The Dutch knew full well what they had, and they were determined to keep it and to exploit it. Their naturalists and agriculturists saw very quickly that most of the wild spices they found could be grown in almost any favorable climate; so the Dutch took steps. They established the death penalty for anyone in Ceylon possessing cinnamon without written authority.

They took measures to make the nutmeg, which is a seed, infertile even if it were smuggled out and planted in the most hospitable soil. They soaked the nutmegs in limewater, which destroyed the life germ without impairing the flavor. Even today nutmegs are soaked in limewater before shipment to market, because housewives think something is wrong unless the seeds have a powdery white coating.

The English were not the sort of people to continue indefinitely paying outrageous prices to the Dutch for the treasures of the Spice Islands. So, in 1600, the astonishing East India Company was formed in London. It was a private corporation with 125 stockholders. Each of these men founded a great fortune upon the exploits of the company's expeditions. And England founded an empire.

The first voyage of the East India Company's merchantmen brought back 300,000 pounds of finest pepper, bought from the seaport merchants of Sumatra—a Dutch possession. That meant war, of course, and the war lasted for fifty years.

Most of it was fought in remote seas of the East. The only episode of this most of us remember was the massacre at Amboina, when the Dutch tortured and killed a thousand Englishmen; but when the war was over, the Dutch monopoly of the spice trade was broken—India and Malaya belonged to the British Empire.

The English did not try to set up a monopoly of the spice trade. Instead, they encouraged the domestic cultivation of all sorts of spices, set up huge plantations of their own and encouraged others to do the same. They were not able to plant the most valuable spice of all, however, for the simple reason that the source of pepper was still a mystery. Merchants in the seaport towns would sell it, of course, but the dried seeds in their bags would not germinate anywhere, and neither bribes nor blandishments would persuade them to tell where the plants might be found.

It was not until 1788 that the source of pepper was discovered, and the discovery was made by an American. In that year Captain William Vans, out of Salem in the brigantine *Cadet*, was trading with native merchants at Benkulen on the southern coast of Sumatra. Two or three ancient characters took a liking to the captain's bluff ways and casually told him that wild pepper was abundant in the northern hills of the island. By 1805, America had taken command of the pepper trade, chiefly because of its merchant fleet of clipper ships.

There is a most considerable difference of opinion about the definition of a spice. Where do spices leave off and herbs begin? Is garlic a spice? Is saffron an herb? Some of the spices are seeds and some are flowers, some are bark and some are roots. There are more than 200 different kinds of spice (although some of them are used parochially and have no place in the world market, and many of those that once held high favor have lost their appeal to modern appetites). Each kind has numerous varieties. There are, for example, more than eighty varieties of the nutmeg tree.

In the kitchens of the world and in the market places as well, by far the most important of all the spices is pepper. It is a more or less common belief that the chief purpose of pepper is to make food "hot," but its actual virtue is far more subtle than that. This spice has the quality of strengthening and emphasizing the natural flavor of almost any food with which it is mixed. Many spices have such pronounced aromas of their own that they mask, or, if used in excess, actually destroy the natural flavor of a meat or vegetable. Pepper, the aroma of which is not overpowering, brings out the best that is in a dish.

The pepper plant is a weak, rather unattractive little vine which, to begin with, grew wild in the uplands of Northern Sumatra. Nowadays, it is completely domesticated and is produced on great plantations in Malaya, the Malabar Coast of India, Ceylon, Thailand and, of course, on Sumatra itself. The seeds of the plant grow in small catkins, and these seeds are pepper. When taken at the harvest they are red, quite odorless, and almost tasteless. But when dried in the sun they turn black and acquire their spicy quality.

Black pepper and white pepper are produced from the identical seed. To make white pepper, the black outer coating is simply taken off by abrasion. The result is a spice that is a little more appealing to the eye but is far less pungent, far less aromatic.

When Columbus discovered the New World he discovered some new spices too. The first of these was an object which he called pepper because it tasted hot to him, and that name has survived in the folk language and even in the cookbooks. In the West Indian islands, in North and Central America, the early explorers noted that the natives were cultivating an incredible variety of these plants. Their seed pods were of all shapes and sizes and colors and degrees of "hotness"—from the sweet bullnose green or red pods that we call sweet peppers and eat as simple vegetables, to the tiny bird or devil pods which would lift the roof off your head.

These plants have no relation whatever to true pepper and are, in fact, closely related to tomatoes. But the planting of them spread very quickly over most of the world, and nearly all people call them peppers. In the spice trade, the dried and processed pod is divided into two categories: when the entire pod—seeds and pulp and skin and all—is ground, the powder is called cayenne or chili pepper or capsicum. When the seeds are discarded and only the skin dried and pulverized, the result is called paprika. The two important varieties of paprika are the Spanish and the Hungarian, which have subtly different flavors. Spanish paprika is ordinarily preferred for fish and fowl dishes, and Hungarian for meat dishes.

The second spice that Columbus discovered was on the island of Jamaica. It was a curious sort of berry, growing wild on gnarled, grotesque trees in the uplands. With a singular paucity of imagination the Spaniards called this pepper, too, and even today its name in the trade is pimento. We call it allspice, because it combines in an elusive sort of way the aromas of cloves and cinnamon and nutmeg and mace. The tree is closely related to the bay tree, and from its leaves a quite passable bay rum is distilled. At the harvest, the berries smell and taste like bay, with no spicy odor at all. But after six or eight days of drying in the sun they become one of the most highly aromatic of all condiments. The trees, which grow to heights of forty feet, cannot be cultivated at all. The world supply of allspice comes from the groves of wild trees that flourish in the Jamaican hills.

Columbus discovered a third product which may or may not be a spice. The definition depends upon the last authority you happened to consult. The plant is an orchid, one of the most beautiful of all orchids. The eight-inch seed pods that it produces are called vanilla.

It grew first in the Mexican swamps and marshes between Tampico and Vera Cruz, and the native Indians have been using it for centuries to flavor their chocolate. Cuttings of the vines, which often rise to a height of eighty feet, were taken to Java and Reunion Island, to Tahiti and Guadeloupe, to the Seychelles and Martinique, where the plant has become a major crop. But the native Mexican vanilla is still at a premium in the trade.

Vanilla lends itself quite readily to distillation into an extract of its essential oils, and most of us use it in that form. But whole beans may be bought almost anywhere and grated for their oddly delicate flavor. The chief advantage of using the whole bean lies in the fact that there are scores of imitations of vanilla which frequently find their way into extracts. None of the substitutes can really compare with the true, vagrant, oddly persuasive aroma and taste of real vanilla.

There is a general agreement among people who travel about the world that the nutmeg tree is the most beautiful of all the trees on earth. It grows naturally in the small islands of the Moluccas, a giant of a tree standing eighty to ninety feet high, with dense, black-green foliage and great clusters of brilliant fruits that resemble big apricots. When the fruits ripen and split open, a jet-black, polished seed the size of a pecan is revealed. The seed is covered with a waxy, scarlet lacework of fibers. That lacework is the spice called mace. Inside the black husk is the kernel itself, the nutmeg.

The natives of the Spice Islands believe two things about the nutmeg tree: It cannot thrive beyond the sound of the sea; it must have meat to feed upon. Even though the tree is widely cultivated now, in Southern Java and Sumatra and Zanzibar and the Celebes—in the British West Indian Islands of Dominica and Grenada, which produce about eighty per cent of the world supply—it remains true that it flourishes best when it is close to the roar of surf. Furthermore, planters confess that burying the bodies of two pariah dogs among the roots of a nutmeg tree has an almost spectacular effect upon its growth and yield.

Most of the clove trees of the world now grow on the islands of Zanzibar and Pemba, whence they were taken from the Dutch Moluccas. The spice itself is the unopened flower bud of the tree, plucked by hand and dried in the sun. There are numerous varieties, but the differences between them would escape the ordinary cook. It is important for the cook to know, however, that good and honest cloves have an aroma that rises quickly at the first sniff, that they are plump and whole, of a reddish brown color, and their oil exudes readily at the pressure of a fingernail.

In the United States, unlike the rest of the world, there is no distinction between cassia and cinnamon, though they are not really the same thing. The natives of Southern China were planting and tending cassia trees at least 3,600 years ago, felling them when they had reached a height of forty feet, and stripping from them their aromatic bark. The cultivation of these trees has now spread to Ceylon, Sumatra and other Eastern islands. Cinnamon was discovered centuries after the cultivation of cassia had become a commonplace in China. "True cinnamon," as it is called in the trade, is a milder form of the spice and is grown in Ceylon.

The harvesting of cassia is usually a crude and highly wasteful operation. But the owner of a cinnamon plantation gathers his crop with the utmost care. Though "true cinnamon" is the premium-priced product, a kitchen would have to take itself very seriously indeed to insist on grinding its own cinnamon from the sticks or quills of "true cinnamon." It is a difficult job, for one thing, and, for another, recipes available in this country are geared to the use of cassia, which is what you get when you buy a can of cinnamon.

It is almost impossible to speak of ginger without saying Jamaica ginger, though the plant is native to Asia and was introduced into Jamaica by the English. Ginger has been cultivated in China for so long a time that its wild origins are completely lost to memory or record, but nowadays the biggest supply for the market, and much the best quality, comes from Jamaica. The plant itself is a dull-looking affair, two or three feet high, and only the roots are used for the spice. These are scalded to remove the outer peel, dried in the sun, and then dusted with lime powder to prevent mildew.

One of the most curious of all the spices is saffron. Since remote antiquity men have used it for three principal purposes: for the dyeing qualities of its deep orange-yellow color; as a perfume; and, of course, as a condiment and coloring agent in food. King Solomon's garden had a plot of saffron. It was strewn as a powdered scent through the Roman streets and baths. It gave us the legend of crocodile tears, for the smell of saffron was the only thing that could make those monsters weep.

The spice comes from the dried yellow stigma of a purple crocus that blooms in the fall rather than the spring. About 70,000 blossoms are used to make a single pound of saffron powder, and so it is not hard to understand why this has always been the most costly of all spices. During the last war, for example, saffron brought $80 a pound on the New York market, despite the fact that it can be grown almost anywhere and is native to all of Europe. Fortunately that absurd cost has been brought within reason now, for saffron is indispensable in the preparation of fish dishes such as bouillabaisse, of certain fish sauces, and of curries for sea food.

The way we use mustard nowadays—the jar of prepared wet mustard or the can of powdered mustard—is something quite new, as time is reckoned in the spice trade. It is true that mustard seeds have always had a place in the kitchen (Jesus made a parable of their trifling size), but it was a limited usefulness until the estimable Mrs. Clements, of Durham, England, discovered in 1720 a method for making mustard flour. Mrs. Clements crushed the seeds, and then pressed them to drive the oil out. She took the hard cake that was left, and broke it up, and bolted it through the finest weave of muslin she could buy. That is still the method used for making mustard flour, which is not only the dry mustard we buy, but also the ingredient that makes possible the various prepared mustards, which are simply the golden yellow or brown flour mixed with vinegar and olive oil and other spices.

So much for the classic spices.

There are scores of others, some of them so widely used in other parts of the world that it seems absurd we have never bothered to import them to America, some of them employed in such highly specialized affairs, the seasoning of beverages and the blending of bitters, that they have no real interest to the cook.

Cardamon seeds, for example, are almost an essential of the diet in the Near East, in Turkish and Armenian cooking, but are used here principally in drugs, scents and perfuming soap.

Turmeric is a root akin to the ginger root, possessing a strong yellow color. In its native state, it possesses an almost revolting odor and flavor. The process for converting this vile article into an appetizing condiment has remained to this day a secret of the Hindus and Malays who gather it. It is essential to curry powders and to many sauces and pickles and chutneys.

Capers are the unopened buds of a wild plant of the Mediterranean, a low prickly shrub with bright flowers that close in the night like a morning glory. The buds are harvested at dawn, just before they open for the first time. They are pickled in vinegar and then sorted for size through copper screens that give them a bright green color. This tint is pleasant to the eye and it does not affect the flavor of the spice.

Coriander is the fruit of a small Mediterranean shrub now widely cultivated in India. It is used for curries and chutneys, but in the United States it is used principally in candy manufacturing and in disguising the taste of unpleasant drugs.

Angelica is the seeds and roots of a small plant, used here in candied or crystallized form for cakes and candies because of its pleasant taste and bright green color.

Fenugreek is the seed pods of a plant widely grown in Morocco, Egypt and India. We rarely see it as a simple spice, but it is the chief flavoring ingredient in many curries. Fenugreek is also the article from which American manufacturers contrive artificial maple flavoring.

The United States now imports, in a normal year, about 137,000,000 pounds of spice. This is indeed an impressive figure, since spices are all dehydrated (and therefore very light) and a pinch is often enough to season a dish. About a quarter of the total import is pepper (black: over 34,000,000 pounds; white: about 3,400,000 pounds). We bring in 18,-000,000 pounds of whole mustard seeds (as well as 940,000 pounds of dry or ground mustard), some 12,000,000 pounds of cinnamon, more than 8,000,000 pounds of paprika, almost 3,000,000 pounds of nutmeg and more than 2,000,000 pounds of cloves.

A very great proportion of these spices is used by the manufacturers of food products. The meat industry buys tons of them for making sausages and spiced meats. The pickle makers, who also bottle ketchups and sauces, use every variety of spice in great quantity. The confectioners and bakers need

their share. Even so, there is no household kitchen in the country which does not have some sort of spice shelf, and it seems appropriate to offer a few suggestions for the keeping of that shelf:

Pepper (white and black), mace and nutmegs should always be bought whole, and ground or grated as they are required. For the rest, ready-ground spices may be used. They are cheap enough to cast away when they have lost their aroma and flavor. Ground spices may be kept for a considerable time if they are in glass jars or bottles with tight-fitting screw tops. But they should be kept in the coolest and dryest and darkest part of the kitchen and its pantries.

There is one other suggestion upon which every cooking expert agrees:

Use spices with imagination, but use them sparingly. A pinch of cinnamon or allspice or ginger or cloves is wonderful. Two pinches are not necessarily twice as wonderful. The generous hand with the spice box may, alas, destroy all the natural flavors of the dish. The thoughtful hand will make the natural flavors of almost any dish taste better.

THE BEST CINNAMON BRUNCH CAKE

1½ cups milk, scalded
1¼ teaspoons salt
1 cup sugar
1 cake yeast
6 cups all-purpose flour, sifted
¼ teaspoon powdered allspice
¼ teaspoon powdered mace

¾ cup shortening, melted
3 beaten egg yolks
1 egg white
1 tablespoon cold water
1 cup brown sugar, packed
1 tablespoon flour
1 tablespoon butter, melted
1 teaspoon powdered cinnamon

Combine hot milk, salt and 2 tablespoons sugar in a large mixing bowl and let cool to lukewarm. Add crumbled yeast, 3 cups flour, sifted with allspice and mace, and mix well. Cover lightly with towel and let rise in a warm, not hot, place until doubled in bulk. Add remaining sugar, the shortening and egg yolks; beat. Add remaining flour, gradually, mixing to a soft sticky dough. Turn dough out on a lightly floured board and knead until dough is soft and springy. Place in greased bowl, cover with towel, let rise in warm place to double its bulk.

Grease 2 8-inch-square cake pans. Roll and pat dough lightly to fit pans. Brush top of dough with egg white beaten with the tablespoon of cold water. Then sprinkle with mixture of brown sugar, flour, butter and cinnamon. Cover pans lightly, let dough rise until doubled in bulk. Start oven at moderate (350° F.) and bake cakes for about 40 minutes. Serve warm or cold. Makes 20 or more servings.

SUNDAY-BRUNCH CODFISH BALLS

Spice and herbs dress this old-fashioned New England delicacy with unusual appeal, giving it a special importance on any brunch menu.

2 cups shredded cooked, canned or quick-frozen codfish
4 cups pared and diced raw potatoes
Boiling water
2 beaten eggs
2 tablespoons butter
2¾ teaspoons ground dill seed

Quick grind black pepper
1½ teaspoons salt
½ teaspoon dry mustard
Dash cayenne
1 cup fine dry crumbs
½ teaspoon celery salt
4 tablespoons shortening or butter

Combine codfish and potatoes in kettle, cover with boiling water that comes 1 inch above foods. Boil for 10 minutes or until potatoes are tender. Drain; add eggs, butter, dill seed, pepper, salt, mustard and cayenne; beat well until thoroughly blended and light. Chill mixture about 1 hour or until firm enough to shape into balls or cakes. Make 2½-inch balls or slightly flattened cakes. Roll lightly in crumbs mixed with celery salt. Brown in about 1 inch of hot fat, frying for 2 or 3 minutes or until lightly browned all over. Drain for a few minutes on thick paper towels. Serve very hot with the traditional tomato sauce, a curry cream sauce or a tartare sauce. Makes about 2 dozen balls or 8 servings.

DELICIOUS PIZZA FOR A CROWD

One of the spiciest delectables of the Italian cuisine is the pizza. A meal in itself, and just right for big parties.

2 cakes yeast	Grind of black pepper
2 cups warm (85° F.) water	1 pound mozzarella cheese, sliced
1 teaspoon salt	
6½ cups all-purpose flour, sifted	2 2-oz. cans anchovy fillets, drained
2 No. 2 cans tomatoes or 4 cans Italian tomatoes	2 3-oz. cans sliced mushrooms, drained
¼ cup tomato paste	½ pound Italian sausage, cut in thin strips or fine dice
1 teaspoon salt	
½ teaspoon garlic powder	
½ teaspoon onion powder	½ pound Parmesan cheese, grated
3 teaspoons whole orégano leaves	⅜ cup olive oil
1 teaspoon sugar	Extra grated Parmesan cheese

Soften yeast in warm water. Sift salt and flour together and add about 2 cups of the mixture to the yeast; mix, turn onto lightly floured board and gradually knead in the remaining 4½ cups of flour. Knead until smooth and satiny. Place in a well-greased bowl, cover lightly with a towel and let rise in a warm place (about 85° F.) until doubled in bulk. Punch dough down, return it to the board and knead a little. Return dough to bowl, cover and let rise for 30 minutes. Roll and stretch dough out on the board to ¼-inch thickness. Cut rounds to fit six 12-inch layer-cake pans and place them in the greased pans or on greased baking sheets.

Start oven at moderately hot (400° F.). Mix the topping. Break up tomatoes with fork and mash in large mixing bowl. Mix in tomato paste, salt, garlic and onion powders, crumbled orégano leaves, sugar and pepper. Spread generously over dough. Lay mozzarella cheese over this mixture. Scatter anchovies, mushrooms and sausage over the cheese. Sprinkle with grated Parmesan cheese and olive oil. Bake for 25 to 35 minutes, or until crust is baked and edges brown. Cut in large wedges and serve. Serves 12 or more people.

SMÖRGÅSBORD SPICED TONGUE

1 medium-sized beef tongue	1 No. 2 can tomatoes
½ bay leaf	Sprig parsley
1 teaspoon celery salt	Sprig thyme
1 quart water	6 cloves
Flour	¼ cup sherry
3 tablespoons butter	

Rinse beef tongue, drain, place in kettle with bay leaf, celery salt and quart of water. Bring to a boil, lower temperature and let cook slowly for about 4 hours. Let cool in liquid. Remove tongue, cut the skin and pull it off. Dredge tongue generously with flour and brown it in a large skillet in hot butter. Combine tomatoes, herbs and cloves; cook for about 10 minutes; add to browned tongue and cook for 30 minutes or longer depending on the size of the tongue. Add sherry, stirring into pan juices for 1 or 2 minutes; then remove from heat. Slice tongue in the sauce and serve or reheat slices and sauce in chafing dish. Serve hot on buffet or smörgåsbord. Makes 10 or more servings.

SUNDAY-SUPPER TURKEY SOUFFLÉ

2 cups finely diced leftover cooked turkey	1¾ teaspoons poultry seasoning
1 cup cooked rice	⅛ teaspoon ground coriander
1 cup soft bread crumbs	
1 cup turkey stock, gravy or consommé	¼ teaspoon onion salt
	4 eggs
1 teaspoon salt	Hot cream sauce with 2 tablespoons chopped truffles added
Quick grind black pepper	

Start oven at moderate (325° F.). Wrap 1½-quart soufflé dish with 3-inch-wide strip of white paper so paper stands high above top of dish. Tie paper in place. Combine turkey, rice, crumbs and the gravy stock or consommé. Mix well; season with salt, pepper, the poultry seasoning, coriander and onion salt. Beat egg yolks until lemon-colored and blend into turkey mixture. Beat egg whites until stiff and fold into mixture. Turn at once into the prepared soufflé dish. Place dish in shallow pan of hot water and bake for about 1 hour and 15 minutes or until well risen and firm on top. Remove paper and serve at once with a well-seasoned cream sauce to which have been added 2 or 3 tablespoons chopped truffles or black olives. Makes 6 servings.

ANISE AND ALMOND PALLITOS

These delicious little cake straws go with a glass of wine, hot tea or coffee, or they accompany a rich frozen dessert.

3 cups all-purpose flour, sifted	6 eggs
½ teaspoon salt	1 tablespoon anisette or pernod
1 teaspoon baking powder	
1¼ cups sugar	2 cups blanched almonds, chopped
4 tablespoons butter	Grated nutmeg

Start oven at moderate (350° F.). Grease baking sheets and dust lightly with flour. Sift flour, salt and baking powder together three times. Combine in mixing bowl with sugar, butter, 5 eggs and the liqueur. Work and mix until well blended into a smooth dough. Roll out on lightly floured board; cut in 4- to 5-inch strips. Twist or roll strips lightly between palms. Mix remaining egg with 1 tablespoon water and brush over straws, sprinkle with almonds and very, very few grains nutmeg. Place on prepared baking sheets and bake for 8 to 10 minutes or until lightly browned. Remove from oven and let cool. Makes 4 to 5 dozen straws.

PANECITOS FOR THE COFFEE TRAY

¼ pound almond paste (from confectioner's)	⅛ teaspoon powdered cinnamon
4 tablespoons rum	Confectioners' sugar
⅛ teaspoon powdered cloves	

Work almond paste with rum and spice in a bowl until it forms a smooth wet paste. Add a little more rum, a teaspoon at a time if paste is not wet. When well mixed, work in a little confectioners' sugar at a time until paste is thick enough to mold. Roll into small balls or ovals. Serve with after-dinner coffee. Makes 12 to 20 pieces.

HONEY SPICE LOAF CAKE

3½ cups all-purpose flour,
  sifted
¼ teaspoon salt
1½ teaspoons baking powder
1 teaspoon baking soda
½ teaspoon powdered
  cinnamon
¼ teaspoon grated nutmeg
⅛ teaspoon powdered cloves
½ teaspoon powdered ginger
4 eggs
¾ cup light-brown sugar,
  packed
¼ cup oil
2 cups liquid honey
½ cup strong coffee
½ cup chopped almonds or
  pine nuts

Start oven at moderate (325° F.). Rub 11 x 16 x 4-inch loaf
pan with oil. Sift flour, salt, baking powder, soda and spices
together three times. Beat eggs, gradually beating sugar into
them, until thick and lemon-colored; beat in the oil, honey
and coffee. Stir flour mixture in, add nuts. Pour batter into
prepared pan. Bake for about 1 hour and 15 minutes or until
browned and cake tester inserted deeply comes out clean.
Let cool on cake rack before removing from pan. Leave plain
or frost thickly with Mocha Frosting. Makes 12 or more
servings.

MOCHA FROSTING

2 tablespoons butter
¼ cup brown sugar, packed
1 tablespoon powdered
  cocoa
1½ cups confectioners'
  sugar
2 tablespoons strong, cold
  coffee

Cream butter with sugar and cocoa. Beat until smooth and
fluffy. Add confectioners' sugar slowly, beating steadily;
gradually add coffee, beating constantly. Makes about 2 cups
frosting.

PECAN GINGER COOKIES

4½ cups all-purpose flour,
  sifted
1 teaspoon salt
½ teaspoon baking soda
1 teaspoon baking powder
2 teaspoons powdered ginger
½ teaspoon powdered
  cinnamon
1 cup shortening
1 cup brown sugar, packed
1 cup light corn syrup
¼ cup milk
½ cup chopped pecans
½ cup finely chopped
  candied ginger

Sift flour with salt, soda, baking powder and spice three
times. Cream shortening until light, beat in sugar and continue beating until mixture is soft and creamy. Add corn
syrup and a little milk and beat thoroughly; stir in nuts and
ginger, mix well. Then stir in about half of the dry ingredients, blend well. Alternately add remaining milk and
dry ingredients; mix thoroughly to a stiff dough. Use wooden
spoon or hands. Turn out onto lightly floured board; divide
dough in half and shape each half into a roll about 2 inches
in diameter. Wrap rolls in foil or heavy waxed paper and chill
2 or 3 hours, or until firm.
  Grease 2 or 3 baking sheets. Start oven at moderate
(375° F.). Cut rolls in thin slices and place cookies on
baking sheets. Bake for 12 minutes or until lightly browned.
Let cool before storing in tightly covered jars. Makes about 7
dozen cookies.

DINNER PARTY BREAD PUDDING

3½ cups milk
4 tablespoons butter
2 cups white-bread cubes
½ cup light-brown sugar,
  packed
2 beaten eggs
½ cup sherry
¼ teaspoon each powdered
  nutmeg, cinnamon
  and ginger
½ teaspoon salt
1 cup currants, softened by
  soaking in warm water
3 egg whites
Light cream or Sherry Sauce

Start oven at moderate (375° F.). Butter a 1½-quart baking
dish. Scald milk, add butter and pour over bread in mixing
bowl. Let stand 10 minutes. Then blend in sugar, the eggs,
sherry, spices, salt and drained currants. Whip egg whites
until stiff, fold into pudding. Pour into prepared baking
dish, set dish in shallow pan of hot water and bake for
about 1 hour or until a silver knife inserted in the center
comes out clean. Makes 6 servings. Serve with light cream
or Sherry Sauce.

SHERRY SAUCE

8 tablespoons butter
1 cup sugar
½ cup sherry
Nutmeg

Cream butter with sugar until light and fluffy; stir over heat
and let come to boiling. Remove from heat and add sherry
and a few grains of nutmeg. Mix and serve hot. Makes about
1¼ cups sauce.

LEBKUCHEN

2¾ cups all-purpose flour,
  sifted
½ teaspoon soda
1 teaspoon powdered
  cinnamon
½ teaspoon powdered cloves
½ teaspoon grated nutmeg
½ cup mixed candied fruit,
  chopped very fine
½ cup finely chopped
  almonds
1 cup light corn syrup
¾ cup brown sugar, packed
1 tablespoon lemon juice
1 teaspoon grated lemon
  peel
1 beaten egg
½ cup confectioners' sugar,
  sifted
1 tablespoon water

Start oven at moderately hot (400° F.). Grease 2 baking
sheets and sprinkle them evenly with light coating of flour.
Sift flour, soda and spices together three times; then combine
in mixing bowl with chopped fruits and nuts. Mix; add
corn syrup, sugar, lemon juice and peel, and the beaten egg.
Mix well. Divide dough in half and turn out each half on
a greased and floured baking sheet. Use ice-filled rolling
pin or palm of your hand moistened in ice water and pat
dough out to ⅛-inch thickness. Dough rises a little during
baking. Bake for 12 to 15 minutes or until lightly browned
and firm to the touch. Remove from oven; brush at once with
a thin icing made with the confectioners' sugar and water.
Cut into oblongs and other shapes while still warm. Remove
from pan. Leave plain or decorate with candied fruits. When
cool, store in tightly covered container to mellow. Makes 3
to 4 dozen lebkuchen.

The Truffle / Joseph Wechsberg

Nobody can cultivate it, and it takes a talented pig to unearth it,
but epicures have been sighing over its flavor for at least two thousand years

EVER since joining the International Brotherhood of *Foie Gras Truffé* enthusiasts—you become a member simply by opening and eating a can of the delicious stuff—I've been wondering about the luscious, piquant black spots in the middle of the velvety goose liver. Of course, they are truffles. Brillat-Savarin, the great epicure, used to call them "the black diamonds of the *haute cuisine*." Somewhere, I'd heard that they were dug up by pigs; but what were they, exactly? Mushrooms? A sort of potato? Colored carrots? Or were they simply something the manufacturers had put in *foie gras* just to get higher prices, or to make *foie gras*—literally, fatted liver—more appealing to the appetite?

My chance to find some of the answers came one day not long ago when, on a trip through the southeast of France, I passed through Périgueux, the truffle capital of the world. Even people coolly disposed toward those expensive delicacies could find no fault with stopping at Périgueux, since it is a town of genuine charm where the ancient past and the present are pleasantly blended. In Puy St.-Front, the old part of the town, you can sit in a small sidewalk café looking out on relics of prehistoric civilization and Roman walls. The *patron*, filling your Dubonnet glass to the brim without spilling a drop, tells you, quite casually, that those hills over there were once occupied by Neolithic man and that this was later the ancient *Vesunna*. The town's miniature boulevards are bordered by Gothic chapels, Renaissance houses, baroque doorways and twentieth-century chestnut trees. Truffles or no, it's a nice place.

Périgueux is the center of the region known to affluent gourmets the world over as "*Le Périgord*," which comprises parts of the departments of Dordogne and Lot-et-Garonne. I had expected to see the local restaurants crowded with people, all of them feasting with abandon on *foie gras*, truffles and *pâté de foie gras*, somewhat as the natives of Detroit always seem to be riding in their cars and the inhabitants of Pilsen used to drink beer most of the time; but the only *foie gras* I saw was in cans in the windows of the more expensive shops. The truth is, of course, that *foie gras* and truffles are too expensive for most Périgourdins, as the people here are called. During a recent poor-crop year one kilo (two and two-tenths pounds, roughly) brought, on the markets of Périgueux, fifty dollars (U.S.)—which is a lot of money in anybody's currency, and certainly a lot to the average Frenchman. In fact, *foie gras* and truffles are served in French homes only on very special occasions: births, christenings, graduations, weddings or deaths—particularly if the deceased has left a nice inheritance.

Some of my friends in Paris, great connoisseurs of *foie gras truffé*, had given me a letter to M. Charles Barbier, one of Périgueux's greatest authorities on the delicacy. "Barbier was once a well-known *chef* who now spends his mellow years surrounded by truffles and *foie gras*," my friends told me.

Late snack de luxe: truffle-studded *foie gras* from France, with ▶
crusty bread and chilled champagne.

NICKOLAS MURAY

"He knows a lot about it. And he's a philosopher to boot."

When I found Monsieur Barbier he was—literally—surrounded by *foie gras*. He stood in the big workroom of the canning factory, Daburon Frères, of which he is the general manager—a large, rotund, placid man with rosy cheeks, a bristling mustache, a double chin and an enormous stomach —as was to be expected. The goose livers had been placed on long tables, one by one, and he was walking from liver to liver, giving them the sharp, merciless glance that drill sergeants have for recruits, making some brief comment to a white-coated assistant who was walking behind him with a pad.

Monsieur Barbier greeted me with enthusiasm. "It's nice to have a visitor from America," he said. "A growing number of people over there are now beginning to appreciate the finer things in life." He pointed at the goose livers. "If you don't mind, I'll just finish my morning parade. This shipment arrived last night and must be canned today. In our business of delicate aromas one has to work fast. A fine goose liver should be moderately fat, not too hard, not too soft. The soft ones lose too much fat during processing and the hard ones get too dry. If they're just right, they'll show the imprint of your fingers like a piece of good, fresh butter. *Voilà!*" He gently pressed one of the livers, applying his thumb from beneath and his four fingers on top. The fingerprints were as clear as if they had been made by J. Edgar Hoover's bright young men. "*Extra!*" said Monsieur Barbier to his assistant, and the liver was whisked off to a special table.

The factory was not big as American enterprises go; there were perhaps fifty men and women, all looking very clean in their white working coats. There are about twenty-five canning factories in Périgueux, Sarlat, Eymet and Bergerac which process truffles and *foie gras*. "We do not have mass production, *mon cher monsieur*. Mass production is the ruin of *la grande cuisine*."

He stared gloomily into space and then he shrugged in a sad, resigned gesture. "When the geese are six months old, they are put into wooden cages and the farmers begin to feed them forcibly, stuffing the maize down their throats. Not very pleasant for the poor animals, but then, monsieur, some of the best things in life don't start out in a pleasant way. Rough diamonds are not a pretty sight, and Madame Du Barry came out of the slums, did she not? After six weeks of being stuffed, the geese get so fat they can't move any more. That is the time to kill them or they might suffocate. Once the merchandise gets here, we have to work fast. Now, during the season from November twentieth to January tenth, we take on extra help and work from six in the morning to eight at night. Unfortunately, there's never enough goose livers. We store them six months, but *foie gras truffé* ought to be in storage at least two or three years until the delicate aroma of the truffles permeates the *foie gras*——"

"The truffles!" I said quickly, feeling that my cue had come. "What *are* truffles?"

Monsieur Barbier's face was transfigured by a sort of unearthly light. "Ah, *le grand mystère*," he said, closing his eyes. Opening them again, he dismissed two goose livers as *choix* and asked me to come to his office. We entered a glass-enclosed room with a large poster showing a couple of geese nibbling happily, if somewhat cannibalistically, at an open can of *Pâté de Foie Gras Truffé Marie*—"Marie" being the trade-mark of the house. On a large desk was a basket filled with what looked like black oranges. I noticed that the room was filled with a strong, piquant scent.

"*Voilà!*" Monsieur Barbier said, pointing at the basket as a guide at the Louvre would present Leonardo da Vinci's *Mona Lisa*. "Truffles. Great mystery of the vegetable kingdom. Highly appreciated by epicures for their flavor and taste long before the day of the Roman emperors. Three hundred years B.C. Theophrastus believed them to be products of thunder. Pliny thought they were the most wonderful creations of nature, since they grow without roots. There are many references to truffles in classical writings. 'Truffles make the women more tender and the men more amorous,' Brillat-Savarin wrote. They grow under the ground, and are found only in the poorest soil where nothing else but a few trees will grow, and they have resisted all attempts at cultivation. Thank God," he added as an afterthought. "Otherwise they would be as commonplace as potatoes and we would be out of business."

The truffles, Monsieur Barbier went on explaining, come in all sizes, from that of a pea to that of an orange. There are white truffles in Italy and chocolate-colored ones in other parts of France, but the finest specimens are black, inside and out. (They are always black on the outside, but white or gray inside until they have fully matured and gained their strong flavor.) They should be firm but not hard and they should have a marble grain. Monsieur Barbier broke one of the truffles in half. "See what I mean? Finely marbled and flesh of a jet-black color. Innocent-looking fruit, but, like the roulette tables of Monte Carlo, they've ruined quite a few people. Truffles are almost as much of a gamble. You see, no one knows exactly how they come into being. The learned books call them saprophytic fungi of the family *Ascomycetes*. The peasants say that they are a product of soil fermentation. Truffles, however, grow only in the vicinity of trees, where the roots protrude from the light soil. There are some truffles near maples, beech trees, junipers, elms, but most of them appear around a species of oak trees called truffle oaks —*chênes truffières*. Our peasants say, 'If you want truffles you must sow acorns.' Unfortunately, it takes twenty years for the oaks to reach sufficient size and even then there remains the question whether you'll find any truffles. Ah, *Monsieur, la nature rait bien des choses!* I have a little property out in Ribérac where I planted oaks twenty-three years ago." He laughed silently, closing his eyes. "Well, I'm still waiting for the truffles.

"Truffles have been found in other regions of France, in the departments of Vaucluse and Basses Alpes and also in England, but none of them compare with the truffles of Périgord (*Tuber melanosporum*) in looks and quality, and before the war exports reached $14,500,000 a year. They grow in open woodland, and you can't miss the formation of a *truffière*—a truffle ground—because gradually all flowers, herbs —even grass—disappear. We say, 'The truffle burns the land.' It's a jealous fruit that doesn't permit anything else to grow in its vicinity. The right climate for truffles is about the same as for wine. Wet springs, hot summers with frequent thunderstorms in July and August. Our peasants say, 'August makes the truffle.' You see, old Theophrastus had something when he called them products of thunder. The autumn should be moderately cool. During harvest-time, from November to February, it must not get too cold. If it goes more than a few degrees below freezing, the truffles will get brittle, fall apart and spoil."

He sniffed at the basket, closing his eyes, and his rosy

cheeks got even rosier. "If you're lucky to find a *truffière* on your territory, you may make *une grosse fortune*—how do you say in America? Hit the ——"

"Hit the jack pot?"

"Exactly. I know a man who made over a million francs last year on truffles. Not bad considering that there is no labor whatsoever involved, though they say a light harrowing of the soil may help. One oak tree alone netted over thirty thousand francs. Ah, but what a gamble! What a whim of nature! The truffles disappear as suddenly as they have come. Last year you may have made a fortune and this year you won't find a single truffle. *Hah!*" Monsieur Barbier puffed up his cheek and exhaled in anger. "We've done a lot of experimenting without solving the problem. No wonder the number of *truffières* decreases steadily. This is an epoch of speed and fast returns. Who wants to plant oaks today in the uncertain hope that there *may* be truffles in twenty years? Of all the truffle people I know there's only one who plants two thousand new trees a year. He's got four sons and *he* cares what's going to happen. The rest say, 'In twenty years I may be dead, so why worry? Let's plant potatoes which we can sell next fall and buy wine with the money.' What a pity! In fifty years there may be no *truffières* left at all in the Périgord." He clasped his hands in despair in front of his chest. "But when that day comes, *I* won't be here either."

That afternoon I found myself riding next to Monsieur Barbier in his small Peugeot through the countryside, past dreamy villages, Roman water towers, prehistoric caves and the ruins of medieval châteaux. Monsieur Barbier was a proud and enthusiastic guide. He loves the country; he was born in the Dordogne, in Laroche-Beaucourt, in 1885. His father owned a hotel in Angoulême, where young Charles started to work in the kitchen. Cooking came easy to him since, like all good cooks, he liked to eat well. "Father wanted me to take over the hotel but I had the wanderlust. I went to England and worked as chef at the Savoy and Carlton in London, and in various places in York and Newcastle. I had to come home to do my military service, but after that I ran out again and became *chef de cuisine* aboard the ships of the P. and O.—Peninsular and Oriental Line—making the Australia, China, Japan and India run. The food was excellent on the ships on which I was chef. We would make everything—even *omelettes aux truffes*. I remember a textile manufacturer from Le Havre and a chap from Liverpool who were great gourmets. They would send me a bottle of champagne once in a while and I would make special dishes for them. One was truffles *à la crème*—you peel them, cut in slices, fry them in butter, season with salt and pepper, add sweet cream and stir over a hot fire until the cream gets thick. There was another French cook on the boat who later became chef of the Taj Mahal Hotel in Bombay. He became so infatuated with truffles that he came to Périgueux and took a few young oak trees to Northern India where, he said, the climate was the same as here." Monsieur Barbier rubbed his nose and laughed in his silent way. "He is still waiting for the truffles to show up, poor boy."

We had arrived in front of a farm on top of a hill. There were the ruins of a burned house, and farther back, a recently built house. Monsieur Barbier explained that the place belonged to the Veuve Merlhiot, who had delivered truffles to his factory, on and off, for twenty years.

"I used to know her husband well," said Monsieur Barbier. "He and their oldest son were shot by the Germans in nineteen forty-four, while his wife and their younger son were forced to look on. The Merlhiots were patriots—they loved their country." He was silent for a moment. "The Boches burned down the farmhouse. For three years the Widow Merlhiot had to live in the stable. Ah, there was a lot of suffering in this lovely country, monsieur."

We walked past the stables and Monsieur Barbier rang the bell of the new house. I heard steps inside and had the uncomfortable feeling of being watched by somebody from behind a curtain. Then the door was opened and there emerged a small, sturdy, suspicious-looking woman wearing a black skirt and scarf.

"*Bonjour*, Monsieur Barbier," she said, without much enthusiasm, shaking hands with him and giving me a sharp, searching glance.

Monsieur Barbier seemed to have expected the lukewarm reception, for he grinned. "You may shake hands with my friend," he said to her. "He is not the tax collector."

The woman shrugged. "I don't like strangers," she said, gruffly. But she gave me a nod and, somewhat reluctantly, her hand. Monsieur Barbier said we had come to look at a *truffière*. Would she permit us to go to her place? He looked a little worried, but the woman said, "I was just going there. You may come with me, if you wish." We walked over to the pigsty and the woman began to shout in her high-pitched voice, "*Viens ici, petite, petite, viens!*" There was a joyful grunt from inside and then a small, cheerful-looking pig came running out and jumped all over the court.

"This is Mignon." The Widow Merlhiot formally introduced the pig to us, with an elegant gesture. "She's my *chercheuse.*"

I asked Monsieur Barbier what a *chercheuse* was. He said, "As I told you, truffles grow only under the ground, anywhere from five to fifty inches below. The human sense of smell isn't able to detect the peculiar flavor of the truffles, but certain animals can find them. Down in the department of Lot they're using small dogs for truffle hunting, and I'm told that they have trained goats in Sardinia and Italy. Here we use sows. A trained sow has a fine nose for the scent of truffles. She'll hunt a truffle as passionately as a foxhound hunts a fox. However, only a few pigs have that talent and they are hard to come by. As a rule, they come from sows who have been *chercheuses* (literally, pursuers). The peasants are always anxious to find a pig with that special instinct and they use quite a few tricks." He laughed and asked the Veuve Merlhiot, "You don't mind my telling the story?"

She shrugged, but I thought there was a smile on her face. "Well, it's no crime, is it?"

"Certainly not. When a peasant wants a *chercheuse*, he goes to the market and cautiously inquires about the prices of young pigs. Then he starts to look at them. He secretly drops a small truffle on the ground and crushes it with his heel. If one of the little pigs gets excited and smells the truffle, it'll be a *chercheuse*." Monsieur Barbier gave a chuckle. "Ah, our people are quite shrewd, monsieur. They wouldn't trust anybody. They'll put their money in one-thousand-franc bills under the mattress. And they'll never tell you whether they've found a lot of truffles."

"You never find a lot of them," said the Veuve Merlhiot. "You thank God if you find just a few."

Monsieur Barbier nudged my elbow and gave me a didn't-I-tell-you look. The woman had hung a white canvas bag over her shoulder. She grasped a stick and we walked toward the woodland behind the farm, followed by Mignon, who seemed as obedient as a dog. There was a stretch of land with groups of oak trees, but no flowers or grass grew on the ground. I noticed that the pig was getting excited. She sniffed over the ground, grunting loudly, behaving like a rabbit dog on a hot trail. Suddenly she stopped and rubbed her snout against the soil. The Veuve Merlhiot watched the pig for a moment, then she bent down and with her stick, gave the animal a gentle tap on the nose. At the same time she dropped a few grains of maize behind her. The little pig grunted happily and began to eat up the maize. Meanwhile the woman very carefully scratched the ground away with a small spoonlike utensil until she found, hidden a good ten inches under the ground, a truffle as big as an apricot. She shook the soil off the truffle and cautiously placed it in her bag.

"*Voilà!*" said Monsieur Barbier. "Looks easy, doesn't it? But you've got to watch the pig or she will dig up the truffle herself and eat it. That is why you divert the animal's attention and give her a little maize or a chestnut for consolation."

"She gets a small truffle once in a while," said the Widow Merlhiot, picking up, with Mignon's help, another couple of truffles. One was close to the surface, the other, a big 150-gram (about a third of a pound) specimen, was fifteen inches down.

"Mignon's a good girl," she said. "I bought her almost two years ago when she was six months old. She'll be good for another three years. When they get over five, they lose their sense of smell. *Allons, Mignon. Viens, petite, petite.*"

"One must be able to determine whether a truffle is ripe," said Monsieur Barbier. "That's not easy, because from the outside ours are always black. You must never touch a truffle that you don't want to take out, or it will rot. It will also rot if you hurt the trees. The pig must be trained not to come near the oaks." Presently Mignon found another.

"Good girl," said Monsieur Barbier, patting the pig. "Giving us so many good things, hams and pork chops and handbags for the ladies, and now even finding truffles for us. Truffles never come in bunches. There's one here and another one there, although they're always within a three-meter distance of the tree." He lowered his voice. "We'd better leave now. The *Veuve* Merlhiot wouldn't like it if we stayed too long and watched her too closely. They are *bien cachetières*, our farmers. If Madame is lucky, she'll bring home two kilos (between four and five pounds) today and make several thousand francs more than a lot of other people here make in a week."

We said good-by to the Widow Merlhiot, who didn't seem sorry to see us go, and drove back to town. Every once in a while I would see a man or woman carrying a bag and a stick, walking with a trained pig through the woodland. "This is the heart of the truffle district," said Monsieur Barbier. "But you go north a few miles and all of a sudden the truffle stops growing. The soil is the same, and the climate, and there are even oak trees—but not a single truffle. Why, monsieur? Ah, *la nature fait bien des choses.* However, our farmers now are smart enough to realize that one must not depend on truffles alone. So they grow grapes for wine, grains, sell their cattle and hope for a *truffière* in the back yard. When the *Veuve* Merlhiot comes home, she will start to clean the truffles and give them a facial, as the ladies say in America, removing imperfections. Better-looking truffles fetch better prices. Then she'll put them into baskets, the smallest on the bottom, naturally, and the nicest on top. And tomorrow, first thing in the morning, she'll take them to the market."

He shook his head. "The truffle market is pretty bizarre, *mon cher monsieur.* During the harvesting season, which they call *cavage*, the farmers meet daily in their little cafés and bistros in Terrasson, Thiviers, Sorges, Brive, Cuzanne, Souillac, Sarlat, Salignac, Montignac, Thenon and Périgueux. They arrive early in the morning and leave their baskets in the home of a friend or in a hotel under guard. *C'est fantastique*—there may be three thousand kilos of truffles on the market on a particular day but you won't see a single truffle anywhere. Everything is done '*en cachette.*' The farmers wander from bistro to bistro, listening to the shop talk, trying to guess what the price will be. I've been here now over twenty-five years but if I went to one of those little dives, I couldn't buy one kilo of truffles. They just wouldn't sell them to me; they would think that something was fishy. They sell only to the established buyers. Everybody has to come to the Périgord to buy truffles, even the big *foie gras* manufacturers from Strasbourg, Lot, Paris, Nantes and Bordeaux. Makes them quite bitter, especially those fellows from Strasbourg."

Monsieur Barbier went on to discuss the bizarre ways of the truffle market. Seems that the buyers are also pretty shrewd traders and won't commit themselves until they have gauged the supply and demand, and sized up the good and bad lots. It's just like the stock market, but then, truffles have always been a steady commodity because they are needed by the practitioners of what the French call *la grande cuisine*.

To be a truffle buyer you must combine the financial instinct of a Morgan with the poker-faced patience of a Talleyrand. You must watch carefully so the competitor won't snatch up the merchandise from under your eyes, and you must prod the peasants until they tell you how much they will take. Sales are made by kilos, on primitive "Roman" scales. Once the deal is closed, the buyers are in a great hurry, for the truffles must reach the factories quickly and a lot of time has already been lost in bargaining.

The big truffle season is just before Christmas, when every restaurant in Paris and many butchers and grocers need truffles which adorn the roast duck that is the *pièce de resistance* of the traditional Christmas or New Year's Eve dinner.

"If I had been smart," Monsieur Barbier said regretfully, "I would have bought lots of truffles twenty years ago, put them into cans and stored them away. What an investment they would have made!"

Before 1914 a kilo of truffles cost ten francs. During World War I when the people of France were occupied with less pleasant matters than *la grande cuisine*, prices fell to an all-time low of three francs per kilo. Scores of farmers in the Périgord region went broke. They chopped down the oak trees, plowed under the *truffetières* and grew wine and potatoes. Many truffle grounds disappeared in those days, production sank sharply and has never completely recovered. At the end of the first war, truffles were up to thirty francs a kilo; in the roaring 'twenties they rose to 100 francs, as more and more French and quite a few Americans, Scandinavians, Belgians, Swiss, Argentinians and British began to clamor for the very special stuff. In recent years the price has fluctuated between 2,000 and 5,000 old francs a kilo.

Monsieur Barbier explained dolefully that, like everybody else, he had failed to stock up on truffles and instead lost his savings in foolish investments. Now he has to go out and spend a lot of money when he wants to regale guests with his own truffle recipes. "My wife and I have a cook," he said, "but on special occasions I like to put on my old chef's outfit and do some of the classical truffle dishes. An *omelette aux truffes*, or scrambled eggs with small slices of truffles which will turn a simple dish into a rare delicacy! Or stuffed truffles, surrounded by a light, fine crust, baked and served with sauce Madeira, and truffles *sous la cendre*, broiled slowly over charcoals on an iron brazier. And did you ever try *truffes au champagne*? Easy to prepare, really. You put the truffles into a casserole, cover them with dry champagne and let them simmer for twenty minutes. At the end there should be no more liquid than a teaspoonful of juice for each truffle. Cover with a light pastry dough and bake in a hot oven for twenty minutes." Monsieur Barbier closed his eyes in supreme delight and the car almost went into a ditch. "Ah," he was saying, "what a dish, what a dish! Truly a feast for Lucullus!"

I observed that it was mainly a feast for extremely solvent gourmets, the prices of truffles and champagne being what they are. Monsieur Barbier chose to treat this remark with lofty indifference. "Perhaps the best truffle dish of all is *truffes à la timbale*. Fill a *vol-au-vent* (puff-paste) or a *bouchée* with peeled truffles that already have been cut in slices or quarters and treated for two or three hours in a marinade of cognac or Madeira. Add salt and pepper, put a slice of ham on top and bake for two hours in a moderately hot oven. Be sure to make a hole in the middle and gradually pour in the marinade. Serve very hot, with a fine, old red wine."

His eyes grew misty. "To appreciate this dish, one must be a truffle merchant from the Périgord. Nowhere in France do people, by and large, eat as well as in our region. It has been said that the Périgourdins were always great fighters and that they stopped warring only when they sat down at the table. Think of the many recipes of *la grande cuisine* which Périgueux has given to the world. Sauce Périgueux, that wonderful concoction of Sauce Espagnole, Madeira wine and chopped truffles that goes so well with a filet mignon, or Tournedos Rossini, which we prepare with slices of *foie gras* and sauce Péregueux. I read somewhere that *pâté de foie gras* was 'invented' by the celebrated Chef Clausse, who worked for Marshal Contades, the governor of Alsace; and that General Daumesnil, the one-legged defender of Vincennes against the Allies in 1814, a native of Périgueux, 'improved' the recipe. Rubbish! Back in the sixteenth century the farmers of the Périgord prepared solid blocks of *foie gras*, embedded in a *pâté de foie gras*. They were the first to put in the truffles, having noticed that the aroma of the truffle will accentuate the flavor of *foie gras* as a fine cheese will accentuate the bouquet of an old Bordeaux wine. Here in town no self-respecting housewife would buy canned *foie gras*. She'll buy raw goose livers and truffles on the market, and put up her own truffled *foie gras*, just as women elsewhere can fruits and vegetables. It's much cheaper too. A one-kilo can of *fois gras truffé* costs about two and a half times as much as a kilo of (raw) extra-fine livers. People here use truffles to stuff geese and ducks, and to prepare their fish. If ever you eat a sole *bonne femme*, with a white-wine sauce, thickened with butter and the yolks of eggs, in which there are not only chopped shallots and sliced mushrooms but a few slices of truffles, you'll never forget it. Not to mention the many kinds of cold *pâtés*, of sausage and ragouts that are vastly improved

by adding a small piece of that fine, black, delicious fruit."

Monsieur Barbier's culinary reveries were interrupted by our arrival at the factory, where everybody seemed to be in a high state of feverish activity. Truffles were being washed in tubs filled with cold water, cleaned of all soil with fine brushes, and carefully dried. Then the best specimens were selected by skilled workers and a group of women peeled them carefully, cutting off paper-thin slices of the skin with sharp knives. Since no part of the truffle, no matter how small, is wasted, even the skins were put in special cans. (They are cheaper and can be used for omelettes or stuffings.) The truffles were placed in cans of different sizes, either with salt water, or in cognac or Madeira which increase the special aroma of the truffle as time goes on. Finally the cans were sterilized in vast vats under steam pressure—a regrettable but necessary process, during which the truffles shrink and lose as much as 30 per cent of their weight.

Some of these canned truffles will find markets in America.

Monsieur Barbier took me into another hall where this morning's load of *foie gras* was being canned. "This is far more difficult than the canning of truffles," said Monsieur Barbier. "Did you ever open a can of *foie gras* and discover that there was more *gras* (fat) in it than *foie* (liver)? *Bien sûr*, it's happened to everybody and people get mad because they've paid a lot of money for the can. Ah, but what can one do? The livers must be precooked a little before they are canned. If you cook them too long, they may lose a lot of fat but they may also get dry. If you undercook them—or if you choose second-rate merchandise which contains too much fat—there will be lots of fat in the can. We have been trying the golden middle way. The livers are cut in half, one half is placed on the bottom of the can, a truffle is put on it, then the other half goes on top. Before the can is sealed, it is baked in the oven for five minutes at less than two hundred degrees Centigrade (392° F.). Now the cans are taken out of the oven and checked for their fat content. As you can see, we take all precautions, but with *foie gras* one is never too sure. We often compare the livers of two animals that were raised by the same farmer under the same conditions, fed the same amount of corn—yet one may be perfect while the other contains as much as fifty per cent of fat. After the livers are cooked, the cans are sealed and sterilized for an hour and a half at one hundred and eight degrees Centigrade (356°F.)."

Monsieur Barbier crossed his fingers, looking at the sterilization vats in which a new load of cans was being placed. "No one knows exactly what he's going to find in those cans a few months or years from now. And there are minor problems. You put in a bigger truffle and right away people will say, 'Aha! Truffles were less expensive last year, so they put in a lot of the stuff!' " Monsieur Barbier uncrossed his fingers. "There are good and bad years in *foie gras*, depending on the climate and the quality of the maize, almost like vintages of wine. Of course, the customer gets what he pays for. All *foie gras* products are graded by government-approved standards."

The people of Périgueux are great connoisseurs of home-made *pâté*. During the *foie-gras-less* season, from February to October, they prepare their own *pâtés*, which they call *ballotine, galantine, terrine, pâté maison*, or *pâté de campagne*. Almost every housewife and every restaurant has a favorite recipe. They use ground meat (beef, veal, pork, chicken) or diced calf's liver, which has been browned in butter, adding chopped, sautéed onions, all kinds of seasonings, and possibly a dash of cognac or Madeira, and then they cook it. If you like a rough-textured *pâté*, you don't even have to pass it through a sieve.

"If you put in good ingredients and season to taste, you can't fail to make a good *pâté*," Monsieur Barbier said. "The trouble starts when people put in stuff which, they say, 'is good for no other purpose than *pâté*.' If you use ingredients that are not fresh how can you expect to create a fine *pâté*?"

It was getting late and Monsieur Barbier took me to his office where a table had been set up with plates and glasses, a dusty bottle of wine and a small block of *foie gras truffé*. Monsieur Barbier eyed the display fondly and carefully filled the wineglasses. "After a hard day's work there's nothing so good as a slice of properly chilled *foie gras* with a glass of fine Bordeaux wine before dinner. Too often people serve

foie gras at the end of a rich meal when the palate no longer appreciates its fine aroma. And never serve salad with it, please! Nothing but a full-bodied, flavory, round, velvety claret deserves to be its companion. A Château Margaux 1899 or a Léoville-Lascases 1926 will do wonders for *foie gras* and vice versa." He began to cut the block with a sharp knife which he dipped into warm water after cutting each slice. "There are people who drink beer or ice water with *foie gras truffé*. No wonder they get stomach trouble! Then the doctors tell you that *foie gras* and truffles are bad for you. Don't you believe them!" Monsieur Barbier fondly patted his stomach. "I've been eating the good things all my life long and I will be sixty-eight next May. Do I look like a man who suffers from indigestion?"

Truffles are suggested as a garnish and in sauces in many recipes throughout this collection. Dishes in which this edible fungus plays a more important role are found not only in epicurean recipe collections of present-day chefs but more notably in the books compiled by 19th-century chefs and gourmets.

Francatelli, one of the great French chefs who worked in London in the Victorian era of splendid dinners, was a pupil of Carême. "Qualified under such favorable auspices," said Charles Elmè Francatelli in the introduction to Francatelli's

Modern Cook, "he (C.E.F.) has subsequently served as chef de cuisine for some of the most distinguished bons vivants among the British aristocracy and gentry . . . and he shall ever consider it the greatest honor to which he could aspire, to have served as Chief Cook and Maître d'Hôtel to Her Most Gracious Majesty the Queen." No wonder he spoke of himself in the third person.

And no wonder his book abounds in luxurious dishes. Here are some suggestions as to what a good cook may do with truffles.

PURÉE OF TRUFFLES

10 ounces canned truffles
2 tablespoons butter
½ bay leaf
Sprig of thyme
⅓ teaspoon grated nutmeg
Sliver of peeled garlic
½ cup brown sauce or gravy
1½ teaspoons meat glaze (approximately)

Drain truffles and peel if necessary. Then pound truffles in a heavy bowl. Combine mashed truffles with butter, herbs, nutmeg and garlic in a saucepan. Stir and heat until mixture simmers, let simmer for a few minutes; stir brown sauce or gravy in, add small piece of meat glaze. Increase heat and cook rapidly to reduce purée by about ⅓ to ½. Should be smooth and thickened. Rub through finest sieve or tamis. Pour into top part of double boiler and keep over hot, but not boiling, water. Add to sauce for fish, meat, game or poultry soufflés or to a sauce for scalloped fish and shellfish entrées. Makes about 1 cup purée.

TRUFFLES À LA PIÉMONTAISE

½ pound canned truffles
2 tablespoons olive oil
1 tablespoon chopped parsley
1 teaspoon chopped fresh thyme
Sliver peeled garlic
½ teaspoon white pepper
¼ teaspoon salt
2 tablespoons brown sauce or gravy
1½ teaspoons meat glaze
Juice ½ lemon
2 hard-crust French rolls, split, buttered and toasted

Drain truffles; wash thoroughly; cut into thick slices. In saucepan, combine oil with parsley, thyme, garlic, pepper and salt. Add truffles; cook over high heat for about 5 minutes, shaking pan frequently. Remove garlic, add brown sauce or gravy, the meat glaze and lemon juice; stir. Shake pan to toss all together and heat for a few minutes. When very hot, pour over the toasted, buttered rolls. Serve at once. Makes 2 to 4 servings.

A fine way to prepare mushrooms, too.

TRUFFLES COOKED IN A WINE MIREPOIX

1 pound beef suet
1 pound fat bacon
Handful of parsley
1 bay leaf
1 sprig thyme
2 carrots, scraped
6 scallions
2 onions, peeled and stuck
    with 2 cloves each

2 lemons, peeled and
    chopped
1 teaspoon peppercorns
½ teaspoon salt
1 pint Madeira
1 pint bouillon or broth
1 pound drained, canned
    truffles
12 to 16 thin slices bacon
Special parsley sauce

Cut suet and bacon in small pieces. Combine in a saucepan with parsley, bay leaf, thyme. Cut carrots and scallions in small pieces and add with onions, lemons, peppercorns and salt to the pan. Cook rapidly a few minutes, stirring continually. Add wine and bouillon; stir. Reduce heat; cover pan and simmer for 1 hour or a little longer. Then strain the mirepoix through a fine sieve or tamis.

Wash drained truffles. Place in a large stewpan lined with thin bacon slices. Pour the wine mirepoix over truffles. Place layers of bacon on top. Cover pan tightly (chefs seal the pan with a thick flour-and-water paste) to concentrate the flavor of the truffles. Let simmer gently on the lowest heat for about 45 minutes. Lift truffles from the sauce to the folds of a napkin-lined warmed serving dish. Serve with the special parsley sauce. Makes 6 or more servings.

PARSLEY SAUCE

1 cup mirepoix, obtained in
    cooking truffles
1 cup olive oil
1 tablespoon chopped
    parsley

Juice 1 lemon
½ teaspoon white pepper
¼ teaspoon salt

Reduce mirepoix by boiling rapidly until only 2 tablespoons remain in the saucepan. Combine with olive oil, parsley, lemon juice, pepper and salt. Beat well to blend. Send to table with the hot truffles.

GLAZED TRUFFLES FOR GARNISH

1 pound canned truffles
1½ tablespoons butter
½ teaspoon salt

1½ teaspoons meat glaze
    (about)

Drain truffles; rinse thoroughly. Cut in various fancy shapes such as small round balls, olives, orange sections, small cylinders and circular slices. Combine with butter in saucepan; season with salt; add glaze. Cover pan, simmer over low heat for about 10 minutes. Shake pan to toss truffles in the hot glaze mixture. Use to garnish center of any meat, fish, poultry, game entrée. Makes 8 servings of garnish.

5. SWEETS AND DESSERTS

Pie: Great American Institution / Herbert Asbury

Pie as made in the U.S.—be it lemon, apple, mince, pecan, coconut custard, Lavender Mist, Shoo-Fly, cherry or Black Bottom— is unlike any other nation's. And our chief claim to cooking fame

WHEN an American says pie, he refers to the noblest and by far the most popular dessert in our national cuisine, a culinary masterpiece which, lovingly assembled and properly baked, makes the fabled ambrosia of the gods seem like leftovers. Lifted piping hot and bubbling from the oven, wreathed in the most appetizing fragrance known to man, it has probably been the cause of more lip-smacking and overeating than any other dish. Other countries have their tarts, turnovers, filled pastries and deep-dish concoctions of meat or fruit, but none has anything comparable to an American pie. Only in the United States, for example, is it possible to enjoy a hot apple pie, redolent with the aromatic juice of ripe apples, rich in fruity flavor, tingling with nutmeg and cinnamon, and tangy with sharp American Cheddar cheese slowly melting on top of a well-

◀ Pie is indispensable to the kind of old-fashioned holiday meal here shown in the kitchen of Sagamore Hill, President Theodore Roosevelt's home in Oyster Bay, New York.

BEN ROSE

browned crust, which for flakiness and buttery tenderness often surpasses the finest French pastry.

The best pies in America, particularly fruit pies, are found in the small towns and on the farms of the Middle West and New England, especially at holiday feasts and family-reunion dinners to which all the women relatives contribute. At these Lucullan festivals there is always a great profusion of pies, for most of these women are expert pie makers and delight in exhibiting their skill. I've attended family dinners in Missouri and Illinois where the long table groaned beneath a dozen kinds of pie—apple, peach and cherry, the old stand-bys, fragrant and spicy; rhubarb, tart and tangy, made of a common garden plant so widely used as a pie filling that for 200 years it has been popularly called pieplant; banana cream, cool and voluptuous, with marshmallows folded into the rich filling and slices of ripe banana lying on top; black-berry, strawberry, and other berries, made with covering crusts, lattice crusts, or open-faced and drowned in whipped cream; luscious lemon, true to the fruit in color, and topped with meringue browned just to the delicate point of perfection; mince, the most flavorful of pies, its modest exterior concealing the heady aroma of half a dozen different spices and almost as many kinds of fruit; coconut custard, meringue-crowned or crested with brown-tipped coconut shreds; pumpkin plain, and pumpkin all prettied up with fancy toppings of whipped cream and preserved ginger finely chopped, or toasted pecan halves marching sedately across a snowy expanse of whipped cream, or a meringue studded with jewels of jelly or marmalade under a golden screen of clover honey. And so on *ad dyspepsum*. Every guest at such a dinner must sample each pie, or risk hurting the feelings of the woman who baked it. I've seen some valiant efforts, but the best score that I recall was eight, made by a tall, thin Missouri farmer. His feat was the more remarkable considering that he had gorged for some two hours on beef, ham, roast pork, turkey, duck, chicken fried and roasted, fresh sausage and headcheese, potatoes white and sweet, boiled, baked, fried and glazed, and half a dozen other vegetables, not to mention gravies, hot and cold breads, cakes and pastries, salads, cheese, relishes, jams, jellies and preserves.

One of the reasons for the superiority of the pies made in small towns and on the farms is the fact that their creators use more tree-ripened fruit and bush-ripened berries than women in other parts of the country. My mother was an extremist in this respect. She used to get everything ready for a pie, even to rolling out the bottom crust and fitting it into the pan, and then she would personally select and pick the apples, peaches, cherries or berries from the trees and bushes which grew in our back yard. As far as she was concerned, there was no such thing as "almost ripe"; fruit was either ripe or green. Nobody could convince her that fruit or berries could ripen properly elsewhere than on the tree or bush. And, although you may mark this a cliché, I'm still convinced she made the best pies I've ever eaten.

Sometimes during the winter months she would make a pie of fruit which she herself had canned, but she always apologized for it. Occasionally my father would hanker for an apple pie at a time when the fruit was not available, and my mother would say she had no apples. He'd suggest dried apples. Then she'd recite an old verse:

> I loathe, abhor, despise,
> Abominate dried-apple pies.
> I like good bread, I like good meat,
> Or anything that's fit to eat.
> But of all poor grub beneath the skies,
> The poorest is dried-apple pies.

We had pie almost every day when I was a boy, and I never tired of it until I went to visit my sister in northeastern Missouri. She became ill while I was there, and since it was impossible to get help, I took over the kitchen. Feeding my sister was easy enough, because she was on a liquid diet, and the women of the town immediately began bringing soups, jellies and other things considered suitable for an invalid. But satisfying the appetites of my brother-in-law and the hired man was another matter. I gave them meat and biscuits and gravy, and for dessert I opened jars of fruit. But soon they began to complain. They wanted pie. So I resorted to trickery. I spread the word around town that my sister would relish a nice pie. Immediately, we were swamped with pies of every description. We ate all we could, but when my sister returned to the kitchen, there were still some twenty pies on our shelves, and we ate them three times a day until the hired man threatened to quit.

American housewives bake more than one billion pies a year, according to careful estimates by the big food-processing companies, and almost as many more are made by commercial bakers. About one tenth of the latter are sold for home use; the remainder are eaten in public places. Many of the commercial pies are excellent, and some of the restaurant pies —most first-class places bake their own—have become famous as house specialties. But they are rarely as good as the best homemade pies, principally because they are produced under handicaps. In the first place, they must look good, and in many cases taste is sacrificed to appearance. Also, many commercial pies are sold by the piece. Therefore, the pie filling must be thick enough to cut cleanly in a tidy wedge. To hold the filling together, too much flour or cornstarch must be used. Actually, this method doesn't work out badly in the case of lemon, pumpkin and other pies of the cream type, but it's ruinous when applied to fruit, berry or mince pies. A commercial blueberry pie, for example, is likely to be dry and gummy; it usually has to be washed down with milk or coffee, and it's lacking in taste and fragrance.

A good homemade blueberry pie is a vastly different affair; it may not be as handsome as a store-bought pie, but it's a great deal kinder to the palate. If possible, a blueberry pie should be made of wild berries; they have a sharper, fresher taste than the cultivated berries, which are often so bland as to require the addition of lemon juice. Wild berries need nothing but sugar, butter and salt, and enough flour to thicken the juice just a little. Blueberry pie is generally made with a double crust, the upper crust delicately pricked with a fork, although some cooks prefer a lattice crust, and there are others who like an open-face pie topped with whipped cream. When the pie is taken from the oven, the fragrant juice should be bubbling gently against the air vents; a little may have seeped out. When you cut this pie and lift out a wedge, some of the juice and berries will run back into the pan. Spoon it out and dribble it over the top of the portion. Then, to eat blueberry pie at its best, top your share with a dab of vanilla ice cream which has begun to soften a bit. Flatten the ice cream gently, so that it covers the crust, and eat the pie with a spoon. Or, instead of the ice cream, try a little heavy cream, thick and richly yellow.

It probably will surprise nobody to learn that apple is the most popular pie in the United States. According to one survey, 26 per cent of the pies baked in American homes in a recent year were apple, with pumpkin a poor second at 10 per cent. Lemon and mince followed with 9 and 7 per cent, respectively. Of the year's total, 68 per cent were fruit pies, and 22 per cent were cream and meringue. Custard, nut and other varieties made up the rest. Apple pie made its worst showing in the Southwest, where apples are sometimes scarce, and in the Southeast, due to the South's traditional fondness for nut pies, mostly pecan, and the soft cream and meringue types. In general, Southern pie eaters prefer one-crust pies, or pies with a strip topping. Sometimes they make even their apple pies without a top crust. In some parts of the country, apple pie yields first place to mince and pumpkin for a few weeks in the late fall and early winter. Cherry pie becomes a serious contender in July, and, owing to Washington's Birthday, enjoys a revival in February. But month in and month out, it's apple all the way, and this is true also in the commercial field.

The men in the armed services prefer apple pie by a large majority; in the Army it is served at least twice a month throughout the year, much more frequently than any other type. In a recent survey, when soldiers were asked to make up a menu around one food commodity—for example, roast beef—almost every man named apple pie as his preferred dessert. Army cooks work from a standard recipe developed by the Armed Services' Food Laboratories, and the soldiers to whom I talked said it was very good. Most of them added—as one might expect:

"It's not as good as Mom's, though."

The home-baked apple pie which Americans find so delicious, and which might well serve as a sign and symbol of our way of life, is essentially the same pie that American housewives baked 300 years ago. Except for the addition of a little lemon juice and grated lemon peel, and a growing tendency to use both cinnamon and nutmeg instead of cinnamon alone, the recipe has not changed, and in most good cookbooks is identical. This doesn't mean, however, that all apple pies are made exactly alike. Some pie makers use just as much cinnamon and butter as the recipe calls for; others, of whom I am one, use more cinnamon and two or three times as much butter. Some sprinkle the sugar-and-spice mixture over the apples, and make sure that all the pieces are well coated before laying them in the pan and dotting them with butter. Others pile all the apples into the pie shell and cover them with the sugar, spices and butter. Some brush the top crust with milk before baking, while others apply a light coating of cinnamon and powdered sugar. In colonial times the pie was baked with nothing in it but the apples, and without sealing the top and the bottom crusts. When it was almost done the top crust was lifted off and the sugar, spices and butter poured in. Then the pie was returned to the oven for a few moments. Apple pies are still made that way in some parts of New England. William E. Broeg, a noted food consultant and an authority on desserts, has recently developed a method which he calls "apple-pie osmosis." He coats each piece of apple with the sugar-and-spice mixture, then stores the lot in the refrigerator overnight. Next day, before putting the slices in the pie, he drains the juice into a saucepan and simmers it with butter until it is the consistency of sirup. When the pie is done he pours the sirup slowly through a one-inch hole cut in the top crust before it was baked.

There are almost as many ways of serving apple pie as there are of making it. Some pie eaters like it cold, some hot; others want to eat it exactly one half hour after it's done. Some like it with whipped cream, others with a scoop of ice cream. In some parts of the Middle West pie fanciers pour orange juice over the pie as soon as it is taken from the oven; those who like it this way insist that the apples must be Jonathans. Most pie eaters, however, like it served with cheese, for, as everyone knows, "Apple pie without the cheese is like a kiss without the squeeze." Whether the cheese is served separately or melting on top is a matter of taste; my own preference is for the latter. The cheese can also be cooked into the crust. Here's how: After you've rolled out the top crust, sprinkle it with American Cheddar cheese, sharp or mild, as you prefer, and either shredded at home or bought grated and ready to use. Then dot the dough with butter and roll it up, folding the ends into the center and folding again in the middle. Then roll out the crust and proceed as usual. This pie should be served warm.

Cooking experts of a hundred years ago, surveying the pie recipes which filled large sections of the cookbooks, and hungrily sniffing the spicy aroma of the innumerable pies which bubbled in thousands of kitchens, were generally agreed that as far as pie making was concerned the American housewife had gone about as far as she could go. Actually, she was just getting into her stride. Today, with vastly improved equipment and cooking facilities, and with quick access to the yield of the lushest fields and orchards in the world, she makes a variety of pies such as her grandmother never even imagined.

It would be difficult to imagine a mixture which an American housewife doesn't bake into a pie. In some parts of the country she even makes pies out of onions. I've found recipes for two such, one of which includes bacon among its ingredients and is far too heavy for anything but a main dish. The other, a famous specialty of the New York Athletic Club, is considerably lighter, but is still not a dessert pie. However, it makes a wonderful between-meal snack with coffee. Here's how to make it: Cook one cup of chopped onions in half a cup of butter for ten or fifteen minutes, until the onions are cooked through but not browned. While the onions are cooking, separate three eggs, putting the yolks and whites into bowls large enough to allow beating the yolks slightly and the whites until they are stiff. Line a nine-inch piepan with rich pastry. Allow the onions to cool slightly, then add to them the beaten egg yolks, a quarter of a cup of light cream, a quarter of a teaspoon of salt, a dash of pepper and half a cup of dry white wine. Mix well. Then slowly add the stiffly beaten egg whites. Pour the mixture into the unbaked pie shell and bake for half an hour in a moderate oven (350° F.) or until the top rises and browns, the filling is cooked and delicately set and the pastry browned. This is enough to serve six to eight people. For a party you can double the quantities and make two pies.

Of course, a pie made of onions couldn't possibly be called anything but onion pie, but many famous pies, obviously the result of a long series of experiments, have been christened with fanciful and romantic names. There's a pie called Lavender Mist, made of grape juice, cornstarch, salt, sugar and eggs, and topped with whipped cream and grape jelly. There's Shoo-Fly Pie, a famous Pennsylvania Dutch dish of many versions, which is really a sort of gingerbread baked in a pie shell. There's White Christmas Pie; according to the cookbooks it's "a pure white heavenly concoction," containing gelatine, flour, milk, eggs, heavy cream, almond extract, sugar, coconut and several other things. There's Pie-in-the-Sky, with a crumb crust of Holland rusk, and a filling of lime gelatine, sugar, salt, lemons and bananas. And there's Black Bottom Pie, which has been called a pie to end all pies. It has a crust of gingersnap crumbs, and the filling contains a dozen or more ingredients, among them milk, sugar, eggs, rum and chocolate. It's topped by a mighty mound of heavy cream whipped with confectioners' sugar, and a generous sprinkling of shaved chocolate. I've never made a Black Bottom Pie, largely because the procedure is quite complicated, but I've eaten it, and I found it a luscious but overwhelming dish. This version is said to have been invented in the Brown Derby restaurant in Hollywood, and is very popular in the moving-picture capital.

Whatever mixture the housewife wants to bake into a pie, probably somewhere there's a recipe for it. Instructions for the making of pies not only bulge the sides of the standard cooking manuals, but the printing presses pour out a steady stream of books, pamphlets and brochures about pie. The newspapers and the women's magazines give an enormous lot of space to pie and there is a continuous stream of pie literature from the food-processing companies, the Federal and state departments of agriculture, and colleges which have home-economics departments.

The gadget makers have also done their part in making the American housewife increasingly pie-conscious. Actually, all the tools needed to make a good piecrust are a round bottle, a board or table top, and a piepan, while most fillings can be prepared with a knife and a spoon. But when an expert pie maker of today goes into her kitchen for a spell of baking, she is likely to have accurate measuring cups and spoons, a spatula, a flour sifter, a pastry blender, pans of oven glass or metal, a blending fork, waxed paper, a canvas pastry cloth, a rolling pin covered with stockinet, a smooth board, a tape measure, pie tape, scissors, a pastry brush, a pastry wheel, aluminum foil, and cooky cutters. In addition, she has on her pantry shelves the pie-crust and pie-filling mixes.

Even with this layout, pie making is far from being a simple matter. Whoever coined the phrase "easy as pie," not only didn't know what he was talking about; he uttered a base slander. It is true that anyone who can read can cook, after a fashion, but baking requires skill. The pie maker is reminded constantly by the experts, and knows from her own experience, that the dough for the crust should be handled as little as possible, that shrinkage in cooking is inevitable if the dough is stretched while being fitted into the pan, that even a trifle too much flour will make the crust tough, that the quantity of sugar used with berries and other fruit varies according to their ripeness and juiciness, that all of the apples in a pie should be of the same variety because some are juicier or require longer cooking than others, that some pies should have air vents and some shouldn't. Unless she is in an experimental mood, when the bars are down and anything goes, she proceeds carefully, following her recipe closely. Even so, she can never know whether a pie is going to turn out well until it has been cooked, cut and tasted. And occasionally, something happens to make her wonder what all the fuss is about. Something like this:

A year or so ago, when my wife and I were spending the summer in the country, we had as guest Miss Edith Barber, a noted food authority, for whom I had promised to bake an apple pie. While my wife drove to the railroad station to meet her, I went to a neighbor's for lunch. I drank three Martinis, and came home feeling very cheerful and efficient, confident that whipping up a delectable pie would be a matter of only a few minutes. So I set to work, using a mix, and soon had the bottom crust in place. Then I discovered that I didn't have any apples. A quick tour of the neighborhood produced half a dozen, of several different varieties. I remember there were a Winesap, a Jonathan, and two McIntoshes. I pared the apples, piled them into the pie shell, affixed a top crust, and put the pie in the oven. Five minutes later I realized that I hadn't put in any sugar, salt, butter or spices. So I hauled the pie out and dismantled it. The dough broke several times, but I squeezed it into a ball. It was a little stiff by that time, but I got it rolled out and proceeded to remake the pie. It looked all right when done, but I wasn't very hopeful about it. Miss Barber had two helpings, and said that she had never eaten a better apple pie; she especially praised the flaky tenderness of the crust!

◀ The pumpkin pie, traditionally American, owes its special flavor to spices. Clippers like the *Flying Cloud*, a model of which is shown here, brought back among their cargoes lovely objects of silver, crystal, mahogany and china that have become cherished family heirlooms.

FOSTER ENSMINGER

Of course, as every cook knows, if this proves anything at all it proves that sometimes people are very lucky. Ninety-nine times out of a hundred, or even oftener, a pie so fearfully abused will scarcely be fit to eat.

Harriet Beecher Stowe once described pie as "an English institution which, planted in American soil, forthwith ran rampant, and burst forth into an untold variety of genera and species." The English didn't invent pie, as Mrs. Stowe seems to suggest, but they developed the dish from which, in time, came the modern American pie. The history of pie is neither clear nor complete, to say the least, but in all likelihood the Romans, who made fruit tarts of a sort, introduced it to the barbarians of Western Europe, whose idea of fine eating was a ripe old mutton bone. Most of the European peoples, especially the French, the Danes and the Italians, have concentrated on the pastry, and have dedicated themselves to making it increasingly light and fluffy. The English, shivering on their cold little island, have neglected pastry in favor of the more substantial part of the pie, the filling. They have always been satisfied to top their pies, meat and fruit alike, with a thick, heavy slab of biscuit dough. It has been suggested that the English never learned to make real pie crust because they couldn't boil it. The truth is, they did boil it. A 17th-century recipe for pie crust instructs the cook to boil together a gallon of flour and a pound of butter, and "make the paste up quick."

In the matter of filling, however, the early English housewives and tavern cooks were very successful; it seems to have been the custom to start all pies with big chunks of meat and then throw in whatever else happened to be on hand. A popular dish served in the taverns and in large households was the "London Pie," which seems to have been quite an affair. The recipe for one of these from the late 17th century calls for eight marrow bones, eighteen sparrows, one pound of potatoes, one-fourth pound of cringoes, two ounces of lettuce stalks, forty chestnuts, three artichokes, a half pound of dates, one peck of oysters, one-quarter pound of preserved citron, twelve eggs, two sliced lemons, a handful of barberries, a half ounce of nutmeg, a half ounce of cinnamon, a quarter ounce of cloves, a half ounce of mace, and a quarter pound of currants. The cook was instructed to "liquor it when it is baked with white wine, butter and sugar."

The settlers who colonized New England brought their knowledge of pie-making with them, but were handicapped by a shortage of materials. They had no wheat flour, except the little that had been sent from England, until the first harvests had been gathered and mills built to grind the grain; and no apples or peaches until orchards had been planted and had begun to bear fruit. They had plenty of venison and other game, but no beef, veal or pork. They had corn meal, but corn meal isn't good for making pie crust. There were good supplies of parsnips, rhubarb and other garden truck in colonial days, but most plentiful of all was pumpkin; there was so much pumpkin that in New England for years it was served at every meal in a great variety of ways.

Perhaps the first pie baked in the New World was made by slicing off the top of a pumpkin, scooping out the seeds, and filling the cavity with milk, spices and maple sugar. A little later the colonial housewife learned to sprinkle corn meal or coarse rye flour on the bottom of a greased pan and pour filling over it. When wheat flour became available, the corn meal and rye were replaced by pastry. Thus was born the bottom crust, one of the distinguishing features of that delectable confection—the American pie.

DEEP DISH CURRANT JAM AND
PEAR PIE

6 cups peeled, sliced ripe pears	¼ cup sugar
3 tablespoons butter	¼ teaspoon salt
½ cup red or black currant jam	¼ teaspoon grated nutmeg
	Pastry for a large 1-crust pie

Start oven at hot (425° F.). Arrange a layer of sliced pears in the bottom of a shallow baking dish. Dot with butter; add almost all of the currant jam, spreading well over the pears. Cover with remaining pears. If fruit is very sweet, sprinkle with only 1 or 2 tablespoons sugar, mixed with the salt and nutmeg. Use more sugar if pears are of a nonsweet variety. Add dabs of currant jam and butter to top layer. Moisten edge of dish with water, adjust pastry top, trim edge and turn it under, pressing it down on the rim of the dish. Use thumb and fingers or tines of fork to make a decorative edge. Gash top with a few lines and leaves. Bake for 35 to 45 minutes, until pastry is browned. Makes 6 servings.

LONDON STRAWBERRY PIE

Baked 9-inch pastry shell	¾ cup currant jelly
2½ cups chilled Soft Custard	½ cup heavy cream
1 quart large ripe strawberries, cleaned and hulled	1 teaspoon Cointreau

Make your best pastry, either puff paste or a rich pie pastry, or use any favorite ready-mix pie crust. Line 9-inch pan and finish the edge with a handsome crimped border. Pour the custard into the cooled, baked shell. Arrange large whole berries in circles filling the shell full. Mound them high in the center by adding more berries. Melt the jelly over warm water, and spread jelly over all berries. Whip the cream, adding the cointreau as flavoring and pipe it in a narrow ribbon edge around the pie. Makes 6 servings.

SOFT CUSTARD

4 egg yolks	2 cups scalded milk
¼ cup sugar	1 teaspoon vanilla extract
¼ teaspoon salt	

Beat egg yolks slightly, combine with sugar and salt in the top part of a double boiler over hot water. Slowly add 2 cups scalded milk, stirring continually. Cook, stirring constantly. When custard coats a metal spoon, remove at once from hot water and place in a pan of cold water to cool quickly. Add 1 teaspoon vanilla extract. When custard has cooled, chill it and use as described in recipe above. Makes 2½ cups custard.

BLACK CHERRY PIE

Substitute large black stoned cherries for strawberries in the above recipe. Fill seed cavities in cherries with a small amount of cream cheese. Make orderly arrangement of cherries in the custard in the pie shell, and build up higher in the center. Complete recipe as described.

BUTTERSCOTCH PIE, CHANTILLY

Baked pastry shell for 9-inch pie	1 beaten egg
2 cups milk	¼ teaspoon salt
4 tablespoons cornstarch	½ teaspoon vanilla extract
2 tablespoons flour	3 tablespoons sliced blanched almonds
2 tablespoons butter	Whipped cream
1¼ cups brown sugar, packed	

Heat 1½ cups milk in top part of a double boiler over hot water. Mix cornstarch, flour and remaining ½ cup cold milk and stir into the hot milk. Cook and stir until thickened. Melt the butter in a saucepan; add sugar and cook until sugar is melted and bubbly. Stir butter-sugar mixture into hot-milk mixture until evenly blended and sugar is dissolved. Add egg, stir, add salt and vanilla, mix. Let cool. Pour cooled mixture into baked pastry shell. Cover top with sliced almonds and decorate with whipped cream. Makes 6 servings.

WALNUT MINCEMEAT PIE
WITH CHEESE PASTRY

Cheese pastry for 1-crust 9-inch pie	2 tablespoons cornstarch
2 cups mincemeat	1 cup heavy cream
⅓ cup brown sugar, packed	¼ cup coarsely chopped walnuts

Start oven at moderately hot (400° F.). Line pie pan with your favorite pie pastry; cheese pastry or spice pastry adds to the good flavor of this unusual pie. If you buy mincemeat, follow directions on package for softening it. Spread mincemeat in pastry-lined pan. Combine sugar and cornstarch and mix well; stir cream in and beat slightly. Pour over mincemeat. Scatter walnuts over the top. Bake for 45 minutes or until pastry is golden. Let cool, or serve slightly warm. Makes 6 servings.

CHEESE PASTRY FOR THIS PIE

Make your usual pie pastry; cut in ½ cup grated Cheddar cheese with the shortening.

BRANDY PUDDING PIE

½ cup butter	Juice 1 lemon
2 cups sugar	Pastry for 2 1-crust 8-inch pies
6 eggs	
¼ cup cognac or sherry	Grated nutmeg
Grated peel 2 lemons	

Start oven at moderate (350° F.). Cream butter and sugar smoothly together. Beat egg yolks until light and combine with butter and sugar. Add brandy or sherry, a few drops at a time, beating well. Add lemon peel and juice and mix. Whip egg whites stiff, fold into yolk mixture. Pour into 2 pastry-lined 8-inch pie plates. Dash top of each with a few grains of nutmeg. Bake for about 40 minutes, until crust is browned. Serve slightly warm or cold. Makes 10 or more servings.

ENGLISH RAISIN PIE

English Pie Pastry for 2-crust
    9-inch pie
1 cup raisins
2¼ cups water
1½ cups sugar
4½ tablespoons all-purpose
    flour, sifted

1 beaten egg
3 tablespoons lemon juice
3 teaspoons grated lemon
    peel
⅛ teaspoon salt

Line pie plate with English pastry. Roll out remaining pastry and cut with knife or wheel into strips for lattice top. Wash raisins, drain, cover with the 2¼ cups cold water and let soak 2 or 3 hours. Start oven at 450° F. Combine sugar, flour and egg; beat well. Add raisins and the water in which they soaked and remaining ingredients. Cook in top part of double boiler about 15 minutes or until mixture thickens, stirring occasionally. Let cool. Fill pie. Cover with pastry strips and make decorative edge all around. Bake in hot oven 10 to 15 minutes, reduce temperature to moderate (375° F.) and bake for an additional 15 minutes. Pastry should be lightly browned all over. Makes 6 servings. Serve warm or cold, with cream cheese or a mild Cheddar.

ENGLISH PASTRY

2 cups all-purpose flour
2 teaspoons baking powder
1 teaspoon salt
1 cup shortening

½ cup hot water
2 teaspoons lemon juice
1 egg yolk, beaten

Sift together flour, baking powder and salt three times. Cut in ½ cup shortening. Dissolve another ½ cup shortening in ½ cup hot water, add 2 teaspoons lemon juice, and 1 beaten egg yolk, mix; combine with the flour mixture. Stir well and knead for 3 minutes. Divide in half and roll out lightly. Makes pastry for 2 large pastry shells, or 1 large 2-crust pie.

CLOUD TOP SOUR CREAM RAISIN PIE

Baked 9-inch pie shell
1 cup sour cream
2 beaten egg yolks
½ cup sugar
1 cup raisins, soaked,
    drained, chopped
1½ tablespoons flour

⅛ teaspoon salt
½ teaspoon powdered
    cinnamon
½ teaspoon powdered cloves
½ teaspoon grated nutmeg
Meringue, optional

Start oven at moderate (375° F.). Combine cream and eggs, add sugar, mix well. Add all remaining ingredients. Pour into baked pie shell. Bake for 12 to 15 minutes. Let cool.

If meringue topping is preferred, let pie cool, as directed. Make meringue just before serving, heap on pie, and brown in slow oven (300° F.), 10 to 12 minutes. Let cool and serve. Makes 6 servings.

MERINGUE FOR THIS AND OTHER PIES

2 egg whites
¼ cup granulated sugar,
    sifted

¼ to 1 teaspoon any
    flavoring

Beat egg whites stiff. Then cut and fold in sugar or beat it in with a whisk. Add flavoring. Spread meringue at once on pie or put through pastry tube. Place in oven for 10 to 12 minutes or until surface is golden.

PUMPKIN PIE

1½ cups canned pumpkin
¾ cup light-brown sugar,
    packed
½ teaspoon salt
½ teaspoon powdered ginger
1 teaspoon powdered
    cinnamon
⅛ teaspoon powdered cloves

1 14½-oz. can evaporated
    milk
2 tablespoons butter
2 eggs
½ teaspoon lemon extract
1 extra egg white
Pastry for 1-crust 9-inch pie
Grated nutmeg

Start oven at hot (425° F.). Turn up to 500° F. when pie is placed in oven. Combine pumpkin, sugar, salt, spices, milk and butter in saucepan. Stir and heat until butter melts. Beat eggs and stir in pumpkin mixture. Add lemon flavoring. Whip egg white until stiff and fold in. Pour into pastry-lined pan. Sprinkle lightly with nutmeg. Bake for 8 minutes. Reduce heat to moderate (325° F.) and bake for 30 minutes longer or until set. Let cool or serve only slightly warm. Makes 6 servings.

LEMON CHIFFON PIE WITH CREAM GARNISH

½ cup sugar
1 envelope (1 tablespoon)
    plain unflavored
    gelatin
⅔ cup water
⅓ cup fresh lemon juice
4 eggs
1 tablespoon grated lemon
    peel

½ teaspoon cream of tartar
½ cup sugar
Baked and cooled pastry
    shell for 9-inch pie
1 cup heavy cream
¼ cup finely chopped
    candied lemon peel

Combine in an enamel or glass saucepan the ½ cup sugar, gelatin, ⅔ cup water, lemon juice and slightly beaten egg yolks. Blend and cook over moderate heat, stirring constantly. Do not boil. Just as mixture comes to a boil, remove pan from heat, stir in lemon peel and set the pan in cold water. Let cool until slightly thickened and a little dropped from a spoon mounds slightly.

Make meringue by beating egg whites with cream of tartar until frothy. Gradually beat in sugar, a little at a time, and continue beating until stiff and glossy and sugar is dissolved. Fold lemon mixture into the meringue; pile into baked pie shell. Chill several hours, until set.

Whip cream until stiff, fold into it about 2 tablespoons of chopped or grated candied lemon peel. Heap the cream onto the chilled pie, swirling it with spatula to completely cover the filling. Decorate around rim with mounds of remaining candied lemon peel. Makes 6 or more servings.

Chocolate / *Karena Shields*

Steaming in a cup, sweet or bittersweet in candies, cakes or pies—
in any form, chocolate is a treat.
No wonder it once was called the drink of the gods

CHOCOLATE by itself is a flavor distinctive and strange, but add to it the aromatic delicacy of vanilla, cinnamon or a bit of nutmeg, and a good dash of rum, and quite suddenly all the romance of tropical forests is in your hand and sweet on your tongue.

There are many ways to enjoy *Theo Broma*, but to taste it native style where it first was grown, you must go to Central America or Mexico. With the grace of a people who move as if they always hear music, a slim girl of Tehuantepec brings you your cup of morning chocolate. "How will you have it, sir?" she asks, her eyes reflecting her hope that you will like it the Mexican way. And when you say, "A la Mexicana," she is pleased.

Once, for Aztec and Mayan rulers, it was served in solid gold chalices with tortoise-shell and mother-of-pearl spoons. But the golden cups have been carried away by the Spaniards, and the spoons broken like the empires they served. This drink of the gods is now for any man to enjoy, but it must be prepared with loving care or the delicacy will go out of it.

Cocoa, since Cortez carried it to Europe, has come to be prepared in almost as many ways as there are nations that use it. The Swiss make it one way, with milk and vanilla; French chocolate has cream and a modicum of rum. English cocoa is very sweet and milky with a bit of nutmeg, and the candy bars and milk shakes consumed by Americans show how they like it best. Since chocolate grows successfully in only about five places in the world, it is one of the rare commodities of our time. It is so costly that it is usually sold mixed with "fillers." Thus, few people who live far from where it is grown know the taste of real chocolate.

Pure chocolate is an oily, rich paste made from the finely ground seeds of the cacao fruit. Its flavor is strong and a little bitter, and it is the oil that gives most of the potency to the taste. Drinkers of the commercial mixes sold as cocoa, which is a powdered residue after the oil is pressed out, get a bland, milky flavor hardly recognizable to one accustomed to true chocolate, which is red-black and strong, with little globules of cocoa butter floating on top.

In the provinces of Mexico the people mix pure ground cacao into a paste with water, cinnamon and sugar, and sell it pressed into little round cakes. Children carry them about the streets on small trays covered with clean napkins, balanced on their heads.

They stand in your doorway and chant in monotone, "Mymothersaysyouwillbuysomechocolatay." If you do, they are pleased, but a little embarrassed at the same time; if you don't, it's all right, too, for they have had a *centavo's* worth of fun at the chance to look you over.

All the people of Central America and Mexico use the little chocolate cakes for hot chocolate and for preparing *atole*, a drink made from sieved rice or corn. Another beverage, as old as corn is on this continent, is *posole*. This is made of corn which has been precooked and ground. A ball of *posole*, wrapped in banana leaves, goes with every workman into the fields or jungle. When snack time comes, he unwraps his ball of *posole*, fresh and fragrant in its smooth green package. Then out comes his chunk of brown sugar, and with water from a nearby creek he mixes a jicara of what is really a very good and cooling drink. If he is lucky, he

Hot chocolate a la Mexicana is made from the black, buttery squares created especially for that drink. The woman of Tehuantepec mixes it in a tall gourd, a *jícara*, with a whirling stick that acts as a churn in her deft hands.

ERWIN BLUMENFELD

carries a little pouch of ground chocolate, and adds some of this to his drink. This *posole*, flavored with chocolate, is sold in restaurants, at soft-drink stands, and is part of the regular diet of all classes.

Mexicans rub the cocoa nibs into a finely ground paste and mix it with chili to season meats; they put a pinch of it into nearly every dish. In rural areas they do this as surely as they drop a bit of corn silk or a kernel of corn into everything they cook, as an insurance against "the evils." If you find corn silk in your soup or chocolate flavor in your chicken, do not complain. The cook considers you worth protecting.

When chocolate was first taken to Europe from the Americas in the 16th century, it was looked upon with considerable uneasiness. All the superstitions that ran riot in a superstitious age grew apace with the introduction of this West Indian drink. Was it a food or a drink, a fruit, a nut or an invention of the devil? When it was discovered that the Mayans planted it with a blood ritual, Europe quickly concluded that there could be no more potent advocate for witchery than a seed that would not prosper unless the ground was prepared with a sprinkling of human blood. So the Spanish and French began to use it in love potions, and in England it was used as a medicine to "settle uncertain stomacks." Once it was even spoken of as "a romantick inflamer worse than the novel." People were admonished to be careful of meddling with such things especially in the month of carnival (May, when the big cacao harvests were celebrated). Not until the middle of the 16th century did *Theo Broma* become a respectable drink in Europe.

In the years since then chocolate in various forms has shared in many of the happier moments in men's lives. As a candy it has become synonymous with "gift." It has presided over fudge parties since great-grandmother's day. As a drink it has played a role in theatrical and literary history. It became an elegant excuse for the English great to sit and talk over profound and not so profound ideas in "cocoa houses." Garrick and Byron drank many a hot cup of it in 'The Cocoa Tree' and 'White's Cocoa House,' forerunners of today's famous clubs of London.

It was the flavor-conscious French, however, who excelled in developing the more savory ways of preparing chocolate. Even in England, it was advertised in London, in 1657: "In Bishopsgate St., in Queens Head Alley at a Frenchmans house is an excellent West India drink, that is called chocolate, to be sold, where you may have it ready at any time at reasonable rates. 10s to 15s a pound."

It is not surprising that some of the best recipes come to us via France. A French candy, the epitome of delicacies, is not difficult to make, but this is urgent: use only the best and richest cooking chocolate.

1 egg white beaten dry	*4 squares chocolate, melted*
2 teaspoons very hot water	*(remember, rich and*
1 cup sifted confectioners'	*dark)*
sugar	*3 teaspoons rum*
	2 to 3 tablespoons heavy
	cream

Blend in order of listing, adding more rum, cream or sugar to make the candy firm enough to roll into little balls. Roll each tiny sphere in dry cocoa, preferably unsweetened. And then let one melt on your tongue.

Here are two more recipes from France, both regarded as classics. I found the first in Louis P. de Gouy's *The Gold Cook Book* (Chilton), and the second in *June Platt's Party Cook-Book* (Houghton Mifflin Company):

FRENCH CHOCOLATE
(Serves six)

Add 2½ squares (2½ ounces) of grated, unsweetened chocolate to ½ cup of cold water and stir till blended. Place over a very low flame and cook, stirring constantly till chocolate is melted. Stir in ¼ cup of sugar and a dash of salt; bring to a boil, remove from the fire and repeat this boiling process 4 times, stirring constantly. Cool. When quite cold, fold in ¼ cup of sweet, chilled heavy cream, whipped. Chill. This will keep a month under refrigeration. When ready to serve, place 1 generous tablespoon of chocolate preparation in each serving cup, and pour scalded milk (6 cups in all) over to fill up the cups; dust with nutmeg or cinnamon, if desired.

POT DE CRÊME CHOCOLAT
(Serves eight)

Melt 3 squares of Baker's unsweetened chocolate in a few drops of water, in a double boiler. Put 3 tablespoons of sugar into 3 cups of cream and heat in a double boiler. Pour on the melted chocolate and stir well. Beat the yolks of 6 eggs and add the chocolate cream slowly. Add a teaspoon of vanilla and strain into cups. Place these in a pan of warm water and put into a slow oven until set.

Like many other exotic foods from the tropics, this nectar of the Indies has a strange and wonderful history. Its name comes from the Mayan and Aztecan languages. In Mayan, chocolate was *xococ*; the drink, *xocochá*. The Aztecs called it *xocohuatl*. It's easy to see how we came by the words chocolate and cocoa, since the x in these languages was pronounced *sh*.

People talk about chocolate beans, so of course their minds run to vines and pods. But it is a tree, not a vine; and it is the nutlike seed, not a pod, that gives us the rich flavor. This product is so precious that it was—and in some places still is—used as money. It also was used as tribute, or taxes. The seeds were counted and put in pouches of different colors, each color designating a different number, and then packed in chests. From the south, during the ruling days of the Aztecs, came the carved chests of red and black filled with the bright-colored pouches of the mahogany-hued "beans." They were carried nearly a thousand miles on the shoulders of especially chosen warriors to the resplendent capital of Tenochtitlán. The law stated that these chests must then be taken by groups of four hundred plumed warriors up the steps to the emperor's palace in a fitting ceremony, which included some sacrifice. Most certainly among the Aztecs the sacrifice was human. Then a great re-counting was done. Both Mayans and Aztecs used the vigesimal instead of the decimal system (that is, they began with units of twenty instead of ten). By their method, four hundred cacao seeds formed a *zontli* (a red pouch). Twenty *zontlis* made eight thousand seeds or a *xyuipilli* (black pouch) and three *xyuipillis* was a *carga*, or chest, which had 24,000 seeds.

Never fewer than four hundred chests were sent from one province.

In the days of the Mayan empires, no human sacrifice attended this tribute, but their ceremonies were none the less fantastic and full of meaning. Today, some of these ceremonies still take place. I have seen blue iguanas sacrificed in the May harvest rituals high in the mountains of the State of Chiapas, Mexico.

Cacao is more than food or money to the people of Chiapas and Yucatán. They believe it to be one of the great gifts brought to earth by the hero-god Itzamná, who is part both of their story of origins and of their prophecies for the future. So the cacao tree, like maiz, is woven into the mystery of Mayan genesis.

The earth and rain gods, Chac and Tlaloc, have responsibility for all growing things. At certain times of the year ceremonies are held to remind these lesser powers of their duty. Then it is that the Sacrifice of the Dog takes place. The dog chosen must be the color of cacao, and if none such is available, one must be dyed that color. Incense is poured upon the altar, the dog and iguanas are sacrificed. The priests wear the plumes of certain birds, and each tribal leader carries as a sacred symbol a branch of the cacao. The people chant songs sung only at this time, songs that echo the long-gone days of majestic empires. For an entire week, each person must partake daily of the chocolate and cinnamon cakes, and drink the pale cacao wine made from the sweet pulp of the cacao pod. This is a time of great laughter, and "a sense of the divine settles upon the land."

It is in the hills of Chiapas, the birthplace of cacao, that the best chocolate grows. The Mayans were exceptional agriculturists. They developed corn from a tiny grass plant, and cacao from a shrub into the full-bearing tree it is today.

Although some chocolate trees grow wild, cacao today is predominantly a cultivated food, and every Indian village or small ranch has a cacao orchard.

Cacao is a prima donna among trees. It either flourishes or quickly dies, and it is even necessary to provide a nursemaid, the madre de cacao, to provide just the right amount of shade. Cacao needs a very hot and humid climate, exceedingly rich but porous soil, heavy rainfall and exactly the right altitude.

Cacao seeds will not sprout unless planted within twenty-four to thirty-six hours after the pods are picked. After that the "fermenting" process will have become so advanced that the seeds will either mold or rot. If they are dried first, the germ will not come to life, as corn germ will. Since cacao is planted in seedbeds first, and then moved to groves, it could be transplanted thousands of miles away. But it will grow in few areas. The only successful large-scale plantations are in Central America, the West Indies, along the west coast of Africa, and in a few South American and South Pacific areas.

The cacao is a most peculiar tree. It grows about ten to twenty feet high, with long, shiny, dark green and reddish leaves. The trunk is mottled gray and white and most of the seed pods (mazorkas) grow out of the trunk instead of hanging from the branches. At harvesttime, the ridged, yellow, red and green mazorkas hang like great lozenges, hodgepodge all along the trunk.

When Humboldt saw a chocolate tree for the first time he wrote: "Flowers were growing so low on the trunk as to be bursting through the roots right up out of the earth." His delight was increased by the tiny delicacy of the flower itself, which he described as a "rose-colored calyx developing into a fruit, five-celled, seven to nine inches in length, three to four inches in width."

The blossoms appear the first year after the cacao is transplanted. The first flowers fall off, and the second year some of the flowers develop into tiny green mazorkas. These also dry up and fall off. The third and fourth year, some of the mazorkas reach maturity. By the sixth year the tree is in full development and, barring accidents, will continue to produce up to sixty years.

The mazorkas are picked ripe, opened, and the seeds scooped out. The washing and drying of the seeds is a crucial operation, for chocolate absorbs flavors from whatever is around it, so the water in which the seeds are washed and the ground on which they are dried (preferably on clean sacking) must be carefully selected beforehand.

When I decided to plant cacao I discovered that there is more to Mayan cacao legendry than meets the eye. It seems that one can't just go into this area and plant chocolate without taking into consideration some of the beliefs of the people. Cacao has been too long in the tradition of those of Mayan descent to be considered only in a purely economic light. I should have known that, for it was here that I spent my childhood and, in planting cacao in the Tumbalas, I was coming home to my father's own plantation and to the Tzendal and Chol peoples I knew as a little girl. I tried very hard not to let sentiment rule my decision of the place, however, for father's finca had been planted in rubber, and chocolate required very different handling.

After looking at orchard land in Nicaragua and Tabasco, I went finally to the San Leandro plantation where I had grown up, and there, with some of the men who had worked for my father, went over acres of jungle, looking for the best location. We found what seemed a suitable place—wild cacao grew there—and settled down to a week's camp in the forest. Meanwhile the jefe sent out word into the hills that I was looking for workmen, and in a day or two they wandered in, a long-haired, wild-eyed lot, each silently coming out of the woods to sit at the edge of the camp. They watched us for a long time without speaking, waiting until they had sized up the situation. Then slowly, they approached the jefe, and in a word or two said they would work for me. Some of them remembered me, others were new, down from the mountains.

So the preparation for chocolate planting was celebrated early in the night with large fires and low singing and chanting in the dark. The strange speech of these descendants of the Mayans and their deep, soft voices reminded me of the days when this was a big plantation, made me wish again to make it a great finca.

Then suddenly something went wrong. The songs died down, the men stirred uneasily and everything was still. The jefe came to me to say the men wouldn't plant in the place we had chosen. When I asked why, he shrugged his shoulders and said they had a reason. This unfathomable refusal was echoed in their songs and their drumbeats as the evening progressed. The workmen sat immobile around their fires. I was puzzled and discouraged. Why hadn't they spoken sooner? What had gone wrong? Brought up in the country, I knew most of its enigmas, but this was something new.

I ended by exclaiming, in their dialect, "Well, where do they want to plant?"

Immediately people came forward and their leader began

talking and pointing. I was urged to go with them, and we started into the surrounding jungle.

Nearly an hour later the men stopped and everyone put out his flashlight. In front of us the thick forest was filled with an eerie green light that seemed to flow upward from the jungle floor. "Here," they said, in a place I had never visited.

All right, I thought, so they want to plant where there is phosphorus. But the next morning when they went to work I discovered something else. As they moved under the trees cutting swiftly with their double-edged machetes, I saw another reason for their choice of this ground. Everywhere, as far as I could see, were the low house-mounds of what had once been the homes of the ancient Mayans. Cacao, it seems, could not be planted just anywhere; if it is to thrive it must have the approval of the ancient peoples.

In this grove, planted under the natural towering jungle, dwarfed by the immensity of mahogany and giant ceiba, the cacao trees now reach upward from clean mossy aisles to catch vagrant splashes of sunlight, their roots anchored deep in the tumbled, ruined abode of the ancient Mayas.

SACHER TORTE

2 tablespoons fine
    breadcrumbs for pan
½ pound cooking chocolate,
    grated
½ pound butter
1 cup plus 2 tablespoons
    powdered sugar

½ pound shelled almonds,
    grated
8 eggs
1 tablespoon cornstarch
Raspberry jam
¼ cup apricot jam, melted
    and sieved
Chocolate frosting

Grease a spring-form mold and dust it with fine bread crumbs. Start oven at moderately slow (300° F.). Melt chocolate in the top part of a double boiler over hot water. Cream butter, add melted chocolate alternately with sugar, almonds and egg yolks, stirring well as each yolk is added. Add cornstarch and beat again. Whip egg whites until stiff and fold into chocolate batter. Pour into prepared pan. Bake for 50 to 60 minutes. Let cool in the mold overnight. Unmold, split, cover lower half with raspberry jam. Replace top layer. Brush top with melted and sieved apricot jam. Then cover with Chocolate Frosting. Makes 6 or more servings. Usually cut in 8 pieces.

CHOCOLATE FROSTING

2 1-oz. squares chocolate
1 tablespoon butter
½ cup milk

2 cups confectioners' sugar
1 teaspoon vanilla

Combine chocolate, butter and milk in the upper part of a double boiler. Cook and stir until chocolate melts. Remove pan from heat and let stand until lukewarm. Beat sugar into mixture; add vanilla. Continue beating until mixture is ready to spread. Spread over torte as described.

CHOCOLATE MOUSSE WITH RUM WHIPPED CREAM

1½ teaspoons plain gelatin
3 tablespoons cold water
2 1-oz. squares unsweetened
    chocolate
¼ cup confectioners' sugar
¾ cup milk
⅔ cup granulated sugar

½ teaspoon vanilla extract
1½ cups heavy cream,
    whipped
Rum-flavored, sweetened
    whipped cream
Ground hazelnuts

Turn refrigerator control to coldest setting. Soften gelatin in the cold water. Melt chocolate in top part of double boiler over hot water, stir in confectioners' sugar, add milk, stirring smoothly. Cook until smooth, stirring constantly. Add soaked gelatin, granulated sugar and vanilla, and mix. Chill until the consistency of egg white, stirring frequently. Fold in the whipped cream. Pour into 6 to 8 individual molds and place in refrigerator till well chilled. Remove from refrigerator a few minutes before unmolding to serve. Decorate with rum-flavored whipped cream and a few ground hazel nuts. Makes 6 to 8 servings.

CHOCOLATE PECAN TARTS

½ cup sugar
1 cup dark corn syrup
¼ teaspoon salt
1 tablespoon flour
2 eggs
1 teaspoon vanilla extract
2 1-oz. squares unsweetened
    chocolate

1 tablespoon butter
1¼ cups pecan halves
8 unbaked tart shells
Evaporated milk
½ cup heavy cream,
    whipped
2 tablespoons grated
    chocolate

Start oven at moderately slow (300° F.). Beat sugar, syrup, salt, flour and eggs together. Add vanilla. Melt butter and chocolate together and stir in, mixing thoroughly. Add nuts and pour into pastry-lined tart shells. Brush edges of pastry with a little undiluted evaporated milk. Bake for about 50 to 60 minutes or until filling is just set. Makes 8 tarts. Let cool before serving. Decorate tarts with swirl of whipped cream dusted with grated chocolate.

DEEP SOUTH CHOCOLATE TAFFY

2 cups light corn sirup
¼ cup water
¼ teaspoon salt
2½ 1-oz. squares
    unsweetened
    chocolate

1 tablespoon butter
¼ teaspoon vanilla extract
¼ cup finely chopped
    pine nuts
Cornstarch

Combine sirup, water, salt and chocolate in a 1-quart saucepan. Cook over medium heat, stirring constantly, until mixture boils. Continue stirring and cooking almost to 260° F. or until a small amount dropped into a cup of cold water forms a hard ball. Remove pan from heat, add butter and vanilla, stir only enough to blend these in. Add nuts and pour onto a buttered platter, let stand only until cool enough to handle. Dip fingers in cornstarch and pull taffy until it has a satiny look, is lighter in color and elastic. Pull into long strips, cut with scissors into pieces. Makes about 1 pound taffy.

It need not be pulled—Instead of pouring this good nut taffy onto the buttered platter, pour it into a buttered square pan, 8x8x2 inches. Let cool and, before it is quite cold, cut in squares. Wrap in foil paper of assorted colors for a gay effect.

MARZIPAN

1½ cups grated blanched
    almonds or almond
    paste
1½ cups confectioners'
    sugar or vanilla
    fondant

¼ teaspoon almond extract
1 cup powdered cocoa or
    grated sweet chocolate
Pure-food coloring
Candied fruit
Whole cloves

Grate or grind almonds very fine or use almond paste if available from a confectioner. Combine with sugar or fondant, working with hands to blend well. Add almond extract. Heat in upper part of double boiler over boiling water for a few minutes or only until slightly warm. Let cool. Add a little extra sugar or fondant and knead well together. When kneaded and smooth, place in a jar, cover tightly and let stand overnight.

Shape into balls and roll them in cocoa or grated chocolate. Or shape into small apples, peaches, plums and pears, decorate with stems and leaves made of candied cherries and angelica. Use a little red color to tint one cheek of apples, peaches, plums and pears. Insert clove in bottom of fruit to make realistic stem end. Marzipan candies are a good contrast in a box of homemade chocolates and caramels. This recipe makes about 1 pound marzipan.

CHOCOLATE MARRON CREAM

1 tablespoon plain gelatin
¼ cup cold water
½ cup scalded milk
2 1-oz. squares semisweet
    chocolate, melted
½ cup sugar

1½ pints heavy cream,
    whipped
1 teaspoon vanilla extract
1 medium-sized jar marrons
    in vanilla-sweetened
    syrup
½ cake sweet chocolate

Soak gelatin in cold water for about 5 minutes. Stir into hot milk until dissolved. Stir melted chocolate and sugar together; then stir into gelatin mixture until sugar is dissolved. Set bowl containing mixture in pan of ice water and stir until mixture begins to thicken. Add 1 pint of cream, whipped, the vanilla, and a few finely chopped drained marrons. Pour into a cold wet mold and chill. Turn out on chilled serving dish, garnish with remaining ½ pint of cream, whipped and containing a few chopped marrons and shaved sweet chocolate. Makes 6 servings.

CHOCOLATE AND WALNUT LOAF CAKE

Butter and flour for pan
6 tablespoons butter
1⅔ cups brown sugar,
    packed
3 eggs
1½ cups milk
2 cups all-purpose flour,
    sifted
1 teaspoon baking powder

7 1-oz. squares chocolate,
    melted
1½ cups grated walnuts or
    almonds
1 teaspoon grated lemon
    peel
½ teaspoon vanilla extract
Chocolate frosting

Grease loaf pan, sprinkle with flour. Start oven at moderate (375° F.). Cream butter, stir in 1 cup brown sugar and beat smoothly together. Beat 2 egg yolks and add to butter and sugar. Add ½ cup milk and blend. Sift in the flour and baking powder and mix well. Beat 3 egg whites stiff and fold in. Combine melted chocolate, remaining ⅔ cup sugar, 1 cup milk and remaining egg yolk. Mix well. Stir into first batter. Add nuts, lemon peel and vanilla. Pour into prepared pan. Bake for 35 minutes or until a cake tester inserted deeply comes out clean. Let cool in pan for 5 minutes; then turn out on cake rack, let cool. Frost thickly with any preferred chocolate frosting. Makes 12 or more servings. A delicious cake.

CHOCOLATE TRUFFLES

4 tablespoons butter
½ cup grated semisweet
    chocolate
1 tablespoon rum

¼ cup coarsely grated
    chocolate crumbs
2 tablespoons finely grated
    pistachio nuts

Cream butter until light; add semisweet chocolate and rum and beat until smooth. Chill. When cold, form balls about 1 inch in diameter. Roll them in chocolate crumbs if an all-chocolate truffle is preferred or in both chocolate crumbs and pistachio nuts for another superbly flavored candy. Makes about 20 truffles. Keep in cool place.

PROFITEROLLES

1 cup cold water	1 cup all-purpose flour, sifted
½ cup butter	5 eggs
¼ teaspoon salt	½ teaspoon sherry
1 teaspoon sugar	¼ cup milk

Combine in a large saucepan the water, butter, salt and sugar and bring to a boil. Stir to mix well and remove from heat. Add flour all at once and stir to mix well. Return pan to heat and stir continually for 2 or 3 minutes or until the paste follows the spoon, forms a ball and leaves the sides of pan. Remove from heat, add unbeaten eggs, 1 at a time, beating thoroughly after each addition. Add sherry, mix. Start oven at moderate (350° F.). Pour paste into a pastry bag with large plain tube; press small portions, about the size of a walnut, onto a buttered baking sheet or drop by teaspoonful. Brush the surface of each with a little cold milk. Bake for 12 to 15 minutes, or until well puffed and a pale golden color. Remove from oven, and let cool. Makes 24 or 30 small puffs.

To fill, make a slit in each puff, fill with chocolate custard, ice cream or any favorite custard or cream filling. Serve on a cold dish, with a lukewarm chocolate sauce poured over. Usually 3 or 4 puffs make 1 serving.

As a grand finale to a buffet supper, arrange the filled profiterolles in a pyramid on a platter and dribble the chocolate sauce over them from the top. Additional sauce is passed with the servings.

HOT CHOCOLATE SAUCE

2 1-oz. squares sweet chocolate	⅛ teaspoon salt
1 cup water	2 tablespoons butter
2 cups sugar	1 tablespoon cognac

Combine sweet chocolate with water, heat, and when smooth and thick, add sugar and salt, stirring continually. Stir until dissolved. Let boil 3 minutes, then add butter and cognac. Stir, and remove from heat. Makes 12 generous servings.

RICH CHOCOLATE SQUARE

1½ cups all-purpose flour, sifted	¼ cup shortening
1 teaspoon baking soda	1 cup sugar
¼ teaspoon salt	1 egg
2 1-oz. squares unsweetened chocolate	1 cup sour milk
	1 teaspoon vanilla extract

Start oven at moderate (350° F.). Grease and flour an 8-inch-square baking pan. Sift flour, soda and salt together three times. Melt chocolate over hot water. Cream shortening and sugar together until light and fluffy. Add egg, beat thoroughly. Add sifted dry ingredients alternately with sour milk, beating well after each addition. Blend in chocolate and vanilla. Pour into prepared pan. Bake for about 35 minutes, or until cake tester inserted deeply comes out clean. Makes 16 2-inch squares. Should be frosted thickly with a rich chocolate frosting.

RICH CHOCOLATE FROSTING

2 1-oz. squares chocolate	1 teaspoon sherry, or mint flavoring
½ lb. butter	2 cups confectioners' sugar, sifted

Melt chocolate over hot water and let cool. Cream butter until fluffy, add chocolate, sherry (or mint flavoring) and sugar. Beat at high speed in mixer bowl until light and fluffy and of good spreading consistency. Makes about 2 cups frosting.

Another superb flavor combination with this chocolate cake, is orange, and it flavors the topping of the famous Sunday night cake of a popular New York hostess. Here it is:

ORANGE BUTTER CREAM FROSTING

4 tablespoons butter	3 tablespoons orange juice
2 cups confectioners' sugar, sifted	1 egg

Cream butter until light. Add sugar, beating steadily until fluffy; add orange juice and egg; continue beating to spreading consistency. Use as a thick frosting on the chocolate cake. Makes about 2 cups frosting.

DELICATE CHOCOLATE SPONGE CAKE

4 egg yolks	¾ cup powdered cocoa
1 cup sugar	4 egg whites
¼ cup water	1 teaspoon baking powder
1 teaspoon vanilla extract	¼ teaspoon salt
¾ cup all-purpose flour, sifted	

Start oven at moderate (350° to 375° F.). Beat egg yolks until lemon-colored and thick, gradually beat in sugar and beat in a little of the water. Add the flavoring, sift flour and cocoa together and add. Gradually add remaining water, beating smoothly. Whip egg whites stiff, with baking powder and salt added. Fold into the cocoa mixture. Pour into an ungreased 9-inch tube pan and bake from 30 to 45 minutes. Remove pan from oven and invert so it stands on the tube. If cake has risen above the top of the tube, invert a funnel and rest the tube on the funnel. Let cake stand until pan feels cool. Run the blade of a spatula between the cake and the tube and around the outer edge of the cake and the rim of the pan, and ease the cake from the pan. Makes 8 or more servings. A wonderful cake to serve with ice cream, a custard sauce or a chocolate sauce.

CHOCOLATE-TOPPED BUTTER CRUNCH

1 *cup butter*
1 *cup sugar*
2 *tablespoons water*
1 *tablespoon light corn sirup*

¾ *cup nutmeats (Brazils, pecans, hazelnuts, walnuts, peanuts or unblanched almonds)*
4 *1-oz. squares bitter or semisweet chocolate*

Melt butter in saucepan. Remove from heat and blend sugar in. Return to heat and, when mixture begins to bubble, add the water and corn sirup. Cook, stirring frequently, to 290° F. (hard-crack stage). Remove pan from heat at once. Quickly stir nuts in, and pour onto lightly buttered baking sheet. Let cool, loosening candy from time to time with spatula.

Melt chocolate in saucepan. Spread half of the melted chocolate evenly over nut brittle. Replace remaining chocolate over low heat. Leave brittle until the chocolate is firm. Then, with a broad spatula, turn the brittle over and spread its other side with the remaining melted chocolate. When the second layer of chocolate is firm, break the candy in pieces and store it in a covered tin or jar in a cool place. Makes about 12 pieces.

FRENCH HOT CHOCOLATE SOUFFLÉ

Butter
3 *tablespoons bread crumbs*
6 *eggs*
½ *cup granulated sugar*

1 *teaspoon powdered cocoa*
½ *cup grated semisweet chocolate*
1 *cup heavy cream, whipped*

Butter the top of a double boiler, sprinkle buttered surface with 2 tablespoons crumbs. Beat egg whites stiff. Beat egg yolks until light, add sugar and beat until lemon-colored. Add 1 tablespoon crumbs, the cocoa and grated chocolate. Fold egg whites into chocolate mixture. Pour into prepared double boiler. Cover, steam over gently boiling water for 1 hour. Serve warm on dessert plates with whipped cream. Makes 6 servings.

6. BEVERAGES

Coffee: The Fragrant Cup
/ Frederic Morton

*Because of its magic aroma half the world starts the day right,
idleness becomes graceful and laziness turns to leisure*

I T WAS the seductiveness of the South American bean that robbed me of the only soccer-playing female cook I ever knew. I remember standing with my mother by the kitchen door at seven one morning, thunderstruck. Usually we weren't up that early, but on Father's birthday we wanted to be sure the gala breakfast was coming along properly. And so we came upon the appalling scene.

"Anna!" my mother gasped.

There had been rumors in Vienna of cooks embezzling the first—and therefore the strongest and best—cup drawn from the drip pot, the one traditionally reserved for the head of the family. But that our Anna, our friend and helpmate, my booting partner, the pearl of the household—that *she*. . . .

"Anna," my mother said, "on his *birthday!*" And then she was stricken with an even more baleful realization: "You've been drinking it *every* morning!"

Thus coffee became an idol smasher of my youth. Yet today for me, as for most other cultured adults, the beverage is a luxurious necessity; after religion, it is coffee that holds civilization together. Without coffee nobody would get up in the morning; executives could not make decisions during their three-hour three-cup lunches; secretaries would have breakdowns instead of breaks. Take away the gregarious aroma of coffee and friendships would freeze, chats bristle

◀ **A sampling from the breakfast menu at Brennan's in New Orleans—a gourmet's delight made complete by the coffee, that staple of even the simplest of breakfasts.**

FRED MAROON

into debates, get-togethers unmask themselves as negotiations. Coffee not only meliorates protracted work but miraculously lends grace to idleness. A single scented cup held properly between forefinger and thumb transforms laziness into leisure.

As final wizardry—though South America produces two thirds of the world's coffee, the brew gives many another country its national flavor. In a coffeeless society France, for instance, would lose the term that rivals *amour* in international fragrance and popularity: I mean, of course, *café au lait*. Austria would be deprived of the very elixir of its *Gemütlichkeit*, Germany of the ingratiating *Kaffeeklatsch*. As for Italy, not even the loss of Vesuvius' smoke plume could rival the extinction of the *espresso*. Britain would survive; but then it always does. No wonder that the world drinks more than 200 billion cups yearly.

It is a wonder how the bean emigrated to South America, the coffee titan, which today dwarfs other producers like Hawaii or Central Africa. Known mythically as the Wine of the Levant, coffee was introduced to Europe by Italian and Dutch sailors. In 1714 the burgomaster of Amsterdam sent France's Louis XIV the coffee plant that was destined to sire the hundreds of millions of trees covering South America today from Santos to the Caribbean. Louis thought the odd fruit would improve neither his gout nor his mistresses, and placed it as a botanical exhibit in his *Jardin des Plantes*.

Nine years later Captain Desclieux of Martinique entered history like a thief in the night. He stole a coffee shoot from the royal greenhouse, put it in a gold chest topped with glass to let in the sun and spirited it onto a Martinique-bound ship. He nursed the young plant back to health after a storm shattered the chest and drenched it in salt spray. When the ship's reservoir ran short and each passenger was allocated a small water ration, Desclieux acted with a solicitude Charles Lamb was to celebrate:

> *Even from his own dry parched lips*
> *He spares it for his coffee slips.*
> *Water he gives his nurslings first*
> *Ere his allays his own deep thirst.*

Desclieux planted the shrub on his Martinique estate. The New World's most succesful greenhorn, it multiplied all over a continent. Its cuttings and seedlings populated the West Indies, Central America, and the South American mainland.

It was another soldier, Lieut. Col. Francisco de Melo Palheta, who carried coffee to Brazil. The Portuguese officer was as accomplished a gigolo as Desclieux had been a kidnaper. When he arrived at the capital of French Guiana to arbitrate a border dispute with the neighboring Dutch colony, he not only mollified both sides of the controversy but he also charmed the governor's wife. Among the presents she gave him was a small bag of coffee seedlings. The colonel returned home to found Brazil's first coffee *fazenda*, which in the course of time fathered seventy thousand other plantations in the state of São Paulo alone and turned the nation into the world's coffee giant.

Another legend explains how the coffee tree was spread over Colombia by Padre José Fulgencio Silva. According to the National Federation of Coffee Growers of Colombia, the padre, who deplored sin almost as much as he enjoyed coffee, required errant members of his flock to do penance by planting coffee trees. In recent years these wages of sin brought Colombians an annual income of half a billion dollars, a figure second only to Brazil's.

Today much of South and Central America is one gigantic coffee grove. Millions of slender green coffee trees cover the endless hills of Brazil, the mountain slopes of Colombia, the tablelands of Costa Rica. Depending on altitude or climate, *coffea arabica* blossoms at almost any time of the year, producing delicate white flowers—the sudden "fragrant snow" that haunts the plantation with its heady jasminelike perfume and then vanishes within forty-eight hours, scent, petals and all.

Some eight months after flowering, the fruit has ripened into a deep purplish berry. This is the moment for picking; the season of the sweat-laced festival of the great god coffee, on whose altar men, women and children offer up their siestas to labor from dawn to dusk.

Next comes the problem of liberating the treasure buried inside the berry. The "wet" method puts the berries through a depulping machine, then immerses the gum-encased beans in water tanks until this covering is fermented away. In the more primitive "dry" method, the fruit is spread on brick patios and the sun bakes away pulp and gum. At last, after a hulling machine removes the parchment husk left by either process, the seed emerges into daylight—the boon, the bean.

It's not that simple, for the flavor and aroma locked inside the bean are perishable and vitally affected by each operation. They are treated by the coffee man as a woman treats her figure and complexion, and the mirror he holds up is his taste buds.

A large coffee importer cup-tests his coffee four times before releasing it to the roaster. First he tastes an airmail sample from the producing country before the lot is shipped.

The shipment is sampled again on arrival at the receiving port. In the processing plant the beans are tested again to make sure no damage has been done in transit. And after a mixture is obtained from several components (they may be drawn from the Brazilian grades that are numbered one to eight, according to quality, or from the strains of Colombia's so-called "mild" Excelso coffee), the blend is savored and judged once more before going to the roaster.

There are a few gourmets who would no more think of buying their coffee preroasted than the cocktail *cognoscente* would buy his Martini premixed.

I've asked Mr. Andrés Uribe, vice-president of the Pan-American Coffee Bureau and the Boswell of the bean, for advice to those who would join their ranks.

After warning that green coffee is not easily purchasable in retail quantities, he recommends blending equal parts of fancy Mexican coffee, Cobans from Guatemala, and the exotic Sumatra variety known as Mandheling. A pungently luscious amalgam consists of one third Java, one third Mocha and one third Colombian Excelso. A slightly milder blend combines, in equal quantity, Excelso and Brazilian coffee (also called Santos) of type 2, 3 or 4. This mixture approximates most of our higher-priced quality-brand coffees.

When it comes to roasting, there is no satisfactory home device, but a heavy iron frying pan with a cover will do. The roast-it-himselfer strives for a medium-brown color best achieved by a temperature of about 400° F. He tests his beans as they brown. They are done if they crack easily and the bean has been roasted through.

As to home grinding, several good mills are available. (In Austria I remember Anna wedging a crank-type model between her capacious knees, like a cellist tuning up. When she began to play, not heavenly music but a celestial aroma filled the air.)

Now, roasting and grinding are the preoccupation of a small culinary cabala, but brewing is a universal problem. Some instant-coffee lovers may challenge this statement, but to drink true coffee, you must brew it.

Here are six simple rules for brewing a rich dark pleasure for your cup:

1. Use fresh coffee. Unless vacuum-packed, it should be tightly covered, kept in a cool place and never more than a week old.

2. Use freshly drawn cold and *not alkaline or hard* water.

3. Measure two level tablespoons of coffee for each cup. If a weaker brew is desired, use less.

4. Employ the full capacity of your coffee maker. For fewer cups, use a smaller pot.

5. Boil as little as possible. At 212° F. flavor-giving oils and ethers are lost. Thus, the optimum coffee-making method is "drip" since it produces the beverage at the ideal range of 185° to 195°.

6. While it is brewing, sniff the aroma of your coffee to alert your taste buds. And serve immediately after brewing.

South America's favorite recipe can be summed up quite simply: black, hot and frequent. The Brazilian reaches for his tiny cup (he calls it, in affectionate diminutive, *café-zinho*) almost as frequently as smokers do for a cigarette. The Colombian resorts no less often to his little *tinto*. Coffee punctuates the hours along the Andes. Below the Panama Canal, you might say that office life consists of taking business breaks during coffee hours. However, in Colombia make sure you're not being served *passilla*—the dregs variety left after better grades are exported. Popular in El Salvador is iced coffee tropical, which constitutes a luscious antidote to dog days: Fill an electric blender half full of finely chopped ice; add one and a half cups strong, cool coffee and one tablespoon granulated sugar. Blend until thick and creamy and pour into four tall glasses.

In Europe the bean cuts a fancier figure. Not only the tastiest but also the loudest coffee is Italian. *Caffè espresso*, made of very dark roast coffee, ground dust-fine, is brewed by steam pressure. The *espresso* machine has the voice of a dragon, the looks of a Martian and the juice of an angel. After each hoarse creative agony it oozes a cup of nutty-flavored nectar. *Caffè cappuccino* is steaming milk added to steaming *espresso*, the whole crowned with cinnamon. *Caffè chocolaccino*, usually served tall, is *cappuccino* glorified by a tiara of whipped cream and feathers of French chocolate.

Caffè espresso is usually available only in an *espresso* (a kind of fluid-drive coffeehouse), but the above-mentioned Mr. Uribe avers that it can be made by any regulation drip or vacuum coffee maker, provided you use two ounces of a dark-roast coffee like *Medaglia d'Oro* for every three ounces of water.

The French have a spectacular called *café royale*, which is staged as follows: Drop a sugar lump into each demitasse. Fill cups half full of strong demitasse coffee. Fill the rest of the cup with brandy; if done gently and lovingly, the brandy will remain on top. Ignite the brandy, say *"Formidable!"* three times, quench, stir—and sip.

Another cup-born bit of Gallic incandescence is *café brûlot diabolique*, which helps keep New Orleans reveling at Mardi Gras time. Antoine's prepares it *comme ça*:

1 *one-inch stick cinnamon*	3 *lumps sugar*
peel of 1 lemon, cut thin	3 *jiggers brandy*
8 *whole cloves*	

Place cinnamon, lemon peel, cloves and sugar in a chafing dish. Place brandy in a large ladle; ignite brandy and pour over ingredients in chafing dish. Keep ladling brandy over ingredients until sugar is dissolved. Gradually add the coffee until the flames fade. Then dim the lights for Wagnerian effect, and serve immediately to carnivalers costumed as fire chiefs.

Less Cinemascopic French suggestions are *café cacao*: add one jigger of *crème de cacao* to each large cup of fresh-brewed coffee, top with whipped cream; and *café Cointreau*: place one teaspoon grated lemon peel in each large coffee cup, add hot, freshly brewed coffee and mix in gently one jigger of Cointreau.

Oh, yes—*café au lait*. It requires hot milk, fresh coffee and

dexterity: the coffee and milk must be poured simultaneously.

A leprechaun cousin of *café Cointreau* is Irish coffee. Into a pre-warmed stemmed glass pour the coffee, hot and black as Satan's soul; insinuate two teaspoons of sugar into the mixture, add a fearless finger of Irish whisky. 'Tis a quarter of an inch of thick cream—if you're in Ireland—you'll be floating on top. In the U.S., 'tis best to whip the cream a bit to make it float. After that . . .

More offbeat is Armenian coffee prepared in the traditional *ibrik*, a brass dipper: Mix one tablespoon powdered sugar with two tablespoons pulverized dark-roast coffee. Add two cups very cold water, and heat until the mixture froths to the top of the *ibrik*. Allow it to froth up three times, then, before serving, let it settle.

Hot Mocha Java, also a heterodox pleasure, results if you combine hot coffee and hot chocolate in equal quantities. Heat thoroughly, but avoid boiling; pour into cups and cap with whipped cream; some people use marshmallows.

Finally we come to Vienna, that old bastion of coffee *gourmandise*. The Viennese are not only choosy but individualistic about their preferences. There exist in all good Viennese kitchens and coffeehouses fifteen recognized proportions in which coffee and milk may be mixed; these range from *Einspaenner* (black coffee topped with whipped cream) to *Schale Licht* (very light coffee, usually topped with you-know-what). Nearly every Viennese has his own favorite shading somewhere between these established norms. Rembrandt was no more careful about the colors on his canvas than the *Wiener* about the shading of his coffee. I once watched a venerable gentleman carry his cup from the dark of the coffeehouse into the light of day to make sure that the chromatic subtlety he favored had been achieved.

My ex-compatriots are also iced-coffee addicts. Viennese coffee frost is a fine way to refrigerate a torrid throat: Brew six cups of double-strength coffee. While still hot, pour it over four crushed cinnamon sticks, eight cloves and eight allspice berries. After an hour strain the beverage and pour over ice in tall glasses. Sweeten to taste with sugar sirup and top with whipped cream. You'll have enough for four.

I don't know if Anna, the cook of my childhood, was much for fancy coffee frost. And I doubt very much that she was aware of her debt to the *fincas* and *fazendas* of South America. But if her love for coffee was simple, it was also dedicated, less articulate than, but just as sincere as, Arthur Gray's sentiment:

> *O, merry, bubbling, berry, bean!*
> *Thou consort of the kitchen queen—*
> *Browned and ground of every feature*
> *The only aromatic creature*
> *For which we long, for which we feel*
> *The breath of morn, the perfumed meal. . . .*

COFFEE-FLAVORED COLD SOUFFLÉ

1½ cups strong coffee
½ cup milk
1 envelope plain gelatin
¼ cup cold water
3 eggs
⅔ cup sugar
¼ teaspoon salt
½ teaspoon vanilla extract
½ cup heavy cream,
    whipped
Cubes of plain coffee jelly

Scald coffee and milk in top of double boiler. Sprinkle gelatin on cold water; let stand for five minutes and dissolve in hot coffee mixture. Beat egg yolks in a mixing bowl, adding 1 tablespoon sugar and the salt while beating. Add hot coffee mixture slowly to egg yolks. Return to double boiler; stir over hot, not boiling, water, until mixture coats spoon. Let cool. Chill until consistency of unbeaten egg white. Beat egg whites stiff and beat in remaining sugar and vanilla; fold into coffee mixture. Fold in whipped cream. Turn into mold and chill until set. Unmold; garnish with whipped cream and cubes of plain coffee jelly. Makes 6 servings.

COFFEE DESSERT RING

1¼ cups all-purpose flour,
    sifted
1 cup sugar
1 teaspoon instant-coffee
    powder
½ cup powdered cocoa
¼ teaspoon powdered
    cinnamon
1 teaspoon baking powder
½ teaspoon baking soda
1 teaspoon salt
⅓ cup shortening
2 eggs
½ cup milk
¼ cup freshly brewed coffee
1 teaspoon sherry
2 teaspoons vinegar
½ cup chopped seedless
    raisins
½ cup coarsely chopped
    pecans

Set oven for moderate (350° F.). Grease and flour a 2-quart ring mold. Sift flour, sugar, instant-coffee powder, cocoa, cinnamon, baking powder, soda and salt into mixing bowl. Add shortening, eggs and ¼ cup milk. Beat with electric mixer at medium speed for 2 minutes or vigorously by hand. Scrape sides and bottom of bowl frequently. Add remaining milk and the coffee, sherry and vinegar. Beat 1 minute more. Stir in raisins and nuts by hand. Pour into prepared pan. Bake for 25 minutes or until done, when cake tester deeply inserted comes out clean. Remove to cooling rack, let stand a minute or so; then turn out on rack to cool. Fill center with coffee ice cream. Serve with coffee sauce. Makes 10 or more servings.

COFFEE, RICE AND RAISIN PUDDING

1 package precooked rice
Regular-strength coffee
½ cup golden raisins
½ cup brown sugar, packed
⅛ teaspoon salt
⅛ teaspoon grated nutmeg
1 cup heavy cream, whipped
½ cup chopped pistachio
    nuts

Prepare precooked rice according to package directions, using coffee instead of water. Stir in remaining ingredients except cream and nuts. Mix well. Let cool. Fold in whipped cream, reserving enough for garnishing. Spoon into dessert dishes. Top with remaining whipped cream and chopped nuts. Makes 6 servings.

FROZEN MOCHA PUDDING
WITH MOCHA CUSTARD SAUCE

½ pound semisweet
    chocolate
2 tablespoons cold, strong
    coffee
½ pound butter
4 egg yolks

Melt the chocolate in the top of a double boiler over hot water; add the cold coffee and stir constantly. When melted and blended, remove from heat; add butter, a little at a time, stirring well. Beat egg yolks until light and lemon colored, stir slowly into chocolate mixture. Pour into buttered fancy mold. Cover mold with waxed paper held in place by rubber band or dabs of gummed tape. Let chill 12 hours. To serve, remove waxed paper and wrap mold in Turkish towel wrung out of very hot water. Let stand about 2 minutes. Cover mold with serving platter, turn mold and platter upside down, and remove mold. Serve with Mocha Custard Sauce. Makes 6 or more servings.

MOCHA CUSTARD SAUCE

3 cups milk
6 tablespoons granulated
    sugar
1 cup strong, freshly brewed
    coffee
6 eggs
1 teaspoon sherry or vanilla
    extract

Heat milk and sugar in top of double boiler. Add coffee and stir well. Beat eggs thoroughly, add a little of the coffee mixture to the eggs, mix; then stir the eggs into the rest of the coffee mixture in the double boiler. Stir constantly and cook over hot water until custard coats the spoon. Remove at once from heat. Let cool. Add I teaspoon sherry or vanilla, chill. Serve on Frozen Mocha Pudding. Makes 6 or more servings.

This is also a wonderful sauce for sponge or angel cake and for chocolate cake and warm gingerbread.

COFFEE CHIFFON PIE

1 envelope unflavored
    gelatin
1¾ cups strong coffee
1 cup sugar
½ teaspoon salt
1 cup heavy cream
3 eggs
1 teaspoon vanilla extract
¼ teaspoon cream of tartar
1 9-inch, baked piecrust
Instant-coffee powder

Soften gelatin in ¼ cup cold coffee. Combine ½ cup sugar, salt, remaining coffee and ½ cup cream in saucepan. Stir over low heat until scalding point is reached. Beat egg yolks slowly adding hot mixture. Return to saucepan and stir over low heat until boiling point is reached. Stir in softened gelatin. Remove from heat. Chill until partially set; then beat until smooth. Add vanilla. Whip remaining ½ cup cream and fold in. Beat egg whites until they form soft peaks; add cream of tartar. Add remaining ½ cup sugar slowly, beating well after each addition. Fold coffee mixture carefully into this meringue. Spoon into pie shell. Garnish with a light sprinkling of powdered coffee. Makes 6 servings.

In place of vanilla, use cognac or rum and this becomes Coffee Eggnog Pie.

COFFEE CHIFFON CAKE SQUARES

2 eggs	½ cup milk
1½ cups sugar	½ cup strong cold coffee
2 cups all-purpose flour, sifted	⅛ teaspoon soda
	⅓ cup cooking oil
3 teaspoons baking powder	2 teaspoons vanilla extract
1 teaspoon salt	French Coffee Frosting

Start oven at moderate (350° F.). Grease and flour 2 9-inch-square baking pans. Beat egg whites until frothy, gradually beat in ½ cup sugar and continue beating until stiff and glossy. Sift remaining sugar with the flour, baking powder and salt 3 times into another mixing bowl. Combine milk, coffee and baking soda. Pour oil into the flour mixture; beat; add half the coffee mixture and the vanilla. Beat for 1 minute at medium speed in electric mixer or 150 strokes by hand. Scrape sides and bottom of bowl constantly. Add remaining coffee mixture and slightly beaten egg yolks. Beat 1 minute longer, scraping bowl constantly. Fold in egg-white mixture lightly but thoroughly. Pour into prepared pans. Bake for 30 to 35 minutes, or until cake tester inserted deeply comes out clean. Remove pans from oven and let stand for 2 or 3 minutes; then remove cake from pans and let cool on cake rack. Place on serving platters and ice generously with French Coffee Frosting. Makes 32 2-inch squares or 20 larger pieces. A superb cake for buffet suppers.

FRENCH COFFEE FROSTING

1½ cups butter	1 teaspoon coffee essence
1 cup granulated sugar	½ teaspoon vanilla extract
½ teaspoon salt	2 eggs
¼ cup cold coffee	

Combine butter, sugar, salt, cold coffee, coffee essence, vanilla, eggs in the bowl of an electric mixer; beat at a high speed until smooth and fluffy or beat by hand with a rotary beater for 10 minutes. Spread on Coffee Chiffon Squares. Makes about 3 cups frosting.

FLUFFY COFFEE AND CHOCOLATE GINGERBREAD

1 cup hot coffee	1 teaspoon powdered cinnamon
⅓ cup shortening	
1 cup molasses	1 teaspoon powdered ginger
½ cup sugar	1 teaspoon powdered allspice
1 beaten egg	½ cup miniature marshmallows
2¾ cups all-purpose flour, sifted	
1 teaspoon baking soda	½ cup semisweet chocolate pieces
⅛ teaspoon salt	

Start oven at moderate (325° F.). Grease 8-inch-square pan. Add hot coffee to shortening and stir until shortening melts. Add molasses and sugar, stirring until sugar dissolves. Add beaten egg. Mix and sift flour, baking soda, salt and spices together; add marshmallows and chocolate pieces. Add to molasses mixture. Bake about 1 hour. Cut into 9 squares to serve.

FROZEN COFFEE MOUSSE

3 egg yolks	⅔ cup strong, cold coffee
⅓ cup light-brown sugar, packed	1 cup heavy cream, whipped
	½ cup chopped pistachio nuts
Few grains salt	

Beat egg yolks until thick and lemon colored. Beat in sugar. Add salt and coffee. Cook over hot water, stirring until mixture coats spoon. Let cool. Fold in whipped cream. Line muffin pans, 2½-inches in diameter, with fluted paper cups. Fill with coffee-cream mixture. Sprinkle with chopped nuts and freeze. Remove paper cups and serve mousse with chocolate sauce, if desired. Makes 8 servings.

MERINGUE RING WITH COFFEE ICE CREAM AND COFFEE SAUCE

4 egg whites	Coffee ice cream
½ teaspoon cornstarch	¼ cup sliced toasted almonds
¼ teaspoon salt	
1 teaspoon vanilla extract	Coffee Sauce for Meringue
1 cup light corn sirup	

Start oven at slow (250° F.). Cover baking sheet with heavy unglazed paper. Beat egg whites, cornstarch, salt and vanilla with rotary beater until stiff. Add corn sirup, a very little at a time, beating continually. Beat until peaks form. Shape with spoon into a ring on the baking sheet. Bake for 50 minutes. Remove pan from oven; let stand for 5 minutes. Remove meringue from paper, with thin sharp knife, to a round serving platter. Fill center with coffee ice cream; sprinkle with almonds and serve with Coffee Sauce. Makes 6 servings.

COFFEE SAUCE FOR MERINGUE

2 eggs, slightly beaten	2 tablespoons finely chopped toasted almonds
¼ cup light-brown sugar, packed	
	½ cup heavy cream, whipped
⅛ teaspoon salt	
½ cup freshly brewed coffee	

Combine eggs, sugar, salt and coffee in the top of a double boiler. Cook over hot water until smooth and thick. Let cool. To serve, fold in almonds and whipped cream. Makes about 2 cups sauce.

COFFEE CRÊPES

2 cups pancake ready-mix	1 cup light cream
1 cup strongly-brewed cold coffee	Fresh or candied orange peel

Measure pancake ready-mix into mixing bowl. Combine coffee and cream; add slowly. Mix and bake on hot, greased griddle until pancakes are golden brown underneath and bubbles on top have set. Turn and brown on other side. Serve with a chocolate sauce or softened vanilla ice cream. Makes enough for 6 servings.

Prince of Brandies / *Paul E. Deutschman*

The intriguing story of the discovery and the making of cognac

IT ALWAYS comes as a great shock when you stop and consider the snobbism and self-consciousness connected with the serving and consuming of the simple aromatic French liquor known as cognac. I know this from my own experience.

Until recently, almost the sum total of my cognac knowledge was that it was a kind of brandy mysteriously labeled "V.S.O.P.," "Three-Star," "V.O." and so on; that St. Bernard dogs served it in small barrels to travelers lost in the Swiss Alps; affluent clubmen sipped it between puffs on rich cigars, while contemplating the masses toiling underneath their windows; and the sexes parted momentarily after dinner parties to huddle ritualistically over scant portions of it— breathing and sniffing before imbibing, like neophytes before a cold and unco-operative holy flame.

Whenever I drank any of the precious stuff I could never rightly enjoy its fragrance and heady taste because, usually, there were some steely-eyed, self-styled cognac *cognoscenti* lurking at my elbow, watching to see if I inhaled when I should have exhaled or twirled it counterclockwise instead of clockwise.

That was before I visited the Charente, on the usually bypassed French west coast. This is one of two provinces (the other is neighboring Charente-Maritime) whose brandy is permitted to be called "cognac."

Roughly twice the size of Rhode Island, the Charente has undulating hills, moist salt air, very special chalky soil and bright diffused sunlight. It is bisected by one of the world's sweetest rivers—the Charente—whose soft green banks seem to melt before your eyes. Also, it has a town called "Cognac" —with musty ramparts and towers tucked behind ancient walls that were battled over for several blood-mingling centuries by English and French troops, and which are now the warehouses of many of the great brandy names.

The only giveaway that anything unusual is happening within these otherwise inconspicuous buildings is the tiny, black spots (actually, a species of mushroom) that freckle their walls. This means there's brandy aging inside. There was no way of hiding this evidence from the German Occupation authorities during World War II, nor can it be hidden today from tax collectors or supervisors at the *Bureau National du Cognac*.

It is here, in Cognac, that you first begin to realize that this is not just a pensive drink for old folks tottering in their armchairs—but a lusty, democratic drink of soil and sun.

My education began at the *Bureau National*. A man there told of the happy, accidental birth of cognac, which sounds like something from Charles Lamb's *Dissertation on Roast Pig*.

In the Middle Ages, fleets from Britain, Scandinavia and Holland came to the banks of the Charente River to load up with salt, fish and wood. The sailors developed a taste for the local wine. Not a great wine; it was a bit too cloudy and dry and acidy. But it sufficed for their northern tastes. So, soon they were loading barrels of "Saintonge" wine to carry home. Thus the great wine fleets began to grow.

But then there were wars; and large levies of taxes on both ends. And, in the early 1700's, an anonymous genius came along with the idea of distilling the wine, to decrease its bulk; and thereby, the taxes. "Let the foreigners add their own water," he said. An *eau de vie* ("water of life") resulted— powerful, clear and fragrant; this was peddled as "*Brandvin*"

Depending on mood or need of the moment, cognac is the ▶ "distilled gleams of the dawn," or a lusty, democratic drink. Here a snifter of Courvoisier, V.S.O.P., gleams headily in Steuben crystal.

ARNOLD NEWMAN

("burnt wine"—referring to the heat of distillation) in Scandinavia, and "brand wine" in Britain. And, eventually, "brandy." Not all this "brand wine" could be sold immediately. The surplus was stored, in barrels of white oak, from the nearby forests of Limousin.

Years passed. Then they opened one of the moldering casks. Inside was not the previous colorless brandy—but, instead, a deep-burnished, amber liquor of fire and fragrance, golden to throat and head. Somehow, "aging" had taken place—with the softness and aroma of this accidental wood worked into the brandy. This, then, became cognac brandy.

Then more foreigners—English, Irish and Norwegians mostly—settled here and began sending casks of cognac to friends at home. But with cognac each year's yield differs from the previous one. Thus, they began blending cognacs from various parts of the province, to achieve the original taste. And this is how the brands you taste today came into being.

"This accidental method," the *Bureau National* man said, "is the one still used—as you will see."

Next stop was a vineyard, a few miles beyond town. Most of the slopes and hills of the Charente are fleeced over with vines (but never the flatlands, where spring frosts can nip the goodness from the grapes). To the farmer, the grapevines are everything. He smirks not a bit when he hears his aging, ambering brandy referred to by the regional poets as "distilled gleams of the dawn," "gold of the Charente," "father and begetter of life," and so on.

This was summer and there were thick, forked clusters of *Colombars*, and *Folle Blanche*, also long, tight-packed *St. Emilions*—all golden-green. No other grapes can be used. They have a peculiar, tart flavor that—with the distilling, aging and praying over that follow—makes cognac brandy. Come October, the grapes will be clipped and loaded into hoppers. The women will wear the traditional, wrap-around harvesttime bonnet—the "*quichenotte*"—as protection against the sun. In the old days, it also protected against occupying English soldiers; the name is a French carry-over of the English term "kiss-not."

These vines were in the *Grande Champagne* region. This has nothing to do with the wine of similar name. "Champagne" means "chalkiness"; it's the chalk in the soil that gives the wine its name. Also, it is the relative amount of chalk in the soil here in the Charente that determines the value of the grapes and the resulting cognac. There's a terrible fatality about it all—or, security—depending on how you see it. More than 70,000 growers and 138,863 acres here are devoted to cognac-destined grapes (new planting is prohibited by law). Come war, fire or high water, the grapes from a certain specified area (or the wine or brandy resulting therefrom) will have a certain relative market value forever after.

This area was set off over seventy years ago by a science professor from the University of Besançon. For twenty-five years (starting as a hobby and continuing by government grant) he studied the soils of the two Charentes; and he drew a map that settled forever exactly which sections could grow grapes for cognac.

There are seven territorial districts, or *crus*, of grapes. In ascending order of importance, they are: *Bois Communs*, *Bois Ordinaires*, *Bons Bois*, *Fins Bois*, *Borderies*, *Petite Champagne* and *Grande Champagne* (the latter lying in a tiny, golden heartland largely between Cognac and Jarnac, the province's two most important towns). So precisely are these gradations worked out, that a farm across the road from yours may well be in a different brandy district. And each of the *crus* brings a brandy that imparts a specific quality to the

carefully computed blends—mellowness, heaviness or lightness, quick or slow aging, and so on. Even within a single *cru*, there are significant variations in the individual brandies. (A warning: when you see a bottle marked *Fine Champagne*, that doesn't mean what it sounds like in English—but rather that all the constituent brandies come from the two *Champagne* districts, *Grande* and *Petite*; which can be confusing to the uninitiated.)

The farmer ferments his own wine. And, since he is one of the 7000 or more *bouilleurs de cru* (those whom the government permits to distill), he distills it himself—generally selling part of the resulting *eau de vie* to a *négociant*, and casking the remainder to be played against future markets. Other farmers may distill through vintners' co-operatives; of which there are ninety-three; or sell their entire wine crop to one of the 227 professional distillers, who sells it in turn to a *négociant*.

Next morning I visited a distillery. The *patron*, a weather-beaten, retired sea captain, led me into a long, stone-walled building busy with huge stone furnaces and alembics (large, shiny copper vessels resembling outsize samovars) all linked together with spirals of copper tubing known as *serpentines*.

You could spend a lifetime trying to decipher the intricacies of the distilling. Basically, the process is exactly that used in the 17th century. Any deviations here (or elsewhere along the carefully toed line) and the product cannot be called "cognac." That is the law.

A vintner, the captain said, gets twenty to twenty-five barrels of wine per acre, each barrel holding seventy-two gallons. Of this, only between one-tenth and one-seventh emerges at the distilling end. And this is only the beginning of the "loss."

All through the winter months, the careful heatings, coolings and condensings take place—slowly, incessantly—with the "ardent soul of the wine" coming out of the still, drop by precious drop. There's the first heating, with the wine converted into raging steam. It is then passed through pipes immersed in cold water at exactly the right temperature, otherwise too much would be lost by evaporation. This first liquid, colorless and surprisingly powerful, is called "*brouillis*."

Then the second heating ("*la bonne chauffe*"), with the *brouillis* resteamed and, over a period of nine crucial hours, condensing into what the French call *eau de vie*.

There's a great art involved here, in deciding just what part of the *eau* goes into the casks for cognac. A first small amount, called the "head," is cast aside—it's too potent. Only the "heart" is permitted to drip through. But the "heart" cannot run too long; otherwise the cognac would end up weak. The distiller must, therefore, taste, smell and fondle his liquor continuously—until he "feels" an alcoholic content of 57 or 58 per cent is reached. Then he cuts the flow, casting off the "tail." This gives a uniform product that averages out to 70 per cent. But weep not for these cast-off portions of the "ardent soul"—they'll be put through with later distillations.

You don't leave anywhere in the Charente without a little *dégustation* (tasting). The old captain offered me a glass of fine, newly distilled *eau de vie*. This turned out to be almost pure, tongue-searing alcohol.

"Go ahead, spit it out!" he laughed. "I wished only for you to taste it. One can develop the *goût*, you know." To prove his point, he gulped down a glassful himself and smacked his lips over it.

Then, to make amends, he drew some private-stock cognac from a cask in the corner. This, apparently, had all the desired cognac qualities: "delicate bouquet," "velvety taste" and "original youthful fire tempered to the firm strength of maturity." But its fire was almost nonexistent compared with the previous conflagration. I sniffed and sipped with appreciation, offered thanks, and was on my way.

Now the really serious *dégustation* began—with visits to the hospitable cognac firms. There are over 160 of these *négociants* that tend, blend, bottle and peddle their individual brands all over the world.

The Cognacers themselves—the men who run these firms —make up an international society. They're all French citizens, of course; but a great many are of foreign extraction. The *Charentais* peasants take special cognizance of this by dividing all *étrangers* (foreigners) into two classes: "*étrangers d'ici*" ("foreigners from here")—meaning the Irish-originated proprietors of the House of Hennessy, the Scottish Otards, the English Martells, Hines and Remy Martins, the Norwegians who run Courvoisier, the German Meukows, and the others whose families came to the Charente anywhere up to 250 years ago—and "*étrangers qui ne sont pas d'ici*" ("foreigners who aren't from here").

As lads, they go traditionally to Oxford or Harvard and then are sent across the wide world to serve apprenticeships with their *papas'* distributors. Back in Charente, they maintain private golf, tennis and flying clubs to vary the slow-moving pattern of village life. Also, they make dozens of sales trips a year to Singapore, Caracas, New York, Jo'burg and the rest—it's not unusual for two rival Cognacers to meet in some Istanbul night club, or peddling their wares from opposite directions across the Finnish snows. (Finland, oddly, is the world's number-five cognac-consuming country, after France, England, U.S., and Sweden—and just before the Malay States.)

Everybody in the Charente is mixed up in the cognac business. As a result, an exceedingly high brand consciousness exists everywhere in the provinces. A story is told of a young Charente peasant newly inducted into the army. He was standing guard one dark night when a general approached. The young man did not salute.

"*Soldat!*" the brass hat barked. "Do you not know who I am?"

"No, *M'sieur*," the lad said.

"Do you not see my three stars?"

The soldier peered. "Oh, *pardonnez-moi!*" he stammered. "I did not recognize you in the dark, *M'sieur* Hennessy!"

My first *négociant* was Hennessy's. There, I was met by James Hennessy, lank of jaw and limb and looking very British (the other Hennessys still bear names like Patrick and Kilian). He asked me to put out my cigarette. There have been no fires in the Charente *chais* in any man's memory, but there easily could be—with all this liquid gold going up into instantaneous ruin; all *négociants* scatter their warehouses, and many even refuse to install electric wiring. I followed him into a large stone building that was steeped with a dank, heady aroma of aging cognac.

We climbed an upper floor, to a kind of ship's runway. Underfoot, there were huge 5000-gallon wooden vats, within which the cognac was blended by being softly agitated with large wooden paddles. Young Hennessy ran his hand over a khaki, blanketlike material stretched tight over the manhole cover of one of the vats. "This is a filter," he said. "We filter every chance we have; it takes certain things out. But we can't filter too brutally. We've tried all kinds of new-fangled means, but it always 'breaks' the brandy. So, we have to stick to the old tried-and-true."

We passed through acres of warehouses, with hundreds upon hundreds of casks sitting around in seeming disarray. "The whole process of cognac making is completely inefficient and idiotic," he went on. "But it works—so we can't be too scientific about it. Nature runs the show. For example, the casks are of oak, only from the Limousin area; the wood must be cut and left to weather outdoors for four years, then shaped by hand over slow fires. Otherwise, no cognac! And no nails can be used. The slightest bit of iron in contact with the brandy would blacken it and give it an 'off' taste."

It's the tannic acid contained in this Limousin oak, you learn, that "ages" the brandy. Through the years, this is gradually "pulled out," giving the reposing liquor its ultimate rich, wonderful, chestnut hue. It's the continuous evaporation, a kind of "breathing" through oaken pores, that gives the deep, concentrated strength.

This evaporation, the constant loss of cognac in volume and alcoholic content, staggers one. Every day in the Charente district the equivalent of 25,000 bottles disappears into thin air.

Evaporation makes it necessary to keep filling and transferring the cognac from cask to cask, which leads to more evaporation. "Let's say you have eighty barrels of Joe Blow's 1947 brandy," Hennessy said. "Well, after a while, the barrels are only about two-thirds full. And we've learned that when there's too little brandy in a barrel it spoils. So we have to juggle them about—to get full barrels. That leaves us with perhaps fifty or sixty barrels of Joe Blow '47. Furthermore, every time you move a barrel the least bit, more brandy evaporates! You have to think years ahead in order to have enough of each individual brandy to go into your blends. Why, some of our blends take as many as two hundred individual 'straights.'"

We went up another set of winding stairs, reaching a glass-enclosed platform that resembled an airport control tower. Here, an intricate switchboard of silver-lined copper pipes was funneling the various blends down to a large, bustling room below, where white-coated men and women were bottling, labeling and crating the cognac.

This seemed the only place where modern, assemblyline methods were used. There was even a machine to rinse each bottle—with *cognac*, not water—before it was filled; this, to remove all alien tastes.

After that, suddenly, we were in "Paradise."

This turned out to be a small back room containing bottles and glass decanters of the firm's best blends and straights. There, we jointly sampled three different cognacs. (All the Cognacers, you learn very quickly, have a fairly strong *goût* for their own product.)

That afternoon, I moved a few hundred yards farther along the inclined banks of the idyllic, unmoving river to the House of Martell which, together with Hennessy, controls almost 60 per cent of all cognac business. There, young Charles Martell showed me through his father's *chais*, which weren't too different from those at Hennessy's. Martell, incidentally, wore an American-style pin-stripe suit, rimless eyeglasses, a button-down shirt and a Madison Avenue tie—though his father's company has its number-one market in England. (Young Hennessy wears heathery English tweeds and flannels, and his father's company has its number-one market in America.)

At the end of the two-hour tour, we reached a small, luxuriously oak-paneled room. There, a uniformed attendant was magically waiting for us with a trayful of assorted Martell cognacs. Every *négociant*, it seemed, has his own private Paradise; and every visit to every *chais* inevitably ends up there. As a result of this important discovery, I found myself visiting probably more *chais* than I actually had to. But, between one Paradise and the next, I learned some important things about cognac.

At Albert Robin (with markets mostly in Canada and Colombia), I learned why cognac must be transferred from wooden casks to glass decanters or bottles.

"It is a matter of aging," I was told. "The cellar master must decide when a brandy reaches its peak of aging. There's no fixed rule about this. Sometimes, full aging takes twenty years; sometimes as long as eighty. It depends on many factors—such as the actual amount of tannin contained in the wood or whether the cellar is dry or damp. But as soon as this peak is reached, we move the cognac into glass. Unlike wine, cognac doesn't age in glass. So, when someone shows you an 'old' bottle of brandy that he says was bottled back in Napoleon's day—it means nothing! Ask him how old the brandy was *before* it was bottled—that's the important thing!"

At the ancient, two-turreted castle of François Premier, headquarters of the House of Otard, they cleared up for me the mysteries of cognac nomenclature: "V.S.O.P." which stands for the words, in English, "Very Superior Old Pale" (going back to the days when both "brown" and "pale" brandy were sold, the former, heavily colored with burnt sugar); "V.O." ("Very Old"); "V.V.S.O.P." ("Very Very Superior Old Pale") and all the other names which the imaginative *négociants* give their blends.

Barnett & Elichagaray is a small house steeped in antiquity. "Here, *M'sieur*, we keep the old ways. We treat our brandy like a beautiful woman—gently." I was introduced as "*Monsieur Holiday*" to a wizened old man who demonstrated the proper drinking of cognac.

He filled some glasses. "Notice, we are using these medium-sized tulip glasses—not those fat balloon ones. Balloons are too big to warm with your hands; and cognac, to be given full justice, must be brought to body temperature. Also, the balloons have very small mouths and they tend to concentrate the aroma too much."

Then he held his glass between his palms, like a praying mantis with some especially toothsome twig. It was only half full "so that the vapor will mix with the air inside the glass before coming up to you." He twirled it slowly. "This brings out the bouquet to fullest flavor." I followed his lead —sniffing the warmed, amber richness and sipping tenderly.

"Now, we will make a little experiment." He signaled the khaki-aproned cellar master, who ceremoniously uncorked two decanters and poured out four glasses. "These are old brandies—not blends, but straights. This one is from 1875 and the other from 1848. We have very little of each left. Tell me what you think of them."

I went through the warming, sniffing and imbibing of each cognac. Both tasted wonderful—but in different ways.

"Now, which do you think is better?" he asked slyly.

"The '75," I said casually, figuring he expected me to say the *older* one was better.

"Ah!" He smiled happily, all the accumulated cognac wisdom of the Charente suddenly lighting his worn old face. "The '48 is better! The other, you will notice, has a more 'wooden' taste. That's because, despite its lesser years, it has aged more rapidly than the older one. Taste it again—can't you feel the difference?"

I tasted the poor old "wooden" brandy again. It still tasted

pretty wonderful to me. So did the other—which I finished in its own turn.

At the House of Hine, I learned about the function of the "taster"—the man who buys the cognac at its various stages and ages and also works out the intricate proportions of the various blends.

François Hine, a bulky, brush-mustached man with the most colonial-British of accents, met me in his "tasting room," which resembled a chemical laboratory.

Right away, Monsieur Hine began to deflate any preconceptions I might have had about the so-called "great noses."

"The story of the man who can put a glass of brandy under his nose," he said, "and tell you where it comes from, who distilled and fermented it, the date it was casked, and so on is, *au fond*, a great deal of nonsense. Perhaps it's true of wine—but cognac is much more difficult to identify.

"Of course, some men are very clever, but to play safe, we have to taste against our samples. Every year, we stock up a new supply of samples of the various brandies, covering the complete range of brandy qualities."

A taster works in the morning, after a very light breakfast. He swishes the fumes about the glass, sniffs deeply, then touches a few drops to the tip of his tongue but never swallows—a man may test some dozen brandies of a morning, and a tipsy taster, of course, could ruin a cognac company. Some tasters take their art so seriously that they avoid tobacco completely—except possibly a single cigar (but never cigarettes) in an evening. They take no strong spices or condiments at weekday meals. (Incidentally, during the time I spent here, I never once saw anybody dip a cigar into his brandy—as so many self-styled *bons vivants* at home delight in doing.)

"Besides looking for the proper flavor, bouquet and strength in buying a new brandy," Monsieur Hine continued, "we have to watch out for a copper taste, coming from certain impurities 'fixed' by copper urns that need cleaning; or a black color, from iron coming into contact with the brandy; also, for evidences of a faulty distillation that removes too little, or perhaps too much, of the sediment.

"Truthfully, we hate to buy brandy anywhere but in our own rooms, tasting out of our own glasses and with our own samples to compare against.

"Even the color of this room is no accident. A light blue background is better to judge a brandy's color against than pure white. Also, we often use dark-blue tasting glasses. That's because—whether you want to or not—you're often very much influenced by your eyes. Sometimes my brother and I have an argument about a brandy. One of us may say: 'It's much *younger* than the other one!'; or 'much more *this*' or 'much more *that*—can't you see?' As soon as that happens, we put the brandy in those dark blue glasses and do some blind tasting.

"And, now," Mr. Hine said, "suppose we do a little tasting ourselves?"

A visitor learns to take these trips to Paradise plus the peripheral imbibing as a matter of delightful course. But there's a great danger—if you concentrate too many visits into too short a time.

I learned this at Jarnac—an aromatic town wrinkled with age. I arrived there around 10 A.M., with a full day's visiting lined up. Over the bridge, the soft, green-draped river was straddled by the warehouses of the six or eight cognac firms headquartered here.

First, there was the aforementioned visit to Mr. Hine's Paradise. Then, lunch with Mr. Hine and Mr. Courvoisier (whose real name is Christian Braasted, Norwegian-born), featuring Martinis beforehand and five bottles of wine (for four of us) during the meal. Afterward, Mr. Hine ceremoniously ordered a glass of Courvoisier, while Mr. Courvoisier countered with a glass of Hine (the Cognacers are *friendly* rivals). As an impartial outsider, I had to have one of each.

Then came a visit to Mr. Courvoisier's *chais*—with en-route tasting plus sampling of the special goodies in *his* Paradise. By now I walked slowly along the riverbank, watching the teetotaling fish cavorting happily within. Too soon I was at the House of Bisquit (pronounced *Bis-kwee*), where Mr. "Bisquit," a dapper, thin-faced gentleman whose name I never caught, was waiting. A daughter of one of the other directors was there with her husband, and her brother-in-law from Mexico City. The daughter, of course, knew all about cognac—but the brother-in-law had never been through a *chais* before. We all embarked on our tour together.

Everything went along swimmingly—but because we were considered visiting royalty, we had to sip every single stage of cognac en route. Then we proceeded to the Bisquit Paradise, where several more prized brandies were sampled.

The visit over, I began to head warily for the exit. But Mr. Bisquit intercepted me. "I would be honored," he said, "if you would join us for a little drink." He led me back into the main office and into a private room with a long table. Everyone else was already seated there, and pretty soon an attendant came in with a bucket of iced champagne. We had two glasses apiece.

Early that evening, I sat in a café in front of the main square of Cognac. It was the promenade hour and practically all 16,000 inhabitants seemed to be parading back and forth around the statue of François Premier. But this is a very quiet town and there isn't much to do of an evening. I'd played Ping-pong the night before and seen both movies the previous nights. So I sat there and watched the pretty girls promenading back to their homes, and the clean-cut boys in French Air Force uniforms (there's a base nearby) watching the pretty girls. And, to pass the time, had a couple of cognacs-and-soda.

Later, at dinner, I had the table d'hôte meal at the town's one good restaurant. And a bottle of wine came with the meal. So I drank that. And, after dinner, there was nothing more to do but sit around the hotel room, drinking cognac. The label on the bottle said: "*Bureau National du Cognac*" —so I couldn't tell which brand it was. But there was nothing to worry about—for, by now, I could twirl the tulip glass, sniff the delicate aroma and sip the heady, aromatic and oh-so-highly-alcoholic "liquid gold of the Charente" with the best of them.

BRANDY REFRIGERATOR CAKE

2 cups boiled custard, cooled	⅔ cup heavy cream
1 pound ladyfingers	¼ cup blanched and
1 cup cognac	shredded toasted
1 teaspoon vanilla extract	almonds

Make custard and let it cool. Line 12-inch spring-form cake pan with waxed paper and butter the paper. Cover bottom evenly and fully with ladyfingers. Place ladyfingers upright in ring around edge of cake. Pour ¼ cup brandy over the fingers a few drops at a time so cake absorbs the liquid. Cover the saturated cakes with a layer about ½-inch deep of custard. Add another thick layer of ladyfingers. Dribble over them ¼ cup cognac. Cover with the rest of the custard; then cover custard with ladyfingers. Dribble brandy over ladyfingers. Place in refrigerator, cover with waxed paper and chill for several hours. To serve, remove cake from pan, tear paper off and slide cake onto serving platter. Whip cream slightly; add vanilla and a few drops of cognac and continue whipping until stiff. Swirl cream over the top of the cake with a spatula; scatter the almonds over the cream. Makes 10 or more servings.

DESSERT OMELET AU COGNAC

6 eggs	3 tablespoons butter
⅛ teaspoon salt	2 tablespoons sugar
½ cup cognac	Shaker of powdered sugar

Break eggs into a bowl, add salt and beat slightly. Add cognac, a few drops at a time, until ¼ cup has been combined with the beaten eggs. Pour into the hot melted butter in an omelet pan. Stir round once or twice with a fork; then let cook slowly. Shake pan frequently. When the omelet is done, lightly browned on the bottom and the top set, fold over with a spatula and slip omelet onto a warm plate. Quickly combine the 2 tablespoons of sugar and the remaining ¼ cup cognac, pour over the omelet and set alight. Carry to the table. Makes 2 or more servings. Some tastes call for a dash of powdered sugar on the omelet after the flame dies down.

LONDON BRANDY SILLABUB

1 cup heavy cream	¼ cup cognac
2 teaspoons lemon juice	6 to 8 small pieces candied
¼ cup granulated sugar	ginger

Whip cream until stiff; fold in lemon juice and sugar; add brandy gradually, beating continually. Pile mixture into 6 or 8 tall dessert glasses. Place on a tray in the refrigerator; cover with waxed paper and chill. The brandy separates out and settles to the bottom of the glass, the cream remains firmly on top. Decorate with a piece of candied ginger. Makes 6 to 8 servings.

WARM BRANDY SAUCE

1 cup sugar	2 or 3 tablespoons chopped
1 cup butter	almonds or pistachios
1 cup light cream	½ cup cognac

Cream sugar and butter together smoothly; stir into cream in top part of double boiler over hot water. Stir until fluffy and light. Stir in nuts; add brandy a few drops at a time, beating slowly. Serve warm over various desserts. Makes about 3½ cups sauce.

American Wines / Frank Schoonmaker

Have you discovered how good our wines can be?
Here's the way you can spot the best of them and bring new joy to your table

IN EVERY wine-growing country, from Austria to Australia, from Portugal to Peru, the wine that most people drink with their meals is the wine of their native soil. Partly this is a matter of economics—among wines of comparable quality, the local product is almost always cheaper; but other factors are involved as well—tradition, climate and, above all, taste.

For nothing ever seems to taste quite as good with the food of a country as the wine of that country. Vintners naturally tend to make wines that go well with their local dishes. It is not by chance that, with Italian food, no wine is as good as Italian wine; that the more complex French cuisine calls for the greater and subtler wines of France; that with our own bounty, our steaks, turkey and fish, all simply prepared, nothing can beat our own, somewhat simpler, American wines.

Despite what the "wine snobs" may tell us, a good many American wines today can hold up their heads in any company. Imported wines bring interest and variety to our tables, as do caviar and Roquefort cheese, and occasionally they provide memorable delights. But nine tenths of what we drink is American wine and probably always will be.

To enjoy wine and buy it intelligently you don't have to be an expert. But wine is like music: the more you know about it, the more you enjoy it. Learning about wine is fun. The ideal system is to stretch your education over years—drinking wine fairly frequently but not always the same wine, tasting comparatively, especially with interested friends, and then discussing what you have tasted. A basic knowledge of wine (which this article provides) will enable you to avoid obvious pitfalls.

The first and most important thing to learn is this: in both the United States and Europe at least three quarters of the wine produced is . . . well, just wine. Honest, passably good, an agreeable mealtime beverage. The really interesting wines, which are collected and laid away in cellars, which can make a passable meal seem good and transform a good meal into an unforgettable one—these make up a fraction of what vintners sell. This is true both here and abroad.

How, then, can you learn to spot the fine wines, the admirable exceptions, on a retailer's shelf or a restaurant wine list? Is choice a matter of price, and are all excellent wines fabulously expensive? No, they aren't: a good wine isn't necessarily expensive and an expensive wine isn't necessarily good. Most European wine prices are up these days (the result of bad recent vintages and short crops) but American wines, even the very best of them, rarely cost $2 a bottle at retail, champagne excepted.

To buy wisely and well, it is necessary to look for certain hallmarks of quality on a wine label—names, statements, phrases. Once you learn their special language, wine labels can tell you a great deal.

A wine label should tell you, first of all, where the wine comes from—France, Germany, Chile, New York State or California. And if California, just what part of California, for this is important. Fine wine cannot—simply can *not*—be made everywhere. Men have been planting grapes and making wine all over the world since the dawn of history, and in France and Italy grapes have been grown, at one time or another, on almost every farm. But the finest Rhine wines and Burgundies, for example, still come from little zones about two miles by twenty or thirty, and if you were to plant

the same grapes a couple of miles outside these zones, you would get different and inferior wines. It is unlikely that grape growers will find and plant another great wine district, and therefore it is safe to say that in the future our best wines, including our fine American wines, will come from districts we already know.

In the United States today nearly 90 per cent of fine wine produced comes from California—from some seven or eight or nine counties grouped around San Francisco Bay. These are our Bordeaux, Burgundy, Rhine Valley and Chianti country, rolled into one. The remainder of our fine wines comes from the Finger Lakes region of New York State, especially Lakes Keuka and Canandaigua, from Northern Ohio, including the Lake Erie islands, and a few scattered precincts in other states.

The San Francisco Bay counties form the heart of America's real wine land, chiefly because of their excellent climate. The cool waters of San Francisco Bay, with deep estuaries running back into the hills, California's unfailing summer sun tempered by cool winds off the Pacific—these produce growing conditions almost ideally suited to the classic grapes of Europe. Five of these counties are of major importance, and their names ought to be as well known to American wine lovers as such terms as Burgundy, Sauternes and Chablis, which are the names of French towns and provinces and almost entirely meaningless when applied to wines made in the United States, five or six thousand miles away.

California's five major wine counties are as follows, from north to south:

SONOMA

Its cooler southern half is potentially an area of great wine; its northern half produces good, rarely outstanding, red wine.

NAPA

Ranks with Santa Clara for top quality. More than half of the premium wine producers have cellars in Napa—Beaulieu, Inglenook, Louis Martini, Chas. Krug and others. The average quality of Napa's wine is at least as high as the average of Bordeaux.

ALAMEDA

The vineyards are in the Livermore Valley, and the district name is *Livermore*, not Alameda. Livermore produces remarkable whites and a few good reds. Wente, Concannon, Cresta Blanca are the outstanding names.

SANTA CLARA

Produces as fine wines as it seems possible to make in the United States. Almadén has the largest vineyards; others include the Novitiate of Los Gatos, Paul Masson, San Martin, and so forth.

SAN BENITO

Very promising and now being developed, although it has produced a few excellent wines for nearly a century. Almadén has vineyards here.

Districts of secondary importance are *Mendocino*, north of Sonoma, promising for red wines; *Contra Costa*; and *Santa Cruz*, between Santa Clara and the Pacific.

We have seen where some of the fine American wines are made; let's now examine the question of what fine wines are made from. Grapes, obviously. But grapes are not just grapes: out of several thousand varieties of grape, only fifteen to thirty ever produced fine wine or ever will. The others have their uses: they make good grape jelly, excellent raisins; many are delicious table grapes; others provide the raw material for first-rate brandy; and still others (usually those that produce huge crops) are made into cheap wine. But these grapes are as different from fine wine grapes as a dray horse is from a thoroughbred. A producer of fine wine would never bring them to his press.

In attempting to judge a wine by its label it is important, therefore, to determine out of what grape or sort of grape the wine was made. This is easy when one buys an imported bottle. It is far from easy when buying American wines, particularly those sold under the old European place names such as Chablis (which is a French village), Sauternes (another French village), Burgundy (a French province), Rhine (a river largely German) and Chianti (a district in Italy). Abroad, these wine and place names have precise meanings, hallowed by tradition and defined by law. Such names indicate that the wines in bottles bearing them have been made in strictly delimited areas from specific, superior varieties of grape, and only these. Producers who violate the rules are prosecuted, often heavily fined, and sometimes even jailed.

Under our much looser American regulations, something called "Burgundy" may be made anywhere in the United States, out of any grape, and a producer may legally ship any wine he pleases as "Chablis" or "Sauterne." On a bottle of American wine such names mean precisely nothing, for, unhappily, more than 60 per cent of the wine produced in California is not even made out of wine grapes but out of grapes designated as "table" and "raisin" grapes by the U.S. Department of Agriculture and the State of California.

Luckily for us, most American producers of fine wine have chosen a more difficult and honorable road. They tell the consumer the straight story; they put the grape names on the labels and the grape names or varieties become, in effect, the names of the wines. Such wines are known as "varietal wines," and they are America's best.

American wine lovers have been slow to realize the assured quality this system offers. Conditioned to think in terms of European wine, we order American Burgundy or American Chablis when we could gaurantee ourselves a vastly better wine by asking for Pinot Noir (which has to be made from the true grape of red Burgundy) or Pinot Chardonnay (which can come only from the true grape of Chablis). Most premium producers will, and all consumers should, welcome the day when all better American wines carry varietal names.

What are the varietal names to look for? Before listing these, we should mention the basic difference between the wines of California and those of the Eastern States. California wines are made from European grapes, varieties brought over from France, Germany, Spain, Portugal, Italy, Hungary, and planted here; they belong to the grape family *vinifera*, the "wine-bearer"; they are blood brothers to the vines of Europe. Eastern vines are not. They have no more to do with Europe than a full-blooded Indian has. They are direct descendants of the vines the first settlers found in America, but of course they have been vastly improved through selection, cultivation and care. The wines are different too. All of them, from worst to best, have a special, unmistakable bouquet and flavor. The French call this a "foxy" taste; others have described it as a "wild, woodland tang"; it recalls the scent of the wild grapes of New England woods, or the flavor of the Concord—the best-known but by no means the best wine grape of the American family. Whether you like this taste or not is a personal matter, about which many people feel strongly. One thing is certain: the white Eastern wines are better than the reds.

Below is a list of the best California and Eastern winegrape varieties. Since the California varieties give a wine comparable to what they produce in Europe, a European equivalent is listed. This cannot, of course, be done for the Eastern wines.

A wine label that has answered clearly and without equivocation, "Where?" and "What?" has already fulfilled its functions. But there are two other less pressing questions to which it may also provide an answer. Who made the wine, and from the grapes of what year?

When it comes to American wines the more important of these questions is "Who?" Although three million tons of grapes are produced in an average year in California, from 440,000 acres of vineyards, the producers of fine wine are not numerous. At least 90 per cent of America's fine wine originates in the cellars of approximately two dozen vintners. For a wine that really deserves to be called "fine" is never an accident. Even granted the best possible climate and soil, the best possible grape varieties, much more is involved —skill, knowledge, patience, proper equipment, and, above all, discrimination and a desire to make the best wine possible. Fine wine making is a personal, often a family operation, in which tradition and pride play a major role. It is a business in which large corporations have never succeeded, in which no large fortunes have ever been made; it is perhaps less a business than a craft. Here, as in Europe, the best wines come from the cellars of men who have planted and who cultivate their own vineyards, who bottle what they make and are proud to have it carry their names. The majority of the wines included in the check-list are precisely such wines.

Finally, what about the question of "When?"—of vintage years? Here, in dealing with American wines, we are on treacherous ground. A good vintage chart is a useful document, almost a necessity, if one wants to buy French or German wines intelligently. But no one has ever published a vintage chart for California. Why? It can't be done.

A 1953 French Burgundy, for example, is worth more than twice a 1954 from the same vineyard, and it is child's play for a taster to tell them apart. But no expert, faced with a collection of Pinot Noirs from California, could hope to distinguish the 1953's from the 1954's. One California winery's product will be better in 1953 than in 1954, but the neighboring winery, as often as not, will come up with a better wine in 1954 than in 1953. Because of this, no quality producer in California ever offers the wine of any given vintage, despite its merit, for a higher price than the wine of the following year. Though the vintage year on a bottle may distinguish varying wines of a single producer, there has been no vintage year in California over the last twenty years that could be described, across the board, as exceptionally good or bad. As a result, many of the best California producers put no vintage year on their wines.

An older wine is not necessarily a better wine. All wines are improved somewhat by aging, but this process does not go on indefinitely, and may be a matter of months, not years. A *vin rosé* is never as good after its second birthday as it was before; most white wines reach their peak prior to the age of five, and of all California wines, perhaps only the Cabernet Sauvignons and Pinot Noirs are really worth laying away.

It is standard practice among the producers of America's premium wines to hold their wines back; age them in the winery, and put them on the market only when they are ready to drink—any time from eighteen months in the case of a *rosé* to five years in the case of a Cabernet. When you buy a bottle of American wine, you may be sure you can pull the cork.

And happy tasting!

A Check List of Outstanding American Wines

Here, listed by category and then alphabetically, are what experts consider this country's most interesting and best wines. Most of these can be purchased in most states. Since the majority of American wines are still sold under European names (Burgundy, Claret, and so forth), under Burgundy, for example, will be found the wines more or less comparable to French Burgundy. After the vineyard name or producing winery and the name of the wine, the country or district where the grapes were grown is given in parentheses.

RED WINES

Claret-Cabernet—*comparable to the red wines of Bordeaux.*

As a group, these are the finest red wines of the United States. Made from the same grape as the famous château wines of the Medoc, they are closer, in quality and character, to the European "originals" than our Burgundies. They can hold their own against all red Bordeaux except wines from truly outstanding vineyards and great vintage years.

ALMADÉN CABERNET SAUVIGNON (*Santa Clara*)

BEAULIEU VINEYARD CABERNET SAUVIGNON (*Napa*)
INGLENOOK CABERNET SAUVIGNON (*Napa*)
CHARLES KRUG CABERNET SAUVIGNON (*Napa*)
LOUIS MARTINI CABERNET SAUVIGNON (*Napa-Sonoma*)

Other Cabernets, of well above average quality, are produced by many other wineries: Concannon, Beringer, Sebastiani, Weibel, Paul Masson.

Burgundy-Pinot Noir—*comparable to the red wines of Burgundy.*

All have more in common with red Burgundy from France than name; they are made from the Pinot Noir, the true Burgundy grape, and almost always sold under this varietal name. While they can hardly compete with the great, rare, and extremely expensive estate-bottled Burgundies of France, they are on the whole much better than imported Burgundies in the same price bracket.

ALMADÉN PINOT NOIR (*Santa Clara*)
BEAULIEU VINEYARD "BEAUMONT" PINOT NOIR (*Napa*)

BUENA VISTA PINOT NOIR (*Sonoma*)
INGLENOOK PINOT NOIR (*Napa*)
LOUIS MARTINI PINOT NOIR (*Napa-Sonoma*)

Other good-quality Pinot Noirs are made by Sebastiani, Weibel, Paul Masson, and so forth.

Miscellaneous—comparable to Beaujolais, Chianti, and so forth.

This large class includes wines that vary greatly in quality and type. Few, if any, are as good as the Cabernets and Pinot Noirs listed above but many compare favorably with the less expensive red wines of France, Italy and Spain.

PAUL MASSON GAMAY BEAUJOLAIS (*Santa Clara*)
LOUIS MARTINI BARBERA (*Napa*)
BERINGER BROS. GRIGNOLINO (*Napa*)
CRESTA BLANCA CHIANTI SOUVENIR RESERVE (*Livermore*)
LOUIS MARTINI MOUNTAIN ZINFANDEL (*Napa-Sonoma*)

WHITE WINES

Chablis-Pinot—comparable to the white wines of Burgundy.

The superior wines in this category are made from the Pinot Blanc, Chardonnay and "white Pinot" (Pineau de la Loire, or Chenin Blanc), which do well in California. They are generally dry without being acid, pale gold, with good bouquet; they are closer to their European counterparts than are our American Rhine wines and Sauternes. They are white wines of which we can be proud.

ALMADÉN PINOT BLANC (*Santa Clara*)
ALMADÉN PINOT CHARDONNAY (*Santa Clara*)
BEAULIEU VINEYARD PINOT CHARDONNAY (*Napa*)
CHRISTIAN BROTHERS WHITE PINOT (*Napa*)
INGLENOOK WHITE PINOT (*Napa*)
CHAS. KRUG WHITE PINOT (*Napa*)
LOUIS MARTINI PINOT CHARDONNAY (*Napa-Sonoma*)
PAUL MASSON PINOT BLANC (*Santa Clara*)
WEIBEL PINOT CHARDONNAY (*Santa Clara*)
WENTE PINOT BLANC (*Livermore*)
WENTE PINOT CHARDONNAY (*Livermore*)

Rhine Wine-Riesling—comparable to German and Alsatian wines.

All the best wines come from the classic European grape varieties, the Johannisberg Riesling, Traminer and Sylvaner of the Rhine Valley, which, in California, produce drier wines, often more alcoholic and with less pronounced bouquet. These wines certainly cannot match the famous vintages of the Moselle and Rhine, but they are much better than most of what is shipped here as Liebfraumilch.

ALMADÉN JOHANNISBERG RIESLING (*Santa Clara-San Benito*)
ALMADÉN TRAMINER (*Santa Clara-San Benito*)
BEAULIEU VINEYARD "BEAUCLAIR" JOHANNISBERG RIESLING (*Napa*)
BERINGER BROS. RIESLING (*Napa*)
BUENA VISTA JOHANNISBERGER RIESLING (*Sonoma*)
BUENA VISTA SYLVANER (*Sonoma*)
BUENA VITA TRAMINER (*Sonoma*)
INGLENOOK RIESLING (*Napa*)
INGLENOOK TRAMINER (*Napa*)
CHAS. KRUG JOHANNISBERG RIESLING (*Napa*)
CHAS. KRUG TRAMINER (*Napa*)
LOUIS MARTINI JOHANNISBERG RIESLING (*Napa-Sonoma*)
LOUIS MARTINI SYLVANER (*Napa-Sonoma*)
SOUVERAIN CELLARS JOHANNISBERG RIESLING (*Napa*)

Dry Sauterne—Semillon and Sauvignon Blanc—comparable to the dry Graves of Bordeaux.

In France a dry Sauternes (note the final "s," even in the singular) does not exist. All French Sauternes are sweet, and they are all made from grapes of the Semillon and Sauvignon Blanc varieties. In California these grapes generally produce wines even drier than the driest Graves and lower in alcohol; most of the best are sold under the varietal names rather than as Dry Sauterne. They are less good than the best Graves but better than many cheap ones and almost always to be preferred to something labeled simply "Bordeaux Blanc."

ALMADÉN DRY SEMILLON (*Santa Clara*)
CONCANNON SAUVIGNON BLANC (*Livermore*)
CRESTA BLANCA SAUVIGNON BLANC (*Livermore*)
LOUIS MARTINI DRY SEMILLON (*Napa*)
WENTE SAUVIGNON BLANC (*Livermore*)
WENTE DRY SEMILLON (*Livermore*)

Sauterne—Sweet Semillon, and so forth—comparable to Sauternes.

In sweet or semisweet table wines we are surpassed by the French. Ours are honorable and good; theirs, due to special climatic conditions during ripening, are better. The following, from California, are wholly acceptable:

BEAULIEU VINEYARDS CHATEAU BEAULIEU (*Napa*)
CONCANNON SWEET SEMILLON (*Livermore*)
CRESTA BLANCA SWEET SEMILLON (*Livermore*)
CHAS. KRUG CHENIN BLANC (*Napa*)
NOVITIATE OF LOS GATOS CHATEAU (*Santa Clara*)
WENTE SWEET SEMILLON (*Livermore*)

ROSÉ WINES

Vins Rosés—Pink Wines—comparable to Tavel and others.

These pleasant, all-purpose wines belong in a special class. They are properly served chilled but they are made from black grapes, like red wines, and are *NOT*, as some people have imagined, simply blends of red and white wines. Informal, fairly inexpensive, almost never "great," they are best when young and should be drunk before they are three years old. Our American *rosés* are as good as all but a few of the very best from France. Many of ours bear a varietal name—note especially Grenache and, in a somewhat lesser category, Gamay. A few interesting *rosés* are now being made in the East from hybrid grapes (crosses of European varieties with our native American vines) by Gold Seal, Widmer, Boordy and High Tor; these have little or none of the pronounced American grape flavor which is so definite in most Eastern wines (see below). Here are a number of America's best roses:

ALMADÉN GRENACHE ROSÉ
BUENA VISTA ROSÉ
LOUIS MARTINI GAMAY ROSÉ
GOLD SEAL KEUKA ROSÉ
BEAULIEU VINEYARD ROSÉ
CRESTA BLANCA RESERVE ROSÉ
SOUVERAIN CELLARS GRENACHE ROSÉ
WIDMER'S SEIBEL ROSÉ

NEW YORK AND OHIO WINES

It is not possible to classify most Eastern wines, however good (and many of them are very good indeed), with those of California or arrange them in terms of European equiva-

ARNOLD NEWMAN

lents. They are as different from what Europe makes, or California, as a pear is different from an apple or a grapefruit from an orange. You may prefer them or like them not at all, and there is no quarreling with tastes. At any rate, they are something quite different, and do not fit easily into categories like Sauternes and Burgundy—at least to those who know what these terms mean in the rest of the world. It is hard, therefore, to say more than this: producers such as Gold Seal, Widmer, Taylor, Great Western (all New York State) and Meier's (Ohio) market wines that are dependable, consistent, well made. Listed below are a few Eastern specialties worth investigating. These are all white and all dry.

GOLD SEAL CHARLES FOURNIER NATURE

WIDMER'S RIESLING

WIDMER'S ELVIRA

GOLD SEAL DELAWARE

MEIER'S ISLE ST. GEORGE SAUTERNES

WIDMER'S DELAWARE

Also the wines of Boordy Vineyard, at Riderwood, near Baltimore, and those of the High Tor Vineyard, on the Hudson, north of New York City.

CHAMPAGNE

"Champagne" is not simply another way of saying "white sparkling wine." Champagne is a special and superior product made in a special way. In the United States, unless the telltale words "Bulk Process" appear on the label (indicating that a speed-up, short-cut method has been used), an American or California or New York State Champagne *must* legally be made by the same slow, costly, laborious method as French Champagne. The rules in France are even stricter, for the wine must come from a specific area and be made only from Pinot Noir and Chardonnay grapes. Perhaps for this reason our American Champagnes are never as good as the best French, but many are better than cheaper, unknown French brands sold at about the same price. In general, California Champagnes taste more like French than do those of New York State, since the latter have the Eastern grape flavor.

Among New York Champagnes, Charles Fournier is regarded by most experts as in a class by itself, followed by Gold Seal, Great Western, Taylor, Widmer. In California, top brands include Almadén, Beaulieu, Korbel and Paul Masson; also Cresta Blanca, Hanns Kornell and Weibel.

PORT

Sweet red wines "fortified" with brandy are produced all over the world; only in Portugal are they of exceptional quality and only in the United States and in Portugal are these wines called "Port." We produce about seven times as much Port as the Portuguese. Their Ports (the name comes from the town of Oporto, center of the trade) are closely defined and delimited—ours are not; theirs are the best in the world—ours are, to say the least, less good.

Only a few American vintners plant the true Portuguese Port grape varieties, make their wine carefully, and lay it away for proper aging in small oak casks. The most interesting Port now made in America is produced by a California family called Ficklin, and sold under that name. A few larger producers, notably Almadén, use a proportion of true Port grapes, and give their wines a chance to develop in oak casks. The result is good, but a long way from what the Portuguese manage to achieve.

SHERRY

Though Americans drink far more Sherry (not only as a national total, but *per capita*) than the Spaniards do, and though American Sherry is cheaper in the United States than Spanish Sherry is in Spain, the Spaniards' is, on the average, vastly better. True Sherry is made largely from a special grape, the Palomino, fermented with special yeasts called *flor*, aged in small oak casks and blended through a complicated system known as a *solera*. Most of ours are mass-produced for a mass market, made from whatever grapes are available and cheap, hardly aged at all, and usually sold when less than two years old; they have little or nothing to recommend them except high alcoholic content and low price.

Fortunately there are a few rare exceptions—American Sherries in which we can take pride—made by the Spanish method. They are surprisingly close in quality and flavor to the very good, if perhaps not the most expensive and best, Sherries from Jerez (capital of the Spanish Sherry country, originally pronounced "Sherris").

The pioneer in this sort of work and the largest producer of such Sherries today is Almadén Vineyards in California. Note Almadén Solera Cocktail Sherry (dry) and Almadén Solera Cream (sweet). Other Sherries made in somewhat the same way, through with less strict adherence to the Spanish tradition, include Louis Martini Pale Dry Sherry, Cresta Blanca Triple Cream, and Widmer's New York State Cocktail Sherry.

WINE-GRAPE VARIETIES

CALIFORNIA	Varietal Name	Rating	European Equivalent
Red	Cabernet Sauvignon	The Best	Red Bordeaux
	Pinot Noir	Excellent	Red Burgundy
	Gamay-Beaujolais	Very Good	Beaujolais
	Barbera	Good	Italian Barbera
	Gamay	Fair	Beaujolais
	Grignolino (or rosé)	Fair	Italian Grignolino
Rosé	Grenache	Excellent	Tavel
White	Pinot Chardonnay	The Best	White Burgundy
	Johannisberger Riesling	Excellent	Rhine
	Pinot Blanc	Very Good	White Burgundy
	White Pinot (really the Chenin or Pineau)	Very Good	Loire
	Traminer or Gewurztraminer	Very Good	Alsace
	Sauvignon Blanc	Very Good	Dry Graves
	Semillon	Good	Dry Graves
	Sylvaner	Good	Rhine or Alsace
	Gray Riesling	Fair	

EASTERN			Comment
All White	Delaware	Excellent	Also a good table grape.
	Elvira	Very Good	Special, pronounced bouquet.
	"Riesling"	Very Good	Not a true Riesling; much like the Elvira.
	Catawba	Good	Largely used in sparkling wine.

The Perfect Match:
Traditional American Delicacies, Native American Wines

WHITE

Certain dishes seem to go with certain wines, though your own taste is what finally counts. But almost everyone finds that fish and shellfish taste better with dry white wine, and most people prefer red with beef, lamb, game and cheese. As for chicken, turkey, eggs—these go with either, or with *vin rosé*.

Three all-American sea-food favorites are superbly complemented by three American wines. The first is a transcontinental marriage of Maine and California: succulent lobster, with one of the subtlest and finest American white wines, Pinot Chardonnay—for instance, Wente's, from the Livermore Valley. Next, with sea bass, a noble American fish, a racier and more piquant wine, Widmer's fresh and aromatic New York State Riesling, from the Finger Lakes. Finally, with fresh shrimp, the Christian Brothers Napa White Pinot, fruity, fragrant and soft.

RED

Traditionally, white wines are served chilled and red wines at "room temperature," but this is a European tradition, poorly suited to our warmer summer weather and our centrally heated homes. No wine is either refreshing or appetizing at over 70°—most reds taste better at 65°, whites at about 50°. Red wines should be opened an hour or so before service: this lets them "breathe," brings out their bouquet.

Served thus, these three red wines do wonders, respectively, for steak, turkey, cheese. Steak-and-mushrooms belongs with a robust, warming, full-bodied wine on the order of a Burgundy: Beaulieu Vineyard "Beaumont" is precisely that, a Pinot Noir from California's Napa Valley. Turkey calls for a red wine (a dry white would be no less acceptable) but one of a different sort . . . a classic—elegant and distinguished—like Louis Martini Cabernet Sauvignon, also from Napa. Cheese and red wine are the happiest of companions;

here are two of the best—Cooper's New York State cheddar, Almadén's soft, sturdy, velvety Pinot Noir, made from the Burgundian grape, in Santa Clara County.

SPECIAL

In our grandfathers' day, when seven courses were par for a holiday meal, when the maid stayed to wash the dishes and there was such a thing as a "stylish stout," people often served five different wines with dinner. There was Sherry with the soup, Sauternes with the fish, Burgundy with the roast, then Champagne, then Port or Madeira. Our tastes today are simpler and one wine or at most two seem enough. If one wine, pick a wine that goes with the main dish. If two, for a festive occasion, add Champagne.

Certain American dishes require special treatment in the way of wine. An excellent choice with Eggs Benedict is a white wine with plenty of flavor, not too dry, such as Meier's Isle St. George Sauternes from Ohio. A California *vin rosé*, fresh and gay, such as Cresta Blanca Grenache Rosé, is perfect with Southern Fried Chicken. And for the special two-wine dinner, it's important to choose a dessert that complements Champagne: An outstanding combination would be Fruit Macedoine and Gold Seal Brut from New York's Lake Keuka.

BEEF RAGOUT PROVENCALE

4 pounds round of beef, cut in serving-sized pieces	12 small onions, peeled
Narrow bacon strips for larding beef pieces	12 small carrots, scraped and cut in shape of olives
Salt and pepper	2 stalks celery, cut in inch lengths
3 whole allspice	4 cloves garlic, peeled and halved
¼ cup wine vinegar	Herb bouquet
2½ cups red wine	2-inch piece lemon peel
¼ pound bacon, finely chopped	

Have meat dealer lard the beef pieces. Mix 1 teaspoon salt, grind of pepper, the allspice, vinegar and ½ cup red wine in a glass or china bowl. Place meat in this mixture to marinade for 3 hours. Add more wine and vinegar if necessary to moisten and marinate all pieces of meat. Turn pieces frequently in the mixture.

Heat the chopped bacon in a large flameproof casserole; brown the onions, carrots, celery and garlic. Add marinated meat. Cook and stir for about 8 minutes; then pour any remaining marinade over the mixture and add 2 cups red wine. Add herb bouquet (parsley, thyme and bay leaf) and the lemon peel. Cover casserole; let mixture cook slowly 6 to 7 hours either on top of the stove or in a moderately slow oven. Remove herb bouquet. Clear all fat from top of pan sauce and serve the stew in the casserole. Makes 8 or more servings.

ESCOFFIER'S BEEF À LA MODE

4 to 5 pounds top round of beef	3 tablespoons suet, oil or butter
6 or 8 slices bacon	3 small, boned and blanched calves' feet
1 cup plus 3 tablespoons cognac	Hot water or consommé
1 tablespoon chopped parsley	4 carrots, scraped, cut in shape of olives and parboiled
Salt, pepper, nutmeg	8 small onions, peeled and sautéed in butter
1 pint red wine	

Marinate the bacon for about 30 minutes in 3 tablespoons brandy combined with the parsley. Drain, cut in narrow strips and lard the beef with them. Rub meat all over with salt, pepper and lightly with nutmeg. Pour the wine and ½ cup brandy in a china or glass bowl; place the meat in this marinade; cover the bowl and let meat stand 4 or 5 hours. Spoon the marinade over the meat frequently and turn the meat a few times.

Heat the suet, oil or butter in a Dutch oven or other heavy kettle. Drain the beef, reserving the marinade. Brown the beef well on all sides in the hot fat. Add the calves' feet and about 2 cups hot water or consommé. There should be about ½ inch of liquid in the pot. Cover the pot; reduce the heat and cook slowly about 2 hours, basting frequently with the reserved wine-and-brandy marinade.

After 2 hours of cooking, transfer the roast to a flameproof casserole (warmed by rinsing with hot water), surround the meat with the carrots, onions and meat from calves' feet cut in small cubes. Strain the liquid from the Dutch oven over the roast; add a little of the wine-and-brandy marinade and continue cooking for about 2 hours longer. Serve from casserole, slicing and adding some of the vegetable garnish to each serving. Makes 8 or more servings.

BEEF CASSEROLE WITH NEW YORK OR CALIFORNIA CLARET

2 pounds round or sirloin of beef, cut in serving-sized pieces	1 teaspoon salt
	⅛ teaspoon thyme
	½ bay leaf
2 tablespoons suet or butter	1 pint good claret or other red wine
4 shallots or 1 onion, peeled and chopped fine	6 slices lean bacon
1 clove garlic, peeled and minced	12 very small white onions, peeled and left whole
1½ tablespoons flour	2 dozen small mushrooms

Start oven at moderate (350° F.). Heat suet or butter in a heavy frying pan and brown meat rapidly over high heat. When browned on all sides, remove the meat to a 3-quart casserole. Add shallots or onion, garlic and flour to the fat left in the pan; stir and cook until the vegetables are lightly browned. Add the seasonings and herbs; then add 1 cup of wine and cook until smoothly mixed. Cook 2 minutes more, stirring; then pour over the meat in the casserole. Add enough more wine to cover the meat. Cook in a moderate oven about 1½ hours. About 30 minutes before the end of the cooking time, cut the bacon in small pieces and cook in the frying pan until lightly browned; add the small onions and mushrooms; stir and cook a few minutes until the vegetables are golden. Add all to the casserole of meat, cover and let cook for a final 30 minutes. Stir occasionally. Makes 4 or more servings.

BOURBON- AND WINE-FLAVORED CHICKEN-LIVER PÂTÉ

1 pound fresh chicken livers	½ teaspoon salt
1 small onion, peeled and minced	⅛ teaspoon Tabasco
1 pound butter	1 clove garlic, peeled and halved
1½ cups clear chicken broth or consommé	⅓ cup bourbon whisky
¼ cup Marsala	¼ tablespoon plain gelatin
½ teaspoon paprika	2 or 3 tablespoons sliced truffles
⅛ teaspoon ground allspice	

Chop livers fine. Cook onion in ½ pound butter in a large saucepan; add livers and cook for 10 minutes, stirring occasionally. Add ¾ cup of the chicken broth, the wine, paprika, allspice, salt, Tabasco and garlic. Cook for 5 minutes more. Remove garlic and discard it. Place mixture in electric blender; blend, gradually adding remaining butter, melted, and whisky, until smooth. Chill.

Heat remaining broth in a saucepan; sprinkle top with gelatin and heat for a few minutes, stirring to dissolve the gelatin. Pour part of the gelatin broth into a mold; add small pieces of sliced truffles as garnish. Chill mold for 10 minutes. Then fill mold with chilled chicken-liver mixture and pour over the top the remaining gelatin broth. Chill mold in refrigerator for about 6 hours. Unmold on a chilled platter; garnish with lettuce or water cress. Makes enough for 20 to 30 guests. Serve melba toast and crisp crackers or French bread with this wine pâté.

CHICKEN MARENGO

2 plump young broiling chickens, cleaned, dressed and cut in serving pieces	1 clove garlic, peeled
	1½ cups sliced mushrooms
	6 medium-sized tomatoes, skinned and chopped
Salt and pepper	¾ cup dry white wine
¼ cup olive oil	1 tablespoon cognac
2 shallots, peeled and quartered	

Season the chicken, fry in hot oil in a large skillet or flameproof casserole until lightly browned. Turn pieces frequently so all are evenly cooked. Lower the heat; cover skillet or casserole and cook for 10 minutes. Remove the chicken to a warm plate and add shallots, garlic, mushrooms and tomatoes to the skillet or casserole. Cook and stir together until mushrooms are done. Remove garlic and discard it. Add the wine and brandy; stir and blend sauce until reduced by about ⅓. Place the browned chicken in the hot sauce; stir sauce around the pieces and spoon some over them. Cover skillet or casserole and cook for 15 minutes or until the chicken is done. Makes 6 servings.

COQ AU VIN

2 plump broiling chickens, cleaned and quartered	1 clove garlic, peeled and mashed
Salt and pepper	2 tablespoons flour
6 slices bacon or salt pork	1 pint red wine
2 tablespoons butter	Herb bouquet
6 onions, peeled and sliced	2 tablespoons chopped parsley
12 mushrooms	
3 shallots, peeled and chopped	

Season the chicken with salt and pepper. Dice the bacon or salt pork and cook for 3 or 4 minutes in a deep flameproof casserole. Add butter, stirring until melted. Place chickens in the hot fat and cook until golden brown. Add onions and mushrooms; cover the casserole and cook over low heat until the vegetables are lightly browned. Spoon off a little of the fat if the amount seems excessive. Add shallots and garlic to casserole; sprinkle them with flour and stir into the sauce. Cook and stir a few minutes over low heat; add the wine. There should be just enough liquid to cover the chicken. If necessary, add a little water or consommé. Add herb bouquet; increase heat a little and bring to a boil, cover the pan and cook for about 40 minutes or until the chicken is tender. Skim the fat from the surface of the sauce; remove the herb bouquet, and serve the chicken in its sauce in the casserole or arrange the chicken on a warmed serving platter and pour the sauce over it. Sprinkle with chopped parsley. Makes 4 to 8 servings.

DELMONICO SHERRIED CHICKEN

2 plump chicken breasts, split in half	4 tablespoons butter
	1½ cups light cream
1 teaspoon salt	¼ cup sherry
½ teaspoon cayenne	1 teaspoon Worcestershire sauce
½ teaspoon celery salt	
3 tablespoons flour	Parsley or water cress

Rinse the chicken; pat it dry. Sift the seasonings with the flour and roll the chicken pieces in the flour mixture until thoroughly coated. Brown the chicken in the hot butter over high heat; then reduce heat and let cook for about 30 minutes or until done. Remove the chicken to a warmed serving dish. Stir the cream into the hot fat in the pan; then slowly add sherry and stir until smooth. Add Worcestershire; mix only until sauce is very hot; then pour over the chicken. Garnish the platter with parsley or water cress. Makes 4 servings.

VENISON STEAK WITH WINE MARINADE

1 or 2 small venison-leg steaks cut ¾-inch thick	1 bay leaf
	1 cup white wine
1 teaspoon salt	3 tablespoons oil
4 peppercorns	
1 onion, peeled and sliced	Gravy:
1 carrot, scraped and sliced	1 tablespoon butter
4 sprigs parsley	1 tablespoon flour
½ teaspoon dried thyme or a sprig of fresh thyme	2 tablespoons wine vinegar
	½ cup hot light cream
	Salt and pepper

Rinse steak, pat dry. Combine salt, peppercorns, onion, carrot, parsley, thyme, bay leaf and wine in shallow glass or china dish. Lay steaks in this marinade; cover dish and place in refrigerator 12 to 24 hours. Turn steaks a few times during the marinating period.

Remove steaks from marinade, let drain. Heat oil in skillet and, when very hot, add steaks. Cook about 3 minutes on each side, longer for better-done steaks. Keep the cooked steaks hot on a serving platter and make gravy in the pan in which they were cooked. Pour off most of the fat from the skillet; add the butter to the pan; stir the flour into it smoothly and let cook until browned, scraping the browned fat from the sides of the skillet. Stir vinegar into the fat and flour; add hot cream, salt and pepper and cook a few minutes, stirring constantly until slightly thickened. Serve hot with hot steaks. Makes 2 or 4 servings of venison and gravy.

FLOUNDER FILLETS BAKED IN WINE

2 tablespoons finely chopped leeks or scallions	1 teaspoon salt
	Grind of fresh pepper
1 young carrot, scraped and sliced	1½ pounds fillets of flounder
3 paper-thin slices lemon	1 cup dry white wine
¼ teaspoon basil	2 tablespoons dry vermouth
2 tablespoons butter	1 tablespoon chopped parsley

Start oven at moderately hot (400° F.). In a shallow, flame-proof baking dish combine the leeks or scallions, carrot, lemon, basil and butter; heat and stir until all are coated with butter and beginning to cook. Add seasoning; then lay fish fillets on the vegetables. Pour wine and vermouth over all. Bake for about 20 minutes. Sprinkle with parsley and serve in the baking dish. Makes 6 servings.

TROUT AU CHABLIS

4 rainbow trout, about 1 pound each, cleaned but head left on	½ teaspoon rosemary
	8 peppercorns
1 quart water	1½ tablespoons plain gelatin
1 pint California chablis	½ cup cold water
2 tablespoons salt	Few fresh tarragon leaves or a few sprigs chervil or dill
1 carrot, scraped and sliced	
1 onion, peeled and sliced	2 hard-cooked eggs, finely chopped
2 tablespoons parsley, chopped	
½ bay leaf	2 tablespoons thinly sliced truffles

Combine water, wine, salt, carrot, onion, parsley, bay leaf, rosemary and peppercorns in a 2½-quart kettle. Bring to a boil; then lower the heat and lay the trout carefully in this court bouillon. Cook gently about 20 minutes or until fish are tender and the flesh flakes easily with a fork. Lift trout out with two wide spoons, and drain them.

Strain court bouillon; then reheat and boil rapidly to reduce by about one half. Soften the gelatin in the ½ cup cold water for 5 minutes; then stir it into the hot bouillon to dissolve. Let the mixture stand until the consistency of an egg white. Place the drained trout on a serving dish. Decorate with fresh tarragon, chervil or dill, mounds of chopped egg and sliced truffles. Pour semi-jelled aspic thickly over and around the trout. Chill until set and firm. Serve very cold. Makes 4 to 8 servings.

MARYLAND CRAB-MEAT CHOWDER

4 tablespoons butter	½ teaspoon salt
4 large mushrooms, finely diced	Cayenne
	2 cups milk
1 tablespoon grated onion	1 cup heavy cream
2 tomatoes, skinned and cut in pieces	2 teaspoons minced parsley
	1 teaspoon minced chives
2 6-ounce packages quick-frozen crab meat	¼ cup dry white wine
	2 tablespoons sherry

Melt butter in a 2-quart kettle. Add mushrooms and cook, stirring gently for about 5 minutes or until lightly browned. Add onion and tomatoes; cook and stir for 5 minutes more. Add crab (all bones removed), salt and a dash of cayenne. Stir gently. After 1 minute stir in the milk, a little at a time; then gradually stir in the cream. When the chowder bubbles, add the parsley and chives. Add wines slowly; then remove from the heat. Serve at once in warmed soup bowls. Makes 4 servings. Small beaten biscuits spread with herb butter are delicious accompaniments for this rich chowder.

PERIGUEUX SAUCE

For hot fish, chicken pies or various fish, chicken and meat soufflés.

¼ cup butter	½ teaspoon salt
2 slices peeled onion	½ teaspoon paprika
2 slices carrot	¼ cup white wine
⅓ cup sifted flour	4 tablespoons chopped truffles
2 cups consommé	
⅓ cup tomato purée	

Melt the butter in a saucepan and cook the vegetables slowly until browned. Stir flour in smoothly and continue to stir and cook until browned. Add consommé, purée, seasonings and mix well; stir until boiling. Strain this sauce; return it to the saucepan; reheat only until steaming hot. Stir wine and truffles in. Remove from heat and serve hot. Makes about 3 cups sauce.

CHATEAUBRIAND SAUCE FOR STEAKS

For broiled filet mignon or for any grilled or broiled steak.

1 tablespoon peeled chopped shallots	½ cup white wine
½ crumbled bay leaf	1 cup veal stock or bouillon
½ teaspoon dried thyme, or 1 sprig fresh thyme	½ cup butter, melted
2 tablespoons chopped mushrooms	¼ teaspoon chopped tarragon

Combine shallots, bay leaf, thyme and mushrooms in an enamel saucepan; add wine and let barely simmer over low heat until the wine has been partly absorbed and almost entirely reduced. Add stock or bouillon and let simmer slowly until reduced by one half. Strain mixture; reheat. Into it beat the melted butter and tarragon. Serve hot. Makes about 1¾ cups sauce.

WHITE-WINE DESSERT SAUCE

1 cup dry white wine	¾ cup sugar
2 eggs	

Heat wine in the upper part of a double boiler over boiling water. Beat eggs with sugar until fluffy and light. Stir steaming-hot wine slowly into the eggs, beating constantly with a whisk. Cook until thickened. Remove from the heat and pour into a bowl. Serve warm with sponge cake, fruit puddings or stewed fruits. Makes about 2 cups sauce.

UNCOOKED WINE SAUCE FOR DESSERTS

2 egg yolks	¼ cup sherry
½ cup sugar	½ cup heavy cream

Beat yolks with sugar until fluffy and light. Add sherry very slowly, beating constantly. Whip cream until stiff and fold into the sherry mixture. Serve with sponge cake, and various cake and pudding desserts. Makes about 2 cups sauce.

CLEAR WINE SAUCE

1½ cups sugar	1 teaspoon vanilla extract
½ cup water	3 tablespoons white wine

Combine sugar and water in a saucepan and boil for 6 minutes. Remove from heat, add vanilla and wine. Serve warm over ice cream desserts, plain cake, raisin pudding and other warm puddings. Makes about 2 cups sauce.

WINE GLAZE FOR BAKED HAM

1 cup good red wine	6 whole cloves
1 cup bourbon whiskey	2 tablespoons grated orange peel
1 cup light-brown sugar, packed	

Combine wine, bourbon, sugar, and cloves. Let stand until sugar has dissolved. Stir occasionally. Add the peel.

When baked ham has been skinned and returned to the oven for its last half hour of baking, pour half of this wine-bourbon mixture over it slowly so the fatty surface of the meat absorbs the flavors. Baste every 10 minutes with remaining mixture and the pan juices. Makes enough for any large ham.

FRUIT COMPOTE WITH WHITE WINE

2 ripe nectarines or peaches	1 cup white wine
2 greengage plums	1 tablespoon cognac
12 oxheart cherries	1 cup sugar
½ cup small tangerine sections (Japanese canned variety)	1 cup water

Peel plums and nectarines or peaches; remove stones; cut fruit in half. Remove cherry stones, leaving fruit whole. Drain tangerine sections. Combine fruits in a glass or china bowl. Pour the wine and brandy over the fruit and let stand for about 20 minutes. Combine sugar and water in a large enamel saucepan and boil for 10 minutes. Then spoon fruit in carefully so as to preserve its shape. Pour any juice remaining in the bowl into the saucepan. Reduce the heat; simmer for about 5 minutes or until very hot, but not boiling. Let cool; then chill in refrigerator for several hours. Serve in wide flat dessert dishes so the fruit may be arranged effectively. Serve mocha or bittersweet chocolate wafers with this compote. Makes 4 to 6 servings.

STRAWBERRIES AND WINE

Wash and hull fine ripe strawberries several hours before you expect to serve them. Sugar them lightly in a deep glass or china bowl. Cover just to the top of the berries with a good red wine. Chill for several hours. When ready to serve, spoon berries out into dessert dishes, stir the wine and sugar in the bowl and pour a little over each serving of berries.

CLARET SAUCE FOR DESSERTS

For baked bananas, banana croquettes, apple fritters, various fruit fritters and other fruit desserts.

1 cup sugar	½ cup claret
⅓ cup water	1 teaspoon lemon juice

Combine sugar and water in saucepan, bring to boiling and boil 6 minutes. Add wine and lemon juice, do not boil, but heat to boiling point. Makes about 1 cup sauce.

BANANA CROQUETTES

Peel ripe bananas and cut in lengths to resemble croquettes. Roll each in beaten egg mixed with 1 tablespoon water and then in bread crumbs. Use frying basket and fry croquettes in deep hot fat (370° F.) for 5 to 6 minutes. Drain for a few seconds on thick paper towels. Serve hot with hot Claret Sauce.

PART II: *The Outdoor Gourmet*

New England Clambake / *Roger Angell*

Purists aver that this is the only true bake,
and that the ideal clam is found chiefly on Yankee shores

NEW ENGLAND'S first great cultural triumph was neither the Bay Psalm Book nor the establishment of Harvard College. It was a gentler achievement, one perpetuated today neither by spire nor by monument but by vast piles of clamshells that lie whitening in the sun from Narragansett Bay to Eastport, Maine. It was the discovery of the clambake. The particular inventor of this institution is unknown, but he was no paleface. He was the New England Indian who, long before the Mayflower was launched, first burned his fingers while pulling a soft-shell clam out of a heap of steaming rockweed and then burned his tongue as he popped the hot morsel into his mouth. As he blew on his fingers and wiped his watering eyes, he probably had no idea that he had just become a Founding Father and something of an immortal, but certainly he needed no such comfort: he knew he had made a discovery.

Today, there are millions of unfortunate Americans who have never breathed a buttery prayer of gratitude to that unknown redskin chef, only because they have never been near the New England seashore. Plenty of these unlucky ones may *think* they have been to a clambake—in the Carolinas, in California and even on Long Island—but, according to purists, they are wrong.

There is only one legitimate New England clambake, for the simple reason that there is only one proper clambake clam—the soft-shell clam, *Mya arenaria*, which lives in the tidewater flats, chiefly north of Cape Cod. There is an impostor that appears at some benighted clambakes, but any salt-water New Englander will spit him out indignantly, recognizing him for what he is—the hard-shell clam, or quahog (*Venus mercenaria*), which is fine when eaten raw as the cherry-stone or littleneck, or put in a chowder, but was

never, never meant to be bedded in a steaming rockweed bake.

The foregoing is about the only point upon which clambake *aficionados* find themselves in agreement; for some reason, the small, damp, innocuous little clam is a born troublemaker. There is the great and unsettled spat about clam chowder, involving the milk-base New England-style chowder versus the stewed-tomato "Manhattan" chowder—a matter which can break up relations between the Boston and New York branches of a family as effectively as Aunt Hester's disputed will. The only difference about clambakes is that there is more room for discussion—and hard feelings. First, the argument about ingredients: do you eat just plain clams, with a few lobsters and fish thrown in, or does the clambake include chicken, corn, potatoes, eggs and even sausages? Then there is the method of cooking: pit or stone platform? Metal sheet or sugar barrel? Stovepipe or pot, without seaweed? There is, of course, no correct answer to these fine points; they are simply variations imposed by taste and local necessity.

For a look at the most authentic clambake in its pristine form, your best port of call is somewhere along the shore of Narragansett Bay, in Rhode Island. This is all bake country. You'll find dozens of commercial beachside establishments advertising "Bake Today!" and probably a few big group bakes.

That party surrounding a steaming canvas on the shore may be anything from a large family to the annual outing of a small-town Democratic Club. If the party numbers in the hundreds it may be a big bake for the personnel of a factory, or one of the famous old community bakes thrown by such organizations as the Hornbine Baptist Church at Rehoboth or the Maple Root Six Principle Baptist Church of Coventry. Let's skip these mass orgies for the moment and go back to the family affair, which is likely to be directed by Cousin Ethan, a purist whose technique has been a proud family possession for generations.

Cousin Ethan may even have ordered his clams from Maine, on the ground that the Down East variety have the greatest flavor. In any case, he will have sluiced and soaked the clams thoroughly, first, perhaps with fresh water to get the sand out, and then with clean sea water. Under his orders you will have dug a shallow but sizable pit in the sand, and have built a huge and roaring-hot fire in it, stoking the flames either with hardwood or with chunks of driftwood. And while the fire burns (for a good two or three hours), you set to and collect a couple of dozen good-sized round rocks. Ethan will insist that they be dry, so that they won't split in the fire; if he is particularly finicky, he may even make sure that they have never been in a fire before, on the grounds that a rock won't "take the heat" twice. While the rocks heat in the fire, you plunge into the sea and collect armfuls of fresh rockweed. By some mysterious divining, Ethan has now decided that the rocks are hot enough so that he won't be faced with the supreme embarrassment of a "raw bake." The time has come for fast work.

Using branches, you sweep the embers off the white-hot rocks and cover the entire pit with your rockweed, about six inches thick. A net of chicken wire on top of this helps if you don't want to lose a single clam. Next come the clams (none with a shell that has started to open), then perhaps some salt and a few onions for flavor. Young potatoes go on next (if Cousin Ethan is a potato man), corn (if he is a corn man), then mackerel wrapped in paper (or cheesecloth) bags, followed by sausages, chicken, eggs and recently caught lobsters—all depending upon Ethan's firm convictions about what is and isn't eaten at a clambake. A white cloth over this helps keep the food clean, and a pailful of sea water will help your steam supply. Finally, you stretch canvases over the middle and sides of the pit, slap a big canvas over all—and wait. In a few minutes a little steam begins to puff out as the canvas heaves and breathes, and you know that you have a healthy bake under way.

While the steam and clam juice is cooking your feast, and your stomach is rumbling hollowly, we will take a moment to consider what Cousin Ethan *might* have done. The most common and simplest variation on the hot-stones bake is the substitution of a permanent concrete-and-stone platform pit for the dug pit. This is customary with professional bake-masters who cook for hundreds of guests at a time. In some Down East quarters a sheet-iron stove is substituted for the rocks, on the grounds that it is simpler to handle and to heat up than the rocks. Even this modest switch shocks a few old-school bake men. The barrel bake is usually described as "next best" to the genuine article, and it's handy. With this technique the hot rocks are placed in a large sugar barrel which has been soaking in water overnight. Sand and some scrap iron will keep the stones from burning out the barrel. Layers of rockweed alternate with layers of food, with rockweed packed over all and topped with damp bags. A good barrel bake cooks for an hour or more and the bake *growls* while it cooks. A simple version of the clambake for a small party is the stovepipe method. An eight-inch-wide stovepipe, stuffed with seaweed at the bottom, is upended in a hot-embered fire. Packed with clams and fixin's, it is then stop-

pered at the other end with rockweed. This neat bake is ready to eat when the rockweed in the top is dried-out and brittle.

The big squabble among clam folk starts when you mention the words "pot bake." Thousands of people, notably in Long Island, have never seen anything but a pot bake, but almost any New Englander will tell you that a pot bake is just not a clambake at all. "It just doesn't have the flavor," says a Maine bakemaster named Joseph W. Larrabee. "They call *anything* a clambake these days, but there's only one real way and that is with steam made by rockweed coming in contact with heated surface and rising up through your food. There is no comparison."

Comparison or not, it is interesting to note that most Maine fishermen, who spend too much of their time near the shore to want to mess around with an open beach fire on Sunday, eat most of their clams steamed in an unromantic kettle on the kitchen stove. Pot bake experts, like M. C. Young of Riverhead, Long Island, turn up *their* noses at the pit method, on the ground that you are apt to come up with a half-baked piece of chicken or a charred ear of corn.

Mr. Young's big bakes in the Hamptons are done over a fire, using grates made of old snowplow blades and set in concrete blocks. He steams the clams, potatoes and fish in a kettle or washtub for about two hours, adding the corn for the last forty-five minutes. Note that these are *steamed*, not boiled, in about two inches of water. Mr. Young claims that this system saves all the juices that are lost in a pit bake. "Besides," he adds, "the seaweed disappeared from around here some years ago. The pit method wouldn't work here, even if we wanted to try it." It must be added, in a whisper, that Mr. Young also uses quahogs. One advantage of the pot bake is that you can hold it anywhere, in a city backyard or even miles from the seashore. Even in New York, though, you don't *have* to use quahogs; the Fulton Fish Market brings in soft-shell clams by the carload from up north.

But let's get back to Cousin Ethan and his genuine Rhode Island family bake, which is now puffing under its canvas blanket. Appetites are getting out of hand, as are the young fry, who have to be chased away from the fireside in their eagerness to lift the canvas and get a whiff of that clam-laden aroma. This, if you insist, is the time for those quahogs. Shucked on the spot and eaten raw, they are a perfect appetizer to their more robust cousins in the fire. For a sturdier prebake course you can serve up cocktails too. Somehow, rum drinks are always recommended before a clambake. Meanwhile, Cousin Ethan is keeping one eye on his watch and the other on his canvas, making sure that the bake isn't going to "blow herself." The guests settle themselves in their best eating positions, belts loosened, fingers supple, eyes aglitter. If there are tables, they sit at tables. If not, they find a comfortable rock or stretch of sand. Paper plates, napkins and plenty of hot butter are distributed. Finally, after the bake has been cooling for anything from half an hour to an hour, Cousin Ethan gives one last look at his watch, pockets it and announces: "She's ready."

The unveiling is the high point. The canvas goes back, a cloud of steam arises, which the eaters sniff hungrily. Clams are rushed onto tin plates, a dozen or so to the plate, and laid in front of the now-frantic eaters. Each clam is bulging open, ready to be plucked. You seize the clam by the snout, shuck off the clinging gray overcoat, dip it in butter and . . . "*slurp!*". . . your clambake has begun. After the clams come more clams, plate after plate of them. In between times, you gnaw away at your corn, eat your potatoes and fish. A cup of clam broth and you're ready for more clams. Only one thing at this point can halt your enjoyment of the bake —your clothing. If you've come wearing anything as foolish as a necktie or a print dress, you will have realized by now that nobody can or should eat a clam without having juice and butter run down his chin and neck. Dress for a clambake as you would for a game of touch football. An occasional paper napkin will keep you from losing traction altogether.

One other matter—some people discard the hard neck of the clam, finding it too tough. Others eat it along with the rest of the clam.

Dessert and side courses are likely to be a matter of small interest to you if you have really done justice to the clams. But for really Falstaffian stuffers and for unfortunates who somehow haven't eaten enough clams, there is usually a plate of cucumbers and tomatoes with radishes and pickles on the side. Finally there's dessert—anything from watermelon to apple pie, along with lots of hot coffee. Some clambake experts insist that coffee is an indispensable last touch to the repast, but there's an equally devout school that plugs beer right through the meal, to be followed by a last brew just before you stretch your bulging form on the beach for a happy nap.

If Cousin Ethan has started his bake in the afternoon, the sun will be going down about now and someone is apt to start a little singing. You don't *have* to join in, though. Just lie there, beer mug in hand, and don't think about anything at all. Before you doze off you might count the shells of the clams you ate and wonder about the world's record. Well, last February, one Joe Gagnon, a Rhode Island man, claimed the title when he downed 167 clams at a sitting out in Seattle. His fellow Rhode Islanders were horrified, however, when it was discovered that he had eaten steamed littlenecks, and it was generally agreed that not only was his record null and void but that he was probably an impostor. Imagine— a Rhode Island boy eating steamed quahogs!

PART II: The Outdoor Gourmet

The Roadside Gourmet
/ J.C. and Helen Furnas

Dining on the road can be a wonderful gastronomical experience

ONE fair spring day not too long ago, on a journey through upper New York State, we tried a certain small restaurant with a silky green view over one of the Finger Lakes and a versatile cold buffet. We started with a truffled liver pâté . . . then a rock-lobster tail with choice of dressings (we took a mayonnaise slightly tinged with curry powder) . . . cold braised celery hearts vinaigrette . . . an old-fashioned dessert of plump ripe pears and Camembert . . . coffee. We finished with a marked sense of well-being in the midriff.

Each item was of elegant quality but the check was only $1.20 apiece. No tipping. We liked the restaurant so much that we took it away with us. When we left, nothing remained but a few tire marks in the grass. Next day's luncheon stop, though not so upstage—it offered merely cold tongue with chutney, and asparagus tips—was quite as good and only seventy-five cents each.

All this means that we have developed a luxurious independence of roadside potluck for lunch and, when we choose, for dinner as well. We first tried the system of using our car as a restaurant—or rather, were driven to it—in West Africa where, the local cuisine being what it is, if roadside restaurants existed, you'd pay for the privilege of staying out of them. The scheme turned out so pleasantly that we have since worked it all over the United States east of the Mississippi and will certainly try it farther west the next time we drive that far from home.

The idea is not at all to picnic in the classic sandwiches-potato-salad-and-pickles way. That is dull two days running, hard to arrange tastily away from home, and dismally inflexible. Nor is it camp-style cookery, which too readily becomes a production. Our idea consists mainly of carrying one's own stock of de luxe provender, largely in cans and bottles, open-ing them wherever circumstances suit and eating high on the hog often for less than conventional highway meals cost. The results are delicious and needn't be fattening if calories are on your mind.

Preliminary planning is needed, true. Soon, however, this shakes down to a permanent check list and a kit of compact gadgets selected for all-season practicality. Thus, when foul weather discourages getting out of the car, the Roadside Gourmet lunches from steel trays, with recesses for his paper cup or tumbler, permanently clamped under the dash and swinging back under when not needed. They can be supplemented with similar trays that hook into the car window, drive-in style. An electric pot that plugs into the cigarette lighter readily produces instant coffee and steaming soup—turtle, say, with the proper dash of sherry; or onion, with the orthodox dusting of Parmesan cheese.

In good weather a neat little hot lunch can be created outside the car on one of those ingeniously small folding stoves fired by alcohol or canned gas—maybe crab Newburg or lobster Thermidor or shrimp Creole, all out of cans, served with French style *petits pois* heated with a nip of powdered onion and fresh-ground black pepper. The adept Roadside Gourmet, however, soon becomes convinced that heat is *not* essential to his enjoyment of many things customarily eaten hot.

Those same fancy peas, for instance, seasoned only with salt, are just as delicious unheated. For the Roadside Gourmet canned boiled pearl onions, when of the best quality, are a treat cold, dipped one by one in soy sauce. Or he baptizes cold canned baby lima beans with a sharp oil-dressing to achieve the equivalent of the cold *flageolets* on a French tray of hors d'oeuvres. Ditto with canned baby carrots or whole canned string beans.

Against a background of Spanish moss and live oaks, a Camp-'n-Wagon tailgate kitchenette takes on overtones of elegance. This compact unit, set up on a Chevrolet Nomad, includes a two-burner stove, a water tank, pump faucet, sink, counter, drawers, grocery compartments and a dashboard icebox. It telescopes for carrying or can be extended into a platform for an air mattress and two sleeping bags.

All this should make sense to any of the millions who like a good smörgåsbord. An age that offers jam in squeeze-out tubes, and cans marble cake, rye bread, cockles, smoked trout, papaya chunks, quail eggs and pheasant consommé—also, for the adventurous, octopus and rattlesnake meat and fried grasshoppers—was bound to revolutionize roadside lunching once the motorist became aware that many, many things are just as good or better cold.

The car designer as well as the food processor now encourages such thinking. Today's wider seats leave ample elbow-room for manipulating can and bottle openers. For good weather the tailgate of a station wagon used chuck wagon-style—and folding stools—make a better outdoor luncheon layout than any traditional picnicker's oilcloth on bumpy ground. There are little fold-up tables, a foot high and under a yard long, that turn a stationwagon's afterdeck into a miniature dining room for small children. The interiors of modern coupés and four-doors show a curious lack of horizontal surfaces. But using the trays and ingenuity, we have not had a serious spill in three years of R.G.-ing. Just in case, however, take along yard-square oilcloth lap protectors.

Our basic equipment item is a rugged 16" x 16" x 10" straw hamper packed before we leave home with canned and bottled items planned to provide lunches of wide versatility. In warm weather we may also carry one of those top-opening, portable metal iceboxes, filling the upper tray with our own cubes to start, and the lower section with soft drinks, a melon or two, canned clam madrilène, Vichyssoise and such. With luck and foresight we may find some old-fashioned chunk ice, which lasts longer, or dry ice to keep such boxes operative throughout the trip. But more often it's simpler to rely on regular pint vacuum bottles for iced tea and coffee from wherever we breakfast, plus a wide-mouth quart vacuum filled with ice cubes as opportunity offers. This sets us up for starting our roadside lunch with canned consommé, bouillon or madrilène "on the rocks."

If you add an insulated carrier-bag, the kind your wife fetches ice cream home in, you can buy special quick-frozen items, such as strawberries or cooked shrimp, as you start in the morning, and take them out to start defrosting at the proper prelunch time—two and a half hours for fruit unless the weather is awfully hot, maybe one and a half hours for the shrimp. Yet high-quality precooked shrimp in glass is about as good as any quick-frozen rival. Actually an expert Roadside Gourmet with hamper packed just right could drive from Bangor to San Diego at moderate speed without icebox or insulated bag, not pay a cent on the way for luncheons, and yet fare sumptuously.

The Roadside Gourmet kit should, of course, include the best twist-it-style can opener money can buy. Next most important is a quart jar of water to rinse things before stowing them or serious washing in the motel or hotel bathroom. We prefer plastic-coated paper plates because they are disposable. But if madame doesn't mind washing them evenings, plastic sectioned plates and cups are admirable. Stainless-steel eating tools, including tablespoons for scooping and fruit knives for paring, are indestructible and easily cleaned.

To avoid finding the contents of the hamper awash in Worcestershire sauce, seasonings should travel in screw-top, plastic bottles such as drugstores sell, packed standing side by side in a cardboard carton of proper size, each tape-labeled for easy selection. We also take dozens of damp-resistant paper garbage bags for the debris—cans, paper napkins, scrunched-up paper plates, odd leavings—until it can be honorably disposed of.

The adept Roadside Gourmet should be able to find imported cheeses at a good specialty shop in his community. With them top-quality dried fruits—pears, apricots, peaches, prunes—are about as good as fresh, more practical at some seasons and always less messy to handle. Lemons and limes keep well and are invaluable for squeezing on cold sea foods and for tingling up de luxe canned fruits. Top-quality canned tomatoes, cold, with salt, fresh-ground pepper, onion powder and a dash of Worcestershire are amazingly good. Even better are what the modern canner labels "stewed tomatoes"— small ones put up with onions, celery, green peppers and odd spices. A can of tomato juice and bottle of Tabasco are a nice standby too—for a quick morning pick-me-up.

Canned, powdered cream-substitutes keep well for cream in coffee. Canned breads are available, but even more convenient are Italian breadsticks, crisp Swedish rye bread, Norwegian flatbread. In season put a few underripe avocados in the trunk to ripen as you roll—use them conventionally or discover that ripe avocado, lightly salted, is a fine butter substitute, as Royal Navy midshipmen knew centuries ago on the West Indian station.

One beauty of it all is that nothing in your basic stock can spoil, so you are committed to nothing. If lunchtime sees you only two miles from a restaurant nationally famous for its passenger pigeons stuffed with minced buffalo tongue, forget R.G.-ing and go there—a thing you are less likely to do when shamefacedly aware of that lumpy paper bag in the back seat full of thick and tasteless roadside-joint "to go" sandwiches, bought where you breakfasted that morning.

But on the frequent days when your trail crosses no such gastronomic landmark, there is always, if you are a confirmed Roadside Gourmet, that cool spot in the shade of a high woods up a side road, and lunch.

◀ **Haven by the highway: the roadside gourmet dines in luxurious independence of crowded hamburger stands.**

PART III: *The Gourmet in the Garden*

A Handbook of Herbs / *Helen Papashvily*

The key to fine cooking: how to use herbs to best effect,
with tips on growing your own, indoors and out

Before history, before agriculture, probably before man himself, there were herbs, for all animals crave some fillip to their ordinary fare; and the cat in catnip, the dog chewing grass, the rhinoceros at the salt lick, the gourmet grinding pepper exemplify the common need.

Five thousand years ago Sumerians flavored their wine with sesame; Egyptians chewed garlic as they built the pyramids; and the seeds of the fennel, orégano, thyme and dill that we sow in our gardens have come to us through time and space from flowers that bloomed in Babylon.

To our ancestors herbs were life itself. Without them it was not possible to worship the gods, preserve food, heal the sick, bury the dead or celebrate a victory. In our society, where we dispel demons through psychiatry, cure diseases with antibiotics and make rose water from coal tar, herbs ought to be obsolete—except that nothing else so adorns the garden, sustains the kitchen and delights the senses.

In gastronomy, as in politics, there is a right wing and a left. To the first, herbs are a devil's brew ("Why spoil the *natural* flavor?"); to the latter, a panacea ("Just a *pinch* turns stew into *boeuf bourguignonne*").

Both are wrong. The function of herbs is to enhance, blend or accent the flavors in a dish, to stimulate appetite and aid

THE ESSENTIAL HERBS

The crisp sprigs opposite represent 26 popular herb varieties that may be grown in any garden. They are identified here, and described in the gardening table on pages 162 through 165.

1. Woodruff, *Asperula odorata* 2. Marjoram, *Majorana hortensis* 3. Cicely, *Myrrhis odorata* 4. Balm, *Melissa officinalis* 5. Sage, *Salvia officinalis* 6. Burnet, *Sanguisorba minor* 7. Parsley (Curly), *Petroselinum crispum* 8. Thyme, *Thymus vulgaris, var. fragrantissimus* 9. Tarragon, *Artemisia dracunculus* 10. Fennel (Bitter), *Foeniculum vulgare* 11. Lavender, *Lavandula officinalis* 12. Orégano, *Origanum vulgare, var. viride* 13. Angelica, *Angelica archangelica* 14. Basil, *Ocimum basilicum* 15. Rosemary, *Rosmarinus officinalis* 16. Dill, *Anethum graveolens* 17. Chives, *Allium schoenoprasum* 18. Clary, *Salvia sclarea* 19. Borage, *Borago officinalis* 20. Savory (Winter), *Satureia montana* 21. Chervil, *Anthriscus cerefolium* 22. Geranium (Skeleton Rose), *P. denticulatum, var. skeleton* 23. Geranium (Rose), *P. graveolens* 24. Basil (Bush), *Ocimum minimum* 25. Mint (Pineapple), *Mentha rotundifolia, var. variegata* 26. Camomile, *Anthemis noblis*.

digestion, to add aroma and perhaps color and texture, to refresh palates jaded by synthetics or bored with the insipidity of mass-produced fodder. Our ancestors' food tasted bad; ours often has no taste at all: such is progress.

Herbs, like everything we eat, have an ethic. There are "right" and "wrong" flavors, classic combinations, immutable methods, too often based only on tradition, sentiment or association rather than actual taste. Do we roast goose with sage dressing because that herb neutralizes fat or because Washington Irving and Charles Dickens assured us it was delicious? Will orégano really give "heart" to tomatoes? Will summer savory complement green beans, tarragon temper vinegar?

Why is one man's flavor another man's "Phooey"? Garden manuals caution readers not to plant coriander lest someone inadvertently pick and eat one of its loathsome leaves. At first acquaintance its astringency might shock provincial palates; yet more than half the world holds this green as dear as we do parsley, and many Americans have discovered and enjoyed it as *cilantro* in Puerto Rico and Mexico, *kotha-milee* and *dhuma* in India, or Chinese parsley in Chinatown markets. (A distinguished visitor from Bombay, told that coriander leaves taste like bugs to Westerners, replied, "Ah, perhaps so, but unfortunately we lack your background for comparison.")

Since there are as many Final Authorities on herbs as eaters of them, the only rule is: Use what you like, how you like, where you like. If you want to put vanilla in cucumbers and dill in ice cream, do so. As a matter of fact, a scoop of dill sherbet, pale green and not too sweet, on a slice of cantaloupe might make an interesting summer dessert.

To discover the distinction herbs will contribute to your cuisine, experiment with not only an open mind but a light hand. Use small amounts at first, a pinch or a "pugil" as the old herbalist called the amount the thumb and two fingers could hold. And remember that coarsely pulverized dried herbs have about twice the strength of fresh herbs, and therefore should be used in approximately half the measure of green leaves. The *exact* ratio depends on such factors as origin, age and concentration, and can be determined only by taste. Steep dried herbs in a small amount of appropriate liquid (water, melted butter, milk) before adding to a dish. Release the volatile oils in fresh herbs before using them by chopping with a knife or pounding in a mortar.

One of the best practice pieces for studying herbs, singly and in combination, is Savoury Cheese, which makes an excellent cocktail spread. Blend a pound of Cheddar (preferably not processed) with three tablespoons of sour cream and a quarter cup of vodka. When smooth, divide into ten or twelve small cups. Add herbs according to taste. This is a way to try such unknowns as rue, camomile, tansy, costmary, hyssop and sorrel, to compare mints, savories and marjorams, and to establish a hierarchy among the anise-flavored.

The earliest methods of using herbs, like most of the plants themselves, came from the Mediterranean countries. Roman colonists carried a taste of home with them—chervil, parsley, rue, borage, sage—when they went to Britain. Crusaders brought sesame seeds, tarragon root, fennel back from the Holy Land. (Many a one, no doubt, infuriated his wife with his epicurean adventures: ". . . spitted chicken, my dear, dipped in marjoram sauce, and anise cake; conserves of roses and mint, lamb with thyme, saffron rice. . . . And so I asked the Arab, infidel though he were, to get the recipe

for you from his wives, and I daresay if you follow the directions and use the seasonings you can make something similar.")

In much the same way *émigrés* and travelers brought from France the methods we now use. We have come to know *fines herbes* as combinations of three or four of the following: parsley, chervil, chives, basil, thyme, rosemary and tarragon, which are added just before serving. *Bouquet garni* consists of whole sprigs of rosemary, thyme, parsley, savory, dill, with a bay leaf, leek, celery stalk and so forth, and is cooked in the dish. For easy removal these are tied with a thread or pinned to the celery or leek with a single clove. When dried herbs are used, they may be added directly. The often recommended method of tying them in a cloth for removal before serving is too reminiscent of the old wash boiler.

Dried herbs serve a purpose, but their limitations are soon discovered. Would you have sweet woodruff for May wine, and grill lamb over rosemary fagots? Would you have rosettes of mint with snow peas, salmon in dill sauce, fresh tomatoes wreathed in basil, a bouquet of thyme and marjoram for the simmering stew, chives and parsley to squander every day of the year? Would you know herbs at their very best, in their full fragrance and flavor? Then you must use them fresh from the garden.

Fortunately this is easy to do, for herbs adapt to a variety of growing conditions and often thrive where other plants fail. Readers who have neither time, place nor desire to re-create the traditional walled garden with knotted borders and formal beds may use a wheel, a ladder length or even the remains of an old foundation as a pattern for planting. Herbs will go into the vegetable, cutting and perennial gardens, border a pool or grow between flagstones. A few pots on a window sill, a box on the terrace or porch, even a space no larger than this page, will produce a creditable crop.

With some effort a very determined do-it-yourselfer might raise *all* his own seasonings. Of the fifty most commonly used, about half are natives of the temperate zone and under certain conditions will grow anywhere within it. The remainder (for the most part what we call spices) are tropicals but may adapt to indoor or greenhouse culture. Ginger with its bold thrust and bright leaf would make a most desirable house plant even without the extra dividends of richly fragrant blossoms and fresh root for Oriental dishes. A bay tree adds so much to the terrace and the soup kettle that it earns warm winter quarters, repotting and regular doles of compost.

But the resins and oils which give any spice or herb its characteristic flavor and aroma reach full development only in natural surroundings. Size, growing habits and harvesting problems make other plants unsuited to home gardens. So the practical-minded must relinquish any dreams of self-sufficiency (Yes, sir, *make the absinthe right on the place from your own wormwood*) and concentrate on more likely subjects.

Few would agree on what six or twenty-six herbs are most important. The twenty-six described in the gardening table were selected because they are common to many cuisines and will grow almost anywhere in the United States, although some must be protected by a mulch or wintered indoors in the North, and others will require supplementary watering and a shaded site in the Southwest and West.

All adapt to ordinary soil. Heavy clays may be improved with plaster rubble, wood ashes or well-rotted compost.

Manure and commercial fertilizers should never be used in herb gardens for they encourage lush growth at the expense of flavor and fragrance.

Herbs also do well in pots and boxes and may be strategically deployed from the outdoor fireplace to picnic table, terrace, entrance and, at the approach of winter, to a sunny window indoors. For indoor cultivation, choose dwarf varieties of the larger plants such as sage, lavender, basil, and so forth. As mints spread rapidly, do not use them in window boxes but pot them alone.

The old earthen crocks once used for cheese and butter make excellent planters, and if a good layer of stones or shards is placed on the bottom, a drainage opening is unnecessary. Slightly richer soil may be required than for field-grown plants, and regular watering is essential.

There are many "wild" herbs—some like creeping thyme, tansy, dill and the mints have escaped from gardens. Others are natives which bear a real or fancied relationship to cultivated varieties. Indiscriminate collection or use of this material by amateurs is always foolish, sometimes fatal. Poison hemlock killed not only Socrates but many others who mistook the plant for "wild parsley" or "wild sweet cicely." Anyone bent on botanizing rather than suicide should study a dependable manual of edible and nonedible plants before collecting herb specimens in the field. (A good one to start with: *Edible Wild Plants of Eastern North America, Rev. Ed.*, Fernald, L. Merritt and others, Harper, 1958, $6.)

With living herbs at hand, the possibilities of the whole plant can be explored. Flowers will give color as well as flavor. Add finely chopped pot marigold (calendula) petals to curries, caramel custard, Irish soda bread (an old specific against nibbling leprechauns). Float stars of borage, blue as the sky, on vichyssoise, or put a circlet of them around *coeur de crème*.

To candy borage and other small flowers, such as violets, select perfect specimens and dip first into slightly beaten egg white and then into granulated sugar. Shake lightly. Dry on a tray in a warm place and store in air-tight containers. Mint leaves can also be candied or, as a bit of 19th-century elegance, chocolate-coated by a process simple enough for a kindergartener to master. Select twenty large, perfect leaves (those from pineapple or apple mint are best). Remove the leaves from the stalk, put them between sheets of uncoated paper or foil and keep them in a warm place until dry. Melt one ounce (a cake) of semisweet chocolate in a double boiler. With a soft brush carefully paint one side of each leaf and slide the leaves into the refrigerator on the paper. As soon as the chocolate hardens, turn the leaves over and paint the other side. When they are lightly coated the pattern of vein, midrib and edging remains distinct. The leaves may be used as confections, on cakes, ice cream and puddings.

To candy the fresh roots of angelica, ginger, lovage, and so on, wash, peel and cut them into half-inch slices. Cover them with boiling water and simmer them in a covered pan until just tender, but not soft; drain them when cool. Make sufficient sirup from equal amounts of sugar and water to cover the roots, and bring it to a boil. Add the roots and simmer them until transparent. Drained and coated with granulated sugar, they look like frosted jewels.

The roots of green ginger, necessary in so many Chinese dishes, and horse-radish washed, peeled, wrapped in foil and quick-frozen, may be grated when needed without thawing.

Seeds of dill, anise, fennel, coriander, sweet cicely, exquisite in form, add a subtle texture and flavor to pastries, and make chopped nuts seem blatant by contrast. Seed heads should be cut after ripening but before shattering—a moment difficult to catch—and spread on a screen or hung in bunches until dry. Then gently shake or rub the seeds from the flower heads and store in jars. An exception is nasturtium seed, which must be used fresh in salad or pickled as mock capers. Crush all large or hard-coated seeds in a mortar or with a rolling pin before using.

A seed's flavor often differs from the flavor of the plant's leaf or flower. Coriander, tasting lemony-clove when crushed, adds such gentility to thin butter cookies that the recipe might be Miss Jane Austen's own.

For a flaky tidbit with a whisper of caraway, cut three ounces of butter and a small package of cream cheese into a cup of flour mixed with a quarter cup of dill seed. Form the mixture into tiny balls, chill them and then bake them at 350° F. four to five minutes, and serve hot or cold with sherry or cocktails.

Seeds may also be added to sweet doughs or sprinkled on the loaf before baking. There is no end to their versatility: dill seed with sauerkraut cooked in white wine, fennel with green mayonnaise on shrimp, lovage in chicken pie, angelica with poached pears.

Thanks to an herb garden, it is possible to explore the full potential of a single herb. Rosemary's affinity for chicken, veal and fish is well known. But also try finely chopped leaves in tiny dumplings with lamb stew, sprinkled on braised celery, in a marmalade of bitter oranges or as a stuffing for broiled mushroom caps. Put a branch into a bottle of vodka for a new kind of liqueur, a second in a jar of mild honey, a third in a cruet of wine vinegar, a fourth in the teapot as a tisane; use a fifth to baste roasting meat.

Dried herbs, if not as good as fresh ones, are, when properly prepared, better than none at all. Friends and family who show little enthusiasm for picking beans or gathering apples will lend willing hands when the time comes to fill the baskets with aromatic shearings. Midmorning on a hot breezy day, preferably just before the plant blooms, is the best time to harvest herbs. (Sage, an exception, is musky unless cut before buds form.) Depending on the season and the age of the plant, a second and sometimes a third cutting is possible. It is not necessary to sacrifice flower for leaf; judicious trimming gives both.

Take only young fresh growth, shake briskly, remove foreign material and damaged leaves, and tie scant handfuls into loose bunches. If necessary, wash trailing plants or those grown in sandy ground and drain thoroughly, but do not bunch.

An old-fashioned, uninsulated attic with low humidity, a temperature between 90° and 100° and no sun to bleach the leaves, fulfills all the requirements for a drying room. Any other place approximating these conditions will serve. String lines four feet apart and hang the bunches fan-wise to dry (hang washed herbs separately). Herbs may also be spread on screens or wicker trays (the Japanese make handsome ones) stacked to permit free circulation of air. Drying by stove can be managed in a warming drawer, a deep-well cooker on a simmer setting, or an oven at lowest setting, but an inferior product results.

Drying time varies with the plant, the weather and the place. Savory, rosemary, thyme, sage, mints take a week or less, and remain pungent. Parsley and dill require more time and lose flavor in the process. Basil tends to reabsorb moisture, molds easily and may turn black if not kept at a constant temperature.

Once herbs have been dried, the problem is to remove stem and stalk but retain the leaf in as perfect state as possible so that its full strength is hoarded until the moment it goes into a dish. This is especially important with herbs used for tea—mint, lemon balm, linden flowers and so forth.

Unfortunately the dream and the reality are difficult to reconcile. Properly dried leaves are brittle. While with patience some may be plucked whole, the bulk is best stripped from the stalk, pulverized by hand and screened through a sieve with a quarter-inch mesh. The goal: a broken leaf rather than flavored dust.

Put a small amount of each herb in a wide-mouthed, airtight container (with either a stopper or screw closure). Check in a day or two. If condensation develops, dry the material further; if not, pack the remainder, label and date.

Herbs hung from ceiling beams or stored in clear glass bottles on open shelves please decorators but not gourmets. Light, dust and humidity diminish flavor; so does time. The day the new herbs are cut everything in the spice cupboard more than a year old ought to be ceremonially discarded. This need not be a loss. Sprinkle rosemary on the coals just before lamb comes off the spit, or orégano to finish off chicken. Green branches, too, produce savory smoke for grills and Chinese ovens.

Herbs may also be preserved by quick freezing. Color and flavor remain, but the greens, when thawed, are too limp for salad or garnishing. They may be used elsewhere, though, in the same manner as fresh herbs. To process, chop them very fine, wrap them in foil and freeze them. Another method is to tie them into small bunches (for example, four to five stalks of parsley) and plunge them quickly into boiling water without allowing the steam to touch the leaves. Blanch them forty-five seconds—in no case longer than one minute—then remove them, chill them in ice water and shake them dry. Pack them in small containers or in foil, folded airtight.

Herb vinegars preserve strength and pungency and add the desired flavor to salads, sauces, marinades, vegetables and soup. Gather your herbs as for drying. Strip the leaves or, if young growth, use the whole stalk. Pack the herbs into a crock or glass jar. Use full-strength cider or wine vinegar, preferably undistilled, adding it at the rate of a quart to three cups of leaves and mixing it well with a wooden spoon. Let the brew stand two to three weeks, stirring it daily, then strain it through cloth, or filter it twice. Use a glass funnel to bottle and put a sprig of fresh tarragon, a dill head, and so forth, in the bottle to serve as a label. Your kitchen by this time may look like the laboratory of Merlin the Magician.

Herb salts are useful where a dash of flavor is desired. Mix a cup of pure salt (not iodized) with one to one and one half cups of chopped or pounded herbs (chives, tarragon, basil, and so on), alone or in combination, in a blender for three to four minutes. Spread the mixture on a flat tray and keep it in the oven at the lowest setting until dry. Reblend if necessary.

Mustard is another vehicle for herbs, but only for those which can challenge its dominancy. A good base is achieved by combining a cup of dry mustard, a cup of flour and a tablespoon of salt. Blend this with a quarter cup of brown

(Continued on page 164)

Guide to Herbs
How to Grow and Use Them

Angelica To 6' high. Coarse-leaved. Small greenish-white flowers in June of second, third year. For back of borders, northern exposures, or naturalizing beside pools, streams.

Balm 1–2' high. Blossom inconspicuous. Lemon-scented foliage. Excellent bee plant. Sometimes called lemon balm.

Basil (Sweet) To 18". Small inconspicuous flower. Fresh green foliage contrasts in mixed border if plant is kept trimmed. There are also dwarf, curly-leafed, purple-leafed varieties.

Borage 2–3' high. Starlike blue flowers (also white and pink). Blooms throughout season. Tendency to sprawl.

Burnet 1–1½' high. Distinctive leaf, rose or white flowers. Attractive in border.

Camomile To 12". Daisylike flowers, fine threadlike leaves. Creeping habit. Excellent ground cover.

Chervil 1–2' high. Small white flowers in clusters, delicate fernlike foliage. Naturalizes well in open woodland.

Chives 8–12" high. Neat clumps. Mauve-pink blossoms throughout season. Attractive in rock garden, or as edging.

Cicely (Sweet) To 3'. White flowers in June, ferny foliage. Attractive in shady border, wild garden, in front of evergreens.

NOTES: *The following are amplifications of terms used in the Propagation column:*
1. *Root division: Break original clumps into smaller ones and reset.*
2. *Cuttings: Cut three- to four-inch-long branch tips at right angles below a node with a very sharp blade. Remove leaves from lower half and set the slip in sand (flats or pots) or directly in an* outside bed. *Either treatment seems equally satisfactory if the cuttings are firmed in very well, kept moist and protected from sun and wind.*
3. *Layering: Peg a low branch to the ground with a flat stone or bent wire and cover it with dirt. If plants are woody, scrape away a small portion of the outer bark of the branch before covering. This "wounding" often hastens root development.*

PROPAGATION	CULTURE	HARVESTING	USE
By fresh seed sown as early as ripe.	Biennial, or if not allowed to seed, a short-lived perennial. Is tolerant, but prefers rich moist soil, half shade, cool climate. Needs feeding or fresh site after few years.	Use second-year plants. Cut stem, leaf stalks in June and Aug. Dry ripened seed. Dig roots in Aug., wash, dry in open air, store.	Has licorice-vanilla aroma and flavor. Fresh stems, leaf stalks, sometimes roots, candied; used as confections, cake decorations, in custard compotes. Seeds in pastry, puddings.
By root division or seed in spring. Self-sows. May be potted for indoor use.	Hardy perennial. Thrives in any soil, sun or shade.	Use green leaves. Dry just before blooming period and again in late Aug.	Lemon flavor and aroma. Fresh leaves used in salad, punch, tea and cold fruit soups; dried, in sachets, potpourri, linen closets.
By seed planted indoors in early spring or outdoors when soil is warm. For winter use, sow seed in pot 3 to 4 weeks before frost, or cut back plants and pot.	Very tender annual. Prefers full sun, ordinary soil. Cut back to prevent legginess.	Matures in 7 to 8 weeks. Use leaves fresh, or dry them in small bunches, turning frequently to prevent mold.	Rich, permeating flavor combines well with tomatoes, fish, salad. Makes an excellent herb vinegar. Essential in Italian, Portuguese, Spanish dishes.
By seed in late fall or early spring. Young seedlings transplant readily. Plant self-sows.	Hardy annual. Prefers dry sunny site, but adapts to partial shade. Cut back sharply to prolong bloom and improve form.	Use blossoms and leaves fresh. Neither retain flavor after drying.	Leaves add cucumber fragrance and taste to salads, freshness to claret cup and punches. Flowers candied or used as garnish.
By root division or seed from early spring to midsummer.	Hardy perennial. Any soil. Prefers sun. Keep cutting out seed heads.	Use fresh leaf tips anytime. Flavor lost when dried.	Adds light cucumber flavor to sandwich fillings, salads, summer drinks, vinegar.
By root division or seed in spring.	Hardy perennial. Prefers dry, sunny location.	Snip leaves and flowers as needed.	A popular tisane in France. Brew as tea or use sparingly in beef or veal stock.
By seed planted late fall or early spring. Less mature plants may be potted in fall for indoor use.	Annual. Prefers moist but well-drained site, partial shade. Seedlings need protection from wind and sun.	Use fresh leaves. Dry in July and Sept.	Likened to tarragon and parsley but more delicate. An important *fine herbe* in omelets, sauces, salads.
By seed in early spring or division of old clump of bulbs anytime during the season. Clumps potted for indoor use need few weeks of low temperature for new start.	Hardy perennial. Prefers light rich soil, full sun, but tolerates shade, withstands drought. Divide crowded clumps annually.	Cut leaves close to ground (never tops). For best flavor, texture cut clump to ground twice yearly.	Chopped leaves give hint of onion to salads, potatoes, soups, sauces, eggs. Small bulbs used fresh, sometimes pickled.
By division spring or fall or fresh seeds sown in fall or after stratification in spring.	Average soil. Likes moisture and shade.	Use leaves, shoots, seeds fresh. Dried leaves lack flavor. Seeds best dried green.	Fresh leaves: salads, cold vegetables. Peeled shoots: raw or lightly boiled as greens. Seeds fresh or dried: cakes, candy, liqueurs.

(Continued from page 162)

sugar dissolved in one cup of herb vinegar. Add herbs as desired: if fresh, very finely chopped; if dried, pulverized and steeped in a tablespoonful of warm olive oil. After bottling this herb mustard, allow it to mellow for ten days before using.

Sugar holds both fragrance and flavor. Eight or ten leaves of rose geranium will give as much character to a jar of it as a vanilla bean. Queen Henrietta Maria, who brought white lavender to England when she married Charles I, made a conserve by pounding lavender flowers with thrice their weight in sugar. Try rose sugar in pound cake and on fruit. For an Elizabethan delectation, warm one cup of lavender sugar with one cup of light cream. Add one envelope of gelatin dissolved in one half cup of cold water and beat in one cup of sour cream. Pour this into molds, and when it has thickened, serve it with wild strawberries.

The delicate flavors of chervil or burnet, as well as the robustness of dill and basil, so often lost in drying, can be preserved in butter. The herbs, alone or in *fines herbes* or other combinations, should be finely chopped and worked into sweet butter at room temperature, at the rate of three to five tablespoons per half pound with a half teaspoonful of brandy added to bless the union. Refrigerate the butter in foil or closed containers, or freeze for later use.

Herbs have gifts for every sense, for every season—a rosemary hung with tiny golden balls at Christmas, "the gilt rosmarie" of Spenser's poem; vases full of dill and borage, bergamot and calendulas all summer; a terrace carpeted with thyme that answers each footstep with the sweet scent, Kipling said, "of dawn in Paradise." Potpourri in the China jars, marjoram for a bubbling pot, a green curl of parsley leaf beneath the snow to promise spring. Fragrance, flavor, flower, form. Who could ask for more?

Clary Sage 3 to 4′. Large-leaved, flowering stalks, whitish blossoms with aromatic odor. Attractive in back of border.

Dill To 3′. Large umbels of yellowish-green flowers. Attractive in flower and vegetable gardens. Dry seed heads handsome in bouquets.

Fennel 4–5′ high. Blooms second year. Resembles dill but bushier. Suitable in borders, as accent plant; attractive in flower arrangements.

Geranium (Rose-Scented) To 2′. Useful in borders or as pot plant. Bloom less profuse than on regular types. Other fragrant varieties: nutmeg, lemon, ginger, apple, mint and cinnamon.

Lavender 1–3′ high. Purple spikes (also rose, white). Useful as border, specimen-tub plant or low hedge. Dwarf varieties attractive in rock garden.

Mint 1–2′ high. Includes peppermint, spearmint and many scented types such as pineapple, apple, orange. Inconspicuous bloom. Crawling, spreading habits do not adapt it to garden use.

Marjoram (Sweet) 8–12″ high. If kept trimmed, useful as edging in border, rockery.

Orégano To 2′. Tends to spread. Good in kitchen garden or dry rocky banks.

Parsley To 8″. Neat habit, bright color, distinct leaf. Good for edging or low border.

Rosemary To 6′ in mild climates, 2′ in north. Inconspicuous flower, gray-green foliage, dynamic form. Attractive in border, pot, rockery.

Sage To 2½′. Blue-purple flowers. A shrub, border or accent plant. Other varieties: dwarf, purple-leafed and pineapple-scented.

Savory Winter savory: To 10″; low hedge edging, rock-garden plant. Summer savory: To 1′; straggles; best in kitchen garden.

Tarragon 12 to 18″. Many-branched. Narrow, twisted leaves.

Thyme 6–10″ high. Almost evergreen. Bush thyme: edging, low hedges, pot border, rockery. Creeping type: ground cover, rockery flagstones.

Woodruff (Sweet) To 8″. White blossoms in early summer. Spreading habit and alert form make it an ideal ground cover.

PROPAGATION	CULTURE	HARVESTING	USE
By seed in spring or Aug.	Biennial. Any soil. Sun. Two-year-old plants should be replaced.	Use fresh leaves.	Used in omelets, fritters.
By seed in late fall, early spring. Self-sows. Very young seedlings will transplant. Plant seeds in pot in August for winter use.	Biennial, usually treated as hardy annual. Prefers average soil, full sun. Extremely tolerant, withstands drought.	Use leaves and seeds. Dried leaves lack flavor, but dried seeds retain pungency.	Leaves, seed heads used in vinegar, pickles, fish salad, vegetables, sauces, soup; seeds, in pastries, cake.
By seed in early spring. Thin seedlings to one per sq. ft.	Perennial, sometimes treated as annual. Prefers light, well-drained, sweet soil and sun, but is adaptable.	Use leaves and stems green. Dried leaves lack flavor. Dry ripened seeds.	Used in salads, cold sauces, fish. Stems eaten raw as relish or blanched as vegetable. Seeds flavor candy, liqueurs.
By cuttings any time.	Perennial only in South and West. Elsewhere wintered indoors. Likes light, well-drained soil, sun. Peppermint-scented variety prefers shade.	Use green leaves. Dry surplus.	Green leaves impart their particular scent to pound cake, puddings, jelly, compotes. Dried leaves used in sachets, linen closets.
By layering or cuttings of new growth in June or July. Also by seed in pots or cold frame, spring or fall.	Shrubby perennial. In exposed position in northern areas may need winter protection.	Snip leaf tips as desired during growing season. Dry surplus. Cut just opening flower spikes and dry.	Leaves and flowers give pleasant bitterness to salad. Fresh flowers garnish fruit desserts, decorate cake. Dried flowers used in sachets.
By runners, cuttings, root division. Spreads rapidly. Clumps potted and cut back need few weeks of low temperature for new growth indoors.	Hardy perennial. Prefers rich moist soil but thrives in average garden in sun or light shade.	Use green leaves. Dry before bloom and again in late summer.	Perhaps most versatile herb. Green or dried with peas, carrots, lamb, potato salad, jellies.
By division, layering, cuttings in spring. Pot before frost for indoor use.	Both marjoram and orégano are perennials, but marjoram is usually treated as an annual. Prefer light, sweet, well-drained soil, sun.	Use fresh young leaves. Dry before bloom in late Aug.	Flavor and aroma of both are similar, although marjoram is considered more delicate. Use in vinegar, salads, with pork, squash.
By seed sown indoors in early spring and transplanted to bed when 3" high.			
By seed, early spring to midsummer. Soak seed few hours to hasten germination. Pot young plants in late fall for indoor use.	Biennial. Sometimes short-lived perennial. Any garden soil. Tolerates light shade, dryness.	Use fresh leaves as desired. Dry leaves in midsummer and late Aug. If protected by cover, plants stay green throughout winter.	Indispensable as potherb, *fine herbe*, garnish, salad green. Enhances almost every dish.
By layering and cuttings. Difficult from seed.	Evergreen shrub. Winter indoors in pots, outdoors in cold frame, pit. Well-drained, gravelly soil, light and sweet. Full sun.	Fresh leaves as desired. Dry branches before bloom or in late summer.	Salad, chicken, fish, veal, vegetables, savories, soup.
By layering, cuttings, root division. Seed in early spring. Renew plants triennially for best flavor.	Hardy shrub Any soil. Sun or half-shade. Withstands drought. Prune sharply after bloom. Cut to ground early winter.	Use fresh young tip leaves. Dry prunings.	Cheese, roast pork, sausage, goose, jelly, tea, creamed onions.
Winter: by layering, cuttings, seed in spring. Summer: by seed sown early in spring.	Winter: hardy perennial subshrub. Light, well-drained soil, sun. Summer: tender annual. Rich, moist but well-drained site. Sun.	Winter: use fresh leaves. Dry branches before bloom in late summer. Summer: sweeter of two, is considered to have more delicate flavor.	Game, eggs, vegetables, particularly beans, soups, stew, stuffings.
By root or branch cuttings in spring or fall. Difficult from seed. Small shoots can be potted for winter use.	Hardy perennial once established. Light sandy soil. Minimum shade or full sun. In North needs winter protection.	Use fresh leaves as desired. Dry upper half of branch. Aroma and flavor decrease rapidly in storage.	Fresh or dried for salad vinegars, marinades, fish, sauces.
By layering, cuttings, root division during growing season. Seed in spring. Pot bush or creeping thymes in late fall for winter use.	Light sandy soil and rocks, sun. Tolerates light shade.	Use fresh leaves. Dry before bloom or in late Aug.	Indispensable in soup, with sauces, stew, meat, fish, poultry, vegetables.
By runners, root division throughout growing season, or by seed sown immediately after ripening.	Shade, rich moist soil. In far North requires winter protection.	Use fresh leaves. Dry after blooming and in late Aug.	Fresh leaves (flavor but little aroma) in May wine, white wine punches; dried leaves (aroma but little flavor) in potpourri.

PART III: *The Gourmet in the Garden*

A Handbook of Gourmet Gardening
/ *Silas and Helen Hoffman Spitzer*

How do you like your vegetables and greens?
Young, tender, at the peak of freshness and flavor? Then grow them.
Down-to-earth tips on the most rewarding form of back-yard gardening

A GOURMET garden has only one purpose, and that a purely selfish one: to bless its owners with a constant supply of young vegetables and greens, picked at the tender, juicy climax of their freshness and flavor.

As any good cook or fastidious eater knows, the only sure way of achieving this is to raise your pet vegetables in your own soil. Certainly you cannot buy peak freshness at the market. There is no comparison between your own lettuces, peas or snap beans, for example, and commercially grown prototypes, which are usually bred oversize to capture the eye, tough-skinned to withstand long exposure, and are sold half-congealed from storage and long hauls under refrigeration.

One of my gastronomical convictions is that vegetables make fine eating on their own. They should be cooked simply to bring out their individual character, not buried in complicated sauces or subjected to other culinary flourishes. But even the most elaborate recipes of *la haute cuisine* are benefited by *fresh* vegetables. Chefs have often remarked to me that the main difference between cooking in France and the same recipes prepared over here is that the French cook is able to use green stuff picked the same day. In that country of passionate *gourmandise*, vegetables are so revered that they are often served as a separate course, after the main dish.

Except for certain commonplace types which require maturity, most vegetables are the better for being eaten while deliciously young and quite small. Among these, I might suggest the following: peas, snap beans, beets, carrots, kohlrabi, lettuce, radishes, spinach (especially in salads), summer squash (cut up in two-inch lengths, steamed and buttered), lima beans, cucumbers and even potatoes (tiny new spuds are marvelous when boiled or baked and served in their vests with butter and a dusting of paprika, especially as a cocktail accompaniment).

The gourmet—a word, by the way, stretched so thin nowadays that it is applied to anyone fastidious enough to avoid pouring ketchup on ice cream—will specialize on his favorites and waste no space in his garden on the so-called "practical" vegetables. These flourish like the wicked and compel one to spend endless tedious hours canning and processing the inevitable surplus for an illusory future use.

In the spring of 1944, my wife and I moved into our first summer weekend home, far out on eastern Long Island. On the first morning, we went around to the back to look things

The Provinces—country markets; the tree-shaded produce is in ▶
Aix-en-Provence.

over and noticed a square patch of ground that obviously had once been under cultivation. We stared at this dreamily for a while and the thought must have struck us both at the same moment—*why not a vegetable garden of our own?* I am not quite sure what this suggested to her, but I still recall my own vivid mental reaction.

In a flash of wishful imagery, a parade of delectable dishes streamed past on the screen of my imagination, in bright Technicolor detail. First I saw a platter piled high with foot-long asparagus, swimming in melted butter. Then tiny sugar peas and infant carrots, nestling like jewels in a brown and fragrant *navarin* of spring lamb. Next appeared a great mound of sweet corn, steaming hot. I bit deeply into three rows of milky kernels and the spurting succulence proved that they had been whisked from plot to pot in a matter of minutes. At least three other mouth-watering visions occurred to me. The delectable Italian vegetable omelet called *frittata con legumi*. A wooden bowl filled with light green lettuce, flecked with olive oil and red wine vinegar and kissed lightly by garlic. And finally, crowning reward of our devoted toil and skill—a great tureen of *minestrone*, crammed with at least ten different vegetables, all fresh from our own miraculous little weekend garden.

Fourteen years have come and gone since that beatific moment in the dream life of an unrepentant glutton. And—glory be—that vision of lovely food, for the most part, has come true. For better or for worse, in triumph and in failure, we have always had a garden.

That first garden set the pattern for all the rest. Earnestly we resolved that our garden would be different from all the others around us. We decided to raise only what we loved to eat, and if we loved it very much, we would raise a lot of it. There were three in the household, and each would indulge his private whims. Our garden would be neither too large nor too small, neither too ambitious nor lacking in experiment. It would reflect our tastes and prejudices in food. It would enable us to prepare food that we hoped would taste like divine dishes we had eaten at the Grand Vefour in Paris, at Papagallo in Bologna or at the home of a rich friend of a friend of ours who has a *cordon bleu* cook in his kitchen. And it would free us from dependence on the market, except for those common staples that we would give no room to because we could buy them cheaper and just as good from Mike, our local dispenser of produce.

Deciding what vegetables should go into a garden is almost as much fun as eating them later on. We planned our present garden in the dead of winter, sprawled on the rug of our city living room, surrounded by notebooks, kitchen memoranda, recipes, seed catalogues and an almost perceptible pink cloud of optimism. This is by far the happiest phase of gardening. It occurs entirely in the mind, and is utterly free from drought, disease, marauding rabbits, pests, headaches and blisters.

The plan was originally a precise rectangle but it has evolved over the years to its present outline, roughly free-form, twenty-five feet wide at the top, sixty feet long, curving on the outer edge to a narrow six-foot tip. Perhaps this flowing shape, resembling the conformation of a Smithfield ham, would not have the approval of the professionals but it blends neatly into our landscape and it is our very own idea, so naturally we are fond of it. The curved side, in summer and fall, is brightened by a sixteen-inch-wide border of annual

flowers, which lends a decorative touch and also helps keep out invading meadow grass.

We selected most of our favorite vegetables from the catalogue of a well-known seedsman in northern New York State. All except a few new vegetables had already been tested in our garden and were adapted to our special soil and weather problems. We are lucky enough to own some of the best truck-garden soil in the Middle Atlantic zone, lavishly productive in potatoes, cauliflower, Lima beans, strawberries and corn. It is sandy loam, neither too light nor too heavy, well drained, slightly on the acid side. (Naturally, any observations on planting or cultivation should be adjusted to suit your own local problems of soil and climate.)

Years ago, we prided ourselves on performing all the heavy duties of maintenance. We used to "double-trench" every spring—as good English gardeners are supposed to do —deeply, thoroughly, spadeful by spadeful. But, as we grew older and wiser, we decided to reduce all strenuous exertion to a minimum. Nowadays we turn all this work over to Frank, our favorite maintenance man.

A year ago last fall, before we closed the house and headed for the city, Frank cleaned up and burned or carted away all trash and debris. When the ground had frozen, he put the garden to sleep for the winter under a thick blanket of well-aged cow manure—that substance as precious to the part-time countryman as sunshine or rain. In early spring, the ground was deeply plowed and harrowed to get it ready for planting.

On the first sunny weekend in April, we drove out to the country and made straight for the vegetable patch. The soft rich brown dirt crumbled easily in our fingers and smelled of moist fertility. We changed to jeans and heavy boots, got out trowels and marking lines and went to work. By late afternoon, with the sun fading and our backs stiff as boards, we had put in both early and late peas, two kinds of red radishes, short rows of dill, parsley, carrots and onions.

From then until midsummer, we were busy every weekend, planting, thinning, transplanting, weeding, dusting and watering. In between times, we could hardly wait to get out there to see what had happened since our last visit. With a garden, there is never an end to surprises.

We are convinced that the three greatest gustatory rewards of gardening are eating young peas, asparagus and green corn. Peas and asparagus have never been missing from our garden. But corn, to our sorrow, we have had to abandon, and for good reasons. We tried it year after year. It always took up more space than it proved to be worth. Worms, borers, smut, ravenous crows and prolonged dry spells kept us frustrated. Most seasons, the total yield of clean, top-grade eating ears was about a third of the original planting, and sometimes it was a complete failure. But fortunately, we can buy all the young, green corn we crave from farms in the neighborhood, where it is usually picked for us an hour or two before mealtime. We like it plain boiled, roasted in ashes, creamed with baby Lima beans, or fried in crisp, thin fritters.

We grow two varieties of peas and eat them very small and young, when they have not only the tenderness of immaturity but also the full flavor of the true pea. Peas should never be fancified in the cooking. Their flavor is intrinsic and not even the most accomplished chef can improve on it. They should be picked and shelled right where they grow and

Garden Plan

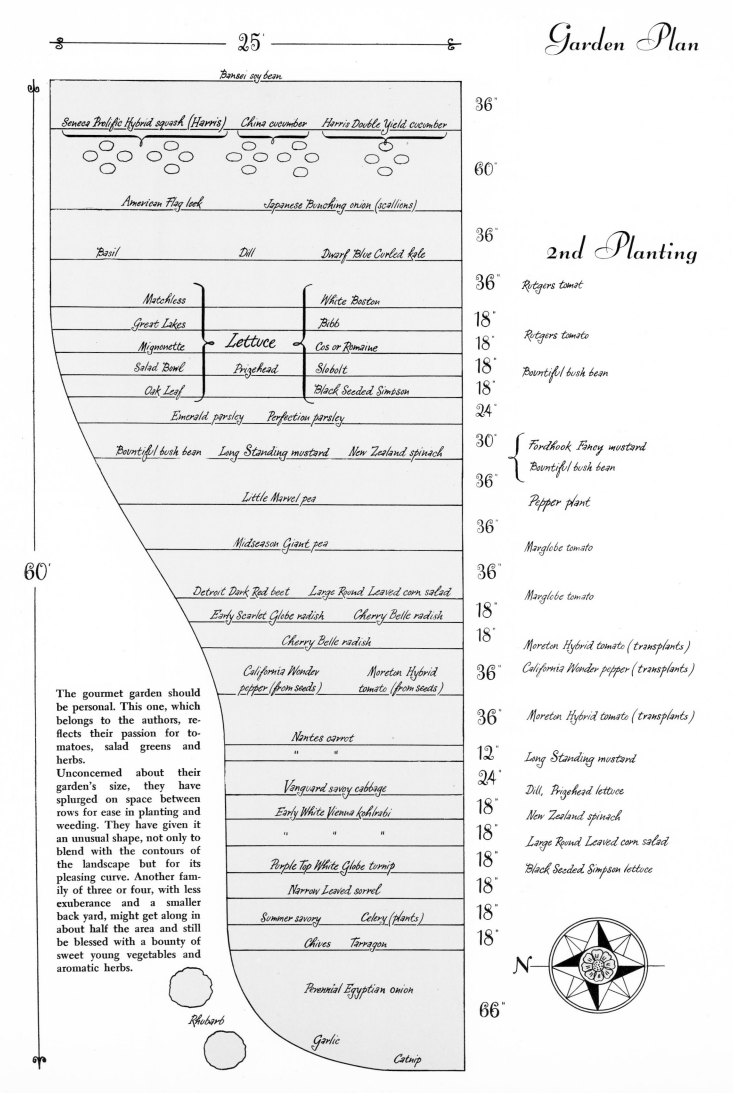

25'

Bansei soy bean

Seneca Prolific Hybrid squash (Harris)   China cucumber   Harris Double Yield cucumber   36"

60"

American Flag leek   Japanese Bunching onion (scallions)

36"

Basil   Dill   Dwarf Blue Curled kale

36"

Matchless   White Boston   36"
Great Lakes   Bibb   18"
Mignonette   Lettuce   Cos or Romaine   18"
Salad Bowl   Prizehead   Slobolt   18"
Oak Leaf   Black Seeded Simpson   18"

Emerald parsley   Perfection parsley   24"

Bountiful bush bean   Long Standing mustard   New Zealand spinach   30"

36"

Little Marvel pea

Midseason Giant pea   36"

Detroit Dark Red beet   Large Round Leaved corn salad   36"
Early Scarlet Globe radish   Cherry Belle radish   18"
Cherry Belle radish   18"

California Wonder pepper (from seeds)   Moreton Hybrid tomato (from seeds)   36"

Nantes carrot   36"
"   "   12"

Vanguard savoy cabbage   24"
Early White Vienna kohlrabi   18"
"   "   "   18"

Purple Top White Globe turnip   18"
Narrow Leaved sorrel   18"
Summer savory   Celery (plants)   18"
Chives   Tarragon   18"

Perennial Egyptian onion

Rhubarb

Garlic   66"

Catnip

60'

2nd Planting

Rutgers tomat

Rutgers tomato

Bountiful bush bean

{ Fordhook Fancy mustard
Bountiful bush bean

Pepper plant

Marglobe tomato

Marglobe tomato

Moreton Hybrid tomato (transplants)

California Wonder pepper (transplants)

Moreton Hybrid tomato (transplants)

Long Standing mustard

Dill, Prizehead lettuce

New Zealand spinach

Large Round Leaved corn salad

Black Seeded Simpson lettuce

The gourmet garden should be personal. This one, which belongs to the authors, reflects their passion for tomatoes, salad greens and herbs.

Unconcerned about their garden's size, they have splurged on space between rows for ease in planting and weeding. They have given it an unusual shape, not only to blend with the contours of the landscape but for its pleasing curve. Another family of three or four, with less exuberance and a smaller back yard, might get along in about half the area and still be blessed with a bounty of sweet young vegetables and aromatic herbs.

cooked very quickly in a small splash of water. After draining, season them lightly, add a large piece of butter and ladle them into individual soup plates. Young June peas are always consumed in a reverent silence in our house. Even though they use up much space, have a short life and provide only two or three man-sized meals per season, we feel that nothing in nature can surpass them.

Every spring, we pat ourselves on the back for having established our own bed of asparagus, ten years ago. A deep trench was dug in a sunny spot close to the garden, thirty-five feet long and about four feet wide. Asparagus are heavy feeders and long tenants, so they require a heavy base of bone meal and organic fertilizer, as well as seasonal doses of the same, plus constant weeding and grooming. But no planting yields as much sheer eating pleasure to the amateur of good food. By early May, a row of sturdy tips thrusts above ground, and when that happens, we cannot wait any longer. We cut a basketful of the tiny green-and-purple sprites when they are no more than three inches long. Then we pile them on a plate of cracked ice and eat them raw with salt as an *hors d'oeuvre*, poetically evocative of the budding spring, especially when combined with an alternate crunching of radishes and young green onions.

For about forty days, the asparagus spikes keep thrusting upward and we keep cutting and eating. There are so many that we bestow fat bunches on our friends and neighbors. Like peas, they are the better for being eaten as plainly as possible. Just steam them, standing upright over boiling water, until they are tender yet firm. Then serve them with melted butter and halves of lemon. For Sunday dinner, they may be dressed with *hollandaise* or *mousseline* sauce. My wife often cooks fresh "grass" as she was taught in her Minnesota girlhood. She chops the tender parts into one-and-a-half-inch lengths, cooks them, drains them and adds plenty of heavy cream, butter and a little salt and white pepper. This lovely country dish should be eaten hurriedly with a tablespoon.

Anyone noticing from ten to eighteen varieties of lettuce in our garden would correctly deduce that we have a weakness for salads. We plant both the heading and leafy kinds in half rows and work hard to keep the late varieties coming even into the hot weather. In June, when the lettuce is spreading and foaming in lacy green masses over the wet earth, our lunch often consists of a loaf of home-baked brown bread, a wedge of yellow cheese and a huge bowl of mixed salad.

The salad might include buttery-tasting Bibb, beautifully designed Oak Leaf, Matchless, Black-Seeded Simpson and Prize Head, loose leaves of young mustard and sorrel, a few sprigs of aromatic basil, a little tarragon and feathery green dill, parsley and very young spinach or kale. The dressing is almost always a simple one of olive oil, wine vinegar, salt, pepper and a pinch of dry mustard, but occasionally we add crumbled blue cheese. Two or three hills of ordinary cucumbers provide another invaluable ingredient for the salad bowl, later in the season. Cucumbers are of course also excellent when thinly sliced, salted, drained and covered with thick sour cream.

High tide in the salad garden confronts us with an embarrassment of riches. My wife solves the problem of overflow rather cleverly by presenting friends and relatives with gift boxes of greens, instead of candy or flowers. She packs symmetrical rows of several kinds of lettuce into a square pasteboard carton, artfully harmonizing the delicate shadings of green. Between the rows, she inserts herbs of one kind or another and in the center puts a few fiery scarlet roses or some other glowing flower in season.

It seems to us that tomatoes, clinging in clusters to tall wooden stakes—green, half-ripe or red-to-bursting—are so beautiful that they justify the time, space and labor we give them, for that reason alone. And that is why you will see more rows of tomatoes in our garden plan than you might expect from its actual size. Apart from their aesthetic value, can anything compare in earthy savor to the taste of a ripe, juicy tomato, warmed by the summer sun, newly plucked from the vine and eaten hungrily out of hand? We grow many rows of tomatoes, both from seed and nursery plants, in order to get successive yields right up to the first frost.

Tomatoes we can't eat at the table, we make into juice— our own kind, which is thicker and richer than commercial products. The fruit is chopped up in chunks, dumped into our biggest pot with a handful of fresh parsley, a few celery leaves, some green onion tops, basil, and one or two green peppers cut up small. To cook, add the liquid from one mashed-up tomato and simmer everything over a low flame for about ten minutes till soft, then run the mass through a vegetable mill, discarding the residue of skins and seeds. Salt and pepper to taste, and do not add any liquid. Chilled, with a squeeze of lemon juice, this is nature's own cocktail, with a concentrated vigor that needs no vodka to add counterpoint. Heated, it makes a beautiful soup for cold weather. Either way, it is a juice for genuine tomato lovers, for it is the whole tomato, undiluted and unprettified.

Tomatoes are invaluable for many other dishes. They form the base for Spanish *gazpacho*, that exotic iced soup made of myriad vegetables, and often referred to as "liquid salad." In late summer and early fall, we eat tomatoes thinly sliced in a French dressing, or wedged into sandwiches of meat or cheese, or stuffed with chopped meat and put into the oven to brown, or baked slowly in a deep casserole between alternate layers of eggplant, Spanish onion and mozzarella cheese.

Baby snap beans, about as long as a boy's thumb, should be prepared in the same simple manner as green peas. A touch of our own is to add chopped walnuts, first grilled in butter and poured over the beans, butter and all, just before serving. A short row of green beans, bush type, can be planted as soon as the ground is warm, and the planting renewed every three weeks, for successive pickings.

We grow many herbs in our garden and have a year-round supply of tarragon, basil, parsley, dill, rosemary and summer savory. At first we tried transferring them to pots for winter growing on the kitchen window sill, but we found that too much trouble both because of the labor and the climatic vagaries of a steam-heated apartment. Now, at the end of the summer, we dry our herbs with infinite care, store them in jars, and enjoy delectable out-season treats like *poulet à l'estragon*, *linguine* with white clam sauce transformed by sweet basil, stuffed eggs in aspic decorated with sprigs of tarragon, spaghetti *al pesto* in the Genoese style (basil, cheese, garlic and olive oil made into a green sauce), and herb-flavored pot roasts, soups and stews. And there is that other sweet reward of a well-employed herb hoard: the aromatic smell of catchup put up in September and eaten at Christmas, as well as the pickles, cauliflower, carrots and other stray bits put up in mustard sauce which to us are

Fresh herbs for savory dishes can be grown indoors on a sunny window ledge. This garden, planted in stoneware crocks, includes sweet basil, thyme, chives, rosemary, dill, orégano and pineapple mint—herbs that take well to indoor cultivation.

HANS NAMUTH

worth their equivalent in truffles or some other expensive exotic.

Like anyone who dabbles in some creative pursuit, the vegetable gardener should indulge his fancy, raising every year a few experimental odds and ends. We have experimented a good deal. Among our ventures, some successful, others merely interesting, and some flat failures, were peanuts, artichokes, Belgian endive, husk tomatoes or "ground cherries," as they are known in the Middle West, water cress, tobacco, miniature watermelons, cantaloupes, snow peas, black horse-radish and, quite recently, China cucumbers, which are climbers, grotesquely thin and oddly curved, growing to a length of twenty inches. We cannot recall where we first obtained sorrel, but we will never be without it. It is a hardy plant that yields a continuous supply of crisp, acid leaves of a beautiful dark green, magically haunting to the palate when added to salads with a sparing hand. We also use sorrel to make one of the most exquisitely delicate of French soups, *crème d'oseille*, with its faintly sour flavor and lovely green-flecked creamy color.

Edible soybeans, another of our experiments, are remarkable, if you, like us, happen to enjoy their nutty, brittle texture and "green" flavor. They should be quickly cooked, pod and all, in boiling water for five minutes, then shelled and heated with butter. Our experiment with kale has resulted in our growing it now mainly for decorative purposes; an entire plant of Dwarf Blue, curled in a vase around lilies or phlox, or arranged with flowers as a table centerpiece, often graces our table.

And that recalls a dinner we gave one fine September evening many years ago, to which came a distinguished elderly Austrian professor and his wife. The table centerpiece was a huge deepsided platter filled with crinkly green kale, a bevy of raw vegetables past their prime, two large whole cabbages, a strangely shaped cucumber, big red onions, and in the very center, yellow squash blossoms, blue asters and a scattering of rose petals. This happened during wartime and we had saved up our ration tickets for weeks so that we could treat our honored guests to a magnificent rib roast of beef. When the roast was served and carved, we discovered to our dismay that both guests were not only vegetarians, but belonged to the slightly odd school that prefers its vegetables raw. But everything went well. Contentedly and with gurgles of delight, they attacked the centerpiece and succeeded in devouring it, to the last leathery leaf of kale, not forgetting to nibble at a few blossoms, presumably for dessert. In our relief, we pretended to eat along with them. Never before were we so convinced that gardening was worth while!

Garden Calendar

JANUARY *and* FEBRUARY

Plan the garden on paper. Keep last year's plan on hand to avoid planting the same vegetable in the same area, which would rob the soil of certain elements and leave others in harmful surplus.

Garden books are stingy with inches. Splurge a little on space between rows to ease cultivation.

MARCH

Have last fall's manure mulch plowed in deeply. Apply lime, if necessary, and have the plot harrowed. Exclude, of course, the perennial section containing Egyptian onions, chives, tarragon and garlic.

Hoe fertilizer into asparagus bed, apply nitrate of soda (about ten ounces to 100 square feet), and rake smooth.

Plant peas as early as the ground is workable (late March or early April). We plant two varieties, early and late, for succession crops. These grow fifteen and twenty-four inches high, without support.

Load a small basket with notebook, pencil, ball of heavy twine, scissors, markers and garden map. Add the packets of seeds that you plan to use that day, and go to work.

Leave one hoe in the garden, handy whenever you decide to have a go at the weeds. If it rusts out, you can throw it away at the end of the season; it will have done more work than any other tool in the shed.

APRIL

Plant head-lettuce seeds as early as possible.

If weather is normal, sow kale, cabbage, radishes, leeks, spinach, turnips, parsley and mustard.

Curled mustard (great for fresh greens—not boiled) should now be planted every few weeks until August in small quantities and eaten young before the taste is too strong. It is loaded with vitamins B_1, C, and G.

Sorrel is a perennial and comes up early every spring; plant some now if you have none.

MAY

At the beginning of the month:

Sow beets, corn salad (mâche), sweet basil, leaf lettuce, dill, carrots, Japanese bunching onions, more radishes, kohlrabi.

Plant pepper and tomato seeds for later transplanting.

About the middle of the month:

Buy tomato plants locally and set them out, three feet apart, in holes that have been fertilized with one tablespoon commercial fertilizer and soaked with water. Pound in poles, five or six feet tall—about four inches from each plant to prevent injuring roots. As the plants grow, pinch off lateral shoots so there will be only one main stem. Attach the stems to the poles with string or cloth strips.

Watch out for those fat, green, six-inch tomato worms.

Side-dress rows of peas with fertilizer six inches from stems and work in to encourage early growth. The younger, the sweeter!

Buy and put in pepper plants, twenty inches apart.

Late in the month:

Sow cucumber and squash seeds ten or twelve to the hill. Later, thin to three or four plants.

Plant more leaf-lettuce seeds, a row of soybeans and bush beans that require no poles.

Buy and plant a dozen or so celery plants. We use celery leaves—not stalks—all summer for seasoning.

Put bands around transplanted seedlings to guard against cutworms.

Use a hoe to weed between rows; pull weeds by hand from between the plants (but pull only after plants are high enough to stand the shock).

Weed young parsley carefully, as the shoots are hard to see. We do not thin our parsley, but use what we want as it grows. By season's end, Perfection Parsley spreads about a foot tall and wide and we pick bouquets of it for decoration.

Transplant leeks when six inches tall to rows six inches apart, and side-dress with fertilizer.

Lettuce needs cool weather. When the heading varieties are three inches tall, thin the row and leave one plant every ten inches. Transplant the strongest thinnings to another row a foot away; eat the rest. We never have trouble making lettuce head, as long as we sow early enough. If a row is delayed and doesn't have time to head before hot weather, we let it grow as leaf lettuce.

Thin rows of mustard, spinach, corn salad, onions, kohlrabi and beets. Kohlrabi should be thinned when about three inches high and then side-dressed with nitrate of soda. Beets should be thinned to stand three inches apart, cabbage eighteen inches. Salads made from thinnings are extra delicious.

JUNE

Weed, weed, weed, especially after rain. It is easier then and also cleansing to the soul.

Sow a hill of pickling cucumbers, ten or twelve seeds, to be thinned later when three inches tall to a stand of three or four.

Put up a trellis of poles and string for China cucumbers to climb on.

Keep thinning perennial Egyptian onions, as they seed themselves and may otherwise get out of hand. When very young, use them as green scallions; when medium grown, pull to use as onions. The plant is reproduced by the cluster of small bulbs at the top.

Plant second crop of snap beans, mustard and radishes.

Transplant five-to-seven-inch-tall tomato plants that were grown from seeds planted in May. Continue transplanting until mid-July in whatever space is available. These tomatoes may crawl unstaked. They will bear late but are prolific.

When about six inches high, set out peppers from previous sowing.

JULY

Stop cutting asparagus on the first of the month. Weed thoroughly and fertilize the bed.

Side-dress with a good chemical fertilizer peppers, beans, cucumbers, squash and scallions (the latter are thinnings from Japanese bunching onions).

Do *not* fertilize tomatoes. If fed too much, they produce a forest of greenery but few tomatoes.

When sweet basil is about a foot and a half high, cut back some plants to encourage new shoots.

After peas are through bearing, pull up plants and hoe them in, as they are packed with soil-enriching nitrogen.

Sow more snap beans and dill.

Spray or dust beans, peppers, squash and cucumbers for bugs, if needed. Rotenone powder is the only pesticide we use. It is harmless to humans and pets and seems to take care of everything.

AUGUST

Last chance to sow more spinach, corn salad, leaf lettuce, and, of course, mustard.

Soybean pods may be ready now. We eat them fresh but they may also be dried for winter.

Weed as usual.

SEPTEMBER

Late this month, dry parsley, basil and celery leaves. First wash, and then dry them slowly on a cooky sheet in a very low-heat open oven, or on top of an oil heater (the best way); parsley will stay emerald green. Put the crumbled dry leaves in glass jars and cover tightly. Tie branches of summer savory, tarragon and other herbs in bunches; hang them from the limb of a tree, let dry in the breeze, and store in jars.

OCTOBER

Put some garlic cloves into the ground in the perennial end of the garden, ready to come up in spring.

Cut off and burn asparagus foliage to avoid disease.

Cover tarragon plants with dry leaves, burlap and an empty bushel basket. Cover some parsley plants with leaves and burlap to keep them alive through the winter.

NOVEMBER

Spread manure on the garden and the asparagus plot and rest your weary muscles until next year.

Calendar based on Northeast climate zone

An arresting feature of the Chambord dining room is a wall of plate glass through which you see Fernand Desbans, *chef de cuisine*, in his gleaming realm. At right, François Monestier, captain of waiters, anoints *canard à l'orange with* Grand Marnier.

PART IV: *A Gourmet Tour of the United States*

Spendthrift Tour of New York / *Lucius Beebe*

A bon vivant *devotes four unforgettable days to re-exploring a special selection of Manhattan's grander dining and sluicing places*

THIS article is devoted to a four-day tour of what the French agreeably term *la vie sporting* in New York, uninhibited by worries of a fiduciary nature and conducted as though neither frugality on one hand nor ostentation on the other were a consideration. It is to be a guided tour of resorts selected on the basis of pleasure and satisfaction alone. More than anything else, the tour reflects the prejudices of a one-time New Yorker who now lives elsewhere and who follows for a few weeks each year in Manhattan a highly discriminating routine.

For almost twenty years in an earlier reincarnation I was a hotel dweller in the howling wilderness of Manhattan. As a newspaper reporter I lived in public quarters and as a private citizen I lived in hotel apartments. I became something of a connoisseur of hotel food, appointments, service and the folklore that comes to surround hotels of consequence, and my wistful souvenirs include many a fragrant name now with the ages: the old Waldorf-Astoria, the Belmont, the Manhattan, the Murray Hill, the Brevoort, the Lorraine and the original Ritz Carlton in the reign of the now almost godlike Albert Keller. My preferences lie with overtones of luxury that are associated with high ceilings, French windows and an opulence of décor now in fashionable decline, and I know nowhere that these pleasures flourish more abundantly than at the St. Regis, strategically located at the corner of Fifth Avenue and Fifty-fifth Street.

My hotel must be managed not by a corps of bookkeepers and cost accountants, but by a personality. The St. Regis is managed by Pierre Bultinck. My hotel must have impeccable room service. The St. Regis has permanently stationed floor waiters who have served the same patrons for, in some cases, decades. My hotel must have the grand manner. None has it more than the St. Regis.

The St. Regis is possessed of excellent restaurants and sluicing parlors, but its outstanding attraction for me is its men's bar, one of the last such institutions anywhere in the land and celebrated alike for the size, potency and excellence of its drinks and the presence over the back bar of Maxfield Parrish's enigmatic painting of Old King Cole. The presence of this splendid premises only an elevator hop from my apartment restores confidence on otherwise grim mornings. Its clientele is as selective as that of a gentleman's club and membership is an accolade. My arrival in New York seldom allows for any great time lag between stepping off the cars at Grand Central and officially registering in town by laying the necessary on the long mahogany in front of Old King Cole.

A two-room apartment at the St. Regis goes for $45 a day, a far cry from the $275 a month I first paid in 1932 for an enormous suite with a triple-size drawing room at the Madison just up the street, but no matter.

An additional reason I cleave to the St. Regis over the years, and perhaps a trivial one, is that it has never attempted to charge me for ice service to my apartment. One of the most miserable of petty larcenies, the practice of charging four bits for cube ice and highball set-ups, came into existence during the years of World War II and has never ceased to arouse me to a state of rage. From the days when Eugene Field wrote his immortal stanzas to "the clink of the ice in the pitcher the boy brings up the hall," free ice to hotel

175

guests has been obviously part of God's scheme of things. It's a safe bet Field never paid four bits for ice in Denver's legendary Windsor and I do not purpose to either.

Here at the St. Regis I leave my suits at a designated place, and the valet takes them out for daily sponging and pressing.

Breakfast at the St. Regis is offered in less variety than luncheon or dinner. Two mornings out of three my companion and I prefer the conventional variations on fruit, eggs, hot bread and coffee purveyed by the hotel at about $2.00, and brought by room service. If either uncommon energy or uncommon appetite demands greater venturing among the chops and omelets, we find that the Madison Avenue Longchamps a few blocks from our hotel is suited to more expansive whims. Here out-of-season strawberries or melon, liver and bacon, creamed codfish or shirred chicken livers, together with fine hot French croissants and superlative coffee, come to about $3.50 each and assure confidence until the noontime martini looms on the horizon.

In the matter of transportation I believe the omnipresent taxicab to be the best solution for the problem of intracity movement, except for such rigidly formal occasions as church weddings, opera openings or other flag raisings of gala dimensions when a chauffeur-driven limousine may be desired. This may be arranged through the carriage starter at one's hotel. In some cases your doorman may have an arrangement with an independent operator who owns a stately vintage Rolls-Royce which you may prefer to the conventional hook-and-ladder-length black Cadillac.

At the St. Regis you will be officially registered in when Chief Bartender Fernand Petiot sets two three-ounce martinis in front of you, and you hoist the first one of the day in the direction of the Fiddlers Three behind the back bar. From here on you have the freedom of the city.

Long habit next directs my steps to that ancient seat of Manhattan hospitality, Jack & Charlie's "21." Greeted by Jimmy and Monti at the door and escorted to the bar by Jerry Berns and Sheldon Tannen, partners of the firm, my companion and I could do no less than dip into half a dozen rounds of superlative martinis compounded by Emil and Henry before sitting down to a modest if late luncheon on English whitebaits, oyster crabs and special "21" Oyster Bay asparagus. This repast came to $28, including a five-dollar tip, and was our opening salute to a spendthrift tour of Manhattan.

Cocktails and dinner our first night were resolved by geographic convenience; for the former we repaired to the new Carlton House at the corner of Madison and Sixty-first, and for the latter, to Gene Cavallero's Colony Restaurant, directly across the street.

Regrettably the décor of the Carlton House Men's Bar, open for ladies after 2:30, has none of the overtones of French glamour crystal elegance that characterized the first Ritz Carlton; it might, in fact, be a well-bred resort anywhere from London's West End to St. Louis. A piano player in an elevated alcove tinkled noncommittally, but the martinis were of the first chop (a $4 tab for four and a dollar for the waiter). Many of the staff were old friends who paused to reminisce about the spacious times of the old Ritz, when its name was a hallmark of international distinction.

Dinner at the Colony, a restaurant which perhaps more than any other in New York maintains an unbroken continuity with the fashionable past, is, as it always has been, an event. The outer, striped-awning-covered café where Marco is head man at the bar, is suitable for lunch, but dinner in the grand manner demands service in the gold-and-white main restaurant that over the years has been the setting for much of Manhattan's social history and many of its greatest culinary triumphs.

Gene himself, Gene Junior, George, then the wine steward, and the conventional battery of captains were on hand to usher us to our old table, the first inside the door on the left. It was like old times and I said so. Terrapin Maryland, a house specialty, came first, with a bottle of undated Bollinger champagne, followed by individual baby roast pheasants, each nesting cozily on its bed of *foie-gras* toast, flanked by a chilly fresh fruit salad and a magnificent bottle of Bordeaux, a Château *Margaux* 1947. For dessert a vanilla soufflé, with a Grand Marnier sauce, ordered when we sat down to give the chef the half hour necessary for its preparation; coffee and two enormous snifters of Hines forty-year cognac. The check came to $58 for two, and we left $10 for the table waiter, $5 each for the captain and wine steward, a total of $78.

We saved Quo Vadis, that East Sixty-third Street resort favored by so many knowing New Yorkers, for an after-the-theater bit of nourishment in the hot-bird-and-cold-bottle tradition of the Lillian Russell age. On arrival in these high-ceilinged, rather old-world premises, we discovered we needed no formal introduction; the senior captain was an old "21" staffer, the bartenders we had known in a variety of oases and the maître d'hôtel had been recruited from the Ritz Carlton in the great days.

An imposing menu hand-written in two colors of ink offered a variety of enticements ranging from Dover sole Dieppoise to pheasant *en plumage*, but we settled for Long Island duck with black cherries, a bottle of 1947 Perrier-Jouet, the champagne beloved of Soames Forsyte in the Galsworthy *Saga*, and shot the works in a gesture toward the Berry Wall era with Peach Melba. The Melba had been created by Escoffier for the diva at the Savoy in London a half century ago, but still seems to us the gala dessert, fraught with opulence, calories and indigestion. This collation at Quo Vadis was a vast success, and the merest bagatelle at $28.50 for two including a tip.

The morning of our second day in New York was occupied with business, and noontime found us ready for tall gin rickeys which we attained by pausing at the Biltmore Men's Bar on the way uptown.

For luncheon this day we selected an old personal favorite, Baroque, in Fifty-third Street between Madison and Fifth. Baroque is extremely stylized, fairly costly and enjoys exacting lunchtime clientele from upper-echelon hucksters, publishers and editors. Its décor is lush Venetian Renaissance and its service is excellent.

We were greeted by Joseph, the owner-manager, and we chose potage Baroque, a fine thick soup based on cream of green peas and clear green turtle with a lick of egg white on top, the whole steaming hot and its egg float quickly browned under the salamander and served in a pottery tureen; supreme of pompano, Volney, that morning air-expressed from New Orleans; and for dessert the chocolate-folded profiteroles for which the house is famed. My companion chose Cotuit oysters, grilled fresh baby calf's liver and a salad of Brussels endive with estragon. We shared a well-chilled bottle of Pouilly-Fuissé and emerged in midafternoon at peace with the world and especially the management of Baroque. This spiritual well-being had been purchased, with suitable *pour-boires*, for $20 for two.

The evening's entertainment of our second day on the town was the most festive and expensive. For dinner we chose Henri Soulé's Le Pavillon, reputedly the finest restaurant in America and certainly one of the most costly in the world. Exigencies of time precluded shopping around for cocktails, but a half bottle of Krug's Private Cuvée sent to the apartment while we were dressing bridged the gap.

Dinner at Le Pavillon is nothing to be undertaken casually; such an attitude may result in one of two catastrophes: a wasted evening in one of the world's truly great restaurants; or, not getting into the Pavillon at all.

Soulé enjoys a fanatic following, with the result that his tables are full for lunch and dinner often weeks in advance. Since he cannot expand his restaurant and will not overcrowd it, it is absolutely necessary to make reservations. The Duke and Duchess of Windsor, Cole Porter, Bernard Baruch and Mary Martin are careful always to have a reservation and you better had too. The chances of presenting yourself at Soulé's without appointment and getting anything but a double brusheroo of arctic proportions are nil.

Having invoked the names of your most influential friends in Texas oil and secured a reservation at Pavillon, dedicate the entire evening to it. Soulé takes dim view of people who are hurrying through dinner with the idea of going to the theater. He prefers patrons who allow a minimum of two hours for dinner. Any other conduct is flying in the face of Providence. Worse, it is flying in the face of Henri Soulé.

Dressed to the nines, we presented ourselves at Soulé's small but admirable bar at eight for just one martini—no more. A minimum of two wines and a limited number of spirits is *de rigueur*; and it's better to be able to walk out. Caviar is the joy of Soulé's life and we ordered it—fresh, pearl-sized medium gray-black eggs, the finest in the market, served with toast and lemon and a snort of chilled Aalborg Aquavit on the side, nothing more. The Pavillon menu bears no price for caviar. For your possible guidance, it is $8 a spoonful if Soulé likes you and you are properly dressed, more if you are in a business suit and have drunk four cocktails at the bar.

Since this was to be a full-dress dinner, we ordered soup—the petite marmite Pavillon, a fine clear broth of chicken and beef stocks with slices of chicken and marrow toast topped with Parmesan cheese at $2.50 the plate.

For fish we had English Channel sole flown in that morning, lightly grilled and served with a hot mustard sauce flanked by a half bottle which provided each of us with one refreshing glass of 1947 Musigny Blanc from the estate of the Comte Georges de Voguë. The sole for two came to $10, the wine $5.50.

We were now beginning to feel our oats, if the phrase may be excused in such august society, and for our entree commanded one of the great specialties of the house—Chateaubriand Pavillon, the most aristocratic cut of beef in the known universe, with one vegetable, *coeur de céleri au beurre*.

To accompany this princely offering, Soulé sent to his deepest cellar for a cobwebbed bottle of equally princely Burgundy, a Grands Echézeaux from the Domaine de la Romanée-Conti. If you are still interested in keeping up with the IBM accounting machines, the Chateaubriand came tagged $17, the celery $4, and the wine $16.

By now lost to all prudence, we plunged into the dessert department and alarmed adjacent tables by splashing happily around in flaming plates of crepes suzette and a bottle of that most regal of all champagnes, Moët & Chandon's Dom Pérignon Cuvée for 1947. Coffee and a snifter of Hennessy's V.S.O.P. seemed anticlimactic. Crepes suzette $6.50, champagne $18, cognac $4.50, coffee $1.25.

If you are still with us, the total tab including cocktails and Aquavit came to $109.25, which is about par for two at Pavillon and which, when we had distributed modest largesse among the retainers, left us barely cab fare home out of $150.

The morning of our third day on this de luxe kick found us with mild shakes, so instead of having breakfast in the apartment we walked around the block to Longchamps. Fresh out-of-season strawberries and cream, liver and bacon, hot French croissants and coffee proved to be just what the doctor ordered and cheaper than a week at Battle Creek.

We occupied the forenoon with professional commitments and a bit of shopping in Fifth Avenue, and found ourselves poised for a matinee of *Around the World in 80 Days*, so we chose the theatrical atmosphere of Sardi's for a brief lunch, in view of a 2:30 curtain. Two Gibsons each, half a dozen Cotuits just in from Wellfleet, a minute steak with O'Brien potatoes, Stilton cheese and coffee with no wine or liqueur stood us $21.50 with the tip.

Hurrying home to change for dinner found us again faced with the necessity for nice timing as it was now 5:30 and we wanted dinner at "21" before attending a Broadway opening with an 8:30 curtain. Showering quickly we solved the cocktail problem with a quick one in the red-and-gold bar of our own St. Regis, while the doorman was calling a taxi.

Any Broadway opening brings to "21" a gathering of names that make news, and we dined downstairs in the grill in order to greet old acquaintances and expedite the service.

For dinner our third evening on the town we selected smoked lake sturgeon, a wonderful green turtle soup with sherry, venison steak *poivrade* with the works, currant jelly, bread crumbs and purée of marrons, and a frozen soufflé with raspberry sauce. To drink, we followed the decree of Mamie Fish when she ruled New York society—one wine is enough if one is going to the opera. We chose an old favorite, Bollinger champagne, *brut*, without a year. With a cup of espresso and a glass of Grand Marnier to sweeten the breath, we went our way rejoicing and just comfortably stuffed—at a cost of $55.

The precise cost of our two seats for the revue opening at the Bijou Theater that night is difficult to record. On one hand we occupied critics' seats, but on the other hand we had invested $5000 in the venture. Perhaps prudence dictates that the $5000, which shortly went up the spout when the show folded, cannot with propriety be included in the evening's legitimate expenses even though, at $2500 each, our seats were about as expensive as theater entertainment can come.

Nothing arouses a man-size thirst more than an evening at the theater, and afterward we taxied across town to the Stork Club for a dish of terrapin Maryland and another bottle of Bollinger. The comestibles, consumed in the Cub Room among old friends, together with tip, made mincemeat of $25 and we walked home up the Avenue to the Sunday papers and bed well fortified against malnutrition.

To the old-time New Yorker, Sunday luncheon in Ed-

wardian state is thinkable only in terms of the glittering Plaza Hotel, which dominates Fifth Avenue at Fifty-ninth Street and Central Park. Tradition gathers thickly around the Plaza, though it is now a property of the ubiquitous Conrad Hilton. The Plaza began being institutional when it opened back in 1907 and has been getting more so ever since. Its sumptuous apartments for a half century have been home to the legendary "thirty-nine widows of the Plaza," opulent dowagers whose *grande dame* until her recent demise was the formidable Clara Bell Walsh, who moved in the week the hotel opened and threatened to leave every time the management laid down a new yard of carpet.

The hotel encompasses a variety of super-de-luxe restaurants, the Edwardian Room, the white-and-gold-and-crystal Palm Court, the Men's Bar, the Persian Room and the Rendez-Vous downstairs where, some three and a half decades ago, youthful cutups of a bell-bottom college generation, including your correspondent, used to tea-dance with Connie Bennett. Sunday luncheon is ritual at the Oak Room where, for years, the monocle of Ferenc Molnar, the walrus mustaches of Jules Bache and the striped trousers of other Sabbath Manhattanites were the hallmarks of a more formal and less urgent age.

Now, save at Christmas and Easter, top hats and tailcoats are largely a memory, but the appointments, service and food of the Plaza remain excellent; things to which perceptive New Yorkers cling as permanent reminders of stability and good manners in a time less familiar with either.

Promptly at one o'clock, the opening hour for Sunday alcohol decreed by New York law, we step up manfully to the Men's Bar just off the Oak Room, for a therapeutic snort with other quivering customers who have been comparing their watches with the wall clock for the past fifteen minutes. The Martinis of the Plaza are things of gelid wonderment served in substantial chalices of crystal, and they provide an elixir of restoration and confidence with which to greet the Oak Room's bedsheet-size menu.

Although the bill of fare bristles with good things—broiled sole Béarnaise, breast of guinea hen under glass Marie Antoinette, chicken pot-pie *maison*—old Sunday patrons of the Oak Room order either eggs Benedict or finnan haddie creamed à la kitchen, a magnificent creation of the best imported Scotch finnan haddie, hard-boiled eggs and potato in rich cream sauce.

All the nice touches of service are taken for granted at the Plaza, a change of napkins after every course, sherry brought to the table in the bottle for green turtle soup, a smiling captain at hand with an enormous mill of Java pepper when it is wanted, a dish of pink peppermints at the door as the satisfied customer eases himself out. Sunday luncheon for two, with two rounds of medicinal cocktails at the bar and a princely Upmann corona as a final panache of ele-

gance, including tip and ransom for our wraps, ran up a tally of $22.50.

Still in sentimental vein, a Sunday-afternoon excursion beckoned in the form of a horse-cab ride around Central Park in a carriage selected from the array of ancient victorias on the Plaza cab rank in Fifty-ninth Street. Gone, long since, are the days when I looked forward to the first snow and Pat Rafferty's sleigh for a dash to the Central Park Casino of ambrosial memory to win the magnum of champagne that much-loved restaurant annually posted for the first arrival in a cutter. But a victoria chartered for the "long circle" ride in the park, enveloped in a rich effluvium of horse, possessed compensations, and off we went for an hour's rediscovery of the park's monuments, memorials and shrines.

For our last evening in New York, and especially because it was Sunday, we elected to dine leisurely at historic Lüchow's in Fourteenth Street. Lüchow's has been doing business at the same stand since 1882 and was a favorite rendezvous of such notables as Victor Herbert, Diamond Jim Brady and Lillian Russell; it is one of the few traces left of what old New Yorkers mean when they mention old New York.

A vast establishment of mirrors and paneled woodwork, Wagner, hasenpfeffer and Würzburger, Lüchow's is an abode of unabashed sentimentality, beloved over the years. We were seated directly below the orchestra, which was playing "Tannenbaum" at the moment. Without reference to such trivial follies as cocktails, we ordered two tall steins of dark Würzburger Hofbrau. This, at Lüchow's, is the wine of the country, and although the cellar boasts of many wonderments in the domain of Rhine and Moselle, the Würzburger is the noblest of all and we stayed with it all evening.

For hors d'oeuvres I ordered filet of Iceland Maatjes herring in sour cream with a blanket of sliced fresh onion, while my companion chose Lüchow's special appetizer which appeared to embrace a complete cold shore dinner of herring, lobster, crab flakes, shrimp and other oceanic oddments under a polar icecap of Russian dressing. Half portions at Lüchow's are the equivalent of a double order in lesser places.

Our entree was larded saddle of Canadian hare in red cabbage with potato balls, together with more Würzburger, and for dessert a monstrous preisselberry pancake flaming in brandy. The bill for this sumptuous tribute to yesterday's way of dining, including twelve steins of Würzburger and a couple of farewell ponies of Hennessy, with a gratuity here and there, came to $42.

This was a fine conclusion to our four days in New York which had included not necessarily the most expensive, but certainly the best, of everything. The over-all tab, not counting speculative Broadway ventures, was $750, take or leave the price of a Bromo Seltzer.

And so to bed.

◀ **Gifts of the sea, arranged at Gloucester House, one of New York's fine seafood restaurants and typical of the best.**

HANS NAMUTH

PART IV: *A Gourmet Tour of the United States*

Sweet's / Joel Sayre

*A homespun portrait of New York's oldest sea-food house,
lying just a stone's throw from the Fulton Fish Market*

SWEET's Restaurant at 2–4 Fulton Street, Manhattan, offers a variety of 116 drinks, some of which I haven't seen since the heyday of Irene Castle, when I first began investigating sin. There are, for instance, Bronx, Orange Blossom and Pink Lady cocktails; Sherry Cobbler, Rock & Rye. Does anybody order such concoctions these days? Probably—at Sweet's; New York's oldest sea-food house, founded in 1845, has a few customers who date back to the Tom and Jerry, made of spiced hot rum and eggs.

Sweet's is now owned by Miss Lea Lake and her brother Charles. I asked Miss Lake what her clients drank with their sea food.

"Some like a split of stout with their oysters," she said. "Chablis is nice with pompano—most good white wines go well with fish."

"What do you do about your drunks?" I asked.

Miss Lake, an alert and friendly lady of middle age, as nice as the pie in her kitchen, looked as though she had been slapped. "Drunks!" she said in a tone of hurt surprise. "This is a serious place."

My question had been thoughtless. Nobody in his right mind would go to Sweet's to tie one on. People drink with their meals there, of course; but the awesome dignity of the thirteen Negro waiters alone would discourage anybody from misbehaving. The eldest of them, Daniel Chisholm, has reached the age of eighty-seven, and several of his colleagues are close behind him. Getting tight at Sweet's would be almost like swigging from a flask in church. Besides, the food is too good. Sweet's regular clients go with a single purpose: to consume and relish the fruits of the boundless oceans, and this attitude pervades the whole atmosphere. It's a serious

place, all right, though Gloria Swanson, dining there alone once, was surrounded by a posse of conventioning Shriners who had got lost and mistaken Sweet's for Sammy's Bowery Follies.

Sweet's is proud of its regulars, and there are many, among them a nimble ninety-three-year-old tobacco importer named Benjamin Hamburger who has been going there for seventy-six years, and his father went before him. One of the main reasons why the regulars love Sweet's is its total lack of chichi. "Not Responsible for Personal Property Unless Checked," says a note on the front page of the menu, although Sweet's hat-check girl is actually a series of hooks and pegs fastened to the walls.

Here and there are nautical relics, including a model of a full-rigged ship in a shadow box, an old harpoon gun and a number of paintings, the kind that everybody beyond fifty has seen, during his childhood, being painted at great speed by a man wearing a smock in the window of a local furniture store. Most of the paintings are marines, but some are pastorals. They are provided by a neighborhood picture framer who eats in the restaurant every day, and all are for sale; now and then a diner makes a purchase. Sweet's draws no com-

Sweet's. The New Yorker—or the globe-trotter, for that matter ▶ —will travel far before finding a better seafood house than Sweet's, which has been situated a stone's throw from the Fulton Fish Market for more than 100 years.

ARNOLD NEWMAN

180

mission on the sales; the pictures are hung as a favor to the framer, and Miss Lake feels that they enhance the décor. When all the tables are set, and the waiters in their crisp, spotless white are at their stations ready for the first customer, and the young bartender with the crew cut, and the oyster shucker are behind the long, old mahogany bar, the dining room presents a fine appearance.

Sweet's is situated downtown near the Brooklyn Bridge, with the huge and fabulous Fulton Fish Market close by. It draws the bulk of its luncheon clientele, overwhelmingly male, from the adjoining financial, coffee-roasting and insurance districts. In summer, whenever chef Peter Cheuces obtains a 300-pound halibut (a Greek, he pronounces it "haliver"), the news flashes up and down Wall Street as though Ford had acquired General Motors. By 8 P.M. when the kitchen closes, the haliver is usually nothing but bones.

Sweet's can seat about 150. It opens weekdays at 11 A.M.; by noon it is almost full, and an hour later there are likely to be customers waiting halfway down the steep stairway— it's on the second floor—to the street. On Fridays and during Lent the queues often extend outside the building. Around 5 P.M. the dinner eaters arrive, and it is then you first see females in respectable numbers—escorted ladies, pairs and trios of fish-loving spinsters, little girls in family groups. It is closed Saturdays, Sundays and holidays.

Families often take their children to dinner there, for the fare is fundamentally simple. Yet, in its 115 years of existence, Sweet's has attracted many astute sea-food lovers. Here are a random few: the Rev. Henry Ward Beecher, that celebrated pulpit orator who was catnip to his lady parishioners; Seth Low, president of Columbia University and the first anti-Tammany mayor of Greater New York; financier Frank Vanderlip; Julian Street, the writer and wine expert; Gov. Alfred E. Smith (who worked as a youth in the Fulton Fish Market), Sen. Robert Wagner, and John Curry, boss of Tammany Hall; Irving Berlin, Beatrice Lillie, Esther Williams, Dave Chasen, Mel Ott of baseball fame, dramatist Marc Connelly and Vincent Astor.

Sweet's main dishes are examples of how delicious American sea food can be without being fancy. In spite of its heavy patronage (between 350 and 550 meals are eaten there on an average day), its service is leisurely, for all of the main dishes are cooked to order. Its methods of cooking are basic: broiling, especially; sautéing, deep-fat frying, baking and boiling. Its sauces are few: tartare, au gratin, Creole, drawn butter, Newburg—and that's about all. There is no pretense of elegance, nothing flossy, but everything done expertly. At least a ton of sea food is served at Sweet's every week.

Miss Lake, her brother Charles, and Chef Cheuces, who has been with them for more than twenty-five years, buy only fresh sea food.

One dawn in early January, I accompanied the chef on his shopping tour of the Fulton Fish Market, which he makes every working day.

The fishermen had spent the Christmas holidays with their families, so the fresh fish that morning were scant. The chef went snorting from stall to stall.

"T'aw out a piece fish and lose its juice," he said. "Then you broil, and it's so dry, it tastes like fire hose." Finally he bought a quantity of fresh sole, flounder and haddock. At the stall of Frank W. Wilkisson, Inc., he rolled up a sleeve and reached deep into a five-gallon can of scallops that had been opened with delicate taps of a fishmonger's hatchet.

Having approved of the succulence of the scallops—or, properly, their dressed-out adductor muscles, which is the part of the scallop you eat—he bought the entire can at the wholesale price of $13.75 a gallon. At Thompson and Potter's, next door to Sweet's entrance, he bought several bushels of Blue Point oysters from Cape Cod, and of cherrystone clams from Long Island.

One of the chef's most successful specialties is clam bisque, served only on Tuesdays and Thursdays. Chef Cheuces is an amiable, bespectacled, rotund man in his late sixties, from the ancient town of Kalamata in the Peloponnesus, a mile from the Ionian Sea. ("Don't snow only once ever' five, ten years; but snow on mountains allatime.") He came to this country in 1907 and signed on shortly after as kitchen apprentice at Whyte's, a famous eating house farther up Fulton Street. After being promoted to its sea-food department he became a specialist in smoking haddock. In 1921 he opened a small place of his own, Finnan Haddie Pete's, at Coney Island. It did well until the crash, when New York sea-food eaters stopped going to Coney Island and started eating in bread lines.

Pete will gladly tell you how he cooks every dish on Sweet's menu except two—the clam bisque and the deviled crab cakes. A taste detective would probably deduce that the cakes are prepared after the fashion of lobster thermidor: the crab lumps mixed with a highly flavored white sauce, breaded with crumbs, delicately deep-fried, then baked. Anyway, however Pete does them, they are certainly glorious eating. The clam bisque is even better. In my opinion, it's a major soup. Pete has never revealed its formula, even to the Lakes. It is understandable that a chef should keep a professional secret. I hope, however, that Pete won't mind my making a guess at how he does it. If any amateur chef who cannot get to Sweet's on a Tuesday or Thursday will follow the recipe below, I think he will find that it will taste pretty good, although it won't, of course, turn out to be exactly what Pete produces. This recipe also works with oysters.

GUESS BISQUE

Reserve the liquor from a pint of clams. Remove hard parts from clams and chop clams fine. Chop fine a couple of stalks of celery, a little parsley and a couple of slices of onion. Put all this chopped stuff into a quart of rich milk or half-and-half, adding a whole clove and a bay leaf, and bring the milk to a scald. Meantime put your chopped clams into the reserved liquor and bring slowly to a boil. Blend 4 or 5 tablespoons of melted butter with 4 or 5 tablespoons of flour, add ¼ teaspoon of curry powder, then stir in the scalded milk mixture until you have a slick, thick sauce. Add the clams in their liquor, blend the whole, and rectify the seasoning with a little salt and pepper. If you don't like curry, omit.

Pete Cheuces became chef at Sweet's in 1935, two years after the death of James Lake, the father of Miss Lake. Veteran Sweet's regulars all knew Mr. Lake as Jimmy, because he had gone to work there at the age of thirteen, the morning after the Blizzard of '88. In a small village near Plainfield, New Jersey, Jimmy's widowed mother kept an eating house. An expatriate Polish count, who had invented a new type of harrow and made a fortune, owned an estate in the vicinity. He had a fierce hawk face, wore a shawl and frequently swooped into Mrs. Lake's, scaring the daylights out of Jimmy. Finally the lad ran away to New York to escape the Slavic hobgoblin. He picked the day of the Great Blizzard.

Abraham Martin Sweet, who had founded the restaurant forty-three years previously, was still living then. But two of his sons, Edwin and Jesse, largely managed it for him. It was Mr. Ed, as the waiters called him, who gave the nearly frozen Jimmy Lake a job as water boy; the lad's duties were to keep the customers' glasses filled with ice water, and make himself generally useful. As the years rolled on, Jimmy became cashier, then manager.

After dinner one evening at Sweet's in the early 1900's, Lillian Russell lighted a cigarette to smoke with her demitasse. Though often described in the press as "the airy fairy Lillian," Miss Russell was definitely a large girl, but that was the way they liked them in those days, and the yearnings of most American manhood during the height of her fame were aimed in her direction. There was scarcely a saloon in the country where the catchy riddle, "If the wind blew, would Lillian rustle?" hadn't brought guffaws and mustache twirls. Diamond Jim Brady, the sensational railroad-equipment salesman and glutton, had given her a solid-gold bicycle and other tokens of his esteem. When Mr. Ed, an austere and eagle-eyed man, saw her exhale a puff or two, he ordered Jimmy Lake to inform Miss Russell that ladies weren't permitted to smoke on the premises. Blushing and gulping, wishing he were anywhere but here, Jimmy obeyed; Miss Russell smiled and extinguished her cigarette.

Mr. Ed retired from Sweet's with a comfortable fortune. His brother Jesse, although he had introduced pompano to New York, wasn't as good a businessman as Mr. Ed. He ran the restaurant until 1916, when he went bankrupt. In 1918 Sweet's was taken over by Jimmy Lake and Axel Anderson, a benign Swede who for decades had been the restaurant's carver. (Sweet's was once almost as famous for meat as it was for sea food. Daniel Chisholm, the eighty-seven-year-old waiter, can remember when double sirloins, of which Diamond Jim Brady could eat no more than half a dozen, sold for 60 cents each. During World War II, the restaurant abandoned meat to save its red points for butter, so essential to fish broiling, and has never served meat since.) For a while Sweet's name was Lake and Anderson's.

In 1920 Christopher Morley wrote in his New York *Evening Post* column of eating swordfish at Lake and Anderson's; it seems to have been the first time he ever tried it, and he reported the taste "reptilian." Jimmy Lake's son, Charles, went to work for his father the following year, after serving in the Artillery in World War I. Lea Lake, after a career on the stage, joined him in 1927, at first washing glasses and keeping the books. When Jimmy Lake died, Charles and Lea inherited his share in the business, and when Axel Anderson retired in 1935, they restored the restaurant's original name.

There have been some confusing inaccuracies published about Sweet's history; especially as to its location. It is still at 2–4 Fulton Street. "Number Four" was the way Abraham Sweet and his sons always spoke of their venture, although in its prime it was spread over a couple of addresses. On the ground floor at No. 4 was a restaurant for men only; on its second floor was the Ladies' Dining Room, but the ladies had to be escorted, and this was where the trembling Jimmy Lake reprimanded Miss Russell; on the ground floor of No. 6 was a saloon. Benjamin Hamburger and William H. Cornell, another old New Yorker, who was once attorney for the Fulton Fish Market Fishmongers' Association, recall all three of these establishments with glints in their eyes. The Sweets

had live sea turtles shipped from Florida for their turtle soups and steaks. In this soup, in addition to chunks of gorgeous turtle meat, were pieces of sausage the size of moth balls, and the resulting subtlety is among the fondest gustatory memories of both gentlemen.

It has also been written that Abraham Sweet was a Quaker, probably by reporters enthralled by the picture of a Quaker selling liquor. Although Abraham married a Quaker girl, he was not a Quaker himself. He was born on Long Island, near what is now the town of Hempstead, on October 8, 1814.

Abraham was not a robust youth. Seeking to improve his health he signed on, at the age of seventeen, for a two-year cruise on a whaling vessel and traveled as far as Madagascar. At first he was assigned to the tasks of an ordinary seaman and apprentice whaler, but when it was discovered that he wrote a clear hand and was clever at figures, he was promoted to the rating of ship's husband, whose tasks were to manage the ship's logistics and keep the books. After his two years at sea he enjoyed good health the rest of his life, living to the age of eighty-seven.

As a ship's husband, young Sweet had become fascinated by the purveying of food and shelter. During the first dozen years after his voyage he clerked for various business concerns in Manhattan and Brooklyn and saved money toward the attainment of his ambition—to run an eating place and small hotel for sea captains. By 1845 he had saved enough and, at the age of thirty-one, opened a place at 8 Fulton Street in partnership with a Vermonter named Whitney. There were a few rooms for the sea captains to bunk in, and to make them feel at home, Sweet decorated the establishment like a ship's wardroom, and specialized in sea food from the fish market, which was so handy.

Whitney found that he hated New York, and that he didn't like seafaring men much better, so he moved back to Vermont. Perhaps it was a mistake; in any case, Abraham Sweet was so successful that he soon expanded to a saloon at No. 6 and another restaurant at No. 4. The expansion was warranted by the bustle and concentration of humanity in the region of Fulton and South Streets, in those days one of the city's busiest corners. In addition to the seafarers off the China and India clippers, carrying tea and spices (Seth Low's father had a spice business nearby), which anchored along the East River, there were New York's prototype commuters —men who worked in the financial district but lived in Northern Manhattan or the Bronx or Brooklyn or on Staten Island.

Dropping in at Sweet's for snacks or drinks while waiting for the ferry or the packet to Harlem became a fixed practice. By 1863 the former ship's husband bought a show place on Brooklyn's Washington Avenue, a select residential district. This house has been preserved in splendid condition by his last remaining descendant, a widowed granddaughter.

I have seen a photograph of Abraham Sweet taken on the day of his golden wedding anniversary; it shows a handsome, upstanding man with cheerful, shrewd eyes and a horseshoe-shaped beard. Although he had little formal education, he was a voracious reader and loved conversation. He had never been to Europe, but strangers, hearing him talk, assumed that he had been there many times.

He became greatly absorbed in the Universalist Church, whose tenets are a good deal similar to those of Unitarianism, and was elected president of the board of trustees of his parish.

For the pleasure and edification of his fellow parishioners he read, from time to time, papers he had written on such themes as Madagascar, whaling in the 1830's, and trips he later made to such then little-known Caribbean islands as Barbados and Cuba. On July 4, 1902, he died, blessed by the years and the esteem of all who knew him. Abraham Martin Sweet was a remarkable innkeeper.

Sea-food lovers who go to New York will find a trip to the restaurant that bears his name more than worth while. For less than a ten-dollar bill a hungry man and the woman of his choice can spend a quietly memorable evening there, eating themselves torpid, with all the appropriate liquid refreshment they require. The evening will be even more memorable if they can manage to reserve one of the coveted window tables.

Sweet's all-year-round perennials are Florida shrimps, Long Island clams and anything you suggest made of crab lumps, which are imported from Virginia and Maryland in the huge refrigerated trailers called reefers. Since freshness, as I have mentioned, is the establishment's fiercest pride, most of the other dishes are seasonal. You may get pompano in June at other New York restaurants, but not at Sweet's: that's the month it starts turning soft; Sweet's pompano in winter or spring, on the other hand, is a definite experience. Also unforgettable are the bay scallops from August through March, the latter also being the great shad-roe month. Sweet's regulars joyfully eat their way around the calendar, for as soon as one outstanding dish leaves the menu, another arrives.

By April, for example, the shad roe and the scallops are gone, but the first great catches of Northern bluefish are coming in; oysters and all smoked fish are finished in May, but there are soft-shelled crabs to drool over, Pete is working magic with eels for his Italian clients, and the haliver starts showing up. Swordfish and butterfish are superb in June, by July the haliver are weighing 300 pounds, and in August the Maine lobsters are at their most toothsome. The following month oysters will be back, and soon there will be smelts again, and so on. Pete's creations revolve in cycle, and Sweet's regulars mark the seasons by their yearnings for them.

Sweet's has a guest book—an old ledger converted by Miss Lake. Having been on the stage, she is always thrilled whenever show people come in, but when she asks them to sign the guest book she is like a shy young autograph hunter, if such a being can be imagined. Noncelebrities are never asked to sign unless they are eloquent about the meals they have just eaten, yet they outnumber the celebrities in the book at least a hundred to one, I'd say. After perusing this book I prefer what the noncelebrities have written in it. I suppose that after a celeb has eaten at Sweet's, he is just too surfeited to come through with anything witty. (Sports columnists Dan Parker, of *The Mirror*, and Arthur Daley, of *The Times*, were evidently spotted by Miss Lake before they had ordered: "Bring on that clam soup," Parker scribbled. "Same here," Daley added.) One signatory of the prewar era I am sorry I was too late to meet was "John H. Dunn, bus boy at Sweet's 70 years ago." The note to her waiter from Miss Mildred Lyons, of Kansas City, Mo., I found appealing: "To William. Thanks for helping me with my first lobster." Two Frenchmen left these testimonials for Pete: "*Un bon dîner, digne d'être baptisé à la française,*" and, "*Dans un cadre purement new-yorkais on trouve une cuisine qui compare avec la cuisine française.*" But my favorite tribute came from a man who added under his name: "He ate up all his onions and his belches sound like chimes."

PART IV: *A Gourmet Tour of the United States*

Where to Eat in Boston
/ Winston Brebner

The home of the bean and the cod has been pampering epicurean appetites
for many years, as you'll discover on this tour of the city's most notable restaurants

ALF a century has passed since John Collins Bossidy proposed his memorable toast at the Midwinter Dinner of the Holy Cross Alumni:

> *And this is good old Boston,*
> *The home of the bean and the cod,*
> *Where the Lowells talk only to Cabots,*
> *And the Cabots talk only to God.*

The result of this indestructible canard is that, while the reputations of the Lowells and the Cabots have survived nicely, the name of Boston has become inseparably and contemptuously wedded to the bean and the cod, and the reputation of New England cooking has suffered a fate that is far from deserved.

Boston's restaurants, in brief, have more to offer than beans and cod, and the fact is that many of them were pampering epicurean palates long before the author of the above doggerel discovered that quahogs were clams and not a variety of New England swine.

Locke-Ober's Café, in the heart of Boston's downtown shopping district, is beyond a doubt the epitome of good dining from the traditional Brahmin point of view. The gist of this philosophy is (1) that a man approaching a gastronomic adventure should not be distracted by social obligations to the opposite sex, and (2) that the art of exciting the gustatory cells does not lie necessarily between the covers of the *Escoffier Cookbook*.

These are sound tenets, but to endorse them without reservation would constitute a short cut to bankruptcy, a condition which Locke's has spectacularly avoided. The recently redecorated Ober Room, and the new Camus Room on the second floor of this venerable building, are graciously coeducational, smartly decorated (the Ober Room has pigskin walls), indirectly lighted, always well populated, and an abomination to the stalwarts of the Men's Bar on the street level, who have successfully defended that sanctum sanctorum against major innovation for eight decades. Here, by day in the pale city light that washes through the windows looking out on Winter Place, and at night under the old-fashioned glow of incandescent bulbs, you find an atmosphere of Victorian opulence compounded of carved mahogany, an honest sufficiency of coat hooks, an enormous Rubens nude, a voluptuous bronze *Gloria Victis*, irreverently used as a hatrack, and the patina of long and satisfactory masculine usage.

The nature of Locke's cuisine derives from the genius who recognized that American regional dishes are not necessarily anathema to a French bill of fare. Originally, Locke's and Ober's were two competitive restaurants, standing side by side on Winter Place. The former specialized in New England cooking and generous drinks; the latter was dedicated to fine French cuisine and a legendary cellar of French wines. (Locke's still maintains the most remarkable cellar of vintage wines in Boston.) In 1894, a firm of wholesale liquor dealers bought out both restaurants and introduced Emil Camus as manager of the new establishment. Gentlemen whose loyalties had been divided celebrated the occasion by unlocking the door which connected the two restaurants. The key was ceremoniously thrown into Boston harbor.

The result of this happy merger, and of the good judgment

of Emil Camus, is that there are on the menu today such contrasting dishes as steamed finnan haddie and *coq au vin* under glass, baked lobster Savannah and broiled honeycomb tripe, planked filet of lake trout and Sweetbreads *Eugénie.*

King's Dictionary of Boston, published in 1883, reported: "The leading French restaurant of the city is Ober's. . . . The viands here are unsurpassed by any place in the city." This brief encomium is as well deserved today as it was seventy-four years ago.

Since Winter Place was inconvenient for possessors of cultivated taste buds in the Copley Square area, Locke-Ober's took over a small restaurant at Dartmouth and Newbury streets in 1949. Bostonians are not notable for their quick acceptance of new institutions, but Joseph's is a felicitous exception, though it suffered during its first years from an excess of feminine enthusiasm.

Even today, uncautioned gentlemen wandering alone into the street-floor dining room are likely to feel they have stumbled into a regional meeting of the Ladies' Aid Society. With typical *savoir-faire*, the Locke-Ober management solved this embarrassment by building in the basement an elegant bar, lounge, and connected dining room which are reserved for men at lunch, while permitting ladies at dinner.

Joseph's menu is substantially the same as Locke's; the wine list is excellent, and the *chef de cuisine*, Domenic Ruzzo, properly served his apprenticeship at the parent *établissement*. The baked oysters Gino, the Rock Cornish game hen, and the Chateaubriand are superb. And you may order the same extra-rich sultana roll with real claret sauce which is the mainstay of the Locke-Ober dessert creations.

With its lengthy and colorful water front and its 300-year history as an East Coast fishing center, it is astonishing that Boston, with one notable exception, is unable to serve a really epicurean sea-food dinner with a view of salt water, sea gulls and fishing boats. The notable exception is Jimmy's Harbor Side Restaurant, on Northern Avenue, situated between the fabulous Boston Fish Pier and the acres of mothballed flattops and destroyers in the Boston Navy Yard Annex.

Formerly known as Jimmy's Liberty Café, the place was for years a mecca for sea-food connoisseurs. Enlarged, renovated and rechristened, it is today one of the most popular eating spots in Boston. James Doulos, a suave, gray-haired Greek in the Pinza tradition, is justly proud that the last five governors of the Commonwealth have paid homage to his cooking. Not too long ago, when Senator Leverett Saltonstall was defending fish chowder New England style against fish chowder New York style, he called upon Jimmy to help him prove his point. The next day the restaurateur flew to Washington with enough chowder for 350 people, which was consumed forthwith in the Senate Dining Room with enthusiasm on both sides of the aisle.

The *décor* at Jimmy's consists largely of the wall of windows overlooking the water, and the gourmet who likes to savor his food while contemplating its natural habitat will wisely make reservations in advance. As an hors d'oeuvre or entrée, the succulent deep-sea scallops, Jimmy's Own Style, are a must. They have cured this writer of a lifelong contempt of the sea scallop as a tasteless substitute for the more dainty and expensive Cape scallop. They are sliced across the grain to the diameter of a half-dollar, rolled in breadcrumbs flavored with a pinch of dry mustard and a touch of garlic,

broiled in butter for five minutes, placed in a hot oven for two minutes to cook the bottoms, and sprinkled with a good sherry just before serving. Also recommended are the finnan haddie—the haddock delicately smoked to Jimmy's own fastidious specifications—and, of course, the fish chowder.

Another excellent sea-food restaurant and one ripe with historical associations is the Union Oyster House at 41–43 Union Street, near Faneuil Hall. On the second floor of this building King Louis Philippe whiled away his years of exile by teaching French to proper Bostonians. For the past 131 years shuckers behind the ancient oyster bar on the first floor have been shelling cotuits and cherrystones for ladies and gentlemen who like their bivalves raw and in quantity. This oyster bar, the old white-painted stalls, the sawdust floor, are authentic survivals of the restaurant's lengthy catering to those with a taste for the finest in sea foods.

Nearby, in the heart of the market district, is Boston's own special temple for gourmands, Durgin-Park. Established by Peter Faneuil in 1742, the restaurant has clung fiercely to the notion that no customer should be served less than the most voracious can consume. The food at Durgin-Park is well cooked, plain and, to put it mildly, plentiful. It is served, in an atmosphere of unimaginable pandemonium, family style, at long community tables, from menus honestly labeled "Dinner Bill" (lunch) and "Supper Bill" (dinner), to a clientele composed of marketmen in white dusters, college boys with unappeasable appetites, out-of-town sight-seers, and a scattering of Boston businessmen. Roast beef arrives in a two-pound slab, the strawberry shortcake (in season) requires a large chowder bowl, and one can dig into the New England boiled dinner of corned beef, cabbage, turnips and carrots for a considerable length of time without discovering the plate beneath it. For the visitor in search of a hearty atmosphere and unadorned New England fare, Durgin-Park promises a robust adventure in eating.

Some years ago, Ruth Brooks, authoress of the Boston *Herald* crossword puzzle, defined the word tripe as an "alleged food." The result of this *faux pas* was a barrage of irate letters from gastrophiles who help consume the ten tons of broiled honeycomb tripe eaten annually at Boston's Parker House. Internationally known as the home of the Parker House roll, this venerable institution celebrated in 1956 an even century of service in the cause of fine foods and worth-while traditions. Rubbing elbows with historic King's Chapel and the Old State House in the retail maelstrom of downtown Boston, the Parker House is patronized by a devoted clientele of salesmen, tourists, shoppers, Harvard undergrads, local businessmen and itinerant celebrities. The Main Dining Room's beautiful wood paneling and colossal crystal chandeliers give an air of satisfying elegance. Incomparable service is provided by aged Negro waiters. The menu is incomparable too. Slipped in periodically among the more standard dishes are such toothsome and offbeat items as codfish tongues and cheeks sauté, rhubarb ice cream and pumpkin drop cookies, as well as the broiled honeycomb tripe.

During the latter part of the 19th century the Parker House was a mecca for such literary figures as Emerson, Longfellow, Whittier, Lowell, Holmes, Hawthorne and Francis Parkman. Dickens stayed at the Parker House when he was in Boston, and Thackeray was introduced to the oyster at the hotel. Asked by an anxious dinner companion how he had enjoyed his first cotuit, Thackeray confessed in a strangled voice: "I feel as if I had swallowed a small baby."

One of the most popular oases in town with department-store executives, newspaper buffs and theatrical folk is Dinty Moore's, located at the end of an alley off Washington Street, Boston's main shopping thoroughfare. Dinty's offers a varied menu, but the steaks and chops grilled over charcoal are a specialty. Both host George Maren and Louis, the head-waiter, are blessed with a gift for making strangers feel like old-timers. The service is excellent, the Franklin Hughes décor is masculine and conducive to relaxed eating, and you can't buy a better Martini anywhere in town. Except, possibly, at the Ritz Bar.

The Ritz is, of course, the Ritz-Carlton, the last genuine survivor of a great hotel nobility. Towering above the brownstones on Arlington Street, the Ritz looks down on the Public Gardens with the dowdy elegance and self-satisfied aloofness of a Beacon Hill spinster, eccentric, independent and dedicated to the defense of morals, manners and good taste.

The simple elegance of its dining room, as well as its menu and wine list, reflects the Ritz credo that good taste is not the sole responsibility of the patron. The wine list is not a long one, since it is not padded with "bargains" and duplications. The menu, likewise, is edited conscientiously to achieve the best possible compromise between maximum variety and epicurean quality. Entrees include such Ritz specialties as young guinea chicken in casserole Chipolata, planked sirloin, creamed finnan haddie and curry of fresh shrimp.

One of the few restaurants in Boston to offer a decidedly Gallic cuisine and atmosphere is the French Room at the Hotel Vendome on Commonwealth Avenue. Patterned after the more luxurious Parisian *salles à manger*, the French Room is presided over by Monsieur Leon, a crotchety and ubiquitous old maître d'hôtel who is as much a Boston institution as Indian pudding and who tosses one of the finest salads in town. For the undecided gourmet, Leon is likely to suggest the Rock Cornish game hen sautéed with grapes, or the pressed mallard with brandy and sherry, a dish for which the French Room is justly famous.

A gastronomic tour of Boston would be incomplete without a sampling of the many fine restaurants catering primarily to the city's Italian, Greek, Chinese and Syrian populations.

Boston abounds, for example, in good Italian restaurants. A personal favorite is Felicia's, at 145-a Richmond Street, a stone's throw from the residence of Paul Revere.

The knowing guest at this delightful restaurant does not wait to be seated and served. Instead, he greets Luigi, Felicia's young assistant who acts as maître d'hôtel, waiter and assistant cook, then he wanders into the kitchen to see for himself what's cooking and to ask Felicia's prescription for his hunger. From this point he is in her capable hands. Visitors with the temerity to *tell* Felicia what they want are guaranteed not to incur her displeasure if they request the veal scaloppine Marsala, the shrimp marinara à *la Felicia*, or the saltimbocca, an ambrosial dish consisting of veal birds stuffed with peppers, scamozza, butter, parmigiana cheese, prosciutto and parsley, dipped in olive oil and broiled on skewers.

The unchallenged colossus of Greek cuisine in Boston is the Athens-Olympia Café, at 51 Stuart Street, in the theat-rical district. Established forty-odd years ago, it has always been a favorite haunt for theatergoers, businessmen, Harvard students and plain fanciers of Greek cooking. George Lyman Kittredge, the great authority on Shakespeare, used to turn up at the Athens two or three times a week and spend half the afternoon reading and eating. Mrs. Jack Gardner, the famous Boston patroness of the arts, was once a steady customer. If the varied menu of the Athens contains a specialty of the house, it is probably the souvlakia à *l'orientale*—barbecued lamb, peppers, onions and tomatoes on skewers.

Just a hop, skip and jump away, on Hudson Street, is another fine Near Eastern restaurant, the Nile. The décor is comfortable, and an Irish waitress, Gertrude Gleason, willingly translates the Syrian menu for neophytes. The jukebox (blessedly tuned low) plays Syrian and Arabic records. For those in a mood to try something different, the Nile offers plentiful opportunities. Unleavened bread, generously spread with Labanee (a yoghurt drained to a creamed-cheese consistency, flavored with olive oil and dried mint), and stuffed with the Nile's special, mint-flavored tossed salad, makes a delectable appetizer. Lamb, lamb hearts, lamb liver and sweetbreads with mushrooms—all on skewers—are equally tasty.

For the sauerkraut and *Apfel Strudel* school of epicureanism, Jacob Wirth's emporium at 31 Stuart Street offers a strictly Herrenvolk cuisine, complete with irascible old waiters, sawdust on the floor and horse-radish on the table. Lentil soup, sauerbraten with buttered noodles, and pigs' knuckles with sauerkraut are local favorites, and it is *de rigueur* to wash the "Milwaukee Specials" down with a schooner of Jake Wirth's special dark beer.

Lovers of the exotic and visitors from the West Coast will be delighted to learn that Boston now has an outpost of that San Francisco institution, Skipper Kent's. It's the Polynesian Village at the Hotel Somerset. The place owes its unique atmosphere to the artistic talents of the "Skipper" himself. Here are carved wooden idols from Easter Island, spears and knives from East Africa, peacock chairs from Hong Kong, tables hand-hewn from Hawaiian monkey-pod trees, glass fishnet floats from Japan. Two of the most popular drinks are the Pagan Bowl, served in a hollowed-out pineapple, and the Headhunter, served in a coconut. The cuisine is built around a tasteful mixture of Cantonese and Polynesian dishes.

Boston is fortunate in possessing a Chinese population second only to those of San Francisco and New York. Located near the theater district, Boston's Chinatown contains the highest concentration of eating places in the city. For connoisseurs of Chinese cookery, the Cathay House on Beach Street, in this writer's view, offers unexcelled service and a felicitous menu. In the twelve years it has been operating under the aegis of owner-manager Gordon Chue and his wife, Anita, the Cathay House has achieved an unrivaled popularity with lovers of Cantonese cooking, particularly those in the entertainment business. After 1 A.M. (midnight on Saturdays), when the city's bistros close, traffic at Cathay House reaches its peak. And you can be sure of finding here a cross-section of those who appreciate a well-prepared meal —Beacon Hill bluebloods, entertainment celebrities, restaurant managers, gourmets. *They'll* tell you there's more to Boston than baked beans and codfish.

Spendthrift Tour of San Francisco / Lucius Beebe

*A student of the finer aspects of San Francisco fleshpots
reveals that the knowing spendthrift still may
wine and dine there in the flamboyant fashion of the nabobs of old*

OF ALL cities in the United States, not excepting
New York in the uninhibited age of the Belmonts,
Vanderbilts and Goelets, not even excepting the
New Orleans of a thousand perfumed souvenirs of Mardi
Gras and the great legend of Creole cooking—none has the
associations of luxury that gather around San Francisco.

The sense of continuity is more compulsive in the shadow
of Nob and Telegraph Hills, and it was only yesterday that
James Ben Ali Haggin, William Ralston and Lloyd Tevis
were indulging themselves in a lavishness suggesting Lucullus
in the days of imperial Rome. Just the other day Sen. William Sharon was chartering private trains from Third and
Townsend to carry his guests twenty-odd miles to galas at
his mansion in Belmont, trains which departed from San
Francisco every hour until midnight and returned thereafter
on each hour until seven in the morning. The memory is still
green in the hallowed precincts of the Sheraton-Palace of
banquets served on gold plate by the lords of creation and
co-owners of everything in sight to conquering heroes and
visiting potentates—Sheridan, Grant, Sherman, the Emperor
Dom Pedro II de Alcántara of Brazil, John C. Frémont and
J. Pierpont Morgan.

Everything about San Francisco smells deliciously either
of money or sauce Mornay. The late O. O. McIntyre remarked that only on the railroads' club cars did he enjoy
ordering mineral water. Similarly, it is only in San Francisco
that I feel like wearing an opera cloak—a garment as appropriate there as a deerstalker hat once was to Sherlock Holmes'
Baker Street.

When I plan a weekend among the fleshpots of California
Street, I think in terms of Rolls-Royces, presidential suites,

oysters Kirkpatrick and breast of capon Kiev. It's the least
one can do without giving offense to the memory of François Pioche, San Francisco's pioneer *viveur*, who imported
from Paris not merely a private chef but an entire boatload
of them.

It had been our intention to drive from Virginia City to
San Francisco's New Montgomery Street in our Silver Cloud
Rolls-Royce, but, alas, U.S. 50 was snowed in. Impervious
to plows, let alone English town carriages, was U.S. 40, and
in these straits we turned to the Southern Pacific, whose
right of way was open to California the Golden.

Fortunately there was ready to hand our private car, *The
Virginia City*, spotted on the house track at Reno. And for
eighteen first-class fares the Southern Pacific would be in-
duced to take us across the wintry Sierra and to Oakland
Pier. This had advantages, since it could include our dog,
T-Bone, whose residence at the Sheraton-Palace would have
been frowned upon by the management. The faithful Mr.
Charlie Yee was installed in the galley, T-Bone was sent to
the dog laundry, and we were off.

A call to British Motors assured us of a stand-in Rolls-
Royce; the dog would be happy in a ninety-ton Pullman car
on the Oakland Mole. All obstacles seemed resolved. To be
sure, the round trip from Reno to San Francisco for eighteen

Lucien of the Palace. Few chefs in America have earned such ▶
fame as Lucien Heyraud, master of the kitchens in San Francisco's glittering Palace.

FRED LYON

is $370, plus forty dollars a day parking charges, but we decided not to include this in our expenses since it accounted for the dog's board and room.

It may be recalled by those readers who stayed with us during a similar skirmish among the fleshpots of Manhattan that my assignment was to concern only the better way of life, uninhibited by considerations of a low economic nature. Well, this seemed fair enough; and by setting up a bridgehead at the St. Regis and living off the Manhattan countryside we contrived in our allotted four days to run up a tab of approximately $750 and perhaps a month off our life expectancy.

"But you can do better than that in San Francisco—you know you can," declared kind friends. "Why, you only ordered caviar three times. Why don't you really put yourself out?"

There are both similarities and differences in opportunities for the good life in New York and San Francisco. In Manhattan, obviously, there is a greater variety of amusement places, yet San Franciscans believe that, per capita, no city in the United States offers so many resorts of culinary excellence. This is, of course, a heritage from the great days of the Gold Rush and later the Comstock bonanzas which made San Francisco the wealthiest community in America, when its cocktail route, French restaurants and theaters made it one of the truly sophisticated cities of the world.

Today the pattern of public life is changed. Following the decline of the drama everywhere, it is no longer the theater-conscious town of playgoers who once knew the Metropolitan and Maguire's Opera in the heyday of such favorites as Adah Isaacs Menken, Lola Montez and Edwin Booth. Only two worth-while playhouses remain, and only infrequently are both the Geary and Curran lighted simultaneously. Theater-going is no longer glamorous, although opera in its season is very grand indeed and starched almost beyond endurance.

Late dining takes the place of theater and virtually monopolizes the gastronomic scene, since few top-flight restaurants are open at luncheon. And, finally, San Francisco boasts no night clubs in the brackets with New York's Stork, El Morocco or Copacabana. There is a wide variety of furnace-room resorts of Bohemian character, but none that will claim the attentions of the truly discriminating.

The Rolls-Royce was waiting when the *Overland* pulled in. In ten minutes we were crossing the Bay Bridge, in twenty installed in the presidential suite at the Sheraton-Palace. For many years this apartment, overlooking the intersection of Geary and Market Streets from the eighth floor, was occupied by Mrs. Nion Tucker, one of San Francisco's great ladies, but recently it has become available—with its forty-foot drawing room, grand piano, and marble bathroom no larger than a skating rink. It rents for $100 a day. Once emplaced, we felt that we had a convenient *pied-à-terre* from which to evaluate the town's more auspicious pleasure domes.

For our first meal, we selected lunch at a comparative newcomer to the ranks of San Francisco's considerable restaurants, the Canterbury Hotel in Sutter Street, the only successful (and it is widely that) patio restaurant in the entire Bay Area. Don Burger, past manager of the Canterbury, visited Broderick's super-swank garden restaurant in New Orleans where the management combats all but the most inclement weather by spotting lamps tastefully among the shrubs, making the place comfortable except in a hard rain. The device worked so well at the Canterbury that the patio is now available to fashionable luncheon customers the year round.

At the suggestion of the maître d'hôtel we went off the deep end with two double Martinis, followed by abalone steak sautéed in lemon butter, and for a salad something called Halekulani Paradise—a half pineapple freighted with sliced Hamburg grapes, avocado and French dressing. Concurrently with these snacks there arrived a tall foiled bottle of well-chilled Liebfraumilch Glockenspiel. Dessert was Roquefort cheese and black coffee with an inhaler of Hennessy's V.V.S.O.P. The damages came for the two of us to $33, the wine ($5.50) being the most expensive single item. With $5.00 to the waiter and a similar sum to the maître d'hôtel, the tab was $43.

After this encouraging beginning, nothing would do for our first dinner but a return engagement at Ernie's, an old favorite which corresponds closely to New York's "21." Ernie's is not only stylish but populated with sincere lovers of fine food.

We felt assured of a welcome from the management, partly on the basis of friendship with Victor Gotti, senior partner in the family-dominated enterprise, and partly because recently we had been instrumental in lending the house even greater fame than it already possessed. Some laudatory paragraphs of ours in HOLIDAY had come to the eye of Alfred Hitchcock, and Ernie's had been selected forthwith as a set in a Hitchcock thriller. Victor played himself in a number of the sequences.

We were not mistaken; Victor escorted us to the bar and then departed to consult with the chef in our best interests, and we knew beforehand that the best would be none too good for old friends.

Ernie's is strictly de luxe, comparable in price and in quality to the best anywhere, and we splashed happily at the bar to the extent of four Martinis apiece before prudence dictated the menu. We chose cracked crab from the cold waters of the North Pacific, Long Island duck à *l'orange* with fresh asparagus and a bottle of the most princely wine on the list, a Richebourg, Romanée Conti, 1934. We were now getting into the proper spendthrift spirit, and dessert was a chocolate soufflé with vanilla sauce, a bottle of undated Bollinger, *brut*, black coffee, Grand Marnier and a Ramon Allones corona.

The tab at Ernie's was substantial. The Burgundy was $18, the champagne $15 and the duck $11, and with incidentals the total came to $57.50, which seemed to indicate about $12 among the staff or an out-of-pocket sum of $70 when we had ransomed our hats.

Things, we remarked, were looking up.

Private commitments occupied the balance of our first evening until nearly bedtime, leaving just the proper amount of time for a visit to old friends, the David Browns at India House. This establishment, located handily behind the county jail in San Francisco, has adequate police protection, such exotic wonderments as real English steak-and-kidney pie and Burra Jhingre Ka Salan, and a menu which characterizes Khorma as "A more important sort of curry." The house staff is recruited from Indian students at the University of California and it is possible to have your Bombay duck served by a doctor of philosophy at no added cost. We were, however, past consideration of solid substance, and David Brown himself mixed us a maharaja's Burra Peg Champagne-

and-Brandy Goblet which turned out to be crushed ice with a split of Mumm's laced with cognac and a shot of Cointreau. It was warranted to induce sleep and it did. The price of two of these imperial arrangements at India House is $5.50 and with this final salute to the Federal Reserve System we were happy to call it a day.

One's breakfast, I aver, should be a matter of seclusion and, if possible, tranquility, best achieved by being served in one's quarters. On our sojourn we breakfasted each morning in our Sheraton-Palace apartment, ordering nothing more exotic than shirred eggs and chicken livers, broiled sand dabs or Minden lamb chops with the requisite grapefruit, coffee and, of course, the Palace sacrament, the raisinbread toast, on the menu since the '70's. This primal collation averaged $3.50 a morning and, with a Nevada silver dollar for the floor waiter, we charged our expense sheet with a flat $4.50 for breakfast each of our four mornings on safari.

For luncheon our second day we arrived on the point of one at Bardelli's Fashion on O'Farrell Street, a sort of combination of Madison Avenue hangout and solid eating house of French-Italian overtones. Editorial writers from the *Chronicle* and advertising executives from Macy's are its customers.

In the interest of a long and absorbent day to come, instead of Martinis we had sherry at the bar, a Pedro Domecq oloroso, and sat down to crab legs au gratin Mornay and fresh artichokes in season directly from the foggy reaches of Monterey Peninsula, the artichoke capital of the world. The wine was a Johannisberger Riesling, and the dessert a Jerusalem pancake in flaming brandy; a businessman's lunch, sustaining but not overpowering, the tab for which came to $19.25 including $3.00 for the boy.

Over our dessert we fell to speculating on whether or not the present San Francisco was really so degenerate in the matter of eating and drinking as compared with the mythical era Before the Fire when the dollar dinner was universal at the Tehama House and Marchand's, and late supper at the Poodle Dog was a ritual with ladies who descended veiled from their cabs and were never introduced to the management.

There was, for example, in the record the welcoming breakfast tendered at the Palace to Lawrence Barrett and the Jarrett & Palmer theatrical troupe which arrived at Oakland from New York aboard the widely heralded *Lightning Express Train* (1876) in the incredible time of eighty-four hours. As the first meal of the day, the Palace had run up the following light snack for the players:

Salmon Grille à la Maître d'Hôtel
Tom Cod Frit   *Sauce Tartare*
Cucumber Salad
Filet de Boeuf, Sauce Béarnaise
Cotelettes d'Agneau Soubise
Escalope de Veau à la Génoise
Pommes de Terre Maître d'Hôtel
Rognons Sauté au Champignons
Poulet Grillé au Cresson
Oeufs Brouillés au Point d'Asperges
Oeufs Frites au Temben
Pré-Salé
Omelettes au Rhum
Apricots, Raspberries, Strawberries,
Cherries

We recalled in our own time in an earlier San Francisco, lunches at the French Club with the late Timothy Pfleugger which lasted until it was time to change for whisky doings and dinner at Izzy Gomez's speakeasy which, in retrospect, assumed proportions little less than Homeric. In the end we decided it wasn't so much the times that changed as our own capacities.

Dinner that evening found us loaded for bear—at least metaphorically—drinking daiquiris and conning the handwritten menu at Mario and Piero's Blue Fox, an extensive eating establishment overflowing into several apartments and doing a land-office business with lofty San Franciscans as well as out-of-town pilgrims. We settled for snails bourguignonne and medallion of tenderloin wrapped in bacon with broiled mushrooms and artichokes with hollandaise; for dessert, crepes Suzette and *café diablo*. Both of the last of these arrived, of course, in flames, an order calculated to please the management, which adores serving anything resembling a major fire hazard. Our wine was Château Haut Brion 1952, at $19.50 the bottle, next to the highest price we paid for wine on the entire project, followed by Hennessy V.S.O.P. with the flaming coffee. The check came to an even $51 and, with $10 distributed where it would do the most good, we called it a deal for $61. We rated the Blue Fox as neither the least expensive nor the most extravagant of San Francisco restaurants.

As an interlude between ingestions of the choicest calories San Francisco offers, we went that evening to the Geary Theater to witness Noel Coward in a piece of personal virtuosity that we had seen in New York when it opened to critical hoots, but on the basis that nothing with Mr. Coward in it can even resemble a bore, we went again and enjoyed ourselves.

After the performance, we persuaded Mr. Coward to accompany us to the new Terrace Room at the St. Francis for a quick one before he went on to a party in his honor at a private Nob Hill home, and recalled a long acquaintance reaching back to his *Private Lives* and *Design for Living* days over a brace of highballs. This pleasure set us back no more than $17.50.

Eleven-thirty o'clock, the clear blue flame of combustion from the Blue Fox having subsided to the merest flicker, we made rendezvous for a late snack with Herb Caen, columnist for the *Chronicle*, at the bar of Grison's Steak House in Van Ness Avenue, a faubourg devoted to the foreign-motorcar trade.

Grison's is a steak palace of notable dimension in a part of the world where the beef critter is king, but the hour of night and the nature of the occasion suggested lobster—not the crustacean of the West Coast, but the McCoy—flown in daily from Rockport, Maine.

We selected a brace of beauties weighing a pound and a quarter each, and ordered them broiled with bread crumbs, butter; cherries Jubilee and Bollinger. The result was all a San Francisco diner, out of the legendary time Before the Fire, could ask of late supper. The addition came to $24.50; $5.00 divided between the captain and waiter brought the total to $29.50.

The third day, a radiant morning without even the conventional mist over the lower city, found us after breakfast in a place that is part of the city's tangible continuity with the past: John Howell's bookshop in Post Street, hard by the St. Francis Hotel. Howell's, managed by Warren Howell, a son of the founder, is a shrine of the Old West, for its stock in trade is Western Americana. We spent an hour among the first editions conversing with Warren Howell and Oscar Lewis, dean of contemporary San Francisco men of letters, and then sauntered to the Sheraton-Palace to pick up the Rolls-Royce for our luncheon appointment on the far side of Telegraph Hill.

Our third luncheon hour of the gastronomic grand tour found us at Julius Castle overlooking the Embarcadero and lower harbor, a perennial favorite for its view. The Castle's promotional deal is its Martinis, easily double the size of conventional Martinis, and a great restorative of confidence too.

Caesar salad, rex sole meunière, which is a house specialty, a bottle of truly elegant Schloss Johannisberger Rotlack of the Prince von Metternich's bottling, and banana fritters, with coffee and cognac each, fetched a tab of $24.60, which, with $5.00 for the boy, came to $29.60, and a dollar for the custodian of the Rolls-Royce made it $30.60.

That afternoon was occupied industriously shopping for tangibles unconcerned with this bill of particulars, but the cocktail hour discovered us near Nob Hill, so we stopped to view the sunset from the Top of the Mark, a tourist spot to which even the most sophisticated San Franciscans also make pilgrimage. Two infusions each of the True Elixir of Life, an old sour-mash bourbon, set us back (including a fee for the boy) an even $5.00, and gave us courage to face the evening.

Dinner our third night out, at Alexis' Tangier at the summit of historic Nob Hill, was almost in the realm of transcendental gastronomy as described by Brillat-Savarin. Tangier came into being a few years ago as the dream child of a management given to Mediterranean tastes; it combines Turkish-Arabian-Moorish-Egyptian overtones both as to cuisine and décor.

It is in the best Before-the-Fire tradition of de luxe leisure and superb service. In fact, if you are one who confuses Cranshaw melon and Parma ham with honeydew and prosciutto you might do better elsewhere. Alexis himself does nothing to discredit the illusion of vaguely Byzantine intrigue connected with the langoustine tails Bagdad.

At the bar with Martinis we had Yalandji Dolma—stuffed grape leaves with a sour-cream sauce—while at the table, the maître d'hôtel, who is strictly French, was running up some caviar blinis Alexis with black Persian Gulf eggs which the management favors for flavor above the larger gray Beluga. With the caviar we had chilled vodka and then hot borsch. My entree was an old favorite, chicken Kiev, which is simple but nutritious: the breast of a suitable bird rolled around a core of butter and foie gras and quickly fried in deep fat. My companion ordered langoustine tails Bagdad—actually tender Australian lobster tails sautéed with mangoes, ginger, white wine and curry. There was a salad and a soufflé Grand Marnier and Turkish coffee. With the dessert we enjoyed Moët et Chandon's Dom Pérignon Cuvée champagne of 1952, and because it is so scarce as to be a collector's item, we had two—at $21 each. The damage was $71. Add $15 for the good of the house and you have our record: $86.

The last day of our skirmish with the fleshpots being Sunday, we did homage to one more San Francisco tradition— one that dates from the years when the town's swells tooled coaches out to the Cliff House at Point Lobos to see the seals; we drove the same route for an eye-opener. With a matchless view of the water, but no seals that day, we ordered a brace of the Cliff House Ramos gin fizzes, paid the barman $3.00, spoke well of the Pacific Ocean and drove back to town refreshed and feeling Old World.

Passing through Golden Gate Park on the way back, we reflected that San Francisco's continuity with the past is less physical than an awareness of grace, a sense of dedication that expresses itself in the presence on half the town's menus of chicken Raphael Weill as an enduring tribute to one of the town's pioneer gourmets. This is the sort of memorial that is pure San Francisco and as endearing as it is enduring. That the past is not exclusively the property of students and antiquaries is evidenced by a perusal of the columns of the universal Herb Caen. Among his properties are not only the politicians and publicans of the moment but gas lamps and opera cloaks, souvenirs of the Barbary Coast, wistful references to long-vanished magnificoes, the Emperor Norton, Lillie Hitchcock Coit, Addison Mizner and Isadora Duncan.

Lunch at the Sheraton-Palace has been institutional in San Francisco since the days of the nabobs and nothing lightly to be approached. Over a preprandial bottle of Bollinger we discussed the menu with Edmund Rieder, the general manager and highest authority we could consult, and came up with the following: cocktail of Olympia oysters, clear double beef consommé en tasse, mignonette of lamb, Bohemian, with mushrooms and tomatoes on a bed of rice, fresh California asparagus hollandaise, and for dessert petites coeurs à la crème aux fraises, a Sheraton-Palace magnificence of thick cream in molds with crushed strawberries. Lamb is a hard dish to complement with wine but we took a chance on a Château Lafite-Rothschild '52 and were not disappointed. Grand Marnier and coffee gave us stamina to last until dinner. The total was $35.20 and the $6.00 between the waiter and captain set us back $41.20.

For our last evening in San Francisco we chose the Fleur de Lys Restaurant Français at 777 Sutter Street, where Chérie and Robert Charles, who have managed French restaurants from Monte Carlo to Marin County, California, are the management, owners and half the fun. Fleur de Lys is enjoying an enormous vogue as perhaps the most purely Gallic resort in San Francisco, an illusion which is heightened by Robert Charles's Existentialist beard and Maurice, the bartender, who is directly from the Hotel Rafael in Paris.

Repudiating cocktails for the occasion and cleaving exclusively to wine, we ordered liberally from a bedsheet-sized menu as follows: vichyssoise, broiled oysters Anna, which are a specialty and resemble Pacific coast oysters, in an enriched poulard sauce beautifully browned before serving, filets de boeuf Périgourdine, blood-rare, white-hot Kansas City filets with truffled foie gras sauce, a green salad served with an assortment of French cheeses, of which we chose a good, runny Brie, and a dessert of the house's suggestion. The dessert was a bombe among whose ingredients it was possible to detect raspberry ice, French vanilla ice cream, fresh strawberries and a chocolate-mint sauce.

Our choice of wines was Pineau de Charente, an apéritif wine, before sitting down to Bollinger's Brut champagne 1952, two Bordeaux, an Alore-Corton 1953 with the filet and a Gruaud Larose 1934 with the cheese, while dessert was flanked by a glittering bottle of Château d'Yquem 1948 —of which we consumed only two glasses, and well worth the price of the bottle! The final bill for two for this classic collation came to $33.50 for the dinner and $33.00 for the wines, to which we added $15.00 for the captain and his assistant for a grand total of $81.50.

As a last salute to the good way of life and its accompanying blood pressure and implications of bankruptcy we paused at Trader Vic Bergeron's for a nightcap comprising an inhaler of forty-year-old Martel's cognac, special *espresso* coffee and an Upmann cigar, which came to $7.40 with largess of $3.00 to waiter and cigarette girl or a total of $10.40.

The Virginia City was attached to the rear end of the *San Francisco Overland* the next morning departing Oakland Mole at 11:20 and giving us just time for breakfast and an accounting with the management of the Sheraton-Palace for our four days on the eighth floor. The amount came to $430 for our apartment, breakfasts, suit pressing and an occasional libation by way of room service. Our bar and restaurant expenses had come to $500 take or leave a bottle of Liebfraumilch Madonna Spätlese, or an over-all total of $930 for the four days, exclusive of the private car which was largely for the dog T-Bone's convenience, and the Rolls-Royce which

was a courtesy from the dealer from whom we purchased our own.

If the sum seems modest for a town as admittedly expensive as San Francisco and moderate in the extreme compared to the casual expenditures of Nevada nabobs in the silver Seventies, it must be recalled that it includes the expenses of but a single pilgrim accompanied by a single companion. A luncheon for twenty guests such as we had had occasion to tender the book trade at the Sheraton-Palace earlier in the year could have accounted for half as much all by itself.

We had, we reflected as the *Overland* crossed the Strait of Carquinez and gathered speed on the long tangent to Sacramento, demonstrated to our own satisfaction that, despite the mutations of time and the ever-declining availability of the best of everything, the perfumed yesterdays of the city by the Golden Gate can still be recaptured by the perceptive seeker. Only the vintages change; the champagne is still there.

PART IV: *A Gourmet Tour of the United States*

Name Your Cut! / *Lucius Beebe*

Chefs in Chicago think in terms of larded filets,
roulades, prime roasts, shell steaks, deviled ribs.
So, of course, do people who eat there

Purely regional food in the United States is largely a thing of the past. There will, obviously, still be Creole cooking in New Orleans, Cape oysters in Boston, scrapple in Philadelphia and sand dabs in San Francisco, and there will survive regional traditions and conventions in the preparation of regional food and drink. But food is no longer geographically exclusive, save in the case of a very limited number of dishes such as shad, which is virtually unprocurable away from the Eastern seaboard, and Sierra cheese, the whole output of which is purchased by the Santa Fe Railroad.

Modern transportation and refrigeration make commonplace Maine lobsters in Cheyenne and fresh California figs in New York. And Mexican shrimp from Guaymas are esteemed the finest available in the fish stalls in Boston's famed Faneuil Hall Market.

In the face of this evidence it is something of an achievement for Chicago to have maintained for more than eighty years its cachet as the beef citadel of the world. Chicago's chefs dream in terms of larded filets, roulades, prime roasts, New York cuts (a steak unknown in Manhattan), shell steaks, deviled ribs and, at the nether end of the social scale, calves' brains, tripe and ground beef. Chicago lives by beef, and the best food you can get in any Chicago restaurant, with few exceptions, is some part of a steer raised on the distant ranges of Texas, Colorado or Nebraska.

Chicago food has been influenced by many factors—Great Lakes fish, the proximity of wonderful game country, the corn-hog economy of adjoining farming states, the dairy industries of Wisconsin, the German and Polish populations, the conventioneer and so on—but to me, the most important

factor is the longhorn steer and its successor, the Hereford beef critter.

The apotheosis of this factor in Windy City gastronomy is to be found in the several restaurants which constitute a subsidiary setup of the Union Stock Yard & Transit Company, of which William Wood Prince, multimillionaire railroad owner, is president. Since its founding in the middle 60's, Chicago's Union Stock Yard has possessed a robust legend, based on the fabulous consumption of choice cuts by persons associated with their production. Famed in the earliest sagas of sirloin was Myrick's Tavern, a scene of prodigious consumption of beef in the years directly following the Civil War. The current generation of Chicagoans recalls wistfully the celebrated Drovers' Inn which was destroyed in the great stockyard fire of the 1930's.

Successor to the traditions of these and several other taverns and hotels among the loading pens is the Stock Yard Inn, which, although mostly plain, is to many a sort of temple of T-bone. It was primarily designed for the accommodation and pleasure of stockmen having business in the Chicago market. The sight of cow ponies tethered to the hitch rack of the Inn alongside custom-built cars is a Chicago commonplace and something of a hallmark of the Yards.

Membership in the Saddle and Sirloin is largely restricted to well-to-do and powerful figures of the cattle industry, shippers, packers and railroad executives. Its collection of portraits of members and former *eminenti* includes such notables as J. Ogden Armour, Calvin Coolidge, Frank Lowden, one-time governor of Illinois, Louis Swift and Dan Casement, nationally known Kansas cattle king and son of the builder of the Union Pacific's original main line; all, it is humorously noted by members, bear a marked resemblance to one another in style and execution and often in beard and Albert watch chain. This is because the original collection was destroyed in the fire of the '30's and its re-creation was executed by a single artist.

Show place and public restaurant of the Stock Yard Inn is the Sirloin Room, which advertises, and probably with ample justification, "where the steak is born!" Steaks are listed and priced by type and weight, the standard single portion of any steak in the two categories, U.S. Prime Sirloin and U.S. Prime Tenderloin, being sixteen ounces for the first and twelve for the second. Based on the reasonable theory that few patrons come there for anything except a superlative skirmish with heavenly Hereford, the menu is generally limited to sirloin and tenderloin in various dimensions and two daily fish dishes.

Patrons at the Sirloin Room select their own cuts from a great ice-filled stand in the center of the restaurant. There is an assortment of miniature branding irons resting in an adjacent charcoal brazier, from which a client may take his choice and brand his cut with the symbol of his fancy: Adair-Goodnight, King Ranch, Capitol Syndicate or any of several others, and it is taken to the kitchen thus tagged and identified, with specific instructions for its preparation. Emerging from the charcoal it is served to the guest on a hot platter from which it is to be eaten. Salad is firmly served on the right-hand side of the entree. Nothing French.

The only fly in the ointment in the conduct of the Sirloin Room is the passion exhibited by late and enthusiastic diners for branding each other with the all-too-handy irons. Nobody seems to mind at the time, but the next day there are likely to be recriminations.

In addition to the white-faced beef critter as an influence on Chicago eating there is another which, to this reporter, is almost as important. That factor is the late Ernest Byfield, of the Ambassador and Sherman hotels.

In saluting the memory of Ernie Byfield, a hotelier who constantly confused Escoffier with Harpo Marx, it must be recognized that not only did he give Chicago a hilarious tradition of gastronomy and laughable good living, but that he was succeeded by Jimmy Hart, a man entirely capable of sustaining the Byfield mantle.

The first Byfield-Hart ventures in the realms of grand-ducal splendor in dining, the Pump Room and the Buttery, situated respectively in the Hotels Ambassador East and West, have been so long established as Chicago institutions that more than their mention is redundant. Amidst their spectacular grandeur, Byfield contrived to evolve a tradition of really fine food which gave a new dimension to the American eating scene.

Byfield's last attack upon the sales resistance of Chicago was in the form of an eye-popping sea-food restaurant in the cellarage of the Sherman. It is called the Well of the Sea, and its Robert E. Lederer decorations give the customers a sense of submergence as they ponder on fresh New Brunswick lobster or Dungeness crab with cold mustard mayonnaise. The cigarette girl is attired in mermaid costume, the bar is built to re-create a sunken ship complete with ribs and planking, and there are luminescent fish, of every variety known to Dr. William Beebe, along the walls.

"Dali will cut his throat when he sees this," Byfield remarked.

The bill of fare for the Well of the Sea, printed in two colors, is approximately the size of the original Magna Carta. It is a most comprehensive document, and it drips with such items as "McGinty's Clam Juice Cocktail or Stiffener Made with Hellfire Bitters from an Old Barbados Recipe," "Bahama Conch Chowder with Barbados Rum, Said to be a favorite with Ernest Hemingway, Believed by the Natives of Barbados to Promote Virility and Longevity," or, if you like, "Green Turtle Soup, Made with a Sixty Year Old Madeira."

Byfield's final contribution to the legend of gay gastronomy was the conversion, accomplished after his death by James Hart, Frank Bering and Pat Hoy, of what had for many years been the famous College Inn at the Sherman. The idea was Byfield's; its execution was a triumph on the part of the dapper and personable Hart, himself a sophisticated hotelier.

The College Inn Porterhouse—the first part of its title is seldom spoken but remains on the menus for identification with the fragrant past—is devoted to beef in a manner, as far as ornateness goes, that outshines the various restaurants of the Stock Yards.

The whole grand design, a sort of El Rancho Pump Room, is such as sometimes to obscure the merits of the menu. The theme of the American West is carried to the last detail. The bar is The Hitching Post; a private dining room, The Corral; there is a Sunday Chuck Wagon Breakfast, and the servitors range in attire from headwaiters in brocaded, white full-dress Hopalong Cassidy costumes through the captains who wear ditto in black suède with silver lamé trim, waiters who are in chaps and varicolored neckerchiefs, and bus boys in blue jeans and checked shirts. The wine steward's regalia includes the war bonnet of an unidentified Indian tribe, probably Ojibway. Finally, there is a troupe of nine fiddlers, in a sort of cowboy dinner dress, who wander through the restaurant playing—with faultless precision—everything from Viennese waltzes to "Home on the Range." The senses of otherwise well-adjusted patrons have been known to reel at the Porterhouse.

The menu, like all Byfield-inspired menus, is of four-sheet proportions. There are cuts of beef for every taste ranging from the lordly Chateaubriand for two at a vaguely astronomical figure to broiled deviled roast-beef bones with hot mustard sauce, which everyone who ever rode a prewar Cunarder knows are one of the noblest if not the most pretentious aspects of the bovine profile.

While it is possible, in some cities, for a stranger to walk into most any small restaurant and obtain an above-the-average meal, Chicago is a place where a newcomer needs to be told where to dine well in the little-publicized establishments.

Of the small, privately operated restaurants in Chicago, Imperial House, featuring classic French cuisine, stands out. It is on East Walton Place, cater-cornered from Don the Beachcomber's (which—not so incidentally—serves Cantonese food that's hard to beat; a specialty is a duck dinner, Cantonese style) and flourishes in the grand manner of intimacy and subdued elegance. Its façade is decorated grandly with royal coat armor, and it boasts an imposing array of local regulars and transient celebrities.

The menu here is imposing and the kitchen performance lives up to the printed bill. With a preponderantly feminine luncheon trade there are fifty desserts alone listed, and in summer months, the management asserts, a substantial three quarters of their luncheon orders are for salads which are named on a separate menu. Almost all Chicago restaurants will, at the drop of an egg yolk, go into a production number of Caesar salad.

There is a legend, never yet denied by the Harvey System management, that, seventy-five years ago when Fred Harvey was bringing civilization to Kansas and New Mexico in the form of the first fine restaurants ever seen in those regions, he discharged a chef because the fellow's kitchen didn't show a loss commensurate with the owner's idea of propriety. Fred Harvey didn't feel he was serving big enough steaks, fresh enough melons or good enough food generally unless his eating houses showed a substantial loss, at least to begin with.

Present heirs to the management may not be as keen on deficits as was the founder, but they still carry on in notable style the most spacious legend of the American gastronomic West. Old Fred Harvey, an Englishman, had nothing but the best. His table linen was specially woven in Ireland; his silverware was made to order in England; his agents and factors throughout the United States were out a job if they didn't discover the biggest strawberries, the most tender Maine lobsters and the thickest Wisconsin cream for Harvey patrons, and the same obtains with the present generation.

The Harveys maintain fourteen Chicago restaurants in four different locations, the greatest concentration being at the Union Station, where six Fred Harvey eating places serve upwards of 10,000 meals a day. Their newest is the Palmolive Building Restaurant, in the middle of the town's "million-dollar mile." Another anniversary project is the Bowl and Bottle Restaurant in the Continental Companies Building in East Jackson, while the oldest Harvey operation in Chicago is the Crossroads Room in the Dearborn Station, which has been gentling patrons with inch-thick slices of rare beef and sluicing them with outsize Harvey Martinis and Old Fashioneds since the turn of the century.

Half a millon dollars, a tidy stake even in inflated times, has been spent on the Palmolive Building venture in the décor alone, but not at the expense of the cuisine. The menu features Escoffier-inspired chafing-dish entrees which are the hallmark of the house much as the rolling tables are the hallmark of the Pump Room. Newburgs, creamed dishes of mushrooms and scallops and such are available in considerable variety and, like all Chicago restaurants, the house caters to iodine-starved inlanders with pompano, red snapper, crab meat Maryland, shrimp Poulette, lobster Thermidor, oysters Benedict and Casino and a multiplicity of other marine fauna.

The walnut-paneled Harvey House Grill, an adjunct of the Palmolive Restaurant, is less formal than the restaurant proper, more masculine in its appointments. It features an open charcoal grill with burnished-copper canopy and the choosy diner can see his T-bone or Maine lobster broiled to his own taste. Specially popular is the new hybrid, semigame what-is-it, generally called a pheasant-chicken, which is a blood combination of Cornish gamecock, ring-neck pheasant and Rhode Island Red; it lends itself excellently to broiling and is possessed of a distinctive flavor and abundance of white meat.

After three-quarters of a century, the Harveys are still a national institution which shows no least sign of lowering standards.

If, as has been suggested, the menus of the Byfield-inspired restaurants approximate the proportions of bed sheets, the menu of the Drake Hotel's Camellia House suggests nothing so much as a carpet woven with an arabesque of Pheasant Souvaroff, breast of chicken Belle Hélène and scallops Poulette. The bemused guest can wander down aisles of lobster Cardinal, coupe Monte Carlo and limestone Bibb lettuce, and explore alcoves devoted to cracked Dungeness crab and mushrooms forestière. In actuality Camellia House menus measure a foot by eighteen inches which, obviously, will put the Pump Room in its place.

The Drake is one of the few notable hotels in the land which is privately owned and under ownership management. Edwin L. Brashears—Naval Academy graduate, of all things—is president, and the place is as socially correct as its physical plan is labyrinthine. It maintains a multiplicity of bar rooms, restaurants and cafés and it would be possible to browse through them for days without ever seeing daylight.

Camellia House, an explosion of decorative whimsey contrived by the florid Dorothy Draper, about whose décors there is nothing either minute or reticent, is the Drake's show-place restaurant. There is also a Cape Cod Room, designed by a Cape Cod artist, Peter Hunt, and devoted, more or less, to Cape Cod matters and the adjoining seas and oceans in its menus; a Club International Restaurant whose members are admitted by card only; and the Oak Room, the management's least-exploited resort but the one which, paradoxically, enjoys the finest view overlooking Lake Michigan and the surging traffic of Michigan Boulevard.

The cuisine at the Drake, all of which derives from a central kitchen, save steaks and chops for the Club International, which are prepared at hand on a charcoal grill, may be described as de luxe hotel fare. Somewhat less costly than the opulent Pump Room and the Buttery, it is classic French in outline and available in the prodigious variety characteristic of almost all better Chicago dining places. The standing menu of the Camellia lists nineteen fish courses, sixteen charcoal specialties and twenty-seven permanent entrees, games and cold dishes in addition to the customary daily specials which vary with the season. The Cape Cod Room augments the fish list with fifty-five regular-standing lakes and oceans entrees and daily luncheon specials and chefs' suggestions past counting.

There are many other restaurants in Chicago where Chicagoans and visitors can dine happily and without fear of being undernourished. Here are a few recommended to this reporter by Chicagoans who do not merely eat to live:

For French fare there are Jacques and Le Petit Gourmet, both on North Michigan Boulevard. Pastries, omelettes and crepes suzette are noteworthy at Jacques, which has a pleasant outdoor garden. Le Petit Gourmet is highly regarded for desserts and pastries. Its atmosphere is quaintly French and rather tearoomish. Another is L'Aiglon, on Ontario Street, which specializes in shrimp and oyster dishes.

Chicago's top Scandinavian place is Kungsholm, at Rush and Ontario streets. Its appointments are beautiful, its smörgåsbord sumptuous and, of course, it specializes in Swedish, Danish and Norwegian dishes. An established Bohemian restaurant is Old Heidelberg, in the heart of the Loop; another, Café Bohemia, serves what is probably the largest variety of wild game in the city; and the Red Star Inn, located in Chicago's German district, is a landmark. Its ample menu includes popular German dishes such as apple strudel, Hoppel Poppel and Sauerbraten; it is also known for fine steaks. Another restaurant of foreign flavor is Riccardo's Studio Restaurant run by an amateur painter named Ric Riccardo. Its walls are hung with paintings by better-than-average amateur artists, and its Italian food and wines are also better than average. Those with a yen for Chinese food unhesitatingly recommend the House of Eng, on East Walton Place.

The Edgewater Beach Hotel has an ardent following that keeps going back for Walter Schrott's chicken *cacciatore*, made with olives, tomatoes, onions, mushrooms, spices, wine and parsley; and the Walter Salad which has been earning acclaim ever since Mr. Schrott (now *maître d'emeritus*) first made it for Cordell Hull almost twenty years ago.

Chicago has its share of hearty eaters, and among their favorite spots are four establishments which have earned reputations for hearty fare: Barney's, in the middle of the market section, is noisy, cheerful and good. Its fine steaks, roasts and sea foods attract a loyal local patronage as well as a large convention and tourist trade. The Charles Harrison Restaurant, on North LaSalle Street, has won friends with its first-class oyster bar, its high-quality steaks and chops. Devotees of Harding's Restaurant on Wabash Avenue are not the least shy about praising the corned beef they eat there. And the Erie Café on North Wells Street for years has been noted for its seven-inch-thick steaks.

When it comes to sea food, much of the local acclaim goes to Ireland's Oyster House on North Clark near Ontario.

A luncheon rendezvous popular with Chicago publishing, advertising and radio executives is the Wrigley Building Restaurant, owned by William Wrigley, Jr. Its patrons boast about the Martinis served there, and when they mention the game and the salads, they are inclined to glow. . . .

When one considers the over-all opportunities Chicago offers a man in search of good food, it is obvious that a visitor who fails to find what he wants should have stayed at home.

Galatoire's of New Orleans
/ Shirley Ann Grau

*To many New Orleanians no restaurant surpasses this modest home
of incomparable crawfish bisque, turtle soup,
Shrimp and Crabmeat Remoulade*

THE address is 209 Bourbon Street, New Orleans, the second block below Canal Street, a block lined with the seamiest of the Bourbon Street clubs. It is a white-painted, three-story building, so narrow that it looks as if it had shrunk. Each of the upper stories has a fringe of iron balcony. The front door and two flanking windows are curtained in white silk. On each side of the door there is a round, white electric globe in the style of thirty years ago, and over the sidewalk hangs a small sign—GALATOIRE'S—in the style of forty years ago.

This is one of two really fine restaurants in New Orleans. The other is, of course, Antoine's, a few blocks away on St. Louis Street. Antoine's is older, dating from the 1840's, and nationally famous. Galatoire's is quite small and, locally, has a reputation that equals or surpasses Antoine's. Like Antoine's, its interior is old-fashioned, extremely plain. It is almost as if the proprietors wanted nothing to detract from the food.

Very little has changed at Galatoire's in the last half century. The floor is white tile, cracked and somewhat uneven; strips of worn red carpet run down the aisles. The walls on both sides are lined with old mirrors with wavering lines in the glass and little brown spots in the silver. On the mirror frames are brass coat hooks. From the very high ceiling hang dozens of two-bladed electric fans, and under each is a circle of glaring, unshaded electric lamps. The fans, now that the place has been air conditioned, are never used. In the back of the restaurant is a towering mirror with an ornate gold frame; across it are shelves of liqueurs. The whole effect is rather like a restaurant in the French provinces.

Shortly after last Christmas, a fire gutted the upper stories of the building, and Galatoire's was closed for two weeks. As soon as it reopened I went back, eager to see what had been changed. Exactly one thing: the elaborate brasswork of the fans was polished.

So the interior of Galatoire's has not changed; nor has the quality of the food that made it famous. This is Creole cuisine, and quite unlike any other. It is rich, heavy, highly seasoned, and excellent. It is as varied as New Orleans' past. All the things Galatoire's does are good, and some are superb.

New Orleanians debate the respective merits of Galatoire's and Antoine's. There is no answer. Each restaurant does different things extraordinarily well. Some friends of mine have solved the problem with a progressive dinner. They start at Galatoire's. First, two Sazeracs, that Pernod-flavored drink which originated in New Orleans. Never more than two, for one must miss no flavor of the food to follow. Then, one of three favorite appetizers: Shrimp Remoulade, Crabmeat Remoulade (though the word is used in all New Orleans restaurants, this spicy red sauce is startlingly different in each), or Oysters Rockefeller—oysters baked on the half shell and covered with a marvelous sauce containing spinach and herbs.

After the appetizers come the soups, the very best of which are the two traditional ones of New Orleans: turtle soup and crawfish bisque. They are both thick red soups, a bit hearty for New Orleans summers, but simply excellent—particularly the piquant stuffed crawfish heads, which are dropped in the bisque just before serving. They taste faintly nutlike, and many people order three or four extra heads in a side plate.

With these courses goes garlic bread—hot French bread, which has been specially baked for this restaurant, with a butter-garlic dressing and a touch of paprika. A word of warning: if you do not like onions, garlic, bay leaf and cayenne, don't go to Galatoire's.

After these two courses everyone slowly walks the half dozen blocks to Antoine's for entree and dessert. The next week the procedure is reversed. For my part, I prefer one restaurant at a time. And I find that I go to Galatoire's more frequently than to Antoine's.

This address—209 Bourbon Street—has had a long history of good food. In the last half of the 19th century it was occupied by Victor's Restaurant, a name some people remember with pleasure even today, for Victor Béro was one of the best chefs in a town that had plenty of good ones. But by the turn of the century he had retired, and Victor's was closed. Then, in 1905, Jean Galatoire took it over. (He had had another place around the corner.)

At that time New Orleans was a fairly small town. Its uptown districts were very proper. But the downtown area, where Galatoire's is located, was rowdy. The Vieux Carré had become a slum area. A lady rarely ventured below Canal Street without an escort. To be sure, some families held onto their old homes and refused to move, but they were a tiny minority. Immigrants crowded into the moldy buildings, strung clotheslines from the lovely ironwork. There were ugly rumors of Mafia activities. A hopelessly corrupt city government made proper law enforcement almost impossible. And a dozen blocks away from the newly opened Galatoire's were the cribs of Storyville.

When Galatoire's opened, my uncle, who lived in a little hotel across the street, decided to try the new place. As he walked down Bourbon Street, he stepped into the middle of a shooting scrape. He left fast; he didn't want lunch that badly. And it was a couple of weeks before he thought of trying the restaurant again. He liked it so much he's been going back once or twice a week for fifty years. There are dozens of old-time customers who have been coming for years on the same day of the week, to order the same food. A waiter pointed out one such couple to me. They were elderly and well dressed. The waiter whispered, "I can tell what they're going to order: Turtle soup in the winter, Shrimp Remoulade in the summer; Chicken Bonne Femme or maybe broiled pompano; head lettuce with vinegar and oil and lemon. Three cups of coffee. And one brandy."

He was absolutely right. It was summer, and they had Shrimp Remoulade, Chicken Bonne Femme (sautéed with potatoes and sweet onions), the salad, coffee and brandy.

The new Galatoire's was only a few blocks from the commercial heart of the city, and it quickly became a favorite lunch place for businessmen. In those days most people had only coffee and perhaps a brioche for an early breakfast; by eleven they were ready to eat heartily.

Today there are very few businessmen in Galatoire's at noon. Mostly, one sees visitors with cameras slung over their shoulders, and smartly dressed women shoppers. On summer nights, before air conditioning, the ceiling fans did no more than stir up the air. "By the end of dinner," old-time Galatoire customers told me, with considerable relish, "your collar was curling. It never stopped us from coming here."

Which is, I suppose, a great compliment to Galatoire's food. Today they come in greater crowds than ever. An old woman in her seventies, tall, thin, and very much the lady, who has been going to carnival balls since she was fifteen and can tell you the name of every queen of Comus for the last half-century, shook her head sadly.

"Why, imagine," she said, tapping me on the shoulder, "you can go in Galatoire's now and not see a single person you know!" In the old days Galatoire's was almost a club.

In spite of the crowds, the restaurant has retrenched rather than expanded. The two upstairs floors contain private rooms and once were reached by an outside stairway. I remember my grandmother giving dinner parties there; each time, as she climbed those stairs, she swore she would never do it again. And each time she forgot. In addition to such staid dinner parties, there were lively college reunions. Earlier and more romantically, Galatoire's was a favorite rendezvous. The social structure of New Orleans was quite rigid, and until the twenties it was not considered proper for a single woman to appear in a restaurant with anyone but relatives. Private rooms were the answer. The separate entrance assured privacy, and the waiters were discreet. The rooms upstairs are empty and dusty now. Their use was discontinued during World War II because of the shortage of help, and they have never been revived.

I once asked Justin Galatoire, a plump, pink-cheeked man who always seems to wear brown suits, why the restaurant did not grow. "It would be nice," he said. (He is French, but his native tongue has acquired a strong Louisiana accent.) "But no . . . we got enough work already." And he is right. Galatoire's is always crowded.

Food in New Orleans is a serious matter. New Orleanians, particularly the older ones, do not like the idea of sharing so small a place with crowds of strangers.

There was the man I noticed last summer. He was sixty-five or seventy, with a small full mustache and dark, heavy-lidded eyes. He wore a white linen suit in the cut of thirty years ago, a type still stylish in the parishes. When he saw the line waiting outside Galatoire's he turned to his companion and said petulantly, in Louisiana French, "I remember when this place wasn't so famous but what you could get in." He spun around on his heel and announced to the city as a whole, "We advance backwards!" And off he marched, straight, stiff, furious.

If you go to Galatoire's in the proper frame of mind—that is, simply starving—the result is rewarding. To me their sea food is the best of all Creole dishes. For an entree you could have, perhaps, Trout Marguery, which is trout in a Hollandaise sauce. This is the most popular dish at Galatoire's, and here's how it's made:

Skin the trout, filet it and fold in half so that it cooks but does not dry. Place the folded fish in a pan and add five tablespoons of olive oil and a glass of water. Bake in a hot oven for fifteen minutes.

For the Hollandaise sauce, consult any good cookbook. To this sauce add 12 lake shrimps; 2 truffles; ½ can of mushrooms. Cut these in small pieces and mix with the sauce. Add condiments to taste; dress the fish on a platter and cover with the sauce.

Then there is the delicately flavored pompano, best of all fish. Galatoire's pompano *en papillote* is baked in a thick sauce of shrimp, crab meat and other, more subtle seasonings. Of course, this would shock many an old-time Creole gourmet; for him there would be only one way of serving pompano: broiled, with a bit of maître d'hôtel sauce.

There are other excellent, less rich dishes: Shrimp Creole, with tomatoes and green peppers, and served over rice. And Redfish Court-bouillon, a kind of glorified fish stew with tomatoes and flavored with thyme, garlic, onions and bay leaf.

Less distinctively Creole in flavor are the chicken dishes: Bonne Femme, or Turenne (with a red-wine sauce containing mushrooms and artichoke hearts). And, to end the proper dinner at Galatoire's, *Crêpes Maison*: pancakes filled with jelly and served in a sauce of orange curaçao, and almonds and tiny curls of orange peel.

Galatoire's is a family business, even today. Three generations have worked there. Jean, the founder, came from France to New Orleans in the 1880's—an energetic man who had an instinctive way with fine foods. Since he had no children, he brought over his brother's three sons—Leon, Justin and Gabriel. Justin, now retired, remembers that time with a wry smile. "My mother wrote to see if he did not have work for us . . . and he had work, yes. Thirteen, fourteen hours a day!" But the restaurant prospered and the boys learned its operation. In 1919 Jean died and the nephews took over. Today there is a third generation at work: Leon's sons, René and Gabriel; Justin's daughter, Yvonne Galatoire Wynne; and Chris Ansel, Justin's son-in-law.

I went to Galatoire's first in the mid-thirties when I was five or six. It was the first time I had ever eaten out, and there was an agreement: I could go visiting with my godmother, but I must behave myself. Galatoire's was the reward.

So my godmother took me to one of the old houses in the Vieux Carré, down a dark passageway, through an arched doorway and into a small, brick-paved patio. Inside there were rooms with high ceilings, plaster medallions and elaborately carved cornices. The furniture had thin, arched, and sometimes gilded legs. There were little old ladies with rustling silk dresses and lips like dry leaves. I was afraid to move.

We walked to Galatoire's. It was very early spring and there was that peculiar lemony smell to the air. We passed a sidewalk stand. "Wait," my godmother said. She left me tugging at the leaves of an artichoke—I always thought they were a kind of puzzle: if you got the right leaf the whole thing would fall open. "Here," she said. She was shaking the water off a large red camellia. And she pinned it to the neck of my dress in the exact center, so that I couldn't bend my head without crushing the petals . . . but it was elegant.

We turned down a side street. There were oyster shells piled in wooden kegs all along the sidewalk (*banquette*, we always said). We turned another corner and she slowed her pace. "Here we are." And there was Galatoire's.

She recognized nearly everyone there. She named them as we sat at the table. I don't suppose I registered a single name, I was so proud to be treated like a grownup. Suddenly

she looked at me, hard. "Sit up, *chérie*." I stretched my back and stuck up my chin—it was still just barely over the edge. The waiter lifted me upright. "A high chair?" he suggested.

"She's too big for that."

He moved off, shaking his head. In a minute he reappeared, grinning broadly and carrying three or four thick books which he put on the chair. They were quite old and crumbling; only one word on the back was legible. I spelled it out: *Balzac*. I've often wondered what those books were doing in a restaurant.

That night was my first experience with coffee, the mark of the grownup. I had some after dinner: black, a demitasse. I had never been allowed any at home. (If you drank it too young, your skin would turn yellow, for sure.) Looking back, I can see that it was a great but subtle compliment to Galatoire's that my aunt decided my first coffee should be of their making. To New Orleanians, coffee must be just so. It must have chicory, but not too much. It must be brown-black, but not bitter. And it must be very, very strong.

One of the best Galatoire foods is crawfish bisque, a thick red soup of those lovely little crustaceans that live in fresh water around New Orleans. Unfortunately, they are available only for a few months each year, February to May—at least in theory. Actually, they are often far too small early in the season, and it is March before they reach the pot.

Nevertheless, each year as soon after February first as he happens to be in Galatoire's, my uncle orders crawfish bisque —confidently, as if it were inconceivable that they should *not* have it.

If the waiter shakes his head my uncle is shocked. He demands a menu and points to it furiously. "It's right here!" The waiter shrugs and throws out his hands. "But there are always many things on the menu that are not in the kitchen!" And he is right; the menu at Galatoire's does not change from year to year.

Traditional Creole cooking is basically, though not purely, French. There are many other elements: the Spanish (in its use of pepper and spices); the African (the word gumbo comes from a Congo dialect and means okra); the Italian (in the liberal use of olive oil); the Indian (the indispensable filé, which is ground sassafras leaves, was a favorite seasoning of the Choctaws).

My elders tell me that I missed the height of Creole cooking. The game laws and the times, I'm told, seriously restrict the art. If I venture to praise a dish at Galatoire's, they patiently correct me. "My dear," they say, "now the waiter goes into the kitchen and in twenty minutes you have your order. Years ago it would take two days. . . . If you could just *taste* the things they did!"

Once, a hostess could have a talk with Mr. Galatoire and work out the menu of the following day's dinner. Today, special dishes can no longer be ordered ahead of time. The menu has been streamlined. Certain elaborate dishes have been eliminated. For example, there was *Poulet Maison d'Or*: stuffed boned chicken in a cream sauce. As Mr. Galatoire

Mr. Justin Galatoire, co-owner of the restaurant which bears ▸ his name, sits with an array of comestibles fit to meet the standards of the most exacting gourmet.

ARNOLD NEWMAN

points out, people just don't eat as much now. A New Orleans cookbook in the early 20th century offered the following as an example of a well-balanced family dinner:

Oysters on the Half Shell
Chicken Consommé
Broiled Sheepshead, Sauce à la Maître d'Hôtel
Potatoes à la Duchesse
Lamb Cutlets, Sauce Soubise
String Beans, Stuffed Cabbage, Spinach
Roast Leg of Mutton, Mint Sauce
Roquette Salad, French Dressing
Lemon Pudding. Strawberry Sherbet

And of course there would be cheese, fruits, nuts and black coffee.

I'm probably lucky not to remember those good old days. I'm happy with the way things are right now—especially at Galatoire's. Take, for example, the Crabmeat Maison—crab with green herbs and a mayonnaise dressing. Served hot or cold, as an appetizer or entree, it simply couldn't be better. The secret is partly in the dressing and partly in the quality of the crabmeat. It is always fresh and firm and delicious.

Then, too, there is Galatoire's Oysters Rockefeller, which I much prefer to the more famous ones at Antoine's. They are served piping hot as an appetizer, and they have a wonderful crunchy texture.

One friend of mine, who believes that balanced diets are nonsense, has a wonderful time in Galatoire's. She invariably orders a dozen Oysters Rockefeller, Crabmeat Maison and turtle soup. And black coffee. Occasionally she will add Crêpes Maison.

New Orleanians are coming to rely more and more on restaurants for traditional cooking. Unless you can spend hours in the preparation of a single dish, Creole cooking is not for you. A good gumbo, for instance, demands a couple of hours standing by the stove, stirring the mixture (with a wooden spoon, experts tell me). Okra scorches easily and the slightest burn will ruin the gumbo. The rice which goes into gumbo and which is, incidentally, one of the staples of the Creole diet, is also a production number. The raw rice must be washed—rubbed between the palms in hot salt water —boiled for exactly the proper time, washed again in cold water and put in a colander to steam. I know one purist who actually keeps a wood stove only for cooking rice. She claims that only a wood fire gives the necessary very slow, very even heat.

Many people consider turtle soup the best thing in New Orleans. One friend of mine says he wants no flowers on his grave, only gallons of turtle soup.

A woman once said to me with a laugh, "Whenever I pass Mr. Galatoire on the street, I don't really see him. I just see his turtle soup." That's a very high compliment indeed. The traditional dishes are left in capable hands.

[Mr. Galatoire's recipes for *Oysters Rockefeller* and *Turtle Soup* may be found on page 206.]

PART IV: *A Gourmet Tour of the United States*

Specialties of Some
Fine American Restaurants

THE SKILL of a great chef is instinctive as well as learned. He *feels* that a dish must have a little more herb, or he *senses* that a sauce has cooked just enough. Translating these ephemeral feelings into recipes which are useful without the chef's having to be on hand for consultation is not a simple matter. Fortunately, however, many of the best restaurants both here and abroad are proud enough of the specialties that come from their kitchens to do just that. The recipes that follow have been worked out by the chefs of some of the restaurants mentioned in the articles in this section. Some may be familiar, others completely new; but in each you will be sure to find the touch of the professional.

BOSTON

Boston is the city whose food is certainly most traditional and probably most American. Here are two recipes from Durgin-Park, one of the city's better-known restaurants, where the plainness of the fare detracts not at all from its delectability. The first is certainly traditional, and it would be difficult to find a more purely American dish than the second.

BOSTON BAKED BEANS

2 *pounds beans (California pea beans preferred or York State beans)*	½ *cup sugar*
	⅔ *cup molasses*
	2 *teaspoons dry mustard*
1 *teaspoon baking soda*	4 *teaspoons salt*
1 *pound salt pork with*	½ *teaspoon pepper*
1 *medium-sized onion, peeled*	½ *cup hot water*

Wash beans, drain, cover with cold water and let soak overnight. The next morning drain; place in a saucepan; cover with water and add the soda. Boil for 10 minutes. Drain and rinse with cold water in a colander or strainer. Dice the rind of the pork in 1-inch squares, cut remaining piece of pork in half. Place half of the meat in a 2-quart bean pot with the whole onion. Pour drained beans into the pot. Place the remaining piece of pork in the top of the beans. Combine remaining ingredients and pour a little over the beans. Start oven at moderately low (275° to 300° F.). Place bean pot in oven and bake for 6 hours. Add more of the basting mixture in 3 or 4 portions during the baking period. Makes 10 servings.

BAKED INDIAN PUDDING

1 *cup coarse yellow corn meal*	¼ *teaspoon salt*
	¼ *teaspoon baking soda*
½ *cup black molasses*	2 *eggs*
¼ *cup sugar*	1½ *quarts hot milk*
4 *tablespoons lard or butter*	

Start oven at hot (425° F.). Mix all the ingredients except the milk; beat well. Add ½ of the milk (3 cups). Mix and pour into a greased 2-quart casserole. Place in oven until mixture boils. Then stir in the remaining 3 cups hot milk. Reduce oven heat to low (200–225° F.) and bake the pudding for 5 to 7 hours. The secret of its excellence, says the Durgin-Park chef, lies in the long, slow cooking. It cannot be hurried. Makes 6 servings.

NEW YORK

To the gourmet, New York means, among other restaurants, the Colony, Voisin, Le Pavillon, and "21." The city means the best in food, the best in service—the greatest variety of fine restaurants to be found anywhere in the country. Sometimes the gourmet's hankerings take him away from the *haut monde* and down to places like Sweet's on Fulton Street, where he knows he can find some of the finest sea-food dishes this side of Marseilles.

Among the many dishes for which the "21" Club is famous are the two made from the following recipes.

BREAST OF GUINEA HEN, SMITANE

2 breasts of guinea hen	*2 teaspoons olive oil*
Salt and pepper	*4 tablespoons sherry*
4 tablespoons butter	*¼ cup hot cooked wild rice*

Season breasts lightly with salt and pepper. Heat butter and oil and sauté breasts for 15 to 20 minutes. Pour sherry on, ignite and continue cooking so meat absorbs butter and sherry flavor. When breasts are done, place in an oven-proof serving platter and set aside. Flank the breasts with 4 tablespoons of cooked wild rice. Prepare Sauce Smitane and spread over the breasts and rice, place under moderate broiler heat and glaze for 2 or 3 minutes. Serve immediately. Makes 2 servings.

SAUCE SMITANE

1 tablespoon butter	*1 tablespoon whipped heavy*
1 tablespoon paprika	*cream*
½ teaspoon salt	*1 tablespoon Hollandaise*
¼ teaspoon pepper	*Sauce*
1 tablespoon flour	*1 tablespoon seedless raisins,*
½ cup chicken stock	*soaked and drained*
¼ cup light cream	

Combine butter, seasonings, flour and chicken stock in a saucepan; simmer for a few minutes; add light cream, stirring, and cook gently until thickened. Remove from heat. Add whipped cream and Hollandaise Sauce and mix well. Add raisins. Makes about 1 cup sauce. Use as described above.

MALLARD DUCK À LA PRESSE

1 mallard duck, carefully cleaned and ready to cook	*1 cup finely chopped cooked goose livers or pâté de foie gras*
1 thin slice fat salt pork	*½ cup port*
Tender top branches 3 stalks celery	*Peel ½ lemon, grated*
3 tablespoons butter	*¼ cup good red wine*
	2 tablespoons cognac

The duck must be carefully cleaned with every feather and root removed. Lay the strip of fat pork over the breast of the bird. Put the pieces of celery (whole) inside bird and fasten vent with skewer; wrap bird with white thread to hold salt pork in place. Place in baking pan.

Start the oven at very hot (450°–500° F.). Brown the duck for 7 to 10 minutes, depending on whether you prefer the bird rare or medium. (Some people prefer a game bird cooked only a few minutes to insure more blood for the pressed sauce.)

Heat the butter in a saucepan; add the goose liver or pâté and sauté until well mixed. Add the port slowly, stirring all the time to thin the mixture. Continue stirring over low heat for 1 or 2 minutes. Add lemon peel, mix, and remove pan from heat.

Remove skewer from bird and take out remains of celery. Remove legs (which are not served). Cut the breast into fine slices and place them against each other in a chafing dish on a warmer. Chop up the carcass and break the spine, so that all the bones fit into the bucket of the press. Sprinkle the carcass in the bucket with the wine. Turn the press so as to mash bones; collect blood and juices in the saucebowl. Add a few drops of cognac to the sauce. Pour the goose liver sauce over the breast meat in the chafing dish and heat over low flame for a few minutes, stirring the sauce over and around the meat. Then pour the blood collected from the press slowly into the pan; continue to heat and stir for an additional 5 minutes. Serve very hot. Makes 1 or 2 servings.

The following two recipes are for dishes served at the Colony. The recipes for the garnish and the sauce in the second are very useful in their own right.

CHICKEN GISMONDA

1 whole chicken breast	*2 cups hot cooked spinach*
Salt and pepper	*¼ cup hot sliced mush-*
½ cup melted butter	*rooms, sautéed in*
½ cup soft bread crumbs	*1 tablespoon butter*
1½ tablespoons butter	

Divide the breast of chicken in two, along the bone; remove skin and cut off each fillet. Slightly flatten fillets by pounding; season with salt and pepper on all sides; dip into melted butter and then into crumbs. Heat the 1½ tablespoons butter in a chafing dish or frying pan and sauté the chicken for 20 minutes, browning well on all sides; for very thick fillets, cook a little longer. Serve on a mound of hot spinach, garnished with mushrooms. Makes 2 servings.

CANAPÉ ARNOLD

4 slices bread	*½ cup fried parsley*
2 freshly boiled medium-sized lobsters	*Mustard Sauce*

Start oven at hot (425° F.). Trim crusts from bread or cut in rounds. Toast slices lightly; place on a lightly greased baking sheet. Slice the lobster meat over the toast. Place in hot oven for a few minutes to heat the lobster. Remove each piece of toast and lobster to a small serving plate. Top each with a generous amount of fried parsley and then with hot Mustard Sauce. Makes 4 servings.

Ernie's in San Francisco is elegant and gratifyingly crowded. Its French-Italian cuisine embraces roast Cornish hen *à l'orange*, *tournedos* Rossini, frogs' legs Provençale.

ELLIOTT ERWITT

FRIED PARSLEY

½ cup finely chopped fresh
   parsley

Oil or fat for deep frying
¾ teaspoon salt

Wash parsley thoroughly; dry well on towel. Heat fat very hot (390° F.). Drop in parsley and fry for a few minutes, until it comes to the surface of the fat and is crisp. Skim it out, let drain a few seconds on thick paper toweling. Sprinkle with salt. Makes ½ cup fried parsley.

HOT MUSTARD SAUCE

1 tablespoon butter
1 tablespoon flour
1 cup hot milk
1 slice onion
¼ teaspoon salt

⅛ teaspoon pepper
1 teaspoon prepared mustard
½ teaspoon lemon juice
1 tablespoon sherry

Melt butter in a saucepan, stir in the flour smoothly, and cook until golden. Add milk slowly, stirring; add onion, salt and pepper, stirring constantly. Stir and cook until thickened. Continue cooking and stirring until reduced by about one-third. Stir mustard, lemon juice and sherry in; heat for 1 or 2 minutes. Strain the sauce to remove the onion. Makes about ⅔ cup. Serve hot as described above.

This recipe is for a dish served at Sweet's.

NEW ENGLAND FISH CHOWDER

1 pound halibut, cleaned,
   and cut in large
   chunks

Bones from a white fish
1½ quarts water
2 teaspoons salt
1 onion, peeled and chopped

½ cup chopped celery
½ pound butter
¼ teaspoon curry powder
½ teaspoon pepper
1½ tablespoons flour
1 cup milk
1 cup light cream
2 cups diced raw potatoes

Wash fish and bones; drain and place in a 2-quart kettle. Add the water with 1½ teaspoons salt. Bring slowly to a boil; reduce the heat; let simmer for 15 minutes. Drain, reserving the cooking liquid. Sauté onion and celery in half of the butter; add ½ teaspoon salt, the curry powder and the pepper. Melt the remaining butter in a 2-quart kettle, blend the flour into this smoothly. Heat and combine the milk and cream; then stir them into the butter-flour mixture. Add the reserved fish-cooking liquid, the sautéed onion-and-celery mixture and the potatoes. Bring to a boil; reduce heat and simmer for 5 minutes or until potatoes are done. Serve in warmed soup bowls. Makes 6 servings.

NEW ORLEANS

New Orleans is the one city in the United States whose native cuisine has a foreign flavor. The French style, changed and refined over the last one hundred and fifty years, still remains. That is one of the reasons the city is so highly thought of by the followers of Epicurus. Galatoire's is represented here with two of the dishes on which its reputation is based.

GALATOIRE'S OYSTERS ROCKEFELLER

4 dozen large oysters in shells	1½ pounds softened butter
Rock salt	½ cup bread crumbs
8 green onions	4 tablespoons Worcester-
1 stalk green celery	shire sauce
1 cup finely chopped parsley	2 tablespoons Pernod
2 or 3 stalks anise, finely chopped	½ teaspoon salt
	½ teaspoon pepper
½ pound spinach	⅛ teaspoon cayenne

Scrub oysters, drain, open and place each oyster on its larger half shell. Arrange these filled half shells on a bed of rock salt about 1½ inches thick in shallow baking pans. Wash, clean and drain all vegetables and greens; grind together very fine. Combine with butter in a saucepan; heat slightly, adding crumbs, Worcestershire, Pernod, salt, pepper and cayenne. Mix and spread generously over each oyster, covering it. Start oven at hot (425° F.). Place pans in hot oven and bake oysters 8 to 10 minutes or until tops of oysters are bubbling and browned. Serve immediately. Makes 4 to 8 servings.

GALATOIRE'S TURTLE SOUP

3 pounds Gulf sea-turtle meat (hard-shell)	2 cloves garlic, peeled and minced
3 tablespoons flour	3 8-ounce cans tomato sauce
1 tablespoon oil	1½ teaspoons salt
3 medium-sized onions, peeled and chopped	Grind fresh black pepper
1 cup finely minced parsley	½ cup sherry
1 bay leaf	4 hard-cooked eggs, finely chopped
1 sprig thyme	2 lemons, thinly sliced

Place the turtle meat in a 3-quart kettle; cover with two quarts of water and boil gently for about 2 hours or until tender (time depends on kind of turtle meat). Skim top frequently during cooking period. When meat is tender, drain it and reserve the broth. Let meat cool; then cut in small pieces. Remove bones and discard. Make a roux by combining the flour and oil in a deep kettle and stirring over low heat for 1 or 2 minutes. Add onions and cook until brown. Add all seasonings, herbs, garlic and tomato sauce; stir and add turtle meat and the reserved broth. Cook gently, over low heat, for about 2 hours. Just before serving, add sherry and garnish each serving with minced hard-cooked egg and thin lemon slice. Makes 6 to 8 servings. (If thinner soup is preferred, use 3 quarts water to cook turtle meat or add 2 cups light bouillon with the tomato sauce.)

CHICAGO

Chicago is the beef capital of the United States—there's no denying that. But in Chicago's fine restaurants you can safely order more than steak. Here are three recipes prepared by the chefs of three of the city's finest hotel restaurants—not an ounce of beef in the lot, but delicious nonetheless.

The following soup-meal is served at the Cape Cod Room of the Drake Hotel.

BOOKBINDER RED SNAPPER SOUP

There are three steps in preparing this delicious soup. First, make the

TOMATO BROWN SAUCE

4 tablespoons lard or butter	No. 2 can (2 cups) tomato purée
3 tablespoons flour	
1½ quarts beef or chicken bouillon	

Heat the lard or butter in a 2½-quart kettle. Stir the flour in until smooth and browned. Add the bouillon and tomato purée. Mix, bring to a boil, reduce the heat and let simmer slowly for 2½ hours. The sauce should be reduced to about 1 quart. (Can be stored in covered glass jar in refrigerator for about a week.)

FISH STOCK

1 medium-sized red snapper, cleaned	6 peppercorns
1½ quarts water	½ bay leaf
1 cup dry white wine	1½ teaspoons salt
1 medium-sized onion, peeled	2 sprigs parsley
	1 carrot, scraped and cut in thin strips
6 cloves	½ teaspoon thyme

Bone the snapper; cut fillets off and dice them, making enough to fill 1 cup. Place bones and all trimmings, and any remaining diced fish (after 1 cup is filled) in 2-quart kettle, add the water, wine, onion stuck with the cloves, peppercorns, bay leaf, salt, parsley, carrot and thyme. Bring to a boil, reduce heat and let simmer for 30 minutes. Strain stock.

VEGETABLE PURÉE

2 tablespoons butter	1 pint (above) Tomato Brown Sauce
¼ cup diced peeled onions	
½ cup diced scraped celery	1 cup (above) diced red snapper fillets
1 green pepper, seeded and diced	
	1 cup sherry
2 pints (above) fish stock	

Heat the butter in a 3-quart kettle; add onions, celery and green pepper. Cook for 2 minutes; add the 2 pints of fish stock; stir and let come to a boil. Stir in a pint of the Tomato Brown Sauce and bring to a boil again. Add diced fish and let boil gently for 12 minutes, until fish is tender. Just before serving, stir sherry in, heat for 1 minute and serve into warmed soup plates. Makes 6 or 8 servings.

This recipe is for a dish served at the Well of the Sea, Hotel Sherman.

SEAFOOD RIJSTTAFEL, CHINESE STYLE

2 tablespoons butter
4 stalks celery, scraped and thinly sliced
1 medium-sized Spanish onion, peeled and chopped
2 cups chicken stock
4 medium-sized mushrooms, peeled and sliced
½ cup freshly boiled lobster meat, cut in small rounds
8 large raw shrimp, shelled and cleaned
½ cup whole raw scallops
½ teaspoon salt
⅛ teaspoon white pepper

2½ tablespoons soy sauce
2 tablespoons arrowroot or cornstarch
2 tablespoons water
2 tablespoons sliced canned water chestnuts
½ cup drained canned bean sprouts
5 Chinese pea pods, cut in thin strips
3 teaspoons Accent
½ cup canned or quick-frozen lump crab meat, cleaned of all bones
4 cups hot cooked rice

Heat the butter in a large skillet; sauté celery and onion for 5 minutes. Add chicken stock, mushrooms, lobster, shrimp, scallops, salt, pepper and soy sauce and cook over low heat for 20 minutes. Add arrowroot or cornstarch blended with the 2 tablespoons of water and stir into seafood mixture. Let come to a boil and boil for 5 minutes. Add water chestnuts, bean sprouts, pea pods, Accent and crab meat and cook for an additional 8 minutes. Serve over hot rice. Makes 4 servings.

From the Edgewater Beach Hotel.

CHICKEN CACCIATORE

3-pound chicken, cleaned, cut in serving pieces
Salt and pepper
Flour
½ cup olive oil
3 shallots or medium-sized onions, peeled and chopped
3 medium-sized tomatoes, seeded and quartered
¼ bay leaf

¼ teaspoon each of thyme, marjoram and orégano
1 clove garlic, peeled and crushed
2 tablespoons chopped mushrooms
¼ cup dry white wine
2 tablespoons cognac
1 teaspoon beef extract
1 tablespoon chopped fresh tarragon

Season chicken with salt and pepper. Dredge lightly with flour. Heat olive oil in a deep skillet and, when very hot, add chicken and cook until browned on all sides. Then add the shallots or onions, the tomatoes, bay leaf, thyme, marjoram, orégano, and garlic. Cover skillet; let cook gently for 1 hour and 15 minutes. Add mushrooms and simmer for about 25 minutes longer. Stir in the wine and brandy, the beef extract and tarragon; serve at once. Makes 6 servings.

SAN FRANCISCO

Next after New York, and occasionally before it, San Francisco is the American city most revered by the gourmet. It is one of those places where it is said that it isn't easy to find a bad meal and where restaurants serving good ones abound. San Francisco is represented here by two recipes—neither of which is difficult to make—both of which make for delicious eating.

This is served at the Fleur de Lys.

ALSATIAN NOODLES WITH CREAM

2 pounds quality noodles
6 tablespoons butter
⅔ cup heavy cream

Grated nutmeg
Salt and pepper
1 cup grated Swiss cheese

Set aside about half a handful of the noodles and cook the rest in well-salted boiling water for eight minutes. Strain in a colander and dry briefly over heat. Then take the noodles that have been set aside, break them into small pieces, and sauté them in 2 tablespoons butter until dark brown. Heat the cream separately and add it to the cooked noodles. Season with salt, pepper and nutmeg and cook for an additional 10 minutes.

Just before serving, add to the boiled noodles the brown fried pieces, with the remaining 4 tablespoons butter and the cheese. Mix all together and serve hot. Makes 4 servings.

A delicious sole fro mChef Gaffney's Cliff House.

DÉLICE DE SOLE, NEPTUNE

2 4-ounce fillets of sole
Salt and pepper
4 cooked and cleaned jumbo prawns or shrimp
¼ avocado
¼ cup oil
1 egg, beaten with
1 tablespoon water

Flour
1 tablespoon butter
2 tablespoons chopped chives
1 tablespoon white wine
Juice ½ lemon

Rinse and dry fillets; season lightly all over with salt and pepper. Slice prawns or shrimp lengthwise and remove dark vein. Pare the piece of avocado and cut it lengthwise into 4 strips. Heat oil in skillet, dip the seasoned fish in egg beaten with the water; then dip into flour. Cook fish until golden brown on all sides. Season prawns or shrimp and avocado with salt and pepper, dip in egg mixture and flour. Remove cooked fillets to a warmed serving platter. Brown prawns or shrimp and avocado lightly in same skillet. Arrange over fish fillets, pouring on any remaining hot oil from the skillet; add butter to skillet and cook the chives for about 1 minute. Splash chives with wine and lemon juice; swirl the skillet and pour sauce over the fish on the platter. Serve at once. Makes 1 or 2 servings.

Holiday Restaurant Awards

FOR NEARLY ten years *Holiday* has been giving awards for dining distinction to restaurants in many parts of the country. The selections are based on the knowledge of, and visits by, *Holiday* personnel.

It is important to point out that these are not necessarily the best restaurants in the United States. If it were a question of choosing strictly the best our search might not take us outside of New York, Chicago, New Orleans, San Francisco and Los Angeles. So, while quality—of food, service and atmosphere—has been the dominant consideration, location also has influenced the choices.

In your travels you need feel no hesitancy in visiting any of these restaurants. All of them are notable; some are among the very best in the world. Good restaurants are crowded today, and, when you decide to dine in one that has been given the *Holiday* award, do it and yourself the considerable favor of telephoning for a reservation, of not being in an unseemly hurry when you arrive, of giving the restaurant the opportunity to prepare and serve you the best of the very good it has to offer.

—*The Editors*

Albany, N.Y.

Keeler's . . . Hearty food, a really fine American restaurant.

Anchorage, Alaska

The Chart Room, Westward Hotel . . . Excellent beef and Alaskan sea food.

Baltimore, Md.

Chesapeake . . . Famed for steaks and Maryland sea food.
Miller Brothers . . . Oysters, crab dishes, terrapin.

Banksville, N.Y.

La Crémaillère à la Campagne . . . One of the great French restaurants, located in the Westchester countryside, 30 miles from New York City; very expensive.

Boston, Mass.

Jimmy's Harbor Side Restaurant . . . Sea food with exciting view of the water front.
Locke-Ober Café . . . A genuine Boston institution.
Ritz-Carlton Hotel . . . One of the last stands of Ritz food in the U.S.

Brooklyn, N.Y.

Gage & Tollner's . . . One of the world's best sea-food restaurants.

Perino's. Alexander Perino is a North Italian village boy who ▶ has come a long way on the basis of a conviction: "Each food has a flavor," he says. "The duty of the chef is to enhance that flavor to the utmost—never to distort it." Distinguished, dignified, dedicated Perino poses with friends, Mr. and Mrs. Ronald Reagan.

FRED LYON

208

Charleston, S.C.

Perdita's . . . Continental cuisine with occasional superb Charleston dishes.

Chicago, Ill.

Blackhawk Restaurant . . . Chicago is the beef capital of America, and many Chicagoans consider this the best steak house in their city.
Café de Paris . . . Very French, outstanding food and wines.
Cape Cod Room, Drake Hotel . . . Superb sea food, nautical atmosphere.
Don the Beachcomber . . . Polynesian and Cantonese food, South Sea atmosphere.
Jacques French Restaurant . . . Chicago's best French food, outdoor dining in summer.
Pump Room, Ambassador East Hotel . . . Fancy food, showmanship, famous guests; very expensive.
Red Carpet . . . Superb French food and wines, small and elegant, make reservations.

Cincinnati, Ohio

Gourmet Restaurant . . . Superb French cuisine and wines.
Maisonette . . . Excellent French food.
Pigall's . . . Outstanding food prepared by a superior French chef.

Dallas, Tex.

Old Warsaw . . . Fine French cuisine.
Twin Tree Inn . . . Beef and sea food, excellent variety.

Denver, Colo.

The Palace Arms, Brown Palace Hotel . . . Rainbow trout, superb beef.

Detroit, Mich.

London Chop House . . . Beef and sea food; crowded because of dance floor.

Falmouth, Mass.

Coonamessett Inn, Jones Road . . . Specializes in fine beef and lobster dishes.

Hohokus, N.J.

The Ho-Ho-Kus Inn . . . Colonial atmosphere, cosmopolitan cuisine.

Hollywood-By-The-Sea, Fla.

Les Ambassadeurs, Diplomat Hotel . . . Luxurious French atmosphere, excellent food, dinner only; expensive.

Honolulu, Hawaii

Canlis Charcoal Burner, Waikiki . . . Superb Hawaiian sea food and cosmopolitan dishes.

Indianapolis, Ind.

The Keys . . . Excellent steaks and roasts, pleasant décor.

Lexington, Ky.

The Campbell House . . . Hearty food in attractive surroundings.

Long Island, N.Y.

Bowden Square, Southampton . . . One of the few places open all year in this year-round community, superb local sea food, excellent wine cellar.
Mont D'Or, Smithtown . . . Excellent food, fashionable.

Los Angeles, Calif.

Chasen's . . . One of the best in U.S.; expensive.
Perino's . . . One of L.A.'s famous; very expensive.
La Rue Restaurant . . . One of very best restaurants in Los Angeles, basically French cuisine, with some Italian dishes; very expensive.
Scandia . . . Friendly, intimate; famous people, excellent food.

Louisville, Ky.

The Old House . . . Fine French cuisine, attractive décor.

Madison, Wis.

Simon House . . . The charm of early Americana, outstanding beef and sea food.

Manchester, Vt.

Toll Gate Lodge . . . Open May 28 to October 18. Continental cuisine in spectacular Vermont mountainside setting.

Marshall, Mich.

Schuler's . . . One of Midwest's finest.

Memphis, Tenn.

Justines . . . Delicious cuisine; bring own wines and liquors, state law prevents sale by restaurant.

Miami Beach, Fla.

Gaucho Steak House, American Hotel . . . Outstanding hotel restaurant, Argentine décor.

Milwaukee, Wis.

Frenchy's . . . Excellent beef and sea food, Gallic overtones.
Karl Ratzsch's . . . Specializes in German food.

Minneapolis, Minn.

Charlie's Café Exceptionale . . . Famous for appetizer tray, plank steak.

New Orleans, La.

Antoine's . . . One of world's famous, make reservations; expensive.

Caribbean Room, Hotel Pontchartrain . . . Fine beef, Louisiana specialties.

Commander's Palace . . . A local favorite.

Galatoire's . . . Perhaps the favorite restaurant of New Orleanians themselves.

Brennan's French Restaurant . . . Best known for Sunday breakfast.

New York City

Baroque . . . Excellent food; very expensive.

Chambord . . . Superb French food; very expensive.

Café Chauveron . . . Delicious French cuisine and wines.

Chauteaubriand . . . Truly French, wonderful wine cellar.

Christ Cella . . . New York's most famous steak spot.

The Colony . . . One of world's great; very fashionable, very expensive.

Forum of the Twelve Caesars . . . Spectacular décor, ancient Roman specialties.

Four Seasons . . . Superb cuisine that reflects seasonal specialties.

Gloucester House . . . Perhaps the best sea food in New York.

Jack & Charlie's "21" . . . One of world's great; very expensive.

Lüchow's . . . Excellent German cuisine; crowded, noisy and gay.

Le Pavillon . . . Considered by some gourmets the best in the world; very expensive.

The Pierre . . . Has one of very best chefs in world today; expensive.

La Potinière du Soir, 47 W. 55th Street . . . Excellent French food and wine.

Quo Vadis . . . Excellent French cuisine.

Robert's . . . An old favorite with New Yorkers. Superb food.

St. Regis . . . Considered by some to serve best food of any hotel in New York, probably in the U.S.; very expensive.

San Marino . . . Superior Italian food.

Veau d'Or . . . Crowded, noisy, advise going at an off hour.

Voisin . . . Superb food; very expensive.

Palm Beach, Fla.

Petite Marmite . . . Excellent French cuisine and wines.

Philadelphia, Pa.

Hotel Barclay . . . Distinguished hotel food.

Warwick Hotel . . . Excellent hotel food.

Phoenix, Ariz.

The Flame . . . Tropical setting, varied cuisine.

Pittsburgh, Pa.

Park Schenley . . . Continental cuisine with accent on French.

Portland, Ore.

The London Grill, Benson Hotel . . . Fine food, good variety.

Reno, Nev.

Eugene's . . . Fine beef and abalone.

St. Louis, Mo.

Mayfair Room, Hotel Mayfair . . . Good food in elegant atmosphere.

San Antonio, Tex.

La Louisiane . . . Fine French food.

San Francisco, Calif.

Alexis' Tangier . . . Continental elegance on Nob Hill, exotic food; very expensive.

The Blue Fox . . . Located on alley across from city prison; fine Italian cuisine.

Ernie's . . . Old-time San Francisco atmosphere, relaxing, varied menu.

Fleur de Lys Restaurant . . . Excellent French cuisine and wines.

India House . . . One of world's fine curry restaurants.

Jack's Restaurant . . . Rich masculine flavor.

Kan's . . . Great Chinese restaurant.

Trader Vic's . . . Wonderful South Seas food and drinks.

Yamato Sukiyaki House . . . Japanese food in authentic atmosphere.

Seattle, Wash.

Canlis' Charcoal Broiler . . . Breathtaking Lake Union view, choice food.

Rosellini's Four-10 . . . Excellent Continental atmosphere and cuisine.

Shaker Heights, Ohio

Gruber's . . . Excellent food and service.

Skaneateles, N.Y.

Kreb's . . . Open from about May 10 to October 31, fine American cooking.

Skokie, Ill.

Le Manoir . . . A great French restaurant, 30 minutes from Chicago's "Loop"; make reservations.

Stowe, Vt.

The Lodge at Smuggler's Notch . . . Superior cuisine. (Overcrowded on ski weekends. Open May 22 to October 15, December 15 to April 15.

Washington, D.C.

Colony Restaurant . . . Popular with Washington's younger set.

La Salle du Bois . . . Fine Gallic menu.

PART V: The Gourmet Abroad

The World's Finest Food / Silas Spitzer

*To those who understand and love fine food, dining abroad
can be as memorable as monuments, cathedrals or masterpieces of art*

AN AMERICAN traveling abroad learns more about the people of Europe by eating their food and drinking their wine than he will get from the guidebooks. For there is a close bond between food and national character. What people eat reveals much about how they live, think and act. And if the tourist is descended from these people, eating their food can bring him closer to his own beginnings.

The cooking of any Continental country differs not only from that of its neighbor but has a special character in every section within its borders. The smallest and humblest community treasures its own typical dishes. Recipes are handed down from generation to generation, and they taste of the good things raised nearby. To a man who dines with a sense of adventure, the finest European memories of all are those of the palate.

The food of Italy is a blend of song, laughter and sunshine. It tastes of lush gardens and silvery olive groves, of fields of ripe wheat and of the sea. No other European food so closely reveals the people and the country of its origin.

Many Americans visiting Italy for the first time are prepared to face mountains of coiled and glistening starch at

◀ **A sampling of Scotland's bounty, arrayed in a ducal banqueting hall in a sixteenth-century castle, 25 miles east of Edinburgh: silvery salmon trout; smoked salmon and kippers, sharing the platter with a haggis; a fresh-killed hare; a veal-and-ham pie; Scotch and its fancy cousin, Scotch liqueur; a pheasant, a grouse, a partridge—and a robust joint of beef.**

ARNOLD NEWMAN

every meal, to find most everything swamped in tomato sauce, garlic and olive oil. But their first good Italian restaurant is a delightful surprise. Its courses are varied, and include dishes prepared as simply as the most delicate eater could wish. True, spaghetti or some other form of *pasta* is always present, usually instead of a conventional entree. But it is cooked with a succulent perfection, and served with an unending variety of imaginative, savory sauces that we rarely experience back home.

Italy's food varies sharply from province to province. Visitors are usually surprised to learn that spaghetti is unknown in the homes of many northern Italians. In Piedmont and the region of Venice, its place is taken by *polenta*, a sort of cornmeal mush. Another widely used northern staple is rice, which is cultivated in the River Po basin. It makes thick, satisfying soup, the indispensable *minestra*. When prepared in a compact mound, juicy but with every grain holding its own, peas, chicken livers, cheese and chicken stock are added and it becomes the celebrated *risotto* of Milan.

For the richest and most artistic cookery in Italy, Bologna is usually awarded first place. Dinner at the Ristorante Papagallo, a time-honored shrine of that region, may well decide you to linger a few days longer in Bologna. Here you may taste the local *mortadella*, a pink-meated sausage of formidable girth, flecked with bits of fat and pepper cloves, and impregnated with garlic. Or try a few thin slices of Parma ham, with a dish of melon or fresh figs.

The people of Genoa vow that they eat better than any other Italians. Their style of cooking is certainly different, with an individual flavor related to the sea and the farmlands about. Genoese families use the finest of olive oil lavishly. With a wizard's touch, the cook adds garlic, other herbs and

213

spices to the seething golden flood. Sage, bay, rosemary, thyme, parsley—all contribute to the aromatic symphony. Cooking "alla Genovese" has sunshine and sea flavors lurking in every pot. It is best enjoyed in some tiny fisherman's *trattoria* along the water front, where you may be offered *zuppa di pesce*, a soup that is mostly stew, crammed with fresh sea food.

The simplest Italian food will be found in Florence and other parts of Tuscany. The art of broiling steak is an ancient heritage among the Florentines, who are blessed with plenty of home-raised beef. The *Fiorentina* is a juicy fillet or other thick cut, grilled to crusty perfection on charcoal or a fire of vineyard fagots, and served with its own dark red juice, nothing else. Fried chicken, Florentine style, is white meat in a delicate, puffy batter. *Tortino* is an omelet in which nestle the tender hearts of artichokes.

Perfectly adequate food of international character is served in the hotels of Rome. The waiter captains in these sumptuous establishments rarely bat an eye when they receive orders for ham and eggs, wheat cakes or liver and bacon, and their kitchens produce reasonable facsimiles of these and other familiar American dishes. They also do a satisfactory job with the more elegant local specialties, but for honest Italian cooking a man should venture forth among the city's hundreds of fine native restaurants. Among typical Roman dishes are *abbacchio*, or baby lamb, and *capretto*, or kid, both roasted with a sprinkle of rosemary, and divinely mated in the spring months with sugary tiny green peas cooked in butter with shreds of smoked ham.

Lombardy cheeses are among the world's finest. One of the most memorable desserts I enjoyed in Milan consisted of an incredibly rich and creamy Gorgonzola eaten with a juicy yellow pear. Lombardy cooking is mostly done with butter, and a crisp veal cutlet, lightly breaded and sautéed in the Milanese style, is a good sample of the technique.

All Italian foods taste better when taken with native wine, and best with the *chianti* of Tuscany. And nowhere on earth is a good dinner so superbly crowned as by Italian coffee— blacker than night, with a powerful aroma that stays long in the memory of the traveler.

Visitors to Spain have to adjust to the late meal hours. *El desayuno*, the light morning collation, occurs at nine, usually consisting of strong coffee or chocolate, with hot milk, buttered rolls or cakes. Lunch, *la comida*, is served at two or three in the afternoon, and dinner is rarely eaten before 10 P.M. Between meals, it is customary to imbibe a few dry sherrys and nibble spicy odds and ends called *tapas*: shrimps, bits of fried fish, hard-boiled eggs, pickled olives, sardines, anchovies, and all sorts of shellfish.

Spain offers a choice of food so ample that the most inhibited eater will find much he will enjoy. Most Americans never fail to be impressed by the lavish *entremeses* which form the first course of most repasts. These tidbits are enlivened by salty and peppery savors, wonderfully conducive to thirst and appetite. The hams of Aragon, Estremadura and the Asturias are served in thin, translucent slices, and have a dry, spicy taste that is unique. There are usually several kinds of *salchichón*, or salami. And fat, luscious Catalan sausage, or black blood sausage mixed with rice, onion or bacon. Shrimps come in several sizes, and there are tiny clams, fresh and preserved sardines, tuna in olive oil and, as a special treat for the gourmet, giant prawns called *langostinos*, six or seven inches long and usually eaten grilled with melted butter.

Most Spanish soups are thick and rich enough to satisfy a hungry stevedore. The Galician *pote gallego* is a heavy mixture of pork, bacon, beans and cabbage.

All the Mediterranean fishing villages have their local versions of bouillabaisse, most of them savagely redolent of garlic, hot peppers and spices. In Barcelona there is an interesting soup called *sopa de albondiguillas*, with fried meat balls the size of hazel nuts afloat in a highly concentrated broth.

Meat lovers will find a plentiful choice in the better restaurants. Homesick Americans are advised to try *solomillo*, a thick cut of grilled beef, with mushrooms or onions. Partridge braised in vine leaves is an epicurean treat. And the menu in Madrid or Barcelona frequently suggests such lordly dishes as roast suckling pig, casserole of hare, roast turkey, roast larded veal and wild duck with rice. As in most southern countries, desserts are limited to custards, fritters and heavily sweetened whipped-cream pastries. But there is a magnificent choice of fruit, especially the green and gold melons, the large black figs, and the wild Aranjuez strawberries.

The universal wine of Spain is Andalusian sherry. There is a type for every thirst, from the exquisitely dry *manzanilla*, which is consumed at all hours and on every occasion, to the sweet brown sherry which makes a perfect dessert drink. In Madrid, most visitors soon learn the pleasant habit of dropping in at a convenient *taberna*, dark and cool on the hottest days, to sip fresh white wines, usually without name or vintage, but always uplifting to the weary spirit.

It is only a short jump from Spain to Portugal, but the traveler will soon discover that Portuguese food is as different from the Spanish as the language. The fiery heat of Spanish cooking subsides in Portugal to a mild glow.

The food seems as bland as the climate, but heavy in content, rich with fat and succulent of flavor. Butter takes the place of oil in much of the cooking. Rice and beans are always present, and eggs occur, in some form or other, with every meal of the day.

In this land so conspicuously graced with sea food, the typical menu lists such dishes as octopus, fried or in a ragout; fresh anchovies and sardines; grilled red mullet; pilaf of lobster, and the national dish of *bacalhao fresco á Portuguesa*, made of fresh cod, eggplant and tomatoes.

Portugal is the land of the sweet tooth, where confectioneries and pastries are contrived with boundless imagination and delicacy. You will be offered miracles in sugar, whipped eggs, fruits and nuts. One of the most popular among them is *croquetes amendoas*, which turn out to be almond croquettes of honeyed sweetness and crunchable texture. There are excellent dry table wines to be had everywhere, but sweet wines are Portugal's special pride. The two best known are port and Madeira, which have achieved their world-wide reputation through British support.

When Americans sit down to dine in Paris, they usually expect the world's fanciest food. And most restaurants do a spectacular job of giving them exactly that. Yet the finest and truest French cooking is simplicity itself. In a talk I once had with the manager of Joseph's, an elegant and "serious" Paris restaurant, he strongly upheld this doctrine.

"True French cooking has no tricks," he said. "The national soup, *pot-au-feu*, takes hours of simmering to bring out the full flavor of beef, bones, vegetables and herbs. When finished, what is it? Only a clear soup of great strength and purity—yet it is the queen of French soups. Simple dishes perfectly executed are the mark of a good chef. A plain omelette, frothy and golden, lamb roasted to the required state of pink juiciness, a young chicken browned slowly in white wine and butter, a vanilla soufflé, light as foam and delicately perfumed—these are simple dishes known the world over, but only in France do they achieve greatness."

Obviously, cooking of that description needs not only skill but the freshest and finest of materials. That is why, if you wish to sample French food at its best, you must tear yourself away from the fascinations of Paris and go forth to the provinces. There you will find inns and eating places which follow the old recipes, and make use of the regional treasures of farm, vineyard, orchard and stream. The chef at some of these shrines of good living is often also the owner. His name may be as well-known in France as that of a cabinet minister. The most famous houses are as luxurious as any in Paris, with prices to match. But you will also be served memorable meals in places that are small, inexpensive and often rude in appearance.

In what part of France do people eat best? Nobody will ever answer that question to the satisfaction of all concerned. But the city of Lyons is most often cited by the *cognoscenti* as the capital of good food. The town is wonderfully favored by its location, within easy reach of the plump chickens of Bresse, the delicate fishes of the lakes, prime beef of the Charollais, fragrant woodland *cèpes* and *morilles* of Bugey, the magnificent cheeses of Dauphiné and Savoie.

The citizens of Lyons are talented eaters—solidly built textile manufacturers and tradesmen who pause at midday for a two-hour lunch, followed by a digestive nap.

Parisians who are driving to the Midi usually stop off at Lyons to visit one of its fine restaurants. Nearly all the famous ones bear a name like "*La Mère Somebody or Other.*" One of the most celebrated of the motherly restaurateurs is *La Mère Brazier,* whose specialty is capon *demi-deuil,* or "half-mourning," a term descriptive of the slices of black truffle inserted just beneath the skin. The chicken is poached in a bladder to conserve the juices, and mantled with creamy sauce. Other sumptuous local dishes are *quenelles de brochet à la Nantua* (small dumplings of finely ground pike in a pink shrimp sauce), braised leg of mutton so tender that it can be eaten with a spoon, and delicious fritters known as *bugnes.* All the illustrious wines of Burgundy are mated to these delicacies in Lyons, but the natives are fondest of red Beaujolais, served in pitchers.

Lyons is the home of genuine *soupe à l'oignon*—the racy liquid soul of the onion, with a thick crown of oven-browned cheese and crusty bread.

But the most important part of a Burgundian repast is not the food, wonderful though it may be, but the wine, which the knowing diner will usually select first, and then build his meal around it. It is thrilling to read the illustrious names of these wines on the list of a restaurant close to the place of their birth. The great reds: Chambertin, Richebourg, Clos Vougeot, Nuits de Cailles, Echézeaux, Beaune, Corton, Pommard, La Tâche, Romanée-Conti, Volnay. And the two noble whites: Montrachet and Meursault. The reds of precious vintage years are subtle of flavor and bouquet; they should be sipped and tasted slowly and reverently.

Along the Mediterranean coast and in the sunny wind-swept lands of Provence, the cooking is utterly unlike any other in France, or elsewhere on earth, for that matter. It is rich in olive oil, garlic, peppers, anchovies and saffron, yet it is unlike Italian or Spanish food. Certain robust dishes are a challenge to the stranger's instinct for experiment. *Pissaladiera* is a tart baked with a filling of onions and tomatoes. *Pan bagna* is a slender loaf of bread, split lengthwise and stuffed with onions, black olives, peppers and anchovies, then drenched with olive oil.

Bouillabaisse is imitated everywhere, but not even in the best kitchens of Paris does it approximate the genuine, which owes its character to freshly caught fish and shellfish native to the Mediterranean. Other dishes worth sampling are: *salade niçoise, ratatouille* (eggplant, tomatoes, peppers, onions, baby squash, garlic, all cooked in oil) and, best of all, to my taste, the *loup de mer,* a large fish resembling our sea bass, baked whole and brushed at your table with flaming twigs of fragrant fennel.

There is space to mention only a few of the remaining regional treasures of the country. Normandy provides the best butter in France, and some of the finest cheeses in the world.

This is the lush dairyland which contributes to our pleasure Camembert, Pont l'Evêque and Livarot. Norman cooks pour cream into practically everything edible.

In Bordeaux, cooking is based on the principle that food serves essentially to bring out the best qualities of a bottle of Haut Brion, Margaux, St. Emilion, or some other magnificent product of that great wine-growing section. A Bordelaise delight is ice-cold oysters of Arcachon, with in-between bites of sausage, fiery with garlic and pepper.

In the charming little restaurants of the château country, there will be specialties like *poulet à la crème, pré-salé* (mutton that has been raised in salt marsh pastures), *rillettes* and *rillons* (creamy *pâtés* of pork or goose breast and white wine), *matelotes* of river fish, *brochets au beurre blanc,* larks and pheasants and other game birds roasted on the spit. And a hundred exquisite little cheeses, nearly all of the goat's-milk variety, with obscure names like *Chavigny, Olivet, Chevrotin, Vendôme de l'Orléanaise* and *St.-Maure de Touraine.*

Wherever possible, provincial French dishes should be experienced in the place of their origin. The next best place to eat them is in Paris, where many restaurants owe their reputation to regional specialties. For that matter you can get anything your appetite craves in Paris, except food that is typically Parisian. But of course in this capital of the culinary art, everything edible is prepared with unsurpassed skill and served with typical elegance.

The most luxurious repasts in Europe, in the opinion of not a few qualified gastronomes, are served in Brussels. The menus and wine lists in the city's many fine restaurants are as distinguished as any in Paris, and the cooking is largely derived from French *grande cuisine.* But the portions are more impressive and the recipes have a Lucullan richness. Belgians eat often, heavily and with gusto. Great quantities of Burgundy wines are imported, but the national drink is beer. The authentic smack of Belgian home cooking may be best savored in the following dishes: Flemish *carbonnade* (a sour-sweet stew of beef, beer, onions and spices); *hochepot* (a variable sort of *pot-au-feu,* with mutton or other meat, green cabbage, potatoes and other vegetables); *côtes de porc Bruxelloises* (smothered pork chops with endives); *beefsteak Américaine* (oddly enough, chopped raw meat with mayonnaise and spices); *potage Brabançonne* (cream soup of Brussels sprouts, onions and egg yolks); herrings served fresh, sour, deviled or in salads, and always with beer: *waterzöie* of boiled chicken and white wine in a creamy sauce, with julienne vegetables.

A Londoner once told me, with a trace of bitterness in his manner, that the only good eating in England today was to be had at French and Italian restaurants. This was perhaps carrying understatement a bit too far. There is still fine food to be had in London pubs, clubs and the better eating places. For the best English cooking, though, you will have to wangle an invitation to some country house where the food is prepared simply and without foreign frills, but is sincerely British.

In olden, golden times the English breakfast was a monument to hearty living. It is still generous compared to the frail Continental affair of café au lait and a roll. But Englishmen who remember those magnificent prewar spreads dream fondly of the smoky kippers and bloaters, the rashers of bacon and platters of eggs, the thick chop, the grilled kidneys, porridge with heavy cream, and the fat sausages of mildly seasoned pork. Visitors, however, will discover that English tea is still strong and fragrant, and the plainest breakfast will be fresh toast kept hot in a napkin, as well as the unbeatable bitter orange marmalade.

The city man's habitual luncheon of grilled chop or rump steak, boiled potato, one "veg," pudding and a bit of Stilton cheese has dwindled in bulk, but its pattern is unaltered. Afternoon tea is an imperishable fixture whether in cottage kitchen, baronial mansion or the favorite teashop of the office worker. A handsome joint, whether of beef, mutton or pork, is still the crowning course of Sunday dinner. Good English cooks of the old school may possess a limited repertoire compared to their French counterparts, but they know how to do a rib roast to pink-and-brown perfection. Meat pies, hot or cold, are unique, especially the richly concentrated beefsteak and kidney, or the wonderful lark pie which used to be featured weekly at masculine haunts like Simpson's and the Old Cheshire Cheese.

But it is during the shooting season that British provender is lifted to epicurean levels. Nothing quite equals the full flavor of a young grouse, hung three or four days, stuffed with a ball of butter and lightly roasted in rashers of fat bacon. The bird is traditionally dished up on a gravy-soaked piece of toast which has been spread with its mashed liver. Grouse pie or grouse soufflé makes a magnificent supper, with a bottle of old claret. Partridge is roasted about the same way as grouse, and pheasant profits by a garniture of puréed chestnuts, braised celery or plain bread sauce.

Here are some British specialties well worth tracking down: Whitstable or Colchester oysters; grilled Dover sole; fresh Scotch salmon with melted butter and thin-sliced cucumbers; poached turbot with egg sauce; Scotch barley broth; Scotch cockaleekie soup; roast beef with Yorkshire pudding and gravy; jugged hare; Yorkshire ham; Devonshire clotted cream; Melton Mowbray pie; Scotch mutton; Lancashire hot pot; Cornish pasties. The five great English cheeses are Cheddar, Cheshire, Stilton, Wensleydale and Double Gloucester, and all of them go down beautifully with a flagon of ale or lager beer.

Holland is the paradise of the solid eater. As in Paris, the busy streets of Amsterdam and The Hague are sprinkled with cafés, always crowded. But, unlike the French, who sip apéritifs or coffee, smoke, chat, or gaze idly at passing ankles,

the Dutch come strictly to eat—before, during and after regular mealtime hours. Yet the Dutch, though noticeably well-upholstered, are among the most energetic and hardest-working people in Europe. The food seems exactly suited to the people.

Dutch cooking is related to both German and Belgian, with exotic tropical strains borrowed from their overseas possessions—hot curries and condiments, ginger, pineapple, cocoa and a whole category of spicy and peppery foods which reach full expression in the vast East Indian feast known as rijsttafel. This intricate ceremonial dinner lasts hours, and is made up of a succession of small dishes containing chicken, shrimp, meat balls, fish of several kinds, curries, fried bananas, pickled onions, chutneys, peppers, grated coconut and peanuts. All of it is bedded down with boiled rice and flooded with good Holland beer. Fish and sea food dominate the national diet, and the herring is king. The Dutch devour herring at all hours of the day; fresh, sour, pickled, smoked or cooked. Plovers' eggs, rarest of delicacies in other lands, are fairly plentiful in Holland during the month of April, when their consumption is legalized. They are boiled rather hard, peeled, flattened in the palm of the hand, and then eaten like a muffin, presumably with closed eyes and a beatific smile. Holland beer is of world-renowned quality, but the veritable essence of good living is Schiedam gin. It is always drunk straight to fully enjoy its aroma and elusive flavor.

Switzerland, vacation spot of the world, sets an international table at which every guest may find the typical dishes of his homeland. Yet every one of the twenty-two Swiss cantons treasures ancient recipes of its own, influenced by German, French or Italian traditions, according to the location. The best known Swiss specialty is probably the fondue, a bubbling symphony of melted cheese, served in a glistening earthen casserole, usually as supper.

Its ingredients vary, but one of the best calls for Gruyère or Emmentaler, or a mixture of both, seasoned and made soulful with white wine, butter, a hint of garlic or onion, a pinch of flour, and often a sizable slug of fiery kirsch.

When I was invited to share a family fondue in Berne years ago, a dozen people, from white-bearded grossvater to the youngest sprig, stood hungrily around the bowl. In turn we dipped into it chunks of bread stuck on forks, twirled the sizzling stuff around to cool it off, and gobbled it with swallows of cold white wine.

Because of its fine pasture and well-bred cows, Switzerland is noted for dairy products of every description from cheese to milk chocolate. Alpine cooking is the substantial kind that puts heat and substance into mountain climbers and winter sportsmen. For rucksack meals on mountain trails there is durable, chewy binderfleisch, which is dry-cured beef, mutton or goat flesh. And for the famished skier at day's end, a bowl of smoking hot cheese soup, a dish of sweet-and-sour calf's liver, or the mammoth Bernerplatte, loaded with salted meats, boiled potatoes and winy sauerkraut.

André Papion, chef de cuisine of the *Liberté*, is shown in the ▶ ship's first-class dining room surrounded by creations of his staff. His *boeuf à la Ficelle*, young pigeon *en casserole* Clamart, Prague ham *en croute*—or any dish requested—will match the best in France.

SLIM AARONS

Of the three Scandinavian nations, Denmark has the richest and most "Continental" cuisine. Nature's abundance makes life easier in Denmark, and the Danes, a sunny and industrious race, know how to take full advantage of their blessings. Their love of the table is summed up in a humorous Danish remark: "Roast goose makes wonderful eating. The trouble is that a goose is too much for one person and not enough for two."

The visitor to Copenhagen usually goes straight to Oskar Davidsen's famous restaurant for his first meal. There he receives an intimation of the lively Danish appetite when he is confronted with a menu more than three feet long, offering 172 dishes on the *smorrebrod* course alone. Most of these temptations are open-face sandwiches whose preparation requires not only an inexhaustible larder but a large staff of culinary workers. Among the popular items is a pyramid of 200 thumbnail-size shrimps in a cocktail sauce.

The cold buffet at many of Copenhagen's 2000 restaurants is a carnival of meats and fishes, arranged in fantastically elaborate designs. Snowy linen, delicate crystal, fine china and soft candlelight are utilized with a charm that will linger long in the memory of foreign guests.

Denmark is the dairy and provision shop of Europe. Bacons, hams and cheeses are exported to all parts of the Continent, and the Danes are especially proud of their butter. After the *smorrebrod* come such notable Danish dishes as beer soup, *frikadeller* (meat balls), roast goose stuffed with prunes and potatoes, *stegt svinekam* (roast pork with red cabbage), *rödgröd med flöde* (currant and raspberry juice thickened with sago), and the fascinating coterie of Danish pastry which is usually heaped with whipped cream, and served with some of the best coffee in Europe. Danes are perhaps the greatest beer drinkers on earth, and anyone who has tasted draught Carlsberg or Tuborg will understand why. The universal hard liquor is *aquavit*, downed ice cold and often chased with beer.

The Swedes and Norwegians are austere trenchermen compared with the Danes. Norwegian climate is harsh, and there is less variety of vegetables, meats and fruits. Freshly caught Norwegian fish and pink smoked salmon, however, are everyday staples which would be rated as delicacies elsewhere. Herring is on every table. The cheeses are remarkable, and include the widely exported *gammelost*, *gjetost* and *mysöst*. And there are the wild arctic raspberries, which are found only in the far north; they are yellow at maturity and taste indescribably sweet.

Sweden's leading contribution to fine eating is the famous *smörgåsbord*, literally "bread and butter table," but actually an enormous buffet of hot and cold edibles. The unlimited *smörgåsbord* of prewar days is now a thing of the past. In the less expensive restaurants it is now called *assietter*, a modest selection of hors d'oeuvres like pickled or smoked herring, liver paste, sliced ham or sausage, vegetables, salad and cheese. In more luxurious places, it is known as *delikatessassietter*, and may comprise several kinds of herring, sardines, smoked salmon, smoked eel, prawns and a tray of assorted cheeses and biscuits. *Ärter och fläsk* (yellow split-pea soup with pork) is a Thursday dish, followed by thin pancakes and lingonberries—the cranberries native to all Scandinavian countries.

Festive eating has returned to Germany, or at least to that western portion which welcomes the tourist. An infallible sign of this national comeback is the forest of sausages which decorates every meat store, filling the counters and dangling fatly from the rafters. The *speisekarte* in restaurants and beer halls is almost as gigantic as in prewar days. Its margins are often decorated with sepia sketches of obese diners stuffing themselves at loaded tables, bosomy mermaids caressing giant lobsters, spitted chickens dripping gravy, Cupid carving a ham, and all the other familiar German symbols of a full stomach and a buzzing head.

The chefs of Munich, Frankfurt, Hamburg and West Berlin are proud of their skill in producing specialties of other nations. On the menu of the famous Restaurant Walterspiel in Munich are listed dishes like roast beef Baltimore, salmon Norwegian style, trout *niçoise*, *risotto Milanaise* and *entrecôte marchand du vin*. But, if you yearn for the flavor of the old Germany, you will have to try the cooking of Bavaria, Baden, Hesse and the Rhineland.

To list German sausages would take a page, but here are a few of them: the delectable *weisswurscht* of Munich (a white sausage filled with calves' brains, spleen and veal); Franconian *rostbratwürste* (crackling pork sausage grilled over hot coals); Nürnberger *bratwürstl*; Westphalian *blutwurst*; Frankfurter *würstchen* (originals of our hot dogs); Bremen *pinkelwurst* (made of cracked oats and bacon cubes); Braunschweiger *mettwurst* and *knackwurst*. Some of these are eaten plain; others come solidly flanked with lentils, sauerkraut, mashed potatoes, dumplings or mashed peas.

Americans are better acquainted with German cooking than any other kind, but at home we rarely encounter true provincial delicacies like *aalsuppe*, the eel soup of Hamburg, or *Himmel und Erde*, a trifling Rhineland delicacy of mashed potatoes and applesauce, eaten with fried black pudding and onions. Westphalian *pfefferpotthast* is a spicy stew of beef, onions, bread crumbs, herbs and hot peppercorns. Bremer *küchen-ragout* is a ragout of chicken with sweetbreads, veal meat balls, asparagus, clams and peas. Notable specialties are the hams and bacons of Westphalia, the lobsters and oysters of Hamburg and Bremen, Pomeranian smoked goose breast, Dresden *stollen*, and the huge apple pancakes served almost everywhere.

Germany is still the heaven of the beer drinker. St. Gambrinus reigns as of old in the beer halls of Munich, and the annual *Oktoberfest* has been revived with all its legendary feats of guzzling and gorging. For more delicate palates, the wines of the Rhineland, Moselle and the Palatinate again pour in golden streams.

The happiest Americans I encountered on my most recent travels were a middle-aged couple who occupied an adjoining table one gay evening at Alfredo's restaurant in Rome. They were mopping up a large platter of the wonderful noodles and cheese. The man caught my eye as he twirled a forkful at arm's length in the approved Alfredo manner, and smiled at me a wide Kansas smile. Then he said: "We visited the Colosseum this morning, lunched at Passetto's and spent the afternoon at the Vatican. And now we're eating this terrific stuff at Alfredo's! All in all, it's been a wonderful day."

Which proved to me all over again that food in Europe, to those who understand and love it, can provide pleasures at least as memorable as ancient monuments, cathedrals and masterpieces of art.

French Food and Wine
/ Pierre and Renée Gosset

*You may learn more about France and the French
from what you eat than from what you see*

IN TRAVELING through France "Where do I eat?" is an even more important question than "What do I see?" In the country which is the primal realm of gastronomy, the proper answer to the first question can give a visitor a greater insight into the spirit of the land than any answer to the second. But you must be adventurous. You cannot discover the greatest French cooking by following the high-roads or the high signs. Not only many visiting Americans but many Parisians forget that the glory of French cooking is in its *regional* variety, and that this must be searched out intelligently on the spot.

Every Frenchman is convinced that he is an authority on French cooking, but all too often he lets that infallible *Guide Michelin* destroy his spirit of adventure. He is led by its stars to eat a *brioche de foie gras* at Vienne in Point's three-star restaurant—even though he is in the homeland of hot sausage and those wonderful fishballs called *quenelles*. He will order a *croustade de langouste* at La Brague, near Nice, instead of tasting a *bourride*, that savory whitefish stew, from the Mediterranean outside his window.

Above all, France suffers from an overdose of Paris. It's true that in Paris you can find anything you want. But someday, perhaps, Parisians will realize that no regional French dish—no Burgundian *pauchouse* (fishes cooked in white wine), no Alsatian *foie d'oie aux raisins* (goose liver cooked with grapes) and no Provençal *agneau au romarin* (lamb cooked with rosemary)—is as tasty in Paris as when you eat it near its home, where the recipe has been passed on from generation to generation, and fresh herbs indispensable to its preparation grow in the restaurant's garden.

THE SOUTHWEST

Here, to be specific, we have in mind a certain *ttoro*—you pronounce it *tioro*—that we ran into one day in the Basque country. This is a smooth half-soup, half-fricassee of fish, dependent for its flavor on thyme, laurel, basil, sage, tarragon and chervil that grow wonderfully in this gentle land where every little valley is washed by blue mists. Our *ttoro* also wouldn't have been the same without the ambience: the cook in rope-soled *espadrilles*, the heavy tablecloth striped in bright colors.

The *ttoro*—as nine out of ten of the most elaborate French dishes—was mothered by necessity. The refinements came later. Centuries later. The *ttoro* goes back to the Basque fishermen who were cruising off the shores of Newfoundland long before Columbus found America by losing his way. They boiled cod heads in garlic and onions (to ward off scurvy) and produced a soup which was then poured over slices of ship's bread rubbed with oil. Then they began to fish off Cape Finisterre, closer to home, where they hauled in tuna, sardines and pollack. The *ttoro* grew into a soup of fresh pollack served first with vegetables and later with aromatic herbs. And, one day after a particularly good catch, someone threw fish steaks into the soup.

Today your *ttoro* arrives at your table further improved by crabmeat cooked in eggs and cream. It is served in big peasant bowls—the same bowls used a little farther north for the *chabrot*, an old custom of the Bordeaux region: just before a winegrower finishes his soup, he pours in a big dose of strong red wine; then he laps it up.

A small country hotel at the river's edge . . . the delightful surprise of never-before-sampled local wines . . . it is just the chance of such a discovery (and in France the chance is excellent) that makes an eating tour of the provinces one of the most rewarding adventures open to a traveler. Would you like to sample the repast shown here? You can find it at the Hotel Bonnet in Beynac on the banks of the Dordogne.

RENE JACQUES

Don't, however, expect to try a *chabrot* in the highly dignified restaurants of the city of Bordeaux itself. Bordeaux restaurants, with their lace and their traditions, are the most self-complacent, self-sufficient, and, strangely, underrated in all of France.

We shall never forget how a Bordeaux *sommelier* put an unhappy customer in his place at a table next to ours. This wine waiter, in his blue apron, had just decanted a dusty, spider-webbed bottle. He had poured a few drops of this Château Margaux 1929 into the hollow of a thin glass, delicately moistened his palate, then rolled the wine around the back of his throat. Ostentatiously, and with all eyes watching for a sign of approval, he had finally declared that he was willing to let his customers drink the wine. It was a rite.

When the customer at the table next to ours saw the *sommelier* draw near with his huge wine list in his hands, he made a terrible blunder. He had decided on a little local wine. "Sommelier, just give me a *petit vin de pays.*"

"Monsieur," said the man in the blue apron, grandly, "in the Bordelais, there is no *petit vin* and there is no *vin de pays*. If you so desire, we have four *premiers grands crus* and fifty-seven *grands crus*. All *crus de château*, naturally. We have one hundred and one *crus bourgeois superieurs*. Two hundred fifty *crus bourgeois*. Ninety-six *crus bourgeois* from the Bas

Medoc. I will not bother to list the *crus paysans*. But a *petit vin de pays*, monsieur, no, I regret . . ."

Our miserable neighbor tried to save the situation: "Well, then, give me a Saint-Emilion. . . ."

"A Saint-Emilion, monsieur? What do you prefer? A *vin de coteau* or a *vin de Graves*? An Ausone or a Cheval Blanc? A Montagne? Saint Georges? Lussac? Puisseguin? Parsac? Lalande? Neac? Fronsac? Canon? Pomerol? Unless you would like to try a Sables, perhaps? . . ."

His drowning victim sank like a stone. For a few seconds, the *sommelier* left him on the bottom before suggesting in his most pleasant voice: "Perhaps monsieur would prefer a good cider?"

By contrast, the wines of Burgundy can be approached heartily and gaily without any suspicion of disrespect. People no longer go in for such majestic tributes to Burgundy as that of the French infantry commander who ordered his men to present arms as they marched by the Clos Vougeot vineyard. Today, affection rather than awe is the keynote of the wealth of expressions Burgundians, from Chablis to Mâcon, use in talking about their wines. A *vin de dentelle* (lace) is light, spiritual and subtle. If a wine "doesn't have enough bone," that's not a major defect. But if it is "short on body," then things become serious! A wine "turns into a peacock's tail" when it spreads all its essences in your throat. But if this aroma remains in your mouth instead, then the wine "sits on your palate." Wine "wears its hat on its ear" when it's just on the point of turning and makes your tongue tingle; it has "a beautiful dress" when its ruby-velvet color gleams; it is a "handkerchief wine" if its scent is light and flowery. Burgundy can also be sumptuous, well-built, dainty or elegant. It can be fruity, charmed, colored, fleshy, musky, tranquil, gentle, well-bred, suffocated, flowery or warm . . . and a host of other, untranslatable things. Even if the Burgundian proclaims that a wine smells like earth, violets, rotten cauliflower or a billy goat, that still doesn't mean he won't drink it.

To do fullest justice to the province we must praise its cooking as well as its wines. In Burgundy the most demanding of gourmets is never disappointed. *Pauchouses* (fishes in white wine); delicious red-wine sauces; crayfish in creamy *sauce Nantua*; eel stews cooked in white wine with garlic, onions, bacon and butter; *farcis aux escargots* (snail forcemeat—though the famed fat "Burgundy snails" have recently had to be imported from Hungary); *chicken fricassee*—these and dozens of other traditional dishes have been brought to perfection.

Of all the great Burgundy chefs, Alexandre Dumaine at the Hôtel de la Côte d'Or in Saulieu is the most famous. This stout, ruddy-faced man is one of the four greatest restaurant men in France, and an artist of such standing asks as much of his customers as they do of him. For example, telephone M. Dumaine and order, for one o'clock sharp, his chicken with truffles (it's his triumph—cooked in the *steam* of a *pot-au-feu* so that it may soak up the aroma of meat and vegetables, with slices of truffles inserted under the skin). Then turn up at half past one. You'll eat a steak—because M. Dumaine will not serve you *his* chicken for anything in the world.

A well-known author once committed the unforgivable sin of asking Dumaine for mustard with his *boeuf en daube*. Dumaine, pale and deathly silent, took his dish back to the kitchen and then seasoned it not with mustard but with these deadly words: "A gourmet? He's just a big eater!"

LYONS REGION

What astounds foreigners about French cooking is not the delicious taste of, say, a *lièvre* (hare) *à la royale* but the thousand-and-one insanely meticulous steps leading to this perfect dish, and the importance the French attach to appreciating it. Outside France, only a Chinese would truly understand the death of Vatel, the Grand Condé's chef, who ran himself through because the fish did not arrive in time for a dinner for Louis XIV.

The hinterlands of Lyons know how to eat. Delicious Savoy with its lake fish that cannot be shipped away from their lakes. Tasty Dauphiné with its *morilles* (noble relatives of mushrooms) *à la crème*, and its *gratin dauphinois* in which the humble potato becomes almost a noble object. Bresse with its fat, fleshy fowl. Bugey, the home of Brillat-Savarin. . . .

We have a weakness for Pérouges, at the threshold of the Dombes, a poetic, medieval town behind ramparts. The upper stories of its old houses hang over the streets and the window bars are of stone. It would be no surprise to see a king's musketeer tether his horse outside the Ostellerie and stomp in to order a *demi-setier* (an old premetric measure) of Roussette.

Our musketeer would feel quite at home in the huge dining room of the Ostellerie, with its carved beams and its monumental fireplace. He would be served his *demi-setier* by a trim maiden, dressed like the maidens he knew, in an ample skirt covered with a white apron, her hair in the headdress of the Old Regime. And, if his heart desired, he could be served a flowing cup of hippocras.

This is a rare amber-colored medieval liqueur, compounded of white wine, honey and spices, and in the old days people believed it was a panacea and elixir of youth. We sampled it after a wonderful regional menu of *gratin d'écrevisses* (crayfish, sauced and browned), *poularde* (a fat pullet) *à la crème*, and a pastry dessert, *galette de Pérouges*. Don't hesitate to try hippocras—it's awful enough to have all the virtues attributed to it.

ALSACE

One morning in autumn, we were driving toward the plains of Alsace. It was quite late. We had purposely strayed from our route and had wandered into a mountain pasture to visit an Alsatian *marcairerie*, one of those little two-room houses to which shepherds drive their flock every May twenty-fifth on St. Urban's Day, carrying on their own backs the utensils for making their Munster or Géromé cheeses.

The sight of so many cheeses had given us a fearful appetite. Unfortunately, it was after two o'clock in this province where the lunch bell always rings at noon. So we set aside hopes for high gastronomy and hunted a table in one of those charming villages of half-timbered houses where storks nest in the chimneys. We were ready to eat anything. Just a snack . . .

But Alsace, personified by a sturdy, apple-cheeked woman in Orbey, was to remind us that even at half past two you don't eat just anything at an Alsatian table.

First, she glared angrily at her clock. "At this time of day, you know . . . and it's not the tourist season either. Well, you might as well sit down. I'll bring you a bit of ham. . . ."

The next time we saw her, she was carrying a huge platter of pink ham, stuffed tongue, saveloy, rabbit *pâté* and thick slices of *foie gras en croûte*. There was a bottle of chilled Gewürztraminer to go with it.

When we had finished this platter, we were ready to call it a lunch. Perhaps a little salad . . .

At this point, the *patronne* surged out of the kitchen with another platter bearing two small trout (they had been alive only ten minutes before) under a cascade of melted butter.

"You'll have to forgive me. They're not very big. That's all I could find . . . but you can't walk in on people at a time like this. Mind you, I've managed to scare up some chicken for you, too, but there's nothing else in the house. I hope it will be enough . . ."

The plump chicken was cooked in Riesling, cream and mushrooms. The red cabbage and chestnuts which followed it, however, remained untouched.

"What's wrong with you? Aren't you hungry? Don't you like it? I know I'm not serving you a real lunch, but it's so late, you know. If I'd only known, I would have cooked you a good *choucroute* with partridges. Well, you'll make up for it with the cheese."

The cheese was the Munster we had seen in the *marcairerie* and it was served with cumin seeds. We were unable to resist it. But then came the *kougelhof*, a big cake all eggs and butter. It finished us.

At quarter past four we managed to empty the last drop of perfumed *Quetsche* from our liqueur glasses, while our inconsolable hostess kept promising us a "real" lunch the next time we passed by, if only we would arrive an hour earlier.

CHAMPAGNE

The gentleman wore his sixty years handsomely and his Legion of Honor ribbon discreetly. We had come to see him about something else, but he was so wrapped up in the subject of champagne we couldn't help listening.

"You don't manufacture champagne," he told us, "you elaborate it. And the wonder is that it has been elaborated in the same way since the 17th century when a monk, Dom Pérignon, discovered its secret. What a discovery!"

He sighed, walked to the window and opened the Venetian blinds which had been casting zebra stripes of sunshine on the walls of his big, modern office. On the wooded hill facing us, we saw strange, imposing buildings.

"Oh," he sighed again, "if mankind had produced only inventors like Dom Pérignon! But I'm not sticking to my subject. You know, of course, that champagne wine is a mixture of wine from white grapes, wine from black grapes and wine from preceding years. It is this marriage—we might call it a triangle—that goes into the vat. The mixture is placed in bottles which are then stored in underground galleries. There the mixture settles out and ferments. Dom Pérignon's secret lay in allowing the wine to ferment a second time in the bottle. To achieve this, he added sugar. The sugar is transformed into alcohol and carbon dioxide—and it's the carbon dioxide which produces the fizz. While this process goes on, the bottle must be stored in a cold place head downward and each bottle must be twirled once a day to prevent a deposit from forming on its side."

The gentleman paused and then continued his informal lecture:

"The last time I visited Rheims, I saw men who could twist as many as 30,000 bottles a day. Thanks to persistent daily twisting, as the wine ages, the deposit settles down next to the cork. Then the bottle is uncorked and the deposit shoots out with all the force of the natural gas in the bottle behind it. Now all that remains is to add a certain quantity of sugar to each bottle to produce a *brut*, a *sec*, a *demisec* or a *doux*. Oh, that glorious French champagne. . . . We use exactly the same method . . . here in California."

You see—and you will excuse our omission—the wine lover wearing the Legion of Honor, who had just spent a quarter of an hour relating with reverence the story of champagne, was none other than the president of the University of California with 16,000 students. His sunny office overlooked San Francisco Bay. And the strange buildings on the hills outside his window housed cyclotrons—the cyclotrons around which five Nobel Prize winners and their hand-picked students were busy disintegrating the atom before one day disintegrating all mankind—the province of Champagne included . . .

BRITTANY

This time, we were really in France. In Breton France, near Josselin. And Josselin is in the very heart of that melancholy Brittany of furze-covered moors . . . that pious Brittany of granite Calvaries at every crossroads . . . that legendary Brittany of stone menhirs, and of Tristan and Isolde.

But by no stretch of the imagination can Brittany be considered a shrine of French cuisine. The Breton peasant's potatoes with bacon, the *lait strengue* (buttermilk) into which an entire family dunks boiled potatoes, fish soup and potatoes (yes, more potatoes) are rather pale figures in the flamboyant arsenal of French gastronomy.

We sat down in the dining room of a small hotel in Josselin to eat *crêpes*—the supreme delicacy of the region. We had watched the preparation of the *crêpes* as you always do in Brittany.

"What do you want to drink?" the waitress asked us.

We had heard about that rare Breton wine grown a stone's throw from Josselin on the Rhuys Peninsula, but we decided against it. According to a local saying, you need four men and a wall to appreciate it: "One to pour, one to drink, two to hold him, and the wall to stop him from running away." It was best to stick to cider . . .

The cider wasn't very sweet and the crêpes weren't very lacy. We still weren't reconciled to Breton cooking.

"You know," said the boss philosophically as he took away our plates, "around here, you should stick to fish."

That night, we followed his advice in a restaurant on our route and, thanks to him, we were able to taste some delicious stuffed clams and a memorable *homard* (lobster) *à la crême*.

NORMANDY

One of us has a memory of Normandy which is all the more precious because it goes back to the invasion of 1944 and a first glimpse of France after four years in exile.

A few days after setting foot on Norman soil, Pierre, who was the only French war correspondent among fifty American correspondents with Patton's army, was shaving in a field under an apple tree. The front was already far off. A neighboring farmer struck up a conversation and ended by saying, "Bring two of your American friends with you Sunday. We'll have lunch at the house. Nothing fancy . . ."

It was a beautiful, squarely built farmhouse. There was an odor of apples in the low-ceilinged dining room and about twenty places had been set on a long table covered with a red-checked tablecloth. All the neighbors had been invited.

Pierre turned up with the representatives of two famous American papers. The three of them arrived groaning under a mountain of American canned foods to help ease the horrible aftermath of the Occupation. Faced with a table already heavily laden with Vire sausage, white *boudin* from Avranchin and rich local butter, they could sniff the odor of *poulets aux petits oignons* (chicken with onions) and *civet de lapereau à la crème* (a stew of young rabbit). They sheepishly deposited their rations on a sideboard.

At the end of the lunch, the farmer suggested to his wife: "And what about the cheese?"

The three Santa Clauses from the press camp beamed. This was their chance. They leaped for the sideboard and returned with their hands full of C and K rations, each one containing a little can of cheese mixed with ham.

Guests and hosts religiously tasted the American cheese

with a polite clacking of the tongue. Then the farmer cleared his throat and said heartily: "I guess it's time for a little change."

Two Camemberts were immediately unfurled, then the Excelsior and the Gournay, the Bondon, the Neufchâtel, the Lisieux, a mountain of cream cheese, and a Pont l'Evêque. The farmer anxiously asked each one of his guests if he preferred his Bondon "stiff" or "giving itself away."

A few bottles of Burgundy had been written off for the cause of Franco-American relations when the farmer suddenly howled: "Great gods, we forgot the Bouille!"

The Bouille had gone astray somewhere on the sideboard between a can of beans and a dozen packages of powdered lemonade.

"Of course, cheese isn't what it used to be before the war," said the farmer later that afternoon. "In those days, we made twenty-one different kinds here in Normandy. Nowadays, though, we just have to make out with what we have. We had to be sly about it too. After all, you can't live without cheese . . ."

PROVENCE

Because we lived a few years in Provence and because we will be stricken with nostalgia for the rest of our lives, we know where perfection lies in southern French cooking. Go to Les Baux, for example, at l'Oustau de Baumanière and try the *gigot des Alpilles en croûte* (leg of mutton in a crust), or the *rouget en papillote* (fish cooked in oiled paper), or the *gratin de langouste* (crayfish) from the kitchen of our friend, Maître Thuilier. We call him "Maître" because he used to be a lawyer. Eating at Les Baux under his ancient vaulted ceiling with its 16th-century stones is a treat for your soul.

But Provençal cooking also means the cooking along the Mediterranean coast. It's based on garlic, tomatoes, pimento and fish. And everything's cooked in olive oil—and we mean *only* in olive oil.

A good woman at Collobrières once apologized as she served us roast thrush: "I didn't have any oil in the house. Not a drop, mind you. So I gave you a little bit of butter. It will be all right, won't it?"

As for fish, everyone knows that while they live in water, they die in oil. Into the oil must go all those rascasse, conger eel and such used in a *bouillabaisse* before they are bathed in white wine and perfumed with saffron, garlic, fennel and tomatoes.

But *bouillabaisse* often is a rare commodity on the French Mediterranean coast. The supply of *bouillabaisse* at any given moment depends . . .

"What? No *bouillabaisse* on the menu today, Mado?"

"Eh, no, none in the market."

"And why?"

"How do I know? Go ask the fishermen. Probably a bit of mistral."

One day, in the middle of a game of bowls, we decided to ask a fisherman.

"Eh," said the mariner. "My poor lady, didn't you see the weather out in the gulf?"

"The weather out in the gulf? Don't you know that the fishermen of Douarnenez go out every day in weather like that?"

Not at all injured in his pride, he lined up his shot calmly. Then he turned back to us, his gaze heavy with the ancient wisdom of his Mediterranean shores.

"Did you ever take a look at a cemetery in Brittany? What do you see in a cemetery in Brittany? It's full of tombstones reading: 'Yves, died at sea,' 'Le Queffelec, died at sea,' 'Le Du, died at sea.' Go see for yourself in our cemetery: 'Titin, died playing *boules*.' That's what you see in our cemetery."

And that day, we decided that, while we loved *bouillabaisse*, we didn't love it to the point of killing a fisherman.

LOIRE VALLEY

Traditional garden of France, blessed and nonchalant valley with its gentle speech and its wines fit for a king—this is Touraine. You go to Touraine to see the châteaux of the Loire, and Touraine gives you a great deal more: its cuisine and its sky, its river and its light.

One of our American friends wandering through France by car allowed himself a week for the châteaux and he began with Chambord. He was duly impressed by the building and also by the *Son et Lumière* (sound and light) show, although regretful that he didn't understand a word that came out of the hidden loud-speakers. Next he went to Blois, where he slipped the guide the required 100-franc piece without daring to admit that his explanations might just as well have been in Greek. Continuing down the Loire, he hunted a quiet little hotel for the night.

That was how he happened to land at Langeais. We never found out what attracted him to that charming little inn . . . whether it was the first part of its sign—"Family Hotel . . ." —or the second—". . . et Duchesse Anne." Or it may have been the strange coupling of the two. It may also have been that, from the tables in the hotel's garden, he had an iron-clad guarantee he would not see another château.

We met Burt MacB⸺ long afterward in his home in upstate New York. He talked to us about France with tears in his eyes. "I'll remember that *brochet au beurre blanc* all my life. And the Vouvray I had there! And the *écrevisse à l'armoricaine*! If we could only get something like it here in the States. Ever have *champignons farcis*? Try it someday. And *escalope à la crème*? And that salmon, my friend . . ."

You see, during the other six days of his seven-day trip through the Loire Valley, Burt MacB⸺ did not budge a millimeter from the shady garden of the "Family Hotel et Duchesse Anne" in Langeais.

For a foreigner who does not happen to be a linguist, this can be a thoroughly satisfying way of discovering France. Judging from the result, there is no better way to become a Francophile.

PART V: *The Gourmet Abroad*

Delicacies of Denmark / Noël Barber

The not-so-gloomy Dane is a hearty diner and winer.
To him a snack is a handsome combination of selected morsels equal
in volume to an entire meal for an ordinary mortal

DENMARK, where eating is a national pastime as well as a national industry, is the only country in the world with a foreign-language dictionary devoted entirely to words and phrases about food.

Other countries offer their tourists phrase books translating: "Where can the bath I discover?" or "What time the train does it depart?" but the Danes spurn these workaday sentences and get right down to proving the maxim that the way to a tourist's heart is through his stomach.

A three-language book with columns in Danish-French-English, Denmark's Gastronomic Dictionary starts with a crisp introduction on the best times to eat, then goes right into a glossary of vital words such as stuffed, boiled and roasted. This is followed by an alphabetical list of foods.

Considering that the menu at one restaurant is four feet long and contains 172 different *smorrebrod* dishes, a pocket gastronomic dictionary is almost as indispensable as a knife and fork.

In Copenhagen alone, a capital with a population of 1,000,000 people and 900,000 bicycles, there are 2,000 restaurants. The city bustles with waiters, the streets are jammed with lorries carrying food and drinks; the harbor is choked with the fruits of the sea; and in the nearby countryside, with its pink-and-white houses, the tables quiver when the farmers sit down to eat.

The basis of Danish food is *smorrebrod*—the "open sandwich"—a sandwich without a top piece of bread, yet it compares to an ordinary sandwich as a diamond from Cartier's compares to a bauble from Woolworth's. The foundation of the sandwich is rye bread, smeared thickly with butter. On this, anything goes—literally anything—including a liberal helping of genius.

Maybe the best way to describe *smorrebrod* is to take an item from the menu of Oskar Davidsen, the famous restaurant with a menu four feet long. Let us consider, for example, No. 61. On the bread are placed pieces of raw scraped meat, Danish caviar, two oysters, the whole flanked by two rows of shrimps. Or No. 52, which was the favorite of Hans Christian Andersen, and consists of crisp cold-bacon slices on tomato, liver paste with truffles, meat and Madeira wine jelly, all topped off with shreds of horse-radish.

Davidsen's epitomizes Danish food, and the genius behind it is shared by two men: young Per Davidsen, who does the buying and managing, and middle-aged, twinkly-eyed Axel Svenssen who, dedicated to the poetry of food, spends his time working out the tastes, colors and eye appeal of new dishes. Since food really is poetry to the Dane, you might say that Axel is the poet and Per the publisher.

Their restaurant was the headquarters of the Danish underground in the war, and when the moment of liberation came, Axel was ready. British troops were the first to enter the city, and awaiting them was a brand-new sandwich—the Union Jack: slices of raw scraped fillet of beef with crossed rows of shrimps and a raw egg yolk in the middle.

Seafood plays an important part in Danish food, shrimps particularly, of which Per Davidsen buys 500 to 800 pounds

Smorrebrod is the Danish name for an open sandwich glorified ▶ with smoked salmon, rare roast beef, breast of duckling, smoked ham, red cabbage, onion rings, sliced beef aspic and/or endless other appetite-provokers—such delectables as to elevate it far above the lowly word "sandwich."

a day. In addition to his 100 cooks, he has twenty-four girls who do nothing all day but peel shrimps at the rate of four pounds an hour. Don't despise a shrimp sandwich at Davidsen's. The smallest has fifty shrimps on it, the largest—the Shrimp Pyramid—has 180 balanced on a slice of bread.

These, of course, are exotic dishes. But there are simple ones too. The Danes cure herrings in dozens of ways and there is nothing more delicious than salted strips of herring smothered in rings of raw onions and doused in vinegar and sugar; or *sildesalat*, a concoction of fish, apple, beet root and mayonnaise spread two inches thick on rye bread, then topped with slices of hard-boiled egg.

The Danish girl is a wonderful cook, and if you are invited out to a *smorrebrod* in a private home, it will be up to restaurant standards. Simple *smorrebrod* may pass for everyday eating, but with a party it's all or nothing.

I own a small Danish cookbook, and the section on *smorrebrod* starts with the following semireligious incantation:

"This is an orgy, nothing more or less. An orgy in food and an orgy in colors. A table of *smorrebrod* that is properly prepared should remind one of the works of the Dutch masters of the Renaissance."

Six pieces of *smorrebrod* may seem far too much when you dine in a restaurant. But eat them anyway. And you can manage them, providing you drink as well. You drink two beverages—Danish lager (Tuborg or Carlsberg), and Danish schnapps; the first out of tall glasses, the latter (for your own sake) out of small ones.

Schnapps is liquid dynamite—a pure white spirit, slightly perfumed—and you'll be wise to toss only half a glass down your throat at the first drink. Then, after a short interval filled with food, somebody will cry: "*Helan gaar!*" That is Danish for "down the hatch," and the gesture is usually followed by a song which has the same name. It's a point of honor to drain the glass. Eating starts again, and a fresh glass of schnapps—ice cold—is poured as you attack the next piece of *smorrebrod*.

Since the Danes have huge appetites, the fixed-price all-you-can-eat meal is a highly dangerous gamble. But, in 1951, Davidsen's restaurant took the plunge and introduced a lobster lunch—two dollars, and eat all the lobsters you can manage. It is featured on the menu every Thursday.

One August day a great hulk of a man arrived from Jutland (where people despise the finicky appetites of the Copenhagers), marched in with his quiet little wife, tucked his napkin round his immense stomach, settled down, and called for lobsters and beer. He went through one, two, three, four, five lobsters before he finally puffed to a stop.

The waiter thankfully grabbed for the empty plates. At which moment the wife, with five lobsters behind her, laid a restraining finger on the waiter's arm and murmured: "More, please!" She kept repeating "More please" until she had eaten eleven—repeat eleven—lobsters.

"Expensive, yes," said Per Davidsen as he showed me the newspaper clippings, "but cheap really—we never got so many headlines."

The Danes dine early—on festive occasions anyway—and finish late. The earliest I ever sat down for lunch was 11:30 on the occasion of a friend's wedding. We ate *smorrebrod* and drank beer and schnapps (and sang) until 5:30. We were then given an hour's grace to bathe and—since as I say the Danes dine early—we sat down for dinner at 6:30.

Dinner is a far more serious affair than the snack lunch; it's a hot meal, a formal procedure. On this occasion we dined at Davidsen's in one of their private rooms and after the consommé, we were served with a tasty titbit called "*Lidt Laekart for To,*" a trifle which translated roughly means "something tasty for two."

There was one for each couple and the plate consisted of two halves of roast chicken, two young fried pigeons, grilled bacon, pork cutlets, smoked ham with pâté, kidneys, sausages, onions, fried potatoes, a mushroom-and-truffle sauce.

The cheese course, I may add, was almost superfluous.

Oskar Davidsen's has the longest menu in Copenhagen, but the famous Wivex Restaurant has one of the longest dining rooms in Denmark. The waiter unlucky enough to serve the table farthest from the kitchen (they take it in turns) must carry his dishes 270 yards.

Wivex is the biggest restaurant of the plush class in Europe. It can seat 1,200 and has a dance floor and string orchestra for lunch. It is more formal than Davidsen's—a lot of gilt and plush and French dishes, and it is characteristic of the place that, though beer is Denmark's drink, 85 per cent of the liquor sold at Wivex is wine.

Even so, democracy rears its pretty little head. I dined there once, a wonderful expensive dinner (for Denmark) costing fifteen dollars a head, given in honor of a visiting fireman. At the next table sat a happy old couple, very, very close to their pension, he in a stiff, black, sharply cut suit, she in velvet and old lace. They ate two pieces of the cheapest *smorrebrod*. They drank water, then coffee. They shuffled round the floor every time the orchestra played. And they were treated like royalty.

Wivex—which was founded in '88 and boasted once that it never closed its doors day or night—makes a double fetish of luxury for the rich and immaculate service for the unaffluent diner.

You can, if you want, go through ten dollars a head in wine and food, but every night there is a set dinner at two dollars and another at one dollar. A couple of dollars equals fourteen kroner, considered a pretty high dinner price by the Danes, even with free dancing thrown in. So those who don't want the whole works eat a couple of pieces of *smorrebrod*, or take only a cup of coffee. I have been to Wivex hundreds of times; I have never seen a waiter give bad service or raise an eyebrow, even for a ten-cent coffee order. If he did, he would be fired on the spot.

The front of Wivex opens onto Vesterbrogade, Copenhagen's busiest street, but the back opens onto a fairyland that is Denmark's own speciality—the famous Tivoli Gardens. Tivoli is New York's Coney Island or Vienna's Prater, and yet it is neither. It is the mirror of Denmark's capacity for simple pleasure.

Here is the real core of Denmark's democracy, crystallized, pin-pointed for everybody. You can be a millionaire in Copenhagen, but you still find it hard to have more fun than you get by paying the ten cents' entrance fee to see the free show the Tivoli offers every night.

The national gardens, open only in the summer, cover acres of valuable land in the heart of the city. They have restaurants, beer houses, miles of parks with files of chestnut trees by pretty lakes and—for extra payment—the usual assortment of Coney Island diversions.

But the point is you don't need these. For in the Tivoli—and for free—there is a first-class open-air theater, one or two symphony concerts, dance halls, a ballet, a pantomime, an open-air variety show (specializing in high-wire and similar acts easily visible by passing crowds) and, at 11:45 every Saturday night, a fireworks display that makes Paris on the *quatorze juillet* look like a damp squib.

The night life of Copenhagen revolves round the Tivoli or some restaurant until midnight and after that in the night clubs. There are not many of these, but most of them have good bands, floor shows, and around 2:00 A.M., when energies begin to flag, the dance floor is usually fairly empty except for waiters surging across with great silver platters of *smorrebrod*.

There is one thing about the night clubs. They are not out to rook you. They are not there for visitors. They are there for the Danes, with all visitors welcome. Many charge a small entrance fee; and after that the drinks are no more expensive than in any restaurant or bar.

Recently I spent an evening at the Ambassadeur, probably the best in the city; at least it's one of the few places where you can't dance without a tuxedo. There is a good

rumba band, a modern revolving floor at one side for adventurous spirits, a first-class floor show.

I took down the prices of drinks: a Manhattan or Martini cost sixty cents; a white lady, seventy cents; a frozen daiquiri or a gin sling, a dollar. A brandy-and-soda was sixty cents.

"And all this," said a proud Dane trying to air his American, "in a tuxedo joint."

Whisky prices are never quoted, but they are high by Danish standards—about eleven dollars a bottle in a night club—and few people drink it. There is Danish whisky, but it is as bad as Danish beer is good. Danish gin—all Europe is making bathtub gin these days—isn't bad when disguised in something like a gin sling, but Martinis are likely to be a deep yellow and just off the boil.

Personally, I always stick to beer and schnapps until after dinner, then try brandy. It goes with the food.

There are other things in Denmark besides food, it is true, but until you know the Danes with their proud, independent spirit, their innate honesty and genuine hospitality to strangers, it is the food that intrigues you.

PART V: The Gourmet Abroad

Dining in Rome / Silas Spitzer

Roast kid, deviled spring chicken, egg noodles frothy with butter and Parmesan cheese; May strawberries, Gorgonzola with slices of juicy pear—such are the delights of dining in Rome

MAY DAY in Rome was a day that began with the threat of violence and ended in peace. It was also a day two hungry Americans discovered *piselli freschi al prosciutto*, a dish to be eaten in all its lovely perfection only in that particular city and in that season.

At eleven o'clock that morning we emerged from our hotel to find the Via Veneto basking under a warm blue sky. The holiday, to our surprise, was not just a political affair but was observed by all elements of the population. Stores and places of amusement were closed, and not a single bus or taxi rolled.

A procession of open-roofed trucks rumbled past the ancient walls at the head of the avenue, red flags flying and fists held high. Clusters of grim-faced policemen, clutching carbines, were stationed at strategic points along the street. Every café terrace was packed to the curb, and the soft breezes hinted of spring flowers, gasoline and strong black coffee. Happy family picnickers sped by in tiny Fiats. Couples clung precariously to motor bikes and scooters, often with a baby in a basket on the handlebars, and a dog guarding the rear. The city presented a curious spectacle, a mixture of angry political excitement and gay vacation mood.

We had a sketchy breakfast on the sidewalk of the Café Rosati, where tables were as thick as planes on a carrier's deck. The orange juice was thin, faintly yellow, and bitter; the coffee a soot-black liquid with a powerful restorative kick. Two stout Germanic ladies were methodically consuming mounds of jelly-filled doughnuts, marzipan dainties and tiny cream puffs, their diamonds glinting in the sun. Prosperous-looking people of a dozen nationalities were munching and chatting, apparently undisturbed by the avenue's ex-

plosive traffic or the shouted slogans of Communist paraders on their way to a demonstration in the Piazza del Popolo. In the busy heart of Rome, this street of well-heeled idlers gave the odd impression of a seaside boardwalk.

For some obscure reason, horse-drawn coaches were exempt from the May Day ban on commercial vehicles. So, for the prearranged sum of 2000 lire, we spent the next hour clop-clopping around town in an open *carrozza*, pulled by the scrawniest horse I ever saw outside a bull ring. We gave him a breathing spell at a curb near the Colosseum, which was still overpoweringly impressive after our last visit fifteen years ago. The Forum, not far away, was closed for the holiday. In the adjacent public square, a red-faced orator, hand on hip, addressed a Neo-Fascist party meeting in obvious imitation of Mussolini. We did not linger long upon this scene, with its uneasy echoes from newsreels of the long ago, but paid off our coachman and went for a walk across town. When we reached the Piazza Navona, we had lunch on the outdoor terrace of a well-known restaurant called Tre Scalini.

· Facing us was one of Rome's loveliest vistas. Lying in a pattern of dappled sunlight was a long rectangle of old

A couple dine alfresco on the terrace of Casina Valadier, a ▶ restaurant in a neoclassic villa built for, but never occupied by, Napoleon's son. The view rolls from the Pincinian Hill to St. Peter's.

BURT GLINN

228

houses, a soft ocher in tint, faded and flecked by time. Above the carved stone doorways was a dark, shadowy line, which our waiter told us was the high-water mark left from feast days of the Renaissance, when the Piazza Navona was often flooded for maritime processions and games. Against this mellow background of antique buildings, at widely spaced intervals in the center of the cobbled square, the three Bernini fountains loomed, green water cascading from their sculptured surfaces.

The day, the place, and the moment seemed magically contrived for our introduction to *piselli freschi al prosciutto*, the first course of our luncheon and the one dish we shall always associate with Rome in Maytime.

It consisted of nothing more than fresh green peas, simmered in butter with just a trace of onion and shreds of raw Italian ham. But these were no ordinary peas. Each was only a little bigger than a healthy grain of caviar. Their color was an innocent vernal green, and they were as sweet as the breath of spring meadows. There was just enough spiciness of ham to point up the sugary sweetness of the baby peas, which must have been picked at the exact second of dewy perfection. We ate them slowly and with muffled exclamations of wonder and greed. Imagine the quantity of pods that had to be shelled by hand to make these two lavish helpings!

Still ruminating upon the delights of fresh *piselli*, we turned to our next course of noodles prepared *al dente*, in a thick russet sauce of mushrooms, tomato purée and ham. We drank a bottle of dry Orvieto, one of the best of Italian white wines. And for dessert, we had a house specialty called *Tartufo Tre Scalini*, a ball-shaped confection of chocolate ice cream, cake and whipped cream. Fuming *caffè espresso* put a strong black period to one of the best of all the many interesting meals we had in Rome. It seemed to embody all the simplicity and succulence of the finest Italian cooking.

The cocktail interlude in the downstairs bar of the Hotel Flora begins about six and builds up to a crescendo around eight. We had been fascinated observers of this animated scene for an hour or more. Most of the guests were elegantly tailored and extremely articulate young men who crowded three deep around the bar. Notable were several strikingly lovely Italian girls who belong to the world of the cinema. Most of them make a fetish of simplicity. They use no make-up, have complexions of warm ivory, and wear their glossy hair boyishly cropped or gathered tightly back from the forehead. There were a few American college students of both sexes, and a number of opulent-looking family groups we took to be Argentines or Brazilians. A scattering of upper-class Romans, wearing their habitual masks of languid irony, drifted in and out.

After a while, we were joined by an American friend who had accepted our invitation to dinner. Aldo, who was of Italian parentage, had been a resident of Rome since the war. He spoke polished Italian and some of the local dialect, and he was full of advice on the subject of restaurants.

"Americans in Rome," he told us, "always eat in the same places. Tonight, why don't we avoid the big expensive joints and the early Roman ones where the waiters wear togas? Let me take you to a little place where the food is cheap, good, and really Italian. The owner's a friend of mine. He'll treat us like the family. But first, promise me you won't give it away. This is one I hate to see spoiled."

We assured him that we could be trusted. A cab outside the hotel took us to the Trastevere, oldest quarter of the city. True to Aldo's description, there was nothing *caratteris-tico* about the little restaurant we entered. It was obviously at home in this ancient working-class section.

A rich smell of red wine, spicy cooking and strong tobacco hung thickly in the air. The ceiling was low, the wooden tables bare. Patrons and waiters were in their shirt sleeves, for the evening was warm. The host, a friendly little man who wore purple suspenders, greeted us warmly and led us to a small crowded room in the back, which was plainly reserved for the family and intimate friends. There was just barely space for the round table where we sat, wedged between a high desk and an immense sideboard littered with wine bottles, fruit, cheese and hunks of broken bread.

We were not offered a menu, but Aldo engaged the proprietor in a lively conversation about food. As the evening advanced, the noise and confusion grew and our spirits rose. We were visited by a small spotted dog and an enormous dirty white cat. Both animals were petted and flung tidbits from our platter of antipasto. The waiters began to clown for our benefit. Eating *en famille* in a *trattoria* of the Trastevere was not the same thing as dining in chandeliered and starchy state at the Excelsior or Ranieri, and they wanted to show us that the difference was all in their favor.

Amidst the din, we heard music. A little girl in a pinafore was singing to her mother's accompaniment on a guitar.

"The wandering minstrels of Rome," explained Aldo, quite unnecessarily. We rewarded the little girl and her mother. They disappeared and their place was taken by a blind man with a violin, and a short, corpulent tenor.

Around midnight, after a substantial meal and several bottles of Valpolicella which we shared with our host and his wife, we had a nip of grappa and went out into the night, hearts singing.

From the gourmet viewpoint, the dinner had not been especially notable. But I recall two high points. One was *Spaghetti alla Carbonara*, made with a hot sauce of bacon, egg and pepper. The other was the pure bliss of combining bites of creamy Gorgonzola cheese with slices of juicy pear.

If you ask an American what restaurants he recalls from a trip to Rome, he will most likely head the list with the distinguished and very expensive Ristorante Passetto, on the Via Zanardelli. Some travelers rate it as good or better than the best in France. It has two memorable features: a fantastic display of food built along the central wall of the main dining room—a culinary monument which I imagine has impressed tourists as much as any other edifice in Rome—and a bartender named Luciano.

The exhibition of food covered many yards of space, and rose, tier upon tier, to the lofty ceiling, twelve to fifteen feet high. On tables and shelving clothed in snowy linen, and imbedded in shaved ice, were masses of hors d'oeuvres, platters of cooked and uncooked meats and poultry, game birds, cold *entremets* of many kinds, towers of fruit and phalanxes of wine and liqueur bottles.

As for Luciano, I consider him the most accomplished bartender I have encountered. I do not refer only to his dexterity with shakers and other commonplaces of the profession. He will be remembered more for his handsome face and dazzling smile, his good-humored charm, and his intimate but never too personal manner with female clients.

It was nearly ten o'clock when we came to dine at Passetto, but there were no tables unoccupied, so we waited in the tiny bar for a half hour, and there made Luciano's acquaintance. He chatted politely in quaintly flavored English as he worked, never missing a beat. We absorbed more valuable information from him about modern Rome in that short space of time than we could have gathered in a fortnight of reading guide books. He brought us menus and recommended not the house specialities but dishes he had investigated and found delightful to his taste.

When we went in to our table, lo, it was Luciano who filled our plates with smoked salmon, who carved the roast kid and unhinged the deviled spring chicken. It was he who plied us with infant green peas (which we had sworn to eat at least once daily during our stay). It was at his suggestion that we chose a fragrant white wine in an extravagantly carved and decorated flask, with the appropriately flamboyant name of *Verdicchio dei Castelli di Fazi*. In a subtle way that was peculiarly Italian, he managed to serve us beautifully without the slightest servility, and everything he did to help us was tinged with delightful humor and tact.

This was one of the most enjoyable meals we had in Europe, not altogether for its food but because of the chance it gave us to make friends with the world's most versatile and talented barman.

Our gastronomical survey covered most of Rome's better-known restaurants, but the only one we returned to a second and a third time was a crowded, clamorous and completely wonderful hangout in the Via Borgognona called Nino's.

It wasn't the epicurean nature of the menu that lured us back, though we had little fault to find with that particular department. Nor was it the beauty of the décor, which at Nino's consisted of bare and rather dingy walls, a quantity of tables and chairs, and a stout lady cashier on a high stool. Certainly it wasn't the rough and far from efficient service. What brought us back to Nino's was its obvious desire to make the customers happy. The fact is that Nino's is one of Rome's favorite haunts for writers, artists, journalists and people of the local theater and films.

On the evening of our first visit, four of us sat at a table halfway down the narrow, crowded room. It was opposite the open doorway of a sort of service pantry that led into the kitchen, and we had a fascinating view of back-stage activities at the height of the dinner rush.

We saw a slender, nervous little man in a well-cut gray tweed suit leave a nearby table and walk quickly into this room, where he seized a huge knife and began slashing away at a quarter of beef on a butcher's block. A few moments later, he rejoined the group at his table as though the interruption had not taken place. We were mystified by this action, but forgot about it in the general commotion around us.

Waiters trotted in and out of the pantry, red-faced, perspiring liberally. Their lips moved soundlessly, and they appeared to be quarreling with some invisible adversary. Occasionally they burst into unaccountable laughter or song. It amused us to note that, for all their panting exertions, they never carried more than a single plate at a time, holding it dramatically at arm's length, high in the air.

Our own waiter, a bald, heavy old fellow in a white shirt open at the neck, was the busiest of them all. He never stopped running or muttering to himself. We were able to attract his attention only by tugging at his trouser leg as he passed. He knew no English, so we talked with him in our dubious Italian. But he had a puzzling trick of darting off in the middle of a sentence, and we were never sure if he understood us.

We learned that at Nino's it is the custom to order one thing at a time, never a complete meal. When your dish is ready, the waiter grabs it piping hot from the kitchen range, trots back to the table, and drops it in front of you. As a result, our meal proceeded in rather haphazard fashion. While one of us ate an appetizer of fennel and artichoke hearts in oil and vinegar, another waited patiently for his grilled sole, and the remaining pair dug deep into a cavernous tureen of soup that was almost solid with rice and red beans. But when the food arrived, it always tasted fine; there was a half-gallon of Chianti in a swinging silver cradle, and after a while we didn't notice the spasmodic cadence of the service.

Aldo, our Italo-American friend, had informed us that the big attraction at Nino's was *bistecca alla Fiorentina*—the thickest T-bone steak east of the Atlantic seaboard, broiled over charcoal in the Florentine style. When we chose steak as our main course, the waiter promptly vanished, as usual, before we had time to question him. He returned almost immediately with the thin, gray-clad gentleman who had puzzled us earlier by his activities with knife and cleaver. This turned out to be Nino himself. We got along beautifully in French, English and Italian. Nino said that in his place the steaks were always cut to the diner's specifications. A kilogram of the classic *biftek Florentine* cost 2000 lire, about $3.30 for two-and-a-fifth pounds of solid beef, and very inexpensive by American standards. Such a cut was usually served for two, but he told us that some of his customers often did away with an entire kilo apiece, and were never the worse for it.

"No steaks in Rome like mine," he exclaimed proudly. "All fresh, tender Tuscan beef. I bring it myself by truck from Florence every week." And he explained in his trilingual dialect that he was a native Florentine, born and raised in the meat trade. We briefed him carefully on details of thickness and rareness, and he hurried to his butcher's block, quickly cut off two steaks, and held them up in the doorway for our approval, bowing and smiling. The steaks were then broiled to a turn and arrived covering two ample platters. Although not the equal of the best American specimens in flavor or tenderness, they tasted reminiscent enough to bring on a slight attack of nostalgia.

When it came time for dessert, we had *fragole*, those tiny May strawberries which are about the size of French *fraises des bois*, but have a pulpier consistency and a haunting flavor and fragrance of their own. They were served plain, with a little lemon juice for contrast. We found their honeyed sweetness unlike any other berry we knew. All that month they were featured on Rome's menus, and the windows of groceries and fruit shops were piled high with the glowing fruit. It didn't seem possible that woodland berries would be available in such quantities. We called Nino over and put the question to him: "Are *fragole* wild or domestic?" He was baffled. "Wait," he said. "If you will excuse me, I will speak to a man who should know—that tall gentleman over there with the young lady. He speaks the beautiful English. He is one of our most popular actors." He left us and returned a moment later with a beaming silver-haired giant whose handsome, deeply lined face we had seen in Italian films. Nino introduced him and repeated our question in Italian. The tall gentleman looked momentarily puzzled. Then his face cleared, and he boomed in a great bass voice: "But of course. These are not at all tame, these *fragole*. They are what you call the savages!"

Nino's is not a great restaurant, in the gourmet meaning of the word. But there is no place in Rome, I am sure, that makes you feel less like a stranger.

The restaurant in Rome most popular with Americans is undoubtedly Alfredo's. Dining there at least once seems to be as inevitable a project as a trip to the Forum. The last time I had eaten at Alfredo's was about fifteen years ago. What remained with me after all those years was the taste of *fettuccine*, a simple dish of egg noodles, butter and cheese that seemed at the time to taste better than all the pressed duck and fancy stuffed lobster in Paris.

I also remembered the eccentric performance of the proprietor, a short, red-faced man of about sixty, who had a prominent mustache and a mock melodramatic manner. He personally blended and served the noodles at every table, assisted by a repertoire of stage tricks which were both naïve and comical. This was at his old place, on the Via della Scrofa, a rather bare and far from impressive room. Since that time, I was told, Alfredo had sold out to one of his waiters, promising the new owner to retire from competition. But years later, during the postwar recovery, he launched a local feud by opening a new establishment. He was then at a fairly advanced age, but being an invincible ham, undoubtedly found himself unable to resist the lure of a new stage and a larger audience. Now, it seems, there were three Ristorante Alfredos. All claimed to be the originators of the unique, the ineffable *fettuccine* of the days of glory. This triplication of Alfredo was a little confusing. However, I decided I would call on the original maestro, provided he still existed.

The address, I learned, was in the Piazza Augusto Imperatore. I will always be haunted by the spectacle that greeted us when we entered the restaurant. There had been a rather agreeable picture in my mind of the old Alfredo's of fifteen years ago, with its modest interior and comfortable shabbiness. The new place was enormous, with a couple of huge connecting rooms and a ceiling at least two stories high. This area was filled from wall to wall with tables. Every seat was taken, the din was terrifying, the crowd was largely American or foreign, and everyone seemed to be enjoying himself immensely.

The decorations were in the most bombastic modern Italian style. Prominently displayed were hundreds of autographed portraits of "celebrities," photos of groups of happy tourists waving forkfuls of noodles, framed mottoes, slogans and caricatures. Just inside the entrance was a coat-checking department, complete with saucy blond attendant, and looking exactly like Broadway and 49th Street. There were half a dozen slick waiter captains who spoke glib American slang, a couple of smart page boys, and nearly as many waiters as guests, all wearing starched white uniforms decorated with Alfredo's signature in blue stitching. A six-piece orchestra in sharp green zoot suits never stopped playing.

After a little difficulty, we were seated at a table brought in and set up in the very center of the nightmare. For the first time in any Italian restaurant, we were asked what cocktails we'd like. Dutifully, we yielded to the custom of the house and requested Martinis. They came, and, surprisingly, they were perfect.

◀ At the witching hour of midnight, waiters on Italian Line vessels bear culinary gifts to the Salle Inverno where the cold buffet is served. Among the festive dishes: antipasto, chicken galantine, truffled duck, pheasant *volante*. This snack is offered to first-class passengers four hours after a lavish dinner.

HANS NAMUTH

The cover of the elaborate menu was decorated with a picture of Alfredo driving a chariot and four rampaging horses. In one hand he held high a great dish of noodles and with the other he clasped the famous gold spoon and fork presented to him years ago by Mary Pickford and Doug Fairbanks. In the distant background there loomed not only the Colosseum but the grandiose Monumento Vittorio Emanuele.

The specialty of the house was listed, with a fine Latin flourish, as *Maestosissime Fettuccine all'Alfredo*.

We were sold. We ordered *fettuccine* for all hands, but agreed to depart the scene if the dish failed to measure up to our memories. Ten minutes later there was a stir, a clatter, and the white beam of a spotlight focused upon a table. There was a roll of drums and a trumpet blast. Alfredo suddenly appeared from nowhere, surrounded by a claque of white-jacketed attendants. It was an extraordinary apparition, and it gave me a queer feeling. Could this be the genuine Alfredo, the old fellow I had seen perform fifteen years ago? The voice, the gestures and the ritual, though shortened and more mechanical, were the same. The mustache was as quirky as before; the hair was still jet black, but the cheeks had bright red spots that surely came out of a make-up box.

We watched him, fascinated, as with incredible vigor he went through the old act, mixing and tossing the noodles with rapid motions, banging on the sides of the plate, shouting in Italian and capering all the while. The squad of dark-faced, cynical waiters clapped their hands with loud insincerity, guests everywhere joined in the applause, and Alfredo—or was it his double?—skipped off, bowing and throwing kisses.

The entire extravaganza took no more than a minute or two. He probably repeated it at least a hundred times every evening.

We tasted our *fettuccine* with understandable skepticism, then glanced at one another with grins of delighted surprise. The noodles were indescribably creamy, frothing with melted Parmesan cheese, soft yet resilient, with a flavor that surpassed any *pasta* in the world. I have requested this dish elsewhere in Rome, in many parts of Europe and America, and have even tried to make it myself on occasion, but there is something about Alfredo's noodles that defies imitation. It may be the purity of his ingredients, or the generous quantities of butter and cheese, or the dexterity and thoroughness with which he blends everything while still foaming hot. Whatever it is, the secret is his, and will probably die with him—that is, if the man doesn't actually prove to be immortal, as I suspect.

Alfredo's tricks are the most obvious tourist bait in town. His show place is the noisiest, the most garish, and the most disconcerting of settings to a man who takes his dinner seriously. But his food is superb. Our dinner that evening included these highly successful dishes: asparagus *parmigiana*; mushrooms *trifolati*; a haunch of roast kid delicately flavored with garlic and rosemary; breast of turkey sautéed in butter with a coat of golden crumbs. For our sweet, we all chose Omelette Flambée, which proved to be a disappointment. The eggs were overdone, and the hot rum tasted like hair tonic. But this was the only flaw in an otherwise satisfactory dinner.

Lunch in the lovely outdoor garden of Capriccio, in the Via Lombardia, occurred on our last day in Rome, and so we had no opportunity to return a second time. It is usually risky to praise any restaurant which you have tried only once. But that single experience was so pleasant in every way that I do not hesitate to put the name at the top of any list of recommended addresses in Rome.

Capriccio is one of those highly civilized and suavely managed establishments that would fit as smoothly into the life of Paris, London or New York as it does in the Eternal City. It has a special fondness for Yankees and proves it by printing its voluminous menu on two facing pages; one in Italian, the other in English. This is definitely not a spot for people who love to bathe in local color. There are no vagrant tenors with guitars, no ropes of onions or sausages suspended from the rafters; no one dances the tarantella, tells fortunes or waits on tables with a jeweled dagger stuck in a Roman-striped sash.

The service is as deft as any that you will encounter at Lapérouse in Paris, Antoine's in New Orleans, or Le Pavillon in New York. Nearly all the traditional Italian dishes appear on the menu, which is unusually varied for Rome, and Americans find such familiar additions as shrimp cocktail, mixed grill, boiled beef, grilled steaks, baked ham, lamb chops, bacon and eggs, and the now thoroughly European-ized hamburger.

If you enjoy serving yourself from the same tray of anti-pasto which has just been offered to Gregory Peck, Sylvana Mangano or Jean Renoir, Capriccio will oblige at almost any luncheon or dinner period. Hollywood and Broadway are as chatty and old-boyish here as ever they were in Chasen's or Sardi's at home. Looking around, you get the impression that all the guests are celebrities.

In spite of its sophisticated sheen, Capriccio's à la carte menu lists nothing that costs much more than a dollar American, except a few rare edibles like caviar, lobster or game. Exceptional was the *Cannelloni Capriccio*, lightest and daintiest of all *pasta* creations, a delicate macaroni of generous girth, stuffed with what might be minced chicken, pork, or both, in a creamy Parmesan sauce that is browned under the flame at the last moment before serving.

For an evening of splendor, no restaurant enjoys such prestige as the Hostaria dell'Orso, a remodeled 14th-century house which Dante is said to have frequented. This is perhaps the only European restaurant with a dance orchestra that I would care to recommend as a place to dine. It has one of the best chefs in Italy, and the resources of its larder are sufficient to satisfy the most fanciful whims of visiting tycoons, statesmen and titled Romans of wealth.

Its fashionable clientele and rich Renaissance décor both seem authentic to a stranger's eye. Everything is muffled in velvet or padded with silk. The music and the lighting are soft, voices are low-pitched and footfalls sink into thick carpets.

There are night clubs on floors below and above the dining room, so that one may find entertainment, if so minded, before, between and during courses. Dell'Orso is the most expensive dining in Rome but the experience is probably worth it.

There are several other eating places which deserve mention. Fagiano, with a terrace facing the magnificent Piazza Colonna, is said to be operated by the same management as Passetto. Here a waiter politely offered a tray of the smallest, pinkest clams in the world, so perfect in their dainty proportions that we promptly ordered them as a first course. They did not appear on the menu, but were entered on our bill at 1800 lire for two portions, or about a hundred lire (almost 15¢) per clam.

The best dish of spaghetti was served to us at Abruzzi, a crowded, businesslike place in the heart of the shopping district. It is difficult to explain why one particular version of spaghetti should taste better than others. This one was heaped, still steaming, in a mammoth soup plate, with a liberal topping of succulent dark red sauce and a large lump of yellow butter. The spaghetti had a nutty, hard-wheat flavor, and was cooked exactly to our taste. The grated cheese was a salt-sweet blend of Parmesan and Romano.

With what any good democratic gourmet might well consider precise justice, the former palace of the late Clara Petacci, mistress of Mussolini, has been turned into a surprisingly good restaurant, the Ristorante Palazzi. This is not exactly in Rome but is on Monte Mario, a pleasant ride of twenty minutes or so outside the city. The building itself is striking and beautiful, modern in architecture but nevertheless rather pleasantly Italian rococo in décor. The rooms are spacious, and the whole atmosphere relaxing. There are a roof garden and a swimming pool which Hollywood might well envy. This is all so terribly touristy that your first reaction would probably be that the food could not be good. You'd be wrong. It is under the knowing direction of Signor Palazzi, who also runs the excellent restaurant in the West Building at Rome's Ciampino Airport, and the food is as good as there is to be had in Rome. The wine, too, is excellent and the prices are reasonable enough to bring the evening to an extremely pleasant end.

Typical Italian cuisine owes comparatively little to the professional cooks of Rome, as far as inventiveness is concerned. Nevertheless, the few traditional Roman dishes featured at most local restaurants possess great character. One of the most appreciated is *saltimbocca alla Romana*, made of thin slices of veal and ham, flavored with sage, sautéed in butter or oil, and served either rolled up or in layers secured by a toothpick. *Saltimbocca* literally means "jump in the mouth," and this dainty morsel is supposed to be so delicious that it will do just that, if you aren't careful.

Stracciatella is a concentrated broth with a flaky content that turns out to be raw eggs, whipped and added to the liquid when boiling hot. A great springtime favorite is *abbacchio al forno*, baby lamb weighing about six pounds when dressed. It is slowly roasted in the oven, after a seasoning of garlic and herbs, and is so tender that eating it may well wound the conscience of an impressionable person. Artichokes are cheap and plentiful, and all classes enjoy the traditional *carciofa alla Romana*—very young specimens, highly seasoned and fried or cooked in oil. But best of all are those wonderful *piselli*, plain with butter, or ideally mingled with the marvelous raw ham of Italy. Of course to enjoy these angelic peas you have to be lucky, or wise, enough to be in Rome in Maytime.

PART V: *The Gourmet Abroad*

The Happy Facts about British Beer
/ Eric Newby

**Let an Englishman fill you in on the pleasant
(and astounding) folkways of British pubs-and-public**

THE other day I was sinking a pint of draught Worthington in the Saloon Bar of my favourite pub when two Americans came in, man and wife hot on the trail of local colour. It was pretty clever of them to find the place and we moved up so that they could get at the barmaid. In this pub, if you want a drink you swivel a little glass window let into the panelling and breathe your order through it. After some slight business with the window, the husband made contact and ordered pints of ale. The barmaid knows about Americans and she looked as though she'd like to talk them out of it, but in England if you order sulphuric acid and they've got it you'll get it. So they got their pints of ale.

After sipping the stuff gingerly they murmured something about having to catch a train and shot out, leaving two almost full tankards behind them. This was a pity because they were bright, freshly pressed people and some interesting conversation might have developed; also because of the waste.

"That's a funny thing to order," someone said, after ten minutes' hard thinking. "I thought they liked something a bit stronger."

This happened because they'd ordered "ale." They thought it sounded Chaucerian and robust but ale or "mild" is the sweetest, weakest stuff that comes out of barrels. Old-age pensioners who get forty shillings a week from the welfare state and can't afford pints of anything else make it their weekly ration because, as they will tell you, "We've got no bloomin' choice, mate." Mild is honest stuff and has its uses, particularly if you're going to drink and drink, but it's unfit for heroes and certainly for visitors.

The question the thirsty visitor asks himself is, "What beer can I drink with an even chance of getting to the bottom of the glass?" Let's face it. For Americans the most putting-off thing about British beer is its temperature. If you're used to drinking your beer ice-cold one of ours, drawn from the barrel at a temperature of 55–59 degrees Fahrenheit, which is the *correct* temperature for beer in this island, will seem almost oven-fresh until you get used to it.

But it is worth taking the trouble; for this business of hot and cold is not just a personal idiosyncrasy of the British. If the temperature is too low the stuff becomes hazy and the flavour is destroyed. Then no one wants to drink it. American beer is highly filtered and pasteurized, so that you can freeze it to death. We regard this with suspicion, perhaps because we have other ways of freezing to death, as anyone who has survived a visit here knows.

Beer is the drink of the nation; there are about four hundred brewers here and if you're set on coming, it's not very kind to ignore them. So the sooner you learn about beer, the better; besides you'll meet such a lot of interesting people.

Assuming that you are already in Britain, the first thing to do is *look at your watch*. If it is between ten in the morning and three in the afternoon, or five-thirty in the evening and eleven at night, *somewhere* they will be open. In the metropolitan area of London it's simple. There are nine drinking hours from half past eleven in the morning to three in the afternoon and from half past five to eleven at night. Of course, if you're staying on the premises you can go on and on.

Everywhere else there are eight hours, which are determined by the licensing justices for the area. The result is pretty crazy. Some places start at ten in the morning, shut at two, go into a retreat until six and finish up at ten at night. Others start at half-past ten or eleven in the morning and go on till half-past two. Then in summer when some of the country boys get an extra half hour, they all finish up at half-past ten on the dot. If it's one second on the wrong side, you'd better take in a Stately Home or two or see about your Ethiopian visa because the whole system dries up outside these hours.* What it boils down to is that either way you have eight or nine hours' practice ahead of you.

The next thing is to *find a place*. Almost every hamlet of more than six houses has at least one. Portsmouth, the home of the British Navy, has more than five hundred licensed premises. You may not come ashore at Portsmouth but don't despair.

Choose a cleanly looking but not necessarily modern place, pluck up your courage and go in. Once you're inside, make for the bar. If it's a little village and the pub's not bursting with people, say "Good evening" (or "Good morning"). Someone is sure to wish you the same. You're halfway to getting a drink. Now you're at the bar. Most probably it will be mahogany. On the other side of it will be a fine girl; the publican (innkeeper), who may be a poet or a gent or someone weighing twenty-two stone (a stone weighs fourteen pounds), in shirt sleeves; his wife or—if it's a house specializing in Guinness' Extra Stout—an Irishman or some biddy of the bog with a brogue as thick as the Liffey.

Whoever it is will be looking at you over some upright porcelain or ebony things like big candles. These are the handles of the beer engines that draw the beer. Somewhere under your feet, away from it all in the darkness, waiting for you at the proper temperature is the beer in thirty-six-gallon oak barrels, two hundred and eighty-eight imperial pints of it. Before the war the best oak came from Memel on the Baltic; now a lot of it comes from Persia, and some even comes from England.

Smile, and in a strong, manly voice say, "Half a best bitter, please." Just that. Not "bitter beer," or they may think you're a Russian spy. The bartender will repeat your order, take a nice clean glass holding half an imperial pint, ten fluid ounces, take a firm hold on one of the handles, give a single long pull and it will come to you full to the brim with best bitter, but not spilling over. A pint takes two pulls, but learn to walk before you can run.

If he (but he will) or she (and she might not if she's learning) doesn't fill it to the brim, bung it back and in the nicest possible way tell her to, because it is the law of the realm that draught in half pints and over must be sold in marked measures. And that means that to get your fair whack your glass must be full.

Before you raise it you'd better pay. The price may be anything from tenpence to a shilling in the Saloon Bar, where you pay a little extra for the pleasure of the company and the superior furnishings. If you're very short of dollars go into the Public Bar; nobody will think any the worse of you. In many places, especially in the country, it's far nicer.

Now you can drink your drink. If it's good stuff and well kept, you will be drinking something that is clear and cool and brilliant, of a glorious colour (I always think of eight-

Except on Sundays when they open at noon, close at two and, in the evening, open at seven and shut at ten. This is England. In Wales and Scotland they don't open at all, except for bona fide travellers. I can't bring myself to speak about this.

eenth-century furniture), not sweet or sugary but not bitter as the name might suggest: a drink for men and the sort of women who like good things but aren't nuts about gentility. I'll deal with the drink for heroes later.

There are lots of names for it: Pale Ale on draught; India Pale Ale (from the time when we had an Empire and thousands of soldiers and civil servants gasped for it); Snooxes (or whatever the name of the brewers may be) Best or Special Bitter; the permutations are almost infinite. The most important thing is, it's the "best bitter." Ordinary bitter, which comes out of another barrel, will be around 1033–1038 degrees gravity. The "best" that you're drinking, unless you've already decided to catch that train, will be about 1050 degrees, the same as American beers. It's deceptively strong because it goes down so easily, so once you get into the swing and start ordering pints, watch out.

A few years ago at a London pub in the Consulate Country around Queen's Gate, Kensington, where they sell a super-variety called Worthington "E," I got into a discussion with a couple of coal heavers, a race of men noted for their capacity for sinking pints quicker than they can be drawn from the wood. After six pints and no lunch I remembered that it was the afternoon for the garden party at my daughter's school and the hundredth anniversary of the death of Friedrich Wilhelm August Froebel, the school's founder. I felt fine until we arrived, then I began to feel peculiar. I implored my wife to let me skulk in a grove of trees on the outskirts.

"You can't do that," she answered, with complete absence of logic. "Think of the children."

I said I was trying to think of the future of all of us; that was why I wanted to hide myself. So I went to the garden party and they told me afterwards that I dived into the swimming pool with all my clothes on during the Girl Guides' demonstration of how to bridge a stream with ash staves lashed together with their neckerchiefs, and lectured the headmistress all through the play about Froebel's life (he lived for seventy years) and the girls' decadent handwriting. I know this is true because next term everyone had to buy calligraphic pens, and now my daughter has the sort of handwriting you see on old tombstones.

That is Worthington "E." Draught Bass is just as good because they both come from Burton-on-Trent, where the water contains a lot of sulphate of lime and something called carbonate of muriate of lime, which means that it is very hard water. This gives the beers brewed at Burton their dry, distinctive quality, duplicated nowhere else. In case you think six pints is overdoing it, perhaps the words of old Tom X, a drayman at a famous London brewery, will restore your perspective. A drayman's job is to deliver the barrels and lower them into the cellar under the pub.

This still life of traditional English food and drink graces the ▶ scarred table of The Golden Galleon, an inn at Cuckmere Haven, Sussex. The composition includes herring with mustard sauce, roast chicken with bread sauce, a basket of Cox's Orange apples with walnuts and mushrooms, a rib roast of beef, a brace of partridges, a hare, Brussels sprouts, Whitstable oysters, Stilton cheese, biscuits, ale and burgundy.

RHYS DORVINE

"Those were the days before 'itler come. We used to take out a drayload. There'd be three of us. At each place the guvnor give us a pint each. We took out three drays a day, five deliveries on a dray—that's fifteen pints each. The brewery allowed us three, that made it eighteen. Then there were little allotments [market gardens] the brewery give us. We'd knock off the deliveries at five and work the market gardens the brewery give us until the pubs opened, when we'd 'ave a few more. Then home to the missus around eight. That'd be about twenty-two a day, regler."

Calcium chloride and carbonate in the London water produce a softer, sweeter brew, but there are some hefty drinks made with it. The water is important. It takes between eight and eleven barrels of water to make one barrel of beer. (This includes two for washing the barrels. If you tell the average Englishman this he will say . . . "and it bloody well tastes like it," but this is because making jokes about beer is a national pastime.)

There are certain imponderables about brewing. Two London breweries belonging to the same firm are seven and a half miles apart. The water used at both places comes from the Metropolitan Water Board, yet one can produce only bitter, the other ale and stout. No one can explain why.

With everyone producing masses of good bitter it may seem a little unfair to single out the productions of any particular brewery, but at the risk of being unpopular I'm going to. They are only personal preferences.

One of the finest, of which the brewers can be proud, is Flower's, brewed at Stratford-on-Avon. Their bitter is smooth and rather dry. They used to issue a map showing the places in the London area where you could buy it, and I knew a man who used to complete the course every Saturday morning. Charrington's Best Bitter, brewed in the Mile End Road, London, is splendid stuff; Young and Company make a special Prize Ale, on draught, at the Ram Brewery at Wandsworth, south of the Thames. The Best Bitter brewed by Groves at Weymouth in Dorset is magnificent; so is Watney's Special Bitter from the Stag Brewery, Pimlico, behind Buckingham Palace. If you're adamant about beer being cold they put out a beer called Red Barrel. It comes in a stainless-steel refrigerated container along with a cylinder of carbon dioxide. When the tap is turned on the carbon dioxide displaces the beer in the container and pushes it into the glass. The whole thing is completely aseptic and the beer is brilliant. Several other brewers are now doing the same thing.

You can drink beer in Scotland but it is a much more austere business. With a few exceptions it is almost unthinkable for a man and woman to go into an ordinary pub together for a drink. The men rush into pubs, drink several whiskeys followed by chasers of beer, rush out again and, for all I know, go home and beat their wives. *This is not civilised drinking.* But the beer is good. Younger's Scotch Ale is one of the finest. It is even exported to England. To make things even more difficult, the Scots don't speak of mild and bitter. Bitter is "heavy beer." They aren't interested in mild.

One of the best places to drink heavy beer is in the downstairs bar of that splendid memorial to Edwardian plumbing, the North British Hotel, Edinburgh. The way in is by a secret-looking door, halfway down the windiest steps in the world, the Waverley Steps, leading from the station to Princes Street. I have never seen an American in this bar. The beer served here is William Younger's Heavy Gravity and the same lady has dispensed it for years. She doesn't drink it herself but she watches over it like a fanatic. It is smooth, cool and has a beautiful head on it.

"Ay, it's real guid beer," she says. "Guid heavy beer, and for why? Because I keep it well and the pipes clean. That's the secret, clean pipes."

Unfortunately, there is no mixed drinking in this particular bar. Your companions will be commercial gentlemen relaxing after another awful day before catching the night train to the south. But you can drink with ladies in a corridor outside, or in an unbelievable Babylonian lounge upstairs with waiter service, where it never tastes the same.

But you're still in England. You've had your half pint of best and you can have another, but why not try a "mild-and-bitter"? You may think I've been reviling mild, but mixed half-and-half with bitter you get the best of both worlds.

If it's winter you can have a powerful variant of mild, called Burton or "old." It has a bittersweet flavour, is strong, and you can drink it mixed with mild, in which case you ask for "old-and-mild"; or with bitter, when you order a "Burton-and-bitter," not an "old-and-bitter," but don't ask me why.

If you've tried all these combinations you should be feeling fine, so let us now pass to the bottled beers.

You'll see them behind the bar, masses of them, in gleaming bottles. All the various draught beers have their bottled equivalents, more or less carbonated. Bottled beer may be just the thing you're looking for. They're mostly far more brilliant in appearance than beer from the wood. The generic name for bottled bitter is "light ale." Just ask for "a light" or, if you know what you want, a Snooxes, or whatever the name of the brewer may be.

Some of the more powerful beers, like Bass and Worthington, throw a deposit and have to be poured as carefully as a bottle of good Burgundy, so watch out that you aren't given the sediment. You can buy a Bass with a blue triangle on the label instead of the familiar red one. There is no sediment and you can drink it iced. The same goes for Worthington. Veteran addicts of Bass and Worthington regard this development with mistrust. "Bound to lose something if there's no sediment," was the gloomy verdict of one I spoke to. Another said he thought it was something to do with television (because you can take it home easily).

Then there are the milds in bottle. I don't think I'm doing the brewers an injustice by saying that I don't think these are for you. But you may like stout. Stout is the darkest beer brewed; it is also the sweetest. Its qualities depend on the degree of roasting of the malt and the quality of the water. An exception is Guinness Extra Stout, which is drier and more bitter than any other. It really is "good for you," and like Imperial Tokay it has the property of raising the near dead, perhaps because the water for it doesn't come from the Liffey but from Kildare Springs. Purists say that the Dublin brew is best, but the Guinness people have even copied the Kildare water at their London brewery, so there's no need to worry. You can get it on draught in many pubs, especially those called Irish houses.

But there are other stouts, magnificent stouts: Whitbread's, Reid's Special, Tollemache's Double. There are stouts made with milk and, going up, very, very strong brews like Simonds' of Reading Archangel Stout and, strongest and blackest in the land, Barclay, Perkins' Imperial Russian Stout, originally brewed for Catherine the Great.

On an empty stomach you've probably had enough. Have some food and afterwards order a "strong ale" or "barley wine" in bottle. This is an extremely esoteric branch of beer drinking, of which many barmaids and some publicans are ignorant, but they will have it even though they may not know much about it. When you order "strong ale" you really are getting something Chaucerian. This is the beer for heroes. It should be served in a fine, stemmed glass. It's expensive but worth it. Here are some I can recommend: Watney's Yorkshire Stingo, named after the brewery that originated it; Barclay's Winter Brew on draught, but preferably in half pints while you're learning; Bass No. 1 Barley Wine, one of the very best; Ind, Coope and Allsopp's Arctic Ale; Simonds' XXXXX Old Berkshire; and the strongest of them all, Colne Spring Ale, brewed by Benskin's of Watford, Hertfordshire. All these beers have a long secondary fermentation in cask before being bottled.

Then there are the unbuyable beers. Until very recently something was brewed up for the Fellows of All Souls College, Oxford, that was served at dinner in very small silver goblets. "I thought it a poor quantity of drink to set before a guest," a good-living don who dined there said to me, "until I tried it. It was the most powerful drink for its size I ever remember." Some College beers are very old and are laid down like port.

There is a King's Ale in existence. A mash tun in Bass's New Brewery bears a plate recording the day in 1902 when Edward VII, that expert in the good things, pulled the levers which started a special mash of four hundred barrels of "an extra strong brew." Bottles are still in existence. The Duke of Edinburgh was handed one in 1956 when he visited Burton. An advertisement in *The Times* a few years back called for "offers over £20" for a solitary bottle.

Once you know about the different kinds of beer you won't go to a pub just to drink. There is no other way in which you can get to know the people of England so well as by visiting a pub. There are pubs where you can sing, play bowls or skittles (with great hunks of *lignum vitae*, called "cheeses"). There is even a pub in Chiswick where you can listen to the organ (Hogarth is buried appropriately in the churchyard next door), but wherever you go you will be accepted. There's no need to lash out a lot of free drinks to people you've just met. Let them offer you one first. When that happens it means you're in.

London's Best Dining / *Ian Fleming*

*A light-hearted lesson on how to get
good English food without bad English cooking*

MY FRIENDS may raise their eyebrows at finding me masquerading as an authority on what are coyly known as the "pleasures of the table," but in fact my credentials are exceptional. To begin with, I am not a card-carrying gourmet. Although I own a first edition of Brillat-Savarin's *Physiologie du Goût*, I opened it only once to read the curious passage relating to aphrodisiacs. Secondly, I will eat or drink almost anything so long as it tastes good. Finally, and most important, I have never received a free mouthful of food or drink from any restaurant in the world. I don't even know the names of too many headwaiters in London.

But I do know the name of the headwaiter on the first floor at Scott's. It is Baker, and I know it because he did his best to have me arrested as a German spy during the war. I was in Naval Intelligence, and a fellow officer from the Submarine Service and I were trying to get the captured captain and navigator from a U-boat drunk at Scott's so as to worm out of them how they avoided our mine fields in the Skagerrak. They had been "allowed out" of their prison camp for a day's "sightseeing" in London, and we were playing the rather clumsy role of brother officers talking chummily about the sea with other brother officers whom we were only fighting because of the politicians.

Baker, then a waiter, became suspicious of our extraordinary conduct and soon we were encircled by harmless-looking couples picking at bits of fish.

It was only when we got back to the Admiralty, befuddled and no wiser about the Skagerrak, that a furious Director of Naval Intelligence told us that the only result of our secret mission had been to mobilise half the narks of the Special Branch of Scotland Yard. But that is the only reason I happen to know Baker's name.

I think good English food is the best in the world. The food I like eating in London and which I regard as unsurpassed is: Colchester and Whitstable oysters; all English fish, particularly Dover soles; Scottish smoked salmon; potted shrimps; lamb cutlets; roast beef; York ham; nearly all the English vegetables, particularly asparagus and peas; English savouries and most English fruits.

The problem in England is how to eat good English food without bad English cooking. Just as I think all Americans cook fried eggs and bacon well, so, in England, I think the best lowest-common-denominator dish is fish-and-chips, and I strongly recommend the adventurous-minded American tourist travelling round Britain to eat his lunch in a fish-and-chips shop rather than in a hotel or a restaurant. If he is dismayed by the slatternly interiors of these places, he can always take his meal out in a paper bag and eat it in the woods or the fields or parks.

Try a London meal, starting with smoked salmon or potted ▶ shrimp; then have turbot or plaice or English sole with fresh vegetables, followed by a savoury such as angels on horseback (oysters wrapped in bacon on toast) or a Scotch woodcock (a dab of scrambled eggs criss-crossed with anchovies). All this and more—plus fine Greek food—is served at the White Tower in Soho.

SLIM AARONS

One other practical hint for the tourist: it is extremely difficult to get a good Martini anywhere in England. In London restaurants and hotels the way to get one is to ask for a double dry Martini made with vodka. The way I get one to suit me in any pub is to walk calmly and confidently up to the bar and, speaking very distinctly, ask the man or girl behind it to put plenty of ice in the shaker (they nearly all have a shaker), pour in six gins and one dry vermouth (enunciate "dry" carefully) and shake until I tell them to stop.

You then point to a suitably large glass and ask them to pour the mixture in. Your behaviour will create a certain amount of astonishment, not unmixed with fear, but you will have achieved a very large and fairly good Martini, and it will cost you about $1.25.

To return to food. I see that Congressman James Tumulty, of New Jersey, on his return home to the U.S., described England as "the only country where it takes ten men in formal clothes to serve you melted mud."

To this I will only quote that even more famous American citizen, Miss Gypsy Rose Lee: "In Europe you have a different taste sensation every ten miles. In America you can travel six thousand miles and you get the same taste every mile. . . ."

But I know what Mr. Tumulty means. He probably tried having luncheon in railway hotels at 12:30. I cannot identify the melted mud. It may have been chocolate mousse or cottage pie. I would have substituted boiled boots.

In fact, I repeat that *good* English food is the best in the world and that you can eat a good meal of it, including a glass of lager beer or wine, coffee and tip (10 to 15 per cent, according to your mood), for something under $3.00.

You should start with smoked salmon, potted shrimps, or *pâté maison*, and then have English sole, turbot, plaice, lobster or crab, with fresh vegetables, followed by cheese or a savoury such as angels on horseback (oysters wrapped in bacon on toast); herring roes on toast; or a Scotch woodcock (a small amount of scrambled eggs crisscrossed with anchovies). Instead of the fish, double lamb cutlets, roast beef or saddle of lamb is nearly always on the menu and, in the best restaurants, except in the case of lamb, these items rarely have been frozen.

Steaks can be had, of course, but in England they are not a usual cut of meat.

Drinking coffee or tea *with* your meal is unheard of in English restaurants, and anyway the coffee is wishy-washy except in the espresso bars. You probably won't care very much for the beer either, but the lagers (English, German and Dutch) are quite like American beer and are frequently served iced(!). Most restaurants have good wines *en carafe*. Wines in bottles and champagnes are first-class but often farcically expensive. Stout, notably Guinness, is an excellent drink with oysters and fish. Even better is Black Velvet, which is half-and-half stout and champagne in a tankard.

If, poor beast, you hope to see "interesting people" during mealtime, you may not be in luck. There are no "coterie" restaurants in London any more, in the sense that the old Café Royal in Regent Street used to be the haunt of artists and writers; after-the-theatre supper at the Savoy Grill is probably your best bet.

Here are my favourite London restaurants, *in alphabetical order:*

> *L'Etoile* (French)
> *The Ivy* (French)
> *Overton's* (Sea food—opposite Victoria Station)
> *Overton's* (St. James's Street)
> *Pimm's* (several of them in the City)
> *Quo Vadis* (Italian)
> *Ritz Grill*
> *Savoy Grill*
> *Scott's* (Sea food)
> *Wheelers* (Sea food—Old Compton Street)
> *Wheelers* (Duke of York Street)
> *Wilton's* (Sea food)

Addresses are in the telephone book, and you'd better book a table.

There are countless other restaurants and hotels where you can eat first-class English, French, Italian or Hungarian cooking. A reliable selection is in *The Good Food Guide* by Raymond Postgate, which you can buy at any London bookstore.

That is about all I have to say about English food. If one eats badly in England—or in any other country, for the matter of that—it is generally one's own fault.

OTHER GOOD LONDON RESTAURANTS

Bentley's, 11 Swallow Street, W.1. Sea food; oyster and shellfish bar; closed 11 p.m. and Sunday. De luxe hotel overlooking Hyde Park.

L'Ecu De France, 111 Jermyn Street, S.W.1. Haute cuisine. Reserve your table. Closed midnight and Sunday.

Majorca, 66 Brewer Street, W.1. Good Spanish specialties, fine Spanish wine. Closed 11 p.m. and Sunday.

Rules, 35 Maiden Lane, W.C.2. Fine food, Edwardian atmosphere. Closed midnight and Sunday.

Trocadero, Piccadilly Circus, W.1. Large, cosmopolitan, probably London's most extensive menu; fine cellar. Closed 11 p.m.

[See also pp. 251–52.]

PART V: The Gourmet Abroad

Specialties of Some Fine European Restaurants

FRANCE

You go to Paris to see the Arc de Triomphe and St. Germain des Prés, but it's just as important that you eat at Grand Vefour, Lapérouse, or the Tour d'Argent. A trip to Copenhagen certainly isn't complete without a visit to the Tivoli Gardens; but it is equally unfinished until you have dined at Oskar Davidsen's or Wivex. A nation's cuisine is as good a clue to national character as you can get. From Scandinavian smörgåsbord to Provençale bouillabaisse the dish reflects the people who made it.

Modern cooking is a French invention—and French cooking is the best in the world. Here are ten recipes from four of France's finest restaurants.

Raymond Oliver of the Grand Vefour, in Paris, originated and serves the dishes made from the next two recipes.

BALLOTINE OF CHICKEN, DUC DE CHARTRE

3-pound chicken, cut in
    serving pieces
Salt and pepper
1 teaspoon chopped thyme
¼ cup plus 1 tablespoon
    cognac
¾ cup port wine
1 cup new peas
4 or 5 lettuce leaves

2 or 3 tender carrots, scraped
    and chopped
Sprig each parsley and thyme
1 tablespoon chopped chives
1 tablespoon butter
Pâté de foie gras
2 cups chicken stock
½ cup water
2 truffles, chopped

5 or 6 thin slices lean bacon
½ cup Sauternes wine
½ cup consommé
2 tablespoons heavy cream

2 tablespoons butter
A few grains cayenne
Slices French bread

Bone the chicken, but preserve the shape of each piece and reserve the bones. Season meat lightly with salt, pepper and thyme. Place in a bowl; pour about ¼ cup cognac and ¾ cup port wine over the chicken and let marinate while making stuffing and sauce.

Place the chicken bones in a saucepan with the vegetables, herbs, butter, 1 tablespoon pâté, the chicken stock and water. Cover and cook gently for about 1 hour; then press through a fine sieve. Drain the marinated chicken and chop about ⅓ of it very fine. Combine this with enough foie gras and the chopped truffles to make a stuffing for the remaining pieces of chicken. Stuff the legs and other pieces. Wrap each around and lengthwise with lean bacon. Fasten the bacon with wooden picks.

Brown the bacon-wrapped chicken in a frying pan, turning the pieces carefully to let both sides brown. Pour the bone-vegetable purée around and over these ballotines. Cook rapidly over high heat for a few minutes. Then baste with the mixture of Sauternes and consommé. Continue to cook, 20 minutes in all after ballotines are browned. Remove ballotines and keep them hot.

Pass pan sauce through a fine sieve; reheat; add cream and butter; stir; add 1 tablespoon cognac and a little cayenne. Keep the sauce hot but do not let it boil.

Sauté slices of French bread in the pan in which the ballotines browned. Serve ballotines on these croutons; cover with hot sauce; garnish with hot potato balls and artichoke bottoms. Makes 4 to 6 servings.

SHRIMP LOAF

Butter
Olive oil
2 shallots, peeled and
    chopped
1 onion, peeled and
    chopped
1 carrot, scraped and finely
    diced
⅔ pound raw shrimp
1 tablespoon tomato paste
1 cup dry white wine

⅓ cup water
Bouquet garni (parsley, bay
    leaf, sprig tarragon)
Salt and pepper
Short, thick loaf French
    bread
¼ cup heavy cream
2 teaspoons cornstarch
2 tablespoons finely grated
    Gruyère cheese

Combine in a saucepan or casserole 1 tablespoon each butter and oil; heat and add the shallots, onion, carrot and the coarsely chopped heads and tail-ends of the shrimp. Stir and let braise for 3 minutes. Stir in tomato paste; mix and stir in about ¾ cup of the wine and the water. Add herbs and a light seasoning of salt and pepper. Cover and cook over moderate heat for 20 minutes. Then press through a fine sieve and reheat over very low heat. Hold until loaf is ready for sauce.

Sauté the shrimp in 2 tablespoons butter for about 2 minutes. Splash them with the remaining 4 tablespoons of wine. Remove from the heat. Cut thick top slice from the loaf of bread; cut out center of loaf leaving a wall about ⅓ inch thick all around. Pass the knife blade through the soft center bread, once lengthwise and then crosswise 2 or 3 times; smooth the inside bottom of the loaf by scraping gently. Brown the soft center bread lightly on all sides in a little hot butter or oil. Return it to the hollowed loaf.

Start oven at hot (475° F.). Pour the cooked shrimp into the loaf. Stir the cream into the waiting herb-and-wine sauce; add about 6 tablespoons butter whipped with the cornstarch; stir and heat almost to a boil. Pour at once over the shrimp in the loaf. Sprinkle with the cheese. Place loaf on a baking sheet and heat in the oven until the crust and top are golden. Serve very hot. Makes 4 servings.

The next two recipes are for game as served in the Restaurant Drouant in Paris.

JUGGED HARE À LA FRANÇAISE

1 hare
¼ cup cognac
Olive oil
Salt and pepper
1 onion, peeled and thinly
    sliced
Good red wine
½ pound butter
½ pound lean bacon cut in
    large dice

20 very small onions, peeled
2 tablespoons flour
Large herb bouquet (thyme,
    bay leaf, sage, basil
    and 2 peeled garlic
    buds)
20 cooked or canned
    mushrooms
Heart-shaped croutons fried
    in butter

◀ Maxim's. A smiling page boy burdened with the accouterments of the frivolous is the symbol for the great Paris restaurant. He is shown in the back room, favorite of the nobility, the rich and the very fashionable.

ARNOLD NEWMAN

If you can get huntsman-fresh hare, skin and clean it at home taking care to collect all the blood available. Put the blood and liver aside. Fresh-frozen hare, skinned, boned and cleaned has recently become available and can of course be substituted.

Cut up hare; put pieces in a bowl with cognac, oil, a little salt and pepper and the onion; add red wine to cover. Cover bowl and let stand in a cold place for several hours. Heat the butter; cook bacon in it; drain the bacon as soon as it browns. Save bacon. Cook small onions in butter-and-bacon-fat mixture; sprinkle with flour; stir and cook until lightly browned. Drain hare; put pieces in with the hot onions and fat; brown well. Moisten hare with some of the wine marinade; add herb bouquet; cover pan and let cook gently over low to moderate heat for 40 to 45 minutes. Add mushrooms; stir until hot; then remove hare to a warmed deep serving dish or terrine. Spoon mushrooms and reserved bacon and onions around hare. Stir liver and reserved blood into cooking pan; mix; cook for 2 or 3 minutes; then strain this hot gravy over the hare and vegetables. Serve garnished with freshly made croutons. Makes 4 to 6 servings.

TERRINE OF PARTRIDGE, LUCULLUS

3 partridges, cleaned and
    ready for cooking
1½ teaspoons salt
1 teaspoon mixed nutmeg,
    cinnamon and ginger
¼ cup cognac
1 glass dry Madeira

1 bay leaf
1 small onion, peeled and
    sliced
1 tender carrot, scraped
    and grated
½ teaspoon dried thyme
2 sprigs parsley

STUFFING

Remaining meat of birds
¾ pound lean pork,
    chopped
½ pound fresh fat pork
½ teaspoon salt

1 teaspoon mixed nutmeg,
    pepper, ginger
1 beaten egg
1 pound pâté de foie gras
4 truffles, chopped
1 bay leaf

Cut breast meat from partridges in generous slices. Combine remaining ingredients and pour over sliced meat. Cover and let stand in cold place for 3 or 4 hours.

Prepare the stuffing by combining the remaining partridge meat with the lean pork and one half of the fat pork. Run all together through the food chopper. Place in a bowl with salt, spices and egg. Add the marinade drained from the sliced breast meat. Mix well together. Line a terrine or game casserole with pâté de foie gras, around the sides and on the inside bottom. Pack in a third of the stuffing; cover with a third of the sliced breast meat; add another layer of stuffing and repeat with sliced breast meat; press down evenly and gently with wide wooden spatula or paddle; add final third of the stuffing; cover with truffles and sliced breast meat. Place bay leaf on top. Cover with remaining pork fat; place cover on dish; seal it with a strip of bread dough if possible. Set dish in shallow pan of warm water. Start oven at hot (425° F.). Bake 20 minutes per pound, or for about 1½ hours. When terrine is done, fat on top is clear. Remove from oven, take dish cover off, replace it with plate with a weight on it which will press the terrine mixture and pack it down. Let cool. Clean outside of dish, cover top of terrine mixture with aspic made with the partridge bones. Let aspic set; chill terrine again. Serve in the dish, cutting slices deeply with a thin knife. Makes 10 servings.

Two typically French ways of stuffing good food as prepared by Paris's La Régence.

BONED CHICKEN LEGS, ALBUFERA

2 thighs-and-legs from an uncooked chicken
4 tablespoons finely chopped uncooked chicken
4 tablespoons cooked rice
Salt and pepper
2 cups well-seasoned chicken bouillon
1½ cups hot cooked rice
1 tablespoon pâté de foie gras
2 tablespoons chopped truffles
1 cup Albufera Sauce
Sliced sautéed mushrooms for garnish

Bone the chicken thighs-and-legs. Mix the chopped chicken, 4 tablespoons cooked rice, salt and pepper, and stuff the legs. Sew opening or fasten tightly with small skewers. Poach the stuffed legs in chicken bouillon for about 30 minutes, or until the chicken is cooked. Combine the 1½ cups hot cooked rice, foie gras and truffles; arrange in a 1-quart mold; place the drained cooked chicken legs on the rice (remove thread or skewers); cover with hot Albufera Sauce and garnish with mushrooms. Makes 2 servings.

ALBUFERA SAUCE

1½ cups strained poultry stock
¼ cup mushroom cooking liquor
1 cup cream sauce made with poultry stock
¾ cup heavy cream
1 tablespoon butter
2 tablespoons pale meat glaze

Combine poultry stock and mushroom cooking liquor in a saucepan. Cook until reduced by a third. Add cream sauce, stirring smoothly. Cook and reduce, stirring with a wooden spoon or spatula. When thickened, stir in ½ cup cream a little at a time. Add remaining ¼ cup cream, a little at a time, stirring continually; add the butter in bits; then add 1 tablespoon meat glaze which has been melted over hot water. Stir steadily. If more intense flavor is wanted, add remaining meat glaze, stirring in well. Makes about 2 cups sauce. Use with poultry and sweetbread dishes.

STUFFED SOLE, PALAIS ROYAL

1-pound sole
2 tablespoons butter
2 shallots, peeled and finely diced
2 teaspoons mixed chopped chives, parsley and basil
½ cup soft bread crumbs
1 beaten egg yolk
1 teaspoon salt
½ teaspoon pepper
1 tablespoon finely chopped peeled onion
1 teaspoon each finely chopped parsley, basil and thyme
½ cup fish stock
1 tablespoon meat glaze

Clean the sole, partially separate the fillets from the bones on the upper side of the fish. Remove as many bones as possible. Mix stuffing of shallots, 2 teaspoons mixed herbs, crumbs, egg yolk and seasoning. Spread stuffing on sole under the fillets. Place fish on a well-buttered baking platter on which is the combined chopped onion and herbs. Add any remaining stuffing over and around the fish. Mix fish stock and the glaze. Pour evenly over fish. Start oven at moderate (350° F.). Cook fish for 18 to 20 minutes. Then place

platter under moderate broiler heat for a few minutes to glaze. Serve very hot. Makes 2 servings.

Two non-Parisian, but marvelously French, recipes from Mme Bertier's Moulin des Ruats, Avalon, Yonne.

CHICKEN DES RUATS

2½-pound chicken, cleaned and ready for cooking
Butter
Salt and pepper
1 cup dry white wine or consommé
1 cup heavy cream
1 beaten egg yolk
2 tablespoons port wine
2 or 3 cups hot cooked rice
2 tablespoons butter

Cut chicken in quarters. Brown lightly in butter over low heat. Add a light seasoning of salt and pepper. Continue cooking, basting frequently with the wine or consommé until the chicken is done, about 45 minutes total cooking time. Place on a heated serving platter. Stir into the sauce in the pan the cream, egg yolk and port; mix well and heat just to the boiling point. Do not boil. Pour this sauce over the chicken and serve at once, with hot rice into which the 2 tablespoons of butter have been stirred. Makes 4 servings.

SNAILS BOURGUIGNONNE, MAISON

40 snails
1 quart cold water
2 cups wine vinegar
1 tablespoon salt

Wash the snails; remove protective membranes at the opening; wash thoroughly again and drain. Repeat washing several times. Cover with a mixture of 1 quart cold water, the vinegar and salt.

Let stand for 2 hours. Drain; rinse snails in cold water; then drop into 2 quarts rapidly boiling water. Let stand for 6 minutes, drain. Remove snails from shells; take the black tips off their tails. Replace snails in their shells. Cook in enough court bouillon to cover with one inch of liquid above the top of the snails. Simmer over low heat for 3 hours. Let snails cool in the cooking liquid.

COURT BOUILLON FOR SNAILS

1 quart white wine
1 quart water
½ cup chopped scraped carrots
½ cup chopped peeled onions
6 chopped peeled shallots
Herb bouquet (parsley, savory, thyme)
1¾ teaspoons salt

Combine all ingredients. Makes about 2 quarts court bouillon.

BOURGUIGNONNE BUTTER SAUCE

1½ quarts Burgundy
5 shallots, peeled and minced
4 sprigs parsley
½ bay leaf
1 sprig thyme
1 tablespoon finely chopped mushrooms
2¾ tablespoons butter whipped with
1 tablespoon flour
10 tablespoons butter
½ teaspoon cayenne
¾ cup dry bread crumbs

Combine wine, shallots, herbs and mushrooms in a saucepan. Heat to boiling and cook until reduced by a half. Strain mixture through a fine sieve. Thicken it with the whipped butter and flour. Stir and boil for 3 minutes; add the 10 tablespoons of butter and the cayenne. Let cool.

When the butter sauce is ready, remove the cooled snails from their cooking liquid and take them from their shells. Fill bottom end of each shell with some of the butter sauce. Return the snails to their shells; close shells with some of the butter mixture. Press well into the shell. Lay snails in 4 shallow baking dishes. Add about 3 tablespoons water to each dish. Sprinkle snails with remaining butter mixture and dry bread crumbs. Place in hot oven (425° F.) for about 8 minutes, or until the snails are very hot and the crumbs lightly browned. Serve at once. Makes 4 servings.

DENMARK

Denmark, almost completely an island country, naturally turns to the sea for the basic elements of its cuisine. Its smörgåsbord (or smorrebrod) is world famous—as is its herring. But the Danes are inventive people and their culinary experimentation has not stopped with seafood. Here are two herring recipes and two uniquely Scandinavian soups which might grace the menu of any fine Copenhagen restaurant.

Two recipes for pickled herring, both from Copenhagen

PICKLED HERRING

3 salt herrings	½ teaspoon pepper
1½ cups vinegar	½ cup each sliced or cubed
1½ cups water	raw carrots, turnips,
½ cup sugar	onions, celery
1 teaspoon crushed allspice	¼ cup chopped leeks
½ teaspoon salt	¼ cup chopped fresh dill

Clean the herrings; cover with cold water and let stand overnight. Combine vinegar, water, sugar, spice and about ½ teaspoon each salt and pepper; heat and stir until sugar melts. Let cool; then pour over the vegetables and dill. Drain the soaked fish. Split, skin, and remove bones. Lay the fillets in a deep dish and cover with the vegetable mixture. Cover dish and let stand in refrigerator for about 1 week. Makes 18 to 24 small servings for the smorrebrod table.

PICKLED HERRING (2)

8 large salt herrings	6 small pieces green ginger
5 medium-sized onions	root
1 large piece fresh horse-	8 to 10 bay leaves
radish	1½ cups vinegar
1 carrot, scraped and grated	1⅜ cups sugar
3 tablespoons whole allspice	2 cups water
2 tablespoons mustard seed	

Wash herrings; scrape well; cut off heads, tails and fins. Wash and drain again; repeat until water runs clear. Cut across each fish making 1-inch slices. In a glass jar or dish, place in layers alternately with the peeled, sliced onions, grated horseradish, carrot, spices and bay leaves.

Heat vinegar, sugar and water together just to boiling. Let cool and pour over fish and pickle mixture. Press the fish down in the marinade with a plate and put a weight on it. Let stand in refrigerator for 5 days. Serve from glass jar. Makes 40 to 50 smorrebrod servings.

CAULIFLOWER SOUP

1 medium-sized head	3 egg yolks
cauliflower	1 tablespoon cold water
Boiling water	Pepper
Salt	3 tablespoons grated
6 tablespoons butter	Gruyère cheese
4 tablespoons flour	Buttered rye bread
2½ quarts bouillon	

Wash cauliflower; cut off stem; remove and discard any large leaves. Cover cauliflower with salted boiling water (1 tablespoon salt to each quart water) and boil gently for 30 minutes or until tender but not too soft. Drain cauliflower and reserve 1 cup of the cooking water. Separate cauliflower into flowerettes and place in a warmed soup tureen.

Stir the butter and flour smoothly together in a 3-quart kettle; stir bouillon and cauliflower cooking water into the kettle; heat, stirring, until boiling. Boil for 3 minutes. Beat egg yolks lightly with 1 tablespoon water; then mix with about ¼ cup hot stock; stir into the kettle. Stir continuously until boiling. Add pepper and cheese; pour soup over the cauliflower in the tureen. Makes 6 servings. Serve with buttered rye bread.

APPLE SOUP

1½ pounds tart apples	¼ cup white wine
2½ quarts water	1 or 2 tablespoons sugar
1 stick cinnamon	¼ cup heavy cream,
½ lemon peel	whipped
5 tablespoons cornstarch	

Wash apples, core, cut in quarters. Cover with 1½ quarts cold water in saucepan, add cinnamon and lemon peel. Bring to a boil; lower heat and cook slowly for 20 minutes or until apples are soft. Rub through a coarse sieve. Add remaining quart of cold water to this thin purée. Heat slowly. Mix cornstarch with a little of the soup; then stir it into the boiling mixture. Stir and let boil for 5 minutes. Remove from heat; add wine and sugar to sweeten to taste. Chill. Serve in chilled soup bowls, with a dab of whipped cream. Makes 6 servings. Cookies are usually served with this fruit soup.

ITALY

Two of the most important ingredients of Italian food, after olive oil, are pasta (of course) and veal. Passetto's in Rome has been a favorite of Americans—and of Europeans as well—for many years. Here are three of their chef's recipes. In them you will find all the important Italian ingredients.

LASAGNE VERDI PASTICCIATE
or
GREEN LASAGNE PIE

2½ cups flour, sifted
2 eggs
½ pound spinach, cooked
   and passed through
   fine sieve

1½ cups Bolognese Sauce
   (meat and tomato)
1¼ cups Béchamel Sauce
   (butter, flour and
   milk)
½ pound mozzarella cheese

Combine sifted flour, slightly beaten eggs and spinach purée into a dough. Roll out in a thin layer. Select a square casserole large enough to serve four. Cut the dough into squares the size of the dish. Cook one at a time in gently boiling salted water for about two minutes. Drain and let cool. Start oven at moderate (350° F.).

Grease the casserole well with buttter; then place in it a layer of lasagne, a layer of Bolognese Sauce, a layer of Béchamel Sauce, and a layer of cheese cut in thin slices. Repeat the layers until all ingredients are used. Place the filled dish in a moderate oven for about 25 minutes. Recipe serves 4 people.

SPEZZATO D'AGNELLO ALLA ROMANA
or
LAMB STEW ROMAN STYLE

1½ pounds lamb
2 tablespoons olive oil
1 onion, finely chopped
1 large clove garlic, minced

1 teaspoon dried rosemary
Salt and pepper
⅓ cup dry white wine
2 tomatoes, peeled

Combine lamb, oil, onion, garlic, rosemary, and salt and pepper to taste. Brown over low heat for about 5 minutes; then add the wine. Raise heat to high and continue cooking for 5 minutes longer. Add the tomatoes, coarsely diced, and turn heat to low. Cover the pan and allow to simmer for about 30 minutes; serves 4 people.

SCALOPPINE DI VITELLO ALLA PASSETTO
or
PASSETTO'S VEAL SCALOPPINE

1 pound veal from leg
Prosciutto, thinly sliced
Sage
Flour

3 tablespoons olive oil
⅓ cup grated Romano
   cheese
4 tablespoons butter

Cut the veal into thin, round slices. They should be 2½ inches in diameter and ⅛ inch thick. On each piece of veal place a slice of prosciutto cut to fit the veal and sprinkle it with a pinch of powdered sage. Roll each piece of veal, dip it in flour and press firmly to hold shape. Brown the veal rolls in the olive oil until they are half cooked. Heat oven to moderate. Then butter a casserole. Put into it the veal rolls, the grated cheese and the remaining butter, in dabs. Place the casserole in the oven for 10 minutes or until hot. Makes 4 servings.

ENGLAND

National cuisine is often as distinctive as national language, and the true gourmet, set down in any part of the world, should be able to locate himself precisely with no other clue than a well-cooked dinner of local specialties. The one place where our blindfolded gourmet might be fooled—is England. The British are famous for their racks and their roasts; but infamous for much of the rest of their cooking. In self-defense their fine hotels and restaurants import their kitchen talent from across the channel; so, if our unsuspecting hero were to take his test. in London, he might miss the mark. In any event, here are five recipes from the land of beef and Yorkshire pudding. The first is traditional—and the others British with a touch of French accent.

Simpson's in the Strand, London's famous shopping street, is known for classic English favorites such as

STEAK AND KIDNEY PUDDING

2 pounds round steak
¾ pound veal kidney
½ pound mushrooms,
   peeled and chopped
1 onion, peeled and
   chopped
2 teaspoons salt

½ teaspoon pepper
3 tablespoons flour
Pastry for a 2-crust pie
   (made with chopped
   suet as shortening)
8 shucked oysters, drained
Hot water or bouillon

Cut steak into thin slices about 3 inches long. Wash kidney thoroughly, cut away fat, slice kidney thinly. Combine beef, kidney, mushrooms and onion. Sprinkle with salt, pepper and flour, mix to coat all ingredients evenly with flour.

Make pie pastry using suet as shortening. Roll out about ⅔ of the pastry in a round piece about ½ inch thick. Line a 2-quart pudding bowl with the pastry, smoothly and evenly. Fill with meat mixture. Add oysters and enough hot water or bouillon to cover. Roll out remaining ⅓ of the pastry; cover bowl, pressing tightly to edge of bottom pastry around the rim of the bowl. Wring a large square of clean muslin out of very hot water, rub flour into it evenly. Place filled bowl in center of cloth, bring up ends and tie securely. Place bowl on rack in a 3-quart kettle, fill with boiling water ⅔ of the way up the sides of the bowl. Boil rapidly for 3½ hours. Replenish kettle with boiling water from time to time as needed. Unwrap bowl; serve hot pudding at once. Or (for American taste) place bowl in a hot (450° F.) oven about 10 minutes to brown pastry top before serving. Makes 6 servings.

Some of the best fish, and other food too, in England, is found, like the dishes made from the next two recipes, at Scott's in London.

Alexandre Dumaine believes that harmony of the inner man is ▶ as important as harmonious décor in the salon. He is chef-owner of the famous Hotel de la Côte D'Or at Saulieu, 184 miles south of Paris on Route Nationale No. 6. Many consider this the finest restaurant in France, a country rich in superb eating places, and it has won the Guide Michelin three-star award since this "worth a special trip" rating was established. Dumaine, a veteran of 45 years' experience, trains his future chefs personally and buys provisions in quantities to serve only a hundred guests daily.

ARNOLD NEWMAN

FILLETS OF SOLE À LA SCOTT'S

1 tablespoon butter	4 large cleaned shrimp,
1 teaspoon chopped shallot	sautéed 3 minutes in
8 large fillets Dover sole	butter
1 cup (approximately) fish	4 hot sautéed button
stock	mushrooms
¼ cup white wine	2 cups White Wine Sauce
1½ cups hot mashed	1½ tablespoons finely
potatoes	chopped cooked
4 large oysters, sautéed 3	prawns or shrimp
minutes in butter	

Start oven at moderate (350° F.). Butter a shallow (metal-based) casserole; sprinkle chopped shallots in bottom; lay fillets on shallots. Barely cover fillets with combined fish stock and white wine. Cover dish; place over moderate heat on top of the range and bring to a boil. Then place casserole in oven and let cook for 10 minutes or until fish is tender.

Pipe a decorative border of hot mashed potatoes around a heated oven-ware serving platter. Remove fish from oven and arrange them on the platter. Add garnish of oysters, shrimp and mushrooms. Quickly reduce stock in casserole to about ⅓ of the original amount. Add this reduced stock with chopped shrimp to the White Wine Sauce. Pour over fish on platter. Place under moderate broiler heat until potatoes are lightly browned. Serve at once. Makes 4 servings.

WHITE WINE SAUCE

2 tablespoons butter	2 egg yolks
1 tablespoon flour	½ teaspoon salt
1 cup strained white-wine	¼ teaspoon pepper
court bouillon	½ teaspoon lemon juice

Melt 1 tablespoon butter in a saucepan; stir flour in until golden. Gradually add bouillon, stirring. Let cook gently for 5 minutes, stirring occasionally. Remove from heat; add egg yolks, 1 at a time, stirring well. Add seasoning and return to heat; stir and let cook for 1 or 2 minutes. Just before it reaches the boiling point, add the remaining tablespoon of butter and the lemon juice. Stir and remove from heat. Makes about 1½ cups sauce.

SUPREME OF CHICKEN PRINCESSE

2 chicken breasts	½ drained canned pimiento
Salt	cut in 8 narrow strips
Pepper	4 slices truffle
Flour	Hot potatoes Parisienne to
1 egg beaten with	serve 4
1 tablespoon water	¼ cup hot Jus Lié
½ cup dry bread crumbs	3 tablespoons hot melted
2 tablespoons oil	butter
1 pound hot cooked fresh or	1½ tablespoons finely
canned asparagus tips	chopped parsley

Remove the skin from the chicken breasts and cut the four thick fillets off the bones. Season with salt and pepper; roll in flour, in egg beaten with water and then in crumbs. Sauté gently in hot oil, cooking until golden on all sides, or for about 20 minutes, and chicken is done.

Place cooked fillets on a warm serving platter; garnish each with 4 short asparagus tips and decorate the asparagus with criss-crossed pimiento strips and slice of truffle. Arrange around dish the hot potatoes. Pour a thin line of hot Jus Lié around all, and pour the hot melted butter over all. Add a sprinkle of parsley and serve immediately. Makes 4 servings.

JUS LIÉ

1 cup poultry stock	1 tablespoon cornstarch

Heat stock to boiling. Mix cornstarch with 3 tablespoons of the hot stock; then stir into the boiling stock. Stir briskly for about 3 minutes until thickened. Makes 1 cup gravy.

The current master chef of the Savoy Grill, Abel Alban, serves this dish.

COLD LOBSTER MOUSSE

2-pound live lobster	⅔ cup heavy cream, lightly
1 quart court bouillon	whipped (for each
2 tablespoons cognac	pound cooked lobster
Salt, celery salt, paprika	meat)
Cracked ice	2 or 3 truffles

Boil the lobster in court bouillon for about 20 minutes. Let cool in the bouillon. Drain lobster and reserve bouillon. Split lobster, remove meat from shell and weigh meat. Leave claws whole, but crack them. Pound lobster shell very fine and add to the reserved bouillon. Reheat bouillon and boil gently to reduce to about one half the original amount. Strain bouillon through a fine sieve; reheat; add cognac, and remove from heat.

Pound lobster meat very fine, adding little by little enough of the bouillon to make a very thick creamy mixture. Add about ¼ teaspoon each salt, paprika and celery salt. Rub mixture through a fine sieve into a bowl or mold. Set bowl or mold in a pan of cracked ice. Use whisk and work whipped cream into lobster mixture, beating well until thoroughly chilled. Place bowl or mold in refrigerator; cover lightly with waxed paper, and leave for 3 hours or longer to set. To serve, decorate top with lobster claws and truffle slices. Makes 4 or 5 servings.

PART V: The Gourmet Abroad

Europe's Fine Restaurants

As it does in the United States, *Holiday* each year selects the fine restaurants in Europe. You will find not only the great eating places of Europe's cities, but also many lesser-known ones in small towns and rural areas. In making our choices we have had the co-operation of the Grand Sénéchal in America of the Confrérie des Chevaliers du Tastevin, one of the oldest and most respected of all the world's societies dedicated to the knowledge and enjoyment of fine foods and wines. We wish there could be more of the "little wonder" restaurants, the kind that serve excellent food at modest prices, which knowing visitors hoard as personal discoveries—but too often they are so small that any increase in their patronage would crowd them severely, or they lack the facilities for service of the larger, more expensive places.

—The Editors

AUSTRIA

Vienna

St. Stephan . . . A view of Vienna's cathedral from the windows of one of the city's best.

Sacher's Hotel Restaurant . . . Traditional Viennese cuisine in a famous but slightly old-fashioned hotel.

Three Hussars . . . Vienna's most elegant restaurant; candlelight and music.

Salzburg

Goldener Hirsch . . . Intimate hotel dining room that draws celebrities.

BELGIUM

Brussels

The Carlton . . . Handsome décor indoors and a garden for summer dining; one of Belgium's great.

Filet de Boeuf et Ambassadeurs . . . A favorite of Belgian gourmets.

La Couronne . . . Rathskeller décor and old-fashioned grilled foods; on historic Grand' Place.

L'Épaule de Mouton (Chantraine) . . . Reservation necessary in this seven-table gastronomic heaven.

DENMARK

Copenhagen

Coq d'Or . . . Famous for Danish hors d'oeuvres and French cuisine.

Divan I . . . Top dining spot in Copenhagen's renowned Tivoli Gardens.

7 Nationer . . . International cuisine in seven different national rooms.

Wivex . . . Hearty Danish food in one of Europe's largest restaurants.

ENGLAND

London

Angus Steak Houses (Kingly St., Blandford St. & Kensington High) . . . English soups, Scottish steaks and chops in friendly, oak-paneled rooms.

Caprice . . . Good value for those wishing to rub elbows with entertainment-arts celebrities. French cuisine.

Connaught Hotel Restaurant . . . Fashionable crowd and perhaps the best hotel food in London.

Coq d'Or . . . Famous for Chicken-on-the-Spit and French specialties. Luxurious tavern décor.

Mirabelle . . . French cuisine in a fashionable Mayfair restaurant.

Savoy Hotel Restaurants . . . World-famous dining rooms especially good for large-scale entertaining.

Simpson's-in-the-Strand . . . Noted for beef carved at your table, for ale in pewter mugs and English tradition.

Wheeler's Old Compton Street . . . Sea food at one of Soho's best.

White Tower . . . Greek cuisine and sea food in a plush Soho restaurant.

Bath

Hole in the Wall . . . Tarragona chicken, sole in cream and Marsala are among unusual dishes in this cellar restaurant.

FRANCE

Paris

Berkeley Hotel Restaurant . . . One of Paris' smartest luncheon and dining spots. Compared to New York's "21."

Grand Vefour . . . Period décor in one of Paris' great restaurants.

Joseph . . . A Parisian stand-by still not too well-known to tourists; elegant and small.

Lapérouse . . . Duck and soufflés are specialties in this series of old-fashioned small rooms.

Lasserre . . . Elegant; sweetbreads and a Cointreau soufflé are specialties.

L'Escargot Montorgueil . . . Snails, fish and meat dishes are specialties in a building that dates from Henry II.

Maxim's . . . Posh showcase of the chic and celebrated.

Plaza Athénée Hotel Restaurant . . . Dine fashionably in spring and summer on courtyard terrace; during cooler months, in elegant dining room.

Taillevent . . . Solidly, classically French with a gargantuan wine list.

Tour d'Argent . . . A floodlit view of Notre Dame on weekends from one of the world's great restaurants.

Ammerschwihr (near Colmar)

Aux Armes de France . . . Alsatian specialties; noted for chicken in Riesling.

Avallon

Hôtel de la Poste . . . An old coaching inn; lobster and trout specialties.

Avignon

Chez Lucullus . . . Famous for Provençal dishes and the celebrated local wine, Château-Neuf-du-Pape.

Beaulieu-sur-Mer

La Réserve Hotel Restaurant . . . Dine on a terrace with a view of Monte Carlo; one of the Riviera's most distinguished hotel-restaurants.

Bordeaux

Dubern . . . Bordeaux's best, with a great carte of regional wines.

Bougival

Coq Hardi . . . Dine on terraces overlooking the Seine; immaculate service.

Cannes

Carlton Hotel Restaurant . . . International celebrities in a dining room of pre-World War I elegance.

Da Bouttau . . . Touristy, but excellent food and good fun.

Col de la Luere (near Lyon)

Mère Brazier . . . View of Lyon countryside from one of France's best.

Eze

La Chèvre d'Or . . . Housed in a medieval building with a sweeping view of the Mediterranean.

Illhausern (near Colmar)

Auberge de l'Ill . . . Country dining; Alsatian wines and specialties.

La Basse-Goulaine (near Nantes)

Mon Rêve . . . Attractive country restaurant overlooking the Loire River.

La Brague (Antibes)

La Bonne Auberge . . . One of Riviera's great; dine in charming Provençal room or on flower-decked terrace.

Les Baux

Baumanière . . . Restful dining on a terrace or in the 16th-century Provençal building. Great classic cuisine.

Nice

Raynaud . . . Elegant dining; overlooking the sea.

Noves (near Avignon)

La Petite Auberge . . . Provençal specialties in an old château.

St.-Paul-de-Vence

La Colombe d'Or . . . Fine Provençal food, carefully prepared. In summer, dine in a flowering courtyard.

Saulieu

Hôtel de la Côte d'Or . . . Perhaps France's greatest cuisine in a small hotel dining room.

Talloires

Le Père Bise . . . Crayfish, trout, lamb and chicken livers are specialties of this charming spot on Lake Annecy.

A Dutch masterpiece in the form of a cold buffet aboard the ▶ *SS Nieuw Amsterdam.*

HANS NAMUTH

Thoissey (near Mâcon)

Chapon Fin . . . Lyonnaise cuisine in one of best small-town restaurants.

Vienne

Pyramide . . . One of the world's truly great restaurants in a provincial town. Reservations a must.

Villeneuve-de-Marsan (South of Bordeaux)

Darroze . . . A gastronomic mecca with a remarkable cellar.

GERMANY

Berlin

Ritz Restaurant . . . A small, exotic room offering exotic fare. Japanese, Chinese, Arabian, Indian dishes.

Assmannshausen

Krone . . . A view of the Rhine and its castles; Rhine salmon and trout.

Düsseldorf

Breidenbacher Hof . . . Gastronomic treats in luxurious German hotel.

Frankfurt

Arnold Grill and Kaiserkeller . . . German elegance and fashion in Frankfurt's best.
Brückenkeller . . . Sea food specialties in an ancient, vaulted, monastery cellar.

Munich

Humplmayr . . . Bavarian elegance in romantic Hunting Castle Room.
Schwarzwälder-Weinhaus . . . One of Munich's oldest and most famous.
Walterspiel (Hotel Vier Jahreszeiten) . . . Continental cuisine in elegant surroundings.

HOLLAND

Amsterdam

Amstel Hotel Restaurant . . . Gracious dining in Holland's top hotel.
Bali . . . Javanese waiters serve ultimate in East Indian food.
Dikker & Thijs . . . Hearty food in a décor combining solid Dutch and equally solid French.

Oegstgeest (near The Hague)

De Beukenhof . . . Garden dining in an Old World village.

The Hague

Hotel des Indes Restaurant . . . Luxurious dining in the heart of the Embassy quarter.
House of Lords . . . Gypsy violinists mingle with celebrities in a smart, modern room.
Tampat Senang . . . East Indian décor and cuisine.

Rotterdam

Coq d'Or . . . A candlelit room, or, in summer, a garden for outdoor dining.

Veenendaal

Koetshuis . . . Provincial cuisine in a woodland restaurant.

Vreeland (near Amsterdam)

Restaurant-Rotisserie Napoléon (Hotel de Nederlanden) . . . Comfortable dining in a charming canal-side hotel.

IRELAND

Dublin

Restaurant Jammet . . . A Dublin tradition; hearty cuisine with French overtones.
Russell Hotel . . . Trout selected from an aquarium and Irish game in a fashionable setting.

ITALY

Rome

Alfredo alla Scrofa . . . Specialties include Saltimbocco à la Romana and chicken cooked with prosciutto.
Boar's Head Grill, Hotel Flora . . . One of Rome's most satisfying.
Capriccio . . . Gay elegance in modern dining room and upstairs terrace; Café Society and cinema celebrities.
Hostaria dell'Orso . . . The magnificence of medieval Italy, from the tavern-bar to the Cabala Room, perhaps Europe's most beautiful night club.
Fontanella . . . Tuscan specialties such as noodles cooked in hare sauce. A great place for game dishes.
Passetto . . . A favorite with Romans.
Tre Scalini . . . Its dining terrace faces the Bernini fountains; the great dessert specialty is Tartufo Gelato, a chocolate ice and cherries sprinkled with chocolate chips.

Bologna

Pappagallo . . . Substantial Bolognese fare in an ancient carriage house.

Florence

Baldini . . . Great Tuscan specialties in this unpretentious room include skewered larks, thrushes, pheasant.
Hotel Excelsior-Italia Restaurant . . . Glamorous hotel dining on banks of the Arno.
Sabatini . . . Substantial food in lovely rooms; popular with Florentines.
Trattoria Sostanza . . . Meals served family style. Situated in an alley near Excelsior Hotel.

Milan

Barca d'Oro . . . Quality cuisine, perhaps somewhat lacking in originality.
Giannino . . . A glass wall exposes a spotless kitchen which prepares Tuscan specialties.
Savini . . . A favorite of native Milanese; faces the famous Galleria.

Naples

Excelsior Hotel Restaurant . . . The very best food in a city shy of first-class restaurants.

San Felice Circeo

Maga Circe . . . Shrimp, mussel and veal specialties in a seaside hotel, halfway between Rome and Naples.

Turin

Cambio . . . Dine in 19th-century red plush and crystal rooms or, in summer, on a terrace facing the Carignano Palace.

Venice

Danieli Royal Excelsior Hotel . . . Dine on its unique terrace with a view of the Grand Canal.
Gritti Palace Hotel . . . One of Venice's most distinguished hotel dining rooms with a canal-side terrace.
Harry's Bar . . . This spectacular bistro attracts gay celebrity crowd, offers surprisingly fine food and drinks.
Taverna La Fenice . . . Close to the Fenice Theater; attracts an opera crowd. Sea food a specialty.

Ventimiglia

La Mortola . . . Pastoral dining in a garden spot off the highway near the French border.

NORWAY

Oslo

La Belle Sole . . . Norway's top gourmet spot; has fascinating aquarium from which you may choose your fish.
Restaurant George's . . . Intimate and subdued. The cocktail lounge is a fashionable meeting place.

Bergen

Bellevue Restaurant . . . In the hills overlooking Oslo with a view of city.

Stavanger

Atlantic Hotel's Restaurants . . . Downstairs room represents old Stavanger square; upstairs rooms an old sail loft.

PORTUGAL

Lisbon

Hotel Aviz Restaurant . . . Absolute tops in Portuguese dining.
Tavares . . . Conservative clientele in this elegantly appointed restaurant.

SCOTLAND

Edinburgh

George Hotel's Ambassador Restaurant . . . Edinburgh's most elegant spot.

Gleneagles

Gleneagles Hotel Restaurant . . . Scottish game dishes in this great resort hotel.

SPAIN

Madrid

Botín . . . (on Calle Cuchilleros). A favorite of bullfighters and aficionados.

Commodore . . . A great spot for Spanish game, also rotisserie dishes.
Hogar Gallego . . . Hearty Spanish fare with sea-food specialties.
Horcher's . . . Elegant Madrid dining among celebrities.

Barcelona

Círculo Ecuestre . . . Smooth service, sound cuisine in club-like atmosphere.
Los Caracoles . . . No grande cuisine here; good, simple Spanish food.
Ritz Hotel . . . Perhaps Barcelona's most satisfying dining spot.

El Escorial

Hotel Felipe II Restaurant . . . One of Spain's most delightful hotels.

SWEDEN

Stockholm

Grand Hotel Restaurant . . . Enjoy great smörgåsbord and dine on terrace or in Winter Garden.
Riche . . . Stockholm's best dining.
Stallmästaregarden . . . This 300-year-old inn, fifteen minutes from town, is famous for hors d'oeuvres.

SWITZERLAND

Basel

Odeon Grill . . . Grilled and sea foods in this fashionable room.
Three Kings Hotel Restaurant . . . The city's finest cuisine.

Berne

Horseshoe Grill (Hotel Schweizerhof) . . . Candlelight, soft music, gourmet food and great wines in this cozy grill.

Geneva

Amphitryon (Hotel des Bergues) . . . Conservative crowd in an elegant hotel restaurant.
Le Gentilhomme (Hotel Richemond) . . . Relaxed dining; worldly crowd.

St. Moritz

Chesa Veglia . . . A celebrity-haunted spot housed in a chalet.

Zug

Aklin . . . Complete dining satisfaction in ancient mountain inn.

Zurich

Ermitage . . . One of the country's best.
Kronenhalle . . . Great food in a friendly room hung **with** original Matisses, Picassos, Bonnards.
Veltliner Keller . . . For years a Zurich favorite; in ancient-mansion setting.

Index